Law and Philosophy Library

Volume 116

The Law and Philosophy Library, which has been in existence since 1985, aims to publish cutting edge works in the philosophy of law, and has a special history of publishing books that focus on legal reasoning and argumentation, including those that may involve somewhat formal methodologies. The series has published numerous important books on law and logic, law and artificial intelligence, law and language, and law and rhetoric. While continuing to stress these areas, the series has more recently expanded to include books on the intersection between law and the Continental philosophical tradition, consistent with the traditional openness of the series to books in the Continental jurisprudential tradition. The series is proud of the geographic diversity of its authors, and many have come from Latin America, Spain, Italy, the Netherlands, Germany, and Eastern Europe, as well, more obviously for an English-language series, from the United Kingdom, the United States, Australia, and Canada.

More information about this series at http://www.springer.com/series/6210

D.A. Jeremy Telman
Editor

Hans Kelsen in America - Selective Affinities and the Mysteries of Academic Influence

Springer

Editor
D.A. Jeremy Telman
Valparaiso University Law School
Valparaiso, USA

ISSN 1572-4395 ISSN 2215-0315 (electronic)
Law and Philosophy Library
ISBN 978-3-319-33128-7 ISBN 978-3-319-33130-0 (eBook)
DOI 10.1007/978-3-319-33130-0

Library of Congress Control Number: 2016943466

Printed on acid-free paper

This Springer imprint is published by Springer Nature
The registered company is Springer International Publishing AG Switzerland

Contents

About the Authors

Christoph Bezemek is an associate professor at the Institute for Austrian and European Public Law at the Vienna University of Economics and Business. He is the editor-in-chief of the *Vienna Journal on International Constitutional Law* and the author of *Die Geschäftsgrundlage im österreichischen Zivilrecht – Strukturfragen und Synopse* (Springer 2009), *Freie Meinungsäußerung – Strukturfragen des Schutzbereichs im Rechtsvergleich zwischen dem Ersten Zusatz zur US Verfassung und Artikel 10 EMRK* (Verlag Österreich, 2015), and numerous law review articles and book chapters on aspects of Austrian and comparative constitutional law.

Brian H. Bix is the Frederick W. Thomas professor of law and philosophy at the University of Minnesota. Professor Bix's published books include *Jurisprudence: Theory and Context* (6th ed., Sweet & Maxwell, 2012); *Contract Law: Rules, Theory, and Context* (Cambridge, 2012); *Oxford Introductions to U.S. Law: Family Law* (Oxford, 2013); *A Dictionary of Legal Theory* (Oxford, 2004); and *Law, Language, and Legal Determinacy* (Oxford, 1993). Among his 100 articles is "Kelsen and Normativity Revisited," which will appear in Carlos Bernal & Marcelo Porciuncula (eds.), *Festschrift for Stanley L. Paulson* (Marcial Pons, Forthcoming).

Joshua W. Felix is a doctoral candidate in philosophy at Binghamton University. His dissertation concerns distributive justice and contemporary debates in egalitarianism. His research interests include justice, equality, practical reason, and jurisprudence.

Michael Steven Green is the Woodbridge professor of law at the College of William and Mary. He clerked for Judge Richard A. Posner on the US Court of Appeals for the Seventh Circuit and practiced law at Paul, Weiss, Rifkind, Wharton & Garrison in New York City. His publications include *Nietzsche and the Transcendental Tradition* (2002) and numerous articles and essays, including publications in the *Duke Law Journal*, the *Michigan Law Review*, the *Northwestern University Law Review*, the *Oxford Journal of Legal Studies*, and the *Virginia Law Review*.

Frieder Günther is the author of *Ideas of the State: West-German Scholars of Public Law Between Decision and Integration 1949–1970* (Munich: Oldenbourg, 2004), which was awarded as one of the five best books of the year 2004 by the German law journal *Neue Juristische Wochenschrift*, and *Heuss on Journeys. The International Representation of the Federal Republic of Germany by Its First President* (Stuttgart: Franz Steiner, 2006). Currently, he is working as a research associate at the Institute of Contemporary History in Berlin, Germany. His articles have appeared in such journals as *Vierteljahrshefte für Zeitgeschichte, Jahrbuch zur Liberalismus-Forschung*, and *Damals* as well as in numerous edited books.

David Ingram is professor of philosophy at Loyola University of Chicago. He is the author of *Law: Key Concepts* (Bloomsbury, 2006) and several books on rights, *Group Rights: Reconciling Equality and Difference* (University Press of Kansas, 2000) and *Rights, Democracy, and Fulfillment in the Era of Identity Politics* (Rowman and Littlefield, 2004). He has also published several books on critical theory, including *Habermas* (Cornell University, 2010), *Habermas and the Dialectic of Reason* (Yale University, 1987), *Critical Theory and Philosophy* (Paragon House, 1990), and *Reason, History, and Politics* (SUNY, 1995). He is currently writing a book on human rights and global justice.

Clemens Jabloner is the Hans Kelsen Professor at the University of Vienna, which is also where he studied law. He then served in the Austrian Federal Chancellery from 1978 until 1991. From 1993 to 2013, he served as president of the Austrian Supreme Administrative Court. Since 1993, he has also served as director of the Hans Kelsen Institute. From 1998 to 2003, he chaired the Commission of Historians dealing with issues of looting of property in Austria during the Nazi regime. He has published broadly in the areas of legal theory, public law, and legal history.

Nicoletta Ladavac studied philosophy and law in Milano, Italy, and earned her Ph.D. in Catania, Italy, with a dissertation on Hans Kelsen's federalism. In 1995, she founded Thémis, Centre d'Etudes de Philosophie du droit, de Sociologie du droit et de Théorie du droit, an institute for research in philosophy of law, sociology of law, and theory of law in Geneva. From 1997 to 2001, she served on the executive board and as secretary of the Swiss section of the Internationale Vereinigung für Rechtsphilosophie and, in 2005, as its vice president. She has been an international correspondent of the Hans Kelsen Institute in Vienna since 2002. Her current research focuses on legal positivism, legal sociology, Hans Kelsen, Norberto Bobbio, Theodor Geiger, and Niklas Luhmann.

Elisabeth Lefort is a doctor of philosophy from the University of Luxembourg and the University of Louvain-la-Neuve. Before that, she studied at the University of Lorraine and at the Ecole Normale Supérieure in Lyon with a double bachelor's degree in philosophy and French literature. Her current research deals with the relationship between moral philosophy, politics, and legal positivism in Hans Kelsen.

Her teaching at the University of Luxembourg includes courses on the philosophy of law, on aesthetics, and on Schopenhauer.

Jeffrey M. Lipshaw is professor of law at the Suffolk University Law School in Boston. He has also been a visiting professor at the Wake Forest and Tulane law schools. Before becoming a full-time academic in 2007, Professor Lipshaw spent 26 years as a lawyer and business executive, both in private practice, and as the senior legal officer of two multinational businesses. He is a 1976 graduate of the University of Michigan and a 1979 graduate of the Stanford Law School.

Thomas Olechowski studied law at the University of Vienna and earned his habilitation there with "Die Entwicklung des Preßrechts in Österreich bis 1918" ("The Development of Press Law in Austria till 1918"). Since 2003, he has been an associate professor at the University of Vienna, and since 2004, he has also been a lecturer at the Pan-European University in Bratislava. In 2008, he was chosen as a member of the Austrian Academy of Sciences, and since 2011, he has served as a director of the Hans Kelsen Institute. He has published five monographs and edited or co-edited numerous volumes on legal history and constitutional history in the nineteenth and twentieth centuries.

Bettina K. Rentsch earned law degrees from the University of Freiburg (2013) and the University of Geneva (Certificat de Droit Transnational, 2010). She currently holds a Ph.D. researcher's position at the Institute for Private International Law and International Commercial Law, University of Heidelberg. Her Ph.D. thesis reevaluates the role of connecting factors in European conflict of laws, taking into account their regulatory function and drawing on, inter alia, Albert Ehrenzweig's lex fori approach.

Daniel F. Rice is professor emeritus of philosophy and religious studies at the University of Wisconsin-Eau Claire. Cambridge University Press recently published Professor Rice's book, *Reinhold Niebuhr and His Circle of Influence* (2013). He is also the author of *Reinhold Niebuhr and John Dewey: An American Odyssey* (SUNY, 1993) and the editor of *Reinhold Niebuhr Revisited: Engagements with an American Original* (Eerdmans, 2009).

Drury D. Stevenson is the Hutchins research professor at South Texas College of Law in Houston, TX, and a Baker Institute scholar at the James A. Baker III Institute at Rice University. He graduated magna cum laude from the University of Connecticut School of Law, where he served as an editor of the Connecticut Law Review. He earned his master of laws (LL.M.) from the Yale Law School in 2002 and became an assistant attorney general for the state of Connecticut until leaving to accept his position at South Texas. Professor Stevenson's publications cover topics ranging from criminal law to civil procedure, with an emphasis on the intersection of law with economics and linguistic theory.

D.A. Jeremy Telman is a professor at the Valparaiso University Law School, where he teaches contracts and various courses in public international law. He earned a J.D. from the New York University School of Law and a Ph.D. in modern European history from Cornell University. His main scholarly and teaching interests lie at the intersection of public international law and US constitutional law, and his scholarship has appeared in Austrian, French, German, Indian, Israeli, South African, UK, and US publications.

Lars Vinx (Ph.D. Toronto, 2006) is an assistant professor in the Department of Philosophy at Bilkent University in Ankara, Turkey, and a visiting professor in the Department of Philosophy at the University of Turku, Finland. Before coming to Ankara in 2007, Dr. Vinx was a Max Weber fellow at the European University Institute in Florence, Italy. His research currently focuses on issues in constitutional theory, as well as on the legal-theoretical and political-theoretical work of Hans Kelsen and Carl Schmitt. He is the author of *Hans Kelsen's Pure Theory of Law: Legality and Legitimacy* (Oxford University Press, 2007) and the editor and translator of *The Guardian of the Constitution: Hans Kelsen and Carl Schmitt on the Limits of Constitutional Law* (Cambridge University Press, 2015).

Jochen von Bernstorff is a professor of public law, constitutional law, international law, and human rights at the University of Tübingen. Prior to joining the faculty at Tübingen, Professor von Bernstorff served in Germany's foreign ministry and represented Germany in various capacities at the United Nations. His publications include *The Public International Law Theory of Hans Kelsen: Believing in Universal Law* (Cambridge University Press, 2010).

Chapter 1
Introduction: Hans Kelsen for Americans

D.A. Jeremy Telman

1.1 Kelsen in America

Hans Kelsen arrived in the United States in 1940. He was, in the words of Roscoe Pound, "undoubtedly the leading jurist of the time" (Pound 1934: 532). When he left his position at the University of Vienna just a few years earlier, the Austrian politician and jurist Karl Renner hailed Kelsen as "the most original teacher of law of our time" (Métall 1969: 59). And yet, when Kelsen arrived in the United States, he was not able to find a permanent teaching position at a U.S. law school. In the end, he took a position in the University of California, Berkeley, Department of Political Science.

He taught, lectured and published in the United States until his death in 1973. After World War II, Kelsen taught and/or held visiting professorships abroad, but also at U.S. universities, and he received honorary degrees from Harvard, Chicago, and Berkeley (Ladavac 1998: 392). However, while Kelsen continues to play a large role in legal education, in jurisprudence and in international legal theory in other parts of the world (Walter et al. 2010),[1] he is almost completely unknown in the legal academy and the legal profession in the United States (Telman 2010: 353). Moreover, Kelsen remains an obscure figure in other parts of the U.S. academy, such as political science, international relations, sociology and political philosophy, despite his extensive writings on those topics and the significant international reception of his ideas in those fields as well (Aliprantis and Olechowski 2014).

[1] Volume 33 of the *Schriftenreihe des Hans Kelsen-Instituts* is the third volume in the series focusing on Kelsen's influence abroad. Earlier volumes on the subject appeared in 1978 (Volume 2) and 1983 (Volume 8). Volumes 12 (1988) and 22 (2001) also include contributions addressing the international reception of Kelsen's pure theory of law.

D.A.J. Telman (✉)
Valparaiso University Law School, Valparaiso, IN 46383, USA
e-mail: Jeremy.telman@valpo.edu

D.A.J. Telman (ed.), *Hans Kelsen in America - Selective Affinities and the Mysteries of Academic Influence*, Law and Philosophy Library 116,
DOI 10.1007/978-3-319-33130-0_1

Many of the chapters in this volume deepen our understanding of the reasons why Kelsen's mode of thought did not find fertile ground within the U.S. academy. At the same time, this volume includes chapters that illuminate unexplored connections between Kelsen and other giants of twentieth century social science and suggests ways in which Kelsenian insights can contribute to a richer understanding of the intellectual milieu in the post-war United States. Inevitably, the narrative explored in those chapters expands beyond the geographic territory of the United States, and we are fortunate to be able to include in this volume contributions that supplement the story of Kelsen's reception in the United States with novel insights into the similar problems involving the reception of Kelsen's work in post-war Europe.

This Introduction explores three distinct modalities of Kelsen's scholarship. Those familiar with Kelsen's pure theory of law are confused—or think that Kelsen is confused—when they read some of his other works, in which Kelsen expressed clear preferences in the realms of moral and political philosophy. While Kelsen believed that legal science must maintain its neutrality in such matters, he did not limit his scholarship to legal science. Many of the contributions to this volume explore Kelsen's relationship with other mid-twentieth century thinkers on subject-matters beyond legal theory. In particular, having lived in times and places where such views were not a foregone conclusion, Kelsen was a vocal supporter of democracy. His ruminations on the nature of justice have less in common with the technical analyses in the pure theory than they do with the philosophical and theological works with which our contributors have placed Kelsen in dialogue. Finally, Kelsen wrote about international law at a time when its modern contours were in the process of being established. As the contributions to this volume indicate, while the international legal order did not arise in Kelsenian form, Kelsen contributed to some of the first international legal institutions to arise in the aftermath of World War II.

The purpose of this volume is to introduce readers who may be unfamiliar or only dimly familiar with Kelsen's work to that work and the man who created it. After a brief review of Kelsen's biography, this Introduction explores some of the constellations of theoretical insights that are at the core of Kelsen's work and thus inevitably arise repeatedly in the chapters that follow.

1.2 Kelsen's Biography

Kelsen was born in Prague in 1881. He received his doctorate in 1906 and completed his *Habilitationsschrift*, which was the first book-length articulation of his legal theory, in 1911 (Métall 1969: 8, 14). Those two milestones roughly corresponded with Kelsen's two religious conversions, first to Catholicism in 1905 and then to Protestantism in 1912 (Staudacher 2009: 46, 48).[2] Also in 1911, Kelsen

[2] Kelsen's conversions seem not to have been motivated by religious belief; he seems to have been agnostic. The second conversion came at the time of his marriage to Margarete Bondi, who con-

received his first appointment at the University of Vienna as a Lecturer (*Privatdozent*) in the fields of public law and legal philosophy (*Staatsrecht und Rechtsphilosophie*) (Métall 1969: 15).

During World War I, while continuing his scholarly research and publication, Kelsen served in the military and began work on drafting what would eventually become the constitution of the new Austrian Republic (Métall 1969: 18–28). In 1918, the law faculty at the University of Vienna named him assistant professor (*Extraordinarius*) and in 1919 full professor (*Ordinarius*) of public and administrative law (*Staats- und Verwaltungsrecht*) (Métall 1969: 28, 38). The establishment of Austria's Constitutional Court, on which Kelsen also sat from 1921 until 1930, is regarded as one of Kelsen's cardinal contributions to the menu of modern, democratic constitutional institutions (Métall 1969: 47–57; Morrison 1997, 323, n.1). While teaching and studying in Vienna, Kelsen produced approximately 200 scholarly books and articles (Métall 1969: 124–134).

By 1930, Kelsen had run afoul of the ruling Christian Social Party, in large part due to his role as a constitutional judge in a lengthy series of legal disputes relating to Austria's policy of permitting Catholics to remarry (Métall 1969: 54–57). In connection with his involvement with these cases, Kelsen was subjected to withering attacks both in the press and from some of his colleagues at the University of Vienna (Métall 1969: 55–56). It was time for Kelsen to move on, and so he took up a position on the law faculty at the University of Cologne.

Forced from his university post because of his Jewish ancestry, Kelsen fled to Geneva in 1933 and to the United States in 1940 (Métall 1969: 63–64, 76–77). While Kelsen seems to have lived happily in the United States, his approach to legal theory never found a following in the United States. Karl Llewellyn, a leading practitioner of the realist school of jurisprudence, regarded "Kelsen's work as utterly sterile," although he acknowledged Kelsen's intellect (Llewellyn 1962: 356, n.6). Echoing Oliver Wendell Holmes' famous dictum that the life of the law is not logic but experience, Harold Laski denounced Kelsen's legal theory as a sterile "exercise in logic and not in life" (Laski 1938: vi). To this day, Kelsen and his ideas are rarely considered in the American academy.

American scholars have dismissed Kelsen's approach to law either because, in short, H.L.A. Hart proved him wrong (Telman 2010: 356–359) or, as Brian Bix puts it in his contribution to this volume, on the ground that "we need not read Kelsen, because H. L. A. Hart said the same things, only clearer." The erudite contributions to this volume by Brian Bix, Joshua Felix, Michael Steven Green, and Lars Vinx all indicate that American scholars have been too hasty in their neglect of Kelsen, with the first two scholars expanding upon the thesis within the specific context of American legal philosophy. I offer four alternative overlapping theories to explain the exclusion of Kelsen's approach not just from American legal philosophy but from the American legal academy more generally.

---

verted from Judaism to Protestantism. Austrian law did not permit intermarriage, and as Anna Staudacher's research indicates, the Catholic conversion ritual included a stark denunciation of Judaism, which may explain why most Jews preferred to convert to Protestantism.

First, Kelsen came to the United States at a time when Legal Realism had established itself as the newly ascendant, dominant paradigm in legal theory. To Legal Realists, Kelsen's approach looked like the legal formalism they had so decidedly rejected and defeated (Telman 2010: 360–362). Interestingly enough, Christoph Bezemek's contribution to this volume takes on the question of whether Kelsen's pure theory is in fact a form of legal formalism. He concludes that it is not.

Second, the American academy (and not just the legal academy) rejected Kelsen's approach as politically anemic. The inability of the Central European legal positivist tradition to stand up to Nazism was cited as evidence that its legal relativism easily elided into moral relativism (Telman 2010: 362–363).

A third set of problems that Kelsen faced in the United States had to do with the differences between legal education in the United States and most of the rest of the world. Legal education elsewhere is part of a general university-style education in which students begin with foundational courses on the nature of law and legal reasoning. In the United States, by contrast, students get their general grounding in the humanities and social sciences as undergraduates and come to law school for professional training (Telman 2010: 365–367). In the current environment, which places increased emphasis on client-centered lawyering, experiential learning and practical skills training, courses on jurisprudence and legal philosophy are moving further and further toward the periphery of the curriculum.

In addition, Kelsen's approach was incompatible with American legal pedagogy, which was based on Langdell's case method. Never having taught before in a common law system, Kelsen did not think about the development of the law in terms of the slow accretion of common law decisions. Kelsen's way of thinking about the law was, to a certain degree, incommensurate with the U.S. approach to legal education (Telman 2010: 367–369). Finally, given that students come to law school with a great variety of backgrounds and trainings, most U.S. law students lack either the ability or the desire to think about fundamental legal principles in Kelsenian terms. It is not that U.S. students lack abilities generally, but very few have philosophical training, and many, by the time they arrive at law school, have a very practical and pragmatic approach to legal education. U.S. law schools are pluralistic and do not inculcate students into any particular way of viewing the law, and most U.S. law schools do not require students to study theoretical approaches to the law in a systematic way (Telman 2010: 369–370).

This book broadens the focus considerably. While some of the chapters explore in greater detail Kelsen's reception in the U.S. legal academy and among U.S. legal theorists, most chapters look beyond the legal academy and beyond law. We explore Kelsen's interactions with political scientists, social critics, sociologists and theologians, and we also look at Kelsen's practical contributions to the development of the law while he was living in the United States. We also are happy to have a contribution from Frieder Günther that details the neglect of Kelsen among West German scholars of public law. The book brings to light some of Kelsen's achievements and influences that have hitherto not been known or highlighted, and it also suggests ways in which Kelsen posthumously still can exert some influence on legal thought.

In order to set up the chapters that follow, this introduction quickly reviews some of the major theoretical themes that make Kelsen's pure theory of law unique.

1.3 Kelsen and the Pure Theory of Law

The idea behind the pure theory of law is not difficult to grasp, but its ramifications can be so unsettling as to render the concept mind-boggling. Kelsen sought to provide a theory of law that was free from impurities derived from theology, sociology, ethics, politics or any other systematic body of knowledge other than logic (Kelsen 1934: 1, 7–8). In the U.S. context, there are two main wellsprings of resistance to the pure theory of law. First, pure theory can be downright obnoxious to those who assume that laws are derived from moral or ethical systems. Second, Legal Realists dismiss the pure theory as naïve, given the tendency among Legal Realists to treat law as a superstructure erected on a conscious or unconscious base. Legal Realism consisted of a diverse group of legal scholars (Green 2005: 1919) committed to the view, as Frederick Schauer put it, that legal decision-making turned on "something other than, or at least much more than, positive law, legal rules, legal doctrine and legal reasoning as traditionally conceived" (Schauer 2013: 756). There was no consensus as to what that "something" was, but Legal Realists rejected (and reject) the idea that law can be an autonomous subject matter, independent from social reality and from politics.

1.3.1 The Relation Between Pure Theory and Legal Positivism

Most people who write about Kelsen take it as a given that Kelsen's pure theory of law is a version of legal positivism. Kelsen himself describes the pure theory as a theory of positive law (Kelsen 1960: 1). That is, Kelsen's pure theory assumes that law is a product of human institutions. Various impulses, including moral and political impulses, may contribute to the substance of legal norms, but the norms are not obeyed because they are moral or ethical. Their force derives from the reality that they were promulgated by an appropriate authority.

Because of its normative character, law has certain formal resemblances to ethics or morality. The structure of legal systems, according to Kelsen, is that they consist of certain normative rules that instruct the subjects of law how they *ought* to behave. Law differs from ethics or morality, however, in that it is indifferent to the substance of those rules and in that the consequence of violating a legal norm is legal sanction rather than moral or ethical sanction (Kelsen 1934: 15–19). Law is for Kelsen an independent normative system. In order to understand how that normative system works, one need not consider it by the criteria of other, non-legal normative systems. This is what we mean when we associate Kelsen's pure theory of law with legal positivism.

In his contribution to this volume, Michael Steven Green makes the important and powerful argument that Kelsen's pure theory is different from both natural law and positivism in that, from the perspective of the pure theory of law, law exists independent of social facts. That is, just as we could hypothesize that certain conduct (for example, murder) is immoral independent of the existence of human beings who might engage in such conduct, law would continue to exist even if human beings did not. This point is important for Green's project of showing that Kelsen's pure theory does not turn on any particular legal regime's efficacy. While Green rejects the term positivism as applicable to the pure theory of law, one need not choose between his understanding of the pure theory and those of other contributors to the volume who routinely refer to the pure theory as a form of legal positivism. Such references describe the pure theory as a form of legal positivism in order to highlight the distinction between legal positivism and natural law approaches to the sources of legal authority.

1.3.2 Elements of the Pure Theory

According to Kelsen's theory, law is to be understood as a hierarchy of norms in which all law derives ultimately from one basic norm, the *Grundnorm*. Within the pure theory, Kelsen rejected any possible linking of the validity of norms to external facts. There is no way to navigate from the "is" to the "ought" or vice versa. "The reason for the validity of a norm can only be the validity of another norm" (Kelsen 1960: 193). Each norm in the chain is valid because some lawful authority has promulgated it. The basic norm is the one norm from which all others derive their authority, and that norm must be presupposed rather than promulgated (Kelsen 1960: 194–195). Kelsen cites, as an example, the basic norm that governs the normative order created by the Hebrew Bible, "One ought to obey God's commands" (Kelsen 1960: 194). In the U.S. legal system, the basic norm would be some variant on "One ought to obey the Constitution."

It is tempting to reject Kelsen's theory as unrealistic or at least as not very useful in understanding law as we experience it in the rough and tumble world in which laws are in fact justified in relation to moral or ethical criteria or with reference to political developments. But Kelsen supplements his "static" description of the law as a hierarchy of norms with a "dynamic principle." The dynamic principle acknowledges that there is something outside of the system of the pure theory that gives rise to the basic norm. That something may be a revolution or a revelation. It does not matter from the perspective of the pure theory.

Thus while Kelsen limited his pure theory of the law to the study of legal norms, he did not rule out the possibility of moral, ethical or political critiques of law. On the contrary, Kelsen considered what he called "legal sociology" to be a worthwhile endeavor, but one distinguishable from the pure theory of law:

> It asks, say, what prompts a legislator to decide on exactly these norms and to issue no others, and it asks what effects his regulations have had. It asks how religious imagination, say, or economic data influence the activity of the courts, and what motivates people to behave or to fail to behave in conformity with the legal system (Kelsen 1934: 14).

Similarly, with respect to the relationship between law and morality, Kelsen rejects not "the dictate that the law ought to be moral and good; that goes without saying… Rather, what is rejected is the view that the law as such is part of morality, and that therefore every law, as law, is in some sense and to some degree moral" (Kelsen 1934: 15). As the natural law theorist John Finnis puts it, Kelsen's position was that "there may be moral truths, but if so they are completely outside the field of vision of legal science or legal philosophy" (Finnis 2000: 1598).

The point is that, from the perspective of the legal system, the original source of the basic norm is generally accepted or not subject to question. The basic norm is the source of the entire legal normative order, and as such it is also the presupposed, not legislated, ground for its own authority. Kelsen thus concedes (not that it is any great concession) that something external to the static legal system gives rise to the basic norm. But once the system of law is set in motion by the establishment of the basic norm, law can function autonomously or at least legal science restricts itself to an analysis of law as such. Because Kelsen views all law as flowing from the basic norm, he regards all law as part of one normative system. This is Kelsen's doctrine of the unity of law.

1.4 Kelsen and the Monism/Dualism Divide

Kelsen's doctrine of the unity of the law leads him to regard international law and domestic (municipal) law as part of one normative system. Kelsen could not accept that legal orders could be in fundamental conflict with one another. That is, local authorities might promulgate lower norms that would contradict higher norms. Such norms could be enforced and would in fact be binding on local authorities. But they would also be subject to review by higher authorities that would test them against higher norms. Lower norms that cannot be reconciled with higher norms are invalid.

1.4.1 Envisioning a Monist System of Law

Kelsen identified three basic theoretical possibilities that might describe the relationship between international and municipal law (Kelsen 1960: 328–347). Within monism, Kelsen entertained two options: either international law or domestic law could be at the top of the hierarchy of legal norms (Kelsen 1960: 332–344). Kelsen associated the primacy of domestic law with the ideology of imperialism and that of international law with the ideology of pacifism (Kelsen 1960: 346–347). Although Kelsen himself claimed not to prefer one form of monism over the other,

Kelsen scholars have identified international supremacy as a hallmark of his theory of international law (von Bernstorff 2010: 93).

Kelsen regarded the third option, a dualist model, as "untenable" (Kelsen 1960: 328). In a dualist model, the international and domestic legal orders are independent of one another. Dualism would produce a world in which behavior that would be permissible in one legal order would be impermissible in another (Kelsen 1960: 329). That is, there would be categories of conduct that, no matter what an actor chose to do, would put that actor in violation of some legal norm. This is not to say that Kelsen believed that domestic legal orders would always enforce international legal norms, but he was comfortable with the notion that legal norms could exist even if they were not enforced—or even if it took a long time for the proper authority to identify a violation and provide a remedy. For example, within the U.S. federal system, a state legislature may pass an unconstitutional statute. Such state legislative action creates a legal norm until it is rendered ineffective by a court or a supervening legislative or executive act. Similarly, the fact that a state may adopt legal rules that are at odds with international legal norms is a temporary anomaly and does not, for Kelsen, give rise to a dualist system (Kelsen 1960: 330–331).

The status of international law as a part of U.S. law, like the status of international law in the municipal law of many states, is something of a hybrid. The U.S. Constitution's Supremacy Clause (U.S. Const., art VI, 2)[3] and the Supreme Court's statement in *Paquette Habana* that "international law is part of our law" (175 U.S. 677, 700 (1900)) suggest a monist system. Kelsen provided a highly plausible gloss on the Supremacy Clause:

> [The] primacy of international law is compatible with the fact that the constitution of a state contains a provision to the effect that general international law is valid as a part of national law. If we start from the validity of international law which does not require recognition by the state, then the mentioned constitutional provision does not mean that it puts into force international law for the state concerned, but merely that international law—by a general clause—is transformed into national law. Such transformation is needed, if the organs of the state, especially its tribunals are authorized (by the constitution) to apply national law; they can, therefore, apply international law only if its content has assumed the form of national law… (Kelsen 1960: 336–337).

However, the Supremacy Clause's reach is severely limited by the Supreme Court's recognition that non-self-executing treaties do not have automatic effect within the domestic system (Foster v. Neilson, 27 U.S. (2 Pet.) 253, 314 (1829); Whitney v. Robertson, 124 U.S. 190, 195 (1888)), a doctrine greatly expanded in *Medellín v. Texas* (552 U.S. 491 (2008)).[4] The status of customary international law as part of

[3]The Supremacy Clause provides that all "Treaties made, or which shall be made, under the Authority of the United States, shall be supreme Law of the Land."

[4]While the majority opinion in *Medellín* is not a model of clarity on this point, the majority position seems to be that a treaty is self-executing and thus effective as domestic law only if the treaty itself, the legislative history underlying the Senate's "advice and consent" to the treaty, or the instrument of ratification expressly indicates a desire or understanding that the treaty was to be self-executing.

law has been severely limited, at least since *Sosa v. Alvarez Machain* (542 U.S. 692 (2004)).[5]

One might be tempted to regard the status of international law as part of U.S. law to illustrate the unlikelihood if not the implausibility of Kelsen's monism. Lars Vinx's contribution to this volume suggests that Kelsen's approach does not require that international law be supreme in a monist system but only recognizes international monism as a possibility. Vinx defends a "weak monism" while conceding that Kelsen's strong monism has found very little support in the world of legal scholarship. Weak monism claims only that, even if Kelsen was wrong to claim that all law *must* be part of one legal system, it is possible and plausible to claim that all law in fact *is* part of one legal system.

In addition, Drury Stevenson's contribution to this volume is also relevant to the question of monism and dualism. Stevenson emphasizes Kelsen's insistence that the law is addressed not to ordinary citizens but to the state actors who implement and enforce the law. If the unity of law is to be realized, the responsibility to do so falls upon such state actors who would prevent any conflict from arising between international and municipal obligations.

1.4.2 Kelsen's Role in the Implementation of a New Legal Order After World War II

As the chapters in this volume by Jochen von Bernstorff and Thomas Olechowski indicate, Kelsen's involvement with international law was by no means merely theoretical. In a manner very different from his approach in the pure theory of law, Kelsen drafted his own plan for a post-war international order. Kelsen's "Draft Covenant" for the Permanent League for the Maintenance of Peace and his "Treaty Stipulations Establishing Individual Responsibility for Violations of International Law" can be found as annexes to his book, *Peace Through Law* (Kelsen 1944: 127–148). Kelsen's disappointment with the international legal order established through the United Nations Charter is evident in his treatise on the Charter (Kelsen 1950).[6]

[5] According the majority opinion in *Sosa*, rules of customary international law can give rise to claims under the Alien Tort Statute only if the rules express norms of customary law as universally recognized today as were the prohibition on piracy, the right of safe passage and protections for ambassadors at the time Congress adopted the Alien Tort Statute in 1789. Very few rules of customary international law can claim such universal acceptance. Norms of customary international law rarely come up in U.S. litigation apart from litigation relating to the Alien Tort Statute.

[6] I am grateful to Jörg Kammerhofer for his skepticism regarding my reading of Kelsen's treatise on the United Nations. Kammerhofer points out that the purpose of treatises in the European tradition to which Kelsen was contributing is to pinpoint all ambiguities in the law so that attorneys and judges can know what they are dealing with. This insight leads me to question my assumption that Kelsen's disappointment with the substance of the Charter informed his view of the weaknesses in its drafting. In my own defense, my reading was influenced in part by Kelsen's preface to his treatise, in which he stated that his ultimate goal was to improve the law governing the United Nations.

There are three main elements to Kelsen's vision for a post-war international order: centralization, collective security, and an international court. Centralization is the key legal technique that Kelsen believed differentiated national from international law and the ultimate means for international law's development. Kelsen's views on collective security are not that different from those envisioned in the U.N. Charter. The most idiosyncratic element of Kelsen's design for a post-war international order was his focus on the establishment of a court of universal and compulsory jurisdiction, as Jochen von Bernstorff details in his contribution to this volume.

Kelsen did not think that a military alliance would be the main engine of international centralization. According to Kelsen, in the national context, the rule of law was not introduced through the executive and legislative branches of government; it was introduced through courts (Kelsen 1948: 161). Kelsen contends that the history of both Roman and Anglo-American law shows that for much of history it was judicial decisions rather than legislatures or executive decrees that made law (Kelsen 1948: 162). Kelsen was convinced that because courts arose first in the domestic context, they must also be the starting point for the global rule of law (Kelsen 1948: 150). Thus, his own design for an international order, which he called the Permanent League for the Maintenance of Peace, had as its centerpiece an international court empowered to exercise compulsory jurisdiction over all member states as well as jurisdiction to try individuals accused of violations of international criminal law (Kelsen 1944: 13).

Despite the fact that the institutions of the international legal order departed sharply from Kelsen's model, he continued to play a role as a consultant to the U.S. government in connection with the establishment of the International Military Tribunals in the aftermath of World War II. Jochen von Bernstorff's contribution to this volume details Kelsen's critique of the Nuremberg Tribunals and highlights the areas in which Kelsen's criticisms overlapped with those of Hans Morgenthau. The two men came to questions of international law from very different perspectives. However, at least when it came to the foundations of the post-war international criminal legal order, they arrived at similar conclusions.

Thomas Olechowski's contribution to this volume discusses previously unknown memoranda that Kelsen composed as an advisor to various U.S. agencies towards the end of World War II. The memoranda illustrate Kelsen's attempts to translate his ideas about international law into reality. It is not clear to what extent the U.S. authorities relied on Kelsen's memoranda in formulating their policies, but the documents are in any case of interest in illustrating how Kelsen, the great theoretician, was able to grapple with the practical problems of international institutions just as he had been willing to grapple with the practical drafting challenges that he faced in his contributions to Austria's constitution after World War I.

1.5 Beyond Law: Kelsen in Conversations About Justice

Kelsen took advantage, as best he could, of his time in the United States. Although, as Nicoletta Ladavac's contribution to this volume makes clear, the continuities in Kelsen's work far exceed the changes, Kelsen's scholarly interests were clearly stimulated by his intellectual exchanges in the United States. It would be difficult to beat Vienna during the first three decades of the twentieth century for the richness and variety of its intellectual and cultural milieu. Still, Kelsen's time in exile brought him into contact with a different cast of intellectual interlocutors, and his scholarship grew in response to these new impulses.

In some instances explored in the chapters that follow, the connections between Kelsen and his contemporaries were largely indirect. Still, they grappled with common problems and often arrived at surprisingly similar conclusions, despite their very different points of departure. For example, Elisabeth Lefort's chapter demonstrates that, in their ruminations on justice, Kelsen and Leo Strauss seemed to reject each other's positions. Kelsen rejected natural law; Strauss rejected relativism. However, Lefort points out, both were in agreement in ultimately concluding that the nature of justice was elusive, insufficiently captured by any one ethical or political perspective.

Bettina Rentsch's narrative has a different flavor. Kelsen was friendly with Albert Ehrenzweig, his colleague at the University of California at Berkeley. Nonetheless, Rentsch suggests that Kelsen's work, especially his attempts to grapple with the concept of justice, would have benefitted from serious consideration of Ehrenzweig's *Pscyhoanalytic Jurisprudence* (Ehrenzweig 1971). Kelsen's inquiries on justice concluded at an impasse. Kelsen could not deny the human need for a satisfactory sense of what is just, but he found the pursuit of a universal definition of justice "irrational." Ehrenzweig's work helped explain the sociological and psychological sources of the impulse for justice. Rentsch contends that Ehrenzweig's theory could have filled some gaps in the pure theory of law by providing a more satisfying grounding for Kelsen's theory of justice.

Other chapters in the volume indicate the ways in which our academic debates about the nature of law, conceptions of justice, and the operations of legal and ethical norms could be enriched were Kelsen's ideas included. Joshua Felix's contribution to this volume also focuses on Kelsen's work on the theory of justice. Felix's work highlights the ways in which contemporary debates, in this case among political philosophers, are enriched by a serious consideration of Kelsen's work. Felix views Kelsen's *General Theory of Norms* (Kelsen 1991) as raising significant challenges to political philosophers, such as John Rawls, who defend the thesis that the objectivity of value judgments can be verified by means of a rational procedure, a position Felix terms "constructivism."

Jeffrey Lipshaw's contribution poses fundamental questions, from a Kantian perspective, regarding the neo-Kantian model at the core of the pure theory of law. As his work so often does, Lipshaw's contribution draws on his extensive experience as a transactional lawyer to test a complex theoretical model for understanding commercial transactions. In so doing, he challenges the distinction between the "is" and the "ought" that is at the heart of the Kelsenian approach. Lipshaw contends that Kelsen's analog to the Kantian categories of cognition is misplaced, at least for an area of law in which legal rules arise in response to real world transactions rather than deriving from higher norms. Lipshaw invites us not to think of contract law as something we *perceive* through Kantian cognition or *know* by way of theoretical reason; he asks us instead to see it as something we *do* with our practical reason.

Finally, living in the United States provided ample material from which Kelsen could draw in developing his understanding of democracy. Daniel Rice compares Kelsen's views on democracy to those of Reinhold Niebuhr, while David Ingram's chapter discusses the interesting connections between Kelsen's views on democracy and human rights and those of Jürgen Habermas. Ingram's contribution to this volume tells a story, much like that of Elisabeth Lefort's discussion of Kelsen and Leo Strauss, of two thinkers who seem to come at a problem from opposite perspectives and yet arrive at similar conclusions. While Kelsen is associated with dogmatic positivism and Habermas is regarded as more of a legal moralist, both embrace a monist view of international human rights grounded in democratic proceduralism.

Rice's contribution completes a conversation that Kelsen initiated with Niebuhr in an essay that Kelsen published in *Ethics* (Kelsen 1955). In that essay, Kelsen criticized some of Niebuhr's writings on the relationships among democracy, justice and Christianity. Niebuhr never responded, but Rice mines Niebuhr's writings and predicts what Niebuhr's response likely would have been. In so doing, he illuminates the positions of these two leading intellectual figures of the mid-twentieth century, while highlighting the limitations and potential blindspots in Kelsen's views.

1.6 Conclusion: Kelsen and Modernity

Kelsen's critique of Niebuhr's views on the relationship between religion and democracy provides a nice segue to the final two contributions in this volume, which are inspired by Kelsen's posthumous book, *Secular Religion* (Kelsen 2012). Clemens Jabloner's contribution devotes some attention to Kelsen's Jewish background, but his primary focus is Kelsen's modernity. Kelsen's resistance to the treatment of modern politics and especially modern social science as ersatz religions is emblematic of his modernity. In my concluding chapter, I expand upon Raphael Gross's observation that *Secular Religion* was Kelsen's most intimate autobiographical work (Gross 2013: 122). Indeed, *Secular Religion* is a passionate defense of Kelsen's scientific project, and, at the same time, an equally passionate defense of a strict rationalism in the Enlightenment tradition. *Secular Religion* was written in conversation with leading intellectuals of the last century.

It is the aim of this volume to introduce or remind contemporary readers of Kelsen's *Weltanschauung*. For U.S. readers, Kelsen's perspective may be rich and strange, but we hope that this volume excites sufficient interest in the reader to encourage further explorations of Kelsen's work.

References

Aliprantis, Nikitas, and Thomas Olechowski. 2014. *Hans Kelsen: Die Aktualität eines großen Rechtswissenschafters und Soziologen des 20. Jahrhunderts*. Vienna: Manz.

Ehrenzweig, Albert A. 1971. *Psychoanalytic jurisprudence*. New York: Oceana Publications Inc.

Finnis, John. 2000. On the incoherence of legal positivism. *Notre Dame Law Review* 75: 1597–1611.

Green, Michael Steven. 2005. Legal realism as a theory of law. *William and Mary Law Review* 46: 1915.

Gross, Raphael. 2013. Der Parallelismus als Gefahr: Zur "jüdischen Biographie" von Hans Kelsen. In *Secular religion: Rezeption und Kritik von Hans Kelsens Ausinandersetzung mit Religion und Wissenschaft*, ed. Clemens Jabloner et al., 113–129. Wien: Mainz.

Kelsen, Hans. 1934. *Introduction to the Problems of Legal Theory*. Trans. B.L. Paulson, S.L. Paulson 1996. Oxford: Oxford University Press.

Kelsen, Hans. 1944. *Peace through law*. Chapel Hill: University of North Carolina Press.

Kelsen, Hans. 1948. *Law and peace in international relations*. Cambridge: Harvard University Press.

Kelsen, Hans. 1950. *The law of the united nations: A critical analysis of its fundamental problems*. New York: Praeger.

Kelsen, Hans. 1955. Foundations of democracy, 66/I, II. *Ethics: An International Journal of Social Political and Legal Philosophy* 66(1), Part 2: 1–101.

Kelsen, Hans. 1960. *Pure Theory of Law*. Trans. M. Knight 1967. Berkeley: University of California Press.

Kelsen, Hans. 1991. *General Theory of Norms*. Trans. M. Hartney 1991. Oxford: Clarendon Press.

Kelsen, Hans. 2012. *Secular religion. A polemic against the misinterpretation of modern social philosophy, science and politics as "new religion"*. Wien/New York: Springer.

Ladavac, Nicoletta Bersier. 1998. Bibliographical note and biography. *European Journal of International Law* 9: 391.

Laski, Harold. 1938. *A grammar of politics*, 4th ed. London: Allen & Unwin.

Llewellyn, Karl N. 1962. *Jurisprudence: Realism in theory and practice*. Chicago: University of Chicago Press.

Métall, Rudolf Aladár. 1969. *Hans Kelsen: Leben und Werk*. Vienna: Verlag Franz Deuticke.

Morrison, Wayne. 1997. *Jurisprudence: From the Greeks to post-modernism*. London: Cavendish.

Pound, Roscoe. 1934. Law and the science of law in recent theories. *Yale Law Journal* 43: 525.

Schauer, Frederick. 2013. Legal realism untamed. *Texas Law Review* 91: 749.

Staudacher, Anna L. 2009. Zwischen Emanzipation und Assimilation: Jüdische Juristen im Wien des Fin-de-Siècle. In *Hans Kelsen: Leben—Werk—Wirksamkeit*, ed. Robert Walter, Werner Ogris, and Thomas Olechowski, 41–53. Wien: Manz.

Telman, D.A. Jeremy. 2010. A path not taken: Hans Kelsen pure theory of law in the land of the legal realists. In *Hans Kelsen anderswo/Hans Kelsen abroad*, ed. Robert Walter, Clemens Jabloner, and Klaus Zeleny, 353–376. Vienna: Manz.

von Bernstorff, Jochen. 2010. *The Public International Law Theory of Hans Kelsen: Believing in International Law*. Trans. T. Dunlap. Cambridge: Cambridge University Press.

Walter, Robert, Clemens Jabloner, and Klaus Zeleny (eds.). 2010. *Hans Kelsen anderswo/Hans Kelsen abroad*. Vienna: Manz.

Part I
Hans Kelsen and American Legal Philosophy

Chapter 2
Kelsen in the United States: Still Misunderstood

Brian H. Bix

2.1 Introduction

Hans Kelsen has been described as "the most internationally famous legal philosopher of [the twentieth] century" (Harris 1996: 95). Yet, in American legal philosophy—even if one narrows one's focus to careful consideration of the sub-category, American analytical legal philosophy—the ideas of Hans Kelsen are generally ignored. And on the rare occasions when Kelsen's ideas are not ignored, they are almost always discussed quickly, and, more often than not, erroneously (there are, of course, prominent exceptions, including works by participants in the Conference on which this Collection is based).

Section 2.2 of this paper gives examples of Kelsen's works being overlooked, offers some misreadings by prominent theorists, and considers possible explanations for this indifference and ignorance. Section 2.3 then turns to some more subtle (and controversial) questions of correct and incorrect readings, focusing on Kelsen's Basic Norm.

B.H. Bix (✉)
Frederick W. Thomas Professor of Law and Philosophy,
University of Minnesota, Minnesota, MN, USA
e-mail: bix@umn.edu

D.A.J. Telman (ed.), *Hans Kelsen in America - Selective Affinities and the Mysteries of Academic Influence*, Law and Philosophy Library 116,
DOI 10.1007/978-3-319-33130-0_2

2.2 Missing the Mark

The usual treatment of Kelsen in contemporary English-language jurisprudence is to ignore him entirely. For example, in Scott Shapiro's recent magnum opus about legal philosophy, *Legality* (Shapiro 2011),[1] a text which spends dozens of pages on John Austin, H. L. A. Hart and Ronald Dworkin (among other theorists), there is only a small scattering of references to Kelsen (almost all of them quite brief, and either critical or dismissive). Even more telling is the thousand-page *Oxford Handbook of Jurisprudence and Philosophy of Law* (Coleman and Shapiro 2002), a seemingly comprehensive and authoritative guide to legal philosophy. While it contains not one, but *two* substantial entries on legal positivism by eminent theorists (one on "exclusive" legal positivism (Marmor 2002), and one on its rival, "inclusive" legal positivism (Himma 2002)), neither legal positivism entry discusses Kelsen at all.[2] The only mention of Kelsen in the full 1039 pages of jurisprudential text is some brief passing references in John Finnis' discussion of Natural Law theory (Finnis 2002: 9–10).

Other standard texts for Jurisprudence fare little better: Feinberg, Coleman and Kutz's *Philosophy of Law* (this is the current version of the text long co-authored by Joel Feinberg and Hyman Gross) contains nothing from or about Kelsen in its section on legal positivism (Feinberg et al. (2014): 74–140); Kelsen is similarly absent from the sections, "Classical Theories of Law" and "Modern Theories of Law" in Adams' *Philosophical Problems in the Law* (Adams 2013: 58–146), and he makes no appearance in any of the sections of Arthur and Shaw's *Readings in the Philosophy of Law* (Arthur and Shaw 2010). I could go on at some length, but will spare the reader the repetition. The basic point is clear enough.

When Kelsen's work is mentioned in texts about legal philosophy, it is usually presented briefly. Consider an otherwise worthy overview of analytical legal philosophy in Murphy and Coleman's *Philosophy of Law*. The authors inform us that we need not read Kelsen, because H. L. A. Hart said the same things, only clearer. What follows is the entirety of the book's discussion of Kelsen—within a 55-page chapter on the "The Nature of Law," Kelsen's work warrants less than a full sentence:

> In *The Concept of Law*, Hart gives the theory of legal positivism the most systematic and powerful statement it has ever received and is ever likely to receive. Though in many respects derivative from the work of the Austrian legal positivist Hans Kelsen, Hart's theory manages to preserve most of Kelsen's central insights [*we are never told what Kelsen's central insights were*] without surrounding them with Kelsen's complex prose and without preserving the obscurity and ambiguity often found in Kelsen's own development of positivism (Murphy and Coleman 1990: 27 (footnote omitted)).

[1] I should note that at this conference Scott Shapiro expressed an intention to write about Kelsen at length in a forthcoming work on international law.

[2] The "exclusive" entry in that text is by Andrei Marmor; the "inclusive" entry is by Kenneth Einar Himma.

There are, of course, overlaps between Kelsen's work and Hart's, and these are well worth noting—though they are best noted in the context of considering the sharp differences as well. However, it is hard to discuss differences between Hart's work and Kelsen's when no effort has been made to summarize Kelsen's work. Both Kelsen and Hart emphasized (each in his own way) the normativity of law, both rejected Austin's empirical approach, and both emphasized the systematic and hierarchical nature (as they saw it) of law. However, Kelsen's neo-Kantian analysis differs sharply from Hart's empirical and ordinary language-based analysis, differences in approaches that are displayed in the different natures of the concepts that might seem similar at first glance: Kelsen's Basic Norm and Hart's Rule of Recognition.

Another very able contemporary theorist, Leslie Green, Professor of the Philosophy of Law at Oxford University, offers the following dismissal of Kelsen's Basic Norm:

> There are many difficulties with this, not least of which is the fact that if we are willing to tolerate the basic norm as a solution it is not clear why we thought there was a problem in the first place. One cannot say both that the basic norm is the norm presupposing which validates all inferior norms and also that an inferior norm is part of the legal system only if it is connected by a chain of validity to the basic norm (Green 2003).

One expects better from a scholar like Green, who is usually very careful in his analyses even of views with which he disagrees. As most of us explain to our students, if you are interpreting a prominent scholar as saying something foolish, the chances are good that you are not understanding that scholar correctly. Contrary to Green's analysis, why would one assume that Kelsen was trying to solve a difficult problem through mere fiat and declaration?[3]

The obvious response to Green's misreading is to point out that Kelsen was working on problems different from those that concern Green and many of his contemporaries. The perspective of contemporary Anglo-American legal positivists on the "normativity" issue is often one that seems analogous to alchemy: how can the "ought" conclusions of law arise from the "is" facts that make up law (Coleman 2001: 70–102; Shapiro 2011: 118–153)? Kelsen is not trying to offer a formula for this alchemical transformation, because he is confident that no such formula exists: he is a firm believer in the Humean division of "is" and "ought" (Hume 1978: Section 3.1.1, at 469–470) (a point I will return to in Sect. 2.3). Because he accepts this sharp division, his theme is not how law can transform "is" to "ought," but what follows (in a neo-Kantian way) from the fact that we *do* treat the actions of legal officials in a normative way, that is, as creating norms (again, more on this in Sect. 2.3).

Of course, many explanations have been offered to account for (some portion of) the lack of interest and attention to Kelsen's work, some of which point to Kelsen's neo-Kantian approach, which is less familiar to American readers than the more

[3] Marmor offers a slight variation of Green's too-quick dismissal: "Instead of telling us something about the foundations of the basic norm, Kelsen simply invites us to stop asking" (Marmor 2011: 146).

empirical and pragmatic approaches of the likes of Hart and Dworkin. One recent and novel explanation for Kelsen's poor reception was offered by Dan Priel in the course of a longer argument for why theories of the nature of law are tied to particular legal systems (in particular, Priel argued that H. L. A. Hart's theory is assertedly connected with the English legal system, and Ronald Dworkin's with the American legal system). Priel commented in passing that the "obvious" explanation for the disregard of Kelsen was that "Kelsen's legal thought, despite his many years in the United States, remained firmly rooted in a particular conception of law that is closer to what one finds in civil law systems" (Priel 2013: 339). Unfortunately, Priel does not develop his argument beyond that mere assertion, and the claim remains far from self-evident. Certainly, Kelsen refers to concepts like "desuetude" (Kelsen 1992: § 30(d), at 63) that are more at home in some civil law systems than they are in the Anglo-American legal systems, and he does not spend much time discussing common law judicial law-making, but the core ideas of Kelsen's theory (*eg*, presupposition of the Basic Norm, the hierarchy of norms, static and dynamic validity, legal norms as authorizations to impose sanctions, etc.) seem as applicable to common law systems as to civil law systems.

One should of course note once again that there are exceptions to the indifference and ignorance to Kelsen in Anglo-American legal philosophy—though the exceptions may be more in Britain than in the United States. Beyond the contributors to this volume, one should certainly mention Stanley Paulson, who has devoted much of his career to explication of Kelsen's works, as well as translation of many of those works into English.[4] J. W. Harris was another influential expositor of Kelsen's works,[5] and Joseph Raz (though some of Raz's readings of Kelsen are subject to challenge) gave Kelsen's work the sort of careful attention that most prominent legal theorists have failed to offer.[6]

2.3 Ongoing Debate

As discussed above, the normative nature of law is central to Kelsen's approach to law. His theory can be seen as responding to the fact that law is, at its essence, a system made up of norms, and this is why his theory differs sharply from empirical theories of law.[7] And, as also already noted, Kelsen's approach assumes or is grounded on the view that there is a sharp division between "is" and "ought" statements, in particular, that no conclusion about what one ought to do can be derived from statements regarding what is the case.

[4] *See, eg*, (Kelsen 1992), (Paulson 1992a), (2012), (2013a).

[5] *See, eg*, (Harris 1977), (1986), (1996); see also (Paulson 2006).

[6] *See, eg*, (Raz 1976), (1980: 93–120), (1986). Raz's reading of Kelsen is challenged in (Paulson 2012).

[7] *See, eg*, (Kelsen 2013: 217).

That division between "is" and "ought" creates certain implications for normative systems like law (and morality and religion). Whenever one asserts a normative claim that something ought to be done, that claim can only be justified by some more basic or more general normative premise. Thus, specific normative claims lead to, or require, or presuppose, ever more general or ever more basic norms, step by step through a hierarchy[8] until one reaches a foundational normative premise.

This structure can be exemplified in a variety of normative systems. For example, the rules in a religious system will be grounded ultimately in the norm, "do whatever the creator God tells you to do"; one's secular ethical standards may be grounded ultimately on either the Kantian norm, "so act that the maxim of your will can be a universal law," or the Utilitarian norm, "maximize the greatest good of the greatest number"; and legal norms may be grounded ultimately on the norm, "act according to what has been authorized by the historically first constitution." Kelsen called this foundational norm for legal normative systems "the Basic Norm" ("*Grundnorm*").[9]

Once one views normative systems as hierarchical structures that are grounded ultimately on a foundational norm that (by definition—as a foundational norm) is not subject to any further (direct) proof, the implications are potentially significant, and potentially skeptical. If the important normative systems of one's life, like morality, religion, and law, are perhaps grounded on an ultimate norm that cannot be proven, and can be accepted or rejected with seemingly equal legitimacy, then those important guideposts of our life suddenly seem less sturdy. However, these implications must be left to others to discuss, or for other occasions.[10]

In Kelsen's "science" of (legal) norms,[11] every "ought" claim implies the (presupposition of the) foundational norm of that normative system—the Basic Norm.

[8] This is the *Stufenbaulehre* that Kelsen adopted from Adolf Julius Merkl. *See* (Kelsen 1992: § 28, at 57), (Jakab 2007), (Paulson 2013b).

[9] There is a common confusion in understanding both Kelsen's "Basic Norm" and H. L. A. Hart's analogous concept, the "rule of recognition" (Hart 2012: 94–95, 100–110). While there is an understandable temptation to equate these fundamental norms with foundational texts of a legal system (like the United States Constitution), this equation is at best imprecise. First, as Kelsen points out, the current foundational text may have been created under the authority of a prior foundational text of the same legal system, so the Basic Norm should refer to the historically first foundational text. Second, there remain questions of how to interpret the provisions of the foundational text, and to determine what priority it has in that legal system in relation to other national and international legal norms. Third, at least with the case of Kelsen's Basic Norm, the norm is an instruction to act in accordance with a particular legal text, a prescription that is in principle separate from the legal text itself.

[10] There are, of course, numerous responses in the philosophical and jurisprudential literature to this potential skeptical challenge.

[11] Kelsen refers more commonly to "the science of law" (or "legal science")—"*Rechtswissenschaft*." The reference to "science" in Kelsen's work, and in German generally, means objective academic inquiry, without necessarily implying all the extra baggage that the term "science" carries in English (such that one might comfortably refer to literary theory in German as a "science," while it would be an unlikely, and certainly controversial, description in English) (Paulson 1992b: 127–129).

And a comparable analysis applies to other normative systems. Every normative system is (thus) self-contained and logically independent of every other normative system. The normative system that is law, with its foundational norm, is necessarily separate from the normative system of a particular religion or a particular (conventional or theological) moral system. This analytical claim in no way contradicts or forecloses the observation that lawmakers are often influenced by the content of other normative system—*eg*, morality and religion.

Kelsen regularly elaborates that the presupposition of the Basic Norm is required to make "possible the interpretation of the subjective sense of [certain material facts] as their objective sense, that is, as objectively valid norms…" (Kelsen 1960a: §34(d), quoted in translation in Paulson 2013a: 50).[12] At the same time, he makes it clear that one need not presuppose the Basic Norm.[13] In particular, Kelsen notes that anarchists need not, and would not, perceive the actions of legal officials as anything other than "naked power" (Kelsen 1992: §16, at 36),[14] with the legal system being for them nothing more than an exercise in brute force, like a gangster's order.[15] He clarifies:

> The fact that the basic norm of a positive legal order *may* but *need not* be presupposed means: the relevant inter human relationships may be, but need not be, interpreted as 'normative,' that is, as obligations, authorizations, rights, etc. constituted by objectively valid norms. It means further: they can be interpreted without such presupposition (i.e., without the basic norm) as power relations…(Kelsen 1967: 218).

The same point can be seen in Kelsen's discussions of the "objective" and "subjective" meanings of lawmaking acts: "For the pure theory strongly emphasises that the statement that the subjective meaning of the law-creating act is also its objective meaning—the statement, that is, that law has objective validity—is only a *possible* interpretation of that act, not a necessary one" (Kelsen 2013: 218–219 (emphasis added)).[16] And in the systematic aspect of legal interpretation: "The Pure Theory aims simply to raise to the level of consciousness what all jurists are doing (for the

---

[12] See also (Kelsen 1949: 116–117): "The basic norm is the answer to the question: how—and that means under what condition—are all these juristic statements concerning legal norms, legal duties, and so on, possible?"

[13] I recognize that there may be other passages in Kelsen's text that support a different reading. For a good overview of the different tenable readings of Kelsen's writings on the Basic Norm, see (Paulson 2012).

[14] In a later edition of the same text, he clarifies that an anarchist who was also a law professor "could describe positive law as a system of valid norms, without having to approve of this law" (Kelsen 1967: 218 n. 82). This idea corresponds with Joseph Raz's idea of a detached normative statement, or statements from a legal point of view (Raz 2009: 156–157), and is fully consistent with the analysis offered in this article.

[15] Kelesen writes:

> The problem that leads to the theory of the basic norm…is how to distinguish a legal command which is considered to be objectively valid, such as the command of a revenue officer to pay a certain sum of money, from a command which has the same subjective meaning but is not considered to be objectively valid, such as the command of a gangster (Kelsen 1965: 1144).

[16] Later in the same passage, Kelsen adds, helpfully: "The concept of normative validity is, rather, an interpretation; it is an interpretation made possible only by the presupposition of a basic norm,"

most part unwittingly) when, in conceptualizing their object of enquiry, they… understand the positive law as a valid system, that is, as a norm, and not merely as factual contingencies of motivation" (Kelsen 1992: § 29, at 58).[17]

Kelsen emphasizes that in legal cognition one starts with the *facts* of actions by officials and interprets or understands those facts in a normative way (or, to change the metaphor, projects onto those facts a normative understanding). He speaks about those who perceive official actions as norms, in some places noting, in other places simply implying, that one can also choose *not* to perceive such actions in a normative way. In H. L. A. Hart's terms, it is the difference between an "internal" and "external" view of the actions of officials, and also the difference between "accepting" and not "accepting" the legal system (Hart 2012: 87–91; *see also* Morawetz 1999).[18] Also, one can understand that a legal institution *purports* to create reasons for actions (for oneself and for other citizens), even if one does oneself not accept the system, and thus does not perceive it normatively.

The perception or interpretation of empirical events in a normative way is not confined to law. When we believe that something is required as a matter of etiquette or religion, we are doing something similar. Equally important, though: many individuals look at the same world and perceive *nothing* normative: etiquette systems may seem like the trivial rules of a pointless game; religious norms may seem like the superstitions of the ignorant and the self-deluded; and legal rules may seem like just one more way by which the powerful control and oppress the less powerful. And, of course, some individuals may perceive in a normative way in some of these areas but not in others (Whether one speaks of perception or interpretation in a normative way, or "acceptance" of the normative system, I think it comes to the same thing).

One can, of course, describe a system as normative (or "as if it were" normative) without perceiving it that way oneself. Here it is useful to refer to Joseph Raz's idea of "detached normative statements." Raz's basic idea is that one can speak of what a normative rule or system requires, without necessarily endorsing or accepting that rule or system (Raz 1990: 170–177). Thus, someone who is not a vegetarian can say to a vegetarian friend, "you should not eat that (because it has meat in its ingredients)," and a non-believer can say to an Orthodox Jewish friend, "you should not accept that speaking engagement (because it would require you to work on your Sabbath)." Analogously, the radical lawyer or anarchist scholar can make claims about what one ought to do if one accepted the legal system (viewed the actions of

and that such an interpretation is well-grounded "*if* one presupposes the…basic norm." (Kelsen 2013: 219 (emphasis in original)).

[17]The omitted text states: "[they] reject natural law as the basis of validity of positive law…." (Kelsen 1992: §29, at 58). And once more: "This presupposition [of the Basic Norm] is possible but not necessary….Thus the Pure Theory of Law, by ascertaining the basic norm as the logical condition under which a coercive order may be interpreted as valid positive law, furnishes only a conditional, not a categorical, foundation of the validity of positive law" (Kelsen 1960b: 276).

[18]For Hart, "accepting" is accepting the legal system as giving reasons for action. As Michael Steven Green pointed out to me, it is probably too strong to see the normative reading of official action within Kelsen as similarly involving any view that the law gives reasons for action.

legal officials in a normative way), even if that lawyer or scholar saw the actions of legal officials only in a non-normative way, as mere acts of power.[19]

As Kelsen sometimes states, and at other times implies, that seeing the actions of officials as (legally) normative is a matter of choice, it may be useful to look at other writers who have written similarly about the normativity of law. In a recent work, John Gardner has observed that law is voluntary in a way that morality is not. Gardner argued that morality's claim upon all of us, as human beings, is "inescapable" (Gardner 2012: 150).[20] According to Gardner, one cannot reasonably ask whether one should follow the dictates of morality.[21] But one *can* reasonably ask that question of law (Gardner 2012: 160–176).[22] However, it may be that the reference to "inescapability" is too vague to be useful here. One might argue that the sanctions pervasively and importantly present in all (or almost all) legal systems (past and present)[23] make law, in a sense, "inescapable."[24] One might choose not to perceive the actions of legal officials as creating valid norms, but law (at least in systems that are generally efficacious) is not something that a practically reasonable person could ignore, the way that she could ignore (say) fashion, etiquette, or chess. Still, while one may be unable to "escape" or ignore the coercive power of the State, one *can* choose not to think of the State's actions in a normative way.

Under the reading offered here, I do not think that Kelsen would declare morality to be "inescapable," for morality (or one's moral system) would be, under this analysis, just one more normative system that one could choose or not choose, internalize or not internalize, assert or not assert. And that conforms, in a way, with a modern view of morality; around us there are a wide variety of (secular and religion-based) moral systems being advocated, practiced, or assumed—with, for example, a broad range of variations on consequentialism, deontological ethics, and virtue ethics (and mix-and-match combinations of the three), just among the secular approaches to morality, even without noting the approaches to morality that are more theologically based. People choose one among the alternatives, and may later change to another (and then another, etc.).

---

[19] When one says that one can *choose* to view the (legal) actions of officials normatively or not, it is important to note that this does not mean that this "choice" is always or necessarily a *conscious* choice. The reference to "choice" indicates primarily that there is an option; one could do (or think) otherwise.

[20] Foot also refers to morality's purported "inescapability" in the course of her discussion questioning the view of morality as a categorical imperative (as opposed to hypothetical imperative) (Foot 1978: 160–164); cf. (Raz 1999: 94–105), on whether reasons are optional.

[21] Gardner here reflects the conventional position, though, of course, thinkers ranging from Philippa Foot to Friedrich Nietzsche have raised exactly the question Gardner's quotation implies cannot or should not be raised: whether one should follow the dictates of morality. See (Foot 1978: 157–173) (on whether morality is merely a "hypothetical imperative"), (Foot 1978: 181–188) (questioning whether moral considerations are "overriding"), (Nietzsche 1998).

[22] Robert Alexy points out similarly that "[o]ne can of course refuse … to participate in the (utterly real) game of law." (Alexy 2002: 109).

[23] Cf. (Schauer 2010).

[24] I am indebted to Frederick Schauer for this suggestion.

Some have tried to explain this approach to normative systems in general, or to law in particular, by exploring the analogy of games. One might say to a person playing chess that she ought not (*eg*) to move the bishop a certain way. However, that person could easily have decided simply not to play chess, in which case prescriptions about how she ought to move the bishop would have no application.[25] The statement of what one ought to do only makes sense once one has taken up the practice.

However, the game analogy is at best imperfect, and it is important to focus on the ways in which it and other proffered analogies differ from law. If someone said that she was not playing chess and did not want to play in the future, it would be clear that "chess rules" and "chess reasons" would not apply to her. By contrast, consider etiquette: someone might reasonably insist that its rules and reasons apply even to those people who insist that they do not "accept" or "participate in" etiquette (Foot 1978: 160). As for religion, our ideas about voluntariness of affiliation have changed significantly over time. On one hand, in many societies today, including most so-called "Western" countries, the normative rules of a particular religion are not thought to be binding on those who are not (self-identified) members of that religious group. However, the way we think about religion today is far different from the way people thought about it in the past. As Jacques Barzun pointed out, "in earlier times people rarely thought of themselves as 'having' or 'belonging to' a religion. … Everybody 'had' a soul, but did not 'have a God,' for God and all that pertained to Him was simply *what is*, just as today nobody has 'a physics'; there is only one and it is automatically taken to be the transcript of reality." (Barzun 2000: 24). And similarly, true believers even today (especially in countries in which fundamentalist views have significant social and political influence) perceive the dictates of their religion not as something chosen, but as "the Truth," binding on all.

Chess, etiquette, and religion are (or contain) normative systems, and thus are like law in some ways, but law remains distinct. If one views legal rules and official actions as things that people may or may not view in a normative way, this understandably affects how one views Kelsen's Basic Norm—the role it plays and how it is justified. As Paulson and others have pointed out, it is common now to view Kelsen's argument for the Basic Norm as a neo-Kantian version of the Kantian transcendental deduction (Paulson 1992a). A transcendental argument (to simplify) goes from an (allegedly) undeniable starting point, and determines what must be true, lest that starting point be false, or, at any rate, unsupported. Kant's transcendental deduction (again, to simplify) went from the unity of our experience to the conclusion that certain categories of thought (eg, time, space, substance, and causation) are projected by us onto sense data.[26] For Kelsen, the relevant transcendental deduction is something along the following lines: since law is (experienced as) normative, the Basic Norm must be presupposed. The difficulty, as Paulson has pointed

[25] Cf. (Marmor 2007: 153–181), comparing law and chess.

[26] See (Kant 1998). The particular way of phrasing the matter in the text above (eg, the reference to "sense data") is likely *not* a way most Kantians would choose, but it should suffice for the rough summary needed here.

out (Paulson 2012, 2013a), is that transcendental arguments depend on there being *only one* available explanation for the matter being examined (in Kant's case, the unity of experience; in Kelsen's case, the normativity of law), and, arguably, Kelsen did not come close to proving that his approach was the only available explanation. Paulson argued, correctly in my opinion, that Kelsen's analysis was far too quick to dismiss natural law approaches and was not convincing in its effort to show that there was no possible explanations beyond the limited number of alternatives he considered (Paulson 2012, 2013a).

However, the approach discussed in this work does not require the full machinery of a (neo-)Kantian transcendental deduction: it needs only the basic and generally accepted Humean division of "is" and "ought," combined with a comparably conventional idea that law is a normative system (with the emphasis both on "normative" and on "system"). Where one asserts the validity of any lower-level norm in a legal system,[27] one implicitly asserts or presupposes the validity of the foundational norm of the system.

In an earlier work, Paulson expressed concerns about the sort of reading of Kelsen's work I am offering here (Paulson 2012). His primary worry was that this reading leaves the basic norm in particular, and Kelsen's pure theory of law in general, doing little work, and not the important task that Kelsen seemed to set for himself.[28] Kelsen seems to offer the Basic Norm (and its presupposition) as the key to explaining the objective meaning of norms generally, not just for those who happen to choose to interpret official actions in a normative way. However, I disagree that my proposed reading of Kelsen leaves Kelsen's theory unimportant, and the reading has the distinct benefit of being more defensible than more ambitious readings of Kelsen's aims.[29] Kelsen's pure theory, as I read it, is offering important insights about *the logic of norms*, about what follows from the fact that someone perceives the actions of officials normatively, and it offers related insights regarding the connections (or lack thereof) between law and morality, and regarding whether (or not) one has an obligation to accept or presuppose the Basic Norm of one's legal system.

2.4 Conclusion

The ignorance and avoidance of Hans Kelsen's approach to law is likely attributable to the usual suspects: foreign-language texts badly served by translators, and a style of writing and thinking too different from the empirical and pragmatic approach that

[27] A comparable point could be made, as earlier mentioned, for a moral or theological normative system, or any other kind of normative system.

[28] My reading of Kelsen is very close to J. W. Harris in (Harris 1996), though Harris—like Paulson—expressed concern that this Kelsenian view of legal normativity might leave the theory with limited practical significance.

[29] As Paulson shows, indirectly, by his sharp critique of other readings (Paulson 2012).

dominates Anglo-American thinking (and not just *legal* thinking). Add to this the fact that Kelsen is a writer from a century ago, rather than being the "new, new thing"—he is at a sharp competitive disadvantage to the fashionable theorists, and legal theorists, of today.

Of course, that relatively few understand, or try to understand Kelsen, does not mean that his works are not worth studying. Kelsen's writings wrestle with central problems about the nature of law that remain equally important and unsolved today, including the nature of legal normativity. In the second part of this work, I suggested a minimalist reading of Kelsen's view of legal normativity—one that is concededly controversial, both on exegetical grounds (though it has substantial textual support) and on its own merits, but one that I assert is both faithful to Kelsen's argument and defensible on its terms.

Acknowledgement I am grateful for the comments and suggestions of participants of the Valparaiso University Law School Conference, *Hans Kelsen in America*. Portions of the second part of this paper were developed from ideas presented in "Rules and Normativity in Law," in *Problems of Normativity, Rules and Rule Following* (Bix 2015).

References

Adams, David M. 2013. *Philosophical problems in the law*, 5th ed. Independence, KY: Cengage Wadsworth.

Alexy, Robert. 2002. *The Argument from Injustice*. Trans. B.L. Paulson and S.L. Paulson. Oxford: Oxford University Press.

Arthur, John, and William H. Shaw. 2010. *Readings in the philosophy of law*, 5th ed. Upper Saddle River, NJ: Prentice Hall.

Barzun, Jacques. 2000. *From dawn to decadence: 500 years of western cultural life, 1500 to the present*. New York: HarperCollins.

Bix, Brian H. 2015. Rules and normativity in law. In *Problems of normativity, rules and rule following*, ed. Tomasz Gizbert-Studnicki, Krzysztof Płeszka, Michał Arszkiewicz, and Paweł Banas, 125–146. Dordrecht: Springer.

Coleman, Jules. 2001. *The practice of principle*. Oxford: Oxford University Press.

Coleman, Jules, and Scott Shapiro (eds.). 2002. *The Oxford handbook of jurisprudence & philosophy of law*. Oxford: Oxford University Press.

Feinberg, Joel, Jules Coleman, and Christopher Kutz. 2014. *Philosophy of law*, 9th ed. Independence, KY: Cengage Wadsworth.

Finnis, John. 2002. Natural law: The classical tradition. In *The Oxford handbook of jurisprudence & philosophy of law*, ed. Jules Coleman and Scott Shapiro, 1–60. Oxford: Oxford University Press.

Foot, Philippa. 1978. *Virtues and vices*. Oxford: Basil Blackwell.

Gardner, John. 2012. *Law as a leap of faith*. Oxford: Oxford University Press.

Green, Leslie. 2003. Legal positivism. In *Stanford encyclopedia of philosophy*, ed. E.N. Zalta. http://plato.stanford.edu/entries/legal-positivism/. Accessed 24 Nov 2014.

Harris, J.W. 1977. Kelsen's concept of authority. *Cambridge Law Journal* 36: 353–363.

Harris, J.W. 1986. Kelsen and normative consistency. In *Essays on Kelsen*, ed. R. Tur and W. Twining, 201–228. Oxford: Clarendon.

Harris, J.W. 1996. Kelsen's pallid normativity. *Ratio Juris* 9: 94–117.

Hart, H.L.A. 2012. *The concept of law*, 3rd ed. Oxford: Oxford University Press.
Himma, Kenneth Einar. 2002. Inclusive legal positivism. In *The Oxford handbook of jurisprudence & philosophy of law*, ed. Jules Coleman and Scott Shapiro, 125–165. Oxford: Oxford University Press.
Hume, David. 1978. *A treatise of human nature*. Oxford: Clarendon.
Jakab, András. 2007. Problems of the *stufenbaulehre*: Kelsen's failure to derive the validity of a norm from another norm. *Canadian Journal of Law and Jurisprudence* 20: 35–67.
Kant, Immanuel. 1998. In *Critique of pure reason*, ed. P. Guyer and A. Woods. Cambridge: Cambridge University Press.
Kelsen, Hans. 1949. *General theory of law & state*. Cambridge, MA.: Harvard University Press. (Transaction Publisher Reprint, 2006).
Kelsen, Hans. 1960a. *Reine rechtslehre*, 2nd ed. Vienna: Deuticke.
Kelsen, Hans. 1960b. What is the pure theory of law? *Tulane Law Review* 34: 269–276.
Kelsen, Hans. 1965. Professor Stone and the pure theory of law. *Stanford Law Review* 17: 1128–1157.
Kelsen, Hans. 1967. *Pure Theory of Law*. Trans. M. Knight. Berkeley: University of California Press.
Kelsen, Hans. 1992. *Introduction to the Problems of Legal Theory*. Trans. B.L. Paulson and S.L. Paulson. Oxford: Clarendon Press.
Kelsen, Hans. 2013. A 'realistic' theory of law and the pure theory of law: Remarks on Alf Ross's on law and justice. In *Kelsen revisited: New essays on the pure theory of law*, ed. Luís Duarte d'Almeida, John Gardner, and Leslie Green, 195–221. Oxford: Hart Publishing.
Marmor, Andrei. 2002. Exclusive legal positivism. In *The Oxford handbook of jurisprudence & philosophy of law*, ed. Jules Coleman and Scott Shapiro, 104–124. Oxford: Oxford University Press.
Marmor, Andrei. 2007. *Law in the age of pluralism*. Oxford: Oxford University Press.
Marmor, Andrei. 2011. The conventional foundations of law. In *New essays on the normativity of law*, ed. Stefano Bertea and George Pavlakos, 143–157. Oxford: Hart Publishing.
Morawetz, Thomas. 1999. Law as experience: Theory and the internal aspect of law. *SMU Law Review* 52: 27–66.
Murphy, Jeffrie G., and Jules L. Coleman. 1990. *Philosophy of law*, rev. ed. Boulder, Colorado: Westview Press.
Nietzsche, Friedrich. 1998. *On the Genealogy of Morality*. Trans. M. Clark and A.J. Swensen. Indianapolis: Hackett Publishing.
Paulson, Stanley L. 1992a. The neo-Kantian dimension of Kelsen's pure theory of law. *Oxford Journal of Legal Studies* 12: 311–332.
Paulson, Stanley L. 1992b. Supplementary notes. In *Introduction to the problems of legal theory*, ed. Hans Kelsen, Bonnie Litschewski Paulson, and Stanley L. Paulson, 127–137. Oxford: Clarendon.
Paulson, Stanley L. 2006. J. W. Harris's Kelsen. In *Properties of law: Essays in honour of Jim Harris*, ed. Timothy Endicott, Joshua Getzler, and Edwin Peel, 3–21. Oxford: Oxford University Press.
Paulson, Stanley L. 2012. A 'justified normativity' thesis in Hans Kelsen's pure theory of law?: Rejoinders to Robert Alexy and Joseph Raz. In *Institutionalized reason: The jurisprudence of Robert Alexy*, ed. Matthias Klatt, 61–111. Oxford: Oxford University Press.
Paulson, Stanley L. 2013a. A great puzzle: Kelsen's basic norm. In *Kelsen revisited: New essays on the pure theory of law*, ed. Luís Duarte d'Almeida, John Gardner, and Leslie Green, 43–61. Oxford: Hart Publishing.
Paulson, Stanley L. 2013b. How Merkl's *stufenbaulehre* informs Kelsen's concept of law. *Revus* 21: 29–45.

Priel, Dan. 2013. Is there one right answer to the question of the nature of law? In *Philosophical foundations of the nature of law*, ed. Wil Waluchow and Stefan Sciaraffa, 322–340. Oxford: Oxford University Press.

Raz, Joseph. 1976. Kelsen's general theory of norms. *Philosophia* 6: 495–504.

Raz, Joseph. 1980. *The concept of a legal system*, 2nd ed. Oxford: Clarendon.

Raz, Joseph. 1986. The purity of the pure theory. In *Essays on Kelsen*, ed. Richard Tur and William Twining, 80–97. Oxford: Clarendon.

Raz, Joseph. 1990. *Practical reason and norms*. Princeton: Princeton University Press.

Raz, Joseph. 1999. *Engaging reason: On the theory of value and action*. Oxford: Oxford University Press.

Raz, Joseph. 2009. *The authority of law*, 2nd ed. Oxford: Oxford University Press.

Schauer, Frederick. 2010. Was Austin right after all?: On the role of sanctions in a theory of law. *Ratio Juris* 23: 1–21.

Shapiro, Scott J. 2011. *Legality*. Cambridge, Mass: Harvard University Press.

Chapter 3
Marmor's Kelsen

Michael S. Green

3.1 Introduction

Kelsen is usually ignored by philosophers of law in the United States (and Anglophone countries generally). But that doesn't mean they are unaware of his existence, the way they are unaware of, say, Fritz Sander's or Alfred Verdross's.[1] They've heard of Kelsen. What is more, they can usually say something about his philosophical views. Kelsen offered, or purported to offer, a *pure* theory of law, that is, a theory in which the law is independent of morality and of social facts.

Given that distinctive voices in the philosophy of law are rare and Kelsen's is unquestionably a distinctive voice, why does he receive so little attention in this country? I think there are two reasons. The first is that American philosophers of law cannot see how a pure theory of law can possibly succeed. The notion that law is independent of social facts is a non-starter. From my own experience, this is the reason that philosophers of law with only a passing familiarity with Kelsen do not give him a more careful look.[2]

The second reason applies to those who have given Kelsen's writings more scrutiny. They conclude that he fails to offer a pure theory of law after all. As they see it, Kelsen believed that the existence and content of the law fundamentally depend upon a legal system's being *efficacious*, in the sense that members of a community

[1] Alfred Verdross was another member, with Kelsen, of the "Vienna School" of legal theory. Fritz Sander, a former student of Kelsen's, became one his most prominent critics.

[2] And to the extent that Kelsen offered insights that can be appreciated without accepting a pure theory of law, they assume that the same insights can be found, more clearly presented, in H.L.A. Hart's writings (Murphy and Coleman 1990: 27).

M.S. Green (✉)
Dudley W. Woodbridge Professor of Law, College of William and Mary,
8795, Williamsburg, VA 23187, USA
e-mail: msgre2@wm.edu

D.A.J. Telman (ed.), *Hans Kelsen in America - Selective Affinities and the Mysteries of Academic Influence*, Law and Philosophy Library 116,
DOI 10.1007/978-3-319-33130-0_3

by and large employ and abide by the system's norms. And that means that law depends upon social facts. There would be no legal system in the absence of an actual human community that makes the system efficacious. Why bother spending time on someone who, while purporting to offer a pure theory of law, unwittingly offered an impure theory?

I begin by describing a genuinely pure theory of law and why it appears so implausible to philosophers of law in this country. Next I offer Andrei Marmor's reading of Kelsen in the first chapter of his book, *Philosophy of Law* (Marmor 2011), as a good example of the second reading of Kelsen, in which he fails to offer a pure theory. I then argue that Marmor misinterprets Kelsen in three ways, each of which makes him look as if he thought the law fundamentally depends upon social facts. Kelsen's theory of law, I conclude, really is pure. But with that conclusion, we return to the first response to Kelsen. What his theory of law gains in consistency it loses in plausibility. As a first step in responding to these doubts, I end by briefly offering evidence in favor of a pure theory of law. There are some legal judgments, I argue, that cannot be made sense of unless the law is independent of all social facts.

3.2 A Pure Theory of Law

American philosophers of law believe that the existence and content of the law fundamentally depend upon social facts about a community. This dependence is something about which both sides of the most prominent debate in the philosophy of law in the United States agree. On one side there are *positivists*, who believe that the existence and content of the law are ultimately determined *solely* by social facts about a community.[3] On the other side there are those, whom we can call *natural lawyers*, who believe that the existence and content of the law are ultimately determined by a combination of social facts about a community *and* evaluative facts (Greenberg 2004: 157–58). For a positivist, if evaluative facts somehow disappeared (say God extinguished them), law could still exist.[4] For a natural lawyer, law would disappear with the evaluative facts. But both positivists and natural lawyers agree that law is fundamentally constituted by social facts about a community to some extent. If human beings disappeared, there would be no law.

By contrast, under a pure theory law would exist even if there were no human beings. An analogy with morality is helpful here. Some philosophers hold a pure

[3] I describe positivists as believing that law is *ultimately* determined solely by social facts, because inclusive legal positivists concede that social facts can make evaluative facts relevant to law's existence and content. For exclusive legal positivists, by contrast, law always depends solely on social facts.

[4] For an inclusive legal positivist, if evaluative facts disappeared, law that depends upon such facts could not exist (or its existence would be indeterminate). But there *could* still be law, for it is not necessary that law depends upon evaluative facts.

theory of morality, in the sense that morality is independent of human beings' beliefs and attitudes.[5] This position is supported in part by our judgments that murder is morally impermissible no matter what our views about murder happen to be.[6] Murder would be morally impermissible even if we thought it was morally permissible, or obligatory. In making such judgments, we are arguably committed to murder's being morally impermissible independent of human beings. Murder would be morally impermissible even if human beings had never existed.

Of course, under a pure theory of law, law is independent of morality too. But, like a pure theorist of morality, a pure theorist of law insists that law would exist in the absence of human beings. And that is not an idea that American philosophers of law think has any chance of success.

Notice that one cannot argue against a pure theory of law simply by pointing to social facts (such as people in a legislative chamber raising their hands) that make a difference to legal facts. The pure theorist can accept that social facts trigger legal norms, by satisfying conditions for the norms' applicability. If there is a legal norm of the form *If social fact X obtains then one legally ought to Y*, the existence of social fact X will make a difference to legal facts. Without X, it would not be a legal fact that one ought to Y. But, the pure theorist can argue, that does not mean that the legal norm that was triggered *itself* depends upon social facts.

Here too an analogy with morality is appropriate. Having promised to take you to the zoo, I arguably have a moral obligation (if only a *pro tanto* obligation) to take you to the zoo—an obligation that I would not have had in the absence of my promise. Recognizing that social facts are relevant to moral facts in this way is compatible with insisting that the fundamental moral norms in the light of which social facts are morally relevant do not themselves depend upon social facts. The social fact that I promised to take you to the zoo made a difference to moral facts because of a moral obligation to keep one's promises—an obligation that existed before there were human beings.

But my guess is that philosophers of law in this country wouldn't think that the distinction between social facts *triggering* and their *constituting* legal norms makes a pure theory of law any more plausible. It is true that we should dissociate the social fact that people in a legislative chamber raised their hands from the law they enacted. The legislators' raising their hands was a social fact that triggered a law, namely a constitutional provision authorizing the legislators to pass statutes. But as one goes back in the history of a legal system, at some point social facts must be understood as constituting laws, for there will be no preexisting law in place to be triggered.

---

[5] An example here is the "robust realist" and non-naturalist David Enoch, who believes that "there is no metaphysically possible world where the basic norms [of morality] are different." (Enoch 2011: 146). It follows that the basic norms of morality were in place when dinosaurs roamed the earth.

[6] An example is Enoch's argument that robust realism about morality is supported by our willingness to "stand our ground" in cases of moral conflict, that is, to not arrive at an "impartial" resolution that seeks to accommodate the disputants' actual preferences (Enoch 2011: 23–24).

Assume, for example, that the validity of the United States Constitution is justified on the basis of Article VII, which was created by the Constitutional Convention and which authorized nine of the thirteen original states, by ratifying the Constitution, to make it law for the ratifying states.[7] One cannot justify Article VII's status as law by other enacted laws. No enacted law authorized the Constitutional Convention to create a new method of constitutional ratification. Indeed, Article VII was contrary to the amendment procedures in the preceding Articles of Confederation, which required consent by the Congress of the Confederation and the legislatures of all the states (Ackerman and Katyal 1995). In that sense, Article VII was revolutionary.

If the Convention's actions triggered preexisting law, there would have to be some unenacted law authorizing the Convention to create a new method for ratifying a constitution. And, to retain a pure theory, this authorizing law would have to be independent of all social facts. It would have to be no less existent when dinosaurs roamed the earth than it was in 1787. Just as it was a moral fact in the Jurassic Era that promises ought to be kept, so it would have to be a legal fact in the Jurassic Era that the Constitutional Convention had the power to create a method of constitutional ratification.[8]

But to American philosophers of law, that sounds crazy. It is much more plausible to understand the validity of Article VII as constituted by or dependent on social facts about American legal practices. For example, one can understand Article VII to be valid law because it is actually used by American officials for assessing the validity of the United States Constitution. Rather than concluding that a law authorizing the Constitutional Convention existed in the Jurassic Era, we can understand the entire American legal system as coming into being only in the late eighteenth century.

Another problem with a pure theory of law is the existence of multiple legal systems. Many legal systems (American, French, Uzbek) currently exist. Many legal systems (Soviet, Prussian, Ancient Roman) have existed in the past. And many legal systems will undoubtedly come into being in the future. This plurality of legal systems suggests that the law of each system must be constituted by social facts about a community. Ancient Roman law must depend upon social facts about the Ancient Romans, because if there had been no Ancient Romans, there would have been no Ancient Roman law.

The pure theorist of law must insist that the multiplicity of independent legal systems is somehow illusory. He need not deny, of course, that there is a *sociological* concept of a legal system (call it a *legal system*$_{soc}$) under which a legal system is reducible to a particular community's beliefs and attitudes. When one employs that

[7] This would mean treating Article VII as, in some sense, independent of the rest of the Constitution. It preceded the Constitution by providing the method for its enactment.

[8] Granted, the positivist can accept that it was a *conceptual truth* even in the Jurassic Era that if the social facts that constitute the American legal system are in place, Article VII will be law. But he would deny that any legal facts existed in the Jurassic Era, in particular, that anyone was legally authorized to create Article VII. For the positivist, the existence of a legal authorization would require an actual human community.

concept, there are as many legal system$_{soc}$s as there are relevant communities. Nevertheless, he will argue, when one speaks about what *is* valid law, as opposed to what people in a community think is valid law, one is committed to a timeless unitary legal system.

Again an analogy with morality is appropriate here. The pure theorist of morality can admit that there is a sociological concept of a moral system (a *moral system$_{soc}$*) under which a moral system$_{soc}$ is reducible to a particular community's beliefs and attitudes. A plurality of moral system$_{soc}$s exists. As one makes one's way around the world or considers the course of history, one encounters different moral system$_{soc}$s. There is, for example, the moral system$_{soc}$ of pre-modern Japan, in which ritual suicide is condoned, and the moral system$_{soc}$ of contemporary Christians, in which it is not. Nevertheless, a pure theorist of morality will argue that when one thinks about what morality actually requires—rather than what various communities *think* it requires—one conceives of the fundamental moral norms as unchanging and independent of social facts.

But if there is only one timeless legal system, how can one make sense of the fact that had France never existed, not only would no one *think* that French law applies to Frenchmen in France, there would have been no French law that *actually* applies to them? Valid French law depends upon the existence of the French legal system$_{soc}$. Here too the pure theorist will have to claim that social facts have triggered preexisting legal norms. The existence of the French legal system$_{soc}$ is relevant to legal facts about Frenchmen in France only in the light of timeless legal norms that make it relevant.

Once more, an analogy with morality is helpful. To say that a unitary and unchanging moral system exists independently of any moral system$_{soc}$, does not mean that the existence of a moral system$_{soc}$ cannot be relevant to moral facts. For example, there might be moral principles of *tolerance*, according to which one must respect the moral system$_{soc}$ of the person affected by one's actions. But the pure theorist of morality will insist that these principles of tolerance are themselves binding independently of any moral system$_{soc}$. The relativity of moral obligation to a moral system$_{soc}$ is not itself relative to a moral system$_{soc}$.

The pure theorist of law can argue, analogously, that the existence of a legal system$_{soc}$ is relevant to legal facts only in the light of legal norms that make it relevant—legal norms that are independent of any legal system$_{soc}$. The existence of the French, American, or Ancient Roman legal system$_{soc}$ simply triggers the timeless legal norms of a unitary legal system.

The pure theorist's strategy is, in essence, the following: For each social fact that makes a difference to legal facts, the pure theorist will explain the social fact's relevance in terms of its triggering legal norms that do not depend upon social facts (von Bernstorff 2010: 91–92). Notice that, by using this strategy, the pure theorist can accept that legal facts *supervene* upon social facts, in the sense that possible worlds cannot differ from one another with respect to their legal facts without also differing with respect to social facts. The pure theorist can explain such supervenience by arguing that any difference in legal facts between possible worlds must be the result of the way that different social facts in those worlds triggered fundamental legal norms—norms that cannot themselves differ between possible worlds.[9]

But to Americans, the notion that there are eternal legal norms waiting to be triggered by the existence of human communities is absurd. That is why I do not think it is fair to chalk up the prevailing attitude toward Kelsen among American philosophers of law to ignorance about his views. Americans have come to the philosophical conclusion that his theory is a non-starter.

To a large extent, Kelsen himself is to blame here, for in his major writings he fails to focus sufficiently on why the law is independent of social facts. Pure theorists of morality take great pains to emphasize moral judgments that are arguably inexplicable if morality is constituted by social facts about human beings (Enoch 2011: 16–49). For example, they point to our judgment that murder would be impermissible even if every human being believed it to be permissible. This suggests that the impermissibility of murder is independent of human beings and their beliefs and attitudes.

The same strategy is pursued by natural lawyers, who emphasize judgments about the law that arguably cannot be made sense of if law is reducible solely to social facts about a community. Ronald Dworkin's preferred examples were theoretical disagreements, in which participants in a legal system consider a legal question to have a determinate answer, even though they disagree about the criteria for law upon which the answer would be based. To do justice to such disagreements, Dworkin argued, we cannot understand the law as determined solely by the social facts to which positivists seek to reduce it, in particular, agreement among participants in a jurisdiction's legal practices. We must instead understand the existence and content of the law as determined conjointly by social facts about a community's legal practices and evaluative facts (Dworkin 1986: 66, 2006: 144).

What would catch the attention of American philosophers of law is if Kelsen had devoted his major works to focusing on legal judgments that cannot be made sense of except through a pure theory of law, that is, judgments in which certain legal facts are understood as obtaining independently of all social facts. To be sure, Kelsen did, at times, attempt to identify such judgments in his writings (Kelsen 1922). But, particularly in his major works, he generally presumed that a theory of law should be pure instead of arguing for this conclusion. His main goal was to explore the consequences of a pure theory, not to convince the skeptic that the law is fundamentally independent of social facts.

I am not sure why Kelsen adopted this approach. Perhaps the general resistance to psychologism and naturalistic reductionism in Viennese philosophical circles at the time he formulated his theory made sustained arguments for the fundamental independence of law from social facts appear unnecessary. But whatever the reason, the absence of such arguments is a big problem for Americans.

[9] The pure theorist of law is analogous to a robust moral realist like Enoch, who accepts that moral facts supervene upon natural facts, but who argues that this supervenience relation follows from moral principles that do not themselves depend upon natural facts (Enoch 2011: 140–50).

3.3 Marmor's Reading of Kelsen

To repeat, I think American philosophers of law with only a passing familiarity with Kelsen are unsympathetic, not out of ignorance, but because they see no reason to adopt a theory in which law is fundamentally independent of social facts. The notion that there would be legal facts in the absence of any human beings has no resonance for them, and Kelsen's writings do not seem to address their doubts.

In this context, let us now consider Andrei Marmor's reading of Kelsen in the first chapter of his book *Philosophy of Law* (Marmor 2011).[10] Marmor's reading is promising, for he takes Kelsen's antireductionism seriously. An overarching theme of Marmor's book is that a great deal in the philosophy of law that purports to be about the proper analysis of the content of the concept of law (that is, the identification of the necessary and sufficient criteria for law wherever it might occur) really concerns reductionism, in particular, the extent to which the law can be reduced to social facts. The two questions are importantly different. Just as a reduction of consciousness to brain states, even if successful, may not be an accurate account of the concept of consciousness, so a reduction of law to social facts, even if successful, may not be an accurate account of the concept of law.

In keeping with this reductionist theme, Marmor's book begins with Kelsen, whom he rightly describes as attempting to offer an antireductionist theory of law (Marmor 2011: 12), that is, a theory in which the law is reducible neither to morality nor to social facts (Marmor 2011: 13–14). To be sure, social facts are *relevant* to law for Kelsen. As Marmor puts it, the social fact that a majority of the members of a group of people that calls itself "the California state legislature" raised their hands can make a difference to what, legally, is the case within the borders of the state (Marmor 2011: 15). But that social fact is not itself law. Rather, it has legal consequences in the light of law—in particular, the California Constitution, which authorizes the California legislature to make law. By the same token, the social facts to which one might point as constituting the ratification of the California Constitution are also not themselves law. They too have legal consequences only in the light of a higher authorizing law.

Marmor describes this law as the United States Constitution (Marmor 2011: 16). Although this is clearly wrong,[11] the important point is that either there is a positive legal norm authorizing the creators of the California Constitution or there is not. And even if there is, the chain of positive authorizations must end somewhere. Eventually one will reach a positive authorization that was created by those who were not themselves authorized by positive law. Kelsen speaks of

[10] I will also occasionally refer to his article on the pure theory of law in the *Stanford Encyclopedia of Philosophy* (Marmor 2010), which overlaps substantially with his book.

[11] The United States Constitution contains no provision authorizing the creation of state law. It presupposes state law's existence. It does contain a provision (Art. IV, § 3) for the creation of new states, but it is not clear that this should be understood as the authorization of state law. And even if it is so understood, this authorization could not apply to the law of the thirteen original states.

this final positive authorization as the "first constitution"—the ultimate positive law in the chain of legal justification.[12]

For simplicity's sake, let us assume that Article VII is this first constitution for the American legal system (including state law). Given that the creators of this first constitution were not authorized by positive law, what makes it legally valid? As Marmor puts it, Kelsen argues that anyone treating the norms of the legal system as valid *presupposes* the validity of the first constitution (Marmor 2011: 16).[13] The basic norm is the content of this presupposition. It is a nonpositive norm authorizing the creators of the first constitution to make law.

So described, Kelsen's theory of law looks pure.[14] Notice that the basic norm must be conceived of as preceding the creation of first constitution. It is in the light of this preexisting norm that the creation of the first constitution can be seen as a lawmaking act. Thus, anyone treating the first constitution as valid is presupposing law—namely the basic norm—that precedes these social facts. Indeed, because the presupposed basic norm is a nonpositive norm, it apparently precedes any social facts. It was no less existent when dinosaurs roamed the earth than it was in 1787. Just as it was the case in the Jurassic Era that promises ought to be kept (even though there was no entity at the time capable of triggering this moral norm by making a promise), it was also the case in the Jurassic Era, according to the presupposed basic norm, that the Constitutional Convention had the power to create Article VII (even though the Constitutional Convention would not exist for well over a hundred million years). There was a legal fact in existence even in the Jurassic Era, namely that *if* the Constitutional Convention created Article VII in 1787, Article VII would be valid.

Despite this apparent antireductionism, Marmor argues that Kelsen did not offer a pure theory of law after all. The reason is Kelsen's doctrine of *efficacy* (or *effectiveness*)—understood as the social fact that the norms of a legal system are "by and large applied and obeyed" (Kelsen 1960a: 210).[15] As Marmor puts it, Kelsen "quite

[12] The first constitution need not be written. Kelsen argued, for example, that the first constitution of international law is that the custom of states creates valid law. Furthermore, this constitution was itself created through custom (Kelsen 1960a: 226, 323).

[13] Marmor argues that, for Kelsen, someone treating the law as valid thereby also treats the law as providing a practical reason for action, that is, "a justified demand on practical deliberation" (Marmor 2011: 25). According to Marmor, Kelsen rejects sociological accounts of the law because of their inability to explain the reason-giving character of legal norms. Later in the chapter, Marmor argues that Kelsen should have distinguished between the question of the validity of law and its normativity (in the sense of its practical reason-giving character). In fact, it is unclear whether Kelsen believed that someone who recognizes a legal norm as valid thereby takes himself to have a reason for action in the sense relevant for practical deliberation (Paulson 2012; Delacroix 2004; Wilson 1982).

[14] Although Kelsen described his philosophy of law as positivist (Kelsen 1960a: 217), he is not a positivist in the sense that I define it, for he does not think law is ultimately reducible solely to social facts about a community.

[15] See also Kelsen 1934, 60 ("[A] normative system to which reality no longer corresponds to a certain degree will necessarily lose its validity. The validity of a legal system…depends in a certain way…on the efficacy of the system.").

explicitly admits that efficacy *is* a condition of the validity of the basic norm: A basic norm is legally valid if and only if it is actually followed in a given population" (Marmor 2011: 20).[16] The basic norm validating the first constitution is not itself valid unless there are people around actually following and applying the first constitution and the laws made pursuant to it. Thus, Marmor argues, Kelsen was ultimately forced into a sociological approach to law, in which the law is fundamentally based upon social facts about a community.

Marmor notes in passing that Kelsen "toyed with the idea that perhaps changes in the basic norms of municipal [that is, national] legal systems legally derive from the basic norm of public international law" (Marmor 2011: 23). If this is true, there would be only one basic norm from which the valid laws of all national legal systems (past, present, and future) are derived. The fact that efficacy is considered a condition for the validity of national legal systems would be compatible with a pure theory of law. The national legal systems would be understood as *sub*systems of the international legal system, which would not itself depend upon efficacy for its existence.

But Marmor quickly dismisses Kelsen's doctrine of the unity of law. First of all, he argues that Kelsen presented the doctrine with "much more hesitation" by the time he wrote the second edition of the *Pure Theory*, in 1960 (Marmor 2011: 23 n.18). This hesitation, he argues, is understandable: "[A]fter all, the idea that all municipal legal systems derive their legal validity from international law would strike most jurists and legal historians as rather fanciful and anachronistic" (Marmor 2011: 23 n.18). But more fundamentally, he argues, the doctrine of the unity of law does not make a pure theory of law any more plausible.

The reason is that "it is very difficult, if not impossible, to maintain both a profound relativist and an antireductionist position with respect to a given normative domain" (Marmor 2011: 23):

> If you hold the view that the validity of a type of norm is entirely relative to a certain vantage point—in other words, if what is involved here is only the actual conduct, beliefs/presuppositions, and attitudes of people—it becomes very difficult to detach the explanation of that normativity from the facts that constitute the relevant point of view (the facts about people's actions, beliefs, attitudes, and such) (Marmor 2011: 23).

Even if Kelsen thought all valid laws are part of a unitary legal system, he considered the laws of this system to be valid only relative to the vantage point in which a basic norm is presupposed. As a result, the validity of law is still due to social facts (namely the facts standing behind the vantage point). What is more, because Kelsen thought that the basic norm of the unitary legal system would not be presupposed unless it was efficacious, efficacy remains a condition for the validity of law.

---

[16] Marmor is not as careful as he could be in describing what efficacy is for Kelsen. The question is not merely whether those subject to the mandatory norms of the legal system generally comply with them but also whether relevant officials *apply* the norms of the system (Navarro 2013: 79 n.12). In Marmor's defense, he might understand such application as officials "following" the norms, however.

Marmor concedes that not all relativism in a particular normative domain leads to reductionism. Morality can sometimes be understood as relative in an antireductionist way: "[S]ome moral reasons for action are relative to some contingent conditions (for example, reasons to care about friendship are contingent upon our psychological makeup and social realities)" (Marmor 2011: 24). But in such cases relativity can be explained in terms of "elements of the theory that are not relative to contingent facts" (Marmor 2011: 24). As we have seen, the fact that my moral obligation to take you to the zoo is relative to my act of promising can be explained in terms of an obligation to keep one's promises that is not relative to social facts. But Kelsen, Marmor argues, is a relativist "all the way down" (Marmor 2011: 24). For this reason, he is compelled to be a reductionist. "If all the elements of a normative explanation are relative to some constitutive facts, then those facts provide you with all the explanation you need. In other words, a position that is relativist all the way down is, ipso facto, reductionist as well" (Marmor 2011: 24).

Things would be different, Marmor acknowledges, if the adoption of a basic norm were rationally inescapable. But choosing a basic norm is "not something that is dictated by Reason" (Marmor 2011: 22). We are free to presuppose no basic norm. For example, we can conceive of political events in a country *alegally*, that is, as "mere power relations" (Marmor 2011: 22).[17] This is why, Marmor argues, Kelsen cannot be understood as offering a Kantian transcendental argument, which would require Kelsen to insist that the basic norm is "something like a necessary feature or category of human cognition" (Marmor 2011: 21).

If Marmor is right, American philosophers of law who are unfamiliar with the details of Kelsen's works have even less reason to be interested in him than they thought. The problem is not merely that Kelsen's pure theory of law is implausible. It doesn't even manage to be pure. Why take a pure theory of law seriously when even its most earnest advocate in the end could not maintain it consistently?

In what follows, I argue that Marmor fundamentally misreads Kelsen's legal theory in three (interconnected) ways. First, he misunderstands Kelsen's doctrine of the unity of law. Rather than being an idea that Kelsen "toyed" with, the doctrine stands at the heart of his legal theory. Second, Marmor misreads how efficacy is relevant to the adoption of the basic norm of the unitary legal system. The fact that only an efficacious basic norm is presupposed does not mean that efficacy is a condition for the validity of the basic norm. Kelsen's statements about the role of efficacy in the adoption of a basic norm are compatible with a pure theory of law. Third, Marmor misunderstands the Neo-Kantian dimensions of Kelsen's thought. When

[17] Marmor quotes *A General Theory of Law and State*: "[A]n anarchist, for instance, who denied the validity of the hypothetical basic norm of positive law…will view its positive regulation of human relationships…as mere power relations." (Kelsen 1945: 413). It is worth noting that Kelsen later explicitly rejected this reading of the anarchist. He concluded that the anarchist, despite rejecting the law politically, could still presuppose the basic norm and therefore understand it as a system of valid norms (Kelsen 1960a: 218 n.82). This is a reason to conclude that Kelsen did not think that someone who treats the law as valid thereby also treats it as providing practical reasons for action. See note 13 above.

his Neo-Kantianism is properly understood, it becomes clear why Kelsen can be both a relativist and an antireductionist about the law.

3.4 Kelsen's Doctrine of the Unity of Law

Let us begin with Marmor's discussion of Kelsen's doctrine of the unity of law. It is important here to distinguish between three positions. The first is *pluralism*, under which multiple legal systems, each with valid laws, are possible (indeed actual) (Kelsen 1960a: 328). For the pluralist, the American, French, and Uzbek legal systems all exist independently of one another. Furthermore, the international legal system can also be understood as existing independently of the various national legal systems. By contrast, under *monism*, all valid laws must be seen as part of the same legal system (Kelsen 1960a: 333).[18]

There are two versions of monism. Under the *international* version—which Kelsen sometimes calls "objectivism" (Kelsen 1945: 386, 1960a: 344)—the unitary legal system is international. This international legal system assigns to all past,

[18] Monism as described here is different from a homonymous term used by international lawyers. If a nation's law is monist in this other sense, international law has a direct effect upon the legal rights and obligations of individuals under national law (Waters 2007; 641). A citizen may, for example, successfully challenge the validity of a statute on the grounds that it is contrary to a treaty entered into by the nation. If a nation's law is dualist, by contrast, such a challenge cannot succeed, unless there is a particular national law that has given the treaty such an effect. In the absence of such a law, the statute is binding on the individual, even though the nation might recognize the treaty's validity as a matter of international law—for example, by acknowledging that the statute's conflict with the treaty makes sanctions against it by other nations legally permissible. Thus, it is sometimes said that under dualism national and international law form two separate systems, with international law's effect confined to the relationship between nations (Henkin 1987: 864).

These positions are not the monism and pluralism described here. Monism, as Kelsen understands it, is compatible with legal phenomena that are described by international lawyers as "dualist." The fact that a treaty recognized by a nation provides individuals with no grounds to challenge the validity of a statute simply speaks to the legal relationship between those two types of law. It does not mean that international law and the domestic laws of each nation are not part of the same legal system.

Likewise, pluralism is compatible with legal phenomena that are described by international lawyers as "monist." Assume that under a nation's law an individual can invoke a treaty against the validity of a statute. The pluralist can still insist that the international and the national legal systems are separate. Facts about the nation's law, she can argue, are reducible to facts about the national community, whereas facts about international law are reducible to facts about an international community (the community of nations or officials of those nations, considered collectively). The individual arguing that the treaty invalidates the statute is making an argument under national law, not international law. Social facts about the national community are ultimately the reason that the statute's conflict with the treaty makes it invalid. To be sure, the fact that the statute conflicts with the treaty is a matter of international law, determined by social facts about the international, not the national, community. But simply because a criterion for the validity of national law refers to international law does not mean that the national and international legal systems are one.

present and future national legal systems, through the principle of efficacy,[19] a certain sphere of lawmaking authority in space and time (Kelsen 1960a: 214–215). Under the *national* version—which he sometimes calls "state subjectivism" (Kelsen 1934: 116, 1945: 386, 1960a: 345)—the unitary legal system is a national order, and international law is valid by virtue of being recognized by that nation's law. The principle of efficacy under international law still validates the laws of *other* national legal orders, but the principle is ultimately valid by virtue of the foundational nation's law.

We can now consider Marmor's claim that in the second edition of *The Pure Theory of Law* Kelsen presented his doctrine of the unity of law with "much more hesitation" (Marmor 2011: 23 n.18; see also Marmor 2010). In the passage Marmor cites (Kelsen 1960a: 214–15), Kelsen does not express any hesitation about *monism*. Nor does he "toy" with the idea. He makes it very clear throughout the second edition that a monistic construction of all valid law is "inevitable" (Kelsen 1960a: 333), and a dualistic or pluralistic construction is "impossible" (Kelsen 1960a: 335) and "untenable" (Kelsen 1960a: 328). To the extent that American, Uzbek, and Ancient Roman law are all considered valid within their own temporal and spatial spheres, they *must* be seen as part of a single legal system. This is the very same position that can be found in Kelsen's earlier works (Kelsen 1934: 111–114, 1945: 363–364, 373).

What Kelsen expresses in the passage is agnosticism concerning the choice between the international and national versions of monism, for either approach brings all valid law into the same legal order. Incidentally, the same agnosticism is present in Kelsen's earlier writings, going back at least to 1920 (Kelsen 1920: 317, 1934: 117, 1945: 388).[20] So Marmor is clearly wrong in claiming that Kelsen changed his position concerning the unity of law in the second edition of the *Pure Theory*.

What is more important, by ignoring the *national* form of monism, Marmor makes it appear as if Kelsen were somehow attracted to pluralism in the second edition. Because he was hesitant about the international version of monism, Marmor suggests, Kelsen must have been sympathetic to the idea that a multiplicity of independent legal systems exists, each system being dependent upon social facts about a particular community. The result is that an absolutely foundational element of Kelsen's legal theory—his doctrine of the unity of law—is falsely treated as marginal.

As Kelsen himself insisted, his pure theory of law and his doctrine of the unity of law are essentially related (Kelsen 1934: 113). Anyone who claims that multiple legal systems exist *independently*—rather than existing as subsystems of a larger legal system that coordinates their relationship to one another—*must* be tying law

[19] That the principle must be one of efficacy is questionable. Because the principle is itself a matter of positive law (Kelsen 1945: 121), there is no reason why it would have to have that particular content.

[20] Kelsen's view that monism did not entail the primacy of international law was the focus of a debate among Austrian legal scholars back in the 1920s (von Bernstorff 2010: 104–107).

to social facts about a community in a way that is incompatible with a pure theory (Kelsen 1934: 114, 1945: 375–376).

The structure of Kelsen's argument in his major works can mislead one into concluding that he is a pluralist. This is because he generally brings up the unity of law toward the end of each work (Kelsen 1934: 111–125, 1945: 363–388, 1960a; 320–347). He begins with a national legal order, understood as having its own basic norm. From that perspective, when he speaks of efficacy as a condition for the adoption of a new basic norm—for example, after a revolution (Kelsen 1960a: 50)—he appears to have accepted a pluralistic approach to the law, in which independent legal systems, each with its own basic norm, exist. But he always ends with the unity of law, where he makes it clear that insofar as we are considering these multiple national legal systems *as each possessing valid laws*, we must be viewing them as subsystems of an overarching legal order.

Because Kelsen insisted on the unity of law, we have reason to believe, contrary to Marmor's reading, that his theory of law is indeed pure. Of course, that also increases the theory's implausibility. To Marmor, the idea that there "is only one basic norm in the world, the basic norm of public international law," is "incredible" (Marmor 2011; 23 n. 18). Things do not appear any better if one notes that legal monism might be national. Under the national version, all valid law would fundamentally be *American* law (assuming the American legal system is the foundational one). The law of other national legal systems would be valid only because they are recognized by principles of international law that are themselves valid only because American law recognizes them.[21] My guess is that Marmor would find this version of monism, under which Ancient Roman law is valid because American law says so, equally incredible.[22]

But the fact remains that Kelsen was a monist. Marmor, in the guise of articulating Kelsen's own views, adopts the very perspective on the law that Kelsen thinks is impossible:

> The problem [that Kelsen's relativism leads to sociological reductionism] stems from the fact that Kelsen was right about the law. Legal validity *is* essentially relative to the social facts that constitute the content of the basic norm of each and every legal order. As noted from the outset, legal validity is always relative to a time and place. And now we can see why: because legal validity is determined by the content of the basic norm that is actually followed in a given society. The laws in the United Kingdom, for example, are different from those in the United States because people (mostly judges and other officials) *actually follow* different rules, or basic norms, about what counts as law in their respective jurisdictions. Once Kelsen admits, as he does, that the content of a basic norm is fully determined by practice, it becomes very difficult to understand how the explication of legal validity he offers is nonreductive (Marmor 2011; 24–25).

---

[21] Curiously, American *subsystem* law would also reappear within the unitary American legal system, because American law as a subsystem would also be recognized by international law.

[22] A national monist might take the position that the law of no other nation is valid. But I doubt that Marmor would be inclined to find that position, under which only American law is valid, any more attractive.

One problem with this passage is that it misdescribes the person to whom the law is relative. Kelsen never says that the validity of the law is relative to the perspective of the participants in a particular set of legal practices. The validity of the law is instead relative to the perspective of the *legal scientist*—the person cognizing the law—who need not be a participant in any legal practices at all (Kelsen 1934; 58, 1960a; 204–205). Kelsen argues that any person who judges norms to be valid law must be presupposing a unitary basic norm. Because Marmor conceives of the United Kingdom and the United States as each possessing laws that are valid within their own time and place, Kelsen would say he is presupposing a unitary basic norm. It is in the light of this norm that the activities of American and British officials can be seen as law-creating acts. But Marmor takes himself to be thinking of the American and British legal systems as *independently* valid, precisely the perspective that Kelsen thinks is impossible.

3.5 Kelsen on Efficacy

To repeat, by marginalizing Kelsen's doctrine of the unity of law, Marmor makes Kelsen appear as if he were attracted to sociological approaches to the law. Once he is understood as a monist, it is easier to believe that his theory of law really is pure. But this still leaves in place Marmor's other arguments that Kelsen lapses into a sociological approach. Even if the laws of various national suborders can be considered valid only in the light of one basic norm (which I will assume is the basic norm of the international legal system), wouldn't Kelsen still admit that *this* unitary basic norm is chosen only if it is efficacious? So can't Marmor still say that, for Kelsen, the law is based on social facts about efficacy?

I will argue that Marmor misreads what Kelsen says about the relationship between efficacy and the choice of a unitary basic norm. Let me begin by drawing a distinction between two types of judgment. The first consists of legal judgments—judgments about the law. The second consists of psychological judgments about people's legal judgments. When Kelsen speaks about efficacy, he is often making a psychological judgment. From such a judgment no legal judgments follow. In particular, it does not follow that efficacy is a condition for the law's validity.

Consider an analogy in connection with morality. Adopting a psychological perspective, it is possible to arrive at numerous conclusions about the causal conditions for our moral judgments. One might conclude that we judge X to be morally good when we have a certain disposition of the will toward X or when our community by and large approves of X. But the truth of these psychological judgments is compatible with the nonreductivist position that the moral states of affairs described by our moral judgments do not depend upon the judgments' causes. Morality does not depend upon our dispositions of the will or our community's beliefs and desires.

The same distinction can be drawn concerning the law. When Kelsen speaks of the relationship between efficacy and the choice of a basic norm, he is often making psychological claims about the causes of our legal judgments. He states, for example, that "a norm that is not effective at least to some degree, is not regarded as a valid legal norm" (Kelsen 1960a: 11) or that "a normative order is considered valid only if it is by and large effective" (Kelsen 1960a: 86). Statements about what is *regarded* or *considered* are psychological, not legal.

Consider as well Kelsen's description of a revolution:

> A band of revolutionaries stages a violent *coup d'état* in a monarchy, attempting to oust the legitimate rulers and to replace the monarchy with a republican form of government. If the revolutionaries succeed, the old system ceases to be effective, and the new system becomes effective…And one treats this new system, then, as a legal system, that is to say, one interprets as legal acts the acts applying the new system, and as unlawful acts the material acts violating it…If the revolutionaries were to fail because the system they set up remained ineffective…then the initial act of the revolutionaries would be interpreted not as the establishing of a constitution but as treason, not as the making of law but as a violation of law (Kelsen 1934: 59, see also Kelsen 1960a: 210–11).

Here too, Kelsen speaks psychologically about how one *treats* the new system or *interprets* the acts of the revolutionaries.

When understood psychologically, Kelsen's statements about efficacy are compatible with a pure theory. It is true that people would not presuppose the basic norm of the unitary legal system if it were not efficacious. But it is also true that we would not judge slavery to be morally impermissible if all sorts of social and psychological conditions were not in place. That does not mean that the moral impermissibility of slavery depends upon those social and psychological conditions.

Indeed, there is substantial evidence in Kelsen's writings that the distinction between psychological and legal judgments was of crucial importance to him. Because legal norms stand outside space and time,[23] they cannot causally interact with human beings. Thus, in his more careful moments, he denied that legal norms can be efficacious at all, because that suggests such a causal connection. What is efficacious is instead a psychological entity, the idea of the norm: "One must therefore distinguish clearly between the *norm*, which is *valid*, and the *idea of the norm* [*Norm-Vorstellung*], which is effective" (Kelsen 1926: 7; see also Kelsen 1945: 43).

A pure theorist of morality would draw an analogous distinction between morality, which exists independently of human beings, and our beliefs about morality. Our beliefs have causes; morality does not. Thus it would not matter to a pure theorist of morality that correct beliefs about morality arose only at a late date. The historical contingency of our beliefs about morality does not mean that morality itself is historically contingent. Analogously, it should not matter for Kelsen if correct beliefs about the law (for example, acceptance of those principles of international law that validate national subsystems) arose at a relatively late date.

So far, I have offered two readings of Kelsen's statements about efficacy that allow us to understand his theory of law as pure. Under the first, efficacy is simply the factual condition for the validity of the laws of a national legal subsystem. The

---

[23] A legal norm, Kelsen argues, "does not exist in space and time, for it is not a fact of nature" (Kelsen 1934: 12).

legal norms triggered by efficacy are part of a unitary legal system, a system that does not itself depend upon efficacy. The second reading addresses those statements in which Kelsen seems to be speak of efficacy in connection with the basic norm of this unitary legal system. Here we can understand him as making psychological judgments about when the basic norm is presupposed, judgments that are likewise compatible with a pure theory of law.

But at times Kelsen speaks of a *justificatory* rather than a causal relationship between the basic norm of the unitary legal system and efficacy. The idea is that when making a choice of how to interpret social events legally, we do so with the *aim* of satisfying the requirement of efficacy. We refuse to presuppose a basic norm with content that would make the resulting legal system inefficacious:

> To understand the nature of the basic norm it must be kept in mind that it refers directly to a specific constitution, actually established by custom or statutory creation, by and large effective, and indirectly to the coercive order created according to this constitution and by and large effective; the basic norm thereby furnishes the reason for the validity of this constitution and of the coercive order created in accordance with it. The basic norm, therefore, is not the product of free invention. It is not presupposed arbitrarily in the sense that there is a choice between different basic norms (Kelsen 1960a: 201).

Here Kelsen describes someone interpreting the law as rationally constrained to presuppose only a basic norm that authorizes an efficacious first constitution.

But even these passages give us no reason to conclude that Kelsen abandoned his antireductionist approach to the law. They too are compatible with a pure theory of law. As Kelsen makes clear, if a basic norm that does not satisfy the requirement of efficacy is chosen, legal meaning will be impoverished (eg, Kelsen 1934: 59–60). Consider someone who interprets events in the territory that we would call "the United States" in the light of an inefficacious basic norm (for example, one under which the Queen-in-Parliament is the ultimate source of valid law). Under such an interpretation, everything that purported officials in the relevant territory have been doing for the last 240 years is without legal consequence (except, perhaps, as treasonous acts). What is more, those authorized to make law (namely the Queen-in-Parliament) have been strangely silent. No laws applicable to the territory have been made for centuries. By contrast, once one adopts a basic norm that validates Article VII, and the U.S. Constitution and laws enacted pursuant to it, a wealth of legal meaning emerges.

We can therefore understand the justificatory role of efficacy as an epistemological requirement in interpreting social events legally (Kelsen 1920: 94–101, 1945: 436–437). One must interpret social events in a manner that maximizes, or at least does not radically impoverish, legal meaning. And that means presupposing an efficacious basic norm.

When efficacy is understood as an epistemological requirement, it is compatible with a pure theory. As an analogy, consider someone who claims that the principle of charity must be used in arriving at judgments about people's beliefs—that is, that one should whenever possible arrive at judgments under which the person interpreted has beliefs that are *true*. Someone adopting the principle of charity need not claim that the beliefs of the person interpreted are actually constituted by or reducible to the principle of charity. She can insist that the beliefs of the person interpreted are independent of our best means of arriving at judgments about those beliefs.

By the same token, Kelsen's principle of efficacy can be understood as the epistemological demand that one interpret the legal meaning of events in a manner that enriches this meaning. It need not follow that law is reduced to social facts. The condition for the validity of the law remains the presupposed basic norm, a norm that stands outside the causal order and so does not depend for its existence upon social facts.

To sum up, there are three methods of reading Kelsen's statements about efficacy as compatible with a pure theory of law. Efficacy can be understood as (1) a legal condition for the validity of a national subsystem under international law, (2) a psychological condition for judgments about the law, or (3) an epistemological condition for arriving at justified judgments about the law. Each method allows us to avoid reading Kelsen as having abandoned a pure theory of law.

3.6 Kelsen's Neo-Kantianism

Marmor has one more argument in the offing. Even if Kelsen is a consistent monist and even if his statements about efficacy are compatible with a pure theory, reductionism about the law still follows from Kelsen's relativism. For Kelsen, presupposing the basic norm is not rationally compelled. Law's validity is relative only to a contingent perspective in which the basic norm is presupposed. And that makes it difficult, as Marmor puts it, to detach the law "from the facts that constitute the relevant point of view (the facts about people's actions, beliefs, attitudes, and such)" (Marmor 2011: 23).

As a preliminary matter, it is worth noting that even if Marmor is correct, Kelsen would be compelled to reduce the law to the beliefs and attitudes of an *individual*—of the person thinking about the law (whom we can call a *jurist*). It would not follow that the law would be reduced to social facts about a community. Marmor's argument that Kelsen reduces the law to social facts about a community relied upon Kelsen's doctrine of efficacy and his (alleged) abandonment of the unity of law. All Marmor is left with now is Kelsen's view that the validity of law is relative to the jurist's presuppositions, which at most suggests that the law should be reduced to the jurist's beliefs and attitudes. An appropriate analogy here is the metaethicist who claims that morality is relative to the presuppositions of the person making judgments about morality. For such a metaethicist, morality should arguably be reduced to that person's beliefs and attitudes.

In addressing the relationship between reductionism and Kelsen's normative relativism, we should distinguish between two questions. The first is whether *Kelsen* thought that the relativity of law to the jurist's perspective leads to reductionism. The second question is whether Kelsen *ought* to have concluded this. I take it that Marmor is primarily seeking to answer the *first* question. Not only does relativism lead to reductionism, Kelsen thought it did, even though this conclusion was uncomfortable for him because it required him to abandon a pure theory of law.

I do not think it could be any clearer, however, that Kelsen did *not* think that the relativity of law to the jurist's presupposition of a basic norm is incompatible with a pure theory, that is, that it is incompatible with an understanding of the law as an objective order not dependent upon human beings. Indeed, it is precisely through the idea that law is relative to a jurist's presuppositions that Kelsen sought to *explain* how the jurist makes objective judgments about the law:

> The question: 'Who presupposes the basic norm?' is answered by the Pure Theory as follows: The basic norm is presupposed by whoever interprets the subjective meaning of the constitution-creating act, and of the acts created according to the constitution, as the objective meaning of these acts, that is, as objectively valid norm (Kelsen 1960a: 204 n.72).

The objective legal meaning about which the jurist makes judgments is a meaning independent of anyone's beliefs and attitudes, including the jurist's own: "The law of normativity is…like the law of nature, in that it is directed to no one and valid without regard to whether it is known or recognized" (Kelsen 1999: 6; see also Kelsen 1960a: 7–8, 20–21).

It is true that Kelsen was a relativist in the sense that he thought that the jurist, in a sense, creates his object of knowledge. This makes the law, in some sense, subjective. But Kelsen thought such relativism was true of *all* knowledge: "[T]he science of law as cognition of the law, like any cognition, has constitutive character – it 'creates' its object insofar as it comprehends the object as a meaningful whole" (Kelsen 1960a: 72). Kelsen's relativism is due to his Neo-Kantianism, which is present even as late as the second edition of the *Pure Theory*.[24]

But how can Kelsen adopt a Neo-Kantian approach, when—as Marmor notes—he accepted that no one is rationally compelled to think legally? One can, after all, simply look at political events as mere power relations.

It is true that Kelsen does not purport to offer a *progressive* transcendental argument of the sort in Kant's first *Critique*, that is, an argument that seeks to refute the skeptic (in Kant's case, the skeptic about the existence of causal relations or substances in nature) by starting with an indubitable fact (for Kant, the unity of consciousness) and showing that what the skeptic denies is a condition for the possibility of the indubitable fact. But Kelsen never claimed to offer a transcendental argument of this sort. Indeed, to my knowledge, he never used the phrases "transcendental argument" or "transcendental deduction" ("transzendentaler Beweis," "transzendentales Argument," "transzendentale Deduction") in connection with his theory of law. The fact remains that he adopted a Neo-Kantian approach, in which the law is dependent upon or constituted by the jurist, to explain how we can know an objective legal order.

---

[24] For example, Kelsen repeatedly speaks of the basic norm as transcendental-logical (Kelsen 1960a: 201–02, 218, 223, 226). Kelsen's Neo-Kantian approach is even more explicit in passages from the German version of the second edition, omitted in the English translation, eg Kelsen 1960b: 208 n.**, where he explicitly draws an analogy between his method and Kant's.

Stanley Paulson has helpfully offered two possible interpretations of the sense in which Kelsen can be understood as a Neo-Kantian. Under the first, Kelsen sought to offer a *regressive* transcendental argument. Under this reading, he took for granted that we make judgments about objective legal norms and tried to explain how such judgments are possible. Kelsen can still be understood as having offered a transcendental *argument* under this reading, because the jurist is understood as creating his object of knowledge, with the basic norm acting as the analogue of a Kantian category (Paulson 2013: 49–57).

The second approach is more closely associated with the Marburg Neo-Kantian Hermann Cohen,[25] as well as the Schopenhauerian intellectual environment in Vienna within which Kelsen—and Wittgenstein (Janik and Toulmin 1973)—wrote. Under this approach, which might be described as *quietist*, Kelsen abandons any transcendental *argument*, although not transcendental idealism. Kelsen's goal is simply to explicate, without any grounding or justification, what jurists in fact do (Paulson 2013: 57–61). The presupposition of the basic norm is a description of what jurists do when they think of valid law. I have argued for this reading myself (Green 2003: 389–405, 2009).

To be sure, Paulson thinks that, under the second (quietist) approach, Kelsen would have to abandon his language about the constitutive role of the knowing subject (Paulson 2013: 60–61). Thus he would likely say that Kelsen's *relativism* presumes the first approach. For the record, I disagree.[26] But even if Paulson is right, Marmor's reading is still mistaken, for Paulson clearly does not think that under the first approach Kelsen thought that his relativism leads to reductionism.

What both approaches have in common is that Kelsen assumes that jurists do indeed take themselves to be cognizing objective legal norms, even if they are not compelled to do so by "Reason" (Marmor 2011: 22) or the requirements of self-consciousness. Kelsen recognizes that our commitment to objective legal norms might be "senseless or merely ideological fallacy" (Kelsen 1960a: 101; see also Kelsen 1934: 33). But he nevertheless thought that denying the existence of such norms would render "[t]he thousands of statements in which the law is expressed daily…senseless" (Kelsen 1960a: 104; see also Kelsen 1945: 436).

Of course, the question remains whether Kelsen's Neo-Kantian approach succeeds.[27] Perhaps Marmor is right that Kelsen should have drawn reductionist conclusions from his Neo-Kantianism. But we have now moved beyond what Kelsen did think to what he should have thought. It is unquestionably true that Kelsen did think that his Neo-Kantian relativism was compatible with nonreductionism.

---

[25] For Kelsen's reliance on Cohen, see Paulson 1992, 2013; Green 2003: 389–402; Edel 1999.

[26] A quietist might speak about the knowing subject creating her objects of knowledge as a means of foreclosing Platonist theories in which the objects of knowledge are given independent metaphysical status. For a discussion of how the quietist must walk a fine line between subjectivism on the one hand and metaphysical realism on the other, see Green 2003: 396–398, 2009: 367–368.

[27] Paulson has argued that the first approach fails, on the ground that Kelsen has not shown that the basic norm is the only means of explaining what is presumed, namely cognition of objective legal norms (Paulson 1992, 2013: 55–57).

3.7 Why a Pure Theory of Law?

So Marmor has given us no reason not to take Kelsen at his word: His theory of law really is pure. But the important question remains: Why accept it? Are there any legal judgments that cannot be made sense of unless the law is independent of all social facts? Such focused arguments for the independence of law from social facts seem lacking in Kelsen's works.

In my own writing on Kelsen, I have tried to fill this gap by identifying judgments about the law that suggest its independence from social facts. Assume, for example, that the validity of the United States Constitution is justified by Article VII. As we have seen, one cannot justify Article VII's status as law by other enacted laws. The creation of Article VII was a revolutionary act. For a positivist, therefore, the validity of Article VII—as well as the validity of the Constitution and laws enacted pursuant to it—must be based upon social facts about American legal practices. Article VII is valid law, roughly, because it is actually used by American officials for assessing the validity of American law. But given the revolutionary nature of Article VII, the requisite legal practices were probably in place in the United States only sometime *after* the ratification process was completed, when American officials had established a practice of justifying the validity of the Constitution and other American law by reference to Article VII. Thus, the positivist would apparently be compelled to say that the Constitution was valid sometime after ratification.

But I doubt many American lawyers would say that the Constitution became valid law when such practices had emerged. They would say that the Constitution became valid on June 21, 1788, when the ninth state (New Hampshire) ratified it. The irrelevance of American legal practices to the validity of American law suggests that American law cannot be reduced to social facts about American legal practices (Green 2003: 387–389, 2009: 361–365).

Although this example is primarily directed at positivist theories of law, it can cast doubt upon natural law theories as well. After all, it is likely that on June 21, 1788, there were insufficient social facts about American legal practices in place to justify the validity of Article VII, even when those facts are combined with evaluative facts.

It is possible, however, that positivists and natural lawyers would be comfortable understanding lawyers' judgment that the Constitution was valid when ratified, not as a statement about the law at the time of the ratification, but as a statement about how events occurring at the time of the ratification ought, legally, to be treated *now*. What is more, there remains the apparent independent existence of legal systems other than the American. Legal pluralism, as we have seen, is incompatible with a pure theory.

In another attempt to give life to the Kelsenian approach, I will briefly consider other judgments that provide, I believe, evidence of a commitment to law that transcends social facts, namely judgments in the conflict of laws (or private international law, as it is known outside the United States). The law of the conflict of laws is conceived of as international law that binds, and so is independent of, particular human communities.[28]

Consider *Holzer v. Deutsche Reichsbahn-Gesellschaft* (277 N.Y. 474 (1938)). The plaintiff was a German Jew who, after being fired from his job with the defendant due to the Nazis' Nuremberg Decrees and spending 6 months in a concentration camp, escaped to the United States. He sued his former employer in New York state court for breach of contract, the alleged breach being the act of firing him solely because he was Jewish. The court dismissed the plaintiff's action on the grounds that it failed to state a claim under German law, because the defendant was legally obligated to fire the plaintiff. The New York Court of Appeals affirmed.[29]

Holzer might appear to vindicate a sociological approach to the law. Holzer failed to state a claim because of social facts about German legal practices. Likewise social facts about New York legal practices would have been relevant to the court's decision, if the events being adjudicated had occurred in New York rather than Germany—if the parties had signed the contract in New York, Holzer had performed his services there, and the defendant had fired Holzer there.

But the fact that a court facing a conflicts problem looks to social facts about a community's legal practices does not show that a sociological approach to the law is correct. As we have seen, Kelsen does not deny that legal facts depend upon social facts. All *Holzer* and other conflicts cases might show is that among the social facts upon which legal facts depend are facts about a particular community's legal practices. Such dependence of legal facts on a community is compatible with there being a single legal system—not dependent upon any community—in the light of which the relativity of legal facts to community obtains. Communities are relevant in conflicts cases only because legal norms make them relevant. And, Kelsen can argue, those legal norms are conceived of monistically.

Of course, a positivist or natural lawyer would respond that conflicts rules are not monistic, but are themselves part of a particular jurisdiction's law. The conflicts rule used by the New York Court of Appeals in *Holzer* was *New York law*—constituted (at least in part) by social facts about New York legal practices.

Our question, therefore, is whether courts addressing conflicts cases think of the legal rules they use monistically or as part of local law. In addressing this question, it is important to distinguish between three types of conflicts rule. First, a rule can be understood as carving up the lawmaking power possessed by various communities

[28] My argument supports the international rather than the national version of monism. Indeed, like a number of Kelsen's Austrian critics in the 1920s—such as Alfred Verdross and Josef Kunz (von Bernstorff 2010: 105)—I find the national version of monism questionable. To the extent that one treats other national legal systems as having validity under principles of international law, I cannot see how one could not consider one's own national legal system as fundamentally subject to those same principles.

[29] The Court of Appeals reversed the trial court's dismissal of a second cause of action, according to which the defendant failed to abide by a provision in the contract that stated that "in the event the plaintiff should die or become unable, without fault on his part, to serve during the period of the contract the defendants would pay to him or his heirs the sum of 120,000 marks, in discharge of their obligations, under the hiring aforesaid."

and their officials. Let us call this a *rule of authorization*. For example, it might say that German officials have exclusive regulatory power over everything that happens within Germany's borders. If so, any court adjudicating a case with facts occurring in Germany is arguably legally obligated to look to German officials to decide the case. That is one way of understanding the rule used in the *Holzer* case. According to the rule, New York officials lacked the power to apply New York law.

Alternatively, we might understand the rule used in *Holzer*, not as claiming that New York officials lacked regulatory power over the event being adjudicated, but only that they chose, at their discretion, not to exercise their power. The New York Court of Appeals was saying, not that New York law *cannot*, but that it *does not* apply to the facts in *Holzer*. Let us call this a *rule of scope*.[30]

Finally, let us assume that two or more jurisdictions have *concurrent* regulatory power over the event being adjudicated and both have chosen to exercise their power. Assume, for example, that German and New York officials both have the power to extend their laws to Germans who enter into contracts in Germany and both have enacted laws that have such contracts within their scope. If that is the case, the forum will have legal discretion to apply German or New York law to the facts. The rule it uses when exercising this discretion is a *rule of priority*.

One might think that a New York state court's decision not to apply New York law to facts over which New York has lawmaking power must mean that the facts are outside the scope of New York law. But such a conclusion is too hasty. It is conceivable that a New York state court might refrain from applying New York law due to a rule of priority. Even though it does not apply New York law, it might accept that the facts are within the scope of New York law, as evidenced by its permitting the courts of other jurisdictions (with different rules of priority) to apply New York law to the facts (Roosevelt 2005: 1874; Kramer 1991: 1029).

Let us now return to the claim that the conflicts rule used by the Court of Appeals in *Holzer* was New York law. Understood as a *rule of scope*, the rule was indeed New York law. When a New York court chooses, at its discretion, not to extend New York law to facts, that decision is a matter of New York law. Even a monist like Kelsen can accept that, understood as a rule of scope, it was New York law, in the sense that it was the result of New York officials exercising their authority.

The same point is true if the rule used by the Court of Appeals in *Holzer* was a *rule of priority*. When a New York court, after concluding that the facts are within the scope of both German and New York law, chooses, at its discretion, to give German law priority, its choice is a matter of New York law. This again is something with which Kelsen can agree.

[30]When conflicts rules are understood as rules of scope, one must then confront the question of whether other jurisdictions ought to respect them. (This is commonly called the problem of *renvoi* or *désistement*.) If New York officials have said, through their conflicts rules, that the facts are beyond the scope of New York law, it would appear that other jurisdictions are not permitted to apply New York law to the facts. I argue, however, that this reasoning is mistaken at Green 2013: 869–884.

But I think it is pretty clear that the Court of Appeals thought it was applying a *rule of authorization*, not a rule of scope or priority. It thought German officials had exclusive lawmaking power over the contract, and thus that it *had* to look to German officials to decide the case. As the Court of Appeals put it, "Within its own territory every government is supreme" *Holzer v. Deutsche Reichsbahn-Gesellschaft* (277 N.Y. 474, 479 (1938)).

Understood as a rule of authorization, it is hard to see how the rule could possibly be New York law. To say that New York officials lack the power to extend their law to such contracts is to say that no change in New York legal practices could make the extension of New York law to such contracts legally permissible. So put, this restriction could not possibly be dependent *itself* upon New York legal practices.

To be sure, the Court of Appeals cited a case from the United States Supreme Court in favor of the principle that foreign governments are supreme within their own territory (United States v. Belmont, 301 U. S. 324 (1937)). What is more, the application of New York law to the facts would pretty clearly be in violation of the Due Process Clause of the Fourteenth Amendment (eg, Home Insurance Co. v. Dick, 281 U.S. 397 (1930)). Thus, one might argue that the rule of authorization it was articulating, although not New York law, was federal law.

But if the rule was federal law, in the sense that it was dependent upon American legal practices, that would mean that those practices could change in a way that would permit the court in *Holzer* to extend New York law to the contract. And my guess is that the rule was not conceived this way. To the extent that the rule was federal law, such law simply recognized preexisting monistic legal restrictions on American officials.

That this division of lawmaking authority was, and is, conceived of monistically is evident in the possibility of intercommunity disagreement. Assume a German court claimed that it possessed the power to apply German law to contracts entered into by New Yorkers in New York. I take it that this is something about which an American court could meaningfully disagree. But under a pluralistic approach, German and American officials cannot meaningfully disagree about the distribution of lawmaking power between them. They can only articulate what the distribution is within their own legal system.

Thus, even if there is significant disagreement between participants in various legal communities about what the correct rules of authorization are, the very existence of such disagreement presumes that the rules bind communities independently of what their legal practices happen to be. And that means that the rules of authorization are conceived of as monistic law.

My argument is not changed if one decides that the New York state court in *Holzer* was not legally obligated to apply German law. Assume, for example, that a court is legally permitted to apply forum law at will. This *still* assumes a monistic distribution of lawmaking authority, namely one in which a community's officials have complete authority over the activities of their courts (including their choice-of-law decisions). This new principle also stands above and binds all communities, for it too is a matter about which meaningful intercommunity disagreement is possible. If a German court were to claim that New York officials lacked the legal power to apply New York law in *Holzer*, New York officials could think the German court was *wrong* (not that it was right for Germany).

I don't want to suggest that either the territorial approach that appeared to be employed in *Holzer* or a forum-based alternative is correct. The proper approach to the distribution of lawmaking authority between jurisdictions arguably cannot be captured by any such simple rule. My goal here is not to get the distribution of lawmaking authority right. It is to render plausible the monist's view that there is such a distribution that stands above and binds every community. This distribution is employed not merely when someone makes a judgment about how a New York court should deal with facts that arise in Germany. It is employed even when one makes a judgment about how a New York court should deal with facts that arise in New York, for it is only in the light of the distribution that one can explain why the court should look to New York rather than German legal practices. Kelsen's monism is not as crazy as its sounds.

Acknowledgments Thanks for helpful comments from the participants in the Kelsen in America Conference, organized by Jeremy Telman. Thanks for further aid to Brian Bix, David Enoch, Andrei Marmor, Stanley Paulson, and Lars Vinx

References

Ackerman, Bruce, and Neal Katyal. 1995. Our unconventional founding. *University of Chicago Law Review* 62: 475–573.

Delacroix, Sylvie. 2004. Hart's and Kelsen's concepts of normativity contrasted. *Ratio Juris* 17: 501–520.

Dworkin, Ronald. 1986. *Law's empire*. Cambridge: Harvard University Press.

Dworkin, Ronald. 2006. *Justice in robes*. Cambridge: Harvard University Press.

Edel, Geert. 1999. The hypothesis of the basic norm: Hans Kelsen and Hermann Cohen. In *Normativity and norms: Critical perspectives on Kelsenian themes*, ed. Stanley L. Paulson and Bonnie L. Paulson, 195–220. Oxford: Clarendon.

Enoch, David. 2011. *Taking morality seriously: A defense of robust realism*. Oxford: Oxford University Press.

Green, Michael Steven. 2003. Hans Kelsen and the logic of legal systems. *Alabama Law Review* 53: 365–413.

Green, Michael Steven. 2009. Kelsen, quietism, and the rule of recognition. In *The rule of recognition and the United States constitution*, ed. Matthew D. Adler and Kenneth E. Himma, 351–378. Oxford: Oxford University Press.

Green, Michael Steven. 2013. Law's dark matter. *William and Mary Law Review* 54: 845–884.

Greenberg, Mark. 2004. How facts make law. *Legal Theory* 10: 157–198.

Henkin, Louis. 1987. The constitution and United States sovereignty: A century of Chinese exclusion and its progeny. *Harvard Law Review* 100: 853–886.

Janik, Allan, and Stephen Toulmin. 1973. *Wittgenstein's Vienna*. New York: Simon and Schuster.

Kelsen, Hans. 1920. *Das Problem der Souveränität und die Theorie des Völkerrechts. Beitrag zu einer Reinen Rechtslehre*. Tübingen: J.C.B. Mohr.

Kelsen, Hans. 1922. *Der Soziologische und Juristische Staatsbegriff*. Tübingen: J.C.B. Mohr.

Kelsen, Hans. 1926. Das Wesen des Staates. *Revue Internationale de la Theorie du Droit* 1: 5–17.

Kelsen, Hans. 1934. *Introduction to the problems of legal theory. A translation of the first edition of the Reine Rechtslehre or pure theory of law*. Trans. B.L. Paulson and S.L. Paulson, 1997. Oxford: Clarendon Press.

Kelsen, Hans. 1945. *General theory of law and state*. Trans. A. Wedberg. Cambridge: Harvard University Press.

Kelsen, Hans. 1960a. *Pure theory of law*, 2nd edn. Trans. M. Knight 1967. Berkeley: University of California Press.

Kelsen, Hans. 1960b. *Reine Rechtslehre: Mit einem Anhang: Das Problem der Gerechtigkeit.* Tubingen: Mohr Siebeck.

Kelsen, Hans. 1999. Foreword to the second printing of the main problems in the theory of public law. In *Normativity and norms: Critical perspectives on Kelsenian themes*, ed. Stanley L. Paulson and Bonnie L. Paulson, 3–22. Oxford: Clarendon.

Kramer, Larry. 1991. Return of the renvoi. *New York University Law Review* 66: 979–1044.

Marmor, Andrei. 2010. The pure theory of law. *The Stanford Encyclopedia of Philosophy*. http://plato.stanford.edu/archives/fall2010/entries/lawphil-theory. Accessed 22 Jan 2015.

Marmor, Andrei. 2011. *Philosophy of law*. Princeton: Princeton University Press.

Murphy, Jeffrie G., and Jules L. Coleman. 1990. *Philosophy of law: An introduction to jurisprudence*. Boulder: Westview Press.

Navarro, Pablo E. 2013. The efficacy of constitutional norms. In *Kelsen revisited: New essays on the pure theory of law*, ed. Luis Duarte d'Almeida, Gardner John, and Green Leslie, 77–100. Oxford: Hart Publishing.

Paulson, Stanley L. 1992. Introduction. In *Introduction to the problems of legal theory. A translation of the first edition of the Reine Rechtslehre or pure theory of law*. Trans. B.L. Paulson and S.L. Paulson, 1997. Oxford: Clarendon Press.

Paulson, Stanley L. 2012. A 'justified normativity' thesis in Hans Kelsen's pure theory of law? Rejoinders to Robert Alexy and Joseph Raz. In *Institutionalized reason: The jurisprudence of Robert Alexy*, ed. Klatt Matthias, 61–111. Oxford: Oxford University Press.

Paulson, Stanley L. 2013. The great puzzle: Kelsen's basic norm. In *Kelsen revisited: New essays on the pure theory of law*, ed. Luis Duarte d'Almeida, John Gardner, and Leslie Green, 43–62. Oxford: Hart Publishing.

Roosevelt, Kermit. 2005. Resolving renvoi: The bewitchment of our intelligence by means of language. *Notre Dame Law Review* 80: 1821–1891.

von Bernstorff, Jochen. 2010. *The public international law theory of Hans Kelsen: Believing in universal law*. Cambridge: Cambridge University Press.

Waters, Melissa A. 2007. Creeping monism: The judicial trend toward interpretive incorporation of human rights treaties. *Columbia Law Review* 107: 628–705.

Wilson, Alida. 1982. Joseph Raz on Kelsen's basic norm. *American Journal of Jurisprudence* 27: 46–63.

Part II
Hans Kelsen and the Development of Public International Law

Chapter 4
The Kelsen-Hart Debate: Hart's Critique of Kelsen's Legal Monism Reconsidered

Lars Vinx

4.1 Introduction

Legal monism is the view that there is only one legal system. Hans Kelsen defended a particularly strong version of that view. Kelsen did not simply hold that there is only one legal system, as a matter of fact. He argued, rather, that it is impossible for a legal science to recognize the existence of more than one legal system. Legal-scientific cognition, as a form of normative cognition, must assume, according to Kelsen, that no two valid legal norms conflict, ie, that there are no two legal norms that make incompatible demands on the behavior of one and the same agent. And the absence or at least the resolvability of such conflict between legal norms can be assured, Kelsen argued, only if all legal norms that exist are understood as belonging to one and the same legal system. Legal pluralism, in other words, is deemed to be juristically inconceivable (Kelsen 1934: 111–125, 1920: 107–111, 1952: 404, 424–428).

This exceptionally strong version of legal monism has found few followers (Somek 2007, 2012). It seems to have been unanimously rejected by the leading Anglo-American analytical legal positivists, in the wake of Hart's highly influential critique of the Pure Theory of Law (Hart 1983).[1] Contemporary constitutional theory generally endorses this rejection and has turned thoroughly pluralist

[1] Hart's arguments have been developed in more detail by Joseph Raz. See Raz (1970: 95–109) and Raz (2009a: 127–129). Hart's and Raz's arguments against Kelsen's theory of legal system are fairly similar. This paper, therefore, focuses on Hart's initial development of the critique. For a discussion of Raz's version of the critique, see Vinx (2007: 184–194).

L. Vinx (✉)
Department of Philosophy, Bilkent University, 06800 Ankara, Turkey
e-mail: vinx@bilkent.edu.tr

D.A.J. Telman (ed.), *Hans Kelsen in America - Selective Affinities and the Mysteries of Academic Influence*, Law and Philosophy Library 116,
DOI 10.1007/978-3-319-33130-0_4

(MacCormick 1993: 8–9; Barber 2010: 145–171).[2] Legal monism, or so it would appear, is clearly the least convincing aspect of Kelsen's theory of legal system.[3]

This paper offers a qualified defense of Kelsen's legal monism against Hart's critique. I concede that Hart managed to establish the falsity of Kelsen's strong monism (Hart 1983: 324—332; Barber 2010: 148–156).[4] But this concession, I argue, does not settle the fate of legal monism in all its possible forms. A Kelsenian, as Hart himself pointed out (Hart 1983: 309), might withdraw to a weaker form of monism: even if monism is not a necessary assumption of all legal-scientific cognition, it might still be true, as a matter of fact, that all the law that currently exists belongs to one and the same legal system. It is this form of legal monism that I want to show to be defensible.

Hart, and other legal pluralists following his lead, would not deny, of course, that it is possible for the whole world to come to be governed by one and only one legal system. This would be a world, according to the Hartian, with only one practice of recognition, carried by one globally integrated system of courts. But Hart forcefully argues, in *The Concept of Law*, that this is not the world we live in. As a matter of fact, there are several practices of recognition, each with its own judicial institutions and ultimate standards of legal validity (Hart 1961: 208–231). According to Hart, monism is not even a remotely plausible description of global legal order as it currently exists.

Despite the alleged descriptive inadequacy of monism, Kelsen, in his numerous works on international law, succeeded in giving a fairly detailed and plausible description of existing global legal order as a monist order.[5] If that description can be shown to be coherent and reasonably true to the facts, monism cannot, *pace* Hart, be brushed off as descriptively inadequate. Rather, it must be regarded—alongside legal pluralism—as one available account of current global legal order. And if monism, as applied to current global legal order, is descriptively viable, we are entitled to ask why a legal-pluralist description of the sort offered by Hart and his followers should be preferred to a monist description. We are also entitled to ask whether Kelsen's monist theory of legal system, though not defensible on the ground of the logical conditions for legal cognition, may not be more defensible than is usually assumed.

Hart's answer to this challenge was to claim that Kelsen's monist description of international legal order is based on a mistaken criterion of the identity of legal systems. Kelsen holds to the view, according to Hart, that all legal norms that are

[2] MacCormick subsequently modified his rejection of Kelsen's monism and argued that the European legal order might be understood as a form of "monism under international law." See MacCormick (1999, 113–121). The view that is advocated here is close to MacCormick's later position.

[3] See for instance Culver and Giudice (2010, 38) who argue—though they sympathize with Kelsen's view that international law is real law—that Hart's criticism of Kelsen's monism is "decisive." This assessment is upheld in Giudice (2013, 161–164).

[4] I have tried to explain why I do not hold Kelsen's strong monism to be defensible in Vinx (2011).

[5] For a comprehensive account of Kelsen's theory of international law see von Bernstorff (2010). A recent defense of the continuing relevance of Kelsen's approach to the theory of international law is given in Kammerhofer (2014).

related to one and the same basic norm by what Hart calls a "relationship of validating purport" form part of the same legal system (Hart 1983: 317–321). It is this criterion of identity, in Hart's view, that allows Kelsen to offer a monist account of global legal order, because it appears to imply that international law validates national law. But according to Hart, it is wrong to claim that all laws related to the same basic norm by a relationship of validating purport must form part of the same legal system. Hence, monism is unsustainable even in its weaker form.[6]

Hart is right to argue that the criterion of the identity of legal systems that he attributes to Kelsen must be insufficient. However, the attribution of the criterion to Kelsen is false. I also argue that, rightly understood, Kelsen's monism can accommodate the observations that Hart takes to establish the falsity of weak monism. Consequently, it is not as clear as Hart makes it out to be that the world is not governed by a monist system. The question why we should prefer a Hartian, legal-pluralist account of global legal order to a weak form of Kelsenian monism therefore persists. An answer to this question, however, cannot be given on purely theoretical grounds, by appeal to considerations of descriptive accuracy or logical coherence. In a somewhat modified form, I will thus uphold Kelsen's view that the choice between monism and pluralism (portrayed by Kelsen as a choice between different monisms) depends on questions of value (Kelsen 1934: 116–117, 1920: 314–320, 1952: 444–447).

4.2 The Identity of Legal Systems and the Relationship of Validating Purport

Weak monism, to repeat, does not claim that all laws belong to one and the same legal system by logical necessity. What it claims is that it is possible (and plausible) to interpret the existing international legal order in a monist way. In his influential article, *Kelsen's Doctrine of the Unity of Law*, Hart rejected Kelsen's monism in its weak variant as based on an inadequate account of what it means for two (or more) legal norms to belong to the same legal system (Hart 1983: 311–321).

Hart's argument rests on the attribution to Kelsen of the following principle, which we can call the "principle of validating purport:"

> **[PVP]** *If two norms are related by a relationship of validating purport, they both belong to the same legal system.*

A relationship of validating purport, according to Hart, exists between two legal norms whenever one of the two purports or claims to validate the other (Hart 1983: 317–321). Hart's attribution to Kelsen of the principle of validating purport is based on passages in Kelsen's work that offer an analysis of the relationship of international and national law. To sustain his interpretation of Kelsen's monism, Hart cites

---

[6] Ronald Dworkin's mild critique of Hart's attack on Kelsen conceded this key point to Hart. See Dworkin (1968).

the following passage describing the "principle of effectiveness" from Max Knight's translation the second edition of Kelsen's *Pure Theory of Law*:

> A norm of general international law authorises an individual or a group of individuals on the basis of an effective constitution, to create and apply as a legitimate government a normative coercive order. That norm thus legitimises this coercive order for the territory of its actual effectiveness as a valid legal order and the community constituted by this coercive order as a "state" in the sense of international law (Kelsen 1960: 215 (cited in Hart 1983: 318)).

Kelsen's point here, as portrayed by Hart, is that there is a norm of customary international law, the principle of effectiveness, that determines the conditions under which the political rule of a person or group of persons counts as legitimate under international law, with the consequence that the rules enacted by that person or group of persons will then have to be recognized as valid law. The condition in question is simply that the coercive order established by that person or group of persons must enjoy actual effectiveness in some territory (Kelsen 1952: 414–415). Through the principle of effectiveness, international law, then, purports to validate national law. And, given the principle of validating purport, this is sufficient, according to Hart's Kelsen, to establish that national laws are validated by international law and that national and international law therefore form parts of one and the same legal system. In Hart's reading of Kelsen, this alleged appeal to the relationship of validating purport is Kelsen's only argument for the view that national and international law form parts of one integrated legal system. If the principle of validating purport can be shown to be false, Kelsen's monism must consequently fail.

To establish that the principle of validating purport is false, Hart introduces a hypothetical example, which is supposed to make it evident that the principle of validating purport can at best be a necessary, but clearly not a sufficient, condition for the membership in the same legal system of the norms that it connects.

> Suppose the British Parliament [...] passes an Act (the Soviet Laws Validity Act, 1970) which purports to validate the law of the Soviet Union by providing that the laws currently effective in Soviet territory, including those relating to the competence of legislative and judicial authorities, shall be valid (Hart 1983: 319).

If the British Parliament passes the act, British law will purport to validate Soviet law. However, it would obviously be false to argue that the Soviet legal system has thereby become part of British law. Hence, the existence of a relationship of validating purport between the Soviet Laws Validity Act and the laws of the Soviet Union is insufficient to make Soviet law part of the British legal system. If a relationship of validating purport is insufficient to ensure that the laws that it relates belong to the same legal system in this case, Hart concludes, the principle of validating purport must be false. It follows that the principle of effectiveness, which purports to validate national law, is insufficient to establish the unity of international and national law.

Hart also offers a diagnosis of what he takes to be Kelsen's "central mistake" (Hart 1983: 318). The reason why it makes no sense to claim that the Soviet Laws Validity Act validates Soviet law is that "the courts and other law-enforcing agencies in Soviet territory do not, save in certain special circumstances, recognize the operations of the British [...] legislature as criteria for identifying the laws that they are to enforce" (Hart 1983: 319). A little earlier in his paper, Hart asks the reader to imagine that the "Vice-Chancellor of Oxford University dispatched to me a document purporting to order me to write a paper on Kelsen's Doctrine of the Unity of Law" (Hart 1983: 312). As Hart points out, it wouldn't follow from this fact, and the fact that he, Hart, did indeed write a paper on Kelsen's doctrine of the unity of law that, in so doing, he obeyed the Vice-Chancellor of Oxford University or that he recognized the Vice-Chancellor's authority to order him to write papers on a certain topic. Hence, we cannot infer from the fact that the Vice-Chancellor purported to order Hart to do something he in fact ended up doing that the Vice-Chancellor had any authority in the matter over Hart.

Similarly, we cannot infer from the fact that the principle of effectiveness purports to validate national law that the validity of national law in fact depends on the principle of effectiveness. Whether that is the case or not must depend, in Hart's view, on whether the legal officials in the coercive order established by national authorities recognize their laws to have been validated by international law. If they do not, the fact that international law purports to validate national law will not suffice to establish that the validity of national law depends on international law.[7]

In accepting the principle of validating purport, Hart argues, Kelsen focused too narrowly on the content of laws purporting to validate others and failed to pay sufficient attention to the circumstances that attend the enactment of such norms, to whether they are recognized as authoritative and by whom. As a result, Kelsen lost sight of the distinction between a norm that merely purports to validate another norm and one that does in fact validate another norm. The pure theory, Hart argues, lacks the resources to draw this crucial distinction. This establishes the superiority, in Hart's view, of a theory of legal system built on the idea of a practice of recognition. A norm validates another norm, in that view, if is recognized to do so, by the relevant legal officials, and does not merely purport to do so (Hart 1983: 312–313, 335–336).

What are we to make of this criticism of the pure theory? At first glance, it is unlikely that Kelsen would have failed to see the distinction between a norm purporting to validate and a norm that really validates, or to appreciate its importance. After all, Kelsen put heavy emphasis on the distinction between objective and subjective legal meaning,[8] and he famously denied that the fact that the Captain of Köpenick managed, for some time, to order people around gave him real legal authority (Kelsen 1934: 9–10). He would therefore surely have rejected the idea that the Vice-Chancellor of Oxford can put himself in a genuine position of normative authority over Hart merely by purporting to give orders to Hart. It is, therefore, *prima facie* implausible to attribute to Kelsen anything like the principle of validating

[7] Needless to say, Hart argues on the basis of his theory of the rule of recognition. See Hart (1961: 97–107).

[8] I have tried to argue elsewhere that the distinction is crucial to Kelsen's conception of legality. See Vinx (2007: 78–100). Kelsen's most interesting and sustained discussion of the issue is Kelsen (1914).

purport, as formulated by Hart, because the principle involves a rather too obvious confusion of subjective and objective legal meaning.

More to the point, Hart's attribution of the principle of validating purport to Kelsen abstracts from the fact that, for the Kelsenian legal scientist, any description of relationships of validation presupposes the prior choice of and commitment to one of several possible variants of legal monism. As is well known, Kelsen argued that there are two different ways, in the framework of a monist theory of law, to conceive of the relationship between national and international law: national monism and international monism. In the first view, the legal scientist assumes a national basic norm and treats international law as valid only to the extent that it has been (indirectly) validated by that national basic norm. It is only in the second version of monism that the legal scientist, by appeal to the principle of effectiveness, comes to endorse international law's claim to validate national law.[9] Both of these options, according to Kelsen, are equally compatible with all available empirical data for which a theory of legal system for the contemporary world would have to account. Both are therefore descriptively possible choices for the construction of a theory of legal system. Hart himself was aware of Kelsen's "choice-hypothesis," but he argued that it had no bearing on his argument against Kelsen's doctrine of the unity of law (Hart 1983: 311–312). In this Hart was quite clearly mistaken.

The availability of two different monist perspectives implies that Kelsen was not committed to the principle of validating purport. To illustrate the point, let us take another look at the example of the Soviet Laws Validity Act. Hart's reasoning here starts out from the claim that the purported validation of Soviet law by the Soviet Laws Validity Act is not really what validates Soviet law (at least if we discount the marginal scenario of the use of Soviet law in British courts). This claim must surely be true, and I do not wish to dispute it. But Hart appears to assume that it follows from the fact that the Soviet Laws Validity Act does not validate Soviet law that British law and Soviet law cannot form part of one and the same legal system. This second step is an obvious a *non-sequitur*. A Kelsenian legal monist can argue, after all, taking the point of view of international monism, that both British and Soviet law form parts of one global legal system, because they are both validated by the principle of effectiveness. This does not commit the Kelsenian to the view that there is a relationship of validation between British and Soviet law (or *vice versa*). He is therefore as free as a pluralist to deny that the Soviet Laws Validity Act validates Soviet law.

It would also be possible, of course, for the Kelsenian legal scientist to adopt a national monist perspective that might be either Soviet or British. In the first case, he would of course deny, as Hart wants him to, that Soviet law is validated by the Soviet Laws Validity Act, because he will hold that Soviet law, validated by the basic norm of the Soviet legal system, or law recognized by Soviet law, is all the law there is. In the second case, he will make the same claim about British law. Perhaps he will then treat the Soviet Laws Validity Act as validating Soviet law within the

[9] On Kelsen's 'choice hypothesis' see ibid., 113–122, Kelsen (1920: 102–320, 1952: 401–447), von Bernstorff (2010: 104–107), and Langford and Bryan (2012).

British legal system. But the claim that the validity of Soviet law within the British legal system might come to depend on a British statute is, as Hart would have to admit, quite obviously true.

The upshot of this discussion is that Kelsen's monist approach can accommodate Hart's example of the Soviet Laws Validity Act as well as other, similar examples that have been put forward in the literature, as I have shown elsewhere (Vinx 2007: 184–194). Hart was right about one thing: If the British Parliament decided to enact a statute validating Soviet law, it would fail to make the validity of Soviet law depend on that British statute. But this is a claim the Kelsenian monist can acknowledge without the slightest embarrassment and without having to abandon monism. Hart's example, I conclude, proves nothing against (weak) monism.

Hart's use of the example of the Soviet Laws Validity Act goes wrong for the reason that it disregards an important element of Kelsen's theory of legal system: the theory of legal hierarchy first developed by Kelsen's pupil Adolf Merkl (Kelsen 1934: 55–75; Merkl 1931). The theory of legal hierarchy claims, in a nutshell, that the norms that belong to one and the same legal system form a hierarchy of authorization in which higher-level norms determine the conditions for the valid enactment of lower-level norms. It follows from the theory of legal hierarchy that a relationship of validation can exist only between a superior and an inferior norm, but not between two norms that are on the same level of legal hierarchy, or between an inferior and a superior norm.

Every construction of legal system makes assumptions about the structure of legal hierarchy, in that it assigns all valid norms to one or another level of hierarchy. These assignments, as we have just seen, will allow us to distinguish, on a perfectly principled basis, between authentic and spurious relationships of validating purport. The Soviet Laws Validity Act, for instance, could not be an authentic validation of Soviet law, in an international monist construction, because British law and Soviet law are, in that construction, situated on the same level of legal hierarchy. It could not be an authentic validation of Soviet law in a national monist Soviet perspective, because that perspective derives all valid law from the basic norm of the Soviet legal system.

It should now be clear that Kelsen is not committed to Hart's principle of validating purport. Whether some relationship of validating purport will have to be regarded as an objective relationship of validation, in the context of legal-scientific description, will depend on which of the different available monist perspectives is chosen by the Kelsenian legal scientist. And these choices impose restrictions on the authenticity of relationships of validation that go beyond the mere existence of a relationship of validating purport, as Hart defines it. Hence, those choices can always be taken in such a way as to accommodate the intuitions about authentic and inauthentic validation that underpin Hart's examples.

Let us now move to a discussion of the principle of effectiveness, and the relation of national to international law. Hart, as we have seen above, challenges Kelsen's claim that international law can be understood to validate national law by arguing that Kelsen's claim is based on nothing more than the principle of validating purport. Because that principle is false, Hart concludes that Kelsen's monism must be rejected as well. For Hart, the practices of recognition in the national context are what determine the nature of the relationship of national and international law, at least in the absence of an international practice of recognition. National practices of recognition, however, typically do not recognize any dependence of the validity of national law on international law.

This attack fails due to Hart's misattribution of the principle of validating purport to Kelsen. The point can be spelled out both from a national monist and from an international monist perspective.

To start with national monism, the mere fact that international law purports to validate national law does not by itself force the Kelsenian legal theorist to accept that international law validates national law. If the legal officials of some nation, and perhaps the population at large, do not recognize that their law is validated by the principle of effectiveness, they will, presumably, come to embrace a jurisprudential perspective akin to national monism. A Kelsenian legal theorist who thinks that a lack of recognition of international law's claim to validate national law on the part of national officials and citizens undermines international law's claim can of course do the same. A monist, then, can go along with Hart's view that the claim that international law validates national law is deeply implausible, and yet hold on to monism, if he is willing to pay the price of embracing national monism.

The fact that Kelsen is not committed to the principle of validating purport also helps defend the viability of international monism. The international monist construction of legal order does not simply claim that national law must form part of a global legal order because the principle of effectiveness purports to validate national law. Rather, it makes the claim that we can conceive of national and international law as forming a hierarchical structure that gives superiority to international law. This claim, *pace* Hart, is not based on an appeal to the principle of effectiveness alone.

Hart's presentation of Kelsen's doctrine of the unity of law fails to take proper account of Kelsen's oft-repeated view that the existence of a legal system—or, rather, the defensibility of a certain construction of legal system—depends on constraints of effectiveness. It makes no legal-scientific sense, according to Kelsen, to postulate the existence of a certain legal system unless the behaviour that it purports to govern exhibits sufficient conformity with the norms of the system (Kelsen 1920: 94–101, 1952: 412–414). International monism, then, will have to meet constraints of effectiveness to qualify as a viable description of legal order.

It would make no sense to postulate the existence of a global legal order that subordinates national to international law if there weren't a system of states that regularly interact with each other, and that tend to do so in recognition of a number of principles—such as the principle that national law cannot derogate from international legal duties—that can plausibly be seen to imply a superiority of international law to national law. It is therefore wrong for Hart to assume that international monism depends on nothing but a relationship of validating purport between the principle of effectiveness and national law. The question, rather, is whether the system of public international law can, under an international-monist interpretation, account for enough state behaviour to make international monism descriptively plausible. Hart has not established that this is not the case.

4.3 The Basic Norm and the Identity of Legal Systems

Kelsen's conception of the identity of legal systems is open, according to Hart, to a second, seemingly decisive objection that has not been discussed thus far. In rebutting Hart's attribution to Kelsen of the principle of validating purport, I relied heavily on the possibility of a choice between different monist perspectives on the relation between national and international law. As is well known, Kelsen consistently argued that the choice between these different perspectives—national and international monism—is not determined, given the current state of development of international law, by objectively ascertainable empirical facts. Both national and international monism, in Kelsen's view, fit the relevant facts well enough to constitute plausible interpretations of global legal order as it currently exists. Legal science, therefore, cannot tell us how to choose between them. The choice, ultimately, must be grounded on one's ideological preferences (Kelsen 1934: 116–117, 1920: 314–320, 1952: 444–447).

This view has an important implication with respect to our aim to distinguish between mere purported validation and real validation. Whether a relationship of validating purport will amount to a real relationship of validation will depend, in some cases, on what form of monism we choose. According to international monism, for instance, the principle of effectiveness does not merely purport to validate norms of national law. It does validate norms of national law. In national monism, by contrast, its validating purport will not be recognized as truly validating. But if the choice between national and international monism is not determinable by legal science, then legal science cannot determine, or so it seems, whether the principle of effectiveness merely purports to validate national law or whether it actually does so. It seems that Kelsenian legal science does not provide us with any way to ascertain the objective legal meaning of the principle of effectiveness. As a result, the question of the identity of legal systems will also remain indeterminate: There is no legal-scientific way to decide whether, say, British law forms part of a global legal system or whether it should be regarded as a self-standing legal system that, from its own point of view, includes all other valid law within it.

One might argue, of course, that a good theory of the identity of legal systems ought to allow us to answer questions like these. Hart's second main criticism of the pure theory's conception of the identity of legal systems takes Kelsen to task for failing to make his theory live up to this criterion of adequacy. This charge is typically framed as a complaint about the emptiness of reference to the basic norm as a criterion of a norm's membership in a legal system (Hart 1983: 338–339; Raz 1970: 100–105). According to Kelsen, as Hart understands him, legal systems are to be individuated by recourse to a basic norm. Two norms belong to the same legal system if and only if they can both be traced back to one and the same basic norm. If, by contrast, two norms are validated by different basic norms, they belong to two separate legal systems. Hart argues, however, that it is sometimes possible to trace back norms to one and the same basic norm, through relationships of validating purport, that do not, in fact, belong to the same legal system:

> The basic norm of the American constitution is (roughly) that the constitution is valid; but unless we have some independent criterion of what it is for laws to belong to one system we cannot trace the validity of laws back to the constitution and thence to its basic norm; we can only trace relationships of validating purport, and these, as we have seen, cut across different legal systems (Hart 1983: 339).

The independent criterion Hart alludes to here is of course a rule of recognition—in this case the set of criteria, whatever they are, that are in fact used by American courts to determine whether a purported law belongs to the American legal system. Once we can rely on a rule of recognition to determine whether some law belongs to the American legal system or not, the appeal to a basic norm validating the American constitution turns out to be superfluous. It makes no contribution to identifying the valid rules of American law.[10] If, on the other hand, we refrain from invoking the rule of recognition as an independent criterion, we are forced to rely on relationships of validating purport. We have to adopt the view, in other words, that two norms belong to the same legal system if there is a basic norm that purports to validate them both. Such an approach, however, must surely go wrong. It would not allow a Soviet court, Hart assumes, to deny that the validity of Soviet laws depends on the British Soviet Laws Validity Act. Hart thinks that the only reasonable course for a legal theorist is to embrace the first horn of this dilemma. Kelsenians should admit that traceability to the basic norm is an empty criterion of the identity of legal system, and accept the theory of the rule of recognition instead.

A Kelsenian might be tempted to give a rather flippant reply to all of this. The question whether some legal norm belongs to this or to that legal system obviously will not ever bother a legal monist. A legal monist is already committed to the view, for good reasons or bad, that there is only one legal system, and that all legal norms that there are belong to it. It thus makes little sense to assume that Kelsen's theory of the basic norm was meant to answer the question of identity, as Hart understands it, ie, that it was meant to provide us with a criterion for deciding whether some legal norm belongs to this or rather to that of several existing legal systems, as though that were an open question. To think that this is an open question is to assume the truth of legal pluralism, which is to beg the question against the monist.

To make this answer a little less flippant, we can re-emphasize a point already made in the discussion of Hart's first criticism. There is a valid concern as to whether monism can provide us with a plausible account of the structure of the one legal system that it holds to exist. Hart is right to argue that it would speak against monism if monism were unable to cast aside and treat as spurious at least some relationships of validating purport. The validity of Soviet law would not have come to depend on British law if Parliament had enacted the Soviet Laws Validity Act. But as we have seen, there is no reason to suppose that a monist view cannot give enough structure to the legal system to avoid such conclusions. A Kelsenian national monist will of course deny that the British Soviet Laws Validity Act validates Soviet law. And a Kelsenian international monist will hardly have a difficult time to come up with an

[10] For Hart's general development of this attack on the rule of recognition see Hart (1961: 107–110).

explanation that relies on norms of international law for why the British Parliament did not have the authority to validate or invalidate Soviet law. According to his view, both British and Soviet law are validated by international law, but not by each other.

To be sure, Kelsenian legal science still does not resolve the choice between national and international monism. In that sense, it fails to give a perfectly determinate answer to the question of the identity of legal system. But is this a shortcoming of the pure theory? Kelsen may well be have been right to argue that the facts and/or examples that Hart considers to be determinative of the question of the identity of legal systems are, in fact, incapable of providing an unambiguous determination of that question. The fact, for instance, that the Soviet Laws Validity Act would not have come to be the validating ground of Soviet law if it had been enacted does not show that monism is false, and it does not help us to choose one version of monism over the other.

4.4 Monism and the Conflict of Laws

There is one final Hartian objection to monism that we have to consider. I conceded at the outset that Kelsen is wrong to claim that all valid legal norms must necessarily belong to one and the same legal system. I do not deny that one can coherently picture a world, from a Hartian external point of view (Hart 1961: 86–88), which contains several legal systems that are not connected in such a way as to provide any basis for a monist construction of global legal order. A pluralist description of global legal order might, given certain circumstances, even turn out to be the only plausible one. It would make no sense, for instance, for a legal historian to argue that the legal system of the Roman Empire and of the Chinese Empire formed parts of one global legal system. But it would make no sense either for the historian to choose the perspective of one of the two and then to deny that the other was a genuine legal system, containing valid norms. Any plausible description of the legal state of the world in late antiquity the legal historian might come up with will have to be pluralist.

In recognition of this point, I have done nothing more than to try to clear the way for the defense of a weaker form of monism, one that merely holds that monism is a plausible and perhaps attractive interpretation of current global legal order. What characterizes the current historical situation is that it has become possible, while taking a Kelsenian normative point of view, as opposed to a Hartian external or a sociological point of view, to interpret all law that now exists on the globe as belonging to one system. But this possibility is historically contingent on a certain degree of global legal interconnection. It is not implied by the conditions of the possibility of legal cognition.

As Hart rightly points out, Kelsen's monism, even in this modified form, is still committed to a "weaker version of the 'no conflict' theory" (Hart 1983: 332). A monist interpretation of global legal order, according to Kelsen, will have to show that there are no legally irresolvable conflicts between national and international law. If an apparent conflict between two norms that are both to be regarded as legally valid were not amenable to a legal solution, through the application of some legal rule or principle that gives priority to one over the other, the two norms in question would, in Kelsen's view, have to be regarded as belonging to separate systems of legal authority, neither of which can claim recognized superiority over the other. In other words, Kelsen would, in describing the relation of the two norms, be forced back into the external point of view and would have to embrace some form of legal pluralism.

Because international monism holds international law to be hierarchically superior to national law, and to authorize the enactment of national law, Kelsen would seem to be committed to the claim that purported national laws that conflict with international law ought to be regarded as invalid. The problem with this view, of course, is that national legislatures often enact laws that appear to conflict with norms of international law, but that are not therefore treated as lacking legal validity. The most natural explanation of this fact, it would appear, is that conformity with norms of international law is not typically a condition of the validity of national statutes. These conditions, rather, depend on a national legal system's own practice of recognition. Such a practice may or may not take account of international law, but, even if it does, international law's standing as a condition of the validity of national laws will itself depend on the national practice of recognition. The national practice of recognition is an ultimate standard of validity that turns the national legal order into an independent legal system.

To deal with this challenge, Kelsen attempts to show that, from a monist perspective, there are no real conflicts between national and international law, ie, that all such conflicts can be shown to be merely apparent (Kelsen 1934: 117–119). Kelsen's main strategy for achieving this goal is to assimilate apparent conflicts between national and international law to apparent conflicts between a constitution and statutes that violate constitutional norms (Kelsen 1929). A statute that apparently conflicts with a national constitutional provision will, unless it fails to pass the threshold of absolute nullity, enjoy legal validity. That the statute is unconstitutional means either that it can be invalidated on grounds of unconstitutionality by a constitutional court or—if the political system does not provide for that possibility—that the organs that enacted the statute can be held liable for violating the constitution, even while the statute itself continues to enjoy validity. As Kelsen points out, there is no conflict between the constitutional norm that allows for the invalidation of the unconstitutional law or for the punishment of its enactors, and the demands, whatever they may be, of the unconstitutional statute.

Similarly for the relationship of national to international law: That a national law fails to conform to a provision of international law that the state is under a duty to observe need not entail that it is not valid, even from a monist and internationalist point of view. The legal significance of the international norm, rather, consists in the fact that its violation makes the violating state liable to a sanction under international law that may be applied by the injured state. Once again, there is no conflict between the national and the international norm. Imagine that two countries A and B enter into a treaty in which A undertakes to grant political rights to the members of a minority. Assume as well that the legislature of A proceeds to enact a national statute depriving members of that minority of its political rights. The treaty-based international norm, in Kelsen's reconstruction, determines no more than that A is now liable to a sanction, and this liability does not conflict with the demands that the national statute, which determines that members of the minority are not to enjoy political rights, makes on its respective addressees.

This defense of the weak no-conflicts thesis raises a host of interesting and complicated questions, and I cannot discuss all of them here. I will focus, rather, on Hart's main criticism that is quoted below:

> This argument is ingenious, but [...] it does not, in fact, banish conflict between international and municipal law; it merely locates such conflict at a different point and shows it to be a conflict not between rules requiring and prohibiting the same action (the treaty and the statute) but between rules prohibiting and permitting the same action, ie the enactment of a statute. It is a conflict of this latter form that arises when a state enacts a statute in violation of its treaty obligations, if its enactment is an offence according to international law, but is not so according to municipal law. There are certainly many systems of municipal law, among them the English, according to which it is not an offence to enact or to procure the enactment of any statute, and so this is permitted. It is logically impossible to conform [...] both to the permissive rule of municipal law permitting the enactment of any statute and the rule of international law relating to treaties which [...] prohibits such an enactment and makes it an offence or a delict (Hart 1983: 334).

Hart argues here that Kelsen's "ingenious argument" does no more than to eliminate the possibility that one and the same act may turn out to be legally mandated by one law, so that its non-performance is the condition for the application of a sanction, and be legally prohibited by another, so that its performance is the condition for the application of a sanction. However, Kelsen's elimination of the possibility of this first kind of conflict, according to Hart, does not rule out the possibility of another, second kind of conflict between national and international norms. The British principle of parliamentary sovereignty permits the enactment of laws with any content, even with a content that constitutes an international delict. As a result, an act of legislation that is permitted under British law, and thus not a condition for the application of a sanction in British law, may turn out to be impermissible under international law, being a condition for the application of an international sanction.

Of course, this second kind of conflict is in one respect less serious than the first: it does not make it impossible for the British Parliament to exercise its power in such a way as not to violate either British or international law. But it does bar Parliament, assuming it wants to avoid breaking international law, from making full use of the permission to legislate granted by the British constitution. Or put differently: One and the same act may still turn out to be legally permissible and legally impermissible at the same time, depending on whether we evaluate it from a national or an international perspective, and that must surely be regarded as sufficient proof of the possibility of conflict between British and international law.

Note, however, that Hart's description of the legal situation seems to presuppose the truth of legal pluralism. Hart, in claiming that one and the same act may turn out to be both legally permissible and impermissible, clearly assumes that British law and international law are independent legal systems with their own ultimate and potentially conflicting criteria of validity. But the internationalist monist view, needless to say, must be that international law and British law are both to be interpreted as parts of one and the same legal system, in which British law is a mere subordinate part of an international system of law. And it is not at all clear whether, in that interpretive context, the principle of parliamentary sovereignty ought to be understood as permitting the enactment of statutes that conflict with international law.

Hart, in the passage just cited, appears to understand permission as the absence of prohibition. Under British law, as Hart points out, "it is not an offence to enact or procure the enactment of any statute." Let us assume, moreover, that it is not possible, under the British constitution, to introduce a law that would make it an offence to do so. From the perspective of international monism this plainly does not entail that it is not an offence for the British parliament to enact or to procure the enactment of any statute. For an enactment not to be an offence, it would of course have to conform to all law that forms part of the legal system, including—from the point of view of international monism—international law. Hence, all that is implied by Hart's observations about the British Constitution is that the prohibition to enact some law, if there is any, cannot be grounded in British law.

Kelsen need not concede that the enactment of a national statute that violates an international treaty is legally permissible. In fact, Kelsen explicitly argues that such an enactment would be an illegal act and, as such, subject to a sanction, notwithstanding the fact that the statute in question may acquire legal standing, as a result of the fact that the system of international law does not provide well-developed guarantees of legality, such as an international legal mechanism to invalidate national statutes that violate international law (Kelsen 1934: 118). From an international-monist perspective, then, it is legally impermissible for the British legislator to enact a law that violates an international treaty. Hence, Hart is simply wrong to claim that the monist must admit that, in the scenario outlined by Hart, one and the same act may turn out to be both permissible and impermissible. That description will only apply to the scenario if we have already adopted a pluralist perspective that treats British law as a separate legal system with its own ultimate standards of validity. However, in doing that, we rather obviously beg the question against the monist.

Hartians are likely to reply that Kelsen fails to take seriously enough the fact that British courts are committed to treating the principle of parliamentary sovereignty as an ultimate standard of validity. It is often held that this supposed fact (as well as analogous supposed facts about the courts of other nations) alone suffices to establish the falsity of Kelsen's international monism.[11]

[11] See, for example, Kumm (2012: 42):

> If the highest court of a legal order insists on applying the law of the more encompassing legal order only under conditions defined by its legal order and the decisions of that court are generally taken as authoritative by other officials of that legal order, then the relationship between the legal orders is pluralist as a matter of fact.

Kumm goes on to argue the relationship should not be pluralist as a matter of right. But I think he concedes the descriptive point too readily. His own cosmopolitan ambitions would be better

The principle of parliamentary sovereignty, however, can be re-interpreted within the monist framework. According to Dicey's classical formulation, to say that Parliament enjoys legislative sovereignty under the British constitution means that British courts will treat all laws enacted by Parliament as valid, which of course implies that they will not enforce constraints of international law against the British legislator.[12]

Kelsen's international monism, however, is clearly compatible with the non-enforcement of international legal constraints in national courts. It does not deny that norms of international law that bind states will often or even typically not be enforceable in national courts. From an international monist perspective, however, this does not settle the question of the legal permissibility of national acts of legislation that violate international law, because the violation of the international norm makes a state liable to an international sanction, to be carried out by the injured state.

As far as I can see, nothing rules out the possibility of a national judge who both upholds the principle of parliamentary sovereignty and adopts international monism as his theory of legal system. Such a judge would hold that the national principle of parliamentary sovereignty bars him from enforcing international constraints on national legislation, but he would nevertheless agree that his state is under a legal obligation not to legislate in ways that violate international law, and he would concede that a state injured by such an enactment on the part of his own state has a legal right to impose sanctions. He may even agree that the laws of his country are validated by the principle of effectiveness. There is nothing at all inconsistent in such a view.

Hence, we cannot interpret the bare fact that national courts, in some states, refuse to enforce international legal constraints as a falsification of legal monism. Or to put the point slightly differently: The fact that a British judge will regard the principle of parliamentary sovereignty as the ultimate standard for the identification of the legal norms that he is tasked to enforce in his own court does not imply that he must regard parliamentary sovereignty as an ultimate standard of legal validity that turns British law into an independent legal system separate from international law. Empirical facts about legal practice, insofar as they are indisputable, are again less determinative than Hart assumed.

served by taking the view that the facts he talks about here do not establish that there is no unified global legal order as a matter of fact.

[12] See Dicey (1982: 87):

> The principle then of Parliamentary sovereignty may, looked at from its positive side, be thus described: Any Act of Parliament, or any part of an Act of Parliament, which makes a new law, or repeals or modifies an existing law, will be obeyed by the Courts. The same principle, looked at from its negative side, may be thus stated: There is no person or body of persons who can, under the English constitution, make rules which override or derogate from an Act of Parliament, or which (to express the same thing in other words) will be enforced by the Courts in contravention of an Act of Parliament.

4.5 Kelsen, Hart, and the Argument from Moral Consequences

The rebuttals of Hart's critique of Kelsen that were offered here leave us with a further question that our dialectical moves on behalf of Kelsen have only made more pressing: Why monism? Let us assume that Hart's specific attacks on Kelsen's weak monism can be parried. Perhaps it is true that Hart implicitly assumes the truth of pluralism and that his arguments thus beg the question against weak monism. Perhaps it is true that the kinds of facts that Hart invokes to establish the falsity of monism fail to lend sufficient support to his rejection of Kelsen's doctrine of the unity of law, for the reason that they can be accommodated by that doctrine. This still leaves a simple and powerful final question in the hands of the Hartian. Why adopt a monist interpretation of global legal order?

What I have argued throughout is that Hart's attempts to establish the descriptive inadequacy of weak monism fail. If such attempts fail, and if it is possible—as Kelsen himself demonstrated—to offer a rich and nuanced description of contemporary global legal order on a monist basis, we are entitled to assume that weak monism is at least a descriptive possibility and that Kelsen's normativist theory of legal system might, *pace* Hart, turn out to be viable. But this is not to say, I concede, that legal pluralism is false. To prove that legal pluralism is false, one would have to defend Kelsen's strong monism, which I did not set out to do, because I am not convinced that this would be a promising endeavor. It is certainly as possible to give a nuanced and rich description of contemporary global legal order on a legal-pluralist basis as it is to give a monist description. In describing contemporary global legal order, then, we appear to have a real choice, as far as descriptive adequacy is concerned, between a Kelsenian monist view and a pluralist account stemming from Hart's theory of legal system.

If both weak monism and legal pluralism are descriptively viable as accounts of contemporary global legal order, then the choice between the two descriptions must, it seems, come to depend on normative factors. Even Hart himself supported the idea, in one of his moods, that the choice of an adequate legal theory might come to depend, within the restrictions set by a requirement of descriptive adequacy, on a theory's practical consequences and thus on our practical interests (Hart 1958: 615–621).

Admittedly, this way of addressing the choice between monism and pluralism conflicts with the purity of the pure theory of law, as it is normally understood, and I certainly would not want to claim that mine is the only plausible way to take Kelsen's ideas on international law forward. But to safeguard the purity of the pure theory, we would either have to defend strong monism, or choose purity over monism and become Kelsenian legal pluralists (Kammerhofer 2009, 2011: 230–240). I am inclined to reject both of these options: The first because I am not convinced that strong monism is defensible, and the second because I would nevertheless like to uphold monism, if it is descriptively viable, for what I suspect may be good normative reasons. At the point where Kelsen's commitment to a value-neutral legal science and his commitment to monism come to pull apart, I prefer to stick to monism and to work out what I take to be its implicit moral content (Vinx 2007).

This approach is open to the charge that one must not make the choice between two different conceptions of law depend on the moral consequences of that choice. Julie Dickson, who has developed this charge most forcefully, claims that to choose a conception of law over another for its beneficial moral consequences must amount to "wishful thinking" and "utopian scheming" (Dickson 2001: 83–102).[13] Dickson argues that the choice for some conception of law can have morally beneficial consequences only if that conception is independently true. Moreover, even if choosing a false conception of law could have morally beneficial consequences, we would, in choosing that conception for its morally beneficial consequences, impair the accuracy of our theoretical understanding of what the law is.

I am perfectly happy to concede that we should not advocate the adoption of a conception of law, on the ground that it has beneficial moral consequences, if that conception can be shown to be descriptively inadequate, ie, if it can be shown to fail to make sense of intuitions or observations that an accurate account of legal system would have to accommodate. Kelsen's monist theory would have to be rejected, even if its adoption had morally beneficial consequences, if it was true that it cannot distinguish between mere relationships of validating purport and genuine relationships of validation. The thrust of my argument, however, has been that Kelsen's monist theory is not descriptively inadequate, or at least that Hartians have so far failed to show that it is. And if considerations of descriptive adequacy do not suffice to distinguish between two conceptions of law or legal system, then it is hard to see how we could make a cognitive mistake, or be accused of wishful thinking, in choosing between them on moral grounds.

Note that Kelsen himself adopted an argument from beneficial moral consequences in advocating the cosmopolitan version of legal monism. According to Kelsen, both national monism and international monism are descriptively adequate: All incontestable facts that a theory of the structure of legal order would have to explain can, in Kelsen's view, be accommodated by either perspective. The choice between the two perspectives must consequently come to depend on one's assessment of the moral consequences of the choice. The problem with the national monist approach, as Kelsen sees it, is that it cannot conceive of different states as equal members of a legal community of nations. The idea of a legal community of nations that enjoy equal standing under international law, irrespective of their size and *de facto* power, however, is described by Kelsen as "an eminently ethical idea and one of the few genuinely valuable and uncontested constituents of modern cultural consciousness" (Kelsen 1920: 204).

Kelsen is concerned that adoption of a national monist perspective is going to have the consequence of impeding the further institutional development of public international law, and in particular of the introduction of a compulsory system of international adjudication, which Kelsen regards to be highly desirable from a moral

[13] Dickson's argument is phrased as a critique of Schauer (1996). See also Schauer's reply to Dickson in Schauer (2005).

point of view. Adoption of the international monist perspective, on the other hand, is likely to favor such a development. After all, if we already agree that there is an objectively valid system of public international law that authorizes national law and to which nation states are already subject, there seems to be no good reason to oppose the introduction of institutions that can efficiently adjudicate and enforce the norms of that system (Kelsen 1942, 1944).

Kelsen's own argument from beneficial moral consequences, to be sure, assumes the truth of what I have called strong monism. It assumes, in other words, that legal pluralism can be rejected on *a priori* grounds of incoherence. Because monism, in either its national or its international form, is, in Kelsen's view, the only logically coherent description of legal order, we can choose only between the two forms of legal monism. Once this is granted, the choice for national monism can be portrayed as a flat denial of international law, ie, of a law that coordinates states that enjoy equal legal status, for the reason that national monism cannot recognize any law that is not validated by, and thus subordinated to, the basic norm of one's own national legal system. International monism is thus made to appear as the only description of legal order that a civilized and progressive person could wish to embrace (Kelsen 1920: 151–204).

I concede that the argument offered here does not allow us to employ this gambit against a Hartian approach. The defense of weak monism offered here does not entail, to repeat, that Hartian legal pluralism can be rejected on *a priori* grounds, or that it is descriptively less adequate than a Kelsenian theory of legal system. A Hartian legal pluralism remains on the menu of available descriptions of legal order. Hart, in contrast to the authors whom Kelsen accuses of embracing national monism, is not committed to a denial of the possibility of the co-existence of national and international legal systems. And though Hart refused to recognize public international law as a paradigm-case of legality, his theory clearly leaves open the possibility that public international law might develop into a full-fledged legal system, and possibly even into one that comes to subordinate and incorporate national legal orders, so as to create a monist global legal order (Hart 1961: 213–237).

A second charge against my suggestion that the choice between a Hartian legal pluralist and a weak monist approach to the description of international legal order ought to be made on moral grounds, then, is that the differences between a weak monist and a Hartian description of international legal order do not run deep enough to make that choice very consequential, as regards its moral consequences. This criticism seems to me to understate the differences between a Hartian and a weak monist perspective.

To begin with, the two views arrive at fundamentally different assessments of the status of the current system of international law. Hart, in the last chapter of *The Concept of Law*, suggested that existing public international law does not amount to a full-fledged legal system, as it lacks a sufficiently developed and unified practice of recognition (Hart 1961: 232–237). The weak monist assessment, by contrast, denies that the system of international law fails to attain the full quality of law. As long as it is possible to construct all law as part of international legal order, and to show that the construction meets a constraint of effectiveness, the assumption that there is a full-fledged system of international law is as tenable, from a Kelsenian point of view, as any other systemic hypothesis (Kelsen 1952: 18–89).

These diverging assessments, in turn, are tied to different views about the relation between law and its institutions. Put crudely, for Hart and his followers, law follows institutionalization. If it is the essential function of law to offer authoritative dispute resolution, Hartians argue, legal systems must be normative systems the norms of which are authoritatively applied by judicial institutions. The practices of recognition of these authoritative institutions must determine what norms belong to a legal system (Hart 1961: 147–154; Raz 1990: 123–148). Kelsen, in marked contrast to Hart, frequently suggests that the development of law can and sometimes does jump ahead of institutionalization, because a coherent and sufficiently descriptive systemic hypothesis may be applicable even in the absence of centralized adjudication and enforcement.[14] Kelsen is quite willing, hence, to acknowledge the systemic and legal quality of "primitive" normative orders that do not possess judicial institutions with compulsory jurisdiction over all questions that might arise under the relevant rules (Kelsen 1944: 3–4, 1952: 13–17). However, Kelsen, of course, does not thereby intend to deny the importance of institutionalization for the efficient functioning of legal order.

The morally salient consequences of adopting a Kelsenian international monist perspective, even if only in its weak form, over a Hartian approach turn out to be very similar to the consequences that Kelsen expected from a choice of international monism over national monism. Once we adopt the weak monist perspective, as opposed to a Hartian approach, jurisprudential questions that Kelsen refers to as "legal-technical" questions—questions, that is, about how to make the international legal system function as efficiently as possible—will naturally take center stage. If our theoretical choice already recognizes the existence of an objectively valid system of public international law that stands above national legal systems and authorizes them, then we are committed, Kelsen suggests, to create the institutions that would make that system function well.[15] In particular, we are committed, Kelsen thinks, to the creation of impartial institutions of adjudication that can offer a "guarantee of legality" other than self-help, ie, other than the unilateral use of coercive

[14] To be more precise, a normative system is a legal system, according to Kelsen, if it successfully claims a monopoly of legitimate force, ie, if the behavior of the purported subjects of the law is sufficiently in line with the principle that the use of coercive force is legitimate only in response to a prior delict or violation of the law. For instance, Kelsen claims, with respect to international law, that:

> international law is true law if the coercive acts of states [...] are, in principle, permitted only as a reaction against a delict, and accordingly the employment of force to any other end is forbidden; in other words, if the coercive act undertaken as a reaction against a delict can be interpreted as a reaction of the international legal community (Kelsen 1952: 18).

This condition could be fulfilled, Kelsen holds, in the absence of centralized adjudication and enforcement of a system's norms, because injured parties (or their allies) could apply sanctions for delicts committed against them by way of (legally authorized) self-help.

[15] Kelsen's line of argument here is strictly analogous to his argument for the introduction of constitutional adjudication in a domestic context. See Kelsen (1929).

force on the part of a state that claims that its rights under international law have been violated (Kelsen 1944; von Bernstorff 2010: 191–220). Adopting the international monist perspective, then, is likely to favor our willingness to institutionally strengthen the system of public international law.

There might be objections that this line of reasoning presupposes a normative standard of the proper functioning of legal order and that it is wrongheaded to attribute such a standard to Kelsen, who often adopted the posture of a hard-nosed demystifier of our understanding of law. But the fact is that Kelsen, at times, rather unambiguously commits himself to such a normative standard, namely to the ideal of legal peace.[16] This commitment is made most explicit in Kelsen's assertion that the essential function of a legal order is to secure peace, by submitting all use of coercive force to constraints of legality (Kelsen 1944: 3, 1952: 17–18). This view is tied to Kelsen's account of the structure of legal norms (as authorizations of the application of sanctions) and to his claim that public international law is complete, in the sense that it provides legal grounds for resolving any possible conflict between states (Vinx 2011). A condition of full legal peace exists where coercive force is used only in response to a prior delict and after an impartial judicial decision. The attraction of international monism, to Kelsen, is that it promises, in contrast to national monism or legal pluralism, to help subject the use of force on the part of states to comprehensive and effective legal regulation and impartial judicial arbitration that Kelsen hopes will pacify international relations (Vinx 2007: 176–207).

In pointing out that Kelsen was committed to the ideal of legal peace, I do not mean to imply that Kelsen embraced international monism over pluralism for the reason that he thought it would serve that ideal. For Kelsen, the adoption of one or another form of monism, as I have emphasized already, is required on *a priori* grounds, in virtue of a demand for the normative consistency of all law that Kelsen considered to be a theoretical and not a practical postulate (Kelsen 1920: 107–111). From that perspective, the fact that the adoption of the international form of monism can be expected to have morally beneficial consequences is a mere by-product, though undoubtedly to Kelsen a highly welcome one, of the only theoretically defensible understanding of the nature of legal order.

My point is that the commitment to the ideal of legal peace must take on a heightened significance for those who think that Kelsen's *a priori* case for monism is unconvincing but who are nevertheless attracted to monism, and in particular to international monism. It might be argued that it is perfectly possible to adopt an international monist perspective on global legal order without thereby expressing a normative commitment to the ideal of legal peace, like the anarchist law professor who adopts an internal point of view to explain to his students what the law is without thereby endorsing its normative claims. But what would be the point of doing that if an institution-centred and pluralist description of legal order is equally available? If a descriptively accurate account of what the law is need not rely on a monist perspective, then why adopt it over a pluralist description that equally serves any purely expository interest? This question will be especially pressing if the adoption

[16] On the importance of the idea of peace for Kelsen's theory of legal system see Notermans (2015).

of monism has morally salient consequences that differ from the consequences of the adoption of the Hartian alternative.

That this is indeed the case appears obvious. For Hart, and authors working in the Hartian tradition, the existence of law is a matter of moral indifference. Whether more law or more unified law—in the international sphere or elsewhere—is better, we are told, depends on whether that law is going to be used as an instrument for good or bad (Raz 2009b). The further strengthening of the system of public international law, from a Hartian perspective, cannot be desirable *per se*. And because public international law, according to Hart, is not as yet a full-fledged legal system, we cannot, on Hartian grounds, argue from the existence of an international legal system to a commitment to make it work. The Hartian perspective, then, like the national monist perspective, is much less conducive than international monism to the goal of the realization of international legal peace. The choice between a weak form of international monism and legal pluralism, I conclude, must depend on one's estimation of the moral value of an international rule of law.

4.6 Why Not Pluralism?

Let me finish by making some tentative suggestions concerning the normative reasons that might come to bear on a choice between monism and pluralism, assuming that both are descriptively viable. Of course, it is by no means obvious that weak monism will prevail over a pluralist theory of legal system once we accept that the choice between the two approaches must depend on moral consequences. In what follows, I do not offer a comprehensive discussion of the question. Rather, I suggest that some common arguments for the moral attractiveness of legal pluralism might be misconceived.

Legal pluralists frequently talk as though monism was inseparably connected to the monolithic and homogenizing political form of state sovereignty.[17] But this portrayal of monism is a clear misrepresentation of Kelsen's monism. If deployed against Kelsen's monism, it is question-begging in much the same way as Hart's descriptive objections. Of course, if we adopt a legal-pluralist point of view that ties the identity of a legal system to an institutionalized practice of recognition, then the development of monism is imaginable only as a consequence of prior political centralization. In order to rely on the theory of the rule of recognition to determine the identity of a legal system, we must know beforehand whose recognition is to count

[17] See for instance Neil Walker (2012: 18–19) who describes monism as "a tendency towards a new manifestation of closure and a new reduction to unity; towards the old familiar of everything deemed constitutional being contained—'constituted' indeed—within the one hierarchically layered legal and political system." Such talk assumes, without offering much in the way of argument, that legal unity must be tied to the kind of political unity we associate with the modern state. It also assumes that all forms of unity and closure are equally bad. Kelsen's willingness to challenge such assumptions strikes me as more progressive and more intellectually enterprising than contemporary legal or constitutional pluralism.

as constitutive of the rule of recognition in question. And we can only know whose recognition counts if we already have an understanding of the boundaries of the political institutions of the legal systems we investigate. Given a legal-pluralist perspective, the call for monism must, then, appear to be a call for a kind of imperialism. Monism must be the arbitrary claim that one of the many institutionalized normative systems or practices of recognition, and thus one particular polity, should lord it over the others.

Kelsen's monism, however, claims that there can be global legal unity without much in the way of political centralization. The only institution necessary for the efficient functioning of the order of public international law, Kelsen argued, is an international court with compulsory jurisdiction over all disputes under international law (Kelsen 1942, 1944). If Kelsen's conception of legality describes a real possibility, a global legal system need not resemble the dreaded world state.[18] And because Kelsen's monism, as I have argued, may well turn out to be descriptively adequate, the normative worry that monism must resemble sovereignty may well turn out to be ungrounded.

My second suggestion is that legal pluralism implicitly disavows the goal of making political conflict between states amenable to legal resolution. In a monist interpretation of global legal order, as Kelsen points out, there are no political conflicts that do not have a legal solution (Kelsen 1931: 184–185). From a monist point of view, all political conflicts between states are in principle open to be settled through the use of legal procedures. The idea here is not, however, that political conflicts are to be made to disappear, perhaps through a prior homogenizing exercise of political violence of the sort that would be needed to found a world state, before legal arbitration begins. Rather, the idea is that they are to take on a different form, one that, hopefully, is going to be more peaceful than purely political conflict, while being open for political difference within legal unity.

Whether hope for such a civilizing power of international law can still be shared today is of course a doubtful question. Kelsen himself may have thought that the danger of the employment of law as a means of oppression and hegemony is less to be feared in the framework of public international law—at least if it comes to be supported by the binding adjudicative settlement of all international disputes—than in the framework of a sovereign nation state that has a legislator who is unhampered by formal constitutional constraints. This stance, in retrospect, may strike us as politically naïve. But it is important to remain aware of the fact that the legal pluralist alternative does little more than to consign the settlement of inter-systemic conflict to the sphere of power politics.

Legal pluralists like to sing the praises of the progressive attitudes that proponents of different systemic perspectives are allegedly going to exhibit to one another as soon as they have come to recognize the inescapable plurality of legal systems. Tolerance, understanding, and mutual respect are regularly portrayed as likely consequences of an adoption of the legal-pluralist mindset (Krisch 2012; Barber 2010: 170–171).

[18] We are perhaps too afraid of this at any rate. See Scheuerman (2011: 149–168).

Pluralism's bottom line, however, must surely be that inter-systemic conflicts have no legal resolution. To demand that the proponents of different systemic perspectives must therefore be nice and respectful to one another, instead of insisting that their perspective must prevail, is all fine and well. But there is no more intimate connection, either logically or psychologically, between the recognition of the relativity of all legal evaluation and such a tolerant attitude of mutual respect than there is between the recognition of relativity and the unreasoned conviction that one's own perspective must, to the greatest extent possible, be imposed on others. The belief in the relativism of legal evaluation does not entail a belief in the duty of tolerance or mutual respect. It might, with equal consistency, lead to the belief that there is no reason why your view should prevail rather than mine. The consequence of an adoption of legal pluralism, as a result, might well lead to a stance that is pragmatically indistinguishable from national monism.

One might reply here—with Carl Schmitt—that we cannot turn political conflicts into conflicts amenable to legal resolution simply by pretending that there is a global legal order. The proper answer to this challenge is that Schmitt was wrong about the limits of legality. Political conflicts do become amenable to legal resolution if the pretence that they are is successful, and the pretence can be successful if enough of us (statesmen, lawyers, academics, journalists, and citizens) think that there are good moral reasons to settle international conflicts through legal procedure rather than through pure politics. If that latter belief is true, then our pretence will be harmless. It will be nothing but the practical expression of our valid moral commitment to the ideal that political conflicts ought to be resolved, wherever possible, through a properly designed legal procedure and not through the unilateral use of force.

Kelsen came rather close to making the same point when he argued that the choice between the two monist perspectives—national and international—depends on ideological conviction. And his personal estimation of the value of the international rule of law, as already pointed out, was highly positive (Kelsen 1920: 314–320). I hope to have provided some reasons for thinking that it would be useful to make the moral reasons for that normative stance, as well as their jurisprudential significance, more explicit than Kelsen himself felt it necessary to do. At any rate, pluralism should not be regarded as the only account of the structure of global legal order that is descriptively viable or that has normative attractions. Kelsen's monism deserves another look.

Acknowledgments This paper was first presented at a seminar on Kelsen's international theory organized by Robert Jan Witpaard at Radboud University in Nijmegen. It was presented again at the 2013 Christmas meeting of the Norwegian Association for Legal Philosophy, at the invitation of Jørgen Stubberud, and then at the workshop in Chicago organized by Jeremy Telman. I am very grateful to Jeremy, Robert Jan, and Jørgen for giving me the opportunity to participate in these events. I received a wealth of feedback on all three occasions: Svein Eng's meticulous comments at Oslo were extremely helpful. I am also indebted to Jochen von Bernstorff, Joseph Fleuren, Michael Steven Green, Jörg Kammerhofer, Christoph Kletzer, Thomas Mertens, Thomas Olechowski, Scott Shapiro, Jørg Stubberud and Jeremy Telman for their valuable questions and suggestions.

References

Barber, Nick. 2010. *The constitutional state*. Oxford: Oxford University Press.

Culver, Keith C., and Michael Giudice. 2010. *Legality's borders. An essay in general jurisprudence*. New York: Oxford University Press.

Dicey, A.V. 1982. In *Introduction to the study of the law of the constitution*, ed. Roger E. Michener. Indianapolis: Liberty Fund.

Dickson, Julie. 2001. *Evaluation and legal theory*. Oxford: Hart Publishing.

Dworkin, Ronald. 1968. Comments on the unity of law doctrine. In *Ethics and social justice*, ed. Howard E. Kiefer and Milton K. Munitz, 200–206. Albany: State University of New York Press.

Giudice, Michael. 2013. Hart and Kelsen on international law. In *Oxford studies in philosophy of law: Volume 2*, ed. Leslie Green and Brian Leiter, 148–174. Oxford: Oxford University Press.

Hart, H.L.A. 1958. Positivism and the separation of law and morals. *Harvard Law Review* 71: 593–629.

Hart, H.L.A. 1961. *The concept of law*. Oxford: Clarendon.

Hart, H.L.A. 1983. Kelsen's doctrine of the unity of law. In *Essays in jurisprudence and philosophy*, ed. H.L.A. Hart, 309–342. Oxford: Clarendon.

Kammerhofer, Jörg. 2009. Kelsen—which Kelsen? A reapplication of the pure theory to international law. *Leiden Journal of International Law* 22: 225–249.

Kammerhofer, Jörg. 2011. *Uncertainty in international law. A Kelsenian perspective*. Routledge: Abingdon.

Kammerhofer, Jörg. 2014. Hans Kelsen in today's international legal scholarship. In *International legal positivism in a post-modern world*, ed. Jörg Kammerhofer and Jean D'Aspremont, 81–113. Cambridge: Cambridge University Press.

Kelsen, Hans. 1914. Über Staatsunrecht. In *Die Wiener rechtstheoretische Schule. Schriften von Hans Kelsen, Adolf Merkl, Alfred Verdross*, eds. Hans R. Klecatsky, René Marcic and Herbert Schambeck, 2010, vol. 1, 785–865. Wien: Verlag Österreich.

Kelsen, Hans. 1920. *Das Problem der Souveränität und die Theorie des Völkerrechts. Beitrag zu einer Reinen Rechtslehre*. Tübingen: J.C.B. Mohr (Paul Siebeck).

Kelsen, Hans. 1929. The nature and development of constitutional adjudication. In *The guardian of the constitution: Hans Kelsen and Carl Schmitt on the limits of constitutional law*, ed. and Trans. Lars Vinx, 22–78. Cambridge: Cambridge University Press, 2015.

Kelsen, Hans. 1931. Who ought to be the guardian of the constitution?. In *The guardian of the constitution: Hans Kelsen and Carl Schmitt on the limits of constitutional law*, ed. and Trans. Lars Vinx, 174–221. Cambridge: Cambridge University Press, 2015.

Kelsen, Hans. 1934. *Introduction to the Problems of Legal Theory. A Translation of the First Edition of the Reine Rechtslehre or Pure Theory of Law*. Trans. B. Litschewski-Paulson and S.L. Paulson, 1997. Oxford: Clarendon Press.

Kelsen, Hans. 1942. *Law and peace in international relations: The Oliver Wendell Holmes Lectures, 1940–1941*. Cambridge, MA: Harvard University Press.

Kelsen, Hans. 1944. *Peace through law*. Chapel Hill: The University of North Carolina Press.

Kelsen, Hans. 1952. *Principles of international law*. New York: Rinehart & Company.

Kelsen, Hans. 1960. *The Pure Theory of Law*, 2nd edn. Trans. M. Knight 1967. Berkeley: University of California Press.

Krisch, Nico. 2012. The case for pluralism in postnational law. In *The worlds of European constitutionalism*, ed. Grainne de Burca and J.H.H. Weiler, 203–261. Cambridge: Cambridge University Press.

Kumm, Matthias. 2012. Rethinking constitutional authority: On the structure and limits of constitutional pluralism. In *Constitutional pluralism in the European Union and beyond*, ed. Matej Avbelj and Jan Komarek, 39–65. Oxford: Hart Publishing.

Langford, Peter, and Ian Bryan. 2012. Hans Kelsen's theory of legal monism. A critical engagement with the emerging legal order of the 1920's. *Journal of the History of International Law* 14: 51–86.

MacCormick, Neil. 1993. Beyond the sovereign state. *Modern Law Review* 56: 1–18.
MacCormick, Neil. 1999. *Questioning sovereignty. Law, state, and nation in the European Commonwealth*. Oxford: Oxford University Press.
Merkl, Adolf. 1931. Prolegomena einer Theorie des rechtlichen Stufenbaues. In *Die Wiener rechtstheoretische Schule. Schriften von Hans Kelsen, Adolf Merkl, Alfred Verdross*, eds. Hans R. Klecatsky, René Marcic and Herbert Schambeck, 2010, vol. 2, 1071–1111. Wien: Verlag Österreich.
Notermans, Mathijs. 2015. Social peace as conditio tacita for the validity of the positive legal order. *Law and Philosophy* 34: 201–227.
Raz, Joseph. 1970. *The concept of a legal system. An introduction to the theory of legal system*. Oxford: Clarendon.
Raz, Joseph. 1990. *Practical reason and norms*, 2nd ed. Princeton: Princeton University Press.
Raz, Joseph. 2009a. Kelsen's theory of the basic norm. In *The authority of law*, 2nd ed, ed. Joseph Raz, 122–145. Oxford: Oxford University Press.
Raz, Joseph. 2009b. The rule of law and its virtue. In *The authority of Law. Essays on law and morality*, vol. 2, ed. Joseph Raz, 210–229. Oxford: Oxford University Press.
Schauer, Frederick. 1996. Positivism as pariah. In *The autonomy of law. Essays on legal positivism*, ed. Robert P. George, 31–55. Oxford: Clarendon.
Schauer, Frederick. 2005. The social construction of the concept of law: A reply to Julie Dickson. *Oxford Journal of Legal Studies* 25: 493–501.
Scheuerman, William E. 2011. *The realist case for global reform*. Cambridge: Polity Press.
Somek, Alexander. 2007. Kelsen lives. *European Journal of International Law* 18: 409–451.
Somek, Alexander. 2012. Monism: A tale of the undead. In *Constitutional pluralism in the European Union and beyond*, ed. Matej Avbelj and Jan Komarek, 343–379. Oxford: Hart Publishing.
Vinx, Lars. 2007. *Hans Kelsen's pure theory of law. Legality and legitimacy*. Oxford: Oxford University Press.
Vinx, Lars. 2011. Austin, Kelsen, and the model of sovereignty. *Canadian Journal of Law and Jurisprudence* 24: 473–490.
von Bernstorff, Jochen. 2010. *The Public International Law Theory of Hans Kelsen. Believing in Universal Law*. Trans. T. Dunlap. Cambridge: Cambridge University Press.
Walker, Neil. 2012. Constitutionalism and pluralism in global context. In *Constitutional pluralism in the European Union and beyond*, ed. Matej Avbelj and Jan Komarek, 17–37. Oxford: Hart Publishing.

Chapter 5
Peace and Global Justice through Prosecuting the Crime of Aggression? Kelsen and Morgenthau on the Nuremberg Trials and the International Judicial Function

Jochen von Bernstorff

5.1 Introduction

At various junctures, Hans Kelsen's academic career was closely linked with that of the Hans Morgenthau, who was 15 years younger than Kelsen. Both had to emigrate from Germany and came to the United States via Geneva in the late 1930s. In Geneva, Kelsen held a professorship at the Institute of Graduate Studies, while Morgenthau wrote his Habilitation at the Institute. Kelsen actively promoted Morgenthau's academic career during this time despite the fact that the two men held fundamentally different positions on the potential of international law as a means of conflict resolution in international politics.[1] One area where these diverging approaches to international law became particularly apparent was the issue of the role of the judiciary in international relations. Despite the experiences of two world wars, Kelsen's wartime publications on the new post-war world order still demonstrate an unwavering trust in the pacifying role of the international judiciary. By contrast, Hans Morgenthau's writings on the future role of the international judicial function in the 1940s became even more sceptical than they already had been at the time of his 1929 dissertation on the "Internationale Rechtspflege."

Conceptually, both authors started from opposing premises. For Kelsen, peace was the potential consequence of a judicially controlled international legal order, whereas for Morgenthau a functioning international judiciary was the potential consequence of a politically secured state of peace in international relations. Kelsen's

[1] For an explanation of why Kelsen (in contradistinction to Morgenthau) after his emigration to the United States did not influence mainstream legal scholarship in the United States, see Telman 2010: 353–376.

J. von Bernstorff (✉)
Constitutional Law, International Law and Human Rights, University of Tübingen, Tübingen, Germany
e-mail: vonbernstorff@jura.uni-tuebingen.de

D.A.J. Telman (ed.), *Hans Kelsen in America - Selective Affinities and the Mysteries of Academic Influence*, Law and Philosophy Library 116,
DOI 10.1007/978-3-319-33130-0_5

"peace through law"-approach can thus be juxtaposed to Morgenthau's "law through peace"-approach. Against this background, it seems at first sight surprising that both authors shared a common critical stance vis à vis the Nuremberg trials, in particular with regard to the fact that the Tribunal convicted high ranking Nazi officials of the newly established "crimes against peace."

The following contribution first explores in more detail Kelsen's belief in the international judiciary in the context of the liberal pacifist quest for compulsory arbitration and adjudication in international relations in the first two decades of the twentieth century. It then deals with the related realist critique of this approach, focusing on Morgenthau's critique of the arbitration movement. The third and last part of the chapter deals with Kelsen's and Morgenthau's critical stances regarding the Allies' move in Nuremberg to criminalize aggressive war.

5.2 Kelsen and the International Judiciary

From the middle of the 1930s to the end of the Second World War, Kelsen devoted most of his scholarly attention to the question of a political reform of the international legal community's institutional structure. Before the outbreak of the Second World War, his publications engaged with ideas for reform of the League of Nations.[2] Later, Kelsen's work on League of Nations reform contributed to the debate over a new, peace-securing world organization that got under way during the war (Kelsen 1941a, 1944a, 1945). At the center of these publications stood the *de lege ferenda* call for the establishment of an international court with compulsory jurisdiction over member states. Kelsen's blueprint of a constitutive document for the new world organization made the court the central organ, the decisions of which would be enforced by a Council of the great powers. The creation of such a court rendering binding decisions was the institutional core of Kelsen's cosmopolitan project.

Having witnessed two world wars, Kelsen saw in the rule of law in international relations, secured by courts rendering binding decisions, the only way to a more peaceful world order. For Kelsen, the state of peace pursued by compulsory jurisdiction[3] did not mean the complete absence of violence, but merely a state of relative peace (Kelsen 1941b: 81). In that sense Kelsen set himself apart from a "utopian pacifism," which he regarded as a serious threat to international politics (Kelsen 1944b: VIII). In the future, the decision to use force would no longer remain within the competency of individual legal subjects, but would be transferred to central organs of the community for the purpose of sanctioning violations of the law. The final, binding decision about the existence of a violation of the law subject to sanction, referred to by Kelsen as a "delict," would be made by a central court organ *ex officio* or at the request of the contending parties.

[2] Kelsen (1934); idem (1939a); with a critical revision of the various provisions of the Charter, idem (1939b); idem (1936).

[3] See the programmatic title of his 1944 book *Peace through Law*, Kelsen (1944b).

The central place that Kelsen accorded compulsory jurisdiction within the legal system had already manifested itself clearly in the twenties with respect to national law in his scholarly analysis of the dispute over the reach of constitutional jurisdiction in the Weimar Republic (Kelsen 1929). Kelsen's approach to the role of courts in both the international and domestic context seems to be marked by his general faith in the peace-creating function of constitutional adjudication, which he helped to develop and introduce in Austria after World War I.

The real originality in Kelsen's works on international law from this period lies in the direct combination of concrete *de lege ferenda* proposals and his own socio-historical studies that buttressed his policy proposals. As a constructive justifying strategy, Kelsen developed his own theory of the evolution of legal systems, which, applied to international law, made the establishment of compulsory international jurisdiction seem like the next step in a progressive development of the international legal order. According to this theory decentralized "primitive" legal orders historically started to centralize their legal functions by introducing centralized, compulsory jurisdiction. A centralized legislature and executive branch followed as a second step (von Bernstorff 2010: Chap. 6A). To further underpin his legal-political convictions, he trained his critical eye on the traditional international legal doctrine concerning the function of international courts in international relations, such as the doctrine of the non-justiciability of political disputes. For him, every political dispute could conceptually be turned into a legal one. Kelsen thus solicited support for the establishment of compulsory jurisdiction on three different levels: first, through the constructive articulation of a draft charter for the new world organization; second, through the equally constructive development of his own general theory of the evolution of legal systems; and third, by deconstructing those doctrinal elements in international legal scholarship that could be marshalled against his *de lege ferenda* proposal.

In 1944, Kelsen published a draft charter for a "Permanent League for the Maintenance of Peace" as the successor organization to the League of Nations (Kelsen 1944b: Annex I, 127–140). Kelsen's new world organization had four main organs: Assembly, Court, Council, and Secretariat (Kelsen 1944b: Art. 2, 127). The charter consisted of clear procedural rules governing the working relationships between the four organs. The only substantive regulation was a comprehensive prohibition of the use of force on the part of members of the new organization (Kelsen 1944b: Art. 34, 134). If a state wanted to enforce international legal rules through war or forcible reprisals against another member state, it was up to the Court, at the request of the affected state or the Council, to decide whether the charter had been violated. Only after the Court had determined that the law had been broken could the Council impose the necessary military and economic sanctions on the responsible member states. In Kelsen's draft charter, the Council could take action on the sanction question only on the basis of and in conformity with the Court's finding that the state conduct in question had been illegal. The Court became the central organ, the actions of which obligated the Council. The eruption of violence in international relations was hereby to be regulated through a judicially dominated and fully institutionalized procedure.[4]

Kelsen's own draft of a charter in 1944 was based on the conviction that the absence of a global court rendering compulsory decisions about any dispute brought to it by states or organs of the League had permanently weakened the international legal order in the interwar period. In his blueprint, the jurisdiction of the court extended to all disputes that arose between members. As laid out above, that also included questions regarding the legality of one member's use of force against another. In Kelsen's conception, war and reprisal were permissible only as legally authorized sanctions against a state that was violating the charter. However, carrying out the sanction presupposed a court's determination that the member had in fact broken the rules. To that extent, not only did the monopoly of force lie with the world organization, but the use of force was possible only to enforce international law on the basis of a court decision. Within his vision of universal law, war and reprisals became acts of law enforcement by the international legal community. This legal community required a central organ that determined the illegality of the behavior being addressed and that reviewed the legality of the applied sanction. In Kelsen's eyes, only a judicial organ could exercise that function.

The substantively unlimited competence of the court also reflected Kelsen's conception of universal law. The political sphere to be regulated by international law was not restricted by a pre-legal concept of sovereignty. A rigid conception of the "*domaine réservé*" or "domestic jurisdiction" in the sense of an untouchable core area of state sovereignty was incompatible with the Vienna School's objective construction of international law (von Bernstorff 2010: Chap. 3 C IV). According to the doctrine of the primacy of international law, the latter could lay hold of and regulate any matter previously regulated by national law. If the judicial organ was to decide all disputes between members brought before it, its jurisdiction could not be subject to any *a priori* substantive limitations. In another Annex to his draft statute, Kelsen added procedural rules on how to punish those individuals who, as organs of their states, were responsible for the violation of the charter (Kelsen 1944b: Annex II, Art. 35a, 144).[5] The court's jurisdiction in criminal matters included the possibility, upon the request by a member state or the Council, to also prosecute and try war crimes committed or ordered by governments (Kelsen 1944b: Annex I, Art. 35b, Section 1, 144). Members of governments were to be punished by the international court as they would have been according to their own state law (Kelsen 1944b:

[4] With this, Kelsen was reviving the Hague Movement's strategy of juridifying international relations through obligatory arbitration. Much to the chagrin of the pacifist movement, the Second Hague Conference in 1907, because of the alleged obstructionist attitude of the Reich government, had been able to agree only on a voluntary form of arbitration by the Court of Arbitration in The Hague. If the pacifists would have their way, the Third Hague Conference would finally remedy this shortcoming. On this see, from the perspective of someone involved in the pacifist movement, Nippold (1917, 12–27).

[5] Excluded from this, according to Article 35c of the draft, were representatives of states belonging to the Council of the organization (Kelsen 1944b: Annex II, Art. 35a, 145).

Annex I, Art. 35b, Section 1, 144). Member states were obligated to hand over individuals prosecuted by the court.

In light of the widespread violations of international humanitarian law and the indescribable horrors of the Holocaust committed during the Second World War, Kelsen did not believe that the doctrine of the functional immunity of state actors was in any way legally sacrosanct. He argued that the new charter could completely revoke immunity of heads of states as a treaty under international law. Direct obligations of individuals, as well as individualized prosecution, indictment and conviction through international courts, were perfectly in line with the concept of international law as articulated by the Vienna School through the concept of a monist global legal order according international law primacy over national law.[6]

The court that Kelsen envisioned was composed of five criminal lawyers and 12 international lawyers. It had not only the power to decide any dispute brought before it by the organs or individual member states but also functioned as a two-tiered criminal court for individual representatives of governments who could be charged with violations of international law. The proposed powers of the new international court were Kelsen's political response to the "failure" of the League of Nations and the need to prosecute and punish war crimes and crimes against humanity committed during the Holocaust.

5.3 Realist Opposition to the Quest for a Strong International Judiciary

In the late 1930s, the international relations realist movement expressed suspicions that the demand for an international court that rendered compulsory decisions was a utopian aspiration out of step with political realities. As early as his 1929 dissertation, Morgenthau had set out his own understanding of the limited role of international adjudication in international politics (Morgenthau 1929; Koskenniemi 2006: 152–158). In Morgenthau's perception of the international judiciary, the interwar reform movement's demand for compulsory jurisdiction in international law was based on a mistaken analogy to national legal systems. His critical assessment of the role of the international judiciary was based on the assumption that the language of international law faced inherent limits when confronted with political "tensions," in which one party sought to transform the existing legal *status quo*. In such situations, the international judge faces the dilemma of either turning the court into a political body by acting (*ultra vires*) as a legislator or rendering a meaningless formalist judgment and thereby failing to ease the political tensions at the core of the dispute.[7]

---

[6] On the individual within Kelsen's doctrine of international law, see J. von Bernstorff (2010, Chap. 4 B).

[7] Later, in a similar vein, E. H. Carr, in his famous book *The Twenty Year's Crisis, 1919–1939*, noted, with reference to Lauterpacht, that the view of international law as a legal system that was

From this perspective, Kelsen's assumption that courts would be able to administer international law to address pressing societal needs in individual cases overtaxed the legal system. For Morgenthau, a legal process is fundamentally different from a political one in that it blocks out the question of power. Before the law, the parties are equal, regardless of the asymmetries of power. This legal fiction contradicts the inherent logic of international politics, where the strength of the individual states has to be considered a crucial factor in the resolution of conflicts of interest. The introduction of a compulsory international jurisdiction encompassing jurisdiction over existential questions of international politics would exceed the capacity of the law. Morgenthau does not per se rule out a functioning international judiciary, but it is dependent on stable and relatively harmonious political preconditions.

As Martti Koskenniemi has convincingly illustrated, Morgenthau's critique of international legal validity as an autonomous concept is based on Weimar intellectual influences. Morgenthau—like Carl Schmitt—developed an approach to international law that tended to treat international legal validity as always dependent on its congruence with the interests of the strongest political actors.[8] For him, effective constraints on state action could only derive from common interests in a given situation or from a balance of power Morgenthau (2006: 10 et seq.). Morgenthau ruled out the idea of an autonomous international legal system guiding the conduct of states, at least for all situations in which diverging and essential interests of strong states were at stake. Despite these realist commonalities with Carl Schmitt, which played out predominantly in questions of adjudicating questions of war and peace, Morgenthau should not be associated with Schmittian authoritarian thinking in general.[9]

For Kelsen, the problem of international jurisdiction before and during the Second World War revolved above all around the future institutional development of international relations; that development could be achieved only by way of an international treaty and thus via international law. Exploiting the theoretical insights of the legal scholar into the specific inherent rationality of highly evolved legal systems, the Vienna School in international law favoured the creation of a court that rendered binding decisions. The reasonableness of applying their system-oriented approach to the law to international law was beyond question for them. Because international law had the quality of law, it had to be conceptualized as a complete system of norms. In this respect, the relatively small number of general international legal norms was no obstacle to the creation of a compulsory jurisdiction. Had the League of Nations not given excessive consideration to the power logic of politics in the structure of its organs? As they saw it, the existing international legal framework was in dire need of better judicial support. Irrational power politics had

institutionally completed by compulsory jurisdiction was another "distinguished international lawyer's dream of an international community whose center of gravity is in the administration of international justice" (Carr 1939: 186).

[8] On Morgenthau and his foundational influence on the post-war discipline of international relations, see (Koskenniemi 2000: 17–34).

[9] See, for his influence as a liberal and progressive intellectual, Scheuerman (2009).

brought war; now a unified international legal system was to bring peace. International legal validity, which came with the criticized notion of formal equality, had an irreplaceable function and value for taming and civilizing the irrational forces of nationalism and unrestrained pursuit of alleged national interests. The last sentence of the lectures on "Law and Peace in International Relations" that Kelsen delivered at Harvard in 1942 epitomized the Vienna School's approach during the Second World War: "The idea of law, in spite of everything, seems still to be stronger than any other ideology of power" (Kelsen 1942: 170).

5.4 Kelsen and Morgenthau on Nuremberg

In 1945, Kelsen must have been deeply disappointed by the position and competencies the founders of the United Nations accorded to the International Court of Justice (ICJ).[10] As in 1918, strong judicial controls were not the central concern of the Allies when erecting the edifice of the new world organization during the last 3 years of World War II. Regarding the jurisdiction of the new Court, the drafters of the U.N. Charter and the Statute of the ICJ relied heavily on the jurisdictional rules of its predecessor from the interwar period, the Permanent Court of International Justice (PCIJ). Hence, jurisdiction of the Court was only foreseen on the basis of voluntary acceptance of the respective state parties, and confined to "legal" disputes as opposed to "political" ones. In addition, individuals had no standing before the court, neither as applicants nor as defendants. Unlike in Kelsen's wartime blueprint, the new court could thus not render judgments in cases of individual criminal responsibility for war crimes. Instead, the Allies opted for a special *ad hoc* tribunal outside the U.N. framework based on a separate agreement concluded amongst them (London Agreement). This agreement foresaw jurisdiction of the temporarily erected International Military Tribunal for individual "crimes against peace," "war crimes," and "crimes against humanity." The notion of the "crimes agianst humanity" made it possible to prosecute crimes committed during the German "Menschheitsverbrechen" of the Holocaust. Only the establishment and application of the first notion—the "crimes against peace" gave rise to Kelsen's as well as Morgenthau's harsh critique of the Nuremberg trials.

[10] On Kelsen's critical stance regarding the UN-Charter, see Telman *Introduction: Hans Kelsen for Americans* (in this volume). I agree that Kelsen's sharp critique of the institutional system erected by the UN-Charter in his methodologically unorthodox Charter Commentary can be explained by his own idiosyncratic methodological beliefs and his vision of the new World Organization (Bernstorff 2010: 225–228).

5.4.1 *Waging Aggressive War as an Individualised Crime*

"Crimes against peace" are defined in the Nuremburg Charter, which was annexed to the London Agreement, as "planning, preparation, initiation, or waging a war of aggression, or a war in violation of international treaties, agreements or assurances, or participation in a common plan or conspiracy for the accomplishment of any of the foregoing." In the first trial against 24 of the most high ranking German war criminals, which began on November 20, 1945, and continued until October 1946, 12 defendants were found guilty of, *inter alia*, either waging "aggressive war" or conspiring to do so. The majority of this group was sentenced to hang, all of them having been convicted on additional charges (Frick, Göring, Jodl, Keitel, Ribbentrop, Rosenberg, Seyss-Inquart) or given life sentences (Hess, Räder and Funk).[11] In the judgment, the Tribunal maintained that individual responsibility for crimes against peace had existed already before the London Agreement gave the Tribunal jurisdiction over these crimes. Otherwise, it would have had to apply Article 6 of the Nuremberg Charter retroactively. In order to avoid the *nullum crimen* problem, the Tribunal thus needed to find a norm, which had stipulated international criminal responsibility of state officials for waging war before the Nazis began their international acts of aggression in 1938.

The first international treaty that attempted to outlaw war as means of national policy was the Kellogg-Briand Pact of 1928 (Roscher 2004). In article 1 of that treaty, the "High Contracting Parties solemnly declare in the names of their respective peoples that they condemn recourse to war for the solution of international controversies and renounce it, as an instrument of national policy in their relations with one another." No explicit references to collective or individual criminal responsibility were to be found in the Kellogg-Briand Pact. Nonetheless, it constituted the only international treaty that could serve as an applicable pre-war rule restricting the *ius ad bellum* for the Tribunal.

But how could the Nuremberg military Tribunal deduce criminal responsibility of individuals from the Pact, which had merely declared war waged by states under specific circumstances illegal under international law? The Tribunal at the outset conceded that the Kellogg-Briand Pact had not explicitly foreseen individual criminal responsibility but nonetheless attempted to develop individual responsibility by interpretation. The main argument for individual criminal responsibility under the Pact was a constructed analogy with existing national practices of individual criminal prosecution for violations of the rules of The Hague Conventions on international humanitarian law. The Tribunal thus sought to transfer legal developments in the criminalization of the *ius in bello* (Hague Conventions) in the early twentieth century to the *ius ad bellum* area (Kellogg-Briand Pact):

> [I]t is argued that the Pact does not expressly enact that such wars are crimes, or set up courts to try those who make such wars. To that extent the same is true with regard to the

[11] Two defendants found guilty of "crimes against peace" successfully pleaded for mitigating circumstances: Neurath was sentenced to 15 years and Dönitz to 10 years imprisonment.

> laws of war contained in the Hague Convention. The Hague convention of 1907 prohibited resort to certain methods of waging war. These included the inhumane treatment of prisoners, the employment of poisoned weapons, the improper use of flags of truce, and similar matters. Many of these prohibitions had been enforced long before the date of the Convention; but since 1907 there have certainly been crimes, punishable as offences against the laws of war; yet the Hague Convention nowhere designates such practices as criminal, nor is any sentence prescribed, nor is any mention made of a court to try and punish offenders. For many years past, however, military tribunals have tried and punished individuals guilty of violating the rules of land warfare laid down by this Convention (The Trial of German Major War Criminals. Proceedings of the International Military Tribunal sitting at Nuremberg, Germany: Judgement of 30th September–1st October 1946: 40).

After having likened national developments in the criminalization and prosecution of violations of the *ius in bello* to the current legal situation under the *ius ad bellum* after the Kellogg-Briand Pact, the Tribunal then pursues the analogy further based on a moral *a fortiori* reasoning: "In the opinion of the tribunal, those who wage aggressive war are doing that which is equally illegal, and of much greater moment than a breach of one of the rules of the Hague Convention" (The Trial of German Major War Criminals. Proceedings of the International Military Tribunal sitting at Nuremberg, Germany: Judgement of 30 September–1st October 1946: 40)

Because waging war in the first place (*ius ad bellum*) has more dramatic political and moral effects then violating specific rules of conduct in war (*ius in bello*), it should also be criminalized. In a later part of the judgment this basically moral *a fortiori* reasoning is argued in universalist terms:

> The charges in the indictment that the defendants planned and waged aggressive wars are charges of the utmost gravity. War is essentially an evil thing. Its consequences are not confined to the belligerent states alone, but affect the whole world. To initiate a war of aggression, therefore, is not only an international crime; it is the supreme international crime differing only from other war crimes in that it contains within itself the accumulated evil of the whole (The Trial of German Major War Criminals. Proceedings of the International Military Tribunal sitting at Nuremberg, Germany: Judgement of 30 September–1st October 1946: 13).

With this justification, which the Tribunal used to overcome the *nullum crimen* problem, for the first time in history international judges tried the "crime of aggression."

5.4.2 *Kelsen's Reading of the Nuremberg Judgment: A Missed Opportunity for the Advancement of International Law*

It needs to be mentioned at the outset that both Kelsen and Morgenthau did not oppose the conviction of Nazi Officials in general. Both defended the need to try high-ranking Nazi officials for the crimes committed inside and outside of Germany since 1933. And neither saw the at least partly retroactive character of the judgment as a legally insurmountable obstacle to the Tribunal. Kelsen expressed two main criticisms of the judgment: first, its flawed attempt to deduce international criminal responsibility from the Kellogg-Briand Pact; second, the insufficient legal foundation of the trial in absence of the consent of the vanquished states and the related lost opportunity for the international community to establish individual criminal responsibility in international law generally via a universal multilateral instrument.

As to "crimes against peace," Kelsen clearly rejected the Tribunal's attempt to justify the assumption, by way of an analogy with the Hague conventions, that criminal responsibility could be inferred from the Kellogg-Briand Pact:

> The differences between the Hague Convention on the rules of warfare and the [Kellogg-Briand] Pact is that the former can be violated by acts of state as well as by acts of private persons, whereas the latter can be violated only by acts of states. The [Kellogg-Briand] Pact does not—as does the Hague Convention—forbid acts of private persons (Kelsen 1947: 161).

Given that the Kellogg-Briand Pact, unlike the Hague Conventions, did not oblige or authorise the state parties to punish under their own laws the individuals, who in their capacity as organs of a State waged war in contravention of the Pact, Art. 6 of the Nuremberg Charter in Kelsen's view had created genuinely new law, instead of applying the Pact.

According to his interpretation of the events in Nuremberg, the application of the newly established "crimes against peace" to acts of aggression that were committed during the "Third Reich" through the Nuremberg judgment was clearly a form of retroactive legislation and punishment. However, international law did not have a clear rule recognizing the prohibition on retroactive legislation, and in most domestic legal systems the rule was only valid with important exceptions. Because it was not an established rule of international law, the Allies in 1945 did not violate international legal rules by authorising the application of these newly established crimes to acts committed during the war (Kelsen 1947: 164). There were simply no applicable rules that prohibited the new rules established by the London Agreement. Kelsen at this juncture did not explicitly refer to the Lotus Principle or the Kantian negative rule according to which, in the absence of a specific prohibition, restrictions upon the freedom of the Allies to establish retroactive legislation through the London Agreement could not have been presumed (S.S. Lotus (Fr. v. Turk.), 1927 P.C.I.J. (ser. A) No. 10 (Sept. 7)). But in the absence of a legal prohibition, the question for Kelsen could now indeed be assessed on moral grounds or based on "general principles of justice." And for him there were good "moral" reasons to allow retroactive punishment of those persons "who are morally responsible for the international crime of the second World War" (Kelsen 1947: 165) The fact that there was no clear rule against retroactive legislation in international law and that there was a demand of moral justice to punish the perpetrators led Kelsen to endorse retroactive punishment in Nuremberg.

Much more worrying for Kelsen seems to have been his second main point of criticism, namely the limited value of the Tribunal for the advancement of international law. Very much in the late nineteenth century German international law tradition, Kelsen had always judged international law against the background of highly developed and formalised Western national legal systems. Hence his labelling of international law as a "primitive" law, which still had to rely on custom and decentralised legislation, enforcement and adjudication.[12] The move from collective to individual responsibility was a decisive evolutionary step in turning a primitive legal order into a developed one. Analogous to the development of the modern state, international law was supposed to move from the phase of privately declared vendettas or blood feuds to the stage of judicially-controlled individual criminal responsibility.

The problem with Nuremberg thus was that the Allies had failed to advance general international law to that desired stage of development. They had failed to do so due to various shortcomings in the legal architecture of the Nuremberg Tribunal. There was first the missing consent to the London Agreement of those states that had lost the war and whose nationals were being tried. The Allies, exercising sovereign rights for Germany through the Allied Control Council, had not made the effort to formally declare Germany's consent to the trial. For Kelsen, the absence of the consent of the European Axis powers was problematic:

> If, however, a tribunal is instituted to make individuals criminally responsible for their State's violation of a treaty, it is not exactly an improvement of general international law to establish that tribunal without the consent of the State accused of the treaty violation.

(Kelsen 1947: 168). While admitting that this was more a formal rather then a substantive charge against the judgment, Kelsen moves on to the main point of his critique. What really impaired the authority of the judgment was that the rules established by the London Agreement had not been established as general principles of international law but as rules applicable only to vanquished states by the victors (Kelsen 1947: 170). Through its asymmetrical establishment and application, the London Agreement had the character of a "privilegium odiosum." This impression was aggravated by the fact that the Tribunal was exclusively composed of representatives of victorious states directly affected by the crimes over which the Tribunal had jurisdiction. Representatives of neutral states were excluded from the bench. The Allies became judges in their own cause.[13]

The Nuremberg trials in their basic architecture had not lived up to the principle of formal equality before the law, which for Kelsen was the very essence and unique

---

[12] Kelsen agrees with the argument put forth by the Tribunal itself:

> In the first place, it is to be observed that the maxim *nullum crimen sine lege* is not a limitation of sovereignty, but is in general a principle of justice. To assert that it is unjust to punish those who in defiance of treaties and assurances have attacked neighboring states without warning is obviously untrue, for in such circumstances the attacker must know that he is doing wrong, and so far from it being unjust to punish him, it would be unjust if his wrong were allowed to go unpunished

(International Military Tribunal (Nuremberg), judgment 30th September–1st October 1946, 39).

[13] It needs to be mentioned here that the Tribunal in several cases reacted to this problem by dropping prosecution, once the defendant could prove that military forces or officials from the United States or United Kingdom acted in a similar manner during the war. International Military Tribunal (Nuremberg) Judgement and Sentences in: 41 *AJIL* (1946), 172 or 13 *International Law Reports (ILR) (1946)* 203.

property of law as a specific social technique that was distinguishable from every other form to exercise power over human beings (Kelsen 1941c: 70 et seq.). All in all, Kelsen in 1947 saw Nuremberg as a lost opportunity to move from collective responsibility to individual responsibility in general international law. Not only had the Allies failed to enshrine this principle in a legal document of general application, such as the U.N. Charter, they also had missed the opportunity of providing a historical example for the neutral application of this principle in line with the ideal of formal equality.

5.4.3 Morgenthau's Comments on the Nuremberg Trial: "Crimes Against Peace" as Allied Moral Hypocrisy

As early as December 1946, Morgenthau published a brief comment on the Nuremberg trials in a non-scientific journal America, December 7, 1946; reprinted in: Morgenthau (1962: 377–379). In his view, the 18 men convicted at Nuremberg "were guilty of many crimes, and they were justly condemned and punished." Like Kelsen, however, Morgenthau took issue with the establishment and application of "crimes against peace" in Nuremberg:

> If the leaders of Nazi Germany are guilty of conspiring to wage, and of planning and waging, a war of aggression and a war in violation of international law, so are the leaders of France, Great Britain, and Russia. (…) German aggression and lawlessness were not morally obnoxious to France and Great Britain as long as they were directed against Russia. If one can believe Ribbentrop's last plea, Stalin wired congratulations to Hitler upon the starting point of the Second World War, which became morally reprehensible in Russian eyes only on June 22, 1941.

According to Morgenthau, the Allies in Nuremberg were not only judging in their own cause, three of them even were accomplices of the Nazi move towards war at one time or another.

By comparing the Nuremberg trial to a "punitive trial" in the scholastic tradition, Morgenthau reminded the Allies that the scholastic just war tradition had limited and qualified the right of the princes to pass judgment on the justice of the enemy's cause in war (Morgenthau 1962: 378). Morgenthau polemically observed a "flood of moralizing legend" and criticized the Allies for mistaking "the voice of the victor for the voice of Divine Justice." A crime of aggression adjudicated by the victors in a punitive trial was inherently problematic in its inclination to hypocritical condemnation of the enemy by those who win the war. A modern and thus secular revitalization of a just war concept in international relations was a dangerous undertaking. The reason was that the foundational circumstances of the scholastic concept had long vanished; namely the moral unity of Christendom and the originally rather strict doctrinal limitations of punitive wars (Morgenthau 1962: 378). Without these preconditions, a modern punitive war was problematic in its inherent tendency to demonise the opponent and to absolve itself of any wrongdoings by moralizing its own cause for, and conduct in, war. Both of Morgenthau's main intellectual reference points, namely Carl Schmitt's concept of the political and Kelsen's pure theory of law, shared his Nietzschean critical sensibility with regard to the moralisation of politics and law.

In his seminal *Politics Among Nations* of 1948, Morgenthau only devotes a few lines to the Nuremberg Trials. According to his reading of the legal debate on Nuremberg there was:

> …no way of stating with any degree of authority whether any country which went to war after 1929 in pursuance of its national policies has violated a rule of international law and is liable before international law for its violation; or whether only those individuals responsible for preparing and declaring the Second World War are liable in this way; or whether all countries and individuals which will prepare for, and wage aggressive war in the future will thus be liable.

Morgenthau (2006: 218). In Morgenthau's view, uncertainties about a question so fundamental as the legality of collective acts of violence demonstrated the weakness of international law as a legal order.

For him both the uncertainty reigning in the *ius ad bellum* area as well as the consistent violation of previously less uncertain rules of the *ius in bello* raised serious doubts as to the validity of international legal rules in these areas. Uncertainty and lack of adherence thus could have repercussions for legal validity itself. In contrast to Kelsen's strict methodological dualism, the effectiveness of the norm—its "*Sein*" does affect its "*Sollen*." In line with Morgenthau's "law through peace approach," international law in his eyes is valid and generally adhered to in all areas where it regulates the delineation of jurisdictions and technical cooperation between states in times of peace Morgenthau (2006: 210–211). However, its validity will be at stake when vital political interests are involved and once war looms under the surface of interstate diplomacy.

After Nuremberg it took more than 60 years before a shaky consensus could be forged in a multilateral setting on how international law could define and prescribe individual criminal responsibility for waging aggressive war. What is being called the 2010 "Kampala compromise" includes a definition of the crime of aggression, which is intended to amend the Rome Statute of the International Criminal Court (Kreß / v. Holtzendorff (2010)). Even though international criminal law has advanced enormously over the last 15 years, the problem of the "privilegium odiosum" through the asymmetrical application of the existing rules remains a fundamental one. The authors of the Kampala compromise deliberately made the new definition of the crime of aggression malleable so that the International Criminal Court would not be obliged to prosecute all acts violating the prohibition of the use of force. Only "manifest" violations of the prohibition of the use of force can be tried under the new definition.[14] Uncertainties arising out of Nuremberg regarding the *ius ad bellum* preconditions of a crime of aggression thus are here to stay. The flexible "manifest"- qualifier plays into the hands of the strongest actors. For the Great Powers—on top of their exceptional political and legal leverage— have been granted a convenient legal justification for evading potential prosecution in cases of

[14]Also critical of the qualification of the breach of the *ius ad bellum* Paulus (2010, 1121).

violations of the *ius ad bellum* in the future. This highly flexible substantive standard comes with the institutional privilege of the Great Power: the ability to dominate U.N. Security Council decisions and to block investigations into alleged violations of the crime of aggression.[15] As long as it seems politically unimaginable or even technically impossible for the ICC to indict leaders of the most powerful nations for waging illegal aggression, the promise of peace and global justice through international criminal law is likely to remain a distant dream at best and another "moralizing legend" at worst.[16]

References

Carr, Edward Hallet. 1939. *The twenty year's crisis, 1919–1939 An introduction to the study of international relations*. London: Macmillan.

Kelsen, Hans. 1929. Wesen und Entwicklung der Staatsgerichtsbarkeit. Überprüfung von Verwaltungsakten durch die öffentlichen Gerichte. *H. Triepel, H. Kelsen and M. Layer (eds.), Veröffentlichungen der Vereinigung der Deutschen Staatsrechtslehrer*, Heft 5, Tagung vom 23. und 24. April 1928 in Wien, Berlin und Leipzig: W. de Gruyter: 30–88.

Kelsen, Hans. 1934. *The legal process and international order*. London: The New Commonwealth Research Bureau Publications.

Kelsen, Hans. 1936. *Sanktionen sind Sache des Gerichts*. Geneva Press Service 10 July 1936: 1–3.

Kelsen, Hans. 1939a. Les resolutions de la S.D.N. concernant la separation du Pacte et des Traités de Paix. *Revue de Droit International et de Législation Comparée* 20: 101–113.

Kelsen, Hans. 1939b. Revision des Völkerbundstatus. In *Legal technique in international law. A textual critique of the League Covenant*. Geneva: Geneva Research Center.

Kelsen, Hans. 1941a. International peace by court or by government? *American Journal of Sociology* 46: 571–581.

Kelsen, Hans. 1941b. The Law as a specific social technique. *The University of Chicago Law Review* 9: 75–97.

Kelsen, Hans. 1941c. The essential conditions of international justice. *Proceedings of the Thirty-fifth Annual Meeting of the American Society of International Law* 35: 70–98.

---

[15] In general, the "determination of an act of aggression by an organ outside the Court shall be without prejudice to the Court's own findings under this Statute" (Art. 15bis (9)) ICC Review Conference, Resolution RC/Res.6, The Crime of Aggression, adopted at the 13th plenary meeting, on 11 June 2010, by consensus and annexes, Annex I. Hence, the Court is not bound by the assessment of the UN Security Council. However, the UN Security Council can always block the investigation (Art 15bis (8)), RC/Res.6 Annex I.

[16] The jurisdiction of the Court over the crime of aggression is further limited by the two following provisions of the "Kampala compromise":

> The Court may, in accordance with article 12, exercise jurisdiction over a crime of aggression, arising from an act of aggression committed by a State Party, unless that State Party has previously declared that it does not accept such jurisdiction by lodging a declaration with the Registrar. The withdrawal of such a declaration may be effected at any time and shall be considered by the State Party within three years.

(15bis (4)) "In respect of a State that is not a party to this Statute, the Court shall not exercise its jurisdiction over the crime of aggression when committed by that State's nationals or on its territory"; (15bis (5)).

Kelsen, Hans. 1942. *Law and peace in international relations. The Oliver Wendell Holmes Lectures 1940–41*. Cambridge, MA: Harvard University Press.
Kelsen, Hans. 1944a. The strategy for peace. *American Journal of Sociology* 49: 381–389.
Kelsen, Hans. 1944b. *Peace through law*. Chapel Hill: The University of North Carolina Press.
Kelsen, Hans. 1945. The old and the new league: The Covenant and the Dumbarton Oaks proposals. *American Journal of International Law* 39: 45–83.
Kelsen, Hans. 1947. Will the judgement in the Nuremberg Trial constitute a precedent in international law? *The International Law Quarterly* 1: 153–171.
Koskenniemi, Martti. 2000. Carl Schmitt, Hans Morgenthau, and the image of law in international relations. In *The role of law in international politics. Essays in international relations and international politics*, ed. M. Byers, 17–34. Oxford: Oxford University Press.
Koskenniemi, Martti. 2006. Morgenthau's books on international law with Kelsen. In *Twenty-five year memorial commemoration to the life of Hans Morgenthau (1904–2005)*, ed. G.O. Mazur, 152–174. New York: Semenko Foundation.
Kreß, Claus, and Leonie von Holtzendorff. 2010. The Kampala Compromise on the crime of aggression. *Journal of International Criminal Justice* 8: 1179–1217.
Morgenthau, Hans Joachim. 1929. *Die internationale Rechtspflege, ihr Wesen und ihre Grenzen*. Leipzig: Noske.
Morgenthau, Hans Joachim. 1948 revised 2006. *Politics among nations. The struggle for power and peace*, revised by K. W. Thompson and W. D. Clinton, 7th ed., New York: McGraw-Hill.
Morgenthau, Hans Joachim. 1962. *The decline of democratic politics*. Chicago: The University of Chicago Press.
Nippold, Otfried. 1917. *Die Gestaltung des Völkerrechts nach dem Kriege*. Zürich: Institut Orell Füssli.
Paulus, Andreas. 2010. Second thoughts on the crime of aggression. *European Journal of International Law* 20: 1117–1128.
Roscher, Bernhard. 2004. *Der Briand Kellogg Pakt von 1928*. Baden- Baden: Nomos.
Scheuerman, William E. 2009. *Hans J. Morgenthau: Realism and beyond*. Cambridge: Polity Press.
Telman, D.A. Jeremy. 2010. A path not taken: Hans Kelsen pure theory of law in the land of the legal realists. In *Hans Kelsen anderswo/Hans Kelsen abroad*, ed. Robert Walter, Clemens Jabloner, and Klaus Zeleny, 353–376. Vienna: Manz.
von Bernstorff, Jochen. 2010. *The public international law theory of Hans Kelsen. Believing in universal law*. Cambridge: Cambridge University Press.

Chapter 6
Hans Kelsen, The Second World War and the U.S. Government

Thomas Olechowski

6.1 Introduction

Does the pure theory of law enable lawyers to solve legal problems, or is it just an academic theory, highly sophisticated, but without practical relevance? Whoever thinks that the latter is true should be aware that Hans Kelsen himself worked not only as a university professor, but also as a legal advisor. In addition to Kelsen's years as an advisor for the Austrian state chancellery, drafting the Austrian federal constitution of 1920, his service during World War I (WWI) and World War II (WWII) must also be highlighted.

Indeed, both wars were of the highest importance for Kelsen's career. During WWI, Kelsen worked in the Austro-Hungarian ministry of war. In its last months Kelsen served as a personal legal advisor to Rudolf Stöger-Steiner, the last minister of war of the Habsburg monarchy. In this capacity, he wrote several memoranda on practical legal problems, which gave him the opportunity to apply some results of the pure theory.[1] The minister was very satisfied and supported him in securing a professorship at the University of Vienna, which was the real starting point of Kelsen's career (Busch 2009).

Twenty-seven years later, much had changed. Kelsen now lived as a refugee in the United States. But, once again, the military and other federal institutions—this time, not Austro-Hungarian, but American institutions—needed the expertise of the

[1] One example: In 1917, Kelsen was ordered to write on some special problems resulting from the seizure of horses for the army – and wrote an extensive memorandum on a highly theoretical level concerning the question whether an administrative decision can be revoked. The text of this memorandum has been published in Oberkofler and Rabofsky (1988: 154–158).

T. Olechowski (✉)
University of Vienna, Vienna, Austria

Hans Kelsen Institute, Vienna, Austria
e-mail: thomas.olechowski@univie.ac.at

D.A.J. Telman (ed.), *Hans Kelsen in America - Selective Affinities and the Mysteries of Academic Influence*, Law and Philosophy Library 116,
DOI 10.1007/978-3-319-33130-0_6

world-famous legal philosopher to solve legal problems resulting from a war. And, once again, they thanked him by helping him to find a university.

6.2 Coming to America

Kelsen came to the United States for the first time in 1936. He came to help celebrate the Tercentenary of Harvard College. On this occasion, Kelsen was to be awarded an honorary degree.[2] His professional and personal situation at this time was very difficult. Dismissed from the University of Cologne by the Nazi Regime in 1933, the 55-year-old scholar could find only temporary shelter at the Institute Universitaire des Hautes Etudes Internationales in Geneva. Of the German-speaking universities, only the German University in Prague offered him a new professorship, where he was supposed to start his lectures in the fall of 1936. But Kelsen knew of the strong anti-Semitic tendencies present also in Czechoslovakia and so he used the occasion of his trip to America to ask if he could stay there permanently—at first without any success.

Back in Europe, his worst fears came true. In Prague, anti-Semitic students not only boycotted his lectures but also started riots, so that the minister had to close the university for several weeks. Kelsen taught in Prague for only three semesters before Hitler occupied Czechoslovakia and Kelsen had to return to Geneva (Olechowski and Busch 2010: 1122). On September 1, 1939—the day Hitler attacked Poland—Kelsen was in the United States again, participating in the International Congress for the Unity of Sciences, and again he tried to get in contact with American universities (Ehs and Gassner 2012). His friends in America also looked for opportunities for Kelsen to stay in the United States, for example at Columbia University, Princeton University or Harvard University. It is notable that they asked the elite universities first, which made the search for a place to stay even more difficult. But lesser-known universities, such as the University of Illinois, also rejected Kelsen. Kelsen and his pure theory of law appeared to be badly suited to American legal education, and there were many younger and more flexible lawyers from Europe, who fled to the United States and competed with Kelsen for the few free positions at U.S. law schools (Feichtinger 2009).

In the end, the New School for Social Research made it possible for Hans Kelsen and his wife to emigrate from Europe. A "University in Exile" had been founded at this New York City college in 1933, with the purpose of bringing scholars from Europe to America (Rutkoff and Scott 1986). It gave them a first engagement—which was necessary for a permanent visa—and supported them in finding a permanent position at another school in the United States. Kelsen indeed never wanted to stay in New York. Only a few weeks after his arrival in the United States (June 21, 1940), he moved on to Harvard, where his friend Roscoe Pound had established the "Oliver Wendell Holmes lectureship," which still exists today, with the support of

[2] The ceremony is documented in The Tercentenary of Harvard College (1937), Cambridge (Mass.).

the Rockefeller Foundation, and Hans Kelsen delivered the inaugural Holmes lecture. He stayed in Harvard for 2 years, from 1940 to 1942, and lectured on the topic of "Law and Peace in International Relations." He was building upon ideas that he had previously articulated during his time in Geneva and then developed further in numerous articles, which finally led to the publication of his monograph, *Peace through Law*, in June 1944 (Kelsen 1934, 1944a; Olechowski 2014: 123).

Kelsen was of the opinion that the law should directly serve the cause of peace. The League of Nations should be replaced by a "Permanent League of the Maintenance of Peace," and this league should be equipped with an International Court of Justice that should have extensive jurisdiction. It would punish war criminals and those who wage illegitimate wars. To put it more precisely, the court would not only have jurisdiction over states but also over individuals. Kelsen's book, which was published shortly after the Allied invasion of Normandy, must have received quite some resonance outside of the world of experts in international law. It must have been these writings that introduced Kelsen's name to Washington, D.C.—how exactly this occurred, we unfortunately do not know. However, there is a letter in Kelsen's estate that was written to him by Michigan professor Lawrence Preuss, who worked for the State Department at that time, in which Preuss informed Kelsen that his book, *Peace through Law*, had been recommended to him by an unnamed U.S. Senator.[3]

At this stage, Kelsen had already ceased to teach at Harvard and had moved on to Berkeley. His endeavors to gain a permanent position at Harvard had failed; in Berkeley, too, he was only a "visiting professor" for 1 year in 1942/43, and then, from 1943 to 1945, a simple "lecturer."[4] In addition, his employment was not at the Law School but at the Political Science Department. His career and financial situation were in a desperate state, and we may assume that the 63-year-old scholar was genuinely happy to accept the invitation to serve the U.S. government in some capacity in Washington, D.C.

6.3 Kelsen and the Future of Germany and Austria After the Second World War

The first governmental agency that asked Kelsen for his cooperation was the Bureau of Areas of the President's Foreign Economic Administration. This office had been established in September 1943 to unify and consolidate governmental activities

[3] Hans Kelsen Institute Vienna, Hans Kelsen Estate 16c9.61. Lawrence Preuss (1905–1956) was professor of international law at the University of Michigan and legal advisor to the State Department as well as the UNWCC; see Bishop 1956. I want to thank Jason Kropsky, participant of the 2014 Kelsen conference in Chicago, for the identification of Lawrence Preuss. The name of the Senator, though, is still an enigma.

[4] University of California, Berkeley, personal files Hans Kelsen, letters from June 30, 1942, July 2, 1943 and May 26, 1944.

relating to foreign economic affairs. The Bureau of Areas made broad program decisions regarding Foreign Economic Administration operations in all areas, coordinating such programs and harmonizing them with State Department foreign policy and with military activities and requests (United States Government Manual Summer 1944, Washington 1944, 68).

On May 5, 1944, Kelsen, by invitation of the Bureau of Areas, took part in a State Department meeting and then also summarized his thoughts in a memorandum.[5] The topic of this meeting was the fate of Austria after the end of the war. Just a few months earlier, the Allies had stated in the Moscow Declaration of October 30, 1943, that Austria "[should] be liberated from German domination." The annexation of 1938 was regarded as "null and void." Surprisingly, Kelsen aimed to narrow the legal meaning of this Declaration as much as possible. If the "annexation" was indeed "null and void" and Austria would only have been "occupied," as a result, then, at the end of the war, Austria would revert to the political status that it had had when it lost its independence in 1938. The legal consequence of this would be that Kurt Schuschnigg's Austro-fascist regime, which had controlled Austria from 1933 to 1938, would return to power! "It is evident that the three Powers do not intend to establish a fascistic State" (Kelsen, Austria (see footnote 5) page 6). Thus, clearly a political motive led Kelsen to argue that the annexation, while illegal, had nevertheless been effective and valid in terms of international law. Accordingly, Austria would have to emancipate itself from Germany by means of a revolutionary act, preferably in a referendum.

As a preliminary question, Kelsen had to deal with the problem of Germany's future after the war. And in this case, too, he argued in favor of a radical breach with the NS regime, which at this point in time was still in power there. Kelsen also warned of making the same mistake as in 1919 by signing a peace treaty with the defeated Germany; such a treaty could once again only take the form of a dictate, as it had been the case with the Treaty of Versailles, and no German politician could sign it without having to fear for his life. Rather it should be the Allies' aim to inflict a complete military defeat onto Germany—he used the term "debellatio"—and then to establish a condominium of the Allied Powers over Germany. This condominium could then build a new German state, which would not be linked to the old regime, and regulate all relationships to this new state at the Allies' pleasure. Also, this would make it possible to bring the German war criminals before an Allied court—Hans Kelsen later also published parts of this memorandum in the *American Journal for International Law*, but only the parts that concerned Germany, not those on Austria (Kelsen 1944b).

Almost exactly 1 year later, on June 5, 1945, the Allies postulated in what came to be known as their Declaration of Berlin that they had gained "the supreme authority and powers with respect to Germany". Kelsen was of the opinion that the Allies

---

[5] The 15-page memorandum bears the title *Austria: Her actual legal status and re-establishment as an independent State* and is dated Berkeley, June 1, 1944. It has been published in Olechowski (2016) 130–140.

had done exactly what he had suggested 1 year ago. He interpreted the wording of the Declaration of Berlin, which stated that the German land and air forces as well as the German navy were "completely defeated," as referring to a "*debellatio*" (Kelsen 1945a: 518). The purpose of assuming "supreme authority" was hence not to avoid further aggression, but to re-establish law, order and administration in the country. He further argued that it was not a "belligerent occupation," because that would necessarily lead to the conclusion that Germany had not ceased to exist. In Kelsen's point of view it was problematic that the Allies had deliberately declared not to intend an annexation of Germany, because according to the traditional doctrine of international law a "subjugation" was only possible after the annexation of the losing party's territory by the winning party. This was obviously not the case because Germany had clearly ceased to exist as a state; therefore, it appeared as if the only solution to this problem was to qualify Germany as "no state's land," which, in Kelsen's opinion, was "simply absurd" (Kelsen 1945a: 521). In order to solve the problem, Kelsen suggested assuming that a condominium of all four Allied Powers had been established.

Unfortunately we know very little about the reactions of the U.S. authorities to Kelsens' approach. In contrast to Kelsen's conception the American military governor Lucius D. Clay declared that Germany still existed as a state. Some members of the Office of Military Government for Germany (OMGUS) were impressed by Kelsen's theories because he denied the applicability of the Hague Convention (Menzel 1947: 1015). Also, an officer of the Judge Advocate General of the U.S. Army stated that Kelsen's suggestions were "excellent" and "appear[ed] to be legally unimpeachable," especially in respect to the punishment of war criminals (Smith 1982: 84). But an official statement does not survive. A series of articles published under supervision of the U.S. authorities in the Berlin daily newspaper "Der Tagesspiegel" seems to have picked up and followed Kelsen's ideas. Apart from that, however, it appears as if the Americans only wanted to exploit some of Kelsen's ideas but not to adopt them (and their consequences) in their entirety (Olechowski 2013: 546). For instance, a legal opinion by the U.S. military government dating from March 17, 1947, only quotes the wording of the Declaration of Berlin, without drawing any conclusions at all. This opinion compared the situation in Germany to the occupation of Cuba by the United States after the war with Spain, which obviously was a poor comparison, as in 1948 the U.S. Supreme Court would declare that the United States was still at war with Germany.[6]

In Germany, Kelsen's propositions were received with far greater skepticism. There, a storm of indignation greeted Kelsen's view that Germany had ceased to exist as a sovereign state. At the first post-war congress of German international law scholars in 1947, the participants overwhelmingly adopted the view that Germany had never ceased to exist. However, at the 1954 congress, only a minority of the participating scholars still thought so (Olechowski 2013: 547).

[6] International lawyers differed on this issue. See for example Kunz (1950). Kunz had been a disciple of Hans Kelsen in Austria and later professor at the University of Toledo, Ohio.

Since then many things, such as the Cold War and the reunification of Germany, have taken place. Nevertheless the German Constitutional Court ruling of 1973, finding that Germany had at all times continued to exist, continues to be valid.[7]

6.4 Kelsen and the Punishment of War Criminals

The second field of studies where Kelsen was quite active concerned the punishment of war criminals. To this end, the Allies had set up the "United Nations War Crimes Commission" (UNWCC) in 1943.[8] The main duty of this commission was to prepare the trials of war criminals that were supposed to take place once the war was over. In addition, the Judge Advocate General of the U.S. Army had set up a "War Crime Office" (WCO) with Brigadier General John M. Weir as its director. The WCO had to prepare the works of Judge Robert H. Jackson, member of the UNWCC and chief prosecutor in Nuremberg in 1946.

Kelsen had already dealt with the problem of the punishment of war criminals, not only in his book, but also in a special article on "Collective and Individual Responsibility in International Law with Particular Regard to the Punishment of War Criminals," published in the *California Law Review* in 1943 (Kelsen 1943).

It is not clear whether the WCO contacted Kelsen, or if Kelsen made efforts to get in touch with it. The only thing known for sure is that Kelsen from April 1945 on—maybe even earlier—was sending letters to the WCO, and in the summer of 1945 he travelled to D.C. twice to participate in meetings.[9] The results of these meetings were eight memoranda published by Hans Kelsen on request of the WCO. The memoranda were:

1. On the Draft Executive Agreement Relating to the Prosecution of European Axis War Criminals,
2. On the Agreement for the Prosecution of European Axis War Criminals,
3. On the Rule against *Ex Post Facto* Laws,
4. On the Definition of Aggression,
5. On the Question: "Is Launching a War of Aggression a Crime?",
6. On the Instrument of Surrender Signed by the Japanese Government,
7. On the Punishment of War Criminals and the Charter of the United Nations,
8. On War Crimes as Related to the Preparation, Launching, and Opening of Hostilities without Previous Warning.

[7] Decision of the German Bundesverfassungsgericht, July 31, 1973, Entscheidungen des Bundesverfassungsgerichts 36, 1.

[8] See the homepage of a new research project of the Centre for International Studies and Diplomacy: www.unwcc.org [online February 5, 2014].

[9] Hans Kelsen Institute Vienna, Hans Kelsen Estate 15p.58.

Memoranda no. 2, 4 and 5 have been located at the National Archives in College Park, Maryland.[10] Memorandum no. 3 could be identical to an article that Kelsen published in the "Judge Advocate Journal" in 1945 (Kelsen 1945b). The list itself was kept with the files and bears no date. It might be the case that Kelsen produced other memoranda as well, which might be identical with his other relevant publications. On the other hand, the contents of some of the memoranda, such as the one on the Japanese surrender, remain unknown.

The individual texts should not be read in isolation. Although they deal with different aspects of international criminal law, they are interrelated in many ways. Some of the propositions go back to ideas published earlier in his book, *Peace through Law*, or in his other, previously mentioned articles on international criminal law. They are of great interest also from the perspective of legal theory, as Kelsen was able to apply his pure theory to address practical problems.

In particular, Kelsen was able to solve one of the main problems of the Nuremberg trials: How can the war criminals be punished if the legal basis for the trial was established after the crimes had been committed? The problem is well known in the United States as the problem of "*ex post facto* laws," as it is regulated in article 1, section 9 of the U.S. constitution: "No Bill of Attainder or *ex post facto* Law shall be passed." Kelsen discussed the genesis of this provision and its meaning in the context of natural law. If the law is "a rule prescribing future conduct of man," the prohibition on *ex post facto* laws would be "a logical necessity" (Kelsen 1943: 8). But legal positivism—Kelsen does not use the term "pure theory" at all—has a different understanding of the essence of law. The law is only "an indirect regulation of the conduct of the subject," but directly a prescription, under which conditions "the organ [is] authorized to execute a sanction" (Kelsen 1945b: 8). So, for legal positivism, the rule on *ex post facto* laws is not a logical necessity but only a provision of positive law.

The next argument, Kelsen was aware, was even more curious: "Retroactive laws are held to be unjust because it hurts our feelings of justice to inflict upon an individual a sanction which he did not foresee, since it was not yet attached to his conduct, and consequently this conduct was not yet illegal," Kelsen stated. But what about the opposite situation? If a law repeals or softens an older criminal law, or is advantageous to the subject in any other way, it would be unjust not to apply it in cases committed before the new law was made. The third argument is that the law must be known in order to applicable. This is also not true, stated Kelsen, quoting Blackstone to the effect that ignorance of the law is no excuse (Kelsen 1945b: 9).

"The result of the preceding analysis is that the rule against *ex post facto* legislation must be interpreted as restrictively as possible" (Kelsen 1945b: 10). From this general statement, Kelsen went on to discuss the London Agreement of the four

[10] See the acknowledgments at the end of this article. Together with the full text of three memoranda, we also found a list including the titles of the others: National Archives and Records Administration (NARA), RG 153, Records of the Office of the Judge Advocate General (Army), War Crimes Branch, General and Administrative Records (Set-Up Files) 1944–1949, Box No. 11.

Allied Powers of August 8, 1945, concerning war criminals. He was of the opinion that it was permitted by international law to establish rules with retroactive force by an international treaty. By passing a retroactive law, it was possible not only to bring the German Empire but also individuals such as politicians, journalists and industrialists to justice.[11] Precedents for this had already been set after WWI, when the "Leipzig trials," in which German war criminals were condemned by the German Supreme Court (Reichsgericht), took place (Segesser 2010: 225; United Nations War Crimes Commission 1948: 48–51). However, concerning the "Leipzig trials," the Allies were of the opinion that the verdicts rendered there had been too mild. Probably for this reason, Article 227 of the Treaty of Versailles stated that Emperor Wilhelm II had to be surrendered to the Allies for trial.[12]

Closer examination reveals that the only problem was to establish international jurisdiction for the prosecution of the crimes, not the prosecution of the crimes as such, because all of the crimes were established as criminal violations long before they were committed. Starting WWII had been a violation of the Kellogg-Briand Pact. Most of the atrocities were "ordinary crimes according to the municipal law of the persons to be accused, valid at the moment they were committed. [...] Even if the atrocities are covered by municipal law, [...] they are certainly open violations of the principles of morality generally recognized by civilized peoples and hence were, at least, morally not innocent or indifferent when they were committed" (Kelsen 1945b: 10).

Only as far as the crime of "starting a war of aggression" was concerned, Kelsen had to admit that so far there had been no law establishing the penal responsibility of a particular person who committed this crime.[13] Generally speaking, Kelsen did not favor the term "war of aggression," as he considered it misleading—international law using the term in a way very different from its original, military meaning.

Kelsen convincingly supported this position with several examples, beginning with the draft Treaty of Mutual Assistance submitted to the member states of the League of Nations by the Council of the League on September 29, 1923, leading to the Geneva Protocol for the Pacific Settlement of International Disputes of October 22, 1924, and ending with the Convention for the Definition of Aggression of July 3, 1933, signed by the U.S.S.R. and seven of her neighbors. Although the first two instruments never came into force and the third was a regional convention only, they

[11] In his book, *Peace through Law*, Kelsen (1944a: 91) had stated that only the "Führer" should be held accountable. When he wrote his memorandum in 1945, the suicide of Hitler was already known in the States; Kelsen did not name the specific persons who should be held accountable and said that this question was "very difficult"; see also Kelsen (1943: 530).

[12] There was never such a trial, because the Netherlands granted asylum to the former Kaiser.

[13] Hans Kelsen, Memorandum "Is'Launching a War of Aggression'a Crime?", in: Letter from John M. Weir to the U.S. Chief of Counsel, dated July 13, 1945, with three documents: The mentioned memorandum, a second memorandum by Kelsen on "The Definition of Aggression" and a third, anonymous memorandum on "Aggression". NARA, RG 0238, World War II War Crimes Records, Office of the U.S. Chief of Counsel for the Prosecution of Axis Criminality, Entry# PI-21 52, Personal Files (Lindenstrasse Files) 1945–1946, Container 2, ARC# 6120160.

all showed that aggression in international law did not merely refer to the "beginning of hostilities" but was defined in a much more complex manner. For example, the Geneva Convention of 1924 established several obligations for states to settle their disputes peacefully. Therefore, the refusal to submit the dispute to a procedure of pacific settlement or the refusal to comply with the decision or recommendation of the agency competent to settle the dispute was an act of "aggression."[14] Wars waged against states that failed to comply with the methods of peaceful settlement of disputes would thus be considered "aggressive wars in the true and original sense of the term," but they would be legal. Even under the Kellogg-Briand Pact, which was supposed to outlaw all aggressive wars, the war against a state that had violated the pact was lawful even if a state not attacked by the violator of the pact initiated war against this violator."[15]

This led Kelsen to the conclusion that the principle of *bellum justum* (just war) still existed in positive international law. This theory had been very controversial, at least since the Kellogg-Briand Pact, when 62 states had "condemn[ed] recourse to war for the solution of international controversies" and declared "that the settlement or solution of all disputes or conflicts of whatever nature or of whatever origin they may be, which may arise among them, shall never be sought except by pacific means." However, Kelsen (who noted that the Kellogg-Briand Pact did not use the term "aggression" at all) showed that the Pact itself required its members to take up arms in defense of peace, as no centralized executive power existed to enforce the law in inter-state relations.

Indeed, when Nazi Germany started WWII in 1939, Germany did not declare war on the United Kingdom and France; rather, these two declared war on Germany (September 3, 1939). But Germany was the real aggressor, as it had attacked Poland 2 days earlier (September 1, 1939). This attack was a violation of the Kellogg-Briand Pact and also a violation of a special non-aggression pact, concluded on January 26, 1934, between Germany and Poland.[16]

"As to the question what kind of tribunal [should] be authorized to try war criminals, national or international, there can be little doubt that an international court is much more fitted for this task than a national civil or military court", Kelsen stated already in 1943, calling to mind the Leipzig trials, which were held after WWI and had very little effect (Kelsen 1943, 562). The punishment should be "an act of international justice, not the satisfaction of a thirst for revenge." Therefore, also the subjects of the victorious states who had committed war crimes should be transferred "to the same independent and impartial international tribunal" (Kelsen 1943, 564).

An international court corresponding to Kelsen's idea was never set up in reality. The Treaty of London, dating from August 8, 1945, which was signed by France, Great Britain, the U.S.S.R. and the U.S.A, only provided for the punishment of German war crimes. On the one hand, this tribunal was not what Kelsen had wished

[14] Kelsen, Definition of Aggression (see footnote 13), p. 6.

[15] Kelsen, Definition of Aggression (see footnote 13) p. 1.

[16] Kelsen, Definition of Aggression (see footnote 13) p. 14.

to create, but—on the other hand—its establishment seemed to support Kelsen's other proposition, namely that the Allies acted as the German sovereign, an idea that Kelsen had already described in his memorandum on the legal status of Germany. In Kelsen's opinion, the Treaty of London was therefore not an international treaty, but an act of the German legislator concerning German war crimes.[17]

6.5 Consequences

Kelsen's work for the U.S. government had some positive effects for him. General Weir, for instance, campaigned for Kelsen so that he very quickly received U.S. citizenship (July 28, 1945).[18] At the same time, the University of California decided that Kelsen—in spite of his age—was a productive and "useful" teacher, and so it offered him a full professorship.[19] On June 21, 1945—more than 12 years after his dismissal from Cologne in 1933—he was appointed full professor.

It is hard to say whether Kelsen's work was an academic or political success. Some developments were disappointing. For example, his memorandum on the concept of aggressive war was forwarded to Justice Jackson, but at the Nuremberg Trials, Jackson made only passing references to the meaning of "aggression," which were obviously not influenced by Kelsen's thesis.[20] On the other hand, Kelsen's opinion that it should be possible to set retroactive laws in force was adopted. The Berlin Declaration of June 5, 1945, through which the Allies gained the supreme authority with respect to Germany, can be seen as the implementation of Kelsen's ideas (although other interpretations are possible). Few lawyers had such a strong influence on the development of international law in the war and post-war periods as Hans Kelsen did.

Acknowledgments The article contains results of my project "Kelsen's life in America (1940–1973) and the diffusion of his legal theory across the globe", funded by the Austrian Science Fund (FWF; Project No. P 23747-G16). With this support, I made two trips to the National Archives in College Park, Maryland, in 2012 together with Dr. Miriam Gassner, and in 2013 together with Dr. Stefan Wedrac. I have to thank both of them for their support. Some parts of this article follow Olechowski and Wedrac (2015). Special thanks also to Ramon Pils, DipTrans for the translation and Dr. Gassner for the proof-reading of large parts of the text.

[17] Kelsen, The Agreement for the Prosecution of European Axis War Criminals, NARA RG 153, Box No. 11.

[18] Hans Kelsen Institute Vienna, Hans Kelsen Estate 16c13.

[19] University of California, Berkeley, personal files Hans Kelsen, Budget Committee Comments, March 1945.

[20] In his closing address at the Palace of Justice in Nuremberg on July 26, 1946, Jackson stated: "We need not trouble ourselves about the many abstract difficulties that can be conjured up about what constitutes aggression in doubtful cases." See Jackson (1947) 127 and also the harsh criticism of Jackson by Kelsen (1947).

References

Bishop Jr., William W. 1956. Lawrence Preuss, 1905–1956. *The American Journal of International Law* 50: 907–909.

Busch, Jürgen. 2009. Hans Kelsen im Ersten Weltkrieg—Achsenzeit einer Weltkarriere. In *Hans Kelsen: Leben—Werk—Wirksamkeit*, ed. Robert Walter, Werner Ogris and Thomas Olechowski, 57–80. Wien: Manz.

Ehs, Tamara and Miriam Gassner. 2012. Hans Kelsen (1881–1973). Legal scholar between Europe and the Americas. In *Transatlantic Perspectives*. [http://www.transatlanticperspectives.org/entry.php?rec=132] (online since 11/8, 2012; read 5/2, 2015).

Feichtinger, Johannes. 2009. Transatlantische Vernetzungen. Der Weg Hans Kelsens und seines Kreises in die Emigration. In *Hans Kelsen: Leben—Werk—Wirksamkeit*, ed. Robert Walter, Werner Ogris and Thomas Olechowski, 321–338. Wien: Manz.

Jackson, Robert H. 1947. *The Nürnberg Case*. New York: Knopf.

Kelsen, Hans. 1934. Die Technik des Völkerrechts und die Organisation des Friedens. *Zeitschrift für Öffentliches Recht* 14: 240–255.

Kelsen, Hans. 1943. Collective and individual responsibility in international law with particular regard to punishment of war criminals. *California Law Review* 31: 530–571.

Kelsen, Hans. 1944a. *Peace through law*. Chapell Hill: The University of North Carolina Press.

Kelsen, Hans. 1944b. The international legal status of Germany to be established immediately upon termination of the War. *The American Journal of International Law* 38: 689–694.

Kelsen, Hans. 1945a. The legal status of Germany according to the Declaration of Berlin. *The American Journal of International Law* 39: 518–526.

Kelsen, Hans. 1945b. The rule against ex post facto laws and the prosecution of Axis war criminals. *The Judge Advocate Journal* 2/3: 8–12.

Kelsen, Hans. 1947. Will the judgment in the Nuremberg Trial Constitute a precedent in international law? *The International Law Quarterly* 1: 153–171.

Kunz, Josef L. 1950. The status of occupied Germany under international law: A legal dilemma. *The Western Political Quarterly* 3: 538–565.

Menzel, Eberhard. 1947. Zur völkerrechtlichen Lage Deutschlands. *Europa-Archiv* 2: 1009–1016.

Oberkofler, Gerhard, and Eduard Rabofsky. 1988. *Hans Kelsen im Kriegseinsatz der k.u.k. Wehrmacht*. Frankfurt et al: Peter Lang.

Olechowski, Thomas. 2013. Kelsens Debellatio-These. Rechtshistorische und rechtstheoretische Überlegungen zur Kontinuität von Staaten. In *Gedenkschrift Robert Walter*, ed. Clemens Jabloner et al., 531–552. Wien: Manz.

Olechowski, Thomas. 2014. Kelsen als Pazifist. In *Hans Kelsen: Die Aktualität eines großen Rechtswissenschafters und Soziologen des 20. Jahrhunderts*, ed. Nikitas Aliprantis and Thomas Olechowski, 119–129. Wien: Manz.

Olechowski, Thomas. 2016. Hans Kelsens Gutachten zur Neugestaltung Österreichs und Deutschlands nach dem Zweiten Weltkrieg. In *Das internationale Wirken Hans Kelsens*, ed. Clemens Jabloner, Thomas Olechowski, and Klaus Zeleny, 121–140. Wien: Manz.

Olechowski, Thomas, and Jürgen Busch. 2010. Hans Kelsen als Professor an der Deutschen Universität Prag. Biographische Aspekte der Kelsen-Sander-Kontroverse. In *Československé právo a právní věda v meziválečném období (1918–1938) a jejich místo ve střední Evropě*, ed. Karel Malý and Ladislav Soukup, 1106–1134. Praha: Nakladatelství Karolinum.

Olechowski, Thomas, and Stefan Wedrac. 2015. Hans Kelsen und Washington. In *Bananen, Cola, Zeitgeschichte. Oliver Rathkalb und das lange 20. Jahhundert*, ed. Lucile Dreidemy and Maria Wirth, 280–295. Wien: Böhlau.

Rutkoff, Peter M., and William B. Scott. 1986. *New School. A History of the new school for social research*. New York/London: The Free Press/Collier Macmillan Publishers.

Segesser, Daniel Marc. 2010. *Recht statt Rache oder Rache durch Recht? Die Ahndung von Kriegsverbrechern in der internationalen wissenschaftlichen Debatte 1872–1945*. Schöningh: Paderborn et al.

Smith, Bradley. 1982. *The American road to Nuremberg*. Stanford: Hoover Institution Press.

United Nations War Crimes Commission. 1948. *History of the United Nations War Crimes Commission and the development of the Laws of War*. London: His Majesty's Stationery Office.

Part III
Kelsen in Unexplored Dialogues

Chapter 7
Arriving at Justice by a Process of Elimination: Hans Kelsen and Leo Strauss

Elisabeth Lefort

7.1 Introduction

Dealing with the lack of reception of Hans Kelsen's writings in the United States (and maybe even beyond its borders), means pursuing at least two goals. The first consists of formulating hypotheses concerning the reasons for such a lack of reception. The second is trying to overcome this situation, at least in part, by rereading Kelsen's texts in order to demonstrate how his thought is still relevant to our contemporary context. In this spirit, the following paper aims at a *philosophical*[1] confrontation between Hans Kelsen and another author from the same period, namely Leo Strauss.

The choice of comparing Kelsen with Strauss requires a justification straightaway. One main justification for such a comparison lies in the fact that, despite their similar backgrounds and experiences, the two thinkers pursued similar subject matters from very different theoretical perspectives.

---

[1] One can find a comparative reading between Kelsen and Strauss in David Novak's article, *Haunted by the Ghost of Weimar: Leo Strauss' Critique of Hans Kelsen* (2012). This chapter obviously benefits from Novak's work, although it takes a different approach. The goal here is a philosophical, not a historical, comparison of the two authors. More precisely, this presentation intends to discover a common view on justice, and to go beyond the differences between Kelsen and Strauss. Therefore, it aims at an *interpretation* of their texts. Moreover, the starting point here is Kelsen's moral relativism, while in David Novak's article, the reading focuses more on Strauss's philosophy. The two respective comparative readings are not in conflict; they pursue different goals and pose different questions.

E. Lefort (✉)
University of Luxembourg, Luxembourg, Luxembourg

Catholic University of Louvain, Louvain-la-Neuve, Belgium
e-mail: Elisabeth.lefort@uni.lu

D.A.J. Telman (ed.), *Hans Kelsen in America - Selective Affinities and the Mysteries of Academic Influence*, Law and Philosophy Library 116,
DOI 10.1007/978-3-319-33130-0_7

On the one hand, they share strong biographical similarities. Both Kelsen and Strauss left Europe around the same time to escape Nazism.[2] On the other hand, a look at their works reveals a strong theoretical antagonism that definitively separates Kelsen from Strauss. This antagonism is so firm that it seems to prevent *a priori* any attempt to reconcile their respective thoughts, especially when they deal with the concepts of law and morality.

Moreover, even though the two scholars never directly confronted one another, the theoretical opposition that divides them is surely well known. Kelsen's name is associated with his *Pure Theory of Law*, a book that had a decisive impact on the juridical tradition of the twentieth century. In this work, Kelsen attempts to build a pure legal science safeguarded from any ideological contamination. In fact, when he mentions ideology, one of the things he is referring to is natural law theory. For his part, Strauss is strongly associated with the denunciation of historicism. According to him, historicism is the discourse responsible for the loss of natural right and its meaning. Historicism holds that the world and human beings are necessarily linked with, and determined by, their historical and cultural context. For Strauss, this idea has contaminated all the modern human sciences and has thereby thrown people into a practical world without any guiding principle(s). For Strauss, historicism leads directly to nihilism.[3] Due to this fact, Strauss calls for a rediscovery of natural right, which can and should be accomplished with the help of philosophy.

From this standpoint, the opposition between the two authors seems to be difficult to overcome. While Kelsen rejects natural law and endorses moral relativism, Strauss calls for a rediscovery of natural right and rejects moral relativism.

How can this evident opposition with Strauss aid one in understanding Kelsen's lack of reception in the United States? Strauss's book, published contemporaneously with Kelsen's writings, is a perfect reflection of the latter's reception in the United States. In his book, Strauss criticizes historicism for introducing moral relativism into the modern social sciences. While doing so, Strauss quotes Kelsen only once, in a footnote, as an illustration of the instrumental nature of modern social sciences. In fact, Strauss claims that Kelsenian legal positivism—because it conducts its knowledge under an imperative of neutrality—does not recognize any differences between democracy and tyranny.[4]

Natural Right and History, precisely because of its scant reference to Kelsen, is a perfect illustration of how the latter's writings were largely ignored and soon forgotten by scholars in the United States. This limited reference to Kelsen cannot be

[2] Strauss left Germany for France in 1932, supported by a grant from Rockefeller Foundation. Then, he went to England in 1934, before definitely leaving Europe for the United States in 1938. See Smith (2009: 18–34). For a more detailed biography on Strauss, see Sheppard (2006). For a biography of Kelsen, see Metall (1969).

[3] Strauss (1953a: 3): "The contemporary rejection of natural right leads to nihilism—nay, it is identical with nihilism."

[4] As David Novak mentions (2012: 394): "the University of Chicago at that time provided Strauss with a congenial atmosphere for his anti-positivism/anti-historicism."

attributed to the fact that Strauss did not know his texts.[5] If Strauss rejects the Kelsenian position but at the same time does not allocate too much space for this rejection, it is because he judges that the latter position is an expression of the dominant *Zeitgeist*.

In the political context of post Second World War, which witnessed the hitherto unseen emergence of totalitarian phenomena, one can clearly see why the Kelsenian position did not excite much popular adherence. At a time when people expected a commitment from their intellectuals, ie, a clear denunciation of Nazism, Kelsen defended scientific neutrality and asserted that a rational moral evaluation is impossible. Even though one should refrain from a "*reductio ad Hitlerum*,"[6] one must nevertheless admit that the Kelsenian legal science does not deliver the expected denunciation of totalitarianism. This failure to offer a clear denunciation of totalitarian phenomena might have contributed to his writings' lack of reception.

If Kelsen's legal theory was a victim of its weak reception, the same thing can be said about his writings that deal with moral questions. The latter, nonetheless, and the Berkeley Farewell Lecture in particular seem susceptible to readings that render them still relevant today for moral and political philosophy. What is particularly interesting in this text is the ambiguity that attends to the kind of moral relativism defended by Kelsen. It is precisely this ambiguity that one can interpret as relevant to contemporary philosophical debates.

Contrary to preconceived ideas about his moral standpoint, *What is Justice*? is not a *radical defense* of moral relativism. In fact, in this lecture, Kelsen explicitly presents moral relativism as a simple personal opinion. The conclusion, in which he expresses his own preferences for democracy and for tolerance, must be read in this light.

> Since science is my profession, and hence the most important thing in my life, justice, to me, is that social order under whose protection the search for truth can prosper. "My" justice, then, is the justice of freedom, the justice of peace, the justice of democracy—the justice of tolerance (Kelsen 1957: 24).

However, if the moral relativism Kelsen defends is merely the expression of his own personal preference, then Jes Bjarup is right to ask: "Why does Kelsen take all the trouble to inform others about his emotional state of mind?" (Bjarup 1986: 298) It is possible to explain the interest in Kelsen's emotional state of mind if one considers that Kelsen's attempt to resolve the moral question matters less than *the question he raises* concerning the essence of justice.

---

[5] It is well established that Strauss had read Kelsen. The preface that he wrote to Isaac Husik's *Philosophical Essays* (Strauss 1953b) is proof of that, because one can find in it many references to Kelsen. Let us remember that at the time, Kelsen already enjoyed a good reputation as a jurist in the United States (see Telman (2008: 2)), while Strauss had only begun his career (see Novak (2012: 393), and Smith (2009: 32)). Strauss's reputation in the United States only got stronger after his arrival in Chicago, and after the publication of *Natural Right and History*: "This book—along with *Persecution and the Art of writing* published the year before—turned Strauss from an unknown into a major voice in American political philosophy."

[6] This is a popular Straussian expression. Strauss uses it in *Natural Right and History* to designate a new form of rhetorical fallacy. See Strauss (1953a: 42–43).

It is essentially the same question Strauss asks. Remarkably, Strauss himself does not appear in *Natural Right and History* as a devoted defender of natural right. He does not pretend that the choice of natural right constitutes the best possible option, or that such a choice would be even possible. On the contrary, Strauss warns his reader: seeking the authentic meaning of nature with the help of philosophy could finally lead to the conclusion of the impossibility of natural right itself. Moreover, Strauss does not define his work as a defense of a particular standpoint.[7] Given how both authors define their own thinking, the main interest of their respective texts does not reside in the answers to the question of justice that they suggest. Instead, it resides in *the fact that they both ask this particular question.*

It is precisely this common question that opens the possibility of a comparative reading of the two authors. What both Kelsen and Strauss demonstrate in the end, is the necessity of questioning the essence of justice. This question is not merely theoretical; it demands human political commitment. Even the act of asking such a question is already a practical commitment. According to Arendt, "justice is something that we think about, talk about, debate about; it is not something that we *know*."[8] Thus, the common question one can find in Kelsen's and Strauss's texts could be interpreted as a call to think and rethink the essence of justice. But how can one find the same question in texts that are the expression of antagonistic standpoints? This fact may be explained by the context of political modernity that is their common background. Maybe it is this modernity itself that is calling for such a question. If one defines modernity *symbolically*,[9] as a time when all human references and certainties are lost, this could make sense. Modernity is an era where the grounds of law cannot be guaranteed absolutely, and indeed, in this era, such grounds were always subject to question. This *indeterminacy* is not necessarily a bad thing. It can be assumed *per se*: for one can think about this indeterminacy as the condition of possibility of democracy itself.

> Thus, the absence of an identifiable ground, the fact that a symbolic place declared empty is not occupied by anybody, engenders the vitality of social relations, since everybody has to seek what should be (Lefort 1986: 563).

A philosophical reading of Kelsen that tries to compare his thoughts with Strauss's seems relevant, when one looks at such a reading as a way to conceive our contemporary political context. Both texts of Kelsen and Strauss reveal themselves as an essential reminder of how important the question of justice is.

---

[7] Strauss (1978: 23): "I myself regard the book as a preparation to an adequate philosophic discussion rather than settling the question."

[8] In his book about Claude Lefort's political philosophy, Bernard Flynn recounts the discussion between one of his friends and Hannah Arendt: the discussion probably dealt with Rawls' *Theory of Justice*, and most certainly with the possibility of determining what justice is. The quotation of what Arendt reportedly said is taken from Flynn (2005: 228).

[9] This conceptual terminology comes from the political philosophy of Claude Lefort. According to him, the symbolic characteristic of a society designates its system of representations. See Flynn (2005: 117–120).

In order to justify this hypothesis, two texts will be considered in this chapter: Kelsen's *What is Justice?* as well as Strauss's *Natural Right and History*.[10] The analysis of these texts reveals three main points of antagonism. Kelsen and Strauss obviously disagree on: the political question (§ 7.2); the question of relativism (§ 7.3); and the question of natural right (§ 7.4). A further reading also reveals that the opposition between Kelsen and Strauss can be overcome if one considers that the two authors are less interested in defending a strong standpoint and providing answers than in formulating the question of the essence of justice (§ 7.5).

7.2 The Political Question

7.2.1 Inconsistencies

Kelsen sought to prove that theories of natural law are inconsistent because natural law theories can potentially justify any political regime. Thus, natural law's defenders never succeeded in agreeing either on which political regime is the best, or even on which one is good. Defenders of natural law have justified different and opposed political regimes. Robert Filmer argued in favor of absolute monarchy, while John Locke was convinced democracy was the only just and legitimate option.[11] Natural law can also defend communism, as well as private property; namely one thing and its diametric opposite. This is the proof that natural law theories fall victim to error and that they are not scientific.

> If nature is supposed to be created by God, the norms immanent in nature, natural laws, are the expression of the will of God. Then the natural-law doctrine has a metaphysical character. If, however, the natural law is to be deduced from the nature of man as being endowed with reason, (…) then the natural-law doctrine pretends to assume a rationalistic character. From the point of view of science, neither the one nor the other view is tenable (Kelsen 1957: 20).[12]

Natural law's history of ideas does not indicate a universal moral criterion. Ironically, the quick genesis of mutually contradictory natural law theories, each of which claims universality, is itself an indicator of the impossibility for human cognition to specify unconditional moral values.

In a symmetrical way, the only reference to Kelsen in Strauss's book, *Natural Right and History*, serves to criticize legal positivism because of its instrumental

---

[10] Concerning the latter, this chapter will only focus on the Introduction and the first chapter that deals with historicism.

[11] See Kelsen (1957: 21). The same argument is also presented in Kelsen (1955: 98 n.70).

[12] Kelsen stated:

> Hence it is not astonishing that the various followers of the natural-law doctrine deduced from nature, or found in human reason, the most contradictory principles of justice (Kelsen (1957:21).

nature. In Strauss's view, Kelsenian legal science can justify any political regime[13] because "it derives its strength ultimately from the generally accepted historicist premise" (Strauss 1953a: 10).

In order to demonstrate that the loss of natural right is a bad thing, Strauss underlines the problems raised by the substitution of nature's sense (a sense implied by such a conception of law) with the historical one. For Strauss, this substitution puts into question the possibility of moral evaluation. Indeed, according to historicism, all moral evaluations are relative to a historical and cultural context. Therefore, moral evaluations can only have a relative weight because a determined moral evaluation can never prevent itself from being contradicted by another. In historicism's view, all moral judgments have, strictly speaking, the same weight and the same value. Modern social sciences:

> (…) [A]ppear to believe that our inability to acquire any genuine knowledge of what is intrinsically good or right compels us to be tolerant of every opinion about good or right or to recognize all preferences or all "civilizations" as equally respectable. Only unlimited tolerance is in accordance with reason (Strauss 1953a: 5).

If all moral evaluations are condemned to have *only* a relative validity, this also means that the moral (or immoral) value of political regimes cannot be determined with certainty. Our modern social sciences are potentially efficient instruments that can serve the interest of any political regime—including tyrannical interests—because of this complete lack of differentiation between what is legitimate and what is illegitimate. However, in actuality, they are not as versatile because they only serve the interest of a "generous liberalism,"[14] and this affiliation with liberalism proves their lack of consistency.[15]

7.2.2 *Strauss's Quotation from Kelsen's* Allgemeine Staatslehre

Precisely after his denunciation of modern social sciences as instruments, Strauss quotes Kelsen. According to Strauss, Kelsenian legal science is a perfect example of the voluntary moral blindness characteristic of the modern social sciences. Strauss

---

[13] Strauss is not the first scholar to criticize the Kelsenian theory in this way. Since its first formulations, legal positivism aroused this suspicion. As Kelsen mentions in his Preface to the first edition of the *Pure Theory Law*, one of the main claims raised against his legal science deals with its independence from politics. Many political orientations have been attributed to his legal science, and he perceives this fact as a proof that it is not politically orientated. See Kelsen (1934: 3). See also: Kelsen (1955: 97 n.70, 1957: 376 n.20).

[14] For Strauss, the only thing that prevents modern social sciences to serve "tyrants" as well as "free peoples" is that they "prefer—only God knows why—generous liberalism to consistency…" (Strauss 1953a: 4).

[15] On the affiliation of the Kelsenian theory with liberalism, see Herrera (1995). In his article, Herrera argues that such an affiliation is not self-evident.

quotes a part of the original German version of *Allgemeine Staatslehre*, written in 1925, wondering why this part has been removed from the English translation published in 1949.[16] This is the quotation from Kelsen included in Strauss's book:

> The assertion that there exists no legal order [*Rechtsordnung*] in despotic regimes, but instead the arbitrariness [*Willkür*] of the despot, is entirely senseless…since a State ruled in a despotic way, also constitutes a certain regulation [*Ordnung*] of human behaviors.…This regulation is precisely the legal order. Denying its legal character is only natural law's naïveté or arrogance.…What is interpreted as arbitrary is simply the despot's legal possibility of making every decision himself, of determining in an unconditional way the actions of subsidiary bodies, and of modifying or repealing at any time the general or even only the particular validity [*Geltung*] of established norms. Such a state is a legal state [*Rechtszustand*], even if it is judged as harmful. It also has positive aspects. The not so unusual call for dictatorship in modern states of law clearly demonstrates this.[17]

The reader familiar with Kelsenian legal science cannot be surprised by the idea contained in this quototation. What is at stake here is, in the end, one of the main claims of his *Pure Theory of Law*, the identity of State and Law. According to Kelsen, a despotic state is, from a scientific point of view, a legal state, and moreover, any state is a legal state regardless of its political nature, as well as regardless of any individual's moral approval of it. Thus, the legality of an existing political regime is not dependent on any individual's moral approval of that regime. This distinction between the legality of a State and its moral standing is a consequence of the Kelsenian definition of legal science.

Indeed, according to Kelsen, knowing the law and evaluating it morally are, *by definition*, two contradictory operations. The former's principles are grounded in the legitimate limits of human cognition, while the latter's principles directly emanate from the human will. The former is rational, while the latter is irrational. Moreover, the first is a descriptive operation, while the second is a prescriptive one. This opposition between description (legal science) and prescription (moral evaluation) is in fact a development of Kelsen's main distinction, the difference between *Sein* and *Sollen*.

This distinction plays a double role in Kelsen's work. We can find it at two different levels. The first is theoretical, concerning the definition of law itself Kelsen (1967: 4–10). The second level is *meta-theoretical*, pertaining to the definition of the *theory* of law. At the meta-theoretical level, the separation between *Sein* and *Sollen* means the limitation of human rational knowledge to the world of *Sein*. Thus, the Kelsenian scientific perspective excludes any evaluative or justificatory aim.[18] It also entails the condemnation of any attempt of establishing natural law.

---

[16] Strauss notes: "Since Kelsen has not changed his attitude toward natural right, I cannot imagine why he has omitted this instructive passage from the English translation" (Strauss 1953a: 4). David Novak notices another passage omitted from the English translation of the *Pure Theory of Law*'s second edition (Novak 2012: 406 n.6).

[17] Strauss directly quotes Kelsen in German (Strauss 1953a: 4 n.2). Therefore, I use and complete David Novak's translation here (Novak 2012: 395).

[18] See how Kelsen characterizes his own legal science in his *Pure Theory of Law* (Kelsen 1967: 9).

This review of Kelsen's legal epistemology is helpful in order to show that, from Kelsen's point of view, being scientific means remaining politically neutral.

7.2.3 The Historical and Political Context[19]

It is significant that it is in the same political and historical context that Kelsen reaffirms axiological neutrality that Strauss denounces the instrumental nature of modern social sciences. To use Strauss's formulation (from another context), the common political climate they shared was "darkened by the shadow of Hitler" (Strauss 1953a: 42). With this in mind, one will easily understand how the Kelsenian reaffirmation of axiological neutrality in 1945 can be problematic, and even unpopular.

In the name of science, Kelsen discredits any moral evaluation of political regimes. His science is therefore an indirect affirmation that all political regimes are undifferentiated. His standpoint leads to the impossibility of any moral denunciation of the mid-twentieth century totalitarian regimes. In this serious context, the expectation of a clear standpoint concerning historical and political events runs against Kelsen's reaffirmation that a neutral standpoint concerning facts is the only rational and legitimate option. This reaffirmation and Kelsen's consequent refusal to intervene intellectually are easily perceived as disappointing, if not rejected as absurd.[20]

It would not be fair however to say that Kelsen did not have a clear perception of this historical and political context or that he did not worry about the questions regarding the moral evaluation of political regimes. Significantly, his writings after 1945 considerably develop his standpoint on the moral question. His Farewell Lecture, which is emblematically entitled *What is Justice?* (1952), was already mentioned. The second edition (1960) of *Pure Theory of Law* was extended in telling ways. First, the chapter dealing with *Law and Morals* is more developed. Second, Kelsen later supplemented the book with two addenda titled respectively *The Problem of Justice*[21] and *Justice and Natural Law*. Finally, there is his *Foundations of Democracy* published in 1955, as well as the collection of some of Kelsen's articles in the book *What is Justice? Justice, Law and Politics in the Mirror of Science* (1957).

---

[19] This part was added to initial drafts, thanks to the suggestions of Peter Caldwell.

[20] The concept of intellectual intervention has different meanings. The one used here is the one Marc Maesschalck points at, namely: contemporary ethical meaning. From this perspective, intellectual intervention means not only to produce discourses but also to take part *in* the ethical field, to consider actions as well as discourses and doctrines. This means adopting a standpoint within the ethical field, within the field of human actions. One can therefore easily understand how Kelsen refused an intellectual intervention in this sense. See Maesschalck (2010: 9–10).

[21] Nicoletta Bersier Ladavac provides a close reading of this Kelsenian article (Ladavac 2008: 19–52). For a detailed bibliography regarding the question of justice in Kelsen's works, see in particular, 38.

The publication of these texts is significant—not because it raises new questions, for, on the contrary, the question of justice and the question of democracy were already present in Kelsen's writings before his immigration to the United States, nor was it because it documented a radical change in Kelsen's theoretical standpoint. The Berkeley Farewell Lecture is nothing more than an extension of the second chapter of his first *Pure Theory of Law* (1934). Rather, this publication is significant because it takes place in the context of post-Second World War. It seems that Kelsen felt the need, at this particular time of history, to get back to these questions, as well as to clarify and develop his answers. This should be proof of Kelsen's strong standpoint on moral and political issues, on which he does not elaborate in his theoretical writings. In those writings, he always tries to preserve consistently the purity of science. Instead, he developed his ideas on justice *outside the theoretical framework of legal science*.

7.3 The Question of Moral Relativism

7.3.1 Kelsen's Relativist Practical View

In his lecture, Kelsen considers five practical dilemmas (Kelsen 1957: 5–7). He explores five situations, each of which requires decision making, and his treatment of these situations illuminates his position on moral relativism. Kelsen uses these situations to prove that human decisions are in fact choices based on preferences. From that perspective, one's decision is nothing more than the election of a certain value. Because each particular decision is a personal preference or a selection based on a determined value, it cannot have enough strength to exclude the possibility of a different choice, which would itself be based on an opposed value. Kelsen wants to prove that the supposition of an absolute value is not a matter of science, because it is not a rational operation, but a matter of choice based on emotions.

One of the five dilemmas is the case of the doctor.[22] A doctor is facing a patient who will soon die. He is therefore facing two contradictory practical options: should he reveal the truth to his patient and tell him about his imminent death, or should he hide this painful truth from him? According to Kelsen, in order to decide which option would be better, the doctor has to establish a hierarchy between two values. In other words, in order to be able to make his choice, the doctor has to decide which value, truth or compassion, is more important. If he judges that truth is a higher value, then he will inform the patient of his health despite the fear of what this news might cause. In this first scenario, the doctor judges that one should always try to be truthful, even if truthfulness can be unpleasant. However, if the doctor considers, for example, fear of death to be the worst feeling one can have, he will lie to his patient,

[22]Even though the figure of the doctor mentioned in *What is Justice?* is quite outdated, this fact does not affect the example, because what Kelsen aims to do here is to show the dilemma in every human practical decision.

intentionally hiding from him the fact that he does not have much time to live. In this second situation, compassion is valued over truthfulness. In Kelsen's opinion, this dilemma illustrates well how value judgments are emotional and not the result of human cognition. The doctor does not decide with the help of logical thinking but by consulting his emotions: the will to be truthful on the one hand, or his compassion on the other.

7.3.2 Strauss's Criticism of Relativism

In *Natural Right and History*, Strauss presents Kelsen's position concerning the lack of objectivity in moral judgments and thus their relativity as a common perspective shared by modern social sciences.[23] In other words, according to Strauss, Kelsen and the modern social sciences hold that the standard one uses to make practical decisions is not rational. Hence, it is also not universal, because it depends on non-universal circumstances. It is relative to one's emotions, culture, time, and place. In short, our moral standard is nothing more than an ideal adopted by our society.

This relativist perspective raises two main problems, according to Strauss. First, this definition of justice makes it impossible to have a reasonable critical distance from society. Furthermore, if one agrees with the idea that the criteria that allow one to make just decisions are given by society, then: (1) this relative standard is not so much superior to society as it is identified with it; and (2) this relative standard is not a way to evaluate society because it derives directly from it. This is obviously not a good thing because political life needs to leave the door open to evaluation and criticism in order to prevent excesses.

> [S]ince the ideal of our society is admittedly changing, nothing except dull and stale habit could prevent us from placidly accepting a change in the direction of cannibalism. If there is no standard higher than the ideal of our society, we are utterly unable to take a critical distance from that ideal (Strauss 1953a: 3).

Moreover, Strauss thinks that this identification between individuals and the moral ideal given by society is a false assumption. The simple fact that one can question one's own social environment is proof that humans are not completely identified with, and determined by, society. If humans were entirely absorbed by society and defined by it, they would be unable to think of society as an object. They would be unable to feel a need for justice (Strauss 1953a: 3).

The second main problem raised by moral relativism concerns the world it builds—a world without references, a world that is confused and absurd. In other words, according to Strauss, moral relativism leads directly to nihilism. From the standpoint of moral relativism, human cognition cannot access knowledge of

---

[23] Others writings of Strauss deal with the same idea. For instance, see *Social Science and Humanism* (Strauss 1956: 3–12), *Relativism* (Strauss 1961: 13–26), as well as *What is Political Philosophy* (Strauss 1957: 343–368).

absolute justice. And this postulate not only condemns human beings to be alone with their choices but also condemns all human choices to be equal and undifferentiated. If it is impossible for people to know what is just and what is not, does this not mean that all possible choices are equivalent? Because there is no unconditional standard, this somehow means that there is no standard at all. A determined choice, or act, is qualified as just only because it corresponds to an ideal that is itself relative. In this world where everything is relative, every behavior and every judgment is weak and therefore meaningless (Strauss 1953a: 3).

Therefore, justice is void of meaning. Herein lies all the irony for Strauss: our modern social sciences are efficient only in determining things that have merely secondary importance for us. This is because they are unable to access what is most important for us, namely, our practical life. Rationality becomes synonymous with voluntary blindness, and we are condemned to choose blindly: all our choices are as good as they are bad.

> We are then in the position of beings who are sane and sober when engaged in trivial business and who gamble like madmen when confronted with serious issues—retail sanity and wholesale madness (Strauss 1953a: 4).

7.4 The Question of Natural Right

7.4.1 Kelsen's Rejection of Natural Law

Regarding the question of whether or not natural law is a legitimate rational option for human beings, Kelsen's negative answer is expected. His rejection of natural law in *What is Justice?* is the rejection of a certain form of moral absolutism.[24] According to Kelsen, natural law requires an absolute ground: this ground is what allows the validity of human moral judgments. An absolute ground means the determination of a non-relative standard, one that is valid in any possible situation and in an unconditional way. Therefore, this standard is a universal concept of justice.

In Kelsen's view, it is precisely this universality that is problematic, because an unconditional moral standard or concept is, by definition, unreachable for human cognition. The rejection of moral absolutism is grounded on a particular epistemology. Because human knowledge is limited, it cannot access absolute values. This limitation also plays an essential role in the knowledge of law. In order to be scientific, one should be aware of the limitations of human reason. This is why Kelsenian legal science uses empirical experience as its raw material.[25] Regarding the question

---

[24] One cannot accuse the Straussian philosophy of being absolutist, if one looks closely at these lines of *Natural Right and History*: "There is a universally valid hierarchy of ends, but there are no universal rules of actions" (Strauss 1953a: 162).

[25] One can find this idea of the theoretical need for empirical facts in Kant's first *Critique* when he deals with the pure categories (Kant 1781: 346). Regarding the question of the Kantian influence on Kelsen, see Wilson (1986: 37–64).

of values, the same principle applies: in order to correctly know the nature of values, one should look at the question of values without ignoring one's cognitive limitations. What human experience shows is not absolute values or unconditional practical standards but multiple, temporary, and changing values or concepts. The world of facts illustrates the relativism of values.

> The absolute in general, and the absolute values in particular, are beyond human reason, for which only a conditional, and in this sense relative, solution of the problem of justice, as the problem of justification of human behavior, is possible (Kelsen 1957: 10).

The second argument Kelsen offers in *What is Justice?* against natural law is the famous "is/ought" logical problem (Kelsen 1957: 20–21).[26] According to him, natural law is constructed under a logical mistake: it tries to deduce norms from the nature of things or of human beings. It deduces from what *is*, how things *ought to be*. It deduces normative statements from factual ones. But the factual world (*Sein*) is ontologically different from the normative world (*Sollen*) (Kelsen 1957: 20).

This is why natural law is nothing but a rationally illegitimate philosophical and metaphysical enterprise that fulfills the same function as religion. In fact, both religion and natural law succeed in satisfying the human need for justification by postulating an absolute justice, albeit through fallacious reasoning. Their reasoning necessarily transgresses the limits of human reason, because the postulate of a transcendent concept is, by definition, beyond our reach. The pretense that one can surpass the limits of human cognition leads both religion and natural law into inconsistency.

Despite his rejection of natural law, Kelsen seems to avoid Strauss's critique of nihilism, because he does not conclude with the absence of moral values. Rather, his conclusion is that tolerance is a moral principle. In Kelsen's opinion, tolerance should be the ultimate value of our moral choices: it is the only rational value possible. It is the only one that can respect the diversity and multiplicity of moral conceptions existing worldwide. One could qualify as tolerant if one welcomes every moral, religious, and political view, particularly opposing ones. Being tolerant means trying to understand the opinions of others, especially those with whom one does not agree. In other words, "[t]olerance means freedom of thoughts" (Kelsen 1957: 23).

7.4.2 Strauss's Answers to the Rejection of Natural Right

Echoing modern social sciences, Kelsen thinks that natural right does not consider the world of facts. Strauss's opposition to this argument is particularly strong. Humans did not wait for historicism and its moral relativism to realize that several

[26] One can find this distinction in Hume's Treatise (Hume 1888: 469–470). Strauss discusses both the Humean and the Kantian influences on modern social sciences in his article titled *Relativism* (Strauss 1961: 22–24).

conceptions of justice exist. In fact, far from being an argument against natural right, this empirical fact is an argument in its favor, because natural right builds itself precisely on this diversity of experience. Its essence is to search beyond this empirical perspective for a universal standard, and this search is conducted with the help of human reason. Therefore, natural right does not ignore empirical facts, but, on the contrary, considers them in order to transcend them.

> Above all, knowledge of the indefinitely large variety of notions of right and wrong is so far from being incompatible with the idea of natural right that is the essential condition for the emergence of that idea: realization of the diversity of notions of right is *the* incentive for the quest of knowledge (Strauss 1953a: 10).

Political philosophy (Strauss 1957: 343–368) and natural right emerged when human beings realized the radical difference between convention and nature. That is the reason that one cannot say that the lack of universal agreement about what natural right states is the proof of its impossibility. Given its essence, the theory of natural right cannot be accessible to every human being. First, it is only an attempt; second, it involves the use of reason (Strauss 1957: 343–344).

Furthermore, from the perspective of modern social sciences, every theoretical position is *historically* determined. Does the claim that all theories are historically determined not imply the adoption of a point of view that is not itself historically determined? Therefore, and by definition, is historicism not a trans-historical perspective? How can one assert such a historicist statement without adopting a *trans-historical* perspective? (Strauss 1953a: 25)

In the best-case scenario, if historicist relativism were true, then it would prove that human cognition could transcend its historical limitations and access a trans-historical point of view. This would obviously contradict the premise of historicism and its moral relativism. This clearly shows that historicism and moral relativism are victims of a logical error. If these theories were consistent, they would not exclude themselves from the historical determination they claim as truth.

In Strauss's opinion, a similar error can be found with the concept of tolerance. This concept is defended by modern social sciences with the hope of escaping nihilism. But in fact, this concept leads them to a contradiction.[27]

Moral relativism has excluded the possibility of absolute values for, from its perspective, all values are relative. Because all values are supposed to have the same legitimacy, why should intolerance be considered a "bad" value? Moreover, why should tolerance be considered better than intolerance? Why does, and how can, tolerance escape relativity? If all human actions are motivated by blind choices or preferences, then why be tolerant?

Historicism chooses here an easy out: it avoids the problem in a dogmatic way. Historicism simply decides, arbitrarily, to place tolerance above all values without any justification. This gesture is an unconscious return to natural right, the very concept that historicism emphatically rejected (Strauss 1953a: 6).

---

[27] Bjarup also raised this problem (1986). For a charitable reading, see Pettit (1986).

7.5 The Question of Justice

7.5.1 A Common Critical Thought: Opening the Debate About Justice

In the texts under discussion here, neither Kelsen nor Strauss appears as a strong defender of moral relativism, or of natural right. Both Kelsen and Strauss are more occupied with discrediting theoretical positions that they judged problematic than with *positively* defending their own positions. Both scholars seem to give a "negative" answer to the question of justice. When Kelsen analyzes classical philosophical concepts of justice in his Farewell Lecture, and when Strauss traces the genesis of historicism in his lectures, both of them say *what justice is not.*

The first argument in favor of such an interpretation is the way both authors themselves define their approaches. Thus, at the end of *What is Justice?*, Kelsen insists that moral relativism and tolerance are only his personal preferences as a scientist. In a similar way, Strauss warns his reader about the question of natural right at the beginning of his book (Strauss 1953a: 6). Finally, the only things the reader can be assured of at the end of this comparative reading are that Kelsen is strongly rejecting natural right and that Strauss is firmly fighting against moral relativism.

7.5.2 The Indeterminacy of Justice: Condition of Our Political and Moral Responsibility

Kelsen's criticism of natural right and Strauss's attack on moral relativism leave us, it seems, with unsatisfactroy theoretical positions. Both natural right and moral relativism appear problematic, and choosing one position over the other seems to be impossible. Nonetheless, one should not consider the value of these writings from this perspective. On the contrary, what is crucial is that they both aim to open a debate by asking the same question. Both affirm the indeterminacy of justice, and that seems the most interesting point for philosophy. Following Claude Lefort, their conclusion relating to justice's indeterminacy is characteristic of modern political philosophy.

According to Lefort, modernity is the era of the dissolution of the ultimate markers of certainty. Monarchy is defined as the system of representations according to which society constitutes a mystical body; one where the king is "both the organic and the mystic unity" of society.

> [T]he society of the ancien régime represented its unity and its identity to itself as that of a body—a body which found its figuration in the body of the king, or rather which identified itself with the king's body, while at the same time it attached itself to it as its head. As Ernst Kantorowicz has shown in a masterly fashion, (…) [t]he image of the king's body as a

> double body, both mortal and immortal, individual and collective, was initially underpinned by the body of Christ (Lefort 1979: 302).

The important idea here, relative to the question of justice, is the fact that Lefort defines modernity in opposition to such a symbolic conception of the political power. Thus, modernity is understood as this new social configuration where the king no longer exists. As such, there is no one to inform the society what is just and what is not. Because of the democratic revolution, modernity can be defined as the theater[28] of the disincorporation of power.

> The democratic revolution (…) burst out when the body of the king was destroyed, when the body politic was decapitated and when, at the same time, the corporeality of the social was dissolved (Lefort 1979: 303).

This means there no longer exists a tutelary figure to give reality's meaning, and to ensure society's unity.

> Democracy inaugurates the experience of an ungraspable, uncontrollable society in which the people will be said to be sovereign, of course, but whose identity will constantly be open to question, whose identity will remain latent (Lefort 1979: 303–304).

This analysis can help in the interpretation of Kelsen's and Strauss's positions. According to the latter, justice is not relative; in Kelsen's view, it is not absolute. Both negative definitions seem to imply in fact, the refusal of a *definitive* definition of justice. Both authors are fighting a common enemy, dogmatism. Both agree on the impossibility of solving the question of justice once and for all. Both reject the claim that justice could be given as "ready-made." In that sense, despite the fact that Kelsen and Strauss's thoughts are antagonistic, they seem nevertheless to demonstrate modernity's embrace of uncertainty and indeterminacy.

In addition, Lefort interprets this indefinite wondering itself as the condition of possibility of democracy. Here, democracy is not defined as a political regime, or as a system of institutions.[29] Lefort gives a symbolic definition: democracy is a way of living modernity.[30] Democracy is the acceptance of modern, radical indeterminacy. The indeterminacy of justice can, therefore, be interpreted as the condition of possibility of our contemporary democracies.[31] Such an interpretation fits quite well with Kelsen's thoughts on the subject, because his works contain a favorable opinion

[28] Claude Lefort uses the word "theatre" since what he tries to do is to analyze the *symbolic* essence of the political, namely, the representations that drive society.

[29] See Lefort (1994: 200):

> Let anyone who doubts that simply observe how difficult it is, for a people accustomed to living under a despotic regime, to regain the will to be free. A change of institutions does not suffice to achieve it. It is Strauss's judgment that the modern philosophers' presuppositions are amoral, but these philosophers have made this difficulty a primary object of their reflection.

[30] See Flynn (2005: 152): "Democracy and totalitarianism are ways of living modernity."

[31] One can find this idea in Kelsen (1955: 70).

of democracy, and maybe even a defense of it.[32] Strauss, however, is more skeptical about democracy.[33]

The fact that the essence of justice is undetermined does not imply that one should believe in moral relativism, or that one should consider natural right as a choice. There is another option: the democratic one, which requires the individual's moral and political responsibility.[34] And this option is precisely what both Kelsen and Strauss point to because they both "firmly [assume] the question that our time imposes on us" (Lefort 1986: 567).[35]

7.6 Conclusion

This chapter had two goals. The first was to remain as close as possible to the respective meanings of Kelsen's and Strauss's texts. In this spirit, it was important not to deny the real opposition separating them. One can restate the opposition between the two authors with the help of Plato's philosophy. Philosophy for Strauss means getting out of Plato's cave, and trying to find a way out can only mean seeking a perspective that goes beyond empirical experience. Kelsen contrarily holds that human beings should be aware of the limits of their own cognitive powers, for, without this awareness, it is impossible to build legitimate and consistent theories. Thus, if people want to achieve any scientific knowledge, they have to admit that

---

[32] Regarding Kelsen's political theory, see Vinx (2007); De Angelis (2009); Baum (2012) and Herrera (1997).

[33] See Strauss (1968: 5):

> [T]he salt of modern democracy are those citizens who read nothing except the sports page and the comic section. Democracy is then not indeed mass rule, but mass culture. A mass culture is a culture which can be appropriated by the meanest capacities without any intellectual and moral effort whatsoever and at a very low monetary price.…Liberal education is the counterpoison to mass culture.…Liberal education is the necessary endeavor to found an aristocracy within democratic mass society. Liberal education reminds those members of a mass democracy who have ears to hear, of human greatness.

Lefort also mentions this difficulty. He deplores that Strauss does not recognize modern democracy as a new form of political society. See Hilb (2013: 71–86).

[34] Despite Strauss's scepticism about democracy, one can still qualify his philosophical fight against dogmatism as "democratic" provided one uses Lefort's symbolic definition of democracy.

[35] One can find an expression of the same idea in his article about Human Rights:

> [T]he view that naturalism and historicism are equally inappropriate tools for conceptualizing the rights of man does not simplify the basic problem; it complicates it. It would seem that we can neither say that these original rights make up a bedrock because we have rejected all belief in human nature, nor that they and the rights that were subsequently won form a chain each link of which is similarly marked by circumstances, because we have discovered in the institution of those first rights a foundation, the emergence of a principle of universality (Lefort 1984: 38).

they can only know with certainty what is empirical. In other words, human cognition is strictly limited to Plato's cave.

The study of the points of antagonism between Kelsen and Strauss revealed one important outcome of their thinking, the absence of a definition of the essence of justice. Regarding this negative approach to justice, their thoughts seem similar. Both note the arguments with which they disagree, question them, and demonstrate their irrelevances and inconsistencies. Both authors appear as fighters against dogmatic thought. In other words, when Kelsen rejects natural law, it is because he considers it a form of dogmatism. Similarly, Strauss criticizes historicism for precluding any discussion, debate, or judgment.

If modernity is this era of the dissolution of the markers of certainty, then the indeterminacy of justice can be understood and accepted. In the end, it matters little if philosophy has an answer to the question of justice; providing such answers is probably not its role (Strauss 1953a: 36). From this perspective, the comparative reading of Kelsen and Strauss appears as a reminder of the authentic meaning of philosophy and of its importance. Its role is to remind us of how important the question of justice is. As long as we are trying to look for an answer to that question, we are actually trying to create a democratic space in which to live together, while also trying to accept and embrace the absence of reference points for our era.[36] If we do not wonder anymore about justice, then we will probably reach "the point at which [we] have become tired of thinking."[37] We will most likely reach the borders of the dogmatic world: the world of "ready-made" thoughts and concepts. And with the same gesture, we will presumably have opened the door to extreme and totalitarian movements. This is the lesson one should retain from this comparative reading of the two scholars. These texts briefly presented are an energetic call to continuously consider and rethink the question of justice. This also means questioning every answer one could give to that question. Because:

> [I]t seems that [the question of justice] is one of those questions to which the resigned wisdom applies that man cannot find a definitive answer but can only try to improve the question (Kelsen 1957: 1).
>
> Genuine knowledge of a fundamental question, thorough understanding of it, is better than blindness to it, or indifference to it, be that indifference or blindness accompanied by knowledge of the answers to a vast number of peripheral or ephemeral questions or not (Strauss 1957: 344).

Acknowledgments This presentation is an extended version of a contribution to "Hans Kelsen in America", a conference sponsored by the Valparaiso University Law School and made possible

[36] See Strauss (1957: 344):

> Philosophy is essentially not possession of the truth but quest for the truth. The distinctive trait of the philosopher is that "he knows that he knows nothing," and that his insight into our ignorance concerning the most important things induces him to strive with all his power for knowledge.

[37] This is a quote of Lessing's letter to Mendelssohn (9th January 1771) as found in Strauss (1953a: 22).

with a grant from the Botsiber Institute for Austrian-American Studies. This academic event took place in Chicago, in June 2014. To revive the philosophy of Strauss in this "geographic context" was an undeniably charming experience. It would not have been possible without Pr. Jeremy Telman. I could never thank him enough for the trust he manifested while accepting me in this common reflection. I am also indebted to the other participants, for their warm welcome and insightful remarks.

I would also like to thank the University of Luxembourg and the Botstiber Foundation for material support of my travel; Pr. Lukas Sosoe and Shaun Colley for their comments on earlier drafts. Thanks to the friendly "invisible hands" for their improvements and corrections: Yara Darwich, Matthew Gardhouse, and Frédéric Seyler. And last but not least, I am grateful to Farhat Chcayra, who helped me translate my thoughts into English.

References

Baum, Sandrine. 2012. *Hans Kelsen and the case for democracy*. Colchester: ECPR Press.

Bjarup, Jes. 1986. Kelsen's theory of law and philosophy of justice. In *Essays on Kelsen*, ed. Richard Tur and William Twining, 273–304. Oxford: Oxford University Press.

De Angelis, Gabriele. 2009. Ideals and institutions. Hans Kelsen's political theory. *History of political thought* 30(3): 524–546.

Flynn, Bernard. 2005. *The philosophy of Claude Lefort. Interpreting the political*. Evanston: Nothwestern University Press.

Herrera, Carlos Miguel. 1995. Kelsen et le libéralisme. In *Le droit, le politique: Autour de Max Weber, Hans Kelsen, Carl Schmitt*, ed. Carlos Miguel Herrera, 37–68. Paris: L'Harmattan.

Herrera, Carlos Miguel. 1997. *Théorie politique et juridique chez Hans Kelsen*. Paris: Kime.

Hilb, Claudia. 2013. Claude Lefort as reader of Leo Strauss. In *Claude Lefort: Thinker of the political*, ed. Martin Plot, 71–86. New York: Palgrave Macmillan.

Hume, David. 1888. *A treatise of human nature*. 1960. Oxford: Clarendon Press.

Kant, Immanuel. 1781. *Critique of Pure Reason*. Trans. P. Guyer and A.W. Wood 1999. Cambridge: Cambridge University Press.

Kelsen, Hans. 1934. *Introduction to the Problems of Legal Theory*. Trans. B.L. Paulson and S.L. Paulson 1997. Oxford: Oxford University Press.

Kelsen, Hans. 1955. Foundations of democracy. *Ethics* 66(1): 1–101.

Kelsen, Hans. 1957. What is justice? In *What is justice? Justice, law and politics in the mirror of science*. 2013. 1–24. New Jersey: The Lawbook Exchange LTD.

Kelsen, Hans. 1960. *Reine Rechtslehre*. 2000. Wien: Verlag Österreich.

Kelsen, Hans. 1967. *Pure Theory of Law*. Trans. M. Knight. 2008. New Jersey: The Lawbook Exchange LTD.

Ladavac, Nicoletta Bersier. 2008. Recht, Moral und Gerechtigkeit bei Hans Kelsen. In *Recht, Moral und Faktizität: Festschrift für Walter Ott*, ed. Sandra Hotz and Klaus Mathis, 19–52. Zürich: Dike.

Lefort, Claude. 1979. The image of the body and totalitarianism. In *The Political Forms of Modern Society. Bureaucracy, Democracy, Totalitarianism*. Trans. A. Sheridan. 1986. Cambridge, MA: MIT Press.

Lefort, Claude. 1984. Human rights and the welfare state. In *Democracy and Political Theory*. Trans. D. Macey 1988. 21–44. Cambridge: Polity Press.

Lefort, Claude. 1986. La dissolution des repères et les enjeux démocratiques. In *Le Temps présent. Ecrits de 1945—2005*. 2007. 551–570. Paris: Belin.

Lefort, Claude. 1994. Three notes on Leo Strauss. In *Writing, the Political Test*. Trans. D.A. Curtis. 2000. 172–206. Durham: Duke University Press.

Maesschalck, Marc (ed.). 2010. *Transformations de l'éthique, De la phénoménologie radicale au pragmatisme social*. Bruxelles: Peter Lang.
Métall, Rudolf A. 1969. *Hans Kelsen: Leben und Werk*. Vienna: Franz Deuticke.
Novak, David. 2012. Haunted by the ghost of Weimar: Leo Strauss' critique of Hans Kelsen. In *The Weimar moment: Liberalism, political theology, and law*, ed. Leonard V. Kaplan and Rudy Koshar, 393–408. Lanham: Lexington Books.
Pettit, Philip. 1986. Kelsen's theory of law and philosophy of justice. In *Essays on Kelsen*, ed. Richard Tur and William Twining, 305–318. Oxford: Oxford University Press.
Sheppard, Eugene R. 2006. *Leo Strauss and the politics of exile: The making of a political philosopher*. Waltham: Brandeis University Press.
Smith, Steven B. 2009. Leo Strauss: The outlines of a life. In *The Cambridge companion to Leo Strauss*, ed. Steven B. Smith, 13–40. Cambridge: Cambridge University Press.
Strauss, Leo. 1953a. *Natural right and history*. 1965. Chicago: Chicago University Press.
Strauss, Leo. 1953b. Preface to Isaac Husik, Philosophical essays. In *Jewish philosophy and the crisis of modernity: Essays and lectures in modern Jewish thought*. 1997. 235–266. New York: SUNY Press.
Strauss, Leo. 1956. Social science and humanism. In *The rebirth of classical political rationalism. An introduction to the thought of Leo Strauss*. 1989.,ed. Thomas L. Pangle, 3–12. Chicago: Chicago University Press.
Strauss, Leo. 1957. What is political philosophy. *Journals of politics* 19(3): 343–368.
Strauss, Leo. 1961. Relativism. In *The rebirth of classical political rationalism. An introduction to the thought of Leo Strauss*. 1989, ed. Thomas L. Pangle, 13–26. Chicago: Chicago University Press.
Strauss, Leo. 1968. What is liberal education? In *Liberalism. Ancient and modern*, 3–8. New York: Basic Books.
Strauss, Leo. 1978. Letter to Helmut Kuhn. *The Independent Journal of Philosophy* 2: 23–26.
Telman, D.A. Jeremy. 2008. The reception of Hans Kelsen's legal theory in the United States: A sociological model. *L'Observateur des Nations Unies* 24: 299.
Vinx, Lars. 2007. *Hans Kelsen's pure theory of law. Legality and legitimacy*. New York: Oxford University Press.
Wilson, Alida. 1986. Is Kelsen really a Kantian? In *Essays on Kelsen*, ed. Richard Tur and William Twining, 37–64. Oxford: Oxford University Press.

Chapter 8
Kelsen and Niebuhr on Democracy

Daniel F. Rice

8.1 Introduction

The following chapter provides an analysis of Hans Kelsen's assessment of Reinhold Niebuhr's views on democracy and what Niebuhr might have said in response if he had known of Kelsen's assessment. The chapter concludes with two subsections relating to democracy on which Kelsen and Niebuhr differ enough to require special attention. These areas are (1): the preconditions and portability of democracy, and (2): justice, liberty, and equality. Given the fact that both Kelsen and Niebuhr were staunch defenders of liberal democracy—thus sharing much political ground—the differences I find assume the character of different emphases rather than sharply polarized views. The differing emphases are largely rooted in Kelsen's three-part distinction between philosophical, political, and legal concerns—a categorization in which he clearly focuses his attention, sometimes exclusively, on the legal area.

In 1955 Hans Kelsen wrote a 100-page essay on the "Foundations of Democracy" that was published in the October issue of *Ethics: An International Journal of Social, Political, and Legal Philosophy* (Kelsen 1955). This essay was based on the Walgreen Lectures Kelsen had given at the University of Chicago at the invitation of his life-long friend, Hans Morgenthau. Midway between addressing the subjects "Democracy and Philosophy" and "Democracy and Economics," Kelsen turned his attention to the issue of "Democracy and Religion."[1] Of the 27 pages given to that subject, a scant, but poignant, nine pages would be devoted to Reinhold Niebuhr,

[1] G. O. Mazur, who has edited two books on Hans Morgenthau, assured me in an April 21, 2005, letter that the Kelsen essay "was the product of Kelsen's and Morgenthau's correspondence of over 25 years since they first met in Europe, and was finally penned by Kelsen himself."

D.F. Rice (✉)
Department of Philosophy and Religious Studies, University of Wisconsin-Eau Claire, Eau Claire, WI, USA
e-mail: d-jrice@att.net

D.A.J. Telman (ed.), *Hans Kelsen in America - Selective Affinities and the Mysteries of Academic Influence*, Law and Philosophy Library 116,
DOI 10.1007/978-3-319-33130-0_8

who, at the time, was the ranking Protestant theologian addressing social and political issues.[2] Kelsen definitely viewed the democracy/religion issue as a problem because he disputed the claims that Christianity had an intimate and constructive connection to democracy.

Nadia Urbinati, who co-edited the recent translation of the 1926 edition of Kelsen's *The Essence and Value of Democracy*, noted that "the article Kelsen published in 1955 in the journal *Ethics*, in which he explicitly reformulated and further expanded his theory of democracy for an English-speaking audience, failed to generate much interest and debate, and has been largely ignored both by the secondary literature on Kelsen's work and by Anglo-American theorists of democracy in general" (Kelsen 1926: 4). Urbinati attributes this to the Cold War ideological confrontation between a form of liberalism conceptually grounded on the notion of "natural law," and the Marxist critique of constitutional democracy as merely "formal." In that context, Ubbinati notes:

> there was not much conceptual space left for a theory of democracy resolutely challenging the premises of *both*. Moreover, throughout the 1950s and early 1960s, American political science departments were dominated by a form of methodological behaviorism which severely restricted the scope of normative political theory itself, due to its insistence on the purely "scientific" and "non-evaluative" dimensions of the discipline (Kelsen 1926: 3–4).

It is thus not entirely surprising that there is no evidence that Niebuhr ever saw or responded to Kelsen's essay. Thus, I am left on my own to formulate a response to Kelsen's criticisms consistent with what I believe to be Niebuhr's views. It is also unfortunate that Kelsen's critique of Niebuhr's view of religion and democracy is confined to Niebuhr's 1944 book, *Children of Light and Children of Darkness*. Because this book involves a direct and sustained treatment of the subject and is subtitled "A Vindication of Democracy and a Critique of its Traditional Defense," Kelsen's choice is, to a large degree, understandable. What proves unfortunate, however, is that Kelsen fails to take into consideration crucial reflections Niebuhr provides on the subject of democracy that were extant prior to the publication of Kelsen's article, eg, *The Nature and Destiny of Man II: Human Destiny*, chapter IX (Niebuhr 1943), *The Irony of American History* (Niebuhr 1952a), and key portions of both *Christian Realism and Power Politics* (Niebuhr 1952b) and *Christian Realism and Political Problems* (Niebuhr 1953a). Would it have altered or moderated Kelsen's criticisms of Niebuhr? I don't know. Would it have increased

[2] Kelsen's section "Democracy and Religion" also included analyses of the views of the European Protestant Emil Brunner and the Roman Catholic theologian Jacque Maritain. Kelsen chose these three men for good reasons. Emil Brunner, second in reputation among Protestant theologians in Europe only to Karl Barth, had published his book on *Justice and the Social Order* in 1945. Reinhold Niebuhr, the ranking indigenous Protestant voice in America during this period, had authored his "vindication of democracy" and "critique of its traditional defense," in *The Children of Light and the Children of Darkness* in 1944. And the French Roman Catholic philosopher/theologian Jacques Maritain, writing to his French compatriots suffering through the Nazi terror, published his little book on *Christianity and Democracy* in 1943. All three books, seeking to connect democracy to Christianity in crucial ways, were published near the end of World War II.

and enriched Kelsen's comprehension of Niebuhr's understanding of democracy? Definitely.

After dealing extensively with Kelsen's critique of Niebuhr, I briefly discuss two issues of importance to democracy on which they differ, at least in emphasis. The first has to do with the pre-conditions and portability of democracy, and the second deals with their respective views of justice in relation to liberty and equality.

8.2 Kelsen on Niebuhr's View of the Liberal Tradition

In turning to Kelsen's criticism of Niebuhr's insistence that there is value in considering the relationship of Judeo-Christian religion's influence on democracy, I first address Kelsen's view of Niebuhr's assessment of the liberal tradition. Initially, Kelsen charges Niebuhr with inconsistency and unfairness in his characterization of the liberal tradition out of which modern democracy emerged. In *Children of Light and Children of Darkness*, Niebuhr stresses that the vindication of democracy depends on surpassing its early bourgeois middle-class ideology. Within that ideology Niebuhr identifies elements, such as naïve optimism, that overestimate the goodness and innocence of man, an excessive individualism, an inability to adequately gauge the vitalities and ambitions of human nature, and the belief that individual egotism does not rise above the limits of nature's impulse for self-preservation. In brief, Niebuhr finds the liberal culture utterly deficient in the kind of realism required for maintaining a viable democracy. As Niebuhr poignantly states "one of the real tragedies of our era is that the very democracy which is the great achievement of liberalism cannot be maintained if liberalism is not transcended as a culture" (Niebuhr 1939: 545). The WWII era in which Niebuhr's book was written reveals both the vulnerability of the democracies and the persistence of those illusions that Niebuhr saw as endemic to democracy. Given the fact that the illusions Niebuhr identified are so prevalent in the American democratic tradition, his highly focused attack on liberalism seems justified. Niebuhr's entire writings on democracy exhibit an overriding conviction that a realistic correction of democratic liberal idealism is *the* pressing requirement of the times.

Kelsen accuses Niebuhr of having used liberalism as an "imaginary opponent" as a foil for claiming the greater adequacy of an understanding of human nature based on a Christian outlook (Kelsen 1955: 55–56). Certainly Kelsen is not alone in this criticism. Niebuhr has been charged with both oversimplifying and misrepresenting various historical alternatives in the process of advancing his own perspective. Kelsen is certainly fair in pointing out that Niebuhr ignored those within the liberal tradition who neither underestimate man's egoistic tendencies nor are ignorant of the need for coercive order. In response to criticisms from Daniel Day Williams, Niebuhr acknowledged that Williams was correct to point out that "my characterizations of 'liberalism' and 'liberal Christianity' are too sweeping and inexact."(Williams 1984: 270–289) However, the excuse Niebuhr offers to Williams is that he was defining "liberalism too consistently in terms of its American versions" (Niebuhr 1984: 517).

It is precisely in the American context that Niebuhr is engaging where one finds liberalism's tendency toward excessive and exaggerated forms of naïve idealism in abundance. Kelsen himself once noted that "there are truths which are so self-evident that they must be proclaimed again and again in order not to be doomed to oblivion" (Kelsen 1944: vii–viii). Although he was speaking in the context of war being mass murder, the content of Kelsen's observation can easily play both ways. For Kelsen misses the point that is crucial for Niebuhr: so pervasive is America's proclivity for sentimental naiveté and for perpetuating illusions about both politics in general and itself as a nation in particular that speaking truth to America is an ongoing obligation. The historical context of Niebuhr's *Children of Light and Children of Darkness* is crucial here. Based on lectures delivered at Stanford in early 1944 as the war in Europe was winding down, Niebuhr's book is responding to diverse attacks on the democracies stemming from fascism, communism, and other forms of radical disaffection. Confronted with what he believes to be a weak and flawed defense of democracy, Niebuhr is convinced that the bourgeois liberal West was ill-prepared to meet the challenge.

Kelsen writes that Niebuhr believes the view of human nature supplied by Christianity is "infected with a sinful corruption." However, Kelsen notes that Niebuhr also partakes of "a Christian belief in man as the image of God, which is certainly more optimistic than any liberal view of human nature could be" (Kelsen 1926: 56). Kelsen does not seem to recognize that Niebuhr leveled the same type of sharp criticisms of the cynical and optimistic tendencies within Christianity as he leveled against the secular extremes. The fact that Niebuhr chooses to employ extremes to illustrate his point seems quite appropriate, for it is in the extremes that the real danger resides. Yet he is aware of the ambiguity of the terms he chooses, for while writing on Augustine's political realism, Niebuhr observes that "the definitions of 'realists' and 'idealists' emphasize disposition, rather than doctrines; and they are therefore bound to be inexact" (Niebuhr 1953a: 120). In the case of his stereotype of liberalism, Niebuhr's juxtaposition of extremes is a typical dialectical device that allows him to focus upon a realistic alternative that avoids the "logic" of the extremes between the Scylla of moral cynicism and the Charybdis of utopian idealism. And while Niebuhr appeals to what he sees as a Christian understanding of human nature as a way out of the extremes, he applies his criticism to the same extremes *within* the Christian tradition as he does to secular culture—a point Kelsen does not appear to recognize. After all, it is Niebuhr who, in a 1958 interview with Mike Wallace, states that "it is significant that it is as difficult to get charity out of piety as to get reasonableness out of rationalism." For Niebuhr the true state of affairs requires the balancing of things. According to Robert Good, for example:

> Niebuhr sees man in part free, and in part bound by necessity; as sinful, yet knowing himself to be a sinner; as capable of justice (which makes democracy possible) and inclined to injustice (which makes the balance of forces by democratic means necessary); as "a lion who devours the lamb," but "a curious kind of lion who dreams of the day when the lion and the lamb will lie down together" (Good 1965: 289).

Kelsen also feels that Niebuhr ought not to have it both ways when Niebuhr insists that modern secular culture is both too cynical and too naively optimistic in its assessment of human nature. Kelsen even seems untactful as he accuses Niebuhr of inconsistency, at once faulting Niebuhr for blaming skeptical secularism for its excessive pessimism, in regard to man's rational capacity for justice, and at the same time accusing liberal culture for being excessively optimistic in its estimates of human nature. Niebuhr is not being inconsistent but is identifying extremes—both of which are clearly evident in Western secular tradition and tend toward the kind of "typology" Daniel Day Williams has noted. Niebuhr's "Children of Darkness" are those within the Western tradition (men such as Machiavelli and Hobbes) who had the wisdom of the serpent in knowing the power of self-interest. Their vision was "evil" in part because it knew no law beyond the self and tended to see human nature in such negative terms that they would opt for a tyrannical order in fear of anarchy. "Children of Light," on the other hand, (John Dewey, for example) do see a higher law than their own will but are "usually foolish because they do not know the power of self-will" (Niebuhr 1944a: 9–10). Both stereotypical extremes can be found in Western history, and Niebuhr's use of this typology aims at what is dominant in the American scene where his "vindication" of democracy is most highly focused. Niebuhr's dialectical balancing act focuses primarily on the sentimentalism and utopian idealism he finds endemic to the American scene. If, in the process Niebuhr gives short shrift to the moral cynics, such as Hobbes, it is because moral cynicism has not been a major problem in American politics.

Kelsen is on somewhat firmer ground when he criticizes Niebuhr for laying totalitarianism at the doorstep of those who disavow traditional religions. For while there is a form of skepticism that, as Niebuhr puts it, "stands on the abyss of moral nihilism," the alleged "demonic religions" that he believes come rushing in to fill the vacuum of traditional faith's "melancholy, long withdrawing roar" (to borrow an image from Matthew Arnold's *Dover Beach*) do not necessarily follow from skeptical relativism. In challenging Niebuhr for blaming secular skepticism for opening up the floodgates to nihilism and the demonic furies of false faiths, Kelsen offers a contrary view. For Kelsen, in agreement with Matthew Arnold, a failed Christianity created the vacuum permitting the inrush of the secular "demonic" religions that Niebuhr so deplores. Whether Kelsen believes this or is merely being eristic, perhaps the truth was more properly grasped by Nietzsche whose announcement of the "death of God" included the double-death of all absolutes, classical and Christian alike. No such final wisdom comes from Kelsen's pen on this point, however. Somewhat pointedly he recommends holding the "relativism of religion, such as advocated by Niebuhr, responsible for the victory of another religion (National Socialism), which in its demonism maintains the illusion of absolutism" (Kelsen 1955: 62).[3]

[3] Two things should be noted here. First, there are certainly instances within the traditional religions (Christian and Islamic, for example) that are as authoritarian, intolerant (tyrannical even) as the "demonic religions" that Niebuhr contends that secularism has spawned. Niebuhr, of course, is acutely aware of this tendency within the religious traditions and has written brilliantly on the need

Niebuhr also resists those secular versions of life that tend to idolatrize either the nation or specific values within the social process. At one point he notes that "we tend to identify our particular brand of democracy with the ultimate values of life" (a tendency most evident in America) and proceeds to caution against those who "know no other dimension of existence except the social one" and whose "loyalty to democracy might dull the critical edge with which they approach their own institutions" (Niebuhr 1947a: 1–2). While believing that no societal arrangement, including democracy, can fulfill the needs of the human spirit (and that, therefore, one's true end is in God) Niebuhr is careful to warn against using religion as a shield with which to sanctify the nation.[4]

8.3 Kelsen and Niebuhr on Christianity and Democracy

Kelsen is perfectly correct in observing that Niebuhr wishes to do far more than merely claim that the absence of religious faith leads to nihilism and totalitarianism. His major criticisms of Niebuhr center upon his twofold judgment that Niebuhr is wrong in thinking that "there is an essential connection between democracy and Christian religion" and that therefore, Christian theology can "furnish a foundation for democracy." Certainly at the very best, Christian theology "can justify democracy only as a relative value" (Kelsen 1955: 41).

There is, of course, no consistent view in Christian history as to how Christians should relate to the political order. Niebuhr's contention that "the most effective opponents of tyrannical government today, as they have been in the past, are men who can say 'We must obey God rather than man'" (Niebuhr 1944a: 82) is certainly questionable. Just because such belief provides a vantage point from which to oppose the pretensions of our mortal Leviathans does not at all guarantee that Christians will draw that conclusion. With sardonic (and appropriate) understatement Kelsen maintains that "If this statement means [that] Christian theology does and always did effectively resist tyrannical governments, its truth is not beyond doubt" (Kelsen 1955: 54). Niebuhr, of course, is well aware that such a vantage point was not always applied in this way. He knows that Pauline tradition augured for subservience to the "powers that be," and that there is a theocratic tradition

for humility, toleration, and self-criticism on the part of a responsible Christianity. Second, there are many relativists and skeptics who neither clamor for substitute faiths nor conclude that discriminatory moral judgments are impossible to make.

[4]Niebuhr insists that a proper understanding of authentic religious belief is crucial for giving meaning to human existence. So strongly does Niebuhr believe that pessimism leads to despair that his writings are replete with the claim (almost a plea) that life is meaningless without the ultimate meaning that only belief in God can provide. Not all religious skeptics lapse into the utter despair Niebuhr believes to be their lot. Bertrand Russell and John Dewey are good examples. Neither would gainsay the fact that a world without ultimate meaning is a tragic world. However, they would dispute the notion that a life devoid of ultimate meaning is a life devoid of meaning.

within Christianity that aims, in the very name of God, to impose a coercive order on society. After all, it is Niebuhr who confesses that even at its best the "Christian tradition itself seldom stated" its position relative "to the political order in such a way that it would give guidance in the complexities of political and social life" (Niebuhr 1943: 278). Not only have the "great portions of Christianity" contributed very little to the development of democracy," as Gordon Harland puts it, but "the story of religious authoritarianism and fanaticism is such a sorry chapter in the history of Western culture that any claims for the necessity of the insights of biblical faith must begin with a contrite confession of the depths of Christian betrayal of those insights" (Harland 1960: 171).

To some extent Kelsen is being somewhat obligatory here. However, he is certainly correct in stating an obvious point that Niebuhr himself has made, namely, that "Christian theology cannot claim to be recognized as an advocate of a definite political regime, because it can and actually did justify contrary regimes, just as it can and actually did defend as well as attack the distribution of property, as Niebuhr's excellent chapter on 'The Community and Property' shows" (Kelsen 1955: 54). Kelsen's viewpoint, therefore, is reasonable enough. What he seems to miss, however, is that Niebuhr is expressing an exaggerated hope, and not a logical proposition. *If* and only *if* the Christian properly understands and applies his or her faith can this transcendent perspective bear the fruit Niebuhr thinks it ought to. Niebuhr, who, as noted earlier, reminded Mike Wallace that "it is as difficult to get charity out of piety as to get reasonableness out of rationalism," seems to have fallen prey to his own form of wishful thinking.

Kelsen also criticizes Niebuhr for having said "democracy is the only alternative to injustice and oppression" (Kelsen 1944: xiv). If that is the case then, as Kelsen sees it, the task of showing "that democracy is the only alternative to injustice… means the realization of absolute justice. For if democracy is demonstrated as relatively just only, it cannot be the 'only' alternative to injustice." Surely only an absolute justice can exclude the possibility of another justice (Kelsen 1955: 56).

Kelsen's way of putting this is curious to the theological reader. Niebuhr, as Kelsen himself recognizes, holds that "there are no living communities which do not have some notions of justice, beyond their historical laws, by which they seek to gauge the justice of their legislative enactments" (Niebuhr 1944a: 67). This statement alone undermines the force of Kelsen's charge. Niebuhr is not saying that there is an absolute justice nor is he so audacious as to claim there is no justice whatever outside democracy. His view of the indeterminacy of human freedom and the resultant openness of history precludes any such notion. Niebuhr is, however, unabashedly willing to maintain that "ideally democracy is a permanently valid form of social and political organization" for the reason that it "does justice to two dimensions of human existence: to man's spiritual stature and his social character; to the uniqueness and variety of life, as well as to the common necessities of all men" (Niebuhr 1944a: 3). And, as a form of social organization that maximizes liberty, the relative freedom of its social and political life corresponds to, and allows for, the endless elaboration of the individual and collective vitalities that rise "in indeterminate degree over all social and communal concretions of life" (Niebuhr 1944a: 49). Indeed, democracy is, for Niebuhr, "a perennially valuable form of social organization" precisely because, by its wisdom, "freedom and order are made to support, and not contradict each other" (Niebuhr 1944a: 1).

Kelsen's formulation of the problem seems, *prima facie*, nonsensical. For Niebuhr justice is not an absolute but only an approximation and expression of love in history; and, as an approximation of love, it is forever open to being drawn beyond any momentary formulation to new heights. Justice, then, has no absolute character or embodiment. It does not even possess a separate status. For Niebuhr, "any definition of moral rules beyond those which mark the minimum obligation of the self to the neighbor are discovered, upon close analysis, to be rational formulations of various implications of the love commandment, rather than fixed and precise principles of justice" (Niebuhr 1949: 189). Moreover, while Niebuhr clearly advances democracy as the best form of government for creating and maintaining structures of justice, he clearly maintains that "the higher possibilities of love, which is at once the fulfillment and the negation of justice, always hover over every system of justice" (Niebuhr 1941: 302). It is arbitrary and irresponsible power from which the injustices of life flow. Thus, Niebuhr is correct in claiming that democracy is that system of government that has most successfully achieved ways of checking power through a separation of powers, balancing conflicting forces and factions within society, and, by means of maximizing freedom and equality, creating the maximum opportunities for social justice. It is his view that there is a transcendent love that is the norm for the embodiment of justice in all historical forms that defies crediting Niebuhr with absolutizing anything within history.

Perhaps Niebuhr is careless in using the word "only" in regard to democracy's role as providing an alternative to injustice and oppression. Elsewhere, while speaking of our "self-righteous attitudes in international affairs," he is still willing to assert that "an open society is…the only condition for justice in society." But he does add that to present the value of "the peculiar form of the open society which has developed in the West" in such a guise as our own "is to make the unique forms of relativism in western life the basis of a false ultimate" (Niebuhr 1959a: 297). Niebuhr does use language carelessly here. He says more than he means and sometimes means something slightly different from how he says it.

Kelsen wants to make the substantive charge that Niebuhr is, theologically, an honest if reluctant relativist in spite of his attempt to argue that the vindication of democracy rests on religion. What Kelsen is really aiming at in his critique of Niebuhr is the issue of relativism and Niebuhr's relationship to it. This issue arises most vividly in Niebuhr's struggle with concepts of natural law—an area where there is enough ambiguity to draw the attention of several critics other than Kelsen, one of whom, Paul Ramsay, I shall consider later. Kelsen makes the case that Niebuhr is a relativist in spite of his disclaimer that "against relativists" a Christian morality "must insist that no man or nation, no age or culture can arbitrarily define its own law" (Niebuhr 1949: 194). Seemingly, Niebuhr's appeal to general principles of justice, ie, in his own terms the "natural law," exempts him by means of his theological convictions from the relativism he so fears and deplores. In Kelsen's understanding, this exemption is only apparent, and in my opinion, Kelsen's point that Niebuhr's views on natural law push him to the edge of some form of relativism is well taken. Niebuhr maligns, for example, those natural law theories "which claim to find a normative moral order amid the wide variety of historic forms or even among the most universal of these forms" (Niebuhr 1952b: 128). When he gets through exposing the contingencies of social history, the relativities of human perspective, and the pretensions of natural law theorists, the ground is largely swept clean of all debris and little is left standing. All natural law theories, for Niebuhr, "introduce contingent practical applications into the definition of the principle" (Niebuhr 1944a: 72). All natural law theories reflect the limitations of reason and the "limited imagination of a particular epoch" (Niebuhr 1944a: 74). All natural law theories are susceptible to having their "truths" appropriated as the special possession of particular historical persons, institutions, and force. And all natural law theories are prone to reflect an ideological taint by becoming the ideology of a particular group. Niebuhr spends much time in numerous places documenting these claims (Niebuhr 1941: 295–317).

Kelsen insists that such views are views "to which the most radical relativist may wholeheartedly subscribe" (Kelsen 1955: 58). He goes on to say that Niebuhr nonetheless "makes the hopeless attempt to soften somehow the impression of his anti-absolutist philosophy of justice by relativizing its relativism" (Kelsen 1955: 59). He supposedly does this by assuming various degrees of validity among moral values. The following quotation from Niebuhr's writings serves as grist for Kelsen's comments: "One might define a descending scale of relativity in the definition of moral and political principles. The moral principle may be more valid than the political principles which are derived from it. The political principles may have greater validity than the specific applications by which they are made relevant to a particular situation" (Niebuhr 1944a: 74–75).

I am not quite sure I would make of this what Kelsen makes of it. Kelsen wants to insist that neither "relativity" nor "validity" are a "quality like heat, which can have different degrees. The relativity of a value consists in its conditional character, and there is no possibility of being more or less conditioned. There are no intermediate stages between the one and the other" (Kelsen 1955: 59). Therefore, Niebuhr's "doctrine of a relative relativism is as untenable as the doctrine of a relative absolutism, that is, the doctrine of a relative natural law" (Kelsen 1955: 59). More than likely, Niebuhr means nothing more than that there is a relational order of higher to lower, of more general to more specific in our attempts to deal with general principles. I doubt if he is imparting ontological status to these relations. Perhaps there is a misuse of the terms relativity and validity on Niebuhr's part. Niebuhr might have been talking about a limited natural law rather than a relative natural law as Kelsen has it. Whether at bottom there would be much difference is an open question. Niebuhr seems to rest his desire to reject the errors of the "moral relativists" on the feeble reed of insisting that there are no living communities that do not have some "general principles of justice"—general principles upon which they base their "notions of justice, beyond their historic laws" (Niebuhr 1944a, 67). But when Niebuhr talks that way he insists that:

> the principles of "natural law" by which justice is defined are, in fact, not so much fixed standards of reason as they are rational efforts to apply the moral obligation, implied in the love commandment, to the complexities of life and the fact of sin, that is, to the situation created by the inclination of men to take advantage of each other.

Consequently, "*[a]ny* definition of moral rules beyond those which mark the minimal obligation of the self to the neighbor are discovered, upon close analysis, to be rational formulations of various implications of the love commandment, rather than fixed and precise principles of justice" (Niebuhr 1949: 188–189 (emphasis added)).

Niebuhr's discomfort with universals and absolutes stems, in part, from his agreement with the pragmatic tradition of James and Dewey. Yet, in basic ways, Niebuhr's position is far more congruent with the temporal-mindedness of historicism than with the illusions of a value-free scientism he finds in Dewey (Rice 1993). In his reply to his friend Paul Ramsey, Niebuhr feels that Ramsey does not do justice to his two main criticisms of both classical and modern versions of the natural law theory. Tellingly, Niebuhr's first point is that natural law "concepts do not allow for the historical character of human experience," being rooted instead "in a classical rationalism which did not understand history." They, therefore, do not understand the uniqueness of historical occasion or the historical biases that creep into the definitions of natural law. This criticism is not met (as Ramsey attempts) by calling attention to the distinctions between the *jus natura*, the *jus gentium*, and the *jus civilis.* Of course, every natural law theory allows for the application of general principles to particular situations, "[b]ut the question is whether its general principles are not too inflexible on the one hand and their definitions too historically conditioned on the other hand." In his second point, Niebuhr faults the Catholic tradition for treating the law of love as a *superadditum*—something added onto as a mere "addendum to the natural law." He concludes by claiming that "[j]ustice is an application of the law of love. The rules are not absolute but relative. They are applications of the law of love and do not have independence apart from it. They would be independent only if they were found in an 'essential' social structure" (Niebuhr 1984: 711).

In 1940 Niebuhr published an article insisting that "it is not possible to state a universally valid concept of justice from any particular sociological locus in history. Nor is it possible to avoid either making the effort or making pretenses of universality which human finiteness does not justify." We reside in "a tragic world, troubled not by finiteness so much as by 'false eternals' and false absolutes, and expressing the pride of these false absolutes even in the highest reaches of spirituality" (Niebuhr 1940: 88). And 6 years later, in an important published sermon, Niebuhr pens the following lines echoing a view consistent with Kelsen's own:

> Just as there are only vantage points of relative impartiality in time from which we view the past, so there are only vantage points of relative impartiality from which we view the present scene. All human justice depends upon the organization of relatively impartial judicial instruments, through which the endless conflicts of interest between men are arbitrated (Niebuhr 1946: 9).

All of this certainly seems to confirm that Niebuhr's unflinching refutation of unalloyed universals (examples of which Kelsen cites from *Children of Light and Children of Darkness*) further corroborates Kelsen's charge that Niebuhr is in agreement with the relativists. Surely all alleged universals are alloyed, first and foremost with the inescapable temporality of history; then, too, by the innocuous fact of limited reason and the inevitable perspectivalism of all human life; and, every bit as important, there are the more noxious aspects of self-interest, self-serving reason, and the ideological taint to which all claims are susceptible.

Yet Kelsen overlooks something, perhaps once again because he did not go beyond the one book in exploring Niebuhr's position. In the end, it is the indeterminate character of the self in its freedom that governs Niebuhr's view—the freedom of a self for whom *agape* is the law of life. Beyond any of its functions, the self has its uniqueness in its radical freedom for self-transcendence. Therein lies human dignity—the self's creative powers. But therein also lie its destructive powers. Both the law of love and the inevitable violation of that law set the tone for Niebuhr's view of human nature. Both the self's grandeur and its misery have the same locus, not in some aspect of the self's identity, such as the rational faculties of the mind, nor in the vitalities of the body, but in its radical freedom. Thus whatever one might regard as permanent and immutable about human life is in tension with, and qualified by, the self's unique freedom understood as the capacity for self-transcendence. To speak of the "nature" of man, as Niebuhr does, is somewhat unfortunate, for it seems to suggest affinity with traditional conceptions of human "essence." For Niebuhr, the "essential nature of man" has reference to "all his natural endowments and determinations, his physical and social impulses, his sexual and racial differentiations—in short his character as a creature embedded in the natural order." Then he goes on to say that "his essential nature also includes the freedom of his spirit, his transcendence over natural processes and finally his self-transcendence" (Niebuhr 1941: 286–287). What Niebuhr is saying here is that the self as "creature" and "spirit" exhibits an indeterminacy at the level of freedom that modifies even its "nature" as "creature." This indeterminacy of the self's freedom rules out interpretations of nature that require an ontology of static, fixed, and immutable elements while at the same time recognizing determinate structures of nature in man from which even his highest flights of spirit-as-self-transcendence cannot dislodge him. As Niebuhr puts it elsewhere, "there is not much that is absolutely immutable in the structure of human nature except its animal basis, man's freedom to transmute this nature in varying degrees, and the unity of the natural and spiritual in all the various transmutations and transfigurations of the original 'nature'" (Niebuhr 1949: 183).

8.4 Religion, Toleration and Democracy

The concluding part of Kelsen's critique of Niebuhr is, I believe even more pointed. He maintains that "since Niebuhr is in favor of democratic tolerance which presupposes a relativistic view, he has recourse to the contradictory construction of religious relativism, because as a Christian he cannot accept the relativism of a rationalistic, antimetaphysical, areligious, skeptical philosophy" (Kelsen 1955: 61). Kelsen insists that Niebuhr knows that democracy presupposes relativism and accuses him of trying valiantly, as the theologian he is, to contend that democratic relativism can be based on religion. Holding that "religion is by its very nature belief in an absolute value" (Kelsen 1955: 59), Kelsen regards such a contention impossible.

Kelsen also has little use for Niebuhr's appeal to religious humility as a basis for democratic tolerance. Given the absolute character of religious belief and insisting that "the Christian religion is, according to its own meaning, not a human but a divine endeavor," Kelsen concludes that the "pride a man takes in []his religion does not and cannot constitute a sin [as Niebuhr argues] because this pride does not at all seek to hide the conditioned and finite character of a human endeavor." Instead, it is the "natural pride of a man who is certain of an absolute a divine truth" and is thus "compatible with, because the compensation for, the most sincere humility which manifests itself in the unconditional submission to this absolute truth" (Kelsen 1955: 61). On my reading, Kelsen's position smacks of the spiritual arrogance that Niebuhr contends is the worst kind of pride—a pride where the "will to power" is transmuted into a spiritual pride that results in "the worst form on intolerance," religious intolerance, "in which the particular interests of the contestants hide behind religious absolutes" (Niebuhr 1941: 213).

Niebuhr does not deny, to use Kelsen's expression, that "religion is by its very nature an absolute value, in an ideal which is perfect, because it is belief in God, who is the personification of perfection, the absolute par excellence" (Kelsen 1955: 60). Niebuhr's position is not, as Kelsen insists, "a contradiction in terms," but is based on two convictions—one of which is the Reformation belief that God alone is absolute and that therefore, the first requirement of the believer is, as the logic of Luther's position would have it, to "Let God be God" (Watson 1966). This is the very conviction upon which Niebuhr bases what Kelsen insists is his contradictory relativism. Niebuhr's relativism is derived from the absoluteness of God in relation to which all beliefs about and formulations of God are at best approximations of the absolute they seek to profess. Such professions, both of believers and institutions claiming to be custodians of truth, are to be uttered tentatively and with great caution and "humility." It is the very conception of God as God that is the basis for Niebuhr's view of humility and its role for the Christian. For Niebuhr one does not *possess* God in either "faith as trust" or in "beliefs" as expressions of that faith. All expressions of faith are fragmentary and partial. Contrary to G. K. Chesterton's view that "tolerance is rather the virtue of people who do not believe anything," Kelsen insists that "tolerance is rather the virtue of people whose religious conviction is not strong enough to overcome their political proclivity, to prevent them from the inconsistency of recognizing the possibility and legitimacy of other religious convictions" and "it is just on such an inconsistency that a religious ideology of democracy is based" (Kelsen 1955: 61–62).

This view leads Niebuhr, as Kelsen puts it, to restrict "relativity to the expression of faith"—a view that he, Kelsen, strenuously denies (Kelsen 1955: 60). For Kelsen, "the very meaning of the expression of the faith in God is that the truth or value expressed is absolute" and "the expression of an idea is absolute if by this expression an absolute truth or value is meant.…Hence if the object to which the expression refers is supposed to be absolute—the object to which the expression of religious faith refers, God, is *the* absolute—the expression cannot be characterized as relative" (Kelsen 1955: 60). To discuss *absolute* symbols or *absolute* language is, in my judgment, utterly nonsensical. *Expressions* are not absolute. Certainly they cannot be meant, but only intended, because language and meaning involve quite another set of relations.

Kelsen equates "having a religious character" with being "in possession of an absolute truth," and "having an absolute truth is" having a truth "founded upon statements or expressions of ultimate truth" (Kelsen 1955: 60). Kelsen, as a consummate legalist, comes across as something of a scholastic fundamentalist (if this is possible). Worse yet, he is unwilling to entertain even the possible discrepancy between God's "revelatory statements" (as he puts the meaning of revelation) and the somewhat distanced role of the believer as an interpreter of those statements. Neither does he pay heed to the context, both literary and historical, in which such expressions are made. Even the Roman Catholic Church, which tends to believe, as does the convert Kelsen, in a propositional theory of faith to which the believer is merely called upon to subscribe, recognizes the problem and purports to solve it by insisting that the Pope, under inspiration of the Holy Spirit, finally interprets correctly God's revealed language.

Nonetheless, Kelsen's contention that the view of toleration that Christianity offers "is not necessarily the most consistent ideology" or "the most effective one" seems well taken (Kelsen 1955: 61). Let us grant that Niebuhr's view of toleration is not as Kelsen represents it, but instead is entirely appropriate in light of the relative forms of all expressions of the ultimate. Still, such a basis for democracy is, indeed, a difficult one. Niebuhr knows full well that the real test regarding toleration is twofold: to possess the "ability to hold vital convictions which lead to action; and also the capacity to preserve the spirit of forgiveness towards those who offend us by holding to convictions which seem untrue to us" (Niebuhr 1943: 227). Moreover, he admits religious tolerance is, without question, a most difficult and rare achievement. Niebuhr laments that not only has the Reformation shown "little advantage over other versions of the Christian faith," but that "Christian history in general has frequently generated fanaticisms as grievous as the idolatries of other cultures" (Niebuhr 1943: 227). He cites Milton's *Areopagitica* and Saltmarsh's *Smoke in the Temple* as examples of those within the tradition who have understood the need for toleration based on "the relativity of human knowledge"—focusing on Saltmarsh's advice given in 1646 that we not "assume any power of infallibility to each other;… for another's evidence is as dark to me as mine to him…till the Lord enlighten us both for discerning alike" (Niebuhr 1943: 244–245). But these are rare voices arising out of the religious struggles in England leading up to the Civil War. They were obvious exceptions to the rule. It is significant that they arose out of the tendencies of left-wing Puritanism, and its evolution in the Levelers and Diggers, to ever more secular modes of thought.

Knowing this, Niebuhr confesses that these provisional understandings were "an integral part of the recovery of the sense of the historical in Renaissance thought" and are causally related to "the ability of the Renaissance to meet one of the two tests of the problem of toleration: the willingness to entertain views which oppose our own without rancor and without the effort to suppress them" (Niebuhr 1943: 244–245). Nonetheless, "it is in meeting the other test: the ability to remain true to and act upon our best convictions" that Niebuhr contends modern culture most frequently fails. "It finds difficulty in avoiding irresponsibility and skepticism on the one hand and new fanaticisms on the other" (Niebuhr 1943: 246).

Niebuhr's sensitivity to the complex historical origins of democracy is evident when he writes:

> [T]he culture and climate, the "ideology" which supports democratic authority in the Western world is thus drawn partly from the peculiar flexibilities and necessities of a technical society, partly from the Christian tradition which valued the individual as transcending any social process and political community, and partly from modern secularism and empiricism which generated the temper of criticism and punctured the religious tensions which were the source of so much political authority (Niebuhr 1959b: 110).

Writing in 1961, Niebuhr stresses that "Christian humanism must make common ground with the different kinds of secular humanism to protect the dignity of the person against the peril of dehumanization in an increasingly technical age." And "it must do so in contrite awareness that the secular humanist may be more honest and courageous in meeting large ethical problems than religious people" (Niebuhr 1961a: 120).

Niebuhr is keenly aware that, because of mixed evidence for both, the debate "waged between Christian and secular leaders on the question whether democracy is the product of the Christian faith or of a secular culture" is inconclusive. And while contending that forces within both traditions helped establish democratic institutions and furnish the resources of modern free societies, Niebuhr reminds the reader that "there are traditional non-democratic Christian cultures to the right of free societies which prove that the Christian faith does not inevitably yield democratic historical fruits" (Niebuhr 1953b: 19).

However he might have misrepresented Niebuhr's view of toleration, Kelsen seems quite right in pointing out what a feeble reed the Christian plea for humility and toleration is as a basis for democracy. When Niebuhr returns to the matter of the relevance of "the law of love to the collective relationships of mankind" 9 years after *Children of Light and Children of Darkness*, he once again contends that only:

> The heedlessness of love, which sacrifices the interests of the self-, enters into the calculations of justice by becoming the spirit of contrition which issues from the self's encounter with God. In that encounter it is made aware of the contingent character of all human claims and the tainted character of all human pretensions and ideals. This contrition is the socially relevant counterpart of love. [Breaking one's pride,] this spirit lies at the foundation of what we define as democracy. For democracy cannot exist if there is no recognition of the fragmentary character of all systems of thought and value which are allowed to exist together within the democratic frame. Thus the *agape* of forgiveness as well as the *agape* of sacrificial love become a leaven in the lump of the spirit of justice (Niebuhr 1953c).

A feeble reed, indeed, such an expectation must be. Niebuhr expects neither perfect love nor perfect justice in this world. What he recognizes, however, is that something more than discrimination and self-interested reason is necessary for the kind of justice to which a democracy aspires.

Kelsen is partially correct in suggesting that Niebuhr's position is "not much different from" what Niebuhr calls that "more sophisticated form of secularism"—a form of skepticism "which is conscious of the relativity of all human perspectives" (Kelsen 1955: 61–62). I, for one, am not much disturbed by the forthrightness of Niebuhr's "perspectival relativism," based as it is on his understanding of history. And I certainly consider it a plus that Niebuhr, unlike those who flirt with irrelevance by staking their claims on abstract revelatory dicta, knows full well that the relevance of religion must make its way in the marketplace of experience where the contest for a genuine hearing resides.

Kelsen suspects that Niebuhr ends up showing that there exists "a relationship between democracy and certain moral-political principles which," by his own light "but without sufficient reason," he identifies with, or considers "to be in harmony, with the evangelical law as the specific Christian morality" (Kelsen 1955: 64). If so, Kelsen seems to miss an important point. He agrees with Niebuhr in holding that there is "only one principle of morality which is specifically Christian…the principle of love." However, unlike Niebuhr, who claims this love has *everything* to do with the relevance of Christianity to political life, Kelsen concludes that "this principle is inapplicable in political reality" (Kelsen 1955: 65). Kelsen's view is, "If love, the love of Christ were really the moving force of democracy, then and only then could it be maintained that democracy is essentially connected with Christianity" (Kelsen 1955: 65). Niebuhr, as we have seen, devotes his entire career to making precisely that case. Avoiding such language as "essential connection" and *the* "moving force," Niebuhr is content to argue that the law of love is related to justice and that, therefore, Christianity has something important to say about democracy.

8.4.1 Niebuhr and Kelsen on the Preconditions and Portability of Democracy

It is important to look briefly at the views of Kelsen and Niebuhr regarding the preconditions for democracy and the prospects of expanding democracy around the world.

Kelsen's view of democracy is inseparable from, and dependent on, his primary aim of establishing what he called a "Pure Theory of Law." By "pure," he means a theory of law that has itself as its sole object, thus freeing "legal science of all foreign elements—elements such as ethics, religion, politics, and sociology" (Kelsen 1934: 7). Kelsen's objective is thus a formal one in that he approaches democracy as "only a form, a method for the creation of the social order" (Kelsen 1926 (2013 ed.: 101)). He felt that the independence afforded by his formal approach to democracy prevented becoming caught up in "the passionate outcry of politics" by embracing "only the cool tones of science," and without becoming embroiled in the value-laden character of social democracy where issues arise that are insoluble or where ideals can as easily be achieved in an autocratic society as in a democratic one (Kelsen 1973: 95). In effect, for Kelsen, independence from ideological conflicts as well as from the ebb and flow of political conflict is crucial for the foundational basis of democracy as a form of governance.

On the strictly formal side, Kelsen insists that he is employing a cognitive science that "must not presuppose any value; consequently he has to restrict himself to an explanation and a description of his object without judging it as good or bad, that is, as being in conformity with, or contrary to, a presupposed value" (Kelsen 1957: 350). However, in turning to politics "as the art of government, that is to say, the practice of regulating the social behavior of men," Kelsen sees politics as "a function of will and, as such, an activity which necessarily presupposes the conscious or unconscious assumption of values, the realization of which is the purpose of the activity" (Kelsen 1957: 350). Given his model of "autonomy" and "autocracy" as encompassing the available types of governance, and convinced that contrasting "world outlooks" are at stake—a critical, relativist, and scientific view for democracy, and a metaphysical/absolutistic view characteristic of autocracy—Kelsen chooses democracy on the grounds that it affords the greatest opportunity for freedom, which is the hallmark of political autonomy.

Kelsen contends that, contrary to science, "politics is an activity ultimately based on subjective value judgments." Kelsen's supreme value is freedom, that is, human beings "should be free" (Kelsen 1957: 355). Freedom here is understood politically as "self-determination." He sees the "Idea of democracy" as the "Idea of freedom as political self-determination. It is found expressed in its relatively purest form where the state order is directly created by those who are themselves subject to it, where a people, in an assembly of the whole population, agrees upon the norms for its conduct" (Kelsen 1955: 99). The core issue, therefore, is establishing a legally grounded constitutional system with parliamentary representation as a basis for social life. Kelsen views democracy as having "an inherent tendency to shift the center of gravity of governmental functions into legislation—to become a government of laws," concluding that "the ideal of legality plays a decisive part here, and hence the idea that the individual acts of state can be justified rationally, through their conformity to law" (Kelsen 1955: 103). As Lars Vinx puts it, Kelsen, in his book, *The Nature and Value of Democracy*, is defending:

> an ideal-type, in the Weberian sense, of the actual constitutional system that has achieved a more or less paradigmatic status in the western world: a political system based on a universal franchise, in which general legislative decisions are taken by majority vote of the people or by majority vote of their elected representatives, that is committed to the rule of law, and that includes a written constitution protecting individual rights and the rights of minority groups (Vinx 2007: 103).

Kelsen's formal, legal emphasis reveals his focus on the constitutional preconditions for democracy. Writing a good constitution, as Kelsen did in helping to draft one for Austria in 1920, is the *sine qua non* for establishing future democracies.

Whether writing a good constitution is sufficient as well as necessary is another question. Certainly the organic preconditions that are so prevalent in Niebuhr's writings on democracy are seemingly lacking in Kelsen's writings.

Although Niebuhr seems to have been unaware of Kelsen's 1955 article on the *Foundations of Democracy*, he did review Kelsen's book, *Peace Through Law*, a decade earlier. It is here that Niebuhr locates Kelsen among those who fail to address the complexity of organic elements in the formation of democratic societies. Niebuhr argues that the reason for this in Kelsen's case lies in his rather abstract constitutionalism. In his 1944 book review. entitled *Sovereignty and Peace*, Niebuhr finds Hans Kelsen's book to be the latest among numerous books that continue to "emphasize the juridical at the expense of political factors." Niebuhr sympathizes with the difficulty Kelsen finds in forming "a unified international political authority, completely transcending national sovereignty" but finds that Kelsen "wrongly imagines that he can evade this difficulty by creating an international court with compulsory jurisdiction over all disputes." According to Niebuhr, Kelsen expects the impossible—that because representatives to the court will be individuals and not representatives of their nations, the nations can be "expected to submit their disputes to it, acquiesce in its judgments, and furnish it with the means of enforcing its judgments should recalcitrance arise." Clearly, in Niebuhr's view, "the author does not understand that courts are not the foundation but the final pinnacle of any system of justice." Niebuhr's conclusion is that Kelsen's treatise:

> is made even more abstract and irrelevant by the addition of an impossible individualism to an unrealistic legalism. The author believes that the nations of the world could enter into an international agreement making their leaders individually responsible for acts of state, undertaken in their representative capacity, which lead to war. The idea not only obscures the complex political forces which underlie the "individual" acts of statesmen but also presupposes the complete abnegation of national sovereignty, without which no nation would deliver its leaders to such a court (Niebuhr 1944b: 623).

A judgment Niebuhr made in the book *Children of Light and Children of Darkness* relates to his earlier assessment of Kelsen. Niebuhr acknowledges that sophisticated idealists recognize "that power is required in the organization of all human communities" and "know that force must provide sanctions for law." However, what they do not understand are "the complex and various elements which compose the authority for which force is an instrument and only an instrument." According to Niebuhr, they:

> also have a too neat view of the organic processes of history by which communities coalesce and communal authorities are established. They estimate the problem of building communities in purely constitutional terms because they do not recognize or understand the vital social processes which underlie the constitutional forms and of which these forms are only instruments and symbols (Niebuhr 1944a: 164–165).

What Niebuhr has to say specifically about the situation in America highlights his emphasis on the organic preconditions to democracy that he finds missing in Kelsen's constitutional focus. Commenting on why America has "produced so many constitutionalists in international political theory," Niebuhr concludes that such a pattern relies on the fact that "American history encourages the illusion that the nation was created purely by constitutional fiat and compact" (Niebuhr 1944a: 166). This is an illusion:

> because the constitution was the end and not the beginning of an historical process which began with a common conflict against an imperial overlord. In this conflict the separate colonial entities gradually coalesced into a single community. In its course a military leader emerged, in the person of Washington, whose prestige was of immeasurable importance as a rallying point for the nation. Most modern nations do not have as clear a constitutional beginning as the United States. It is therefore the more significant that even in the history of the United States the real beginning is more organic and less constitutional than is usually assumed (Niebuhr 1944a: 166–167).

According to Niebuhr, the highly developed degree of integration that both imperial and national communities worldwide have achieved have:

> all have had some core of ethnic homogeneity, though various and heterogeneous elements may be on the periphery. They have also been bound together by particular and unique cultural forces and by the power of a common tradition and of common experiences. The authority of the government in such communities is not infrequently derived from the same history from which the community derived its unity (Niebuhr 1944a: 165).

Such considerations raise the question as to the exportability of democracy.

Niebuhr was not very sanguine regarding the ease with which democracy could spread and flourish. He certainly agreed with Kelsen regarding the constitutional preconditions for democracy as basic to a process by which democracy could achieve a lawful and workable embodiment. However, as Niebuhr views it, democracy is not a universal panacea easily transported around the world. Writing in the 1960s—the last decade of his life—Niebuhr concludes that however venerated democracy is for its multitude of virtues, the "question remains whether democracy is not…a luxury which only advanced nations can afford" (Niebuhr 1962: 8). What should "be obvious is that Western-style democracy is not immediately relevant to non-European culture. They lack the standards of literacy, political skill and social equilibria which would make viable political freedom as we have come to know." And, however ideal democracy is, it "requires greater political skill, cultural adequacy and a fortunate balance of social forces that are not available for many non-European or, more accurately, non-technical nations" (Niebuhr 1961b: 11–12).

Thus, the issue of "organic" factors in the development of community resurfaces as to why Niebuhr regards the exportation of democracy as having minimal chances of success. Free and democratic societies can neither be established nor flourish until the soil has been prepared—unless certain conditions are met. The democracies grew gradually out of bloody soil and are highly intricate systems requiring complete political institutions, an acute sense of justice, and highly developed notions of individual freedom, rights, and responsibilities. Moreover, democratic nations "have a culture which demands self-criticism in principle; and institutions which make it possible in practice" (Niebuhr 1944a, 183). In one of Niebuhr's last books, co-authored with Paul Sigmund while jointly teaching a course at Harvard University, the authors claim that:

[The] [s]tudy of European democracy has shown three constant prerequisites of free governments: (1) the unity and solidarity of the community, sufficiently strong to allow the free play of competitive interests without endangering the unity of the community itself; (2) a belief in the freedom of the individual and appreciation of his worth; and (3) a tolerable harmony and equilibrium of social and political and economic forces necessary to establish an approximation of social justice (Niebuhr and Sigmund 1969: 73).

8.4.2 Niebuhr and Kelsen on Justice, Liberty, and Equality

8.4.2.1 Justice

Niebuhr and Kelsen differ in terms of the time and attention they give to the issue of justice. This reflects a different emphasis between them. For Niebuhr, the dominant theme of social justice in democracy arises out of his primary emphasis on the political sphere; whereas Kelsen chooses to separate the question of justice for philosophical and metaphysical reflection in order to allow his pure theory of law to stand on its own two feet.

In Kelsen's essay, *What is Justice*?, based on his May 27, 1952, farewell lecture as an active member of the University of California at Berkeley, he surveys history for answers to the question of justice without finding any resolution. Convinced that "absolute justice is an irrational ideal or, what amounts to the same, an illusion—one of the eternal illusions of mankind," (Kelsen 1957: 21) Kelsen claims we are left with only a conditional solution of the problem of justice as "a judgment of value, determined by emotional factors, and therefore, subjective in character—valid only for the judging subject and therefore relative only" (Kelsen 1957: 4). In his final reflection on justice Kelsen concludes:

> I cannot say what justice is, the absolute justice for which mankind is longing. I must acquiesce in a relative justice and I can only say what justice is to me. Since science is my profession, and hence the most important thing in my life, justice, to me, is that social order under whose protection the search for truth can prosper. "My" justice, then, is the justice of freedom, the justice of peace, the justice of democracy—the justice of tolerance (Kelsen 1957: 24).

In the end, Kelsen settles on opting for the relative justice that democracy can guarantee in bringing about the greatest possible degree of individual freedom. Kelsen regards freedom as a spiritual matter. He writes that "The life principle of every democracy is…spiritual freedom, freedom to express opinions, freedom of belief and conscience, the principle of toleration, and more especially, the freedom of science, in conjunction with the belief in its possible objectivity. The constitutions of all democracies bear witness to this spirit" (Kelsen 1973: 101–102).

Niebuhr agrees with Kelsen that absolute justice is a chimera and that whatever justice is attainable in history is tentative and temporary, relative to a never-ending balancing of social forces. Niebuhr also probes the spiritual element of democracy in claiming that, speaking ideally, "democracy is a permanently valid form of social and political organization which does justice to two dimensions of human existence: to man's spiritual stature and his social character; to the uniqueness and variety of life, as well as to the common necessities of all men." However, in emphasizing the "common necessities of all men," Niebuhr seeks to emphasize that while "the community requires liberty as much as does the individual," it is also true that "the individual requires community more than bourgeois thought comprehended." It is precisely for this reason, Niebuhr concludes, that democracy cannot "be equated with freedom. An ideal democratic order seeks unity within the conditions of freedom; and maintains freedom within the framework of order" (Niebuhr 1944a: 3). For Niebuhr freedom is required for social organization on the grounds that man is essentially free—namely, capable of indeterminate transcendence over nature to which he also belongs. However, while "a free society is justified by the fact that the indeterminate possibilities of human vitality may be creative," the limitations society places upon freedom are also justified "by the fact that the vitalities may be destructive" (Niebuhr 1944a: 63–64).

For Niebuhr, injustice, rooted in the destructive forces of inordinate self-love, is the fundamental problem in social and political life. He claims that democratic societies seek to bring political power into the service of justice in three ways. First, "they have tried to distribute economic and political power and prevent its undue concentration" (Niebuhr 1952a: 135) Second, "they have tried to bring it under social and moral review." Third, "they have sought to establish inner religious and moral checks upon it" (Niebuhr 1952a: 135). In Niebuhr's view this "effort to coerce competitive and contradictory human aspirations and interests into some kind of tolerable order and justice" is "a highly moral one" (Niebuhr 1959c: 116). While Niebuhr maintains that "there is no Christian economic or political system," he does claim that there is "a Christian attitude towards the claims of all systems of justice." This consists of maintaining "a critical attitude towards the claims of all systems and schemes, expressed in the question whether they will contribute to justice in a concrete situation," and also in adopting "a responsible attitude, which will not pretend to be God nor refuse to make a decision between political answers to a problem because each answer is discovered to contain moral ambiguity in God's sight" (Niebuhr 1957: 253–254).

When Kelsen attends to the question of what is just and what is unjust in a society, as a matter of diverging value judgments, he concludes on the basis of rational judgment that:

> there are only interests of human beings and hence conflicts of interest. The solution of these conflicts can be brought about either by satisfying one interest at the expense of the other, or by a compromise between the conflicting interests. It is not possible to prove that only the one or the other solution is just. Under certain conditions the one, under others the other may be just. If social peace is supposed to be the ultimate end—but only then—the compromise solution may be just, but the justice of peace is only a relative, and not an absolute, justice (Kelsen 1957: 21–22).

Niebuhr certainly concurs with Kelsen's viewpoint, as far as it goes, but he is not willing to let matters rest here. For Niebuhr the issue of balancing conflicting interests is precisely the point where a serious concern with justice surfaces in political life. Justice, for Niebuhr, comes down to the issue of balancing power among groups holding opposing interests in order to achieve a modicum of social harmony. While

Niebuhr sees "no neat principle which will solve the relation of power to justice and of justice to freedom," (Niebuhr 1952a: 100) he insists that we have:

> achieved such justice as we possess in the only way justice can be achieved in a technical society: we have equilibrated power. We have attained a certain equilibrium in economic society itself by setting organized power against organized power. When that did not suffice we used the more broadly based political power to redress disproportions and disbalances in economic society (Niebuhr 1952a: 101).

Insofar as democracy has proven itself capable of holding all cultural viewpoints under criticism and of achieving an uncoerced harmony among the various social and cultural vitalities, it has demonstrated itself to be the most adept political answer to the problem of accommodating and balancing the interests of competing groups. To the degree that democracy succeeds in holding "all claims to truth under critical review" and balancing "all social forces, not in an automatic, but in a contrived harmony of power…it distills a modicum of truth from a conflict of error" (Niebuhr 1952b: 51).

Niebuhr sees justice as something beyond the mere balance of power. He views it as an approximation of love, as the relative embodiment of love in society. Kelsen clearly understands the radical nature of Christian love. However, he re-categorizes the discussion of justice for the philosophical domain so as to separate it from legal science. This results in disregarding the possible relevance of love to the realities of human nature that is so prominent in Niebuhr. Kelsen is convinced that Jesus proclaimed a justice that "is beyond any social order to be established in reality; and the love which is the essence of this justice is evidently not the human instinct we call love.…The love taught by Jesus is not human love" (Kelsen 1957: 12). Kelsen's view finds him in agreement with the position Anders Nygren took in his highly influential book, *Agape and Eros*, published in 1969. Niebuhr's understanding of Nygren would also apply to Kelsen. Niebuhr points out that the "rigorous distinction" Nygren makes "between the 'unmotivated' self-giving love which the Gospels ascribe to a merciful God and the classical idea of *eros* which, according to Nygren, is always a calculating love, seeking to complete the self from the standpoint of the self and which therefore makes love the servant of self-love" results in Nygren's *agape* as "a complete impossibility and irrelevance for man. It describes the character of God but has no real relation, as source and end, toward *philia* and *eros*, toward either mutual love or expressions of love, tainted with self-interest, which are the actual stuff of our human existence" (Niebuhr 1949: 178). Niebuhr, as opposed to both Kelsen and Nygren, finds *agape* as having perpetual relevance to the structure of human existence:

> in the fact that it is both the fulfillment of the self's freedom and the contradiction of every actual self-realization insofar as every actual self-realization is partly an egoistic and therefore a premature closing of the self within itself. *Agape* is thus, as the final norm of the self as free spirit, a perpetual source of judgment upon every other norm which may be used tentatively to describe the self's duties and obligations. At the same time, it refutes the lawlessness of those theories which imagine that the freedom of the self entitles it to have no law but its own will. Such a proud assertion of the self's freedom and disavowal of its finiteness leads to self-destruction (Niebuhr 1949: 179).

What this involves for Niebuhr is a conviction that there is a dialectical relationship between love and justice in which love fulfills justice by calling us to seek wider and more inclusive structures of justice than that of merely balancing power. At the same time, love negates justice by always rising above the calculations that justice inevitably requires. Love demands that we surpass the minimal requirements of justice. As Niebuhr sees it, love is:

> the end term of any system of morals. It is the moral requirement in which all schemes of justice are fulfilled and negated. They are fulfilled because the obligation of life to life is more fully met in love than is possible in any scheme of equality and justice. They are negated because love makes an end of the nicely calculated less and more of structures of justice. It does not carefully arbitrate between the needs of the self and of the other, since it meets the needs of the other without concern for the self (Niebuhr 1941: 313).

8.4.2.2 Liberty and Equality

Kelsen sets his view of democracy in sharp contrast to democratic theories based on the principle of "equality." While not opposed to recognizing the value of "political" equality, Kelsen wants to point out that those who insist on grounding political legitimacy on the notion of justice—understood as equality—end up contrasting a formal notion of equality with a substantive notion in a way that undermines democracy itself. Kelsen views democracy as a process, not as a fact—a process in which equality has the appropriate political meaning that everyone should have an equal right in participating in the process of collective self-government. According to Kelsen:

> The idea of equality certainly plays its own role in democratic ideology. Yet, as we have seen, it does so only in a completely negative, formal, and secondary sense. The demand for preferably universal, and therefore equal, freedom requires universal and therefore equal participation in government. Historically the fight for democracy has been a fight for political freedom, that is, for popular participation in the legislative and executive spheres. Insofar as the idea of equality is meant to connote anything other than formal equality with regard to freedom (i.e. political participation) that idea has nothing to do with democracy. This can be seen in the fact that not the political and formal, but the material and economic equality of all can be realized just as well—if not better—in an autocratic-dictatorial form of state as it can in a democratic form of state (Kelsen 1926: 97).

Consistent with his emphasis on "pure" law, Kelsen's focus is on a notion of equality that conforms with his notion of political freedom. Kelsen claims that the very "Idea of democracy is the Idea of freedom as political self-determination." Such freedom is thus the primary foundation for democracy itself. For Kelsen the word democracy relates to a specific method for creating a social order and not to the content of that order. The notion of equality fits into the democratic equation for Kelsen only in that "the ultimate meaning of the democratic principle is that the political subject should will the freedom that is aimed at, not only for himself, but also for others; that the 'I' wills freedom also for the 'thou', because it feels that 'thou' to be of the same nature as itself." It is in this sense, for Kelsen, that "the Idea of freedom must be supplemented, and restricted, by the Idea of equality"

(Kelsen 1973: 99). What is at stake for Kelsen is the goal of achieving equality, ie, universal freedom, for all members of society. Kelsen rules out any other notion of equality as relating to the foundational meaning of democracy.

Niebuhr's views on justice within democracy are much more complex and nuanced than those of Kelsen. Niebuhr insists that both liberty and equality are involved as "regulative principles of democracy and fraternity" (Niebuhr 1947b: 65). He expands on this thought as follows:

> Without liberty a community ceases to be a community of persons and becomes a forcibly unified mass. Without equality as the regulative principle of justice, the community allows either ancient or hereditary or newly created inequalities of privilege and of power to destroy the community of persons. If the middle-class democratic movement of the eighteenth and nineteenth century emphasized primarily the value of liberty as contrasted with the two repressive cohesions of feudal society, the modern democratic impulse borne primarily by the industrial workers in expressing itself in socialism has emphasized particularly the value of equality. The emphasis was important because one of the ironic effects of an industrial society which had promised emancipation from the inequalities of a feudal agrarian society, was the creation of more dynamic forms of inequality than were possible in an agrarian society (Niebuhr 1947b: 68).

Niebuhr knew that, if taken to extremes, liberty and equality would negate the other. Total liberty—because of the wiles of the wise, the powerful, and the cunning—results in gross inequalities. Total equality—because of its need to be coerced—destroys liberty. Healthy democracies involve recognition of both liberty and equality as components of justice in the perennial struggle of balancing power and interest with the body politic.[5] They are consistently in tension with each other in the conflicting give and take of a viable democracy.

As Niebuhr sees it, the "principle of 'equality' is a relevant criterion of criticism for the social hierarchy, and the principle of 'liberty' serves the same purpose for the community's unity. But neither principle could be wholly nor absolutely applied without destroying the community" (Niebuhr 1958: 62). He is aware that while inequalities of privilege are somewhat proportioned to prestige and function, they never correspond exactly to these inequalities of function. In the end:

> We thus confront the two basic realities of the community's social hierarchy. The one is that such a hierarchy is necessary, and the other is that the prestige, power and privilege, particularly privilege, of its upper levels tend to be inordinate. That is why there can be no simple solution for the problem of social gradation. That is why equality must remain a regulative principle of justice and why equalitarianism is the ideology of the poor. They resent the inequalities, rightly because of their inordinate character; but they wrongly imagine that all inequalities could be abolished (Niebuhr 1958: 64).

---

[5] For Niebuhr, justice demands something more than merely balancing power. Central to his thought is the claim that the quest for justice be related to the norm of love. Niebuhr is well aware that what he calls the "law of love" (*agape*) is a normative ideal and not something historically realizable. Such love is heedless, uncalculating, sacrificial—devoid of the careful calculations so essential to adjudicating conflicts of interest. Niebuhr once called such love an "impossible possibility"—and recognizes that its "impossibility" is far more obvious in collective life than in individual life.

In the final analysis Niebuhr cautions against believing liberty and equality to be simple historical possibilities. The two are "in paradoxical relation to each other and that it is possible to purchase the one only at the price of the other" (Niebuhr 1958: 69).

References

Good, Robert C. 1965. National interest and moral theory: The 'debate' among contemporary political realists. In *Foreign policy in the sixties: The issues and instruments—essays in honor of Arnold Wolfers*, ed. Hilsman Roger and Robert C. Good. Baltimore: The Johns Hopkins University Press.

Harland, Gordon. 1960. *The thought of Reinhold Niebuhr*. New York: Oxford University Press.

Kelsen, Hans. 1926. *The essence and value of democracy*. 2013 edition by Nadia Urbinati and Carlo Invernizzi Accetti. Trans. B. Graf. Plymouth: Rowman & Littlefield Publishers, Inc.

Kelsen, Hans. 1934. *Introduction to the Problems of Legal Theory*. Trans. B.L. Paulson and S.L. Paulson 1996. Oxford: Oxford University Press.

Kelsen, Hans. 1944. *Peace through law*. Chapel Hill: University of North Carolina Press.

Kelsen, Hans. 1955. Foundations of democracy. In *Ethics: An international journal of social political and legal philosophy*, ed. Charner Marquis Perry, Supplement, 1–101. Chicago: University of Chicago Press.

Kelsen, Hans. 1957. What is justice? In *What is justice: Justice law, and politics in the mirror of science*. Berkeley: University of California Press.

Kelsen, Hans. 1973. State-form and world-outlook. In *Hans Kelsen: Essays in legal and moral philosophy*, ed. Ota Weinberger. Boston: Reidel.

Niebuhr, Reinhold. 1939. Ten years that shook my world. *Christian Century* 56: 545.

Niebuhr, Reinhold. 1940. Christian faith and natural law. *Theology* 89: 88.

Niebuhr, Reinhold. 1941. *The nature and destiny of man, volume I, Human Destiny*. London: Nisbet & Co. Ltd.

Niebuhr, Reinhold. 1943. *The nature and destiny of man, volume II, Human Destiny*. London: Nisbet & Co. Ltd.

Niebuhr, Reinhold. 1944a. *Children of light and children of darkness*. New York: Charles Scribner's Sons.

Niebuhr, Reinhold. 1944b. Sovereignty and peace. *The Nation*, November 18.

Niebuhr, Reinhold. 1946. *Discerning the signs of the times: Sermons for today and tomorrow*. New York: Charles Scribner's Sons.

Niebuhr, Reinhold. 1947a. Democracy as religion. *Christianity and Crisis*, 1–2. August 4.

Niebuhr, Reinhold. 1947b. Christianity as a basis of democracy. *The Listener* 37.

Niebuhr, Reinhold. 1949. *Faith and history*. New York: Charles Scribner's Sons.

Niebuhr, Reinhold. 1952a. *Irony of American history*. New York: Charles Scribner's Sons.

Niebuhr, Reinhold. 1952b. *Christian realism and power politics*. New York: Charles Scribner's Sons.

Niebuhr, Reinhold. 1953a. In *Christian realism and political problems*. New York: Charles Scribner's Sons.

Niebuhr, Reinhold. 1953b. Democracy, secularism, and Christianity. In *Christianity and Crisis*, March 2.

Niebuhr, Reinhold. 1953c. Christian faith and social action. In *Christian faith and social action*, ed. J.A. Hutchison. New York: Scribner.

Niebuhr, Reinhold. 1957. Theology and political thought in the western world. *Ecumenical Review*, April 1957.

Niebuhr, Reinhold. 1958. Liberty and equality. In *Pious and secular America*. New York: Charles Scribner's Sons.

Niebuhr, Reinhold. 1959a. *The structure of nations and empires*. London: Nisbet & Co. Ltd.
Niebuhr, Reinhold. 1959b. Power and ideology in national and international affairs. In *Theoretical aspects of international relations*, ed. W.T.R. Fox. South Bend: University of Notre Dame.
Niebuhr, Reinhold. 1959c. Education and the world scene. *Daedalus* 88(1): 107–120.
Niebuhr, Reinhold. 1961a. How my mind has changed. In *How my mind has changed*, ed. Harold E. Fey. New York: Meridian.
Niebuhr, Reinhold. 1961b. Well-tempered evangelism. *New Republic*, June 26.
Niebuhr, Reinhold. 1962. Can democracy work? *New Leader*, May 28.
Niebuhr, Reinhold. 1984. Reply to interpretation and criticism. In *Reinhold Niebuhr: His religious, social and political thought*, ed. Charles W. Kegley. New York: Pilgrim Press.
Niebuhr, Reinhold, and Paul Sigmund. 1969. *The democratic experience: Past and prospects*. New York: Frederick A. Praeger.
Rice, Daniel. 1993. *Reinhold Niebuhr and John Dewey: An American Odyssey*. Albany: State University of New York Press.
Vinx, Lars. 2007. Kelsen's theory of democracy—reconciliation with social order. In *Hans Kelsen's pure theory of law*. Oxford: Oxford University Press.
Watson, Philip. 1966. *Let God be God: An interpretation of the theology of Martin Luther*. Minneapolis: Fortress Press.
Williams, Daniel Day. 1984. Niebuhr and liberalism. In *Reinhold Niebuhr: His religious, social and political thought*, ed. Charles W. Kegley. New York: Pilgrim Press.

Chapter 9
Hans Kelsen's Psychoanalytic Heritage—An Ehrenzweigian Reconstruction

Bettina K. Rentsch

9.1 Introduction

The significance of Hans Kelsen's impact in Europe is evident both in his influence on numerous scholars in a wide range of fields and in the widespread acceptance of his substantial findings (Cf. *Jestaedt* 2008: XXII). Conversely, in the United States of America, there was never a second generation of U.S. scholars who explored Kelsenian approaches to the law or even commented, whether appreciatively or critically, on Kelsen's body of work. Also, while some of his contemporaries show great respect for Kelsen's outstanding qualities,[1] most of American scholarship is, at best, critical with regard to the pure theory of law (cf. Meiklejohn 1958: 543 (545); Northrop 1958: 815; Halbach 1973:957).

From a scholarly perspective, controversies involving Hans Kelsen in the United States prove very useful for a thorough understanding of his work. Putting one of the most renowned European legal scholars of the twentieth century under the considerable pressure of justification, American scholarship not only motivated Kelsen to refine the pure theory of law (Meiklejohn 1958: 543; Ross 1957: 564) but also forced him to reconsider the jurisprudential underpinnings of his legal theory. In response to the challenges he faced in the United States, Hans Kelsen adopted more of a legal realist point of view than the orthodox label "normative legal positivism" captures (Jestaedt 2008: XXII).

[1] As Halbach stated: "A giant of the law has left us" (Halbach 1973: 957).

B.K. Rentsch (✉)
Institute for Private International Law and International Commercial Relations, University of Heidelberg, Heidelberg, Germany
e-mail: bettina.rentsch@gmail.com

D.A.J. Telman (ed.), *Hans Kelsen in America - Selective Affinities and the Mysteries of Academic Influence*, Law and Philosophy Library 116,
DOI 10.1007/978-3-319-33130-0_9

9.2 Why Psychoanalytic Jurisprudence and Hans Kelsen?

To review Hans Kelsen's scholarship in light of psychoanalysis may seem an odd undertaking at first glance. Indeed, while there are striking biographical parallels between Hans Kelsen and Albert Ehrenzweig, the two scholars do not seem to stand on the same academic ground. Having received his education in Vienna, Kelsen adhered to normative positivism and, throughout his academic career, concentrated on constitutional and public international legal issues. Ehrenzweig, who also graduated from the University of Vienna, concentrated on private and insurance law and, later in his career, became an adherent of legal realism (Zaremby 2014), although he maintained a strong, albeit sometimes critical, identification with European legal sociology. How can there be an intersection between two jurists, given this level of divergence in their academic interests and approaches?

As I will point out, Ehrenzweig's psychoanalytical concept fills one of the pure theory of law's most striking substantive gaps, the question of how to define justice. Kelsen confronted this question on various occasions,[2] but, whenever interrogated as to his justice conception, Kelsen denied that justice is a necessary basis of the law. Kelsen's argumentation on this subject often failed to convince his critical audience. A psychoanalytical and realist approach to the law clarifies and justifies Kelsen's argument, especially his acquiescence in the impossibility of providing scientifically sound definitions for the question of justice. According to psychoanalytical jurisprudence, justice is an objective, normative basis of the law but stems from the human desire to be provided with external control on one's own behavior. Kelsen, who enjoyed a close relationship with Sigmund Freud's academic circle in the early twentieth century, certainly would have been happy to join the psychoanalytical jurisprudential movement. Doing so, he would have been very likely to end up in a dialogue with Ehrenzweig, whose jurisprudential contribution would have helped shield Kelsen's scholarship against criticism.

9.3 Albert Ehrenzweig: Vita and Academic Record

Before I proceed to a further elaboration of how Ehrenzweig's sociology can be used to supplement and fortify the pure theory of law, I will provide a brief overview of Albert Ehrenzweig's biography and academic record.

[2] Cf. the subtitle to Kelsen (1957) essay collection *What is Justice?—Justice, Law and Politics in the Mirror of Science*.

9.3.1 Ehrenzweig: Biographical Cornerstones

Albert Armin Ehrenzweig's biography is part of Johannes Feichtinger's piece *Wissenschaft zwischen den Kulturen* (*Science in between Cultures*) (Feichtinger 2001: 276). Indeed, Ehrenzweig can be labeled bi-cultural, at least when it comes to his legal education, because he was one of the few European emigrants who supplemented their legal studies in their domestic countries with a full education in the American (and, along the way, the British) system. Born in Vienna in 1906, Ehrenzweig, who had studied in Vienna, Heidelberg, and Grenoble, completed his J.U.D. degree in 1928 and his habilitation in 1937 at the University of Vienna,[3] specializing in tort liability and insurance law. Forced to leave the country in 1938, Ehrenzweig first moved to Great Britain and then, in 1939, to the United States, where he continued his legal studies at the University of Chicago and Columbia University, earning a J.D. from the former in 1941. Ehrenzweig's appointment to UC Berkeley in 1948 came only 6 years after that of Hans Kelsen, who, discharged from his dean position at the University of Cologne, spent several years "exiled" at the Geneva Graduate Institute and Harvard Law school and was appointed professor for Political Science and International Relations at UC Berkeley in 1942. Ehrenzweig and Kelsen, who most certainly knew one another from their Vienna days, formed a loose and not especially academic, but durable and amicable relationship. Among other things, Ehrenzweig hosted the well-known 1961 symposium, the first face-to-face encounter between Hans Kelsen and H.L.A. Hart, the two leading figures in analytic legal theory at the time (Hart 1962–1963: 709).

9.3.2 Ehrenzweig as a Stranger to Contemporary Jurisprudence

Ehrenzweig's academic record does not evidence strong ties to either jurisprudence or to legal theory. In contrast, Ehrenzweig's treatise on the conflict of laws (1962), together with several publications on the subject matter, elaborated the so-called *lex fori* approach, a prominent, though nowadays minority realist position within the "Conflicts Revolution" (Siehr 1957: 585).

Adhering to legal realism, the *lex fori* approach departs from the finding that courts tend to neglect foreign elements when adjudicating legal issues. Consequently, courts apply the law of their own jurisdiction, the *lex fori*, to a much higher number of cases than they should (Ehrenzweig 1962: § 21 ff). As a remedy, Ehrenzweig first develops normative and inclusive criteria for finding the appropriate forum. In so doing, Ehrenzweig treats together two questions—jurisdiction and applicable law—that are usually kept separate by all possible means. In Ehrenzweig's opinion, questions like those of jurisdiction and choice of law not only tend to raise the same

[3] *Barton/Hill/Riesenfeld*, 1977, University of California: In Memoriam.

issues, they also tend to influence one another in practice. Ehrenzweig next establishes criteria for how to appropriately identify foreign elements (data) in a case with foreign elements, and provides guidance as to the question of how to determine whether foreign law or forum law should be applied to those foreign elements.

9.3.3 *Ehrenzweig's Legal Sociology*

The *Psychoanalytic Jurisprudence*, published in 1971, is the Ehrenzweig's only jurisprudential treatise. From a contemporary (*ex post*) point of view, the piece does not mark a substantial turn in his academic orientation. Rather, it gives us an insight into the theoretical justification and methodological background to Ehrenzweig's tort, insurance, and conflicts scholarship (Friedmann 1972: 1720). The piece is thus both explanatory and self-referential. Ehrenzweig was not attempting to develop a new "school" of jurisprudence; rather, the psychoanalytic jurisprudence was rooted in Ehrenzweig's private law scholarship.[4] From a contemporary point of view, the piece, therefore, could be read as an outline and general guide to the author's scholarly contributions. Ehrenzweig most certainly initiated and has been an important promoter of the psychoanalytic approach to common law jurisprudence.[5] However, his single treatise is too concise and lacking in specificity to provide a satisfactory foundation for a thorough or influential contribution to the jurisprudential dialogue (Friedmann 1972: 1718, 1721).

9.3.3.1 The Psychoanalytic Jurisprudence as a Comparative Treatise on Legal Realism

Despite its negligible scholarly impact, Ehrenzweig's treatise is of great value for current discussions, as it offers a thorough comparative analysis of contemporary scholarship on legal sociology and legal realist jurisprudence in Europe and the United States (Ehrenzweig 1971; Friedmann 1972: 1718, 1721). Indeed, Ehrenzweig's policy objective was to initiate a transatlantic dialogue on legal methodology (Ehrenzweig 1971: § 75). In order to achieve his objective, Ehrenzweig first concisely summed up the leading ideas of German-speaking legal sociology (Friedmann 1972: 1718, 1720) and second introduced his readers, through a comparative study, to contemporary analytic U.S. scholarship, such as critical legal studies and legal realism (Ehrenzweig 1971: § 75). He intended to get U.S. scholars to become more receptive to current developments in European legal theory. By means of a German translation of his treatise (Ehrenzweig 1972: Vorwort des

[4] This may also be due to the criticism in the treatise's substantial vagueness (Friedmann 1972: 1718, 1721).

[5] For direct references to Ehrenzweig's influence, see Bienenfeld 1965: 957; Part II: Analysis, 1254; Goldstein (1968: 1053).

Verfassers, 18 ff), Ehrenzeig also thought to introduce scholars working in the tradition of European legal sociology to U.S. versions of the legal realism and critical legal studies (Ehrenzweig 1972: Vorwort des Verfassers, 18 ff).

In sum, the psychoanalytical jurisprudence tends to combine both: A comparison and a transatlantic reunion of jurisprudence. Beyond a new approach to jurisprudence, the author intended to create the foundation to a transnational school of legal sociology (Ehrenzweig 1965: 1331, 1335, 1971: § 75f.).

9.3.3.2 The Psychoanalytic Jurisprudence as New Meta-Discipline to Legal Realism

Despite this harmonizing objective, Ehrenzweig's work maintains a critical distance to both legal sociology and legal realism (Ehrenzweig 1972: § 76). Instead of choosing one side as a scholarly ground for his inquiry and then comparing it to the other, Ehrenzweig synthesizes both by means of psychoanalytical categories derived from Freudian methodology. He does so in order to decode the contemporary jurisprudential "Tower of Babel," disclosing all existing schools' common, unconscious presuppositions (Ehrenzweig 1965: 1331, 1335, 1971: Synopsis, § 7).

The psychoanalytic jurisprudence has a scope similar to that of the pure theory of law. Like the latter, it is dominated by a clear *Leitmotiv*. Ehrenzweig, through the categories and perspectives of modern psychoanalysis and behavioral science (reframed as "Psychosophy"), intends to re-evaluate and identify the genuine roots of past and contemporary legal and jurisprudential discourses (Ehrenzweig 1971: § 75). From a legal sociological point of view, this task had not yet been accomplished by legal scholarship or by jurisprudence, nor by inclusive social science approaches to the law (Ehrenzweig 1971: Synopsis § 7). Instead, the existing jurisprudential scholarship was characterized by its indifference towards the psychology and deficiencies of humankind, its generator. As a result, and regardless of the approach chosen and the arguments formulated, Ehrenzweig was not satisfied by the existing attempts to thoroughly define the law, as it is or should be. First, existing jurisprudence analysis departed from false assumptions, such as the existence of absolute principles of justice and rational human actors (Ehrenzweig 1971: Synopsis § 7). Second, in his opinion, existing approaches failed to take into account human instinct and its influence on the roots of each respective approach to jurisprudence (Ehrenzweig 1971: Synopsis § 7).

Ehrenzweig identifies the conflict between the main assumptions in natural law and legal positivism as "false,"[6] a finding that clarifies his scholarly intentions: He intends to show that both schools are not contradictory in content, but provide two alternative explanations for the validity of human-made legal rules (Ehrenzweig 1965: 1331, 1337). However, the validity of an existing legal norm, the very thing both theories claim to verify, appears to be inaccessible by means of conventional

[6] By using "false conflicts," this article borrows from contemporary conflicts of laws methodology, following Currie (1963: 33, 159, 181, 582; reflection see Cavers 1983: 471).

methods of legal and jurisprudential inquiry (Ehrenzweig 1965: 1331, 1337). Both schools, as Ehrenzweig concludes, are rooted in unsubstantiated, hence unreliable hypotheses (Ehrenzweig 1965: 1331, 1337).

The author then argues that psychoanalytical jurisprudence can overcome these uncertainties. It does so first, by means of an explicit disclosure of its hypotheses, and second, by the express relativity of its presumptions. Psychoanalytical jurisprudence avoids the use of normative arguments. Hence, by using psychoanalytic methodology, Ehrenzweig does not intend to find the right answer to an open value controversy or support one among several jurisprudential positions on a given question. His main objective is instead to disclose the underlying emotional conflict between the three categories of psychoanalysis, id, ego, and super-ego, to which controversies among competing jurisprudential schools can be reduced. Like other partisans of psychoanalytical approaches (Bienenfeld 1965: 957, 1254; Goldstein 1968: 1053), Ehrenzweig considered his method a unique and, therefore, revolutionary attempt to build up a sustainable meta-order to legal and trans-legal discourse (Ehrenzweig 1971: Synopsis § 7, § 75). For Ehrenzweig, psychoanalysis embodied and improved upon all other methodologies previously used to evaluate or describe legal phenomena and discourse.

9.4 Kelsen and the Boundaries to the Pure Theory of Law

In what regard can the psychoanalytical jurisprudence be considered suitable as an underpinning to normative legal positivism? First, we must identify the common ground between legal sociology on the one hand and analytical legal theory on the other. Indeed, these shared hypotheses can easily be identified, if we take into account the often claimed "realist underpinnings" of Hans Kelsen's positivist and, even more, the relativist perception of the law (Jestaedt 2008, XL; Christoph Bezemek 2016). The descriptive and seemingly neutral framework of Kelsen's argument is evidenced by various examples from his public international legal scholarship (Bezemek 2016). However, important parts of Kelsen's jurisprudence also go beyond mere "realism," especially when the purpose of legal scholarship is under discussion. In Kelsen's opinion, legal scholarship was not created to define justice, because the law itself does not necessarily need to satisfy the normative claims it creates. In fact, justice is neither a necessary condition nor a reliable justification for the law. In short, law can legitimately fall short of defining and granting justice. This is because justice is not a necessary condition of law, but a human expectation *with regard to* the law. This last argument moves Kelsen's reasoning from the normative to the descriptive and, beyond, indicates a semi-conscious shift from realism to psychology that allows us to link up Kelsen with subsequent psychological approaches.

9.4.1 What Is Justice?

As he raises the question of justice, Kelsen sets the stage for fundamental criticism of his approach to legal science. Reviewing *What is Justice*, the 1952 essay collection that starts by a print version of Kelsen's farewell lecture, Donald Meiklejohn (Chicago) states that:

> ...Kelsen himself clearly feels the need to find the normative principle which can underline the law, though not at the cost of corrupting the scientific study of the law. I propose to raise the question, in considering the book as a whole, whether in his enthusiasm for science he has not improperly rejected or repressed his concern for justification (Meiklejohn 1958: 543).

Meicklejohn's critique ignores the fact that not only Kelsen's *Pure Theory of Law*, but also the essay collection that Meiklejohn reviewed were dedicated to logic-based, analytic inquiry that does not seek to prove but to confront normative claims.

9.4.2 The Uselessness of Enquiries on Justice (What Is Justice?)

Indeed, Kelsen's farewell lecture, *What is Justice?*, formulates an argument against a definition of justice and attempts to refute any possibility of providing one. Kelsen develops three major points to state his argument. First, from a rational point of view (Kelsen 1957: 1, 10), justice can only be determined in reverse; that is, by means of justification. On this hypothesis, justice is necessarily predetermined by individual needs (Kelsen 1957: 2, 9). These needs can, second, by no means be predetermined exhaustively (Kelsen 1957: 1, 9) nor objectivized (Kelsen 1957: 1, 5 f., 17, 18 f). Justice, if understood as the result of individual justification processes, can, therefore, only be determined by a case-by-case comparison of means. Its results thus may differ, depending on the individual in question (Kelsen1957: 1, 6, 8). In many cases, however, even the comparison of means and ends becomes impossible, as the ends chosen cannot be objectively analyzed, but directly derive from human consciousness. Consciousness, though, is directly linked to human emotion (Bienenfeld 1965: 1254; Kelsen: 1957, 1, 9). Besides being irrational, justice, third, is only valid in a concrete, not in an abstract, sense. Hence, at least from a logical perspective, it is impossible to trace it back to an absolutely valid, objective principle (Kelsen 1957: 1, 8), as the degree of abstraction necessary to grasp the different phenomena of justice necessarily ends up in "empty formulas," such as the Kantian categorical imperative and the Platonic *mesotes* (Kelsen 1957: 1, 13 ff., 18 f., 2008: 14). In consequence, generalizing a concept meant to provide substantive values to the law to this extent proves useless.

To sum up, efforts to access scientifically the concept of justice are fruitless from a scholarly perspective. What can be subject to an analytical explanation is the need to ask for and define justice: This is the irrational assumption of a divine power that dictates duties of justice and injustice (Kelsen 1957: 1, 10 f.). If we assume absolute justice to be, on the other hand, profane and not divine in its nature, we come to grips with a human need to externally justify and, by doing so, falsely rationalize individual, and by their very nature, subjective needs (Kelsen 1957: 1, 10 f.).

9.4.2.1 Justice Equals Individual Happiness

Kelsen introduces his analytical enquiry with a thorough rephrasing of Platonic observations on justice (Meiklejohn 1958: 543). Justice, according to Kelsen's interpretation of Plato, equals individual happiness (Kelsen 1957: 1, 2). One might object, Kelsen notes, that if individual happiness be presumed as a ground for and measure of justice, we cannot generalize about the latter by its very nature. If justice, according to Kelsen, equals individual happiness, it can only be determined through an inductive, case-by-case analysis (Kelsen 1957: 1, 2). All abstract definitions of justice thus far offered either suffer from refutable metaphysical foundations or, like the Hartian Justice formula, avoid a substantive definition of justice and instead identify a competent authority that can develop a working definition of justice on a case-by-case basis.

Kelsen at first deliberately remains silent regarding the grounds on which Plato bases his arguments. However, later in the essay, Kelsen uses Platonic ideology as an example to show how metaphysics can fill the gap between the human need for justice and its lack of objectivity (Kelsen 1957: 1, 11). Eclectic in his axioms, Plato shares the assumption of Stoicism, according to which all people have the capacity to understand justice by listening to their consciences (pneuma). From a Kelsenian perspective, however, this results in a contradiction. If justice equals individual happiness, it is, from a rational point of view, simply individual (Kelsen 1957: 1, 2) and, therefore, cannot provide a guiding principle for or even a condition providing content for lawmaking. To follow one's nature may guarantee happiness, but doing so cannot dictate substantive duties or provide objective guiding principles, neither for oneself nor for others.

9.4.2.2 Justice Is Irrational as a Claim

Kelsen's criticism against Jeremy Bentham's formulation of justice is identical in its substance. For Bentham, a just order can be defined as the sum of the greatest possible degree of happiness for the greatest possible number of individuals.[7] To Kelsen, this objectivity-in-sum-formula is as useless as other attempts to formulate a general theory of justice. Admitting that happiness is necessarily subjective

---

[7] Rephrasing cf. *Kelsen*, Justice (1957, 1, 3); on the original *Bentham*, A Fragment on Government, preface, 393: "*it is the greatest happiness of the greatest number that is the measure of right and wrong*, been as yet developed."

undermines any possibility that it could be used to calculate the highest shared set of values in sum (Kelsen 1957: 1, 3). The soundness of Kelsen's opposition becomes manifest when considered in the light of Bentham's heritage in modern welfare economics. Pareto (2014 (summarized by Cirillo 1979: 94 ff)) efficiency, located at the highest number of intersecting sets of individual happiness, builds upon the faulty assumption that human behavior is rational and that degrees of happiness are readily quantifiable (Kelsen 1957: 1, 9). "If a man is a more or less rational being...," Kelsen states, "he tries to justify his behavior, motivated by the emotions of his fear and desire, in a rational way, that is to say, through his intellect" (Kelsen 1957: 1, 8). The attempt to rationalize fear and desire, however, does not end up changing their irrational nature.

As a result, even an inter-subjective and concrete definition of justice, such as any attempt to define its content analytically, cannot generate reliable results, as it carries the bias of humankind's expectation. In fact, any human expectation regarding justice ends up being created by human consciousness, which itself is inaccessible to analytic research (Kelsen 1957: 1, 10). The longing for an objectively accessible version of justice is irrational, as trying to define justice means trying to rationalize the irrational.

9.4.2.3 Justice as a Set of Relatively Valid Values

Although he rejects the rational nature of justice in principle, Kelsen admits that "... very many individuals agree in their judgments of value" (Kelsen 1957: 1, 7). Value concepts, therefore, may happen to be similar in substance if the societal and cultural circumstances that generate them converge (Kelsen 1957: 1, 7). The substantial coherence of a purely subjective value set can generate a moral order of quasi-absolute coercive command that can be equivalent to what is considered to be justice in substance (Kelsen 1957: 1, 22). A relativist concept of justice, therefore, is neither amoral nor immoral (Kelsen 1957: 1, 22).

These systems of justice, despite being born out of parallel human needs, can by no means be objective or absolute. Instead, they are fugitive constructions that prove justice as a concept to be relative in scope, time, and substance (Kelsen 1957: 1, 21): "If the history of humankind proves anything, it is the futility of the attempt to establish, in the way of rational considerations, an absolutely correct standard of human behavior..." (Kelsen 1957: 1, 21).

In a later essay, Kelsen would use the Holy Scriptures to exemplify the relativity of morals (Kelsen 1957: 25). The intrinsic relativity of justice, according to Kelsen's reading of the *Bible*, is displayed in the gap between God's omnipotence and his absolute justice (Kelsen 1957: 25). Kelsen also highlights the difference between the moral convictions displayed in biblical times and their alteration in modern societies.

9.4.3 Absolute Justice as an Irrational Means of Behavioral Control

While rejecting the existence of absolute justice and moral orders, Kelsen acknowledges the practical difficulties in accepting relative concepts of justice (Kelsen 1957: 1, 22).

> [R]elativism imposes upon the individual the difficult tasks of deciding for himself what is right and what is wrong. This, of course, implies a very serious responsibility, the most serious moral responsibility a man can assume (Kelsen 1957: 1, 22).

The impossibility of defining justice objectively thus increases human responsibility. Indeed, relativist conceptions of justice may result in difficulties for the individual. By acknowledging this difficulty, Kelsen provides a realist explanation for humankind's obvious longing for an external corrective order. However, as the following subchapter shall explain, he fails to identify an explicit link between the longing for external corrective mechanisms on the one hand and the human psyche on the other.

9.4.4 Filling in the Gaps by Means of Psychoanalytic Jurisprudence

9.4.4.1 Readers' Dissatisfaction with Kelsen's Relativism

Kelsen acknowledges that relativist conceptions of justice challenge and dissatisfy human beings. However, his argument is empowering insofar as every individual is deemed able to decide by himself what is right and what is wrong, because his answer to the eternal question of what justice is turns out to be as unsatisfying to his readers as admitting the relativity of justice itself. Because he fails to pursue his initial reasoning on the need for justice, Hans Kelsen misses an important opportunity to shield his scholarship against criticism.

How can a more satisfying answer be provided if not by a thorough investigation of the human need from which the concept of justice stems? Whatever the answer—by doing so, Hans Kelsen would certainly have convinced his audience to acknowledge and, in consequence, critically reconsider the irrationality underlying the human desire for justice.

9.4.4.2 Discovering the Irrational Need for Justice by Using Ehrenzweig

Ehrenzweig, having written the most thorough treatise on psychoanalytical methods and the law published to date, might have been able to finish the story and satisfy the readers' expectations at least insofar as it comes to the provenance of justice.

As mentioned above, my principal scholarly objective here was not to pursue the question of justice but to show that Kelsen saw that the underpinnings of the claim for absolute justice are rooted in human emotion. On this basis, Ehrenzweig's analysis begins where Kelsen's ends.

9.4.4.3 Kelsen and Ehrenzweig's Shared Assumptions

Ehrenzweig shared Kelsen's views on justice in many respects. Like Kelsen, he admits that justice can only be determined on a case-by-case basis and by means of justification. Also, he concedes that justice concepts have been witnessed significant variations in substance throughout the years (Ehrenzweig 1971: § 125). There is no "one Justice" but different ones (Ehrenzweig 1971: § 130), and any attempt to reduce the various concepts of justice to one uniform formula will end up being void of content. He points to the famous "*suum cuique*" as just a paramount illustration of this point (Ehrenzweig 1971: § 126). Like Kelsen, Ehrenzweig, following Konrad Lorenz, acknowledges that social interaction can generate shared sets of values (Ehrenzweig 1971: 198, § 167). As he put it, "through the synthesis of individuals there can be gained super-individual totality" (Ehrenzweig 1971: 199, § 167).

On the other hand, Ehrenzweig's and Kelsen's approaches differ significantly in their details. Ehrenzweig neither rejected the concept of justice as irrational and relative, nor did he attempt to unify all existing concepts of justice. Instead, Ehrenzweig's scholarly objective was to discover the emotional roots behind the law's, moral philosophy's, and ethics' inclination towards justice. By doing so, he discovered the motivation fueling fights over conceptions of justice even among legal positivists and natural lawyers.

9.4.4.4 Disguising Instinct by Using Justice

To Ehrenzweig, humankind's longing for absolute Justice stems from an attempt common to all humans: to disguise one's instinct, the id (Ehrenzweig 1971: 157, § 130). Like the behavior of animals, the instinctive behavior of humans can be observed, and multiple observations can help to establish rules describing behavior. Many instinctive acts derive from a basic need of human life: maintaining and increasing human population is one of them (Ehrenzweig 1971: 155, § 129). Instinct is not informed by reason.

If they were to admit to the existence of an uncontrollable instinct dictating their behavior, human beings would have to accept that they answer to an animal component in their nature. For this very reason, they reject their instinct or sublimate it into a broad, blurry, and, therefore, useless formula, such justice or divine power (Ehrenzweig 1971: 156, § 129).

From Ehrenzweig's perspective, the main purpose behind jurisprudential discourses throughout the centuries has been to disguise the false assumption that reason, not emotion, dictates human behavior (Ehrenzweig 1971: 155, § 128).

> We have undertaken to still the battle between those claiming and those denying the "existence" of a natural law as a "valid" legal order based on justice. Any such undertaking must accept that this battle, insofar as it is not one of words, is based on and carried by deep-seated emotions (Ehrenzweig 1971: 197, § 166).

Based on this finding, Ehrenzweig develops a normative plea: Philosophy, social science, and, especially, jurisprudence should engage in a higher degree of self-reflection when it comes the emotional underpinnings of their discussions. Subconscious motivations should be identified and, though they cannot be fully appreciated by rational means, be accepted as determining factors.

9.4.4.5 Retracing Absolute Justice Through a Disentanglement of Human Consciousness

Ehrenzweig's second claim is by far more important for this chapter. To understand what the need for justice is based on means to analyze and investigate the origins of as many of the different justice conceptions as we are able find in human interaction. In sum, these justices may disclose the basic principle from which they stem (Ehrenzweig 1971: 198, § 167).

In doing so, we identify the same conflict in different shapes and contexts. Reason fights un-reason. The super-ego fights the id. Acknowledging that an individual's longing for objective categories, such as justice, results from an internal conflict between different categories of human consciousness enables us to explain why we desperately seek an external justification of our behavior. It also explains, why Kelsen, admitting the irrationality in justice and obliging the human being to individually justify his behavior, neither answers our question nor fulfills its underlying needs. The same is true for his inclination towards democracy as a political system, which, due to its value neutrality, is a feasible means to maintain and develop individual justice (Kelsen 1957: 1, 23).

Finally, Ehrenzweig's reasoning offers an alternative option of conflict resolution regarding the relationship between diverging conceptions of justice and the political systems generating them: According to a psychoanalytical approach to the law, different understandings of "just" societal organizations can be traced back in their divergence as analogies to human beings' mental development (Ehrenzweig 1971: 199 f., § 169). Borrowing from Rudolf Bienenfeld, one of Ehrenzweig's leading sources on psychoanalysis and the law (Bienenfeld 1965: 1254), Ehrenzweig outlined possible parallels between a child's continuous emancipation from its mother (Bienenfeld 1965: 1254, 1255) and political systems. The first stage of development is analogous to a theocracy, where the child lives under omnipotent parental authority, which the child cannot overcome because it lacks independent critical reasoning skills (Bienenfeld 1965: 1254, 1257). Next, a child's physical (Bienenfeld 1965: 1254, 1257) and emotional emancipation from its mother first results in anarchy (Bienenfeld 1965: 1254, 1259). Finally, a model of social cooperation between mother and child emerges (Bienenfeld 1965: 1254, 1260; Ehrenzweig 1971: 200, § 170). Likewise, after a phase of declared communism ignorant towards values like property, children, developing a sense of privacy, adopt a more individualistic position to delimit their sphere from that of others (Ehrenzweig 1971: 197, 200 f., § 171). To sum up, one might argue that every social order and the justice concept on which it is based mirrors the development of human consciousness. The more we understand human consciousness, the better we can analyze the foundations of what we establish as a social order.

9.5 Conclusion

One might ask whether the relativism that results from Ehrenzweig's work and the ecclecticism it seems to justify is even less satisfying than simply admitting that absolute justice is irrational. I share Ehrenzweig's view that it is not.

"Our vital task is to reduce our ancestors' conflict of justness by reconquest" (Ehrenzweig 1971: 197, 198, § 169), he states. Investigating the determining factors for individual conceptions of justice reveals psychological processes that have thus far been run in disguise. Thanks to psychoanalytic jurisprudence, we no longer have an excuse to end the inquiry when it bumps up against irrationality. Just as analytical legal theory can help us find appropriate conclusions to how law works, a discipline dedicated to the irrational can explain why we have expectations that a just legal order could and does exist. This appreciation for the psychological origins of our conceptions of justice helps us not only to understand but also to acquiesce in the relativity of a given social norm. Hence, Ehrenzweig's perspective is supportive of Kelsen's concluding argument: A social order has to be as open as possible to allow the development of multiple individual conceptions of justice.

Psychoanalytical jurisprudence assists us when we wish to discover whether a time-resistant and society-neutral, and thus absolute concept of justice is possible. This task does not seem impossible, but it certainly requires a significant amount of further research (Ehrenzweig 1971: 200, § 169). Altering Hans Kelsen's answer to the question of what justice is, one might dare say, "We don't know—but we will find out."

Acknowledgments This essay is a contribution to *Hans Kelsen in America*, a conference sponsored by the Valparaiso University Law School, supported by the Botstiber Institute for Austrian-American Studies, and held in Chicago on June 27–28, 2014. I am truly thankful to Jeremy Telman for the invitation to present my ideas in this forum and to Jörg Kammerhofer for the encouragement to further investigate my almost accidental discovery of Ehrenzweig's supplementary function to Kelsen's scholarship. Besides that, I am grateful to Matthias Jestaedt, to whom I owe my interest Hans Kelsen's legal theory. Finally, I owe many thanks to my thesis supervisor, Marc-Philippe Weller, who invited me to present my ideas on Hans Kelsen's importance for private international law in his colloquium in February 2014. In doing so, he gave me a forum to present a first draft of the ideas I will elaborate in this chapter.

References

Bezemek, Christoph. 2016. Pure formalism? Kelsenian interpretive theory beyond textualism and originalism. In *Hans Kelsen in America: The anxieties of non-influence*. Ch. 13, ed. D.A. Jeremy Telman. Springer (forthcoming).

Bienenfeld, Rudolf. 1965. Prolegomena to a psychoanalysis of law and justice: Preface. 53 *California Law Review* 53: 957; Part II: Analysis. *California Law Review* 53:1254.

Cirillo, Renato. 1979. *The economics of Vilfredo Pareto*. London: Routledge

Cavers, David F. 1983. A correspondence with Brainerd Currie, 1957–1958. *Mercer Law Review* 34: 471.

Currie, Brainerd. 1963. *Selected essays on the conflict of laws*. Durham: Duke University Press.

Ehrenzweig, Albert. 1962. *Treatise on the conflict of laws*. Berkeley: University of California Press.

Ehrenzweig, Albert. 1965. Psychoanalytical jurisprudence: A common language for Babylon. *Columbia Law Review* 65: 1331.

Ehrenzweig, Albert. 1971. *Psychoanalytic jurisprudence*. Berkeley: University of California Press.

Ehrenzweig, Albert. 1972. *Psychoanalytische Rechtswissenschaft*. Berlin: Springer.

Feichtinger, Johannes. 2001. *Wissenschaft zwischen den Kulturen—Österreichische Hochschullehrer in der Emigration* 1933–1945.

Friedmann, Wolfgang. 1972. Review Ehrenzweig, Psychoanalytic jurisprudence. *California Law Review* 60: 1718.

Goldstein, Joseph. 1968. Psychoanalysis and jurisprudence. *The Yale Law Journal* 77: 1053.

Halbach Jr., Edward C. 1973. In memoriam Hans Kelsen. *California Law Review* 61: 957.

Hart, H.L.A. 1962–1963. Kelsen visited. *UCLA Law Review* 10:709.

Jestaedt, Matthias. 2008. Hans Kelsens Reine Rechtslehre—Eine Einführung. In *Kelsen, Reine Rechtslehre, Studienausgabe zur 1. Auflage 1934*. I-LVII.

Kelsen, Hans. 1957. The idea of justice in the Holy Scriptures. In *What is justice?* ed. Hans Kelsen. Berkeley: University of California Press.

Kelsen, Hans. 2008. *Reine Rechtslehre*, Studienausgabe der 1. Auflage 1929.

Meiklejohn, David. 1958. Book review: Hans Kelsen, "What is Justice?". *The University of Chicago Law Review* 25: 543.

Northrop, F.S.C. 1958. Book review: Hans Kelsen, "What is Justice?". *Virginia Law Review* 44: 815.

Pareto, Vilfredo. 2014. *Manual of political economy*. Oxford: Oxford University Press.

Ross, Alf. 1957. Book review Hans Kelsen, "What is Justice?". *California Law Review* 45: 564.

Siehr, Kurt. 1957. Ehrenzweigs lex fori-Theorie und ihre Bedeutung für das deutsche und amerikani-sche Kollisionsrecht. *Rabels Zeitschrift für ausländisches und internationales Privatrecht* 34: 585.

Zaremby, Justin. 2014. *Legal Realism and American Law*. New York: Bloomsbury.

Chapter 10
A Morally Enlightened Positivism? Kelsen and Habermas on the Democratic Roots of Validity in Municipal and International Law

David Ingram

10.1 Habermas and Kelsen: Two Neo-Kantian Positivists Confronting Schmittian Decisionism

Renowned are the many writings in which Habermas excoriates positivism in general and legal positivism in particular. So the following tribute to a founding figure in modern legal positivism requires some parsing.

> Hans Kelsen is best known for his legal theory. But he is equally important as a political philosopher and intellectual of the social sciences. During the Weimar period he was one of the few prominent academics who were engaged in the defense of liberal democracy. In a famous controversy with Carl Schmitt, Kelsen was an early advocate of the idea of a Constitutional Court. Even in advance of the foundation of the United Nations, Kelsen developed the design for a cosmopolitan model of compulsory jurisdiction…As much as I admire the fervent spirit of the interventions of the democratic law professor and legal pacifist, so much also can I appreciate Kelsen's philosophical motivation for developing a theory of legal positivism. I agree with his arguments against classical natural right theories, in particular against the Platonist idea of a normative order that is founded in nature rather than invented by the will of human beings. (Habermas 2012a: 1)

Habermas's tribute to Kelsen is noteworthy for being one of the very few places where he discusses Kelsen's positive contributions to legal philosophy at any length. Indeed, most of his scattered references to Kelsen in writings leading up to and including *Faktizität und Geltung* (Habermas 1992), were largely critical in tone, underscoring the normative deficits of and inconsistencies in Kelsen's legal positivism. That changed once Habermas shifted his attention to international law and human rights. Here he enlists the support of Kelsen as an ally against a common nemesis, Carl Schmitt, whose attacks on liberal democracy, constitutional courts,

D. Ingram (✉)
Loyola University of Chicago, Chicago, IL 60660, USA
e-mail: dingram@luc.edu

D.A.J. Telman (ed.), *Hans Kelsen in America - Selective Affinities and the Mysteries of Academic Influence*, Law and Philosophy Library 116,
DOI 10.1007/978-3-319-33130-0_10

international law, and human rights continue to draw support from both Left and Right. In keeping with Habermas's change of heart, we will here examine how Habermas further develops Kelsen's "scientific" analysis of democracy, international governance, and human rights in advancing Christian Wolff's vision of a *civitas maxima*. Conversely, we will examine how Habermas's embrace of Kelsenian legal monism forces him to confront the political nature of constituting and applying international law in all of its humanitarian dimensions.

To situate our comparison of these thinkers it might be useful to recall Schmitt's argument against liberal democracy and human rights (Dyzenhaus 1997). Schmitt argued that law is an empty vessel that derives its entire force from the sovereign will of a person, group, nation, or other extra-legal source of power. This "might makes right" argument seemed especially plausible to Schmitt in light of his Hobbesian analysis of the impotence of the rule of law in modern liberal democracies. In liberal democracy riven by unresolvable ideological conflicts between parties who view the world through the bipolar lens of "friend and foe," the indecisiveness of legislative will inclines toward a permanent constitutional crisis. In such a state of national emergency—which Schmitt imputed to the Weimar regime - only a chief executive who has the supreme power to "decide the exception" can rise above the law, suspend part or all of the constitution, and restore through martial decree the political order and unity without which legal order itself is meaningless (Schmitt 1996: 46, 1985: 5–35). For Schmitt, this "commissarial dictatorship" is legitimated by the presumption of a political will, personified in the nation state, the identity and membership of which is defined solely by a majority that exists in its own right, independent of, and therefore sovereign over, the law. Schmitt also argued, like Hobbes and Hegel before him, that beyond the plurality of national wills there can be no sovereign, for each nation possesses an identity and will that is also irreducibly unique. The impossibility of assimilating nations to a single humanity, possessing its own universal will and sovereign power to decide, renders talk of international law and human rights utterly meaningless, except as an ideological rationale covering up acts of aggression that are undertaken exclusively to advance national interests (Schmitt 1923/1988: 11–17, 1987: 73–89).

Kelsen and Habermas counter Schmitt's realist assault on the rule of law with realist arguments of their own. Departing from the same Hobbesian premises as Schmitt, they acknowledge the weakness of moral motivations and the inadequacy of abstract ideals in resolving modern conflicts between self-interested individuals who subscribe to opposing conceptions of justice and human goodness. But like Kant (Kant: 1996), they insist that the only solution to a state of war wherein persons are disposed to seek unlimited power over others is the rule of law, fully instituted in liberal democracy at the level of state law and in a cosmopolitan human rights regime at the level of international law.[1]

[1] In *Zum Ewigen Frieden* (Kant 1900), Kant departed from Hobbes's hypothetical state of nature, which Hobbes famously characterized as "a war of all against all," in arguing—along thoroughly realist lines—that even a "race of devils" would find it in their mutual self-interest to establish a lawful republic in which their individual rights would be protected. Continuing this realist argu-

Kelsen and Habermas argue that such "idealism" appears eminently more suitable to realizing the psychological aspirations underlying Hobbes's political realism than Schmitt's political-theological postulation of a homogeneous, metaphysical source of national sovereignty that exists above the law. While the Kantian project promises a realistic framework for achieving peace and freedom, the Schmittian project portends imperial warfare and totalitarian genocide in the service of ideology. In the wake of so many horrors that have been committed in the name of national security conducted under the banner of absolute sovereignty, it is no wonder that Habermas looks to Kelsen's monistic theory of law as the pre-eminent exemplar of Kant's project for the twenty-first century.

Kant's argument in defense of an international legal order as a pre-requisite for the secure enjoyment of any rights whatsoever (and therewith, as a pre-requisite for morality as such) is often described as a variant of natural law reasoning from moral premises. Habermas and Kelsen subscribe to this judgment as well, albeit in a qualified way (Kelsen 1946: 445; Habermas 1996: 101).[2] The status of Kantian legal theory is important for both thinkers given their rejection of what Habermas, in the passage cited above, refers to as the Platonism underlying natural law reasoning. For them, law is a human technique (to use Kelsen's terminology) that can be used for many ends besides those conformable to morality, and even laws that originate from just procedures or are supported by moral reasons need not, upon further reflection, be morally justified. But given the important role that natural law reasoning has played in the human rights movement and in the social contractarian defense of liberal democracy, denying the importance of moral justice as a basic requirement for legal validity and legal duty seems antagonistic to their support for a global *civitas maxima* based on democracy and human rights. Leaving aside their own

ment further, Kant observed that republican governments protect the freedom of their citizens by enabling them to channel their acquisitive urges through mutually beneficial economic competition. The appetite for commerce, in turn, inclines republican nations to seek peaceful relations among themselves. By promoting general freedom and happiness, liberal democracy cultivates the peaceful *moeurs douces* observed by Montesquieu. As Kelsen remarks, "the democratic type [of foreign policy] has a definite inclination towards pacificism, the autocratic, towards one of imperialism" (Kelsen 1933/1973: 106). Indeed, according to Michael Doyle, since 1800 no liberal democracies have warred against one another, although powerful democracies have engaged in imperialist ventures against weaker governments with less secure liberal democratic credentials. Kant culminates his realist vision by defending a cosmopolitan legal order as the ultimate guarantor of peace and basic rights. However, against Hobbes's narrow realism, Kant (Kelsen and Habermas concurring) insists that the social contractarian idea underpinning his theory of law cannot be adduced from the empirical psychology of strategically calculating egoists but requires an a prior normative foundation (Doyle 1997: 277–284).

[2] In defense of Kant's legal positivist credentials, Ingeborg Maus (2009: 53) notes that Kant's use of "moralisch" in the opening passages of the *Metaphysik der Sitten* designates all "Gesetze der Freiheit" in opposition to deterministic laws of nature. Kant subdivides morality into ethics (natural morality) and law. Contrary to a natural law theorist such as Locke, Kant insists that the moral right to possession (first occupancy) is superseded by the legal right to acquire and own property: "Original acquisition can only be provisional—Conclusive acquisition takes place only in the civil condition" (Kant 1996: 52). According to Maus, Kant's concept of "morality" occupies a neutral status between law and ethics not unlike Habermas's own discourse principle (D).

questionable understandings of natural law theory[3]—depending on what we mean by the term, Kelsen and Habermas might be characterized as natural law theorists of a sort[4]—it is difficult to understand their rejection of this theory when we recall positivism's poor reputation in the aftermath of the Second World War.

Former positivists such as Gustav Radbruch embraced natural law reasoning as providing the only legal rationale for prosecuting officials of the former Third Reich for humanitarian crimes committed in the course of carrying out legally authorized duties (Radbruch 1946; Paulsen 1994).[5] Justice Robert L. Jackson's opening statement at the Nuremberg Tribunal contending that such crimes were already implicitly, if not expressly, forbidden by international treaty and custom, did not seem particularly compelling on positivist grounds. Indeed, some of these treaties and customs appear to endorse natural law reasoning. The Martens Clause inserted into the preamble to the 1899 Hague Convention governing Regulations on the Laws and Customs of War on Land, for example, appeals to the "laws of humanity" and the "requirements of the public conscience" as compelling and peremptory grounds of international law possessing the status of *jus cogens*. So, in the wake of positivism's massive failure to provide an obvious legal ground for resisting and prosecuting evil acts that were committed in the name of obeying orders commanded by legally authorized superiors, it fell to natural law theory to rebut Schmitt's "might makes right" sanctioning of such commands in its metaphysical appeal to natural rights.

Leaving aside the familiar theoretical counterarguments Kelsen and Habermas marshal against natural law theorizing,[6] it must be conceded that whatever approach they propose in its stead should provide a substitute grounding for cosmopolitan human rights law. Kelsen's defense of a "monistic" conception of law under the supreme aegis of a centralized, hierarchical system of international law takes a

---

[3] John Finnis criticizes Kelsen's view that natural law theorists "from church fathers down to Kant" derive the entire validity and content of positive law from morality and therefore enter into a contradiction when they derive the authority to make law from natural law (Kelsen 1946: 412–413, 416). Finnis rightly notes that this description does not apply to Aquinas's natural law theory, which allows law makers discretion to make laws for all sorts of useful ends, so long as they stay within the broad framework of morally just procedure (Finnis 2011: 26–29). This view is consonant with Habermas's proceduralist (and otherwise positivist) account of legal validity, which I argue is not (pace Habermas) fundamentally different from Kelsen's own.

[4] See n.3. Indeed, in *Between Facts and Norms*, Habermas expressly rejects an argument he developed in *Law and Morality* (1988) that, in natural law fashion, assimilates the discourse principle (D), which according to Habermas founds the democratic legitimacy of law, to the Kantian moral principle of universalizability (U) (Habermas 1996: 108–109).

[5] H.L.A. Hart (1959) criticized the German Courts' post-war deployment of the principle of humanitarianism involving cases where Nazi informants were convicted for following statutes that were (in the opinion of one court) "contrary to the sound conscience and sense of justice of all decent human beings."

[6] Natural law reasoning allegedly runs afoul of scientific reason in deriving an "ought" from an "is" while its "derivation" of law from unchanging morality ostensibly limits or violates positive law's essential instrumental flexibility and alterability (Kelsen 1934/67: 64–69, 219; Habermas 1996: 106). As Kelsen notes, without the law/morality distinction civil disobedience makes no sense (Kelsen 1934/67: 69).

necessary step in this direction, while his and Habermas's arguments for liberal democracy invoke a procedural, rather than directly moral, justification for equal rights (including the equal rights of states under international law). This procedural positivist manner of grounding human rights potentially counters one Schmittian objection that natural law, with its appeal to moral intuitions of a vague and uncertain nature, fails to address: the alleged abstractness, indeterminacy, and political contentiousness of human rights. Once we show that basic rights are procedurally embedded in modern law and democracy, we can then account for their legitimacy and concreteness through their own reflexive application.

But a problem still remains. According to Habermas, Kelsen's positivism is incompatible with a proceduralist defense of human rights and, in fact, unintentionally converges with Schmitt's decisionism. He accuses Kelsen of "sharing with his opponents a genetic account of normative validity" (Habermas 2012a: 1). Because "the source of norms explains the kind of validity that is claimed for them" and the ultimate source is nothing other than the "will of the legislator," viz., his original "decision to establish and enforce them," the ultimate source for the binding power of norms would appear to be nothing more than "a threat of sanctions."

There is some truth to this claim. Kelsen distinguishes moral norms, which take the form of an unconditional duty (or a conditional duty backed by the immediate sanction of conscience), from legal norms, which are backed by the socially organized threat of depriving someone (not necessarily the lawbreaker) of possessions ("life, health, freedom, or property") against that person's will (Kelsen 1957: 233, 35). They are conditional duties that take a hypothetical form: If a person X commits delict A, s/he should suffer punishment P. Importantly, in contrast to Hobbes and Austin, Kelsen insists that laws are not reducible to personal commands backed by threats, because on this reading the highwayman's command "[You should] hand me your money or I'll injure you" is subjectively (psychologically) indistinguishable from a similar command issued by a monarch. But threat of sanction in this sense amounts to the factual prediction that harm will be done unless conditions are met, and the meeting of the condition is understood as a prudential—viz., subjective—obligation contingent on the factual existence of a preference to avoid said harm. The highwayman's command "obligates" subjectively, contingent on the psychological fact, which may not obtain, of a preference to avoid harm, but not objectively, based on a norm. Coercion alone does not obligate compliance with the command—might does not make right; at best it physically compels compliance, and the fact that the addressee "should" obey it means only that s/he would be acting against his/her own interest not to, if his/her interest is to avoid harm. By contrast, the same command issued by a monarch should be obeyed for the additional reason that the threat of coercion has the meaning of law. What makes it a law is not the fact that it is commanded and backed by threat of sanction (which cannot generate a normative obligation, permission, or authorization to punish) but the fact that the command asserts an obligation, ie, embodies a norm.

Habermas himself alludes to a more genuine source of legal validity, namely, "the cognitive authority of some enabling 'procedure' or 'process'…[the] intrinsic features [of which]…rather than the more or less arbitrary choice of the lawmaker," qualifies the result's having a "presumption of validity, or the reasonable expectation of intersubjective recognition" based on "rational acceptability" (Habermas 2012a: 2). Connected to this observation is Habermas's additional concern that "[i]n Kelsen's analysis the moral content of individual rights expressly lost its referent, namely the free will (or 'power to rule') of a person, who from the moral point of view, *deserves* to be protected in her private autonomy" (Habermas 1996: 86).

Kelsen is here alleged to believe that a dictator's command is as binding as a law authorized by a fair democratic procedure. This allegation, I submit, is true only if we focus, as Habermas does, on Kelsen's theory of law in its pure form, abstracted from his legal sociology. Kelsen orients his pure theory of law around a *normative* understanding of legality that reflects the austere assumptions of a *jurist* who is tasked with distinguishing laws from other types of norms. In explaining the special way law obligates, a jurist must assume that law comprises a hierarchical system of valid authorizations anchored by a constitution. This *static* aspect of law concerns law "only in its completed form and in a state of rest" as a system of norms. It concerns the essence of law as a normative system distinct from other normative social systems in its attachment of "a criminal or civil sanction" to norm violations (Kelsen 1946: 39, 122). The validity of the first constitution, not having been authorized by a prior law, must be presupposed as having been authorized by a basic norm (*Grundnorm*).

In the normative syllogism leading to the foundation of the validity of a legal order, the major premise is the ought-sentence which states the basic norm: "One ought to behave according to the actually established and effective constitution"; the minor premise is the is-sentence which states the facts: "The constitution is actually established and effective"; and the conclusion is the ought-sentence: "One ought to behave according to the legal order, that is, the legal order is valid"(Kelsen 1934/1967: 212).

As formulated above, the basic norm appears to endow any constitution—however despotic—with binding force so long as it meets a threshold of effective recognition. But, as we shall see, meeting this latter threshold in modern societies may require that a constitution be democratic rather than despotic.

This becomes apparent when we turn to Habermas's legal theory. In contrast to Kelsen's juridical standpoint, Habermas, orients his thinking around the more robust moral expectations of *legal subject*s inhabiting a modern society who are tasked with finding good reasons why they should voluntarily submit to the law. From this normative perspective, the procedure by which the constitution is generated must satisfy minimal democratic requirements.

Here we encounter an additional layer of validating reasons that pertain exclusively to the *dynamic* creation of law. According to Kelsen, the dynamic aspect of law "furnishes an answer only to the question whether and why a certain norm belongs to a system of valid legal norms, forms part of a certain legal order" (Kelsen 1946: 122) Key to understanding the dynamic aspect of law "in its movement" is the fact that law "regulates its own creation" through legally authorized acts of legislation and adjudication (Kelsen 1957: 245).

Despite their different points of departure—the universal essence of law as a valid form of coercion versus the capacity of a democratic form of legislation to uniquely motivate voluntary compliance with the law—both philosophers regard static and dynamic aspects of law as referring to two inseparable (if analytically distinct) dimensions of legal validity. Both concede that, from the static perspective of a jurist tasked with identifying law, a legal act is validated only if it is constitutional. Both further concede that, from the dynamic perspective of a legal subject tasked with submitting to law, a legal act is validated only if the manner of its generation gives rise to an expectation that said law is prudentially and morally reasonable enough to motivate a legal subject's voluntary compliance. Noting that the moral reasons that motivate people to abide by the law vary within and between societies, Kelsen shares Habermas's opinion that the moral expectations inclining legal subjects inhabiting modern societies to comply with the law principally refer to democratic procedures of lawmaking.

Because these dynamic legal expectations determine not only the normative legitimacy but also the effectiveness (or positive legality) of a constitution, one might doubt whether Kelsen's basic norm is needed to explain our obligation to obey valid law. Again, to recall Kelsen on this point:

> To the question why we ought to obey its [i.e., the historically first constitution's] provision a science of positive law can only answer: the norm that we ought to obey [its] provisions must be presupposed as a hypothesis if the coercive order established on its basis and actually obeyed and applied by those whose behavior it regulates is to be considered a valid legal order binding on these individuals; if the relations among these individuals are to be interpreted as legal duties, legal rights, and legal responsibilities, and not as mere power relations; and if it shall be possible to distinguish between what is legally right and legally wrong and especially between legitimate and illegitimate use of force. This is the basic norm of a positive legal order, the ultimate reason for its validity, seen from the point of view of a science of law (Kelsen 1957: 262).

By 1952, after decades of defending his doctrine of the *Grundnorm*, Kelsen expressed doubts about its necessity: "I have abandoned it seeing that a norm (*Sollen*) must be a correlate of a will (*Wollen*). My basic norm is a fictive norm based on a fictive act of volition…In the basic norm a fictive act of volition is conceived that actually does not exist" Kelsen (1952: 119–120; Paulsen and Paulsen 1998). By the time he wrote the second edition of the *Pure Theory of Law* (1960) he again reversed course, distinguishing the basic norm, as a pure cognitive presupposition, from any constitution or other positive act of will (Kelsen 1934/1967: 204 n.72). Doing so perhaps saved him from the objection that Habermas levels at him, that despite his insistence on subordinating will to norm, he had in fact subordinated norm to will, thereby falling prey to decisionism. But if I am not mistaken, Kelsen's momentary abandonment of normative transcendentalism brought him closer to Habermas's own position, which despite its appeal to transcendental argumentation in grounding a discourse principle (D), is not a foundational theory of moral or legal rights and duties. We may agree with Jochen von Bernstorff that abandoning the *Grundnorm*, with all its foundational and hierarchical aspects, comports better with Kelsen's understanding of law as a reflexive (circular) procedure not dissimilar from Habermas's own (von Bernstorff 2010: 270). And we may then further agree with Hauke Brunkhorst that "we should read Kelsen's theory no longer primarily as a scientific theory of pure legal doctrine, but as a practically oriented theory that anticipates the global revolution of the [twentieth century]" (Brunkhorst 2009: 232).

It may well be that this understanding of the relationship between morality, law, and democracy, which incidentally very few critics have sufficiently appreciated in Kelsen's writings,[7] reaches beyond the purely descriptive status that Kelsen himself accords his scientific legal philosophy.[8] However, if we take seriously his functional definition of law as a tool for securing peaceful cooperation as well as his theory of legal evolution, it becomes clear that the totality of his legal theory strongly inclines

[7] Many critics of Kelsen repeat Habermas's (in my opinion, mistaken) criticism that "Kelsen's type of legal formalism is not sufficiently dynamic to ensure that the imperatives of administrative power remain accountable to the democratic will" (McCormick 1997: 737). Others (Kalyvas 2006: 584–586) argue that Kelsen traces the legitimacy of the constitution to "the contingent act of a first legislator," despite the fact he and Habermas both conceive modern constitutional law as a reflexive learning process that draws its full legitimacy from in-built normative expectations. Also see Gümplová (2011: 17).

[8] Lars Vinx, for example, asserts that "Kelsen's position, is in some important respects, not positivist because it affirms, rather than denies, a necessary connection between legality and legitimacy" (Vinx 2007: 214–215). In arguing that Kelsen "tries to…read autocratic legal systems as anticipations of a legal order that more fully realizes the ideal of the rule of law" (Vinx 2007: 212)—what Vinx elsewhere refers to as a "utopia of legality" (Vinx 2007: 73–74)—Vinx in fact comes close to interpreting Kelsen as a natural law theorist. In Vinx's opinion, to presuppose a basic norm "is to postulate that exercises of coercive force that take place under the authorization of that basic norm are, in some sense and to some extent, morally justified" so that "without this assumption, Kelsenian normative legal science would be pointless" (Vinx 2007: 56). As Neil Duxbury (2007) notes, the main textual evidence Vinx offers to support this revisionist interpretation of Kelsen's theory (which he concedes flies in the face of Kelsen's own self-understanding as a legal scientist) is a passage from Kelsen's early *Rechtsstaat und Staatsrecht*, where Kelsen writes, "Die Rechtsstaatsidee aber ist noch nicht überwunden, ihre allseitige rechtslogische Entwicklung bleibt aufgabe der Zukunft" (The "idea of the rule-of-law state…is not yet vanquished (überwunden); its comprehensive legal-logical development remains the task of the future") (Kelsen 1913/2010: 155). Duxbury correctly notes that whatever this statement might have meant prior to Kelsen's mature development of the pure theory of law in 1920, the meaning Vinx attributes to it stands in stark contrast, not only to Kelsen's vision of legal science as purely descriptive and value free but also Kelsen's belief that majoritarian governments may be lawfully replaced by autocratic governments—objections to his interpretation that Vinx himself notes (Vinx 2007: 56, 131, 217). In fact, Vinx's interpretation of Kelsen would better apply to Habermas's reconstructive approach to law, which sees a kind of normative (even moral) teleology at work in legal evolution (see below), one that enables him to establish a conceptual co-originality between rights and democracy, while at the same time acknowledging that this necessary link remains implicit and undeveloped (or anticipated) in the pre-liberal, pre-democratic *Rechtsstaat*. I suggest that a better way to defend Kelsen's support for a "utopia of legality" is by appealing to Kelsen's sociology of law and especially his Weberian account of social evolution (modernization). According to this reading, liberal democracy is the legal form that best accords with the peace-seeking motivations and moral expectations of modern, rationalized (scientifically enlightened) societies. Of course, this argument—which matches normatively imbued, legal ideal types (autocracy v. democracy) with social, ethico-political *Weltanschauungen*—also relies on purely descriptive premises, which is to say that its "defense" of liberal democracy is premised on the latter's empirical (adaptive) efficiency in response to integration problems peculiar to modern social complexity. I think a similar kind of reading can be extended to Kelsen's earlier "ethico-politico" preference for a *civitas maxima* anchored in a world state; for here, too, evolutionary changes in international relations leading to the universal aspiration for equality and independence among all nations flies in the face of the older, Westphalian regime of unrestricted state sovereignty.

toward a positive moral assessment of liberal democracy and cosmopolitan law as twin pillars of a fully realized rule of law.

10.2 Kelsen and Habermas on Democracy

Habermas and Kelsen develop their theories of democracy in the shadow of Schmitt's attacks on liberalism as a sterile ideology of rational, consensual discussion, the parliamentary institutionalization of which allegedly evinces all the anti-democratic evils of majoritarian class-based tyranny (Schmitt 1923/1988: 3–6).[9] They accordingly reject the assumption of an undivided sovereign will that informs Schmitt's notion of democracy as incompatible with modern social differentiation and value pluralism, insisting instead that a democratic will can at best assume the form of a non-hegemonic compromise constituted by open and inclusive deliberation among free and equals.

This deliberative model of democracy is famously developed by Habermas as an extension of his discourse theory of normative validity. Like Kelsen, Habermas grounds legal validity in a basic norm. Unlike Kelsen's *Grundnorm*, Habermas's principle of discourse (D) designates a norm that informs only those modern legal systems in which members are permitted the freedom to pursue individual aims. (D) reflects this accent on modern subjective freedom in its emphasis on individual consent as a criterion of validation: "just those action norms are valid to which all

[9] In *Strukturwandel der Öffentlichkeit* (Habermas 1962) Habermas accepted much of Schmitt's indictment of mass democracy as well as Schmitt's concern about the tendency of liberal ideology to "suppress" politicized conflict behind the veneer of a transcendent rational harmony of interests or, conversely, behind the veneer of an atomization of private interests (Habermas 1962/89: 81, 205). In this respect he followed in the footsteps of earlier critical theorists. Despite Schmitt's disdain for Marxism, which espoused corporatist conceptions of representation that he thought were corrosive of any unified state, some of his most famous students were Marxists who shared his critique of the modern state. Franz Neumann and Walter Benjamin both came under Schmitt's spell. Otto Kirchheimer, who, along with these thinkers, would later associate himself with the Frankfurt School, argued in his dissertation (written under Schmitt's direction) that parliamentary democracies instituted on a capitalist base inevitably lack legitimacy. In his opinion, the sphere of private law allows capitalist enterprises to contest the sovereignty of the state in asserting their own partial interests in the form of statutory protections. The solution to this problem, Kirchheimer argued, was the abolition of an autonomous sphere of private law immune from democratic regulation by the state. Thirty odd years later Kirchheimer's Schmittian diagnosis of capitalist democracy would resurface in Habermas's *Strukturwandel*, which documented the decline of a liberal public sphere grounded in rational, open debate in the face of propagandistic class democracy. Habermas's later masterpiece, *Legitimation Crisis* (1973), continued to frame this diagnosis in terms of a vaguely Schmittian conception of legitimacy, understood as a process of democratic will formation having legal results that reflect a unitary consensus on common interests, as distinct from a strategic compromise that balances plural interests according to their relative degree of political power. This notion of legitimacy —which Habermas has since considerably qualified—was presented in a way that opposed the separation of powers, the private law/public law distinction, the grounding of legal policy in class compromise, and other liberal principles.

possibly affected persons could agree as participants in rational discourse" (Habermas 1996: 107). More precisely, Habermas adduces (D) from the requirements of a "post-conventional" ethos of individual accountability. This ethos requires that persons coordinate their actions by offering to defend the reasonableness and reliability of their commitments to each other beyond asserting a desire to pursue personal ends. In so doing they claim (tacitly if not expressly) that the facts and norms around which they orient their behavior reflect beliefs, the truth (or rightness) of which, can be justified to others.

Justification of such claims (*Geltungsansprüche*) here has both a vertical (hierarchical) and horizontal (symmetrical) structure. The substantive arguments persons present to each other must be capable of being made at ascending levels of generality and depth. Most importantly, within a post-conventional moral setting, persons will typically suppose some higher normative principles (such as human rights) in justifying the permissibility or necessity of their actions. A moral principle of universalizability (U) thus functions as a kind of foundational basic norm, which follows "abductively," Habermas believes, from other assumptions regarding rational discourse and communicative interaction (Habermas 2012a: 17).

Superficially, Habermas's appeal to one of these assumptions, the principle of discourse (D) noted above, looks suspiciously like the social contractarian principle of self-authorized obligation:

> With the loss of the religious promise of salvation…"validity" now signifies that moral norms could win the agreement of all concerned [as being] in the equal interest of all. This agreement expresses…the freedom of legislating subjects who understand themselves as the authors of those norms to which they subject themselves as addressees (Habermas 2012a: 13).

Stated thus without further qualification, the argument contained in this passage appears to succumb to Kelsen's following objection:

> The doctrine of the basic norm is not a doctrine of recognition as is sometimes erroneously understood. According to the doctrine of recognition positive law is valid only if it is recognized by the individuals subject to it, which means: if these individuals agree that one ought to behave according to the norms of positive law. This recognition, it is said, actually takes place, and if this cannot be proved, it is assumed, fictitiously, as tacit recognition. The theory of recognition, consciously or unconsciously, presupposes the ideal of individual liberty as self-determination, that is, the norm that the individual ought to do only what he wants to do. This is the basic norm of this theory. The difference between it and the theory of the basic norm of a positive legal order, as taught by the *Pure Theory of Law*, is evident (Kelsen 1934/1967: 218 n.83).

Kelsen here reiterates his familiar logical point that an "ought" cannot be derived from an "is." The fact that people all want something and therefore agree to it, as in the fiction of the social contract, does not mean that they ought to want it. Will or collective might cannot constitute right. For the social contractarian conception of legal validity to get off the ground, logically speaking, some prior basic norm would have to be presupposed, such as "the individual ought to do only what he wants (agrees) to do." This "basic norm," however, is entirely incompatible with any system of positive law. Self-obligation (self-determination, self-legislation, self-authorization) are metaphysical conceptions that traditionally define conceptions of divine sovereignty, but which are logically incoherent and, in any case, conflate volition with normativity (cognition).

Does Habermas's principle (D) commit the is/ought fallacy Kelsen describes? A closer reading of Habermas suggests that it does not.

> [P]rocedural characteristics of the process of argumentation itself must ultimately bear the burden of explaining why results achieved in a procedurally correct manner enjoy the presumption of validity. For example, the presuppositions of rational discourse demand that all relevant contributions have their say and that the unforced force of the better argument alone determines the "yes" and "no" responses of the participants (Habermas 2012a: 14).... Instead of an objective world presupposed to exist independently of us, what is not in our power to accept or reject here is the moral point of view. In communicative action, the moral point of view is imposed on our minds. It is not the social world as such that is not at our disposal but the structure and procedure of a process of argumentation which facilitates both the production and discovery of the norms of a properly regulated existence (Habermas 2012a: 15).

In light of modern value pluralism, the only neutral (universally shared) normative principle people can rely on for settling disputes and reaching agreement must be "some intrinsic feature of the practice of deliberation" itself—Habermas's principle (D). But an agreement reached according to this principle "cannot be understood as a contract (*Vereinbarung*) which is rationally motivated from the egocentric perspective of each individual" (Habermas 2012a: 17). For (D) refers to a conception of procedural justice that captures not only the equality and autonomy of speakers but also their empathetic solidarity (or friendship) toward each other (Habermas 2012a: 8, 9, 12); viz., their willingness to alter their interests and perspectives to reasonably accommodate the interests and perspectives of consociates.

More precisely, (D) requires:

> (a) that nobody who could make a relevant contribution may be excluded, (b) that all participants are afforded an equal opportunity to make contributions, (c) that the participants must mean what they say, and only truthful utterances are admissible, and (d) that communication must be freed from external and internal compulsion so that "yes"/"no" stances the participants adopt on criticizable validity claims are motivated solely by the rational force of better reasons (Habermas 2012a: 19).

The defense of (a)–(d) as intrinsic features of (D) appeals to a "transcendental argument," which shows that the "*argumentative* duties and rights" implied in (a)–(d)—duties and rights that are not moral duties and rights, but enabling rules that are "constitutive for the game of argumentation"—cannot be denied by participants in discourse without entering into a "performative contradiction" (Habermas 2012a: 1). Thus we have, as in Kelsen, the transcendental-logical defense of a basic norm (D) underlying validity—a defense that appeals to a vertical, non-circular, conception of validity.

According to Habermas, because "moral insight is based on the weak force of epistemic reasons and does not itself constitute a rational motive as in the case of pragmatic reasons," the "weak motivating force of morality in many areas needs to be compensated by coercive law" (Habermas 2012a: 13). Indeed, (D) itself is neutral between the kinds of norms—moral, ethical, and legal—to which it might apply. When applied to moral discourses, it assumes the role of a principle of argumentation (U) that requires a *strong cognitive* orientation toward reaching universal consensus. When applied to ethical discourses, (D) loses this strong cognitive orientation in recognition of the fact that values and other desired ends are intersubjectively valid only for a specific group or community. As we shall see, contrary to Habermas's depiction of him as a value skeptic, Kelsen himself generally interprets ethical life as evincing just this kind of weak cognitivism (Habermas 2012a: 4–7).

When applied to law rather than to moral or ethical deliberation, (D) loses its status as a principle of argumentation. Linked to the modern legal form of "subjective" (or permissive) rights, it becomes a principle of democratic *legitimation* (PD) which asserts: "Only those [freedom-granting] statutes may claim legitimacy that can meet with the assent of all citizens in a discourse process of legislation that in turn has been legally constituted" (Habermas 1996: 110). (PD) thus presupposes a system of basic rights: a legal code specifying, in addition to subjective rights (freedom from non-interference), rights to membership and legal due process. Giving determinate meaning and prescriptive force to this abstract legal code requires legislation, and (pursuant to PD) democratic participatory rights. Finally, securing the "fair value" of these rights requires social rights to education, health, and welfare (Habermas 1996: 123).

Constitutions entrench these rights as well as the legislative, judicial, and executive institutions that apply them according to institution-specific democratic procedures. Following Habermas, we detect a kind of Kelsenian monism in the way that the constitution authorizes all law (even customary or common law), as well as in the way that "communicative power" authorizes state power generally. On one hand, validation descends from (D) through (PD), the system of basic rights, the constitution, and the various levels of law creation and application. On the other hand, a uni-directional constitutional flow of political power is set in motion from the "periphery," located in the informally organized public sphere, and directed toward the formally organized legal system, or "center." Thus, public opinion remains the supreme authority for setting the legislative agenda (Habermas 1996: 150, 170, 182). Social concerns originating in the periphery are suitably reformulated as policies and modified on the basis of negotiated compromises by the center. However, to comply with the stringent procedural justice embedded in (D), compromises that balance competing interests should only be negotiated after good-faith attempts at reaching consensus on generalizable interests have failed. Habermas accordingly rejects the skeptical presumption that competing interests cannot be transformed into harmonious or shared interests. This presumption would permit the imposition of "pseudo-compromises" that enable the majority to impose its will unilaterally without considering the minority's interests (Habermas 1975: 112). By contrast, (D) requires "an equal opportunity for pressure, that is, an equal opportunity to influence one another during the actual bargaining, so that all the affected interests can come into play and have equal chances of prevailing"(Habermas 1996: 167).

Finally, Habermas warns that this impression of a Kelsenian *Stufenbau* (or hierarchical authorization of subordinate acts) within a legitimate circulation of legal power should not obscure the genuine circular (or reflexive) nature of the legal system. Not only do official decision-makers unavoidably reformulate the concerns and arguments drawn from public deliberation, but judges and administrators reformulate and develop the laws that limit their individual actions. Far from being a mechanical process of application that rigidly preserves legal contents without addition, such decision-making, Habermas insists, is unavoidably interpretative (Habermas 1996: 182).

As I noted above (and as I shall argue below) Kelsen's own understanding of the reflexive creation of law as a process involving judges and administrators departs from the image of a *Stufenbau* to the point of rendering otiose any practical presumption of a *Grundnorm*. That said, Habermas's philosophical reconstruction of the conceptual linkage of law, democracy, and justice finds no parallel in Kelsen's writings. But a parallel does exist when we turn to the functional linkages between democracy and modernity elaborated in their respective sociological treatments of law. Drawing from Weber's account of modern law, Habermas and Kelsen regard liberal democracy as a logical correlate to cultural "rationalization." For Kelsen and Habermas, bureaucratic administration and parliamentary systems of political representation—no less than the constitution of the individual as a legal holder of rights—emerge as adaptive responses to cultural changes that accompany revolutionary socio-economic transformations. Citing Weber against Marxists and Schmittian romantics, Kelsen warns that "the abolition of a professional bureaucracy (*Berufsbeamtentums*), no less than the rejection of parliamentarianism, is simply a negation (*Aufhebung*) of the division of labor and therewith of that progressive development, that cultural differentiation within political life" (Kelsen 1920b: 24). No doubt Marxists and their reactionary counterparts are right to worry that the stratification and ideological fragmentation of capitalist societies premised on the rational notion of a modern legal subject threatens to undermine the legitimacy of the legal order. But Kelsen maintains that social and political integration based on shared moral principles can be advanced by means of democratic institutions that protect minorities and vulnerable economic classes while encouraging discursive will-formation through compromise. In a remarkable passage that could have been penned by Habermas, Kelsen writes:

> Here precisely resides a decisive advantage of democracy and its majoritarian principle, that it nonetheless secures by means of the simplest organization a certain political integration of a society legally regulated by a state (*Staatsgesellschaft*)...That the "will of the state" created juristically is supposedly the "will of the people" is thus itself a fiction—albeit a fiction closest to reality—*so long as the procedure for creating the will is democratically organized* (Kelsen 1920b: 28 (emphasis added)).

It should be added that, although Habermas and Kelsen reject proletarian democracy as a regression to premodern *Gemeinschaft*, they regard social welfare as an *inevitable* compromise required by the egalitarian solidarity underwriting democratic citizenship.[10]

[10]After criticizing the Marxist idea of a radical workers democracy, Kelsen makes the following comment: "Doubtless the ideal of the greatest economic equality is a democratic ideal. And therefore social democracy is a perfect (*vollkommene*) democracy" (Kelsen 1920b: 35).

Habermas and Kelsen thus defend liberal democracy as the most optimal regime for integrating polities premised on modern, rationally enlightened, cultural expectations (Habermas 1996: 139–146; Kelsen 1957: 31–38, 244–256). As a manifestation of cultural modernity, legal evolution obeys the same logic of functional differentiation and formal integration typical of other institutional spheres. Just as universalistic morality extrudes empirical and religious grounds in its systemic hierarchy of norms, so law extrudes partisan moral grounds in its specialized hierarchy of judicial, executive, and legislative procedures. Yet both Habermas and Kelsen insist that, despite their functioning as coercive techniques for achieving non-moral social and political ends, these procedures retain a residual link to post-conventional ideas of moral justice (Kelsen 1920b: 26). As we shall see, Kelsen no less than Habermas insists that modern legal orders can be stabilized only by institutionalizing toleration, individual rights, and solidaristic deliberation as a way of negotiating reasonable compromises.

To be sure, Habermas is less convinced that democracy is functional for stabilizing modern class societies. One need only recall his notorious indictment of capitalism for privileging the functional imperative of bureaucratically administered economic growth over the moral imperative of democratic deliberation to appreciate how far more problematic his understanding of modern democracy under late global capitalism is than Kelsen's (Habermas 1987: 356–373). Habermas's understanding of modern democracy, informed as it is by a dialectical opposition between different processes of cognitive learning (scientific-technical versus moral-practical) and social integration/reproduction (systemic-functional versus communicative-lifeworld-embedded), situates law at the crossroads of both sides of this opposition.

As one might expect, Habermas's distinction between law as a medium of administrative power and law as a normative institution underscores the dialectical connection between these aspects. As always, the normative aspect—here reflected in a constitutional system of rights—grounds the administrative aspect, which regulates a civil society of strategic actors governed by private law. In his Tanner Lectures (1988), Habermas especially emphasized the crucial link between modern normative legal institutions and early modern natural law theory. In order for law to be conceived as an "autonomous" system of *norms* distinct from the power–backed commands of a ruler it must have the force of *unconditional morality*. Kelsen's demarcation of the legal from the moral in terms of the coercive form of law alone —the central thesis of Kelsen's static account of law—fails, Habermas notes, because the concept of *valid* coercion that distinguishes legal coercion from coercion *simpliciter* must be conceived as emanating from a source that transcends the factual threat of sanction (Habermas 1988: 263). The motivation to obey the law out of respect for its intrinsic goodness would require grounding the authority of law in the sacral realm of absolute ends. Contrary to Kelsen's evolutionary account of law out of tribal custom, Habermas insists that tribal societies that resolve internal conflicts through magical oracles, trials of endurance, ritual combat, self-defense, vendetta retribution, or non-binding peaceful arbitration, have yet to evolve any distinctly *normative* conception of law, because they have not infused their preconventional morality with an understanding of divine ends that transcend immediate interests. In order to become a medium of normatively sanctioned coercion, law needed to be infused with an evolutionarily more advanced morality that judges actions by their intentions and not solely by their consequences and that places cosmic justice and the highest good above the immediate satisfaction of interests (Habermas 1988: 264–267). Compelled by an internal logic of rationalization, such conventional moral-legal systems, eventually evolved (Habermas speculates) into post-conventional, natural law-founded, legal orders.

From this perspective, Habermas claims, positivists like Kelsen fail to appreciate the extent to which morality is not simply exported into law by positive fiat but constitutes law's very normativity. In modern conceptions of the rule of law, this normativity encompasses a basic respect for the dignity of the individual legal subject as an autonomous agent (Habermas 1988: 274). Conceptions of legal due process in Anglo-American law emerging as early as the seventeenth century already embody an argumentative procedure that evinces this respect. Civil and political rights likewise constitute the procedure of democratic legislation from within (viz., conceptually) and not merely as adventitious moral contents that just happen to be legally posited by a first legislator (Habermas 1988: 268–279) Despite this internal connection between law and morality, which liberal natural law theory conceptualizes in its foundational understanding of human rights, basic rights (including "intrinsically valuable" liberal rights to life, property, freedom of movement, etc.) are not external limits upon democratic procedure, as liberal natural law theory would have it; they are rather its enabling conditions (Habermas 2001a: 770–771, 776–780). Every subsequent legal act "reflexively" expands the inclusiveness, equality and freedom vouchsafed by this foundational right, so that we may speak of the constitution as a learning project, the binding force (justice) of which actually increases over time (Habermas 2001a: 774–776).

Although we might concede Habermas's point that Kelsen under-appreciates the *conceptual* link between post-conventional morality and constitutional law,[11] it would be wrong to conclude that Kelsen overlooks the *functional* conjunction of these terms within modern democracy. Kelsen observes that legal institutions become democratic in response to modern social complexity; furthermore, he agrees with Habermas that basic rights and minority protections are *intrinsic* qualities of modern democracy. Finally, like Habermas, he notes that modern democracies are dynamic learning processes that reflexively realize their emancipatory potential:

[11] Kelsen's legal theory, Habermas claims, converges with the legal systems theory developed by Niklas Luhman and his epigones (Habermas 1988: 263, 1996: 86), thereby offering no resistance to the "colonization of the lifeworld" (Habermas 1975: 40–50, 71–92, 1987: 356–373). Notwithstanding this objection, Habermas concedes that"autochthonously functioning" subsystems depend on democratic input for their optimal coordination and functioning (Habermas 1996: 350–352). What Habermas adds to Kelsen's functionalist defense of democracy is his grounding of modernization in a distinctly normative theory of communicative action (Habermas 1987: 142–43, 341–342, 359–360).

> If we define democracy as a political method by which the social order is created and applied by those subject to the order, so that political freedom, in the sense of self-determination, is secured, then democracy necessarily, always and everywhere, serves this ideal of political freedom. And if we include in our definition the idea that the social order, created in the way just indicated, in order to be democratic, must guarantee certain intellectual freedoms, such as freedom of conscience, freedom of press, etc., then democracy necessarily, always and everywhere, serves the ideal of intellectual freedom (Kelsen 1955: 4).

Later, in the same work, Kelsen continues:

> Modern democracy cannot be separated from political liberalism. Its principle is that the government must not interfere with certain spheres of interest of the individual, which are to be protected by law as fundamental human rights or freedoms. It is by the respect of these rights that minorities are safeguarded against arbitrary rule by majorities (Kelsen 1955: 28 (emphasis added)).

At the center of Kelsen's conception of modern democracy is "political liberalism," or the idea of basic human rights that cannot be infringed upon by the majority. The most important of these rights are civil rights, such as freedom of speech, of press, of conscience, and of association, that serve the "ideal of intellectual freedom." Intellectual freedom includes freedom from domination as well as positive self-determination. Without the protection of dissenting voices, the discussions necessary for generating an autonomous, unified political will would be incapable of integrating groups of widely opposed interests and ideologies. Indeed, with Schmitt no doubt in the back of his mind, Kelsen maintains that citizens of a liberal democracy are procedurally committed to relating to each other as friends bound by mutual cooperation and benefit.

> The principle of majority, the greatest possible approximation to the idea of freedom in political reality, presupposes as an essential condition the principle of equality…that all individuals are of equal political value and that everyone has the same claim to freedom… *The personality whose desire for freedom is modified by his feeling of equality recognizes himself in the other.* He represents the altruistic type, for he does not experience the other as an enemy but is inclined to see in his fellowman his friend. Because the permanent tension between majority and minority, government and opposition, results in the dialectical process so characteristic of the democratic formation of the will of the state, one rightly may say*: democracy is discussion* (Kelsen 1955: 25, 26 (emphasis added)).

The coincidence of Kelsen's idea of democracy and Habermas's is amply borne out by their common emphasis on the role of discussion. Despite Kelsen's concession to the "disenchanted" scientific spirit of the modern age, which promotes skepticism regarding all dogmatic ideologies and an awareness of the relativity of value orientations,[12] his reference to discussion as a medium of mutual recognition and solidarity holds open the possibility that skepticism can give way to knowledge, or

[12] Habermas and Kelsen assess the cognitive advantages of deliberative democracy somewhat differently. For Habermas, democracy generates an ideal expectation that laws and official decisions are (or could be) singularly just and correct. For Kelsen, by contrast, "[o]nly if it is not possible to decide in an absolute way what is right and what is wrong is it advisable to discuss the issue and, after discussion, to submit it to a compromise" (Kelsen 1955: 39). I discuss the implication of this disagreement in Part 8.4.

at least to a reasonable understanding of what is good and right sufficient to transform antagonistic ends into a common political will. Such a will need not (and typically does not) express a consensus on the rationales or interests that ought to be served. Consequently, Kelsen adds that:

> ...the content of [democratic] legal order may be a compromise. Because [democracy] guarantees internal peace, it is preferred by the peace-loving, non-aggressive type....[T]he respect for science corresponds perfectly to that kind of person which we have described as specifically democratic. *In the great dilemma of volition and cognition, between the wish to dominate the world and that to understand it, the pendulum swings more in the direction of cognition than volition...because with this type of character the will to power, the intensity of ego experience, is relatively reduced and self-criticism relatively strengthened* (Kelsen 1955: 28 (emphasis added)).

The above citation strongly suggests that Kelsen and Habermas share remarkably similar views about how democratic procedural justice advances a rational learning process in which mutual (self-) criticism leads to moderation and accommodation of differences. Thanks to the mutual enlightenment of one's own and others' interests vouchsafed by deliberative democracy, citizens have a right to expect that the law will respect, if not advance, each of their interests equally.

10.3 Habermas and Kelsen on International Law and Human Rights

Habermas's failure to acknowledge the proximity of Kelsen's thinking to his own reflections on democracy and law is not repeated in his writings on international law. Indeed, Kelsen himself anticipates the relevance of democratic theory to international law:

> *The democratic type (of government) has a definite inclination towards an ideal of pacificism, the autocratic, towards one of imperialism....The aim of [a] war [may be the] final establishment of peace through a world organization which bears all the marks of democracy: a community of states having equal rights under a mutually agreed tribunal for the settlement of disputes, if possible a world court, as a first step to the evolution towards a world state*; a notion which is not only of no political value to an autocratic and imperialistic outlook, but which, owing to the dreary leveling and weakening of national differences involved, implies, in effect, the downfall of culture (Kelsen 1933/1973: 106–107(emphasis added)).

To paraphrase Kelsen, if liberal democracy within a local jurisdiction has proven to be essential for guaranteeing peace among free and equal citizens, its global extension through a world-wide organization may be presumed to be likewise essential for guaranteeing peace among free and equal states. Indeed, Hobbesian realism teaches that states are assured of their sovereign independence only when a higher sovereign protects them from aggression (Kelsen 1944b: 207–208, 1934/1967: 34). The worry that a world state will destroy the sovereignty of its subordinate members is therefore as groundless as the worry that lawful order is inimical to individual freedom. Far from destroying national cultural differences, a world state provides the cosmopolitan shelter of human rights and toleration that enables such individual differences to flourish.

Kelsen's defense of cosmopolitan legal order also reflects a realistic (Hobbesian) assessment of the limits of morality in securing human rights. These limits were cited by Schmitt as a reason for rejecting human rights *in toto*: "When a state fights its political enemy in the name of humanity, it is not a war for the sake of humanity, but rather a war wherein a particular state seeks to usurp a universal concept in its struggle against its enemy" (Schmitt 1932/1996: 54). Schmitt's challenge to cosmopolitans, however, goes beyond demonstrating the emptiness of human rights moralizing. It denies the very possibility of meaningful human rights law as something distinct from the lawful rights recognized by nation states.

Kelsen's definition of the state as a system of legal norms (the identity thesis) and his argument that territorially overlapping systems of law logically imply a higher, overarching system of law from which they derive their authority (the monism thesis) lays the foundation for a response to Schmitt's challenge. Kelsen's articulation of this response in *Das Problem der Soveränität (1920)* demolishes the state/law dualism prevalent among jurists at the time, to wit, that the state embodies a political identity and will independent of its legal constitution. By doing so, it further demolishes the idea of legal pluralism, or the idea that states constitute themselves as independently self-contained and sovereign loci of legal authority. For Kelsen, on the contrary, the rights of a state conceived as a geographically and temporally bounded legal person interacting with other such persons must be conferred upon it by an authority other than itself: international law (Kelsen 1920a: 9–53).

The fact that a state does not exist until it has been legally recognized by other states only shows that, from the standpoint of these other states, it cannot be regarded as legally self-authorizing.[13] However, each state regards itself as legally self-authorizing (sovereign). Hence the question returns in a slightly different form: Why can't a state claim its rights in defiance of international recognition?

[13] Kelsen's monism, in both its domestic and international applications, has come under attack by pluralists such as F. Rigaux, H.L.A. Hart, and Joseph Raz (Rigaux 1998; Hart 1983: 309–342; Raz 1979: 122–145). Raz, for instance, raises two main counter-examples to the thesis: the presence of distinct customary and statutory sources (basic norms) of law within the same legal system and, in the case of former colonies being granted independence, the authorization of a new state constitutional order (basic norm) by another state constitutional order, in which both orders (basic norms) are considered distinct yet equally authoritative. As Vinx notes, for Kelsen, the first counter-example is not compelling because any legal system will designate a higher (constitutional) authority as a common source specifying how conflicts between customary and statutory law are to be resolved (usually in favor of the latter) (Vinx 2007: 184). The second counter-example fails because it can be interpreted in two ways that comport with Kelsenian monism: if a former colony sees itself as breaking with the mother country in a revolutionary manner, it will not regard its constitution as standing in a relationship of continuity with the constitution of the mother country, in which case its constitution will be seen as grounding an entirely separate order. If it does not see itself as breaking with the mother country (as perhaps exists in the case of British Commonwealth countries today), then by definition it recognizes its order as in some sense co-extensive with the basic norm of the mother country (some British Commonwealth countries may recognize the British monarch as the titular if symbolic authority behind their law).

Kelsen demonstrates the absurdity of such a notion by attacking the idea of legal pluralism that resides at its center. Because a legal system is presumed to be absolutely sovereign over its jurisdiction in all matters that affect it, internal as well as external (Kelsen 1920a: 45), only one truly sovereign (self-authorizing) legal system can exist. But which system? Does the system of international law delegate rights to state organs or do these organs delegate rights to international law, in the manner of a social contract (or treaty ratification)? The conventional answer affirms the second alternative. But this alternative is improperly stated. If state law were absolutely sovereign, the state would not be legally bound by international treaties. In that case, a system of international law would be impossible (Kelsen 1920a: 196). But a state of nature composed of multiple states would also be impossible. Because each state would interpret the legality of any action affecting it from the standpoint of its own system, the legality of any action affecting multiple states would not be decidable (Kelsen 1920a: 206). In order to avoid this result, each state must deny the sovereignty of all other states and regard its own law as globally supreme. Although Kelsen concedes the coherence of this kind of legal monism (Kelsen 1920a: 129, 134), he notes that it would logically entail an imperialistic power politics at odds with the rule of law (Kelsen 1920a: 317 ff); for the destruction of an objective legal order would unleash a solipsistic will to power *incompatible with normativity as such* (Kelsen 1920a: 315, 317).[14]

Having demonstrated the logical absurdity of a global order composed of multiple sovereign states, Kelsen observes that only a single world state can guarantee the rights of subordinate legal regimes and their legal subjects (Kelsen 1920a: 319). Indeed, social evolution consists in nothing but the humanistic overcoming of subjectivism in all its forms. If normativity is what distinguishes the objective rule of law from the subjective rule of violence, then it is not exaggerating to say that law first appears with the advent of the *Rechtsstaat* and comes to full fruition with the creation of a *civitas maxima.* Advocating on behalf of a legal order he originally sought only to describe, Kelsen concludes his treatise on the problem of sovereignty with the admonition that "all political striving must be put to the infinite task of realizing such a world state as a world organization" (Kelsen 1920a: 320).

Defending "a [global] monistic constitutional political order" almost a century after these words were penned, Habermas observes that "[t]he classical meaning of sovereignty has already shifted in a direction anticipated by Hans Kelsen (Habermas 2008b: 449). Today the sovereign state is supposed to function as a fallible agent of the world community; under the threat of sanctions, it performs the role of guaranteeing human rights in the form of basic legal rights to all citizens equally within its national borders" (Habermas 2008b, 453). Habermas could have called this world community that lawfully compels governments to respect the human rights of persons within their jurisdiction a world state but for the fact that its capacity to threaten sanctions is limited to certain rights violations and depends on the willingness of

[14]The trajectory from Schmittian subjectivism to Kelsenian objectivism laid out here defines the career of the founder of the realist school of international relations, Hans Morgenthau (Morgenthau 1948; Jütersonke 2010; Koskenneimi 2002; Engel 1964).

governments to offer up their sanction of last resort: military intervention. The precedent for this model of a primitive world state is thoroughly Kelsenian.

In his first detailed proposal for transforming the League of Nations into a Permanent League of the Maintenance of Peace, *Peace Through Law* (1944), Kelsen conceives this primitive world state as a non-voluntary league of nations consisting of members' whose rights and duties have already been authorized by an even more primitive form of international law, the ancient custom of respecting treaties (*pacta sunt servanda).* In primitive legal systems, this custom is enforced through the principle of self-help; in the absence of international courts and enforcement mechanisms aggrieved states must take it upon themselves to sanction delicts through war. Because neither the League nor the U.N. Charter (1945) provided proxies for these mechanisms, Kelsen again enlisted the support of a *bellum justum* doctrine to remedy this shortfall, a position that placed him at odds with the Kellogg-Briand Pact (1928) and the Charter, both of which permit only defensive warfare (Kelsen 1944a: 18, 1952/1966: 16–87; Landauer 2003). Conceding the danger and illegality of such a doctrine, he advocated strenuously on behalf of a more impartial application of the war sanction that would require the creation of an international tribunal (Kelsen 1944a: 12). Because the Moscow Declaration (1943) had insisted on the (equal) sovereignty of states, Kelsen proposed only the creation of international courts coupled with the compulsory adjudication of all inter-state and state-individual disputes as the centerpiece of his proposal (Kelsen 1944a: 12–15, 19–23). According to Kelsen's proposal, the international court would have jurisdiction over all disputes *including political disputes* and decisions would be made by majority principle, thereby overcoming the chief weakness of the Council of the League of Nations, in which binding decisions had to be unanimous (Kelsen 1944a: 23–32, 43, 50).

Like Kelsen, Habermas views human rights courts as the centerpiece of any currently feasible global legal regime. That said, his own proposals for a global constitution go well beyond Kelsen's vision of an international regime headed by international courts, albeit in a direction Kelsen himself anticipated. The democratic principles underlying his theory of legal legitimation have pushed Habermas to advocate changing the U.N. General Assembly into a legislative body. The unresolved tension between republican and liberal tendencies in his thought over the last two decades—which explains his vacillation over the institutional design of world governance—stem, in part, from the multiple functions he ascribes to international law. In the mid-nineties he defended a more state-centric, republican design in response to the economic realities of globalization (Habermas 1998: 187). In the years following he proposed a less radical, more liberal conception that focused the centralized energies of global governance on pacification and human rights enforcement (Habermas 2006: 128–138; 2008a: 312–352). This period witnessed a skeptical turn in Habermas's thinking regarding the direct democratic legitimation of global governance. He was convinced that the solidarity requisite for legitimating global economic redistribution would be difficult to achieve beyond national and regional levels (Habermas 2006: 79, 139, 177). The realities of multicultural and economic conflict instead led him to settle upon a tripartite model of international law delegating centralized peacekeeping and humanitarian functions to international courts and a more democratically structured Security Council. Today, his renewal of the more ambitious democratic project—under the banner of Kelsenian monism—still retains important elements of this tripartite scheme.

Departing from a realistic assessment of national and international affairs, Habermas prefaces a recent statement of his project by noting that:

> Nation states have in fact lost a considerable portion of their controlling and steering abilities in the functional domains in which they were in a position to make more or less independent decisions until the most recent major phase of globalization (during the final quarter of the twentieth century). This holds for all of the classical functions of the state, from safeguarding peace and physical security to guaranteeing freedom, the rule of law, and democratic legitimation. Since the demise of embedded capitalism and the associated shift in the relation between politics and the economy in favor of globalized markets, the state has also been affected, perhaps most deeply of all, in its role as an intervention state that is liable for the social security of its citizens (Habermas 2008b: 444).

Rejecting state-centered responses to global insecurities in favor of international legal remedies, Habermas proposes a "three-level system" of global governance wherein statehood, democratic legitimation, constitutional governance, and civic solidarity are carefully distinguished. As noted above, Habermas does not deny the importance of states as sanctioning agents within this system: "whereas the political constitution…can also extend across national borders, the substance of the state—the decision-making and administrative power of a hierarchically organized authority enjoying a monopoly of violence—is ultimately dependent on a state infrastructure" (Habermas 2008b: 445). There is an additional sense in which this system authorizes states to negotiate matters touching on global distributive justice. At the highest *supranational* level of global governance, a *hierarchical* organization would be

> specialized in securing peace and implementing human rights [but]…would not have to shoulder the immense burden of a global domestic policy designed to overcome the extreme disparities in wealth within the stratified world society, reverse ecological imbalances, and avert collective threats, on the one hand, while endeavoring to promote an intercultural discourse on, and recognition of, the equal rights of the major civilizations, on the other (Habermas 2008b: 445).

Because there is no "*institutional framework* for legislative competencies and corresponding processes of political will formation" (Habermas 2008b: 446) in dealing with these problems in a way that could directly satisfy democratic demands for legal legitimation, such problems would instead be treated in *heterarchically* structured "*transnational* negotiation systems" uniting governmental actors (powerful, regionally extensive states, such as the United States, China, and Russia, as well as regional governing bodies, such as the EU) and non-governmental entities. Non-governmental bodies would include entities that address specifically political issues, such as non-governmental organizations (NGOs) and global economic multilaterals (the World Trade Organization, the World Bank, the International Monetary Fund, etc.) as well as entities that address technical coordination problems concerning international health, energy, telecommunications, and so on (Habermas 2008b: 446). Owing to the dearth of democratic institutions of legislation at this level, states with elected representative bodies would retain a vital legitimating role at the bottom rung of global governance.

From a Kelsenian perspective, this model leaves several questions unanswered. As Rainer Schmalz-Bruns and others (Scheuerman 1994) have observed, delegating responsibility for negotiating treaties on trade, greenhouse emissions, and other matters of global domestic policy to persons representing the interests of states and their corporate clients creates a legitimation gap (Schmalz-Bruns 2007: 269–293; Scheuerman 2008: 133–151). Even if these negotiators indirectly represent the interests of their own fellow citizens, whose livelihood depends on the governments and businesses that provide them with services and jobs, they do not represent the interests of foreigners, much less the interests of humanity—especially the poorest two-thirds of the world's population who have a greater stake in reducing poverty and greenhouse emissions. Although the distribution of benefits and burdens regarding global development and environmental security raises sensitive political questions that must be negotiated, the reigning imbalances in power between rich and poor nations, and between powerful and weak clienteles, hardly inspire confidence that the terms agreed upon will fairly advance the interests of humanity, let alone the most vulnerable portion of it.

The legitimation gap becomes even wider if, following the Universal Declaration of Human Rights and other United Nations' proposals, we include rights to subsistence, environmental security, and development among the basic human rights, the severe and widespread lack of enjoyment of which amounts to a human rights violation. If Habermas was once unclear about whether these rights deserved protection at the highest supranational level, his recent pronouncements on the matter suggest that he no longer is. Having linked the concept of human rights with the concept of a dignified human life in which human development and environmental security are guaranteed, he can no longer convincingly argue that supranational human rights protection and transnational global domestic policy are neatly separable.

Habermas must now endorse something closer to Kelsen's world state once matters of global domestic policy are acknowledged as impacting the basic rights of a world citizenry. That means that political negotiations over global domestic policy must be democratically institutionalized and regulated at the supranational level as well. For,

> only in a world state would the global political order be founded upon the will of its citizens. Only within such a framework could the democratic opinion- and will-formation of the citizens be organized both in a *monistic* way, as proceeding from the unity of world citizenry, and *effectively*, and hence have binding force for the implementation of decisions and laws (Habermas 2008b: 448).

However, in light of the fact that the international arena is currently organized around states, the governments of which ought to advance the interests of their own citizens, Habermas recommends a more realistic vision of global governance that would allow for the equal representation of a world citizenry *and* a nationally identified citizenry. Any "thought experiment" regarding the possibility of constituting a world state out of a "second state of nature" composed of legitimately recognized nation states must serve three major ends. First, the contradiction between the normative orientations of cosmopolitan and national citizens "must be defused in a monistic constitutional world order." Second, this monistic construction should not implement a world republic that would violate "the loyalty of citizens to their respective nations." Finally, "consideration of the distinctive national character of states…must not, in turn, weaken the effectiveness and the binding implementation of the supra- and transnational decisions (Habermas 2008b: 449)."

Habermas proposes the following institutional design for implementing these ends:

> A General Assembly, composed of representatives of cosmopolitan citizens, on the one side, and delegates from the democratically elected parliaments of member states, on the other (or alternatively, of one chamber for the representatives of the cosmopolitan citizens and one for the representatives of states) would initially convene as a Constituent Assembly and subsequently assume a permanent form—within the established framework of a functionally specialized world organization—as a World Parliament, although its legislative function would be confined to the interpretation and elaboration of the Charter (Habermas 2008b: 449).

A Habermasian World Parliament would address "principles of transnational justice from which a global domestic politics should take its orientation" (Habermas 2008b: 449) in order to secure the "equal value" of political and civil rights as well as to ensure performance of "duties that citizens of privileged nations have towards the citizens of disadvantaged nations, where both are considered *in their role as cosmopolitan citizens*" (Habermas 2008b: 449–450). However, the divided loyalties of representatives in a unicameral parliament—or the multicultural divisions present in a bicameral parliament—would probably *not* permit "philosophical discussions of justice" (Habermas 2008a: 449–450), or discussions of justice that theoretically bracket national cultural differences and the potential, discursively testable, overlap and/or convergence between them.

The democratic deficit plaguing Habermas's tripartite scheme would be solved through electing representatives who would be sensitive to global public opinion. Yet, despite the fact that Habermas asserts that supranational governance "would be *more judicial than political*," with courts and executive bodies taking a leading role in interpreting and applying humanitarian law, it is significant that he changes course in midstream and designates the General Assembly as elaborating "the meaning of human rights" in its legislation—an elaboration that is essentially political and not judicial. Although legitimation of such legislation in the first instance might be secured through the direct election of representatives, legitimation of judicial and executive decisions would be indirect, passing through global public opinion. Habermas suggests that the legitimation of executive decisions be enhanced through the "veto rights of the General Assembly against resolutions of the (reformed) Security Council (UNSC), on the one hand, and rights of appeal of parties subject to Security Council sanctions before an International Criminal Court equipped with corresponding authority, on the other" (Habermas 2008b: 451). Indeed, as of 2009, thanks to the unprecedented judicial review and reversal of Security Council sanctions, as well as pressure from lobbying groups in the wake of *Kadi I*, *Kadi II*, and similar cases, reform of the UNSC had partly met Habermas's stipulation, albeit by non-judicial means, through the creation of an ombudsperson to address individual challenges to the UNSC's 1267 sanction's regime.[15]

Finally, Habermas believes that the legitimation deficit plaguing transnational negotiations could also be reduced by submitting them to supranational regulation. Given the political nature of such negotiations, which unavoidably advance national as well as cosmopolitan interests and cultural perspectives, legitimation will mainly be indirect (contingent on the approval of global public opinion) rather than direct (contingent on the approval of legislatures and judges).

> Power politics would no longer have the last word within the normative framework of the international community. The balancing of interests would take place in the transnational negotiation system under the proviso of compliance with the parameters of justice subject to continual adjustment in the General Assembly. From a normative point of view, the power-driven process of compromise formation can also be understood as an application of the principles of transnational justice negotiated at the supranational level. *However, "application" should not be understood in the judicial sense of an interpretation of law. For the principles of justice are formulated at such a high level of abstraction that the scope for discretion they leave open would have to be made good at the political level* (Habermas 2008b: 452 (emphasis added)).

I will return to the italicized part of this passage at the conclusion of this essay insofar as it suggests a qualification of and departure from the monist world order Habermas and Kelsen ideally endorse. It suffices to note in summation that Habermas proposes to strengthen the democratic legitimation deficit of the current world order by increasing centralized regulation on behalf of the often-neglected domestic interests of world citizens without sacrificing the domestic interests of national constituencies. This combination of realism and cosmopolitan idealism finds a precedent in Kelsen's thinking as well. In his discussion of the U.N. Charter and the U.N. Declaration of Human Rights (Kelsen 1950; 1951), Kelsen urges legal recognition of individuals as cosmopolitan subjects of international law. Such recognition would require granting individuals rights to bring claims against other individuals and states before international courts. Yet neither the United Nations Charter nor the Universal Declaration of Human Rights defines human rights as actionable claim rights; for although Article 8 of the Declaration states that "[e]veryone has the right to an effective remedy by the competent national tribunals for acts violating the fundamental rights granted to him by the constitution or by law," no international tribunal is suggested for adjudicating such claims. The European Convention for the Protection of Human Rights fares somewhat better by allowing individuals to file complaints to the European Commission for Human Rights—but not directly to the European Court of Human Rights—and even then it requires that they must first prove that they have exhausted all domestic legal remedies.

Delegating states as the sole subjects of international law leaves the enforcement of human rights on very precarious ground, for as Kelsen observes, "[a]gainst a state violating its obligations, the enforcement of human rights will be undertaken when

[15] UNSC Resolution 1904 (adopted 1 December 2009 and most recently extended by Resolution 2161 in 2014). For further discussion of the *Kadi* case and recent changes in oversight of the UNSC sanctions regime, see Ingram (2014).

such action serves the state(s) taking enforcement action" Kelsen (1952/1966: 241). Departing from his earlier defense of *bellum justum* he adds: "[e]ven if enforcement action should be undertaken it is likely to pose as much a threat to human rights as a promise, for the enforcement measures open to states are of a collective character; as such, they may prove to be as injurious to human rights as the actions of a government in response to which they are taken. Indeed, the most characteristic, and the most important, of these measures—war—has surely proven in this century to be most destructive of human rights Kelsen (1952/1966: 241).

Kelsen concedes that this latter defect in the enforcement of human rights would still exist in a cosmopolitan regime in which individuals were subjects of international law. However, at least the politicized nature of enforcement "would be largely obviated, at least in principle, if the law constituting individuals the subjects of international rights at the same time constituted individuals the subjects of international duties, duties corresponding to the rights in question" Kelsen (1952/1966: 242). But to presuppose a situation where enforcement of individual duties does not follow in the aftermath of a successful war but involves policing interventions analogous to municipal law "is not to presuppose the transformation of international law but the disappearance of this law through the replacement of the present system of states by a world state" Kelsen (1952/1966: 242).

Today we can now describe peace-keeping and human rights enforcement as "policing actions" that have shed some but certainly not all elements of "just war," as evidenced by the murderous trade embargo that was imposed on Iraq during the 1990s (Gordon 2010). Human rights still remain moral aspirations subject to selective politicized enforcement. Although the arguments in support of human rights intervention "feed off the outrage of the humiliated at the violation of their dignity" (as Habermas puts it) they cannot be compelling when delivered outside the framework of international legal institutions. Far from being vague moral aspirations that provide blank checks for self-aggrandizing intervention, human rights are (again citing Habermas) "designed to be *spelled out in concrete terms* through democratic legislation, to be *specified* from case to case adjudication, and to be *enforced* in cases of violation. Thus human rights circumscribe precisely that (and only that part) of morality which can be translated into the medium of coercive law" (Habermas 2010: 470); viz., their "epistemic status is *beyond state control*" (Habermas 2010: 469)

To summarize: Habermas today develops his formulation of global governance in a decidedly Kelsenian (monistic) direction. Whereas earlier formulations sharply distinguished a transnational regime oriented exclusively to negotiating politically sensitive issues of global domestic policy from a supranational regime oriented exclusively to guaranteeing security and protecting against gross human rights violations, his current formulation integrates all three levels of global governance around *integral* human rights enforcement. Unlike in earlier writings, where he grounded civil and political rights directly in democratic procedure, grounded classical economic liberties and property rights in the legal form, and subordinated social, economic, and cultural rights to contingent enabling conditions for achieving the "fair value" (as Rawls would have it) of these other rights (Habermas 2001b: 125), he now insists, in conformity with the Vienna Declaration (1993), that all three categories of right are "indivisible" or equally necessary (complementary) for realizing *human dignity* (Habermas 2010: 468–469).[16]

Although the U.N. General Assembly has specified these different categories of human rights in various covenants and their institutionalization has been furthered through the establishment of procedures granting individual petition, periodic compliance reports, and adjudication in international courts, war crimes tribunals, and the International Criminal Court, rights to subsistence, environmental security, and human development remain largely unprotected. Indeed, enforcement of rights against genocide and other atrocities remains hostage to the strategic calculations of geopolitical *Realpolitik*. To this extent Habermas concedes Schmitt's point that the current "program of human rights consists in its imperialistic abuse" (Habermas 2010: 477). It is tempting, of course, to mitigate this abuse by limiting the list of human rights to be protected by supranational intervention to just those whose violation is most easily quantified and most easily ascribed to definite state actors. It was this temptation that led Habermas to his original separation of politicized and non-politicized levels of global governance (and that led Rawls to endorse a culturally neutral schedule of human rights as a threshold for non-intervention). This kind of trimming strikes at the very universal foundation of human rights, the integral dignity of the individual. The importance of guaranteeing all categories of human rights equally as a necessary step toward honoring this dignity brings to the fore a universal moral monism, the logical correlate of which is a fully developed *civitas maxima* (Habermas 2010: 478).[17]

[16] Habermas's use of human dignity here—as an inventive source for human rights that grows out of and unifies the "plethora of human experiences of what it means to get humiliated and be deeply hurt" (Habermas 2010: 467–468)—finds earlier mention in *Between Facts and Norms* (Habermas 1996: 426) without, however, designating the evolving complementarity of rights (Ingram 2010: 171).

[17] Although Habermas accepts a monistic understanding of the complementarity of moral elements underlying the concept of human dignity and, therewith, of human rights (see n16), he rejects a monistic understanding of human rights as having a common *moral foundation* in, for example, a "right to justification" of the sort proposed by Rainer Forst (Forst 2012). Such a monism of morality and law, Habermas argues, neglects the essentially *juridical form* of human rights as specifying, first and foremost, "subjective rights," or *permissions to act without need of justification* that can be *enforced* against government and non-government agents. Moral rights, by contrast, derive directly from moral *duties*, so that, properly speaking, the moral right to justification follows from a prior moral duty to justify one's actions to others (Habermas 2012b: 296–298). By conceiving human rights as permissions to act without interference, Habermas commits himself to interpreting human rights violations as violations of reciprocal *negative* duties to desist from causing harm, specifically by interfering with the agency of others. Human rights to subsistence, by contrast, have traditionally been understood as entailing reciprocal *positive* duties to aid others in need. This distinction (typically exemplified in the difference between civil and social rights), however, is hardly decisive; for Habermas, like many others, observes that fulfilling negative duties generally requires that agents do more than refrain from interfering with others. Legal agents, especially, must actively *protect* against rights violations as well as *aid* those whose rights have been violated. Finally, besides showing how negative duties imply positive duties, Habermas argues that "violations" of human rights to subsistence, human development, and environmental integrity *are* violations of *negative* duties insofar as legal and economic institutions effectively harm the poor by denying them free access to resources necessary for a minimally decent human life (Ingram 2010: 170–189).

Taking legal monism this far would require rethinking the role of international courts in a way that neither Habermas nor Kelsen envisages. Human rights courts would no longer be conceived exclusively as criminal tribunals for prosecuting crimes against humanity. They would also be conceived as fora where individuals could sue governments, global economic multilaterals, and other entities for violating (or inadequately securing) their rights to subsistence, environmental security, and human development. The European Court of Justice's (ECJ) recent decision (18 July 2013) to uphold the European General Court's earlier removal of Yassin Abdullah Kadi from a UNSC-imposed sanctions list targeting suspected terrorists (*Kadi I* and *Kadi II*), shows that the courts have asserted their prerogative to subject UNSC decisions to substantive and procedural review.

The ECJ's decision is ambiguous: Does it reflect a regional rebellion against an international legal order or a move to bind an international executive body to international norms of legal due process and human rights? Interpreting the ECJ's decision in this latter sense suggests a stronger analogy between global and domestic models of governance and the peculiar problems of constitutional hierarchy that attend all governmental regimes. In particular, the ever-present worry that vulnerable persons of all categories—not just the poor but immigrants, aboriginal peoples, ethnic minorities, women, children, and ostracized castes—will remain marginalized in transnational negotiations and other forums where human rights are debated, defined, and applied suggests that a system of higher courts for appealing decisions *and* reviewing legislation may also be necessary. But, as in the domestic case, a perennial question arises: if judicial review is problematic from the standpoint of democratic legislation in general, is it not more so when conducted at the level of supranational democratic governance?

10.4 Constitutional Courts in the Shadow of Legal Realism

Habermas and Kelsen defend judicial review not only in dealing with appeals and inconsistent rulings but also in reviewing the constitutionality of legislative and executive resolutions. Constitutional review, they argue, is not opposed to democracy when properly limited to guarding the institutions, rights, rules, and discursive processes (formal and informal) that make up democratic procedure. But because such review addresses matters of justice normally taken up by the legislature (eg, the impact of electoral map-drawing on minority representation) and because annulment of a statute typically accompanies a reinterpretation of constitutional language, constitutional review makes (legislates) as well as applies the law. It is this impression—that electorally unaccountable courts are legislating from the bench—that generates the legitimation problem.

Constitutional review abrogates the relatively strict separation of powers that Habermas, in particular, feels must be respected in order to retain the democratic legitimation of laws. The Austrian Constitution of 1920 that Kelsen helped design mitigated the democratic deficit attendant on having Platonic philosopher kings legislate from the bench in its provision for the election of constitutional judges by the House and Senate. At the same time, it rendered more visible the political nature of review. But executive appointment of judges with legislative approval is also political, and reducing political pressures on the judiciary through life appointments or term limits without opportunity for future political advancement does not eliminate the impact of politics on judicial decision-making. For this reason, Kelsen and Habermas contemplate review of pending legislation by a constitutional advisory committee, initiated, perhaps, by a special prosecutor or a legislative minority. Combined with delayed enforcement of judicial annulments, these provisions mitigate the intrusive nature of constitutional review (Kelsen 1942: 183–200; Ingram 2014).

Because Kelsen and Habermas defend the rights of individuals and states to appeal to international courts based on an analogy with the state model of constitutional law, it would seem that they should endorse constitutional courts at the supranational level for these same reasons. Is this realistic?

To answer this question it behooves us to revisit their response to Schmitt's rejection of constitutional courts. Schmitt's rejection of constitutional courts hinges on the theoretical assumption that abstract review violates the logic of judicial application, according to which courts apply a general norm to a particular "fact situation." Schmitt argued that constitutional review "makes comparisons among general norms, but does not subsume one norm under another or apply one to another" (Schmitt 1931: 42). In Schmitt's reading, judicial review appears to be either an imaginary exercise of philosophical interpretation without application to the factual world (and hence irrelevant to resolving real political disputes) or a disguised act of political legislation. Schmitt accordingly recommended that the supreme executive (eg, the President, exercising dictatorial powers under Article 48 of the Weimar Constitution), and not the judiciary, be entrusted with "guarding" the constitution against the threat of parliamentary politicization and anarchy by dissolving parliament or suspending the constitution.

Kelsen rejects the idea that the supreme executive is better positioned to guard the constitution than the judiciary. To quote Kelsen on this score: "Since precisely in the most important cases of constitutional violation the parliament and the executive branch (*Regierung*) are the disputing parties, to decide the dispute it makes sense to call upon a third authority that stands apart from this conflict and is not itself involved in any way in the exercise of power" (Kelsen 1931: 609). Habermas, of course, agrees with Kelsen, but defending the supremacy of the judiciary because it is less political than the supreme executive and the legislature depends, once again, on the dubious assumption that judicial review, like any ordinary act of adjudication, involves applying the law and not creating it. Habermas's occasional tendency to construe adjudication as a technical form of applying rather than creating law not only runs afoul of common law jurisprudence (judge-made law) but it occludes the way in which constitutional courts unavoidably develop the law by providing novel justifications and interpretations not expressly contemplated in legislative debates and subcommittee hearings (Zurn 2007: 243–252).

In his response to Schmitt, Kelsen likewise falls back on the idea that judicial review, no less than ordinary adjudication, is a species of law application, albeit with a difference: "the fact situation that is to be subsumed under the constitutional norm in decisions about the constitutionality of a legal statute is not the norm…but the production of the norm" (Kelsen 1931: 590). Following Habermas's paraphrase, Kelsen here argues that it is not the *political content* of the statute that is in question in abstract review, but the factual *act* by which it was made. The legislative act under review must not only be undertaken by a body that has been specifically authorized as competent to act in this way by the constitution (the legislature), but the act must respect constitutional rights, which as Habermas argues, are constitutive of the very procedure of democratic lawmaking. Habermas and Kelsen thus reject Schmitt's contention that judges on constitutional courts legislate from the bench. Their function is to guard a legal procedure that ensures respect for the rights of minorities, mainly by nullifying statutes that threaten to undermine them.

That said, there is no disputing that constitutional courts do not stop at nullifying statutes but undertake acts of interpretation that extend and deepen the meaning of the constitution (Habermas 1996: 243). It might therefore be asked why this creative dimension of interpretation is not itself a political act of legislation. Habermas responds to this concern (following Ronald Dworkin's (1986) narrative conception of law) by insisting that the discretion exercised by constitutional judges in interpreting the constitution is constrained by other, largely non-political normative principles that inform a tradition of legal reasoning. To quote Habermas at length on this subject:

> When Dworkin speaks of arguments of principle justifying judicial decisions externally, in most cases he has legal principles in mind in any case, that is standards that result from the application of the discourse principle to the legal code. The system of rights and constitutional principles are certainly indebted to practical reason, but they are due in the first instance to the special shape this reason assumes in the principle of democracy (Habermas 1996: 206)….This explains why landmark decisions and important precedents usually admit reasons of extralegal origin, hence pragmatic, ethical, and moral reasons, into legal discourse (Habermas 1996: 207)….Rules and principles both serve as arguments in the justification of decisions, though each has a different status in the logic of argumentation. Rules always contain an"if" clause, specifying the typical situational features that constitute the features of application, whereas principles either appear with an unspecified validity claim or are restricted in their applicability only by general conditions that require interpretation (Habermas 1996: 208)….From Dworkin's perspective, positivists are forced to reach decisionistic conclusions only because they start with a *one-dimensional* conception of law as a system of rules without principles (Habermas 1996: 209)….Referring to my critique of Gadamer, Dworkin characterizes his critical hermeneutical procedure as a "constructive interpretation" that makes the rationality of the interpretative process explicit by reference to a paradigm or purpose…By following such a procedure of constructive interpretation, each judge should be able in principle to reach an ideally valid decision in each case by undergirding her justification with a "theory," thereby compensating for the supposed "indeterminacy of law." This theory of law is supposed to rationally reconstruct the given legal order in such a way that that existing law can be justified on the basis of an ordered set of principles and thereby displayed as a more or less exemplary embodiment of valid law in general (Habermas 1996: 211).

Presumably it is the more substantive layer of principled reasoning noted above that prevents constitutional interpretation from descending into the void of political casuistry. However, Habermas doubts whether a positivist jurisprudence restricted to rule application of the sort he imputes to H.L.A. Hart (Hart 1961)—and by extension to Kelsen—can avoid such extra-legal reasoning:

> The priority of legal certainty [over rightness] is evident in the positivist treatment of "hard cases." In these cases, the hermeneutical problem becomes especially clear: how can the appropriateness of unavoidably selective decisions be justified? Positivism plays down this problem, analyzing its effects as symptoms of unavoidable vagueness in ordinary language....Insofar as existing norms do not suffice for an exact specification of cases, judges must decide according to their own discretion. Judges fill out their discretionary leeway with extralegal preferences and orient their decisions, if necessary, by moral standards no longer covered by the authority of law (Habermas 1996: 202–203).

At stake in this discussion is whether constitutional law embodies a substantive morality (or historicized natural law) in the tradition of legal reasoning that has determined a path upon which its concrete application must follow. If it does not, then, as legal realists argued, its general provisions would require supplementation from extra-legal sources, such as the judge's personal morality and political ideology, in order to signify meaningfully.[18]

Kelsen concedes that "the content of an individual norm can never be determined completely by a general norm" so that "there is always a certain degree of discretionary power left to the organ bound to apply the general norm," which is to say that "a certain degree of arbitrariness is inevitably involved in the application of the law which is also a creation of the law" (Kelsen 1955: 78). Kelsen thus concludes, in keeping with Justice Oliver Wendell Holmes Jr. and other realists, that "absolute legal security is an illusion, and it is just to maintain this illusion in the law-seeking public that traditional jurisprudence denies the possibility of different interpretations, which are from a legal point of view equally correct, and insists on the dogma that there is only one correct interpretation ascertainable by legal science" (Kelsen 1955: 79). For Kelsen, the difference between applying the law and creating the law is thus a matter of degree, with judges having less discretion for creative interpretation than legislators (Kelsen 1946: 130, 144).

As we have seen, this reflexivity (circularity) in the way law is validated, interpreted, and created belies the hierarchical image of a self-contained legal system grounded in a basic norm. The infusion of indeterminacy in the meaning of law generated by its reflexive application is nonetheless subject to several qualifications. First, although Kelsen accepts the realist critique of formalist (or deterministic) conceptions of legal certainty, he rejects the view that the law is unknown until the judge decides its application to a particular case (Kelsen 1946: 150). Even in hard cases a judge's discretion is limited by the law. Second, one can affirm that there are no gaps in the law and yet allow that judges sometimes legislate. Such "retroactive laws" (precedents) are the natural products of constitutional review (Kelsen 1946: 145, 150).

---

[18] For Habermas's confrontation with legal realism and critical legal scholarship (CLS), see Ingram (2002).

Whatever else one might say about Kelsen's jurisprudential philosophy, it is clear (*pace* Habermas) that it does not privilege legal certainty over rightness. At most, it can be charged with allowing for more than one right decision. This concession, of course, runs afoul of Habermas's Dworkinian view of law as a coherent system of general moral principles and concrete rules that ideally determines precisely one right decision for any given case.

Whether Habermas's or Kelsen's model of jurisprudence is to be preferred as a more realistic model for domestic (let alone international) law is a question to which I shall return shortly. It suffices to note for our present purposes, that Habermas himself harbors a few Kelsenian doubts about Dworkin's model of jurisprudence. To begin with, it is impossible to conceive a system of law that retains its ideal unity, identity, and determinate meaning throughout historical acts of reconstructive interpretation.

> In criticism of Dworkin's version of the coherence theory, it has been objected that a rational reconstruction of past decisions requires their revision from case to case, which would amount to a retroactive interpretation of existing law.... [T]he element of surprise in each new case now seems to draw theory itself into the vortex of history. The problem is obvious: the political legislator must adaptively react to historical processes, even though the law exists to erect walls of stable expectations against the pressure of historical variation (Habermas 1996: 219).

Added to this problem is the practical difficulty of conceiving such a coherent system of law in its relationship to the political and social system. The full range of arguments that enter into judicial decisions include the very same pragmatic, ethical, and moral arguments that enter into legislation, albeit within the context of "discourses" of applying—rather than of justifying—norms (Habermas 1996: 230). But pragmatic and ethical arguments are not straightforwardly true or right but probable or maximizing relative to some taken-for-granted purpose, value, or good (Habermas 1996: 232).

In sum, Dworkin's principle of hermeneutical charity requires that the historical body of law be conceived as ideally coherent. Only from this perspective can we say that a legal system "gives for each case exactly one right (ie, appropriate) answer." For Habermas, this "absolutist ideal of a closed theory" not only resembles metaphysical, natural law reasoning but is not entirely plausible, empirically or practically (Habermas 1996: 219, 227, 233). In his opinion, the "counterfactual" presupposition of "an ideal coherent system" has heuristic value "only as long as a certain amount of 'existing reason' in the universe of existing law meets it halfway. According to this presupposition, then, reason must already be at work—in however fragmentary a manner—in the political legislation of constitutional democracies" (Habermas 1996: 232). In other words, the degree to which law possesses integrity at any given moment is a function of the shared reasons that legislators bring to bear in defending it. But legislators as well as judges are divided on the substantive background theories of justice—Habermas mentions liberal and welfare paradigms—by means of which they defend and interpret the entire body of law "as a coherent narrative."

Each of these paradigms helps mitigate the problem of indeterminacy by predefining the meaning of certain general types of application situations in accordance with a fixed ranking of competing normative principles. For instance, in American law questions regarding the scope of individual civil liberties and questions regarding equal protection of minorities are framed in opposing ways, one limiting the regulatory power of the state, the other extending it. In many situations calling for legal regulation (eg, hate speech) it is far from clear which of these paradigms claims priority. Applying them in tandem is ruled out by the fact that each retains its internal narrative integrity by excluding the other (Habermas 1996: 221).

The ideological rigidity characteristic of legal paradigms, Habermas remarks, provides "sufficient incentive for a *proceduralist understanding of law* to distinguish a level at which reflexive legal paradigms can open up *for one another* and *prove themselves* against a variety of competing interpretations mobilized for the case at hand" (Habermas 1996: 221–222) A proceduralist (discourse theoretic) paradigm of adjudication should thus determine which contexts call for a given paradigm and which call for hermeneutically fusing multiple paradigms in a novel synthesis.

Yet even with this reflexive turn in the judiciary, there is no reason to believe that judges must interpret legislation as if it embodied a single conception of justice. In order to avoid imposing a single conception ideologically, judges must mediate liberal and welfare paradigms by being attentive to the most extensive information available. For Habermas, this will require converting their courts into quasi-political fora, in which (to paraphrase Klaus Günther) all relevant perspectives that bear on the interpretation of disputed facts are represented. The outcome of deliberation, with judges mediating multiple legal paradigms and multiple perspectives (and, at higher levels doing so in communication with fellow judges, jurists, and the various "publics" impacted by the decision), is far from certain—so much so that it stretches credulity to think that those involved will presume that the decision reached is the only right one that could have been decided. Hence, Habermas himself concludes that what remains of our "certainty" that legal decisions are right is the expectation that "in procedures issuing judicial decisions only relevant reasons will be decisive, and not arbitrary ones" (Habermas 1996: 220, 224, 232).

Kelsen seems to endorse a similar proceduralist jurisprudence: judges facing hard decisions will be reluctant to read any single theory of justice into the law. Kelsenian judges serving on constitutional courts will therefore do what Habermas says judges generally ought to do, which is mediate adversarial contests between competing justice paradigms wherein all affected have equal standing to argue and appeal.

For Kelsen, the "most radical way to satisfy legal-political interests (*rechtspolitische Interesse*) following the [constitutional court's] setting aside of unconstitutional laws and decrees (*nach Beseitigung rechtswidrige Akte*)" is to require that the constitutional court institute a procedure of constitutional review (*Verfahrung der Prüfung der Rechtmässigkeit*) "pursuant to an appeal made by or on behalf of any private party (*auf jedermanns Antrag*)" (Kelsen 1929/1968: 1857). In addition to allowing an "acto popularis" of this sort, it is of the greatest importance, to permit a "qualified minority within parliament" to challenge parliamentary resolutions that may be deemed unconstitutional—"all the more so, as constitutional courts in parliamentary democracy must necessarily serve to protect minorities" (Kelsen 1929/1968: 1859). This stipulation regarding constitutional procedures complements Kelsen's insistence that parliamentary procedure guarantee representation of electoral minorities. Finally, Kelsen shares Habermas's discourse theoretic understanding of judicial decision-making as a public process of joint deliberation:

> The principle of publicity and oral argument (*Mündlichkeit*) is generally to be recommended for courtroom procedure in cases involving constitutional review, although it chiefly deals with pure questions of law...The public interest concerning the affairs of the constitutional court is so weighty that in principle oral argumentation before the court might be necessary to fully guarantee the publicity of the proceedings. Indeed it might be necessary to guarantee the publicity of judicial deliberation and judgment by considering extending said deliberation to include an assembly of lectures and hearings (*Gerichtskollegium*) (Kelsen 1929/1968: 1860).

Given that judges must interpret the constitution principally as setting forth the procedural conditions of liberal democracy and not as specifying a single conception of justice, they will be reluctant to nullify statutes unless it is necessary to protect basic rights. This position—which in American jurisprudence is associated with the view espoused by John Hart Ely—receives a ringing endorsement from Habermas in the following passage, where Habermas highlights the dangers of jurisprudential idealism.

> Ely is justified in taking a skeptical view of a paternalistic understanding of constitutional jurisdiction (Habermas 1996: 266)...[I]t is the exceptionalistic description of political practice—how it really ought to be—that suggests the necessity of a pedagogical guardian or regent....the exceptionalist image of what politics should be is suggested by...[ethically] virtuous citizens...oriented to the common good....[D]iscourse theory insists, by contrast, on the fact that democratic will formation does not draw its legitimating force from the prior convergence of settled ethical convictions...[but from] procedures that secure fair bargaining conditions (Habermas 1996: 278–279).

The jurisprudential idealism Habermas warns against imposes an exceptionally high standard of what counts as a constitutionally acceptable democratic process. Such idealism is almost always accompanied by an understanding of what counts as a constitutionally acceptable level of background justice. By denying that a constitution prescribes a singular paradigm of social justice, Habermas also refutes a jurisprudence guided by an expectation that hard cases have only one right answer. Indeed, such an expectation encourages precisely the kind of natural law reasoning that both he and Kelsen oppose to democratic proceduralism.

10.5 International Courts: A Test Case for Legal Monism

Kelsen's jurisprudential philosophy, which rejects judicial activism inspired by belief in the one true justice, appears more attractive when we turn to international law. Here one must agree with Rawls that national cultural differences do not currently permit an unequivocal endorsement of the liberal democratic understanding of human rights that Habermas believes is conceptually required by the rule of law. Put simply, Kelsen's less conceptual understanding of the linkage between modern law and liberal democracy is better suited to the current state of legal pluralism that reigns in the international arena, in which different legal systems occupy different stages—and different pathways—of modernization. Indeed, the problem of pluralism at this level is both cultural and institutional, shaped as it has been by highly specific challenges of systemic complexity and historical development.

Consideration of such legal diversity might induce skepticism about the possibility of realizing the monistic utopia of a *civitas maxima*. Legal realists and critical legal scholars have long highlighted the multiplicity of reasons validating international treaties (factual consent of sovereign states versus conformity to norms). Today's skeptics focus additionally on conflicting legal practices (Crawford and Koskenneimi 2012). Competing systems of law—trade law, environmental law, human rights law, security law, etc.—describe the same event under incompatible legal descriptions. As Martti Koskenniemi points out, each system of law is further subdivided into competing internal paradigms; we may speak of a minimalist approach to human rights (of the sort put forward by Rawlsian pragmatists) or a maximalist approach (of the sort defended by Habermas), and we may speak of conservative and progressive variants of each of these, as well as culturally differentiated sub-variants representing, for example, American and Chinese practices (Koskenneimi 2009: 7–19).

The fragmentation of international law into legal sub-specialties, each with its own ideological centers and peripheries (which are again traversed by competing schools, national practices, etc.) explains why international courts are wary of intervening in legal disputes involving competing areas of law. Citing numerous cases in which international courts were forced to choose between competing legal perspectives from which to interpret a conflict, Koskenniemi notes that the shift from the old power politics of state sovereignty to the new rule of law has not led to a corresponding constitutional privileging of human rights over power politics (Koskenneimi 2007, 2009).[19] If anything, it has obscured the politics of "forum

[19] For example, in opposition to the Israeli government's insistence that building the Palestine Wall flowed from its right to defend against terrorist attacks, the International Court of Justice's Advisory Opinion on the Legal Consequences of the Construction of a Wall in the Occupied Palestinian Territory (2004) interpreted this act as a violation of the Palestinians' right to self-determination as well as a violation of their human rights to liberty of movement (as specified under Article 12 of the International Covenant on Civil and Political Rights [ICCPR]) and to work, to health, to education, and to an adequate standard of living (as specified by the International Covenant on Economic, Social, and Cultural Rights). In the *Al Jedda* case (2005), by contrast, the High Court of Justice of Britain appealed to the law of security in denying relief under the British Human Rights Act of 1998 to the plaintiff—a dual Iraqi-British citizen, who had been detained for 10 months without charge. In another case, *Legality of the Threat or Use of Nuclear Weapons* (1996), the ICJ observed that both the law of armed conflict and the ICCPR applied equally to the strategic use of nuclear weapons. In deciding that the law of armed conflict was more directly relevant to the use of nuclear weapons (applying the principle of *lex specialis*), it favored a narrow interpretation of ICCPR Article 6's clause concerning the "arbitrary deprivation of life." Critics of

shopping" and global influence peddling behind the façade of institutional expertise, as if law were the "technical production of pre-determined decisions by some anonymous logic" (Koskenneimi 2009: 29).

Koskenniemi places hope in the redefinition and democratization of functional legal regimes ("giving voice to those not represented in the regime's institutions"). However, he remains dubious about whether instituting a legal hierarchy of the sort proposed by human rights monists such as Kelsen and Habermas would circumvent elitism or politicization. Unfortunately, there are no simple, unproblematic recipes for implementing global constitutional review. Instituting this function within the legislature or executive administration threatens politicization; instituting it within the judiciary threatens politicization *and* elitism.

Even when intervening in disputes that center on a single legal vocabulary, such as human rights, courts are loath to enter into philosophical or cultural debates about interpretation. At most, they condemn as violations only those criminal actions on which there is broad agreement: slavery, torture, ethnic cleansing, genocide, and so on. In many cases, such as the U.S.-backed sanctions regime against Iraq (Gordon 2010) or the decision by the U.N. High Commissioner for Refugees to forcibly repatriate refugees to war-torn areas in central Africa, the line separating legal violation from legal enforcement is vague, which just goes to show how much more politicized human rights enforcement is in comparison to humanitarian assistance (Barnett 2010).

Fragmentation of international law clearly threatens legal monism. But the utopian image of a centralized legal hierarchy commonly associated with Kelsenian and Habermasian monism is misleading.[20] Given the logical gap between higher-order norms and their lower-order applications, any constitutionalization of international law will perforce permit flexibility in the choice of which legal systems are best suited for addressing legal problems. However, it will also have to recognize that the choice of system is itself largely political. And when a situation clearly falls

---

this interpretation argued that the ICJ had made an error in its judgment about which legal regime was more relevant to the "arbitrary deprivation of life" inasmuch as nuclear weapons are weapons of mass destruction that technically have no strategic military use. Finally, the case involving the environmental impact of the MOX Plant nuclear facility at Sellafield, U.K. illustrates how different legal institutions, each with its own jurisdiction, frame the issue of impact from their own perspective. Is the issue to be decided by the Arbitral Tribunal responsible for adjudicating matters that pertain to the United Nations Convention on the Law of the Sea (UNCLOS), the tribunal established by the Convention on the Protection of the Marine Environment of the North-East Atlantic (OSPAR Convention), or the European Court of Justice (ECJ) under the European Community and Eurotom Treaties? As the Arbitral Tribunal for UNCLOS observed, even if the other two tribunals applied rights and obligations that were similar or identical to those of UNCLOS, they would do so relative to their own peculiar context, objective, purpose, case law, and historical experience (Koskenneimi 2007: 7).

[20] "Monism" can mean either the *constitutional* incorporation of international law into domestic law (as in the case of the Netherlands or South Africa) in contradistinction to its selective domestic inclusion by way of treaty ratification (as in dualist systems such as the United States), or it can mean the centralization (constitutionalization) of an international legal order analogous to the state-centered organization of domestic law—the meaning intended here.

under the jurisdiction of human rights, it will have to recognize that the concrete application of such rights will be institutionally and politically conditioned. Practically speaking, the development of human rights will be from the ground up—dispersed among many institutions—rather from the top-down.

The same might be said for institutionalizing constitutional review in the legislation, adjudication, and execution of international law. The reasons that compel instituting constitutional review in a separate court, namely, that doing so facilitates philosophical examination of human rights impartially, also compel institutionalizing such review in legislative and executive bodies (Ingram 2014).[21] Although these latter institutions lack the greater political autonomy of a separate court, they are better equipped as sensors of injustice and discontent, and can respond to concrete cases of conflict more readily. Ultimately, a global public sphere will also share in this review. It goes without saying that global social movements representing cosmopolitan concerns should have the right to initiate formal review at the level of the highest court.

This realism in the flexibility of human rights application may still not counter all objections to monism. One might object that there remains an inextricable tension between human rights and domestic rights. Even stalwart monists like Kelsen and Habermas concede that the juridification of human rights at the international level works at cross purposes to their juridification at lower levels of regional and state governance. Trade-offs between multicultural flexibility and centralized juridification are thus to be expected. Given current political realities, that means postponing centralized juridification. But without this further step toward constitutionalizing international law, we find ourselves once again staring at the Schmittian abyss (Koskenneimi 1990: 4–32; Fischer-Lescano and Teubner 2004).

Acknowledgement The author thanks George Mazur, who greatly helped in navigating the subtleties of Kelsen's legal theory.

References

Barnett, M. 2010. *The international humanitarian order*. London: Routledge.

Bernstorff, Jochen von. 2010. *The public international law theory of Hans Kelsen: Believing in universal law*. Cambridge: Cambridge University Press.

Brunkhorst, H. 2009. Dialectical snares: Human rights and democracy in the world society. *Ethics and Global Politics* 2(3): 219–239.

Crawford, J., and M. Koskenniemi (eds.). 2012. *The Cambridge companion to international law*. Cambridge: Cambridge University Press.

Doyle, M. 1997. *Ways of war and peace*. New York: Norton.

[21] As noted above, Kelsen's understanding of the reflexive continuity (*Stufenbau*) linking legislation and application undermines notions of institutional supremacy and separation and also disperses democratic accountability in a way consonant with Habermas's tri-level institutionalization of international law under aegis of a centralized (monistic) human rights regime (Kelsen 1920b: 19–26; Brunkhorst 2009: 232; Zurn 2007).

Duxbury, N. 2007. Review of Lars Vinx, Hans Kelsen's pure theory of law. Legality and legitimacy. *The Modern Law Review*, 71/4 (July 2008): 647–650.
Dworkin, R. 1986. *Law's empire*. Cambridge: Harvard University Press.
Dyzenhaus, D. 1997. *Legality and legitimacy: Carl Schmitt, Hans Kelsen, and Herman Heller in Weimar*. Oxford: Oxford University.
Engel, S. (ed.). 1964. *Law, state, and international legal order. Essays in honor of Hans Kelsen*. Knoxville: University of Tennessee.
Finnis, J. 2011. *Natural law and natural rights*, 2nd ed. Oxford: Oxford University Press.
Fischer-Lescano, A., and G. Teubner. 2004. Regime-collisions: The vain search for legal unity in the fragmentation of global law. *Michigan Journal of International Law. Vol.* 25: 999–1046.
Forst, R. 2012. *The Right to Justification*. Trans. J. Flynn. New York: Columbia University.
Gordon, J. 2010. *Invisible war: The United States and the Iraq sanctions*. Cambridge, MA: Harvard University.
Gümplová, P. 2011. *Sovereignty and constitutional law*. Baden Baden: NOMOS Verlagsgesellschaft.
Habermas, J. 1962/1989. *The Structural Transformation of the Public Sphere: An Inquiry into a Category of Bourgeois Society*. Trans. T. Burger and F. Lawrence. Cambridge, MA: MIT.
Habermas, J. 1975. *Legitimation Crisis*. Trans. T. McCarthy. Boston: Beacon Press.
Habermas, J. 1987. *The Theory of Communicative Action. Volume Two. Lifeworld and System. A Critique of Functionalist Reason*. Trans. T. McCarthy. Boston: Beacon Press.
Habermas, J. 1988. Law and Morality. *The Tanner Lectures on Human Values: Volume 8*. Trans. K. Baynes. Ed. S.M. McMurrin. Salt Lake City: 217–279.
Habermas, J. 1992. *Faktizität und Geltung*. Frankfurt am Main: Suhrkamp.
Habermas, J. 1996. *Between Facts and Norms: Contributions to a Discourse Theory of Law and Democracy*. Trans. W. Rehg. Cambridge: MIT Press.
Habermas, J. 1998. *The inclusion of the other: Studies in political theory*. Cambridge, MA: MIT Press.
Habermas, J. 2001a. Constitutional democracy: A paradoxical union of contradictory principles? *Political Theory* 29(6): 766–781.
Habermas, J. 2001b. *The postnational constellation: Political essays*. Cambridge: MIT.
Habermas, J. 2006. *The divided west*. Cambridge: Polity Press.
Habermas, J. 2008a. In *Between naturalism and religion*, ed. C. Cronin. Cambridge: Polity Press.
Habermas, J. 2008b. The constitutionalization of international law and the legitimation problems of a constitution for world society. *Constellations* 15(4): 444–454.
Habermas, J. 2010. The concept of human dignity and the realistic utopia of human rights. *Metaphilosophy* 41/4 (July 2010): 464–479.
Habermas, J. 2012a. Law and the cognitive content of morality. In *Thirty year commemoration to the life of Hans Morgenthau*, ed. G.O. Mazur, 1–20. Paris: University of Paris.
Habermas, J. 2012b. *Nachmetaphysisches Denken II. Aufsätze und Repliken*. Frankfurt am Main: Suhrkamp.
Hart, H.L.A. 1959. Positivism and the separation of law and morals. *The Harvard Law Review* 71: 593–629.
Hart, H.L.A. 1961. *The concept of law*. Oxford: Oxford University Press.
Hart, H.L.A. 1983. Kelsen's doctrine of the unity of law. In *Essays in jurisprudence and philosophy*. Oxford: Oxford University Press.
Ingram, D. 2002. The sirens of pragmatism versus the priests of proceduralism: Habermas and American legal realism. In *Habermas and pragmatism*, ed. M. Aboulafia, M. Bookman, and C. Kemp. New York: Routledge.
Ingram, D. 2010. *Habermas: Introduction and Analysis*. Ithaca: Cornell University Press.
Ingram, D. 2014. Pluralizing constitutional review in international law: A critical theory approach. *Revista Portuguesa de Filosofia: Special Double Issue on Philosophy of Law* 70(2–3): 261–286.
Jütersonke, O. 2010. *Morgenthau, law and realism*. Cambridge: Cambridge University Press.

Kalyvas, A. 2006. The basic norm and democracy in Hans Kelsen's legal and political theory. *Philosophy and Social Criticism* 32(5): 573–599.

Kant. 1900. Zum Ewigen Friede: Ein Philosophischer Entwurf. Gesammelte Schriften. Band VIII, 341–386, Berlin.

Kant, I. 1996. *The metaphysics of morals*. Cambridge: Cambridge University Press.

Kelsen, H. 1913/2010. Rechtsstaat und Staatsrecht. In *Hans Kelsen Werke. Band 3. Veröffentliche Schriften 1911–1917*. Ed. Matthias Jestaedt with the cooperation of the Hans Kelsen Institut. Tübingen: Mohr Siebeck: 147–155.

Kelsen, H. 1920a. *Das Probleme der Souveränität und die Theorie des Völkerrechts: Beitrag zu einer reinen Rechtslehre*. Tübingen: Mohr.

Kelsen, H. 1920b. *Vom Wesen und Wert der Demokratie*. Tübingen: J.C. Mohr.

Kelsen, H. 1929/1968. Wesen und Entwicklung der Staatsgerichtsbarkeit. In *Die Wiener Rechtstheoretischer Schule. Ausgewählte Schriften von Hans Kelsen, Adolf Julius Merkl und Alfred Verdross*. Zweite Band, ed. Hans. Klecatsky, René Marci, and Hans Schambeck: 1813–1872.

Kelsen, H. 1931. Wer Soll der Hüter der Verfassung sein? *Die Justiz* 6: 576–628.

Kelsen, H. 1933/1973. State-form and world-outlook. In *Essays in legal and moral philosophy*, ed. O. Weinberger. Dordrecht/Boston: Reidel.

Kelsen, H. 1934/1967. *Pure Theory of Law. 2nd and Rev. Edition*. Trans. M. Knight. Berkeley: University of California.

Kelsen, H. 1942. Judicial review of legislation. A comparative study of the Austrian and American constitutions. *Journal of Politics* 4(2): 183–200.

Kelsen, H. 1944a. *Peace through law*. Chapel Hill: University of North Carolina.

Kelsen, H. 1944b. The principle of sovereign equality of states as a basis for international organization. *Yale Law Journal* 53(2): 207–220.

Kelsen, H. 1946. *General Theory of Law and State*. Trans. H. Wedberg. Cambridge, MA: Harvard University.

Kelsen, H. 1950. *The law of the United Nations*. London: Stevens & Sons.

Kelsen, H. 1951. *Recent trends in the law of the United Nations*. New York: Stevens.

Kelsen, H. 1952. Was ist ein Rechtsakt? *Österreichscher Zeitschrift für Öffentliches Recht*.

Kelsen, H. 1952/1966. *Principles of International Law*, 2nd edn., ed. R. Tucker. New York: Holt Rinehart &Winston.

Kelsen, H. 1955. Foundations of democracy. *Ethics* 66(1): 1–101.

Kelsen, H. 1957. *What is justice? Justice, law, and politics in the mirror of science. Collected essays*. Berkeley: University of California.

Koskenneimi, Martti. 1990. The politics of international law. *European Journal of International Law* 1(4): 4–32.

Koskenneimi, Martti. 2002. *The gentile civilizer of nations. The rise and fall of international law 1870–1960*. Cambridge: Cambridge University.

Koskenneimi, Martti. 2007. The fate of public international law: Between technique and politics. *Modern Law Review* 17: 1–30.

Koskenneimi, Martti. 2009. The politics of international law—Twenty years later. *European Journal of International Law* 20(1): 7–19.

Landauer, C. 2003. Antinomies of the United Nations: Hans Kelsen and Alf Ross on the Charter. *European Journal of International Law* 14(4): 767–799.

Maus, I. 2009. I. Recht und Kant. In *Habermas Handbuch*, ed. H. Brunkhorst, R. Kreide, and C. Lafont. Stuttgart: Metzler.

McCormick, J. 1997. Habermas' discourse theory of law: Bridging Anglo-American and continental legal traditions? *The Modern Law Review* 60(5): 734–743.

Morgenthau, H. 1948. *Politics among nations: The struggle for power and peace*. New York: Knopf.

Paulsen, S.L. 1994. Lon Fuller, Gustav Radbruch, and the 'Positivist Thesis'. *Law and Philosophy* 13: 313–359.

Paulsen, S.L., and B.L. Paulsen. 1998. *Normativity and norms: Critical perspectives on Kelsenian themes*. Oxford: Clarenden Press.
Radbruch, G. 1946. Gesetzliches Unrecht and Übergesetzliches Recht. *Süddeutsche Juristen-Zeitung* 1: 105.
Raz, J. 1979. *The authority of law. Essays on law and morality*. Oxford: Oxford University Press.
Rigaux, F. 1998. Hans Kelsen on international law. *European Journal of International Law* 9: 325–343.
Scheuerman, W. 1994. *Between the norm and the exception. The Frankfurt School and the rule of law*. Cambridge: MIT.
Scheuerman, W. 2008. Global governance without global government? Habermas on postnational democracy. *Political Theory* 36(1): 133–151.
Schmalz-Bruns, R. 2007. An den Grenzen der Entstaatlichung. Bemerkungen zu Jürgen Habermas's Modell einer Weltinnenpolitik ohne Weltregierung. In *Anarchie der kommunikativen Freiheit*, ed. P. Niesen and B. Herborth, 269–293. Frankfurt am Main: Suhrkamp.
Schmitt, C. 1922/1985. *Political theology. Four chapters on the concept of sovereignty*. Cambridge, MA: MIT.
Schmitt, C. 1923/1988. *The crisis of parliamentary democracy*. Cambridge, MA: MIT.
Schmitt, C. 1931. *Der Hüter der Verfassung*. Tübingen: Mohr.
Schmitt, C. 1932/2007. *Constitutional theory*. Durham: Duke University.
Schmitt, C. 1934/1996. *The concept of the political*. Cambridge, MA: MIT.
Schmitt, C. 1978/1987. The legal world revolution. *Telos* 72: 73–89.
Vinx, L. 2007. *Hans Kelsen's pure theory of law. Legality and legitimacy*. Oxford: Oxford University.
Zurn, C. 2007. *Deliberative democracy and the institution of judicial review*. Cambridge: Cambridge University.

Part IV
Kelsen's Legacies

Chapter 11
The Neglect of Hans Kelsen in West German Public Law Scholarship, 1945–1980

Frieder Günther

11.1 Introduction

> Mass murder, concentration camps, expulsions from home, tortures, tears of innocent people, bold lies of public institutions, all this is legally acceptable for Kelsen, because for him the order of the state and the legal order, law and justice are identical. At the same time you can find here the practical consequences of a theory of the state, that cannot differentiate between good and evil, justice and injustice.

This dismissive judgment of Hans Kelsen and his legal theory comes from Ernst von Hippel's popular textbook "General Theory of the State" ("*Allgemeine Staatslehre*") in 1963 (Hippel 1963: 154). Hippel's opinion of Kelsen was widespread among West German scholars of public law between 1945 and 1980. The majority of scholars of public law in Germany refused to either discuss or work with the ideas of Hans Kelsen, because they considered his theory ideologically inadequate and wrong. Among the German members of the renowned Association of German Scholars of Public Law (*Vereinigung der Deutschen Staatsrechtslehrer*), which meets annually and publishes its academic discussions,—with two exceptions that I will discuss later—no single statement was made about Kelsen's theory between 1949 and 1980. Hence, Kelsen's ideas existed in a vacuum or a non-space in the debates about public law. Since the mid-1980s, Kelsen's scholarship has enjoyed a renaissance among German scholars of public law, which raises questions as to the reasons underlying this decades-long silence and disregard of his legal theory. In this chapter, I argue that it is not enough to concentrate just on Kelsen's work to answer this question. Rather, in order to understand the contempt for Kelsen's ideas among West German scholars, we also need to consider Kelsen's

F. Günther (✉)
Institute of Contemporary History, Berlin, Germany
e-mail: guenther@ifz-muenchen.de

D.A.J. Telman (ed.), *Hans Kelsen in America - Selective Affinities and the Mysteries of Academic Influence*, Law and Philosophy Library 116,
DOI 10.1007/978-3-319-33130-0_11

biography, social circumstances, and the intellectual atmosphere in West Germany after the Second World War.

11.2 Anti-Semitism Among Scholars of Public Law

Historical research has shown that anti-Semitism was widespread within bourgeois and national-conservative circles during the Weimar Republic. In the field of public law during that time, scholars could assume anti-Semitic prejudices among their colleagues even if such views were not explicitly pronounced in everyday conversations (Berding 1988; 165–225; Peukert 1987; 161–163; Wehler 2003; 495–511). Carl Schmitt is only the most prominent figure among the legal scholars with an abiding hatred of Jews (Mehring 2009: 113–302; Gross 2000). This widespread anti-Semitism helps explain the often sharp reactions to Kelsen's legal ideas during the Weimar period. The level of hostility to Kelsen's ideas was academically motivated in part but it must be understood against the background of racism that pervaded the legal academy during the Weimar Republic.

After the Nazi seizure of power, a large number of scholars of public law included decisively anti-Semitic statements in their academic works (Günther 2010: 141–142; Stolleis 1999: 250–299; Lösch 1999). Such statements should not be trivialized as minor adaptations to Nazi ideology but must be understood as expressions of deeply-rooted racist mentalities among scholars of public law. The majority of legal scholars thought that the influence of Jews in law should be diminished and that the number of Jewish students at universities should be reduced. Hans Kelsen himself was the victim of anti-Semitic measures. Despite the efforts of many of his colleagues in the department of law at the University of Cologne who tried to intervene on his behalf, Kelsen was forced to retire in the summer of 1933.

Anti-Semitic resentments did not disappear with the end of the Nazi rule, although racial arguments could no longer be found in the publications of the scholars of public law. In order to further advance their careers, anti-Semitic scholars made subtle adjustments in the new editions of their books and erased all racial references. Anti-Semitism, however, remained an undercurrent in their legal thinking. For example, in the letters of Ernst Forsthoff or Carl Schmitt, one can still notice that they used anti-Semitic phrases such as "canine behavior" ("*hündische Beflissenheit*") or "deficient abilities to fit in" ("*mangelnde Anpassungsfähigkeit*") when they characterized their Jewish colleagues (Meinel 2011: 312; Forsthoff and Schmitt 2007). In an article of 1960, Rudolf Smend, one of the most recognized scholars after 1945, reproduced anti-Semitic stereotypes when he characterized the appointment of his colleague Hermann Heller at the Humboldt University of Berlin in the year 1928 as "politically motivated." Smend objected that Heller's appointment destroyed the homogenous and consensual atmosphere at the department, because Heller was a social climber, a Social Democrat, and most importantly a Jew (Smend 1994: 542; Sälzer 2010: 81–83).

Apart from anti-Semitic resentments, there also existed feelings of guilt among the scholars who had stayed in Germany during the Nazi period. They simply had a bad conscience in respect to those who were forced to emigrate, because they had not protested loudly enough against the dismissal of their Jewish colleagues. They had not supported them on their way to emigration and did not even try to contact them afterwards. Many also had used the forced Jewish emigration to accelerate their own careers, as they succeeded to the academic positions of those who were forced to leave. And nearly everybody had concealed the achievements and intellectual contributions of former Jewish colleagues or identified such former colleagues as Jews if they decided to cite them in their publications.

Kelsen and his ideas were thus disregarded based on his Jewish descent. He was a prototype of an assimilated Jew, and that undermined his reputation before and after 1945.

11.3 Kelsen as a Legal Positivist

In addition to his Jewishness, Kelsen's legal positivist position also prevented his ideas from being taken seriously after the Second World War. After 1945, West Germany experienced a renaissance of natural law. In order to avoid the perverseness of law under the Nazi rule, the majority of the scholars believed that law should be subordinated to some general principles of justice. Therefore, they extensively discussed legal concepts such as a system of eternal values, ethical principles of justice, or a continuous right to revolution. However, legal positivism, with which Kelsen was associated, was considered responsible for the lack of legal defense against the injustice of National Socialism. Many scholars argued that, by considering "law just as law," lawyers had become defenseless against the arbitrary and criminal content of Nazi laws (Radbruch 2002; Hippel and Voigt 1952; Walther 1998; Rückert 1998; Kühl 1998: 614–619).

But this argumentation deserves reconsideration. It was not the positivist understanding of law that enabled the Nazis to influence the legal system with their ideology; rather, it was the willingness to leave positivism behind and be open to methods of interpretation based on general values and natural law. In general, Nazi legal scholars, including Carl Schmitt, were hostile to legal positivism and saw its former popularity as a result of Jewish influence (Schmitt 1934, 2006; Rüthers 1988: 91–322; Stolleis 1999: 323–325).

Legal positivism played the role of a scapegoat in West German legal discourse after 1945. By blaming legal positivism for the aberration of law during the Nazi years, legal scholars avoided facing the question what really made their works susceptible to Nazi ideology and to what extent they bore individual responsibility for Nazi rule. Blaming positivism also provided some measure of relief of personal guilt, which scholars had accumulated during the Nazi years. The association of positivism with complicity with or passivity in the face of the Nazi legal regime led to the further repudiation of Kelsen's legal theory because he was a major advocate for legal positivism. As a result, the end of the Nazi regime did not mean a positive reevaluation of his legal scholarship. On the contrary, scholars continued to accuse him of ignoring the necessities of reality and relativizing the values of democracy. As we have seen in the passage of Ernst von Hippel's textbook at the beginning of this chapter, West German legal scholars criticized Kelsen's ideas on two grounds: their susceptibility to totalitarianism and their inability to differentiate between good and evil legal normative systems.

The work of a younger scholar of public law argued in the same way as von Hippel. Horst Ehmke, who later became the West German Minister of Justice under Chancellor Kurt Georg Kiesinger, wrote in his dissertation in 1954 that Kelsen's pure theory of law showed a lack of connection with reality and a relativism of values, which did not fit the necessities of modern democracy. For Ehmke, Kelsen's theory—in accordance with the ideas of Carl Schmitt—failed to differentiate between law and power. Instead of Kelsen's formal relativism, Ehmke called for general integration and an orientation towards values in order to create cohesion and solidarity in a society that was still shaped by deprivations and economic shortages as a consequence of the Second World War (Ehmke 1981: 37–42).

11.4 Kelsen as Emigrant

In general, emigrants who had left Germany for political reasons during the Nazi years were treated with suspicion and seen as traitors to the fatherland. In addition, emigrants were regarded as not being able to understand the specific situation in post-war Germany. The most prominent target of such resentments was the writer and Nobel Prize laureate Thomas Mann. At the same time, emigrants, who decided to return to Germany, had difficulties reintegrating into their old home country and revitalizing their old networks. People assumed that the emigrants sought some form of revenge against the Germans who had remained in Germany during the Third Reich, and they were not viewed as representatives of a morally "better Germany" (Krauss 2001).

Kelsen, too, must have realized that West Germans did not welcome him with open arms. As early as 1945, the British occupying authorities asked him to return to the University of Cologne, where he had been dismissed in 1933, but he declined. Apart from this early initiative, no other German university offered Kelsen a position afterwards. Search committees preferred expelled persons, refugees from the GDR and dismissed colleagues who had lost their job due to their Nazi past, because these people were seen—in comparison to returning emigrants—as more reliable in questions of national interest.

In this context, Kelsen seemed especially unreliable because of his statements about the end of the Second World War and the legal status of defeated Germany. In two articles published in the renowned *American Journal of International Law* in 1944/45, he argued that the allied powers had not just occupied Germany at the end of the war but had taken over—in the sense of a condominium—its territorial sovereignty. Therefore, with the Berlin Declaration of the allied powers of June 5, 1945, the German state had ceased to exist and had to be re-established at a later date (Kelsen 1944, 1945). Kelsen argued here as an emigrant who wanted the allied powers to be as free and legally unfettered as possible so that they would be able to reconstruct a democratic order and punish the Nazi perpetrators in their sole discretion. His position was the result of his experience after the First World War when the Germans proved to be incapable of solving the problems of the post-war era by themselves.

Kelsen's opinion, however, was incompatible with the conviction of the majority of West German scholars of public and international law at that time (Diestelkamp 1985; Rückert 2006; Möllers 2008: 34–37; Stolleis 2003: 283–287, 2012: 32–37; Dreier 2001: 27–28). Among German lawyers, nationalism and etatism were still so strong that an end of the unified German state was simply unimaginable. They developed a theory that the German Empire in its boundaries of December 31, 1937—despite its military defeat—continued to exist. Hence these scholars aimed to establish strong legal limits for the allied powers, contending that the rules of the Hague Convention respecting the laws and customs of war on land applied. They argued that the allied powers should treat their control of Germany as a temporary occupation and administer the territory with an eye to returning it to the Germans in the same condition it was in at the outset of the occupation. Scholars of international law unanimously adopted this opinion at a conference in Hamburg in 1947. At a conference of the Association of German Scholars of Public Law on the legal status of Germany in 1954, the vast majority again confirmed this idea. They directly attacked Kelsen in absentia. On the one hand, they contended that his views on Germany's legal status resulted from his inadequate formal theory. On the other hand, they argued that his ideas about the end of the German state were incompatible with his own theory of pure law, because his conclusions followed from the facts and not from legal data (Dürig and Heydte 1955).

Inadvertently, Kelsen's statement about the legal status of the German state confirmed the prejudice about the unreliable patriotism of emigrants and Jews, which was widespread among the majority of West German scholars of public law. Kelsen supported the position of the allied powers and, therefore, positioned himself outside the national consensus.

11.5 Kelsen as a Liberal and Pluralist

The disregard for positivism among scholars of public law was accompanied by a de-liberalization of political opinions that already started during the 1920s. The political system of the Weimar Republic experienced a continuous decline of political liberalism (Langewiesche 1988: 233–286). The younger generation of scholars of public law who began their academic careers during the 1920s regarded the liberal political system of the Weimar Republic with critical eyes. Politically, they stood at the far right and, academically, they followed an anti-positivist method of legal interpretation in order to politicize the debates in their field and promote anti-liberal concepts. The determining feature of their ideas was holistic thinking, which juxtaposed the chaotic political reality to a visionary expectation of salvation, promising an alternative stable, value-based, united, and harmonious order (Lepsius 1994; Stolleis 1999: 171–186).

After the Second World War, the anti-positivist concepts that were developed during the Weimar Republic were revitalized. These concepts lost their original anti-parliamentary orientation and were no longer directed against the democratic constitutional system. But they were still determined by a yearning for harmony, unity, and stability. At the same time, the revitalized anti-positivist concepts of the Weimar period maintained their anti-liberal and anti-pluralist orientation. They aimed to reinforce the "conserving forces" ("*haltende Mächte*") that could limit the negative aspects of modernity and absorb the de-personalization and alienation that they associated with modern mass society. In general, scholars of public law tried to promote conservative concepts such as community, state, order, traditional values, and eternal justice by referring to the anti-positivist legal concepts of the Weimar period (Günther 2004: 191–192; Schildt and Siegfried 2009: 122–161; Hacke 2009: 17–24).

A good example of this development is Rudolf Smend's theory of integration. The main thrust of Smend's theory is that the state constitutes itself by a quotidian integration of the individuals into the state. The process of integration was the essence of the constitution in order to overcome the separation of individual and collective, between ego and state in the dis-integrated political culture of the Weimar Republic. In contrast to its original anti-parliamentary and folkish orientation, the theory of integration was reinterpreted after 1945 in a normativistic way and became a popular theory of the reformable West German state. Still, the theory of integration did not lose its focus on unity and integration and thus remained indebted to the harmonistic and nationalist ideas that informed theories of public law in the Weimar Republic (Korioth 1990; Günther 2004: 159–191; Stolleis 2012: 216–246).

As part of this development, liberal ideas were pressed onto the defensive during the 1950s. The debate about basic rights reflected this development. In this context, the majority of scholars of public law emphasized the necessity to limit individual legal protection in order to ensure the interests of the community. During the 1950s, the Federal Constitutional Court consciously established an understanding of basic rights as an order of values as an alternative to a liberal and positivist understanding of rights (Schmidt 1994; Günther 2004: 193–195, 202–204). Liberal and neo-liberal attitudes, which dominated West German economic policy during the 1950s, were also in a minority position in the debate about the economic system that was derived from the Basic Law. The majority of scholars of public law argued that the Federal Republic should be a strong state and that the government should not refrain from interfering in society in order to secure social justice and the interests of the community (Scheuner and Schüle 1954; Kübler 1994; Günther 2004: 204–206).

The scholars of public law also had reservations about pluralist ideas during the 1950s. In fact, they gradually accepted the central role of the political parties and pressure groups in the process of political decision-making, but they also emphasized that political parties and pressure groups had to subordinate themselves to the common good and that their influence should not surpass a certain degree (Günther 2004: 200–202; Möllers 2008: 47–50). The field of public law resisted sociopolitical and legal developments in which the rest of West German academia largely acquiesced. As a result, other academic disciplines regarded scholars of public law with deep mistrust. Political scientists frequently dismissed the majority of public law scholars as conservative partisans of the authoritarian state who refused to come to grips with the fact that West Germany was developing into a modern democracy (Fraenkel 1990: 297). This opinion is slightly exaggerated, but it remains an acute observation of the situation at that time.

Kelsen stood in contrast to nearly everything the scholars of public law wanted to reestablish during the 1950s. Due to his liberal and pluralist political opinions, he had formulated a radical alternative to many legal problems that were discussed during the Weimar years, and this situation did not change during the 1950s. Whereas the scholars of public law emphasized the necessity for harmony, unity, and stability of state and society, Kelsen understood society as a pluralist entity. His democratic theory was based on liberty and emphasized the relativity of all values.

11.6 A New Generation of Scholars of Public Law and Hans Kelsen

The atmosphere of the 1950s, which I have just described, changed gradually during the 1960s. A new generation of scholars of public law now raised their voices because they aimed to break from the stifling situation in their discipline. These younger scholars, who were born around 1930, had different experiences from the older generation during the Nazi years, the Second World War, and the years of reconstruction, and they accordingly offered different perspectives on that era. After experiencing the defeat of the Weimar democracy, the older generation considered the vulnerability of parliamentary democracy the most important topic for their work. For the younger generation, the Basic Law was the appropriate response to the Nazi past. In contrast to the older generation, which had accepted the Basic Law only with reluctance and reservation, the new generation saw no better alternative than the present constitution and thus embraced it with muted enthusiasm (Günther 2004: 211–234; Stolleis 2012: 317–322, 395–403).

This generation developed a methodological and theoretical basis for their discipline that differed sharply from that of their teachers. They discussed such fundamental questions as methods of interpretation, the doctrine of basic rights, the expansion of the welfare state, and the understanding of the state, of the rule of law, and of democracy in general. They were open to discussing and reviewing the old doctrines of the Weimar period instead of completely discarding them. Accordingly, they advocated continued modernization and progress, in which people still believed during the 1960s (Günther 2004: 243–264, 277–283, 295–309; Stolleis 2012: 379–394).

The new generation was no longer skeptical about the role of political parties and pressure groups in the decision-making process. In their eyes, state and society were closely linked. Therefore, parties and pressure groups should have a public character when they participate in elections or advise government agencies (Hesse and Kafka 1959; Leibholz and Winkler 1966; Günther 2004: 295–298; Stolleis 2012: 322–332). While the theories of Carl Schmitt and Rudolf Smend had dominated the theoretical debates of the 1950s, the new generation started to work with other classic theorists of the Weimar period including Hermann Heller, Erich Kaufmann, and Heinrich Triepel (Häberle 1962: 76–80; Lerche 1961; Hollerbach 1966).

The reception of Kelsen, however, has continued to follow a difficult path since the 1960s. Some members of the new generation started to have a closer look at the Kelsen's ideas. In particular, two scholars of administrative law, Hans Heinrich Rupp and Dietrich Jesch, referred to Kelsen in their books in order to expand the provision of legality (*Gesetzesvorbehalt*) to all acts of administration. Yet these books were widely challenged and received very critical reviews, in part because they referred explicitly to Kelsen (Jesch 1961; Rupp 1965; Schönberger 2006: 79; Ipsen 1972: 409–413; Günther 2004: 257–267; Stolleis 2012: 249–250). Something similar happened 20 years later, when Norbert Achterberg referred several times to Kelsen's theory in a presentation at the annual meeting of the Association of German Scholars of Public Law in 1980. His colleagues reacted either with strong criticism or deliberately ignored Achterberg's presentation (Bernhard and Achterberg 1980; Schulte 2013).

Apart from these sporadic examples, there was no other positive reception of Kelsen's ideas among scholars of public law. At first glance, this is surprising, because the breakthrough of a more pluralist opinion in the Federal Republic would have been compatible with Kelsen's theory of pure law. I explain the continued disregard for his ideas with respect to the social networks among scholars of public law and the sociology of knowledge within that field. Legal concepts and theories are not timeless designs of an independent and grand genius; rather, they are developed in a process of exchange with teachers, students, and colleagues on the basis of political and social circumstances (Fleck 1999). Since the teachers of the new generation had been hostile toward Kelsen's positivism, their students avoided direct reference to his work because they knew that doing so could provoke sharp criticism and hurt their chances for a successful academic career. Kelsen himself did not have any students in Germany after the beginning of the 1930s, and he also had no followers or supporters of his ideas in his own discipline after 1945. Moreover, the majority of the new generation continued to argue on the basis of values in order to implement the main ideas of the Basic Law in state and society (Günther 2004: 264–276, 309–319; Meinel 2011: 400–429; Stolleis 2012: 356–361, 506–510). But, Kelsen's relativistic theory was regarded as completely inadequate for such battles over proper values. The disregard for Kelsen demonstrated that the yearning for unity continued to be popular even after the 1950s.

This disregard for Kelsen prevailed until Horst Dreier published his dissertation on Kelsen's theory of democracy in 1986 and received very positive reviews (Dreier 1986). From then on, a rethinking of Hans Kelsen's ideas started to take off among scholars of public law and spread widely during the 1990s. This new open-mindedness towards Kelsen took place in a context of growing interest in questions of legal theory and the publication of Anglo-American legal literature in the German language (Dreier 2001: 30–33, 2013; Lepsius 2003: 371–372).

In retrospect, if I may comment as a historian, Kelsen's liberal and pluralist theory should have been well-suited to the atmosphere of the transition in the 1960s. But the field of public law proved to be much more oriented toward the past than the self-understanding of the younger generation of scholars would suggest. Additionally, the systematization of the decisions of the new Federal Constitutional Court precluded extended theoretical debates which would have become conducive to a positive reception of Kelsen (Schlink 1989). Still, the period between 1960 and 1985 was decisively different from the 1950s, and resentments against Jews, emigrants, pluralists and liberals no longer dominated German public law. In general, the disregard for Kelsen is a vivid example of how the legacy of the Weimar Republic and Nazi Germany still dominated the history of the Federal Republic of Germany after 1949, and the decisive break only happened after the 1980s.

References

Berding, Helmut. 1988. *Moderner Antisemitismus in Deutschland.* Frankfurt/Main: Suhrkamp.

Bernhard, Rudolf, and Nobert Achterberg. 1980. Deutschland nach 30 Jahren Grundgesetz. *Veröffentlichungen der Vereinigung der Deutschen Staatsrechtslehrer* 38: 7–111.

Diestelkamp, Bernhard. 1985. Rechtsgeschichte als Zeitgeschichte: Historische Betrachtungen zur Entstehung und Durchsetzung der Theorie vom Fortbestand des Deutschen Reiches als Staat nach 1945. *Zeitschrift für Neuere Rechtsgeschichte* 7: 181–207.

Dreier, Horst. 1986. *Rechtslehre, Staatssoziologie und Demokratietheorie bei Hans Kelsen.* Baden-Baden: Nomos.

Dreier, Horst. 2001. *Rezeption und Rolle der Reinen Rechtslehre: Festakt aus Anlaß des 70. Geburtstags von Robert Walter.* Vienna: Manzsche Verlags- und Universitätsbuchhandlung.

Dreier, Horst. 2013. Die (Wieder-)Entdeckung Kelsens in den 1980er Jahren—Ein Rückblick (auch in eigener Sache). In *Hans Kelsen und die deutsche Staatsrechtslehre: Stationen eines wechselvollen Verhältnisses*, ed. Matthias Jestaedt, 175–192. Tübingen: Mohr Siebeck.

Dürig, Günter, and August Freiherr von der Heydte. 1955. Der deutsche Staat im Jahr 1945 und seither. *Veröffentlichungen der Vereinigung der Deutschen Staatsrechtslehrer* 13: 6–87.

Ehmke, Horst. 1981. Grenzen der Verfassungsänderung. In *Horst Ehmke: Beiträge zur Verfassungstheorie und Verfassungspolitik*, ed. Peter Häberle, 21–141. Königstein/Taunus: Athenaeum.

Fleck, Ludwik. 1999. *Entstehung und Entwicklung einer wissenschaftlichen Tatsache: Einführung in die Lehre vom Denkstil und Denkkollektiv*, ed. Lothar Schäfer and Thomas Schnelle. Frankfurt/Main: Suhrkamp 1999. English Edition: Fleck, Ludwik. 1979. Genesis and development of a scientific fact, ed. Taddeus J. Trenn and Robert K. Merton. Trans. F. Bradley and T.J. Trenn. Chicago: University of Chicago Press.

Forsthoff, Ernst, and Carl Schmitt. 2007. *Briefwechsel 1926–1974*, ed. Dorothee Mußgnug, Reinhard Mußgnug, and Angela Reinthal. Berlin: Akademie.

Fraenkel, Ernst. 1990. Der Pluralismus als Strukturelement der freiheitlich-rechtsstaatlichen Demokratie. In *Ernst Fraenkel: Deutschland und die westlichen Demokratien*, ed. Alexander von Brünneck, 297–325. Frankfurt/Main: Suhrkamp.

Gross, Raphael. 2000. *Carl Schmitt und die Juden: Eine deutsche Rechtslehre*. Frankfurt/Main: Suhrkamp. English Edition: Gross, Raphael. 2007. Carl Schmitt and the Jews: The "Jewish Question," the Holocaust, and German Legal Theory. Trans. J. Golb. Madison: University of Wisconsin Press.

Günther, Frieder. 2004. *Denken vom Staat her: Die bundesdeutsche Staatsrechtslehre zwischen Dezision und Integration 1949–1970*. Munich: Oldenbourg.

Günther, Frieder. 2010. Ein aufhaltsamer Niedergang? Die Rechtswissenschaftliche Abteilung in der Zeit des Nationalsozialismus. In *Die Universität Tübingen im Nationalsozialismus*, ed. Urban Wiesing et al., 178–198. Stuttgart: Franz Steiner.

Häberle, Peter. 1962. *Die Wesensgehaltsgarantie des Art. 19 Abs. 2 Grundgesetz: Zugleich ein Beitrag zum institutionellen Verständnis der Grundrechte und zur Lehre vom Gesetzesvorbehalt*. Karlsruhe: C. F. Müller.

Hacke, Jens. 2009. *Die Bundesrepublik als Idee: Zur Legitimationsbedürftigkeit politischer Ordnung*. Hamburg: Hamburger Edition.

Hesse, Konrad, and Gustav E. Kafka. 1959. Die verfassungsrechtliche Stellung der politischen Parteien im modernen Staat. *Veröffentlichungen der Vereinigung der Deutschen Staatsrechtslehrer* 17: 11–117.

Hippel, Ernst von. 1963. *Allgemeine Staatslehre*. Berlin/Frankfurt/Main: Franz Vahlen.

Hippel, Ernst von, and Alfred Voigt. 1952. Ungeschriebenes Verfassungsrecht. *Veröffentlichungen der Vereinigung der Deutschen Staatsrechtslehrer* 10: 1–73.

Hollerbach, Alexander. 1966. Zu Leben und Werk Heinrich Triepels. *Archiv des öffentlichen Rechts* 91: 417–441.

Ipsen, Hans Peter. 1972. Die Verhandlungen von 1949 (Heidelberg) bis 1971 (Regensburg). *Archiv des öffentlichen Rechts* 97: 375–417.

Jesch, Dietrich. 1961. *Gesetz und Verwaltung: Eine Problemstudie zum Wandel des Gesetzmäßigkeitsprinzips*. Tübingen: Mohr.

Kelsen, Hans. 1944. The international legal status of Germany to be established immediately upon termination of the war. *The American Journal of International Law* 38: 689–694.

Kelsen, Hans. 1945. The legal status of Germany according to the Declaration of Berlin. *The American Journal of International Law* 39: 518–526.

Korioth, Stefan. 1990. *Integration und Bundesstaat: Ein Beitrag zur Staats- und Verfassungslehre Rudolf Smends*. Berlin: Duncker & Humblot.

Krauss, Marita. 2001. *Heimkehr in ein fremdes Land: Geschichte der Remigration nach 1945*. Munich: C. H. Beck.

Kübler, Friedrich. 1994. Wirtschaftsrecht in der Bundesrepublik: Versuch einer wissenschaftshistorischen Bestandsaufnahme. In *Rechtswissenschaft in der Bonner Republik: Studien zur Wissenschaftsgeschichte der Jurisprudenz*, ed. Dieter Simon, 364–389. Frankfurt/Main: Suhrkamp.

Kühl, Kristian. 1998. Kontinuitäten und Diskontinuitäten im Naturrechtsdenken des 20. Jahrhunderts. In *Erkenntnisgewinne, Erkenntnisverluste: Kontinuitäten und Diskontinuitäten in den Wirtschafts-, Rechts- und Sozialwissenschaften zwischen den 20er und 50er Jahren*, ed. Karl Acham, Knut Wolfgang Nörr, and Bertram Schefold, 605–658. Stuttgart: Franz Steiner.

Langewiesche, Dieter. 1988. *Liberalismus in Deutschland*. Frankfurt/Main: Suhrkamp.

Leibholz, Gerhard, and Günther Winkler. 1966. Staat und Verbände. *Veröffentlichungen der Vereinigung der Deutschen Staatsrechtslehrer* 24: 5–124.

Lepsius, Oliver. 1994. *Die gegensatzaufhebende Begriffsbildung: Methodenentwicklung in der Weimarer Republik und ihr Verhältnis zur Ideologisierung der Rechtswissenschaft im Nationalsozialismus*. Munich: C. H. Beck.

Lepsius, Oliver. 2003. Die Wiederentdeckung Weimars durch die bundesdeutsche Staatsrechtslehre. In *Weimars lange Schatten—"Weimar" als Argument nach 1945*, ed. Christoph Gusy, 354–394. Baden-Baden: Nomos.
Lerche, Peter. 1961. Stil, Methode, Ansicht: Polemische Bemerkungen zum Methodenproblem. *Deutsches Verwaltungsblatt* 76: 690–701.
Lösch, Anna-Maria Gräfin von. 1999. *Der nackte Geist: Die juristische Fakultät der Universität Berlin im Umbruch von 1933*. Tübingen: Mohr Siebeck.
Mehring, Reinhard. 2009. *Carl Schmitt: Aufstieg und Fall. Eine Biographie*. Munich: C. H. Beck. English Edition: Mehring, Reinhard. 2014. Carl Schmitt: A Biography. Trans. D. Steuer. Cambridge/Malden: Polity Press.
Meinel, Florian. 2011. *Der Jurist in der industriellen Gesellschaft: Ernst Forsthoff und seine Zeit*. Berlin: Akademie.
Möllers, Christoph. 2008. *Der vermisste Leviathan: Staatstheorie in der Bundesrepublik*. Frankfurt/Main: Suhrkamp.
Peukert, Detlef J. K. 1987. *Die Weimarer Republik: Krisenjahre der Klassischen Moderne*. Frankfurt/Main: Suhrkamp. English Edition: Peukert, Detlef J. K. 1993. The Weimar Republic: The Crisis of Classical Modernity. Trans. R. Deveson. New York: Hill and Wang.
Radbruch, Gustav. 2002. *Gesetzliches Unrecht und übergesetzliches Recht*. Baden-Baden: Nomos.
Rückert, Joachim. 1998. Zu Kontinuitäten und Diskontinuitäten in der juristischen Methodendiskussion. In *Erkenntnisgewinne, Erkenntnisverluste: Kontinuitäten und Diskontinuitäten in den Wirtschafts-, Rechts- und Sozialwissenschaften zwischen den 20er und 50er Jahren*, ed. Karl Acham, Knut Wolfgang Nörr, and Bertram Schefold, 113–165. Stuttgart: Franz Steiner.
Rückert, Joachim. 2006. Die Beseitigung des Deutschen Reiches—die geschichtliche und rechtsgeschichtliche Dimension einer Schwebelage. In *Strukturmerkmale der deutschen Geschichte des 20. Jahrhunderts*, ed. Anselm Doering-Manteuffel, 65–95. Munich: Oldenbourg.
Rupp, Heinrich. 1965. *Grundfragen der heutigen Verwaltungsrechtslehre: Verwaltungsnorm und Verwaltungsrechtsverständnis*. Tübingen: Mohr.
Rüthers, Bernd. 1988. *Die unbegrenzte Auslegung: Zum Wandel der Privatrechtsordnung im Nationalsozialismus*, 3rd ed. Heidelberg: Müller.
Sälzer, Gerd. 2010. Martin Drath: Ein Bericht über Lebensabschnitte mit vorwiegend hessischem Einschlag und über Draths Verhältnis zu Rudolf Smend. In *Moderne Staatswissenschaft: Beiträge zu Leben und Werk Martin Draths*, ed. Michael Henkel and Oliver W. Lembcke, 29–122. Berlin: Duncker & Humblot.
Scheuner, Ulrich, and Adolf Schüle. 1954. Staatliche Intervention im Bereich der Wirtschaft. *Veröffentlichungen der Vereinigung der Deutschen Staatsrechtslehrer* 11: 1–152.
Schildt, Axel, and Detlef Siegfried. 2009. *Deutsche Kulturgeschichte: Die Bundesrepublik von 1945 bis zur Gegenwart*. Munich: Carl Hanser.
Schlink, Bernhard. 1989. Die Entthronung der Staatsrechtswissenschaft durch die Verfassungsgerichtsbarkeit. *Der Staat* 28: 161–172.
Schmidt, Walter. 1994. Grundrechte—Theorie und Dogmatik seit 1946 in Westdeutschland. In *Rechtswissenschaft in der Bonner Republik: Studien zur Wissenschaftsgeschichte der Jurisprudenz*, ed. Dieter Simon, 188–226. Frankfurt/Main: Suhrkamp.
Schmitt, Carl. 1934. Nationalsozialistisches Rechtsdenken. *Deutsches Recht* 4: 225–229.
Schmitt, Carl. 2006. *Über die drei Arten des rechtswissenschaftlichen Denkens*. 3rd ed. Berlin: Duncker & Humblot. English Edition: Schmitt, Carl. 2006. On the Three Types of Juristic Thought. Trans. J.W. Bendersky. Westport: Praegar.
Schönberger, Christoph. 2006. "Verwaltungsrecht als konkretisiertes Verfassungsrecht:" Die Entstehung eines grundgesetzabhängigen Verwaltungsrechts in der frühen Bundesrepublik. In *Das Bonner Grundgesetz: Altes Recht und neue Verfassung in den ersten Jahrzehnten der Bundesrepublik Deutschland (1949–1969)*, ed. Michael Stolleis, 53–84. Berlin: Berliner Wissenschafts-Verlag.

Schulte, Martin. 2013. Juridischer Relationismus—Norbert Achterberg auf Kelsens Spuren. In *Hans Kelsen und die deutsche Staatsrechtslehre: Stationen eines wechselvollen Verhältnisses*, ed. Matthias Jestaedt, 99–112. Tübingen: Mohr Siebeck.

Smend, Rudolf. 1994. Zur Geschichte der Berliner Juristenfakultät im 20. Jahrhundert. In *Rudolf Smend: Staatsrechtliche Aufsätze und andere Abhandlungen*, 3rd ed, ed. Wilhelm Hennis, 527–546. Berlin: Duncker & Humblot.

Stolleis, Michael. 1999. *Geschichte des öffentlichen Rechts in Deutschland. Volume 3: Staats- und Verwaltungsrechtswissenschaft in Republik und Diktatur 1914–1945*. Munich: C. H. Beck. English Edition: Stolleis, Michael. 2004. A History of Public Law in Germany 1914–1945. Trans. T. Dunlap. Oxford: Oxford University Press.

Stolleis, Michael. 2003. Besatzungsherrschaft und Wiederaufbau deutscher Staatlichkeit 1945–1949. In *Handbuch des Staatsrechts der Bundesrepublik Deutschland, Volume 1: Historische Grundlagen*, 3rd ed, ed. Isensee Josef and Kirchhof Paul, 269–312. Heidelberg: C. F. Müller.

Stolleis, Michael. 2012. *Geschichte des öffentlichen Rechts in Deutschland. Volume 4: Staats- und Verwaltungsrechtswissenschaft in West und Ost 1945–1990*. Munich: C. H. Beck.

Walther, Manfred. 1998. Hat der juristische Positivismus die deutschen Juristen wehrlos gemacht? In *Juristische Aufarbeitung des Unrechts-Staats*, ed. Redaktion Kritische Justiz, 299–322. Baden-Baden: Nomos.

Wehler, Hans-Ulrich. 2003. *Deutsche Gesellschaftsgeschichte. Volume 4: Vom Beginn des Ersten Weltkriegs bis zur Gründung der beiden deutschen Staaten 1914–1949*. Munich: C. H. Beck.

Chapter 12
Philosophy of Law and Theory of Law: "The Continuity of Kelsen's Years in America"

Nicoletta Ladavac

> Within the history of Western thought, in particular its modern currents, [...] the natural law school has amounted to the greatest attempt ever made to construct a rational theory of morality and law (Norberto Bobbio 1972)
>
> If a man could write a book on Ethics which really was a book on Ethics, this book would, with an explosion, destroy all the other books in the world (Ludwig Wittgenstein 1989)
>
> Two scientific structures are conceivable: one determined by natural laws and the other by rules. Which of these two structures will be chosen by men is dependent upon their level of rationality. The more irrational man is, the more he tends towards a natural law structure (Friedrich Dürrenmatt 1991)

12.1 Introduction

When Hans Kelsen decided to leave Europe in 1940 and to emigrate to the United States, he knew that he was leaving behind a world full of certainty, and that he was seeking refuge in a new world that was unknown and foreign to him. This decision—which Kelsen hoped would perhaps not be definitive—represented a radical departure in his animated life, although he would never have grounds to regret it, as he himself acknowledged in his autobiography (Kelsen 2006: 92). It was not easy for him to adapt because, especially at the start, he ran up against a number of difficulties, including those relating to the English language, which Kelsen could read, but he could not speak fluently, let alone write. However, the American academic world, which exhibited a striking intellectual resistance, showing scant interest for his theories or his writings, imposed the greatest obstacles on him. For Kelsen, it

N. Ladavac (✉)
Thémis Centre d'Etudes de Philosophie du droit,
de Sociologie du droit et de Théorie du droit, Geneva, Switzerland
e-mail: nbersier@iprolink.ch

D.A.J. Telman (ed.), *Hans Kelsen in America - Selective Affinities and the Mysteries of Academic Influence*, Law and Philosophy Library 116,
DOI 10.1007/978-3-319-33130-0_12

was therefore not easy to find tenured employment and a suitable position within a university.[1] Kelsen ended up being highly disillusioned at this lack of appreciation, in addition to his many concerns related to his precarious financial circumstances (Nitsch 2009: LVIII–LXXII).

The first university to welcome him during the initial years was Harvard Law School, where Kelsen gave the Oliver Wendell Holmes Lectures in 1940 and 1941.[2] He stayed in Harvard into 1942 as a research associate teaching sociology of law, after which he taught at Wellesley College near Cambridge as a visiting professor. During the years spent at Harvard, Kelsen dedicated himself intensely to research, writing mainly in English. Out of a desire to adapt to his new environment, Kelsen also displayed an interest in English-speaking legal science, for example in his essay *The Pure Theory of Law and Analytical Jurisprudence* (Kelsen 1941c), which was published in the *Harvard Law Review*. As he had already taught at Harvard, albeit only for a short time, Kelsen hoped very much that he would be hired there on stable terms, and he found it very hard to understand the university's reasons for not acceding his request. He thus decided to accept an appointment as visiting professor in the Political Science Department at the University of California Berkeley, even though it was not a law school. He taught at Berkeley until 1945 as a fixed-term Political Science lecturer, teaching international law, jurisprudence, and the origins of legal institutions. It was only in 1945 that he was appointed as a full professor at the University of California, where he remained until his retirement in 1952. The experience of teaching at Berkeley was gratifying (he would continue to teach mainly international law, the origins of legal institutions, and elements of jurisprudence), although Kelsen would have preferred to teach at a law school. As he himself said:

> With my Pure Theory I would fit in better at a law school. However, American law schools aren't particularly interested in a scientific theory of law. They are training schools; their function is to prepare students for practical work as an attorney. They teach almost exclusively American law, which they do according to the case method. Since the American courts base their decisions essentially on precedents, it is understandable that the law schools see it as their goal to acquaint their students with as many cases as possible.[…] The law as an object of scientific knowledge would perhaps be more at home in a faculty of law, history or social science (Kelsen 2006: 94)

He also stressed that his students had very little interest in scientific research, above all in jurisprudence, given that they were students in the Political Science Department.

During the years he spent in the United States, Kelsen was able to dedicate a great deal of time to scientific research and to publish, also in English (Kelsen 1942b, 1943), various new works that brought him success and recognition. In order to introduce the pure theory in his adoptive country, he published *Law as a Specific*

[1] See the detailed account and introduction by Nitsch in Kelsen (Kelsen 1942b, 2009: V- LXXX), Nitsch (2012: 71–135), Métall (1969: 77–94), and Kelsen's autobiographical notes in Kelsen (2006: 92–94).

[2] The Oliver Wendell Holmes lectures were published in 1942 in the book *Law and Peace in International Relatio*ns, see Kelsen (1942b).

Social Technique (Kelsen 1941b) and the essay entitled *Value Judgments in the Science of Law* (Kelsen 1942c). In 1941, he published in English, albeit in abridged form, the previously published paper *Causality and Retribution* (Kelsen 1941a), followed in 1945 by the English language version of *General Theory of Law and State* (Kelsen 1945), a publication that Kelsen considered to be of central importance. During his years in America, he published widely above all in the area of international law (Kelsen 1944), a field that undoubtedly lent itself better to his new academic life. His most renowned works on international law include *Principles of International Law* (Kelsen 1952), published in 1952. The interest in positive law, including in particular legal theory, in any case went hand in hand with the study of international law.

Alongside his numerous publications, Kelsen participated in various conferences[3] in both the United States and in Europe, and it was around 1954 that American academics, including above all international law scholars, started to take an interest in his work. In 1953/1954, Kelsen participated in various conferences on the issue of justice and legal theory, including the important conference on the foundations of democracy, as part of the Walgreen Lectures at the University of Chicago in 1954. Alongside theoretical problems, he also studied political theory and the relationship between natural law and positive law, to which he dedicated a range of important papers published in English (Kelsen 1957). He continued to work relentlessly up until the end. The two principal works published late in life were the second edition of the *Pure Theory of Law* (Kelsen 1967) in 1960 and the *General Theory of Norms* (Kelsen 1991), published posthumously in 1979 by the Hans Kelsen Institute (Kelsen 1979) in Vienna. Several years ago, after resolving various complex editorial issues, the Hans Kelsen Institute published *Secular Religion* (Kelsen 2012), a study on which Kelsen had worked for many years, but which he had decided against publishing.

12.2 Kelsen's Contact with the Common Law

When Kelsen came to the United States, he was already in his sixties and had a markedly central-European cultural mindset along with legal training rooted in the Austro-German tradition and European civil law. It was obviously inevitable that he would engage with the common law and the analytical jurisprudence of his new country, although it would have been naive to expect Kelsen to cast aside his classically-informed theories. Because the legal cultures and legal traditions of

[3] In 1948 he contributed to a conference at Stanford University, which resulted in the later publication on *Absolutism and Relativism in Philosophy and Politics* in *The American Political Science Review*, vol. 42; the year before he expounded his theoretical interest in an important essay in honor of Roscoe Pound on *The Metamorphoses of the Idea of Justice* in *Interpretations of Modern Legal Philosophies. Essays in Honor of Roscoe Pound* (New York: Oxford University Press, 390–418).

Europe and America were so different, it was inevitable and evident from the outset that they would be radically irreconcilable (Telman 2010). Nevertheless, Kelsen made an effort to understand analytical jurisprudence and expressed his ideas concerning it in various articles, such as *The Pure Theory of Law and Analytical Jurisprudence* (1941), in which he analyzes in detail the thinking of John Austin and Anglo-American analytical jurisprudence.

The article on Austin include's Kelsen's detailed analysis of English speaking analytical jurisprudence and a comparison between it and his own theories. The study also contains a broad analysis of justice (an issue that Kelsen would consider in greater depth during the years spent in the United States) and its relationship with law, as well as a digression into American Legal Realism. Kelsen does not reject Legal Realism entirely; rather, he takes issue with its claim to be the exclusive science of law:

> The Pure Theory of Law by no means denies the validity of such sociological jurisprudence but it declines to see in it, as many of its exponents do, the only science of law. Sociological jurisprudence stands side by side with normative jurisprudence; neither is able to replace the other because each deals with different problems (Kelsen 1941c: 268)

Analyzing the theory of John Austin (Kelsen 1941c: 271–283), Kelsen makes an even more interesting observation, pointing to a parallel between his theory as presented in the *Reine Rechtslehre* and analytical jurisprudence. Although analytical jurisprudence did not have any influence on the pure theory of law, the two ideas coincide in various important ways, and the discrepancies are due more to the different premises on which they are grounded than on how they are developed. Kelsen states:

> While the pure theory of law arose independently of Austin's famous *Lectures on General Jurisprudence*, it corresponds in important points with Austin's doctrine. It is submitted that where they differ the Pure Theory of Law has carried out the method of analytical jurisprudence more consistently than Austin and his followers have succeeded in doing (Kelsen 1941c: 271).

This is true above all as regards the concept of norm.

For example, criticizing Austin's definition of the law as a rule and of the rule as a command ("Every law or rule…is a command") (Austin 1885: 89 f.), Kelsen expounds the relationship between legislative volition and the content of the legal norm with even greater clarity than in the *Reine Rechtslehre*. He states:

A norm is a rule stating that an individual ought to behave in a certain way, but not that such behavior is the actual will of anyone.…A command which has binding force is, indeed, a norm. But without the concept of the norm, the law can be described only with the help of a fiction, and Austin's assertion that legal rules are "commands" is a superfluous and dangerous fiction of the "will" of the legislator or the state (Kelsen 1941c: 273–274).

He also adds that Austin's notion that the law is enforceable provides further demonstration of the necessary status of the sanction within the structure of law and the resulting need to adopt the legal proposition as a hypothetical judgment in order to introduce consistently the coercive element, because anything else would end up—as with Austin—promoting a sociological jurisprudence rather than a normative jurisprudence.

> Austin and his followers characterize law as "enforceable" or as a rule "enforced" by a given authority. By this they mean that the legal order "commands"...and "forces" men in a specific way to obey the commands of the legal order....The "coercion" which according to this view is characteristic of the law is a psychic one;...And psychic coercion is not a specific element of the law....We are here in presence of a problem of sociological, not analytical or normative jurisprudence....Hence the law is not, as Austin formulates it, a rule "enforced" by a specific authority, but rather a norm which provides a specific measure of coercion as sanction. Analytical jurisprudence takes into consideration...only the connection between delict and sanction (Kelsen 1941c: 274–275)

In fact, only the norm considered as a hypothetical judgment as it is understood by Kelsen, enables unlawfulness to be justified, because the person who commits an unlawful act is not always responsible for his own conduct, in the sense that duty does not always coincide with responsibility.

By contrast, the norm understood as a command, as Austin conceived it, does not allow for any distinction between responsibility and duty.

> The Pure Theory of Law is only drawing an obvious conclusion when it formulates the rule of law...as a hypothetical judgment, in which the delict appears as an essential condition, the sanction as the consequence....It is precisely by establishing this relation that the legal norm imposes duties and confers rights upon the individuals subjected to the law (Kelsen 1941c: 276)

In fact, Kelsen argues that Austin does not clearly distinguish between the concept of duty and responsibility. He argues that "[t]he liability rests upon the individual against whom the sanction is directed. The duty rests upon the potential delinquent who may by his behavior commit the delict" (Kelsen 1941c: 276). However, says Kelsen, according to Austin it is not the legal norm that establishes a legal duty; it is the command that obliges the individual, and this concept of command prevents Austin from distinguishing between duty and liability. Austin's theory also contains no concept of right different from that of duty.

While there are certain overlaps between Kelsen's and Austin's approaches, there is an absolute difference with respect to at least two questions. The first concerns nomodynamics. For Austin, the concept of nomodynamics does not exist, just as his theory offers no legal concept of the state. For Kelsen on the other hand, the opposite is the case:

> Analytical jurisprudence, as presented by Austin, regards law as a system of rules complete and ready for application, without regard to the process of their creation. The Pure Theory of Law recognizes that a study of the statics of law must be supplemented by a study of its dynamic, the process of its creation (Kelsen 1941c: 278–279)

According to Kelsen, nomodynamics, the notion that the law regulates its own production, is necessary in order to move beyond the limits imposed by a static normative system. This is due above all to the two jurists' differing concepts of the state.

For Austin, the state, or rather the concept of the state, is structured according to the sovereign/subject framework, namely according to a division between two distinct entities:

> One characteristic of Austin's doctrine is its lack of a legal concept of the state. The concept of an "independent political society" plays a certain role in his teachings, but it is not a legal

> concept, and Austin himself does not call this "independent political society" a state. By it he means a society consisting of a sovereign and subjects" (Kelsen 1941c: 280)

For Kelsen on the other hand, the state is the system that brings together in unitary form, without any hierarchical distinctions, all of the subjects who belong to it. In contrast to Austin, Kelsen thus wished to assert the absolute unity and identity of the state and the law, and the subjection of individuals to one single legal order. Kelsen's pure theory of law:

> shows that a number of individuals can form a social unit, a "society" or, better, a "community," only on the basis of an order, or, in other words, that the element constituting the political community is an order. The state is not its individuals; it is the specific union of individuals, and this union is the function of the order regulating their mutual behavior. Only in this order does the social community exist at all (Kelsen 1941c: 273–281)

Kelsen's interest in the common law was in any case always limited more to a cultural interest. Kelsen engaged with Anglo-Saxon law almost certainly in order to reassert his own viewpoint. The reasons why Kelsen was never truly able to integrate into the American legal world, in terms of both teaching and legal reasoning, have been clearly illustrated in an interesting article by Jeremy Telman (Telman 2010). Other scholars have focused on Hans Kelsen's reception in the United States,[4] the problems and difficulties encountered, as well as the criticisms, disinterest, and stark rejection by Anglo-American academics. The difference between Kelsenian and Anglo-Saxon legal thinking was the main reason that Kelsen was never integrated into American law schools and was practically "relegated" to teaching only in political science faculties, even though opinions differ on this issue.[5] The criticisms, and a substantial refutation of Kelsen's thought, up until the decisive engagement with H.L.A. Hart, continued even after his death in 1973.[6]

12.3 Kelsen's Concept of Justice

Kelsen in any case engaged with his adoptive country's legal community above all through his numerous important writings in English on international law, even though these too did not meet with any great success or receive the recognition they were due from American academics. However, in the area of philosophy of law and legal

[4] For the reception of Hans Kelsen in the United States of America, see Nitsch (2012) and Kelsen (2009), in particular the detailed introduction by Carlo Nitsch to the Italian translation of *Law and Peace in International Relations, The Oliver Wendell Holmes Lectures, 1940–41*; see also Paulson (1988). See Losano (2011).

[5] See the introduction by Carlo Nitsch describing the many problems concerning his career that Kelsen encountered when he moved from Europe to America in Kelsen (2009: V–LXXX).

[6] See Tur and Twining (1986). In this volume, leading experts in Kelsen from different countries present and discuss interpretations and evaluations of Kelsen's work not only as a whole, but especially his ideas on law, logic, social theory, legal science, legal sociology, jurisprudence, justice, and international law.

theory, Kelsen's interests remained unchanged compared to the European period. In the United States, Kelsen continued to develop certain fundamental concepts of law, such as justice and politics. He analyzed in depth above all the issue of justice, publishing 15 important essays in 1957 in *What is Justice? Justice, Law and Politics in the Mirror of Science*, two of which were new publications (Kelsen 1957).[7]

The problem of justice is just as classic an issue in Kelsen as those developed in the *Reine Rechtslehre*. It should be stressed in particular that, for Kelsen, the problem of justice relates to individual convictions and the individual and autonomous conduct of the individual and not the objective structure of law, because the law as a social technique and justice as a subjective moral problem fall into different fields. Thus, in the writings on justice Kelsen analyzes the relationship between law and value, while in the *Reine Rechtslehre* he sets out his ideas on the structure of law, including in particular its validity. The problem of justice is present throughout Kelsen's works,[8] in which it is continuously measured against natural law, and within the convinced assertion of a rigorous legal positivism. Kelsen included a broad essay on justice (Kelsen 1960: 355–444) in the second edition of the *Reine Rechtslehre* (1960) (Kelsen 1960) with the intention of expounding his thinking on "why this problem is of capital importance within law," although he detached it from the main body of the text and presented it as an appendix "because the problem of justice, as a problem related to values, lies outside a legal theory that is limited to an analysis of positive law understood as the reality of law" (Kelsen 1998: XV, n.2). Therefore, the problem of justice was of interest to Kelsen insofar as it intersected with the law and in particular when dealing with the pure theory of law.

As we know, Kelsen attempted to found a theory that, while presenting itself as purely descriptive, sought to circumscribe any value judgment in the description of the law. Relating to the problem of justice, it should be stressed that Kelsen sought to circumscribe the law with regard to the problem of value, while by no means intending to remove all ethical reflection from the law, arguing simply that ethical reflection on the law is not the task of legal science. Thus, while the jurist's task is not to evaluate the law but only to describe it, when confronted with the problem of justice, he must consequently remain neutral. For example, when considering a certain norm, the jurist must describe the content of that norm and must not make any assertion regarding the value of justice on which it is based, in the sense that the jurist must not express value judgments within a descriptive argument. In fact, the *Reine Rechtslehre* does not assess, no less to judge the merits of other disciplines, and only seeks to trace out the limits between various disciplines. However, Kelsen recognized the importance of other scientific subjects in all of his writings and stressed that formalist discourse must therefore be supplemented by sociological and axiological discourse. In 1948, undoubtedly influenced by American Empiricism, Kelsen argued that "[t]he Law may be the object of different sciences;

[7] The two new publications are *Aristotle's Doctrine of Justice* and *Why should the Law be Obeyed?* (1957). See also the important review of *What is Justice?* by Alf Ross (Ross 1957).

[8] Kelsen (1998), see in particular about Kelsen's concept of justice the introduction by Mario G. Losano (XXXIV–XLI). See also Losano (1981, 152–175).

the Pure Theory of Law has never claimed to be the only possible or legitimate science of law. Sociology of law or history of law are others. They, together with the structural analysis of law, are necessary for a complete understanding of the complex phenomenon of law" (Kelsen 1957: 294).

12.4 The Relationship Between Justice and Values

When engaging with the issue of justice, Kelsen applied to the theory of values the same methodology used when elaborating his theory of law. In fact, in comparing the problem of justice with the problem of law, Kelsen identifies a common characteristic, discerning both to be scientific in nature by virtue of their non-evaluativeness. In this way, arguing in favor of the non-evaluative nature of this theory, Kelsen claimed that it is possible to describe all possible values of justice without characterizing any particular value as preferable or superior to others.

The premise upon which Kelsen bases his position, and the entire conceptual framework of the *Rechtslehre*, is his relativist conception of values. For Kelsen, it is not possible to decide rationally which value is objectively superior because the value is based on an internal subjective and psychological choice, and is not related to an objectively and universally valid norm of justice. Moreover, Kelsenian relativism is premised on an all-inclusive and even more fundamental value, namely the value of tolerance. For Kelsen, such tolerance not only has political value, but, on the contrary, also entails a liberation from all politics and the assertion of politics as the "foundation of a universal order of peace and rationalization of human existence."[9]

As Kelsen repeated time and again, justice is an irrational ideal, which cannot be accessed by rational consciousness (Kelsen 1957: 21). Thus, Kelsen's neutrality with regard to values, which was already asserted in the *Reine Rechtslehre* in relation to the distinction between law and morals (Kelsen 1934: 12–18, 1960: 60–113), is taken to extremes within the analysis of justice, because for him absolute justice cannot be apprised by human reason (Kelsen 1957: 20–21). Consequently, the ideal of absolute justice is an irrational and subjective ideal for Kelsen. Indeed, according to his radical non-evaluative conception of law, any value judgment will be irrational, as it is based on faith and not on reason (Kelsen 1957: 20–21). It is therefore impossible to assert that any one value is scientifically, ie rationally, preferable over any other. Thus, a scientific theory of justice must be limited to indicating the possible values of justice, but without stating that any one is better than the others.

In his essay on justice, contained in the second edition of the *Reine Rechtslehre*, Kelsen identifies and analyzes various principles of justice from which all norms of justice may be inferred. Moreover, polemicizing with natural law, Kelsen does not deny that human beings have always been searching for an answer to the problem of absolute justice, but only asserts that the *Reine Rechtslehre* is unable to provide such an answer, thus acknowledging the limits inherent within the methodological purity

[9] See introduction by Agostino Carrino in Kelsen (1989, XII).

preached by him. In reality, according to Kelsen, the question of justice must be directed at a science of law and justice *tout court*, and not at a legal science that purports to be pure.

The above arguments also apply to the interpretation of norms. In fact, because the activity of interpretation involves interaction between the relative values of justice and the legal system, Kelsen could not avoid concluding that different interpretations were possible, each corresponding to possible values of justice. Consequently, according to this viewpoint, the jurist's task must be to describe all possible interpretations of a norm, without, however, indicating any interpretation as being preferable over others, in order to avoid making a value judgment, in which case it would no longer be a scientific exercise (Bersier Ladavac 2013; Losano 1981: 92–116).

While the application of the non-evaluative approach to law enabled Kelsen to engage in structural reasoning concerning the legal order, when applied to justice it led Kelsen to conclusions that were uncertain and unclear. In fact, by virtue of its aim of describing and not prescribing, listing and not choosing, the *Reine Rechtslehre* presented itself as a doctrine of the legal status quo, of the decision not to make social and existential choices. This is because, for the *Reine Rechtslehre*, all legal systems are acceptable insofar as they are reduced to pure forms devoid of content. In pursuing his formal theory, Kelsen leaves substantive study, and hence decisions about choices, to others.

In relation to natural law, Kelsenian relativism is used to support the position that an internally consistent pure theory of law cannot tolerate absolute value judgments within it. It was natural that he thereby imposed the limit that historical and social reality must be disregarded, whereas values perform highly precise social and contingent functions when they express themselves. Kelsen himself pointed to the lack of answers in the *Reine Rechtslehre* to these important questions, which are by contrast the very precondition for human social existence, when he gave his last lecture at Berkeley prior to retiring from teaching, entitled *What is Justice?*. In this lecture, he clearly explained that the Platonic idea of good and the Aristotelian principle of the "right means" are non-substantive foundations of justice, which may be filled with any moral or political content, and which may therefore justify any social order, admitting that:

> I started this essay with the question as to what is justice. Now, at its end I am quite aware that I have not answered it. My only excuse is that in this respect I am in the best company. It would have been more than presumptuous to make the reader believe that I could succeed where the most illustrious thinkers have failed. And, indeed, I do not know, and I cannot say what justice is, the absolute justice for which mankind is longing. I must acquiesce in a relative justice and I can only say what justice is to me. Since science is my profession, and hence the most important thing in my life, justice, to me, is that social order under whose protection the search for truth can prosper. "My" justice, then, is the justice of freedom, the justice of peace, the justice of democracy—the justice of tolerance (Kelsen 1957: 24)

For Kelsen, the ideal of justice thus becomes an ideal of peace and the social task of positive law is to guarantee peace between the individual subjects of the legal order (Kelsen 1985: 103–105), whereby the legal order transforms the ideal of absolute justice into the relative justice of legality, of compliance with positive legal norms (see Carrino in Kelsen 1989: XI).

12.5 The Sociological Concept of Justice

But Kelsen has also analyzed a sociological concept of justice, which is connected more with politics than with law. In particular the book, *Society and Nature* (Kelsen 1943), and especially its preface, is important because Kelsen sets out in it what Renato Treves has correctly referred to as a "sociology of the idea of justice" (Treves 1981). In this book, he distinguishes between a normative theory of law and a sociology of phenomena understood in terms of cause and effect for natural events, ie, the interplay between legal and natural reality. The legal order, ie, the normative order, determines how people ought to behave. However, the actual behavior of men is determined by the laws of nature according to the principle of causality. Kelsen defines this as natural reality and claims that, insofar as sociology deals with this reality, sociology is a branch of natural science. Moreover, just as actual behavior may or may not comply with the legal order, positive law may or may not correspond to an ideal law of justice, which means that it should be conceived in terms of a sociology of the idea of justice, of an idea which is conceived as an ideal. Thus, a science of law is only possible if the theory of law is separated from a sociology and philosophy of justice (Treves 1981: 10 n.8). In particular, in *Society and Nature* Kelsen stresses the sociological origins of natural law theories when explaining how the animist interpretation of nature, based on the principle of retribution, gives rise to the idea of nature as an ideal society and how this in turn leads to the idea of a natural law understood as an absolutely just law. While on the one hand Kelsen assesses and criticises natural law theories and sociological theories in the same terms, on the other hand he takes account of the needs to which these theories must provide an answer, namely the requirements of a legal policy that is interested in issues related to ends and values.

In the important preface to *Society and Nature* and also in the important introduction to the *General Theory of Law and State* (Kelsen 1945), Kelsen argues in relation to a sociological idea of justice. The sociology of justice is undoubtedly a discipline that deserves to be investigated with reference to the ideas that effectively determine it, or, at the very least, from a moral point of view, should determine the formation of the norms that we call legal. For Kelsen, moreover, a study of the sociology of justice proves to be useful in that it also identifies the social function of certain ideas that exist in the minds of human beings and function as a cause for their behavior. In particular, in the second edition of *Reine Rechtslehre* (Kelsen 1960; see *Anhang*), he stresses the fact that the idea of justice is of crucial importance for legal policy and that the sociology of the idea of justice must analyze a broader field, as does the sociology of knowledge and the sociology of values.

The sociology of the idea of justice cannot give any objective and absolute value to any theory and must conceive of values in relativist terms. It is well known that Kelsen's relativism from the 1930s was no different from his relativism in the 1960/1970s, which argues in favor of a sociology of the idea of justice that is based on relativism. Kelsen inferred his viewpoint regarding the relativity of values, which he always defended, from that concept. That idea may be used to infer the principle of tolerance, which is closely related to the principles of freedom and democracy and, ultimately, also to science, in relation to which Kelsen asserts that the soul of science is tolerance.[10]

12.6 The Existential Concept of Justice and the Critique of Ideology

Until this point, we have analyzed Kelsen's concept of justice within the *Reine Rechtslehre* as related to the legal order. In fact, Kelsen was a great jurist and saw the world above all through the eyes of a legal scholar. However, Kelsen was also a man of culture, hailing from that deep-rooted central European culture that profoundly shaped the Viennese milieu. He was also typical of the Jewish intelligentsia, a typical example of the Viennese elites predominant at the time, driven on by continuous attempts at inclusion due to previous marginalization. The culture and values of Great Vienna thus constituted a fundamental element of Kelsen's intellectual baggage, and it is certain that this way of being and of feeling continued to mark his personality, even after his emigration. While his world view remained predominantly that of a jurist, his legal reasoning concealed a deeper *Weltanschauung*, which was philosophical in nature, and which undoubtedly continued to guide his legal thinking. His thought is thus a synthesis of philosophy, specifically moral and social philosophy, and legal theory. One is inconceivable without the other, even though Kelsen the jurist has prevailed within the collective imagination of legal doctrine.

Moreover, if analyzed over and above the context of the *Reine Rechtslehre* and the standard interpretation of Kelsenian thought, the issue of justice covers an idea that Kelsen has of justice that goes beyond its legal and social aspect, revealing profound reflections related to the issue of ideology. As Friedrich Dürrenmatt once remarked, "An ideology is not a science" (Dürrenmatt 1991: 371), which is what Kelsen appears to be saying in all of his writings (Kelsen 1947, 1957) on the issue of justice. This is because, if analyzed in detail, Kelsen's entire thinking—and not solely that concerning justice—runs against any ideology. Examining significant religious, political and metaphysical texts, Kelsen directed his rigorous critique of ideology in an extremely decisive manner, classifying all that is ideological as lacking in substance and logical support in the face of scientific criticism in general, and more specifically, the *Reine Rechtslehre*. His critique of ideology is predominantly directed against religion (any religion), and seeks to purify science—and for Kelsen legal science in particular—from all theological and metaphysical remnants that perform an anti-scientific role. It would be misleading if we were to consider Kelsen's criticism exclusively as part of his broader theoretical project, which only provided for the abandonment of metaphysics and theology. In reality, the critique of ideology was also made within the context of a highly precise political project,

[10] Kelsen (1953 and 1973), in particular the introduction by O. Weinberger, XXV-XXVI regarding Kelsen's legal positivism and value-relativism, and the ideological and democratic consequences.

which went beyond the abandonment of metaphysical and theological claims, ie, as a necessary way of overcoming the dichotomies of good/evil, true/false, being/not being, science/magic, and rationality/irrationality. Thus, Kelsen's critique of ideology was the critical annulment of everything related to mythology, magic, archaism, and totemism and, on the other hand, the assertion of the law as a structure based on logical and scientific propositions: in short, science as a process of self-determination of reason (see Carrino in Kelsen 1989: XII), the pure theory as a means of destroying all mythological, metaphysical and mystic residues inherent within human society.

Moreover, for Kelsen, the critique of ideology, of which the critique of justice is a constituent element, is the result of an atavistic and magical vision man has of himself, which is rooted in his primitive origins, and, as Agostino Carrino has correctly noted (see Carrino in Kelsen 1989: IX), leads him to adopt a social ideology and an ideology of retribution as an instrument of justice (Kelsen 1985: 248). Within Kelsen's analysis, which is focused on good and evil, analyzing above all Plato (Kelsen 1942a) from the starting point of justice, this vision transforms into a vast discourse on ethics, which is juxtaposed with the dissolution of existential relations due to European affairs of the time, focusing on the normative as a value as such. Kelsen's discourse on justice is thus primarily critical of classical and traditional views. We recall the concise critique of religions, including in particular secular religions and philosophies (Kelsen 2012), along with Platonic and Aristotelian philosophies, which are regarded as ideologies and, as such, as having a negative social function. Kelsen directs a central criticism against Plato, whom he studied assiduously. It is aimed in particular at the metaphysical conception of the soul and the belief in its immortality, which is typical of Greek and Christian philosophies.

For Kelsen, souls considered in a metaphysical sense are conceived of ideologically and hence perform an anti-scientific and anti-rational function. Kelsen's entire discourse on the soul is a discourse on superstition, on magic, and on ideology as a magical vision with social ends. In fact, he writes that "faith in souls is first and foremost an ideology of retribution and as such an instrument of justice" (Kelsen 1985: 248). Thus, the soul is directly related to ethics and must engage with a need for justice. For Kelsen, all other illusions, such as the existence of God or justice, are born out of the soul as a primitive and totemic concept. Moreover, when understood in this way, for him the soul and other illusions belong to an irrational metaphysics, which is seen as an emotive postulate and a moral requirement stemming from a subjective need, which has nothing to do with the objective reality. Thus, justice too is born out of an internal need of the individual, who in this way seeks to justify a subjective value by associating that subjective value with a value, or a norm of justice, that is regarded as objective and universally valid. The lack of objectivity, of possible corroboration within an external reality not merely constrained to the subjective sphere, renders the ideal of justice an irrational ideal which, like all other ideals, is inaccessible to human consciousness (Kelsen 1957: 10) and anti-scientific. For Kelsen, such a conception of justice is alien to a rational science, the only form of science capable of providing true knowledge.

Although justice may be classed under irrational ideals and ideologies, it nevertheless performs a useful and socially positive function for Kelsen as it promotes the ideal of peace, which is without doubt a consistent and mandatory aspect of a positive legal order. In order to ensure good social cohabitation, the legal order seeks to promote peace. In attempting to manifest itself within the practice of social reality, the ideal of absolute justice transforms itself into an ideal of relative justice, attempting to engage with positive legal norms. When understood in these terms, Kelsen's positivism and natural law, which endorse the concept of justice in its two principal forms—the metaphysical-religious concept of Plato and the rationalist concept of Aristotle (Ross 1957)—arrive at the same postulate, namely the meaning of justice as legality and obedience to the laws of the state. However, as Agostino Carrino explains, "...while natural law ideology is forced to engage in a *metamorphosis* of its starting postulates, Kelsen remains consistent from the outset with the postulate of the value of veracity and thus has no need to abandon the scientific method in order to champion requirements of possible justice" (see Carrino in Kelsen 1989:, XIX, and Kelsen's article on justice and metamorphosis in Kelsen 1947).

The complexity of Kelsenian doctrine, also as regards the discourse on justice, is due to a complex interaction between various ideals, which sought to satisfy two types of requirement. On the one hand, the *Reine Rechtslehre* has a neo-Kantian philosophical basis in the purely descriptive and non-evaluative meaning of its conception; on the other hand, his theory is tied to historical values and must therefore be interpreted also in an ideological light, as the reflex of a political vision and a certain political design of Kelsen. These two opposing visions, which have perhaps not been fully acknowledged, have hindered an understanding of the true meaning of the historical and theoretical project of the Kelsenian construction. It would be a mistake to regard the two conceptions as countervailing. In reality, they are perfectly in tune with and complement each other. Moreover, it would be limiting to consider Kelsen's theory as legal or political only because it was also a philosophical enterprise, characterized by a strong moral valence. It must, of course, be considered as a reflection on what is normative, on that which must be. However, it must also be viewed as being juxtaposed to a conception of existence understood as pure contingency, as having a merely mutable nature, as the "is" juxtaposed to the "ought."

When understood in this way, Kelsen's project, which is characterized by various aporias, is without doubt ambiguous, and almost contradictory. Indeed, on the one hand, there is the rigorously formal side to the Kelsenian conception expressed in the pure theory of law, such as purity, system, order, norm, ought, coercion, validity, efficacy, etc.; yet, on the other hand, there is a clear political and legal theory designed for the achievement of particular legal and political ideals. Here Kelsen's variegated and unstinting commitment related to his legal and political activity, including in particular the important involvement in constitutional issues and his work as a legal consultant during the years spent in Europe, needs to be recalled and not downplayed. Perhaps this contradiction within his theory simply expressed the contradictions within Kelsen himself. In fact, his existential and cultural roots were also grounded in a theological and religious conception of life and history. As was rightly hypothesized by Agostino Carrino in an interesting study (see Carrino in Kelsen 1989), perhaps Kelsen elaborated his legal and political theoretical conception in order to counter the setbacks of human society and history, opposing the formal categories of the pure theory of law with history itself and religious archaism, ie, the ought against the is, form against fact, purity against the contradictory reality of being, and order against disorder. It is only in this way that the absorption of God into nature (along with its natural law ramifications) and of the state into pure normativity and formal abstractness can be understood. In rejecting any substantive conception of the state—thereby taking an intellectual step that was by no means insignificant—Kelsen used his pure, rational, and formal concepts to destroy any residual mythological and archaic element present within an archaic-substantive state characterized by age-old ideologies, which also required de-substantivisation, as occurred, for example, with justice. For Kelsen, in fact, mythological thinking, and with it ideology, acted as a brake on the emancipation of a critical view of the human sciences. Moreover, a normative conception of the state is only possible against a conception of the world and of life that resulted in a de-substantivisation from any substantive category, including in particular that of God.

If this interpretation is correct, we have to ask why Kelsen wanted to debunk all metaphysics, all theology, all ideology, and all archaic sacredness. We can hypothesize that his project was not only theoretical-philosophical but also ethical, because in deconstructing the absolute values of absolute ideologies Kelsen in fact advanced his own relativist view of values with the goal of promoting more peaceful and more ethical cohabitation (the idea of *civitas maxima*), which was morally better. Thus Kelsen did not want to engage in an absolute deconstruction of values, ethics and morals, but attempted to change the viewpoint from which ethics, morals and values were to be considered. He simply proposed another vision, a relativist vision of values, ethics and morals (Bersier Ladavac 2008). This relativist vision was consistent with the requirements of modern science and was in keeping with Kelsen's legal and philosophical construct. With his concise critique, Kelsen undoubtedly sought to debunk and desacralize existing ethics and morals, not in order to destroy but in order to propose different morals and ethics. The aim of this was to promote tolerance and an improved social order, and probably also to promote interests regarded as socially useful. Yet its purpose was not to guarantee a utopian well-being—Kelsen naively defines it as happiness (Kelsen 1957)—for all subjects as an ethics based on absolute values seeks to achieve. Kelsen thus relativized absolute values, reducing them to relative values. In reducing values from an absolute level to a relative level, Kelsen achieved an epistemological shift: from value absolutism to gnoseological relativism.

This relativization of values also implied a different concept of the state, which transformed it from a state of substance and sovereign into a legal norm. The conceptual transformation of the state is perhaps the most deep-seated and revolutionary legal argument proposed by Kelsen. The traditional concept of the sovereign and substantive state is superseded by the pure law, the pure norm according to the canons of the *Reine Rechtslehre*. Consequently, this demetaphysicalization, desacralization and demystification of the state (Herrera 1997, 2001: 13–28), also entailed a metamorphosis in the concept of justice: from an absolute value, as an expression of state and substance, it transformed into a category of positive law.

The Kelsenian ideological reduction of the state and of values was possible because it was essentially based on a dual vision of reality. God on the one side and the world on the other; the state on the one side and the law on the other; justice and values on the one side and positive law on the other, thereby positivizing the former. This is not a pure and simple cancellation of the archaic-ideological reality, but its incorporation into a new gnoseological dimension; in other words, for Kelsen there can be two parallel truths, as the science of nature is in any case a value, a positive value which cannot be demonstrated by reason, just as its opposite—evil—is also indemonstrable. In Kelsen's view, the values of natural science appear on the same plane as the formal values of legal science, there being no clear distinction within them. However, Kelsen claims that it is necessary to distinguish between them. As a positivist, Kelsen endeavors to make that distinction a typological division. For example, the legal value of justice is different from the value of justice of traditional ethics. Values are relativized and compared and contrasted with one another, with the result that all values are broken down and reconstructed within one single plurality. Agostino Carrino explains:

> [T]his conscious departure from the classical systems, from all forms of thinking under such systems, encapsulates the legal positivism of Kelsen and the very positivity of law, which as such appears as the product and result of the "disintegrating" scientific method, which separates, tears, divides and analyses what was once part of the universality of things, the totality of the world, including also the world of values and their hierarchy (Carrino in Kelsen 1989: XVI)

Kelsen's position and his relativist theory of values is therefore a vast and detailed proposal because it includes an infinite possibility of values and possible choices and decisions. However, at the same time it is ideologically neutral in that it is able to endorse a pluralist view of values and to promote *weltweit* the ideal of tolerance within a society inspired by democratic ideals (Bobbio 1992). Within that perspective, the pure theory and its positivism may be regarded as "the highest and most consistent point of a worldly rationalization, of a definitive immanentization of the vital processes of man" (Carrino in Kelsen 1989: XII).

12.7 Conclusions

Kelsen's discourse was certainly an expression of a special intellectual and original development—undoubtedly unique within the history of legal thinking. Kelsen developed his ideas against an ideologically turbulent and dramatic historical and cultural backdrop, which posed novel questions to which the *Reine Rechtslehre* sought to give answers. However, Kelsen's ideas fell on deaf ears and were overwhelmed by the force of European tragedy. He himself understood the tragedy that was playing out in Europe and decided to go into exile. However, Kelsen did not want to remain on the sidelines and always felt the need to engage with political and social issues. Above all, he understood that the West had attempted to save itself from nihilist internal and external pressures within the eternal order of nature, creation and absolute values. Inspired by democratic political ideals, Kelsen thus considered the problem of dominance (*Herrschaft*), seeking to unmask the ideologies of dominance (*Herrschaftsideologien*), which had long dominated society through positive law in order to implement the absolute norms of natural law (Cf. Kelsen 1964, in particular the introduction by Ernst Topitsch). Analyzing the reasons at the base of religious and social ideologies, which had endured through the archaic depths of human consciousness, Kelsen had identified the role played by myth, which on an ontological level does not admit any difference between nature and society. In fact, the nature of mythological *Weltanschauung* had found its natural outlet in the social community (*Gesellschaft*), that is within a union between human beings, an entity that must abide by a universal system of norms. Within this social universe, Kelsen conceived of humans in an ethical and normative sense as *Normadressaten* (ie, addressees of norms).

However, such a conception of the world did not enable Kelsen to draw a distinction between social and religious elements, and the society with which individuals were confronted also represented divine authority, which may authorize and prohibit. Natural law is naturally derived from the same dynamics, ie, the conception of the universe as a social community dominated and regulated by a superior being. Moreover, it was this superior being's laws that held together the cosmos, the legal community, in a regulated and ordered manner. These norms, which were posited by God, reason or nature, had supreme status—that which is truly good and truly right, over and above positive law. Kelsen thus highlighthed the close link between theories of natural and metaphysical absolutism.

His critique of ideology undoubtedly sought to deconstruct the use by positive law of substantive norms of natural law which, according to the *Ideologiekritik*, was regarded as a right law and compliant with justice. Moreover, it sought to debunk the authority that defended positive law by asserting that it maintined the norms of natural law, and of justice in particular, thus attempting to legitimize positive law with reference to natural law. On this view, positive law and natural law authority overlapped with each other.

Kelsen demonstrated with many examples drawn from history that natural law ideologies were systems essentially based on empty formulae, which were used in order to legitimize any legal and political order whatsoever, and above all in order to legitimize structures of social domination. With his analyses of the mythical and religious foundations of natural law ideologies, with his analyses of the metaphysics of morals of Plato and Aristotle, along with his studies on the sociology of the *Seelenglauben*, Kelsen directed his critique against the convictions that made up the core of European spiritual life. The ideological critique revealed the weaknesses within those ways of thinking. Kelsen sought above all to demonstrate in his work *Causality and Retribution* (Kelsen 1941a) from 1946 that the social metaphysics of the West was derived essentially from the sociomorphic *Weltdeutung* (interpretation of the world) of primitive thought, from the conception of the world understood as a vast social structure.

Paradoxically, Kelsen's opponents objected that his relativism could legitimize any legal, political or social order whatsoever—not only positive systems such as democracy but also authoritarian, autocratic and other systems based on coercion.

This was an unfair charge against a man who, with the *Reine Rechtslehre*, had only sought to give prominence to the *Wertfreiheit* (value freedom) of science by placing it in the service of a liberal and humanitarian political ideal, theorizing a liberal and democratic state as the maximum political expression of humanity. As Karl Larenz, accusing Kelsen from his National Socialist perspective, put it, "It was objected that the liberal-democratic theory of the state found its purest and most consistent expression in Kelsen's theory of law, and that as the ultimate conceptual pinnacle of positivism it was in actual fact nothing other than an embodiment of spiritual alienation (Überfremdung)," and could no longer conceptualize the metaphysical sense of the concepts of national spirit (Larenz 1934: 11).

The role and function of Kelsen's theoretical contribution to Austro-German—and European—spiritual history is beyond doubt, including in particular the fact of having raised the question of value relativism, which had far-reaching consequences for the political and social philosophy of the twentieth century, contributing to disenchantment with modernity and nihilism, value polytheism and the crisis of universalism (Bolaffi 2002: see in particular n.4, XXV). Although natural law doctrines have always dreamt of being able to demonstrate their premises with precise certainty, those doctrines are self-defeating and hence untenable. However, if everything is relative and nothing can be demonstrated, then the same too applies for Kelsen, and we can consistently conclude with Werner Maihofer:

> Nevertheless, the proposition that natural law ideologies cannot be proven must be placed alongside the corresponding proposition for positivism. Positivism too has proved to amount to an approach to science that is ultimately based on a value decision (the decision of not wanting to make value judgments). The attempt to achieve objectively valid knowledge in this manner reveals itself to be a pretext, which can only be formulated by constraining the concept of reality. On the contrary, all new knowledge obtained in this manner as a continuation of exact natural science does not show the principal revealability, but the essential immunity from disclosure of the deepest relations of being (Maihofer 1969: 113)

Acknowledgements This paper, including all quotations, was translated by Thomas Roberts, Edinburgh, to whom I would like to express all my gratitude. I would like to express my gratitude to Jeremy Telman for having organized such an interesting event about Hans Kelsen. I had the opportunity not only to attend to the conference in Chicago but also to learn a lot more about Kelsen. I am especially grateful to Carlo Nitsch and Jürgen Busch for the detailed information and the many discussions we have had about the life of Hans Kelsen. These discussions proved to be very useful in clarifying the difficult period of his career following his move from Europe to the United States. I am also grateful to Stanley L. Paulson and Agostino Carrino whose long discussions helped me to understand the complex thought of Hans Kelsen. However, I am especially grateful to Morris L. Ghezzi for introducing me to the work of Hans Kelsen many years ago.

References

Austin, John. 1885. *The Province of Jurisprudence Determined.* All references are to the fifth and last edition published in 1885, reprint in 1995. Cambridge: Cambridge University Press.

Bersier Ladavac, Nicoletta. 2008. Recht, Moral und Gerechtigkeit bei Hans Kelsen. In *Festschrift für Walter Ott*, ed. Sandra Hotz and Klaus Mathis, 19–52. Zürich-St. Gallen: Dike.

Bersier Ladavac, Nicoletta. 2013. Zur Interpretationstheorie von Hans Kelsen. Die Auslegungslehre im Verhältnis zur Reinen Rechtslehre. In *Gedenkschrift Robert Walter*, ed. Clemens Jabloner, Dieter Kolonovits, Gabriele Kuckso-Stadlmayer, Hans René Laurer, Heinz Mayer, and Rudolf Thienel, 51–67. Wien: Manz.

Bobbio, Norberto. 1972. *Giusnaturalismo e positivismo giuridico*. Milano: Edizioni di Comunità.

Bobbio, Norberto. 1992. *Diritto e potere. Saggi su Kelsen*. Napoli: Edizioni Scientifiche Italiane.

Bolaffi, Angelo. 2002. *Il crepuscolo della sovranità. Filosofia e politica nella Germania del Novecento*. Roma: Donzelli.

Dürrenmatt, Friedrich. 1991. *Das Dürrenmatt Lesebuch*. Zürich: Diogenes.

Herrera, Carlos Miguel. 1997. *Théorie juridique et politique chez Hans Kelsen*. Paris: Kimé.

Herrera, Carlos Miguel (ed.). 2001. *Actualité de Kelsen en France*. Paris: L. G. D. J.

Kelsen, Hans. 1934. *Reine Rechtslehre. Einleitung in die rechtswissenschaftliche Problematik*. Leipzig/Wien: Franz Deuticke.

Kelsen, Hans. 1941a. Causality and Retribution. *Philosophy of Science* 8: 533–556. Reprint in: *What is Justice? Justice, Law, and Politics in the Mirror of Science. Collected Essays*. Berkeley and Los Angeles University of California Press: (1957, 533–556).

Kelsen, Hans. 1941b. The Law as a Specific Social Technique. *University of Chicago Law Review* 9: 75–97.

Kelsen, Hans. 1941c. The Pure Theory of Law and Analytical Jurisprudence. *Harvard Law Review* 55: 44–70. Reprint in: *What is Justice? Justice, Law, and Politics in the Mirror of Science. Collected Essays*. Berkeley/Los Angeles: University of California Press: (1957, 266–287).

Kelsen, Hans. 1942a. *Platonic Love*. Trans. G.B. Wilbur. The American Imago. A Psychoanalytical Journal for the Arts and Sciences 3: 3–110.

Kelsen, Hans. 1942b. *Law and Peace in International Relations. The Oliver Wendell Holmes Lectures, 1940–41*. Cambridge, MA: Harvard University Press. Italian Edition, Hans Kelsen, *Diritto e pace nelle relazioni internazionali*, a cura di Carlo Nitsch, Milano, Giuffré 2009.

Kelsen, Hans. 1942c. Value Judgments in the Science of Law. *Journal of Social Philosophy and Jurisprudence* 7: 312–333. Reprint in: *What is Justice? Justice, Law, and Politics in the Mirror of Science. Collected Essays*. Berkeley/Los Angeles: University of California Press: (1957, 209–230).

Kelsen, Hans. 1943. *Society and Nature. A Sociological Inquiry*. Chicago: The University of Chicago Press.

Kelsen, Hans. 1944. *Peace through Law*. Chapel Hill: The University of North Carolina Press.

Kelsen, Hans. 1945. *General Theory of Law and State*. Trans. A. Wedberg. 20th Century Legal Philosophy Series vol. 1. Cambridge, MA: Harvard University Press.

Kelsen, Hans. 1947. The Metamorphoses of the Idea of Justice. In *Interpretations of Modern Legal Philosophies. Essays in Honor of Roscoe Pound*, ed. Roscoe Pound and Paul Lombard Sayre, 390–418. New York: Oxford University Press.

Kelsen, Hans. 1952. *Principles of International Law*. New York: Rinehart.

Kelsen, Hans. 1953. *Was ist Gerechtigkeit?* Wien: Franz Deuticke.

Kelsen, Hans. 1957. *What is justice? Justice, law, and politics in the mirror of science. Collected essays*. Berkeley/Los Angeles: University of California Press.

Kelsen, Hans. 1960. *Reine Rechtslehre. Mit einem Anhang: Das Problem der Gerechtigkeit*, Zweite, völlig neu bearbeitet und erweiterte Auflage. Wien: Franz Deuticke.

Kelsen, Hans. 1964. Aufsätze zur Ideologiekritik (ed. by Ernst Topitsch). Neuwied am Rhein/Berlin: Luchterhand.

Kelsen, Hans. 1967. *Pure Theory of Law*. (Without the appendix *DasProblem der Gerechtigkeit*). Trans. by M. Knight, Second Revised and Enlarged German Edition. Berkeley/Los Angeles: University of California Press.

Kelsen, Hans. 1973. *Essays in Legal and Moral Philosophy*. Selected and Introduced by Ota Weinberger. Trans. P. Heath. Dordrecht/Boston: D. Reidel Publishing Society.

Kelsen, Hans. 1979. *Allgemeine Theorie der Normen*. Edited from the estate of Hans Kelsen on behalf of the Hans Kelsen-Institut by Kurt Ringhofer and Robert Walter. Wien: Manz.

Kelsen, Hans. 1985. *Die Illusion der Gerechtigkeit. Eine kritische Untersuchung der Sozialphilosophie Platons.* Edited from the estate of Hans Kelsen on behalf of the Hans Kelsen-Institut by Kurt Ringhofer and Robert Walter. Wien: Manz.
Kelsen, Hans. 1989. *L'anima e il diritto. Figure arcaiche della giustizia e concezione scientifica del mondo.* Trans. and ed. A. Carrino. Roma: Edizioni Lavoro.
Kelsen, Hans. 1991. *General Theory of Norms.* Trans. and edited by M. Hartney. Oxford: Clarendon Press.
Kelsen, Hans. 1998. *Il problema della giustizia.* Trans. and edited by M.G. Losano. Torino: Einaudi.
Kelsen, Hans. 2006. *Hans Kelsen im Selbstzeugnis.* (ed. Matthias Jestaedt). Tübingen: Mohr Siebeck.
Kelsen, Hans. 2009. *Diritto e pace nelle relazioni internazionali. Le Oliver Wendell Holmes Lectures, 1940–1941.* Trans. and ed. C. Nitsch. Milano: Giuffré.
Kelsen, Hans. 2012. *Secular Religion. A Polemic against the Misinterpretation of Modern Social Philosophy. Science, and Politics as "New Religions."* Edited from the estate of Hans Kelsen on behalf of the Hans Hans Kelsen-Institut by Robert Walter, Clemens Jabloner and Klaus Zeleny. Wien/New York: Springer.
Larenz, Karl. 1934. *Deutsche Rechtserneuerung und Rechtsphilosophie.* Tübingen: J. C. B. Mohr.
Losano, Mario G. 1981. L'interpretazione, ovvero come descrivere una prescrizione. In *Forma e realtà in Kelsen.* Milano: Edizioni di Comunità.
Losano, Mario G. 2011. Gli anni americani di Hans Kelsen. *Materiali per una storia della cultura giuridica* XLI(1): 253–258.
Maihofer, Werner (ed.). 1969. *Ideologie und Recht.* Frankfurt: Vittorio Klostermann.
Métall, Rudolf Alàdar. 1969. *Hans Kelsen, Leben und Werk.* Wien: Franz Deuticke.
Nitsch, Carlo. 2009. In Hans Kelsen, *Diritto e pace nelle relazioni internazionali.* Milano: Giuffré.
Nitsch, Carlo. 2012. *Diritto e forza nella comunità degli Stati: Studio su Hans Kelsen e la teoria del diritto internazionale.* Napoli: Satura.
Paulson, Stanley L. 1988. *Die Rezeption Kelsens in Amerika.* In: Reine Rechtslehre im Spiegel ihrer Fortsetzer und Kritiker. Edited by Ota Weinberger and Werner Krawietz. Wien/New York: Springer (179–202).
Ross, Alf. 1957. Review of *What is justice? Justice, law and politics in the mirror of science. Collected essays.* In *California Law Review* 45(4): 564–570.
Telman, Jeremy D.A. 2010. A path not taken: Hans Kelsen's pure theory of law in the land of the legal realists. In *Hans Kelsen anderswo. Hans Kelsen Abroad. Der Einfluss der Reinen Rechtslehre auf die Rechtstheorie in verschiedenen Ländern, Teil III*, Schriftenreihe des Hans Kelsen-Instituts 33, ed. Robert Walter, Clemens Jabloner, and Klaus Zeleny, 353–376. Wien: Manz.
Treves, Renato. 1981. Sociologia del diritto e sociologia dell'idea di giustizia nel pensiero di Hans Kelsen. In *Sociologia del diritto*, 7–24. Milano: Franco Angeli.
Tur, Richard, and William Twining (eds.). 1986. *Essays on Kelsen.* Oxford: Clarendon.
Wittgenstein, Ludwig. 1989. *Ein Reader.* Frankfurt: Suhrkamp Verlag, 354.

[illegible]

Chapter 13
Pure Formalism? Kelsenian Interpretative Theory between Textualism and Realism

Christoph Bezemek

13.1 Back to School

As a graduate student in the United States I was quite surprised at how often I found myself in a position defending my positivist theoretical approach. A surprise, it may be argued, owed to a quite guileless view: "The faculty of Yale," as Frank Easterbrook stated in 1998, "little loves positivists" (Easterbrook 1998: 119). At least to a certain extent, this proved to be true still 10 years later. I guess some of my professors had fun bantering me that some of my remarks in class were owed to me being a positivist of the Kelsenian variety. And the discussions following such attributions proved to be quite entertaining, particularly as I, an Austrian lawyer, trained in a Kelsenian perspective on law, never really saw the problem.

Perhaps that was naïve, undertheorized even, given the tradition of the law school I attended: Yale Law School, so closely related to the realist movement,[1] was at least not destined to be eager to embrace arguments suspicious of being based on Kelsen's pure theory of law (see, in particular, Telman 2010: 362); as legal positivism and legal realism, so often described as opposing views in legal scholarship, would just not match.[2]

---

[1] See the classical account by Myres McDougal (1947). For the interesting background of the establishment of legal realism at Yale in opposition to "formalism [...] practiced most successfully at Harvard" by former YLS Dean Harry Wellington, see Posner (1980: 1118–1119).

[2] And, of course, the Kelsenian seems to be particularly opposed to realist ideas:

> [P]ositivists, especially those of the Kelsen school, have adopted an extreme conceptualism: Consistency of legal norms is for them the only criterion of legality once a sovereign lawmaker is postulated. At the opposite pole of positivist jurisprudence, self-styled American legal realists and many adherents of the Critical Legal Studies movement treat

C. Bezemek (✉)
WU (IOER), Welthandelsplatz 1, D3, 1020 Vienna, Austria
e-mail: christoph.bezemek@wu.ac.at

D.A.J. Telman (ed.), *Hans Kelsen in America - Selective Affinities and the Mysteries of Academic Influence*, Law and Philosophy Library 116,
DOI 10.1007/978-3-319-33130-0_13

Thus, many of my assigned readings implied that things were not as simple as I thought. And the consequences of positivist deficiency, it seemed, were crucial; in particular with regard to method: A formalist, or even "hyperformalist" theory, positivism, it was suggested in one of my favorite assigned readings, was destined to entail a "hypertextualist" approach to interpretation.[3]

Such assumptions, to borrow from Frederick Schauer, are generally based on the following consideration:

> Formalism merges into ruleness, and both are inextricably intertwined with literalism, i.e., the willingness to make decisions according to the literal meaning of the words or phrases or sentences or paragraphs on a printed page, even if the consequences of that decision seem either to frustrate the purpose behind those words or to diverge significantly from what the decisionmaker thinks—the rule aside—should be done. (Schauer 1988: 538)

Such a reception of positivist theory seems to be, if not common, widespread in U.S. academia,[4] even among quite prominent jurists who taught or teach at quite prominent law schools.[5] To make matters worse, among the positivist theories of law, the Kelsenian variety seems especially prone to a diehard textualist method, or so writers like Ronald Dworkin obviously tried to convince their readers.[6]

All this made me wonder: Is Kelsenian thought based on a "hyperformalist," or at least a "formalist" theory? And even if so: Does such a theory entail a "hypertextualist," or at least a "textualist" method of interpretation? An answer to this needs to be developed in several steps in order to avoid the confusions and misapprehensions that seem to dominate at least some parts of the discourse.

> legal rules as rationalizations of the empirical behavior of legal officials and find the sources of that behavior in economic, political, and other non-legal factors. (Berman 1998: 781) (footnote omitted)

See, for further references of the wide spread claim that positivism and realism are opposing theories, Leiter (2001).

[3] Ackerman (1998: 92): "[M]y hypertextualist interlocutor builds on a jurisprudential school that has been (more or less) dominant throughout the twentieth century: legal positivism."

[4] Hardly a novel claim, of course. See, ie, Gardner (2001: 518) or Schauer (1996: 32).

[5] See, for example, Ely (1980: 1): "'interpretivism' [...] indicating that judges deciding constitutional cases should confine themselves to enforcing norms that are stated or clearly implicit in the written Constitution." Continuing in the annotation to this remark: "Interpretivism *is* about the same thing as positivism."

[6] Dworkin states:

> Could the advocate of the 'text' do better by appealing, not to political theory, but to the concept of law? None of the standing philosophical theories of law supplies the necessary arguments. Not even positivist theories, which seem the most likely. Neither Bentham's nor Austin's theory of positivism will do. Nor even Kelsen's (Dworkin 1985: 37).

A belief held not only in U.S. academia of course—see, for example, Brugger (1994: 405 n.22): "Positivism, formalism, and textualism form the main elements of Begriffsjurisprudenz and Hans Kelsen's Reine Rechtslehre." For further references as to the allegation in European academia that Kelsen's theory of law was particularly formalist, see Paulson (2005: 213–214).

13.2 First Things First

The question that needs to be raised in order to address the problems outlined above in the first place is, of course: What does the appreciation of a lawyer or a method as "formalist" actually mean? It hardly comes as surprise that it is far from simple to answer this, as the term "formalism does not really have an identity of its own" (Sebok 1998: 57). It does rather exist as a target to be attacked than a goal to be achieved. It has opponents rather than proponents.[7] And it thus, generally speaking, serves as an umbrella term for a plurality of intermingled reproaches, differing, while not in their core, still at least on their fringe—and quite a fringe that is[8]: "Formalist," Richard Posner (1986" 180–181) found nearly 30 years ago, "can mean narrow, conservative, hypocritical, resistant to change, casuistic, descriptively inaccurate (that is, 'unrealistic' in the ordinary-language sense of the word), ivory-towered, fallacious, callow, authoritarian—but also," focusing on the political stance underlying a formalist position,[9] "rigorous, modest, reasoned, faithful, self-denying, restrained."

In any case: "[a]ccording to the Realists," Jeremy Telman (2010: 361) tells us, "[f]ormalist legal theorists […] believed that judges mechanically applied the law without reference to their own policy preferences or ideological beliefs."[10] Still it does obviously come in nuances: "At its most extreme," so Jim Chen (1995: 1270) stipulates, "formalist dogma posits that identifying all of the 'established' canons of interpretation and subjecting them to brute Euclidian logic will yield one and only one answer to every legal problem." Finally, "Pure Formalists," to refer back to the title of this essay, as Burt Neuborne (1992: 421) explains, "view the judicial system as if it were a giant syllogism machine with a determinate, externally-mandated legal rule supplying the major premise, and objectively 'true' pre-existing facts providing the minor premise."

It may suffice to leave it with those impressions that allow for a general idea of the direction the diverse criticism of the formalist approach takes. Against that backdrop it seems preferable, rather than to give another definition of formalism, to sum up by again quoting Frederick Schauer's approximation to the problem (1988: 510): "whatever formalism [actually] is, it is not good." I think all the critics of a formalist

[7] Even though there obviously are, (few) "self-described formalists in America today" (Leiter 2010: 131).

[8] To give just a few examples of the variety of definition in legal scholarship: While Malkan (1998, 1393) holds that "formalism usually refers to the claim that wellcrafted rules embodied in authoritative texts will constrain the choice of an impartial decisionmaker" (For a quite similar appreciation, see, ie, Eskridge 1990: 646); "Formalism," according to Burton (2007: 3), "insists that legal reasoning should determine all specific actions required by the law based only on objective facts, unambiguous rules, and logic." According to Strauss (1987: 488) the formalist approach is thus essentially anti-functionalist. For a further display of a wide number of different accounts of formalism, see Leiter (1999: 1144–1145) or Schauer (1988: 510).

[9] For these arguments, see Hayek (1944: 117–123).

[10] On this approach, see in particular Kennedy (1973: 359).

approach to legal interpretation can agree on that, whatever their particular position or quarrel might be. In fact, one has to add, it is *so not good*, that even those authors like Ernest Weinrib, who try to defend an approach closer to one or another definition of formalism, feel obliged to justify their endeavor as "not merely a perverse theoretical indulgence" (Weinrib 1988: 951).

Fighting formalism, broad coalitions had been formed in the first half of the twentieth century to tackle legal positivism: "Both the natural lawyer and the realist said they disavowed legal positivism" (Sebok 1995: 2068). Little one has to wonder then, why even non-realist academics like Morris Cohen (1927: 237–38) already back in 1927 sneered at "formalists like Kelsen" and their "fiction that the law is a complete and closed system, and that judges and jurists are mere automata to record its will or phonographs to pronounce its provisions." And little one has to wonder then, why "'Formalism' is, like 'Positivism' frequently used as an ephithet" (Leiter 1999: 1144).

One has to wonder, however, how all this adds up: H.L.A. Hart dedicated a whole chapter of his seminal *Concept of Law* to battle formalist simplifications (Hart 1961: 121–150),[11] which seems strange, not only because Hart is arguably the most important representative of legal positivism in the English-speaking world, not only because Hart evidently drew on Kelsenian thought (see, ie, Summers 1963: 631), but also because Kelsen himself on the other hand, openly remarked that he agreed with Hart's general position (Hart 1963: 710).

This is quite confusing, taking into account what has been stated before: How can positivism join the choir of critics of formalist approaches and at the same time stand accused of having forged the archetype of formalism?

But is Kelsen's pure theory of law actually a formalistic theory? And does that make Kelsen actually a formalist according to the definition provided above? The correct answer needs to be twofold: yes, of course, but no. Such an ominous statement evidently is in need of specification.

13.3 A Formalistic Theory

Let us start with the affirmative part of the answer. When Ota Weinberger (1982: 31) weighed, as the title of the essay here referred to states, "the Pros and Cons of the Pure Theory of Law" back in 1979, he described its method as "anti-ideological and formalistic"; candidly, one may add, as this appraisal did not refer to the allegations sketched above nor to the "methods" of interpretation some critics construe from them.

---

[11] See in particular Hart's critique: "The vice known to legal theory as formalism or conceptualism consists in an attitude to verbally formulated rules which both seeks to disguise and minimize the need for [...] choice, once the general rule has been laid down" (Hart 1961: 126). Also see Hart (1958: 606–615).

Obviously Kelsen's approach to law is formalistic.[12] It needs to be, as this formalistic approach roots deep in his positivist perception of what law is and what legal science can achieve.[13] As Kelsen himself put it:

> As a general theory of law the Pure Theory of Law establishes the fundamental concepts by which every positive law can be conceived and described. Consequently, the Pure Theory of Law must disregard the contents of the legal norms insofar as they differ in time and space. In this sense the Pure Theory of Law has—and by its very nature must have—a formalistic character. This [...] means [...] that the concepts defined by the theory must hold what is common to all positive legal orders, not what separates them from each other (Kelsen 1966: 4).

These thoughts—albeit translated—evidently reproduce parts of two prior essays, the first of which was published already in 1929. In both texts, however, Kelsen had supplemented this statement by the remark that

> it is self-evident that a system of concepts must have a relatively formal character because by these very concepts the ample material of positive law is to be coped with cognitively. Like any cognition, the cognition of law has to formalize its object. And nobody may hold this kind of formalism against it. As in this formalism lies what virtuously counters the vice of the 'formalist' method generally frowned upon: Its objectivity (Kelsen 1929, 1723).[14]

Jeremy Telman (2008: 17–18) surely is correct when he observes that against that backdrop Kelsen's "legal positivism could only have struck his Legal Realist colleagues as a return to the naïve formalism of [...] previous generations."[15] But it becomes clearer now that the ample and variant use of the term "formalism" may be one of the chief causes for some confusion,[16] as "[i]t has to be ascertained whether the derogatory value judgment implied in the claim of formalism is directed at the conception of law and consequently against a theory of law or whether this claim is intended to apply to the generation of law, its creation and evolution, ie, legal practice." (Kelsen 1929: 1723).

Depending on the perspective, the allegation that the pure theory of law takes a formal/formalist/formalistic approach is either a presumably unwarranted accusation or a truism, both of which—this is important to note—are not necessarily connected to one another. The formalism Kelsen talks about is a necessary precondition to define the object of his pure theory, "confining jurisprudence to a structural analysis of positive law" (Kelsen 1961: XV). Kelsen argues in favor of a formalistic

[12] For a short account focusing on this "formalistic" character, see Stewart (1990: 273).

[13] See, for a more recent account, Kammerhofer (2011): 147–148).

[14] My—quite literal—translation. Kelsen continues by referring verbatim to Hermann Cohen (1922, 587): "Nur das Formale ist sachlich[;] je formaler eine Methodik ist, desto sachlicher kann sie werden. Und je sachlicher in der ganzen Tiefe der Sache ein Problem formuliert wird, desto formaler muß es fundamentiert sein." [Only what is formal is objective; the more formal a method, the more objective it can be. And the more objective a problem is defined in its depth, the more formal it has to be founded]. Kelsen then continues by stating: "Whoever does not grasp that, does not know what science is about." For the second essay mentioned above, see Kelsen (1953: 512).

[15] For the historical background of this claim, see Tamaha (2010: 60–62).

[16] My—quite literal—translation.

theory of *law*, not a formalist theory of *legal interpretation*.[17] His approach is about formalizing the concept of law, not its content (see Schreier 1927: III). Thus, because, as Kelsen (1929: 1723) explicitly stated, "the allegation of formalism as a negative value judgment is directed at some specific legal practice,"[18] "'[f]ormalism' can be no objection to a general theory of law, although, as a matter of fact, it is frequently brought forward against the Pure Theory of Law." (Kelsen 1966: 4).

This argument, however, has another edge: "Realism," as Brian Leiter (2001: 301) pointed out, itself "a [...] theory of adjudication,"[19] does not *per se* have to be an objection to a general theory of the Kelsenian variety: "[T]he typical interest of a genuine legal positivist is in logic and form, while the interest of the legal realists in these aspects of law is in a degree incidental to their interest in the function, operation, and consequences or, in other words, the substance, of law." (Yntema 1941: 1164).

13.4 A Formalist Theory?

Specifically addressing the allegation he would argue in favor of a formalist approach to interpretation, Kelsen did not tire of pointing at this misapprehension, which he already tried to refute in the preface to his "Hauptprobleme der Staatsrechtslehre" in 1911 (VIII–X).[20] In the aforementioned essay from 1929, he eventually took a broad (perhaps even the broadest, in any case the most passionate) stand against it (Kelsen 1929: 1723–1726). The essay, additionally, is particularly interesting for the topic at hand, as Kelsen, as he himself points out,[21] at that time

[17] Which is, of course, generally true for the relation of formalism and positivism—see, for example, Leiter (1999: 1150) "Positivism is a *theory of law*, while formalism is a *theory of adjudication*."

[18] My translation. Continuing: "Judgments or decisions by administrative bodies are referred to as formalist in order to point to some specific deficiency" [my translation], showing quite the same understanding as Posner or Schauer quoted above. For [nearly] the identical remark, see Kelsen (1953: 511).

[19] Also see Jeremy Telman (2013: 6).

[20] Kelsen, however, did later consider some of his remarks in that preface as "unfortunate" ["verunglückt"] (Kelsen 1929: 1725).

[21] In the essay mentioned above, however, Kelsen indicated that the "Pure Theory of Law had [...] until recently not commented on the problem of interpretation" [my translation] (Kelsen 1929: 1725). For this "recent comment," Kelsen refers to Fritz Schreier (1927: III), who also points to the fact "that the Vienna School had disregarded the problems of interpretation to some extent" [my translation]. It seems worth noting that unlike Schreier (Schreier 1927: 6), Kelsen does not mention Adolf Merkl, Zum Interpretationsproblem, Grünhutsche Zeitschrift für das Privat- und Öffentliche Recht der Gegenwart 1916, 535, even though later scholarship on this question (see Mayer 1992: 63 or Günther Winkler 1990: 208) treats this essay as starting point of the pure theory's stance on interpretation.

had not yet published his thoughts on interpretation.[22] Still, he remarks "the Pure Theory of Law [had] never opposed any of the possible methods of interpretation in the first place[; while at the same time] in no way arguments in favor of a formalist interpretation may be derived from the Pure Theory of Law." (Kelsen 1929: 1725).

Examined from the angle of his personal credibility—already at that time this claim is quite impressively corroborated by the way Kelsen acted as a member of the Austrian Constitutional Court[23] as well as by his doctrinal work[24]—Kelsen was emphatically not a representative of a dreary as well as short-witted mechanical approach to legal problems.[25]

And this is clearly reflected in his theoretical encounters with the problem of legal interpretation published from 1934.[26] Not to be misunderstood, Kelsen never actually did expound a theory of interpretation,[27] which scholars as intimately acquainted with his work as Robert Walter (1983: 189–190) or Stanley Paulson (1990: 136, 137) already emphasized (also see Thaler 1982: 18 n.38 or Mayer 1992: 61).[28] What Kelsen did was (merely) to point at the imponderabilia of the result of interpretation, which are—at least to a certain extent—inevitable according to his opinion.[29]

In order to be able to relate to this position, it is important to see that Kelsen's approach to interpretation is essentially based on the hierarchical perception of the legal system (see Bersier 2013: 53) originally developed by Adolf J. Merkl (1931: 252–294). "Interpretation," Kelsen (1934: 9) defines against this background, "is an intellectual activity accompanying the law-creating process as it moves from a

[22] Which he published separately for the first time 1934. For Kelsen's prior "phase on interpretation," see Paulson (1990: 141–143).

[23] Where he at one point was even defamed to act based on political motives—see Christian Neschwara (2005: 368) which, albeit quite simply put, eventually led to Kelsen not being re-appointed to the Constitutional Court after the Constitutional reform of 1929 (BGBl 392/1929, 393/1929) in 1930. *Id.* at 374–382.

[24] To link both aspects of his professional life at that time (cf. the prior note), see, for example, Kelsen's defense of the Court's approach in a highly controversial question of jurisdiction (Kelsen 1928a: 105–110, 1928b: 583–599).

[25] To give just one example that proved to be particularly important for Austrian Constitutional doctrine: It was Hans Kelsen who drafted the Constitutional Court's judgment introducing the non-delegation doctrine to Austrian Constitutional Law (VfSlg 176/1923)—(Öhlinger 2008). The wording of Article 18 § 1, however, on which this judgment is based does not state any requirements to be observed by the legislator when providing a legal foundation of administrative action (also the earlier commentary by Kelsen, Fröhlich and Merkl (1922: 85) does not make any reference to such an assessment).

[26] These—generally speaking—do not differ significantly regarding their core assessment as to the "achievement potential" of legal interpretation (see Christoph Schwaighofer 1986: 233).

[27] Kelsen, overall, gave limited attention to the problem of interpretation as such (see Jackson 1985: 88 with further references).

[28] Which makes it pointless to elaborate on this here any further.

[29] This is not necessarily common to any positivist theory of law (see Leiter 1999: 1150).

higher level of the hierarchical structure to the lower level governed by this higher level."[30]

This may be confusing, at least at first glance, given the effort made in this essay to argue in favor of the non-formalist character of a Kelsenian view of interpretation, as to perceive interpretation embedded in this hierarchical system would indeed indicate a mere deductive process of legal reasoning typically proclaimed "formalist,"[31]; applying law "all the way down" as Elena Kagan put it during her confirmation hearings (see Leiter 2010: 128 and n.76).

However, this is not Kelsen's thinking. He explains:

> [t]he relation between a higher and a lower level of the legal system—as between constitution and statute, or between statute and judicial decision—is a relation of determining or binding. The higher-level norm governs the act whereby the lower-level norm is created. [...] This determination, however, is never complete, for a norm cannot be binding with respect to every detail of the act putting it into practice. (Kelsen 1990: 127–128)

Indeterminacy is therefore inevitable (Grimm 1982: 151; also see Paulson 1990: 143); according to Kelsen "no legal decision is completely determined by the law" (see Schauer 2004: 1949). This, of course, may be intended by the lawmaker in the first place, granting discretion to whomever is to act based on his commands. Putting that aside, however, indeterminacy is owed to "the ambiguity of a word or a phrase used in expressing the norm," Kelsen (1990: 129) argues closely related to what H.L.A. Hart (1961: 124–125) should term later as the "open texture [as a general feature of human] language."[32]

In addition to that, Kelsen continues (1990: 129–130), "discrepancies between the linguistic expression of the form and the will of the norm-issuing authority are to be assumed," as "[i]n spite of every effort, traditional jurisprudence has not yet found an objectively plausible way to settle the conflict between will and the expression of will. Every method of interpretation developed thus far invariably leads merely to a possible result, never to a single correct result."[33]

One has not to wonder that theorists of the Dworkinian kind have their quarrel with such statements, particularly with regard to Kelsen's anticipative rejection of the right answer thesis. One has to wonder, however, why such statements should necessarily contravene realist thought, or at least some of its adepts of the less extreme kind; we shall get back to that after having finished the survey of Kelsen's thoughts on interpretation:

Given this predicament the "result [of interpretation]," so Kelsen continues:

> can only be the discovery of the frame that the norm to be interpreted represents and, within this frame, the cognition of several possibilities for implementation. Interpreting a statute,

[30] I will rely on and refer to the English translation by Bonnie Litschewski Paulson and Stanley L. Paulson (1990: 127–135) unless explicitly stated otherwise. *Id.* at 127.

[31] For the perception of "formalism" as a mere process of legal deduction, see Sebok (1998: 57–112).

[32] For a deeper discussion, see, ie, Brian Bix (1991: 51–72).

[33] Lastly, to give a full account, Kelsen argues, "purportedly valid norms [may] contradict one another wholly or in part" (Kelsen 1990: 129–130).

then, leads not necessarily to a single decision as the only correct decision but possibly to several decisions, all of them of equal standing measured solely against the norm to be applied, even if only a single one of them becomes, in the act of the judicial decision, positive law. That a judicial decision is based on a statute means in truth only that the decision stays within the frame the statute represents, means only that the decision is one of the individual norms possible within the frame of the general norm, not that it is the only individual norm possible (Kelsen 1990: 129–130).

To be clear, the question whether the frame referred to has to or can be defined in the first place is subject to dispute,[34] even among his followers (Ringhofer 1971: 205; Paulson 1990: 151; Mayer 1992: 65–67; also see Jackson 1985: 86–88). It is not for this essay to address the rigor of Kelsen's approach.[35] For more important are the conclusions he draws from it, emphasizing that:

[f]rom the standpoint of [...] positive law [...] there is no criterion on the basis of which one of the possibilities given within the frame of the norm to be applied could be favored over the other possibilities. In terms of [...] positive law, there is simply no method according to which only one of the several readings of a norm could be distinguished as "correct"—assuming, of course, that several readings of the meaning of the norm are possible in the context of all other norms of the statute or of the legal system (Kelsen 1990: 130).

"For if a norm can be interpreted," Kelsen continues,[36] "then the question as to which is the 'correct' choice from among the possibilities given within the frame of the norm is hardly a question of cognition directed to the positive law; it is a problem not of legal theory but rather of legal policy." (Kelsen 1990: 131).

Already these extracts show that Kelsen, far from advocating a formalist approach to interpretation, actually rejects it, has to reject it, as he—based on his formalistic conception of law—has to reject the notion of "ruleness" as a reliable indicator of correct solutions to legal problems. Thus, interestingly it was Kelsen's "formalist-pessimist" approach, as Günther Winkler (1990: 208) critically put it, that makes formalist interpretation incompatible with Kelsenian theory.

Just like Hart (1958: 611), or perhaps even more so, Kelsen emphatically argued against a mere mechanical view of jurisprudence—so emphatically, in fact one must add, that by some scholars he is accused of "methodological nihilism" (Adomeit and Hähnchen 2012: 57; see also Öhlinger 1978: 258), which is not only quite a

[34] For more recent encounters, see, for example, Lindahl (2003: 769) or Kennedy (2007: 296).

[35] It is important to note, however, that in his later writings on interpretation Kelsen emphasized that in cases of authentic interpretation (ie interpretation by a law applying organ—see, for example, Kelsen (1960: 351)), norms—albeit cognitively outside the frame—are to be considered valid; also see Kelsen 1950: xv—for this argument see Paulson's (1990: 151–152) analysis.

Taking this into account, of course, Richard Posner (2003: 270) is correct in stating that in Kelsen's thought "law does not dictate the outcome of judicial decisions." See, for an earlier version of this argument, Posner (2001: 23) adding: "provided only the judge does not stay outside the boundaries of his jurisdiction. [...] He may be mistaken, but he is not lawless."

[36] This was particularly emphasized by Kurt Ringhofer (1971: 205) who argued that "in order to interpret the norm its meaning must not be clear from the very outset." [my translation]

It is, however, not certain (or rather, far from certain) that Kelsen adhered to the principle "in claris non fit interpretatio." For this maxim, see Meder (2004: 17–21) or Tosato (2000: 157 n.94). For background and origin, see Masuelli (2002: 402).

distance from the claim he was a formalist, but also quite unfair. Kelsen—to draw from Feyerabend (2010)—was not "Against Method," and he would agree, it is to be assumed (see in particular Walter 1983: 191), that there are indeed "easy cases" (see Schauer 1985).

What he did was to emphasize the limited capacity of legal methodology when evaluated by a standard of cognition (Walter 1990: 51–52)—particularly so by taking a stand against embellishing interpretative arguments as focal point of objective discovery thereby often disguising mere political preferences:

> The conservative professor—strictly scientific, of course—deduces from the concept of the state that democracy is impossible and some kind of fascism or "corporate state" is necessitated; while the revolutionary Marxist argues—based on some equally "scientific" socialism—that the law of causality is to bring about the dictatorship of the proletariat." (Kelsen 1929: 1724).[37]

13.5 A Realist View on Kelsen

If, however, "[t]he most important of Realism's multiple facets is its denial of [the] traditional [formalist] view" (Schauer 2013: 754), not only is Kelsen's pure theory of law not in conflict with aim and scope of core arguments of the forerunners and members of the legal realist movement,[38] his views on interpretation and on what may be achieved by its means at some point take quite the same direction as their critique.

Of course this claim is bold as well as it is naïve, as most bold claims are, particularly because—as common wisdom has it—the term "Realism" is as much undefined, maybe even undefinable as the term "Formalism" proved to be.[39] It is perhaps even more so due to the fact that realism not only had opponents but—albeit quite diverse —proponents as well.[40] And, of course, as we have seen, Kelsen would not concur with the more extreme forms of rule-skepticism[41]; the claim, as Hart (1961: 133) describes it, "that talk of rules is a myth." He would not say that the outcome

[37] My translation. Hart's argument, analyzing the allegation of "formalism" takes the same direction. (Hart 1958: 611).

[38] As generally "[t]he pure theory of law by no means denies the validity of [...] sociological jurisprudence" (Kelsen (1941: 52).

[39] See, for the classical account, Llewellyn (1931).

[40] Citing some of the more common definitions, Brian Leiter (1997: 267–268).

[41] Which—as Brian Leiter (2001: 294) explains—few realists would in the first place.

of a case may merely depended on "what the judge had for breakfast,"[42] even though it seems that nobody, not even Jerome Frank,[43] really assumed that.[44]

But, as we have seen, the critical view of how adjudication actually works, beyond what has been the formalist caricature, common to the Realist movement (Leiter 1999: 1147), is not alien to Kelsen. He would easily agree with Oliver Wendell Holmes that "general propositions do not decide concrete cases" (Lochner v. New York, 198 U.S. 45, 76 (1906) (Holmes, J., dissenting)—judges do, Kelsen would submit,[45] by their decisions effecting what he should term "authentic interpretation" in his later work (see, in particular, Kelsen 1960: 351–352). And Kelsen would agree that in adjudicating, there is indeed "a concealed half conscious battle on the question of legislative policy" that cannot "be settled deductively" (Holmes 1997: 999). "Even the judge," Kelsen would argue:

> creates law, even he is relatively free in his capacity.[…] In applying a statute, there may well be room for cognitive activity beyond discovering the frame within which the act of application is to be confined; this is not cognition of the positive law, however, but cognition of other norms that can now make their way into the law-creating process, the norms, namely, of morality, of justice—social value judgments customarily characterized with the catch-phrases "welfare of the people," "public interest," "progress." and the like (Kelsen 1990: 131).

Kelsen, therefore, would not be troubled by what Frederick Schauer describes as common denominator of a realist position, that "judges typically make decisions on the basis of something other than, or in addition to existing legal doctrine," (Schauer 2009: 134) as he would not be troubled, Jochen von Bernsdorff (2010: 215) pointed that out, by a realist critique as to the potential of legal interpretation, specifically such as by Karl Llewellyn's allegation that "the correct unchallengeable rules of how to read statutes […] lead in happily variant directions" (Llewellyn 1950: 399). And, as we have seen, he would not wrestle too hard with many of the issues raised in Llewellyn's *Theory of Rules* (2011) such as the inadequate determination of hard cases by the legal framework formally applied.

Kelsen's sympathy for such skeptical accounts—we may call them in accordance with Brian Leiter (2001: 293–300), "empirical rule skepticist"—comes hardly as a surprise. Already, in the aforementioned essay from 1929 (1726), he frankly

[42] For a quasi-empirical take on this question, see Kozinski (1996): 993).

[43] See, however, Jerome Frank's statement:

> Out of my own experience as a trial lawyer, I can testify that a trial judge, because of overeating at lunch may be so somnolent in the afternoon court-session that he fails to hear an important item of testimony and so disregards it when deciding the case. "The hungry judges soon the sentence sign, And wretches hang that juryman may dine," wrote Pope. Dickens' lovers well remember Perker's advice to Pickwick: "A good, contented, well-breakfasted juryman, is a capital thing to get hold of. Discontented or hungry jurymen, my dear sir, always find for the plaintiff." (Frank 1973: 162)

[44] However, empirical evidence suggests that there is indeed some truth to this claim (see Danziger et al. 2011: 6889–6892).

[45] Even though judges, of course, would typically present the result as conclusion based on a "sophisticated formalist" manner (Brian Leiter 2010: 112).

considers "the Pure Theory of Law [was] not in conflict with the German Free Law Movement (Freirechtsschule),"[46] a movement related to (or rather, preceding) legal realism (see Herget and Wallace 1987). In fact, Fritz Schreier (1927) dedicated a whole book to the effort to realign the Free Law Movement and the pure theory of law, in order to complement one with the other. Kelsen (1929: 1725) approved.

All this is not to say that Kelsenian thinking and Realism are to be natural allies, they may be to some extent—possibly, to quote Frederick Schauer once more, in a rather "tamed version" (Schauer 2013: 774). They surely don't have to.

It is to say, however, that Kelsen shared many of the core concerns articulated by members of the realist movement and that the pure theory of law does provide the structure to act on them.[47] Let us not forget that, even if not natural allies, legal realism and legal positivism were fighting a common enemy of the formalist kind: "The view that interpretation is cognition of the positive law, and as such is a way of deriving new norms from prevailing norms," so Kelsen (1990: 132) explains, "is the foundation of the so-called jurisprudence of concepts (Begriffsjurisprudenz), which the Pure Theory of Law also rejects. [...] The illusion of legal certainty is what traditional legal theory, wittingly or not, is striving to maintain."

Kelsen, however, sure was not.

Acknowledgments This essay was originally drafted as a contribution to "Hans Kelsen in America," a conference held in Chicago on June 27–28, 2014, sponsored by the Valparaiso University Law School, supported by a grant from the Botstiber Institute for Austrian-American Studies. I am most grateful to Jeremy Telman for organizing this event and inviting me to take part in it as well as to the participants for their most helpful comments. Particular thanks to Michael Potacs for his willingness to discuss an earlier draft of this essay and to my late friend Heinz Peter Rill who generously shared his most valuable insights on the topic.

References

Ackerman, Bruce. 1998. *We the people*. Cambridge, MA: Transformations.

Adomeit, Klaus, and Susanne Hähnchen. 2012. *Rechtstheorie für Studenten*, 6th ed. Heidelberg: C.F. Müller.

Berman, Harold J. 1998. Toward an integrative jurisprudence: Politics, morality, history. *California Law Review* 76: 779–801.

Bersier Ladavac, Nicoletta. 2013. Zur Interpretationslehre von Hans Kelsen. In *Gedächtnisschrift für Robert Walter*, ed. Clemens Jabloner, 51–67. Vienna: Manz.

Bix, Brian. 1991. H. L. A. Hart and the "Open Texture of Language". *Law and Philosophy* 10: 51–72.

Brugger, Winfried. 1994. Legal interpretation, schools of jurisprudence, and anthropology: Some remarks from a German point of view. *American Journal of Comparative Law* 42: 395–421.

Burton, Steven. 2007. *An introduction to law and legal reasoning*, 3rd ed. New York: Aspen Publishers.

[46] For some of the core writings of the Free Law Movement, see Rümelin (1891) or Ehrlich (1903).

[47] On the compatibility of Legal Positivism and Legal Realism in general, see Brian Leiter (2001: 278).

Chen, Jim. 1995. Law as a species of language acquistition. *Washington Law Quarterly* 73: 1263–1309.
Cohen, Hermann. 1922. System der Philosophie Vol. I. In *Logik der Reinen Erkenntnis*, 3rd ed. Berlin: Cassirer.
Cohen, Morris. 1927. Positivism and the limits of idealism in the law. *Columbia Law Review* 27: 237–250.
Danziger, Shai, Jonathan Levav, and Liora Avnaim-Pesso. 2011. Extraneous factors in judicial decisions. *Proceedings of the National Academy of Sciences of the United States of America* 108: 6889–6892.
Dworkin, Ronald. 1985. *A matter of principle*. Cambridge, MA: Harvard University Press.
Easterbrook, Frank. 1998. Textualism and the dead hand. *George Washington Law Review* 66: 1119–1126.
Ehrlich, Eugen. 1903. *Freie Rechtsfindung und freie Rechtswissenschaft* (Reprint 1973). Leipzig: Scientia.
Ely, John Hart. 1980. *Democracy and distrust*. Cambridge, MA: Harvard University Press.
Eskridge, William. 1990. The new textualism. *UCLA Law Review* 37: 621–691.
Feyerabend, Paul. 2010. *Against method*, 4th ed. London: Verso.
Frank, Jerome. 1973. *Courts on trial*, 3rd ed. Princeton: Princeton University Press.
Gardner, John. 2001. Legal positivism: 5½ myths. *American Journal of Jurisprudence* 46: 199–227.
Grimm, Dieter. 1982. Zum Verhältnis von Interpretationslehre. *Verfassungsgerichtsbarkeit und Demokratieprinzip bei Kelsen, Rechtstheorie Beiheft* 4: 149–157.
Hart, H.L.A. 1958. Positivism and the separation of law and morals. *Harvard Law Review* 71: 593–629.
Hart, H.L.A. 1961. *The concept of law*. Oxford: Oxford University Press.
Hart, H.L.A. 1963. Kelsen visited. *UCLA Law Review* 10: 709–728.
Hayek, F.A. 1944. *The road to serfdom*. Ed. Bruce Caldwell 2007. Chicago: University of Chicago Press.
Herget, James, and Stephen Wallace. 1987. The German free law movement as the source of American legal realism. *Virginia Law Review* 73: 399–455.
Holmes Jr., Oliver Wendell. 1997. The path of the law (Reprint). *Harvard Law Review* 110: 991–1009.
Jackson, B.S. 1985. Kelsen between formalism and realism. *The Liverpool Law Review* 7: 79–93.
Kammerhofer, Jörg. 2011. Hans Kelsen's place in international legal theory. In *Research handbook on the theory and history of international law*, ed. Alexander Orakhelashvili, 143–167. Northhampton: Edward Elgar Publishing.
Kelsen, Hans. 1911. *Hauptprobleme der Staatsrechtslehre entwickelt aus der Lehre vom Rechtssatze*. Tübingen: Mohr.
Kelsen, Hans. 1928a. Der Begriff des Kompetenzkonfliktes nach geltendem öffentlichem Recht. *Juristische Blätter* 57: 105–110.
Kelsen, Hans. 1928b. Zum Begriff des Kompetenzkonfliktes. *Zeitschrift für Öffentliches Recht* 7: 583–599.
Kelsen, Hans. 1929. Juristischer Formalismus und reine Rechtslehre. *Juristische Wochenschrift* 58: 1723–1726.
Kelsen, Hans. 1934. Zur Theorie der Interpretation. *Internationale Zeitschrift für Theorie des Rechts* 8:9–17. Trans. B.L. Paulson & S.L. Paulson 1990. On the Theory of Interpretation. *Legal Studies* 10:127–135.
Kelsen, Hans. 1941. The pure theory of law and analytical jurisprudence. *Harvard Law Review* 55: 44–70.
Kelsen, Hans. 1950. *The law of the United Nations*. New York: Praeger.
Kelsen, Hans. 1953. Was ist die Reine Rechtslehre? In *Demokratie und Rechtsstaat. Festgabe zum 60. Geburtstag von Zaccaria Giacometti*, 143–162. Zürich: Polygraphischer Verlag.
Kelsen, Hans. 1960. *Reine Rechtslehre* (2d ed—Reprint 2000). Vienna: Verlag Österreich.

Kelsen, Hans. 1961. *General theory of law and state*. New York: Russel & Russel.
Kelsen, Hans. 1966. On the pure theory of law. *Israel Law Review* 1: 1–7.
Kelsen, Hans, Georg Fröhlich, and Adolf Merkl. 1922. *Die Bundesverfassung vom 1. Oktober 1920*. Vienna: Deuticke.
Kennedy, Duncan. 1973. Legal formality. *Journal of Legal Studies* 2: 351–398.
Kennedy, Duncan. 2007. A left phenomenological critique of the Hart/Kelsen theory of legal interpretation. *Kritische Justiz, Vierteljahresschrift für Recht und Politik* 3: 296–305.
Kozinski, Alex. 1996. What I ate for breakfast and other mysteries of judicial decision making. *Loyola of Los Angeles Law Review* 26: 993–999.
Leiter, Brian. 1997. Rethinking legal realism: Toward a naturalized jurisprudence. *Texas Law Review* 76: 267–315.
Leiter, Brian. 1999. Positivism, formalism, realism. *Columbia Law Review* 99: 1138–1164.
Leiter, Brian. 2001. Legal realism and legal positivism reconsidered. *Ethics* 111: 278–301.
Leiter, Brian. 2010. Legal formalism and legal realism: What is the issue? *Legal Theory* 16: 111–133.
Lindahl, Hans. 2003. Dialectic and revolution: Confronting Kelsen and Gadamer on legal interpretation. *Cardozo Law Review* 24: 769–798.
Llewellyn, Karl. 1931. Some realism about realism—Responding to Dean Pound. *Harvard Law Review* 44: 1222–1264.
Llewellyn, Karl. 1950. Remarks on the theory of appellate decision and the rules and canons about statutes are to be construed. *Vanderbilt Law Review* 3: 395–406.
Llewellyn, Karl. 2011. *The theory of rules*. Ed. Frederick Schauer. Chicago: The University of Chicago Press.
Malkan, Jeffrey. 1998. Literary formalism, legal positivism. *Cardozo Law Review* 19: 1393–1439.
Masuelli, Saverio. 2002. In claris non fit interpretatio'—Alle Origini del brocardo'. *Rivista di Diritto Romano* 2: 401–424.
Mayer, Heinz. 1992. Die Interpretationstheorie der Reinen Rechtslehre. In *Schwerpunkte der Reinen Rechtslehre*, ed. Walter Robert, 61–70. Wien: Manz.
McDougal, Myres. 1947. The law school of the future: From legal realism to policy science in the world community. *The Yale Law Journal* 56: 1345–1355.
Meder, Stephan. 2004. *Mißverstehen und Verstehen—Savignys Grundlegung der juristischen Hermeneutik*. Tübingen: Mohr Siebeck.
Merkl, Adolf. 1916. Zum Interpretationsproblem. *Grünhutsche Zeitschrift für das Privat- und Öffentliche Recht der Gegenwart* 42: 535–556.
Merkl, Adolf. 1931. Prolegomena einer Theorie des rechtlichen Stufenbaues. In *Festschrift für Hans Kelsen zum 50. Geburtstag*, 252–294. Vienna: Springer.
Neschwara, Christian. 2005. Kelsen als Verfassungsrichter. Seine Rolle in der Dispensehen-Kontroverse. In *Hans Kelsen—Staatsrechtler und Rechtstheoretiker des 20. Jahrhunderts*, ed. Stanley L. Paulson and Michael Stolleis, 353–384. Tübingen: Mohr Siebeck.
Neuborne, Burt. 1992. Of sausage factories and syllogism machines: Formalism, realism, and exclusionary selection techniques. *N.Y.U Law Review* 67: 419–450.
Öhlinger, Theo. 1978. Bemerkungen zur Verfassungsdogmatik. *Zeitschrift für Verkehrsrecht* 23: 257–261.
Öhlinger, Theo. 2008. Hans Kelsen—Vater der österreichischen Bundesverfassung? In *Festschrift für Wilhelm Brauneder zum 65. Geburtstag*, 407–424. Vienna: Manz.
Paulson, Stanley L. 1990. Kelsen on legal interpretation. *Legal Studies* 10: 136–152.
Paulson, Stanley L. 2005. Zwei radikale Objektivierungsprogramme in der Rechtslehre Hans Kelsens. In *Hans Kelsen—Staatsrechtler und Rechtstheoretiker des 20. Jahrhunderts*, ed. Stanley L. Paulson and Michael Stolleis, 191–220. Tübingen: Mohr Siebeck.
Posner, Richard. 1980. The present situation in legal scholarship. *The Yale Law Journal* 90: 1113–1130.
Posner, Richard. 1986. Legal formalism, legal realism, and the interpretation of statutes and the Constitution. *Case Western Reserve Law Review* 37: 179–217.

Posner, Richard. 2001. *Kelsen, Hayek, and the economic analysis of law*. Lecture at the XVIII. Annual meeting of the European Association of Law and Economics in Vienna, Sept 14.
Posner, Richard. 2003. *Law, pragmatism, and democracy*. Cambridge, MA: Harvard University Press.
Ringhofer, Kurt. 1971. Interpretation und Reine Rechtslehre—Gedanken zu einer Kritik. In *Festschrift für Hans Kelsen zum 90. Geburtstag*, 198–210. Vienna: Deuticke.
Rümelin, Gustav. 1891. *Werturteile und Willensentscheidungen im Civilrecht*. Freiburg: Lehmann.
Schauer, Frederick. 1985. Easy cases. *Southern California Law Review* 58: 399–440.
Schauer, Frederick. 1988. Formalism. *The Yale Law Journal* 97: 509–548.
Schauer, Frederick. 1996. Positivism as pariah. In *The autonomy of law* ed. Robert P. George (Reprint 2005) 31–56. Oxford: Oxford University Press.
Schauer, Frederick. 2004. The limited domain of the law. *Virginia Law Review* 90: 1909–1956.
Schauer, Frederick. 2009. *Thinking like a lawyer* (Paperback 2012). Cambridge, MA: Harvard University Press.
Schauer, Frederick. 2013. Legal realism untamed. *Texas Law Review* 91: 749–780.
Schreier, Fritz. 1927. *Die Interpretation der Gesetze und Rechtsgeschäfte*. Vienna: Deuticke.
Schwaighofer, Christoph. 1986. Kelsen zum Problem der Rechtsauslegung. In *Untersuchungen zur Reinen Rechtslehre*, ed. Stanley L. Paulson and Robert Walter, 232–251. Vienna: Manz.
Sebok, Anthony. 1995. Misunderstanding positivism. *Michigan Law Review* 93: 2054–2132.
Sebok, Anthony. 1998. *Legal positivism in American jurisprudence*. Cambridge: Cambridge University Press.
Stewart, Iain. 1990. The critical legal science of Hans Kelsen. *Journal of Law and Society* 17: 273–308.
Strauss, Peter. 1987. Formal and functional approaches to separation of powers—A foolish inconsistency? *Cornell Law Review* 72: 488–526.
Summers, Robert. 1963. Professor H. L. A. Hart's concept of law. *Duke Law Journal*: 629–670.
Tamaha, Brian. 2010. *Beyond the formalist-realist divide: The role of politics in judging*. Princeton: Princeton University Press.
Telman, Jeremy. 2008. The reception of Hans Kelsen's legal theory in the United States: A sociological model, *Valparaiso University Legal Studies Research Paper* No. 08–03.
Telman, Jeremy. 2010. A path not taken: Hans Kelsen's pure theory of law in the land of legal realists. In *Hans Kelsen Anderswo/Hans Kelsen Abroad*, ed. Robert Walter, Clemens Jabloner, and Klaus Zeleny, 353–376. Vienna: Manz.
Telman, Jeremy. 2013. International legal positivism and legal realism, *Valparaiso University Legal Studies Research Paper* No. 13–9.
Thaler, Michael. 1982. *Mehrdeutigkeit und juristische Auslegung*. Vienna: Springer.
Tosato, Angelo. 2000. The Catholic rule for interpreting the Bible. In *Journal of Legal Hermeneutics ed. Giuseppe Zaccharia*, 129–206. Münster: Lit.
von Bernsdorff, Jochen. 2010. *The public international law theory of Hans Kelsen: Believing in universal law*. Cambridge: Cambridge University Press.
Walter, Robert. 1983. Das Auslegungsproblem im Lichte der Reinen Rechtslehre. In *Festschrift für Ulrich Klug zum 70. Geburtstag*, 187–197. Cologne: Dr. Peter Deubner Verlag.
Walter, Robert. 1990. Philosophische Hermeneutik und Reine Rechtslehre. In *Beiträge zur juristischen Hermeneutik*, ed. Helmuth Vetter and Michael Potacs, 41–52. Vienna: Literas.
Weinberger, Ota. 1982. Reine Rechtslehre: Pro und Contra (Bilanz aus Anlaß eines Doppeljubiläums). In *Memoria del X. Congreso Mundial Ordinario de Filosofía del Derecho y Filosofía Social Vol. VI, Symposia II*, 23–37. Mexico City: Universidad Nacional Autonoma de Mexico.
Weinrib, Ernest. 1988. Legal formalism: On the immanent rationality of law. *The Yale Law Journal* 97: 949–1016.
Winkler, Günther. 1990. *Rechtstheorie und Erkenntnislehre*. Vienna: Springer.
Yntema, Hessel. 1941. Jurisprudence on parade. *Michigan Law Review* 39: 1154–1181.

Chapter 14
Cognition and Reason: Rethinking Kelsen in the Context of Contract and Business Law

Jeffrey M. Lipshaw

14.1 Introduction

One rarely finds an essay that links academic consideration of a legal philosophy like Hans Kelsen's positivism with the rough-and-tumble world of an American business lawyer's practice. As Tevye said in *Fiddler on the Roof* (with regard to intermarriage), a bird may love a fish, but where would they build a home together? (Stein et al. 2004). Rather than bemoaning the fact that finding an audience for the topic is as likely as finding guests for the bird-fish marriage, I am going to press ahead. Thinking explicitly about legal positivism, and particularly Kelsen's version of it, is a salutary exercise not just for legal philosophers, but also for those of us who educate Anglo-American deal-making lawyers.

To use a corporate expression, there is an unexpected bit of synergy here. Kelsen's conception of positivism is particularly appealing to those of us who traffic in contract and business law. The usual philosophical debate revolves around law and morality, ie, whether the justification for contract law—the state's involvement in the resolution of wholly voluntary and private transactions—arises from the moral affirmation of promise keeping, the welfare-maximization that voluntary contractual commitments promote, or something else entirely.[1] The more mundane aspects of contract law doctrine often have less to do with grand theories about promise-keeping and more to do with determining how the parties meant to order their interests or, alternatively, with the imputation of what, as a rule, their objective manifestations are understood to signify about that ordering (Craswell 1989). In this more prosaic arena, one of Kelsen's reasons for articulating a pure theory of law

[1] For a review of this debate, see Lipshaw (2012a) and the essays that follow in the symposium issue dedicated to Charles Fried's iconic book.

J.M. Lipshaw (✉)
Suffolk University Law School, Boston, MA 02108, USA
e-mail: jlipshaw@gmail.com

D.A.J. Telman (ed.), *Hans Kelsen in America - Selective Affinities and the Mysteries of Academic Influence*, Law and Philosophy Library 116,
DOI 10.1007/978-3-319-33130-0_14

resonates with those of us who teach and practice it. Law, as the parties use it in private ordering, is indeed separate from morality. As he observes, "there are only interests and thus conflicts of interests…That only one ordering of interests has absolute value (which really means 'is just') cannot be accounted for by way of rational cognition" (Kelsen 1934: 17). As I often tell my first year law students, the courts' articulation of contract law doctrine in hard cases may well reflect a tension between coherence and consistency, on one hand, and fairness, on the other, but from the litigants' standpoint, the rules of contract law are merely arrows in a quiver meant to advance the underlying interest of the parties. Not surprisingly, each of the opposing parties argues its application of the rules fits more coherently within the system, promotes fairness, and just *happens* to dictate a result in favor of that party.

Reading Kelsen again,[2] it has dawned on me that the interesting insight in the pure theory for contract and business law involves not the usual positivist focus on the separation of law and morality, but Kelsen's additional emphasis on the separation of law—part of the normative realm of the "ought"—and fact—the empirical realm of the "is." As Stanley Paulson's instructive matrix showed (Paulson 1997: xxvi), Kelsen was ambitious. He sought not only to isolate pure law from questions of morality, but also to create a science of positive law, even while recognizing that the science will operate on the ideal and normative reality that is the law, and not on natural or physical reality (Kelsen 1934: 15). In short, "a cognitive science of the law is what the Pure Theory aims to be." (Kelsen 1934: 19). The key to that science—indeed, to the very idea of "pure" law—was Kelsen's analogy to the *a priori* categories in Kant's schematic of cognition.

To make my thesis clear, I need to review briefly the significance of the "categories" in Kant's epistemology. Under David Hume's radical empiricism (to which Kant was reacting), the only *a priori* judgments we make about objects or things are *analytical*. That means the predicate of our thought about the object says no more than what we thought in the subject of the judgment. "All bodies are extended; they take up space." That is an analytical judgment because everything I need to know about a body taking up space is already subsumed in the concept of a body (Kant 1783: 14). Knowing that something is a ball or even that it is a moving ball does not, however, *in and of itself* dictate the predicate of movement of another ball. Hence a judgment that one thing causes another—that the cause of the billiard ball striking the rail was its collision with another ball—is an example of a *synthetic* judgment, one in which the predicate of the proposition is not implicit in its subject (Kant 1783: 15). Hume contended there are no synthetic *a priori* judgments; what we perceive, for example, as cause-and-effect is simply the result of "common experiences marked with a false stamp" (Kant 1783: 4)—ie, with (false) metaphysics of causation. In his view, all such judgments are *a posteriori*—they derive wholly from experience (Kant 1783: 15). There is no necessary or metaphysical reason why the ball has to carom that way; our ability to predict that it will occurs only because of our repeated experience that billiard balls always so carom.

[2] In Lipshaw (2007), I discussed the difference between an "ought" of moral freedom and the "ought" of legal compulsion implicit in Kelsen's pure theory.

Kant's fundamental contribution was to assert, *pace* Hume, that synthetic *a priori* judgments must be possible in order even to be skeptical (as was Hume) about knowledge itself (Kant 1783: 26–31). How we make sense subjectively of an objective world depends on an *a priori* cognitive faculty that does not derive from experience. Kant's "categories"—concepts like substance, plurality, unity, existence, and causation—are what constitute the cognitive faculty (Kant 1781: 210–213). That faculty corresponds to, and is in harmony with, an objective world of experience and possible experience that exists independently of our perception of it.[3]

Kelsen contended there is an *a priori* faculty in making legal judgments akin to Kant's *a priori* faculty of cognition. In Kelsen's pure theory, this is the human ability to recognize a *legal* (as opposed to moral) norm as a specific linking of conditioning material fact and conditioned consequence. Kelsen wrote:

> Just as the laws of nature link a material fact as cause with another as effect, so positive laws [in their basic form] link legal condition with legal consequence (the consequence of a so-called unlawful act). If the mode of linking materiality is causality in one case, it is imputation in the other, and imputation is recognized in the Pure Theory of Law as the particular lawfulness, the autonomy, of the law (Kelsen 1934: 23).

This was Kelsen's crucial step. He saw the imputation of an "ought," a normative connection between conditioning fact and legal outcome, as an *a priori* category for comprehending the reality of law in the world (in his words, "empirical legal data"), different from causality in nature, "but just as inviolable" (Kelsen 1934: 24–25). Moreover, like Kant's categories, this faculty for imputing legal consequence purports to be "transcendental" not "transcendent." It tells us nothing about metaphysical or natural law; instead, the faculty acts formally to have us identify what is a legal and not merely a moral norm, just as Kant's categories act to order our sense perceptions of manifold reality (Kelsen 1934: 25).

Others before me have questioned this move.[4] What I intend to do here, in my bird-fish incarnation as a business lawyer, contract law theoretician, and Kant-influenced epistemologist, is different. I want to focus on the difference in Kantian

---

[3] Kant wrote:

> Thus although in synthetic judgments we cognize *a priori* so much about space in general or about the shapes that the productive imagination draws in it that we really do not need any experience for this, still this cognition would be nothing at all, but an occupation with a mere figment of the brain, if space were not to be regarded as the condition of the appearances which constitute the matter of outer experience; hence those pure synthetic judgments are related, although only mediately, to possible experience, or rather to its possibility itself, and on that alone is the objective validity of their synthesis grounded (Kant 1781: 282–283).

This is about as pithy a statement as we get in the *Critique of Pure Reason* on the relationship of our subjective cognition to the objective world. What follows thereafter is Kant's extensive and difficult argument—the balance of the Transcendental Analytic—why the assertion is necessarily true. As Paulson notes (1997: xxix–xxx), this is Kant's argument "that the notion of 'a world of the senses existing of itself'—existing absolutely—amounts to a self-contradiction, and must be replaced by the notion that the world exists not 'of itself' but only in relation to mind."

[4] See the discussion below of Paulson (1997) and Wilson (1986).

epistemology between the kind of knowledge that arises, on one hand, merely by the faculties of cognition and, on the other, through the exercise of theoretical reason. The most problematic aspect of legal positivism, whether Kelsen's or Hart's, is the sense that law cannot be studied merely by observations of patterns of actors' behavior. Rather, the idea of something being imbued with legal significance invokes the subjective point of view of the legal actor. To me, the most significant "Kantian" benefit of the pure theory is precisely this grappling with the relationship between, on one hand, the actor's subjective assessment of the legal consequence of a set of conditions and, on the other, the objective existence in the world of something characterizable as "law." But the most significant "Kantian" problem in the pure theory is not the *a priori* nature (or not) of such subjective legal judgments, but Kelsen's focus on cognition rather than reason as the source of any knowledge that purports to be science, whether of law or anything else. And the key to understanding the problem in the context of contracts and contract law is returning directly to Kant to challenge Kelsen's separation of fact and law—the dichotomy between the "is," the empirical and natural, on one hand, and the "ought," what is normative, on the other.[5]

Transactional lawyers create contracts as a matter of empirical fact, but that is a trivial observation. Resort to contract law in business transactions, it turns out, whether before- or after-the-fact, is an odd amalgam of descriptive and normative undertakings. The prevalent mythology among academics and practitioners alike is that resolution of contract disputes is a search for an empirical "is"—either the expressed mutual intention of the parties or the inference of such intention by way of default rules reflecting what, as a rule, the objective manifestations of the parties would mean. What makes contract law unique, as Kelsen observed, is the minimal intrusion of the state into the creation of the specific legal norm at issue. "Here the parties who are subject to obligation participate in creating the norm that imposes obligations, and therein lies the essence of the contractual creation of law" (Kelsen 1934: 93). But, as Kelsen also observed, this is not a wholly normative inquiry. Ironically, to decide a contract case a court has to determine the applicable norms as a matter of fact.[6]

As a contract law teacher and business lawyer, I wholly concur in Kelsen's skepticism about the connection between law and justice. As an epistemologist strongly influenced by Kant, I am not wholly satisfied with H.L.A. Hart's adoption of the "internal point of view" so as to explain the subjective impact upon actors of the law qua law (thus distinguishing law as experienced subjectively from mere patterns of

[5] As Alexander Somek suggested to me, I am confronting Kelsen directly with Kant systematically, and not intermediated by the historical circumstance of Kelsen's relationship with neo-Kantians like Hermann Cohen. For a short and readable account of that history, see Green (2003: 395–398).

[6] "Exercising powers delegated to them by statute, [private] parties set concrete norms for their own behavior, norms that prescribe reciprocal behavior and whose violation constitutes the material fact to be established by the judicial decision" (Kelsen 1934: 70).

behavior) (Hart 1997: 56–57, 89–91). Kelsen was onto something when he analogized to Kant's epistemology. Yet I am troubled by his appropriation of the Kantian categories of *cognition* to what I understand contract and business lawyers to be doing when they practice law. The problem with transposing the Kantian categories to law, at least in contract law, is the implication that what one knows *a priori as a result of the categories* is meaningful in any way other than trivially so. Instead, what is significantly meaningful in contract law is the knowledge we obtain by exercise of the faculty either of theoretical or practical reason, an aspect of Kant's epistemology that Kelsen does not appear to have adopted (or even considered) in the pure theory. As Kant viewed it, our faculty of reason is a regulative process—a way of thinking that may or may not produce knowledge. It is distinct from cognition—the process of judgments by which we have constitutive knowledge of the objective world of experience. The problem with reason when not used merely as a way of assessing experience or possible experience, as Kant inveighed in the First Critique, is that it is capable of creating transcendental illusion, having us think we know things that truly must be consigned to faith.[7] In other words, when we focus on reason rather than cognition, the line between the "is" and the "ought" blurs.

My aim in this essay is therefore to reconsider the pure theory in the context of contract and business law. In Sect. 14.2, I discuss what the experience of contract and business law really *is*. Kelsen was right: there is a separation of fact and law. Transactions are observable empirical events. Whether undertaken after the fact in litigation or before the fact in planning a transaction, law is an exercise of mind, consistent with the basic norm, in which we apply particularly *legal* rules of inference in *modus ponens*[8] logic to particular circumstances—those observable empirical events—to impute legal conclusions from antecedent conditions. The very core of *modus ponens* logic may well be *a priori* in the same sense as is pure mathematics. But the actual rules of law (at least in contracts and business) constituting the connection between "if" and "then" in the major premise must be *a posteriori*, ie, derived wholly from experience.

In Sect. 14.3, I attempt something not often done, which is to reconsider the core analogy in the pure theory, and to examine the relationship of cognition and reason

---

[7] Hence, Kant's oft-quoted statement from the Preface to the Second Edition of the *Critique of Pure Reason*:

> Thus I had to deny knowledge in order to make room for faith;...to see this we need merely to compare the culture of reason that is set on the course of a secure science with reason's unfounded groping and frivolous wandering about without critique, or to consider how much better young people hungry for knowledge might spend their time than in the usual dogmatism that gives so early and so much encouragement to their complacent quibblings about things they do not understand, and things into which neither they nor anyone else in the world will ever have any insight...(Kant (1781: 117).

[8] *Modus ponens* is a rule of inference as follows:

If *a*, then *b*.
a.
Therefore *b*.

as they relate to knowledge, not as Kelsen or his critics might or might not have done it, but in a way I believe is more faithful to Kant.[9] This is necessary if we are going to think of contract and business law as a kind of science, whether descriptive or normative, under Kantian conceptions of cognition and reason. While giving credit to Kelsen for understanding that there was something about the relationship of subject and object that evoked Kant, there is a problem with treating the core of Kelsen's basic norm as a Kantian category of cognition. Thinking legally is an exercise of entirely different faculty: reason, of which the law's *modus ponens* logic is perhaps one of the best examples.[10]

In Sect. 14.4, I consider the practical implications of the foregoing somewhat obscure and arcane distinction if not for the contract and business lawyers who actually do the practicing then at least for those who teach them. Facing reality before one decides on a course of action is often the hardest task for lawyers and their clients. I am thus skeptical of a legal "science" that seeks an ironically and paradoxically abstract positive law of contracts, an ideally coherent doctrine that exists somewhere "out there," removed from its application to real world experience. When we use theoretical and practical reason to solve problems, whether normatively or descriptively, we are lawyers. When we reason speculatively on the coherence of the doctrine, removed from the reality of a set of facts, as though we could know the law as a "thing-in-itself," we are theologians.

Finally, I conclude with some brief thoughts on legal positivism in the context of "lawyering as doing" rather than the more academic project of the demarcation and classification of law.

[9] I cannot say "as Kant did," because Kant's views on the "role reason plays in his theoretical philosophy" is less clear than in his moral philosophy, and those views are the subject of a good deal of secondary work by Gerd Buchdahl, Susan Neiman, and others, much of which I adopt here (Williams 2013). I acknowledge that I am adopting a particular view of what Kant meant, whether or not he meant it, but my aim here is not to resolve that issue. I do find these interpreters' distinctions between cognition and reason both consistent with my own reading particularly of Kant's Appendix to the Transcendental Dialectic in the *First Critique* and the Critique of Teleological Judgment in the *Third Critique*. Indeed, because I think Kant is clearer on these points than his reputation for abstruse writing would make one think, I have quoted him liberally in the footnotes to this essay. More importantly, I find the distinction between cognition and reason to be powerful in assessing my own bouts of transcendental illusion as well as what seems to me to be the conflation of truth and belief in others. Undoubtedly there is a distinction between cognition and reason in Kant's work, and my aim is to explore how that distinction, in light of Kelsen, might inform, if not contract jurisprudence, then the role contract law and contract lawyering play in light of all the other norms that operate among contracting parties.

[10] It is perhaps only incidental to my analysis of Kelsen that Kant himself probably thought so (Weinrib 1987: 478–491).

14.2 What Contract Law Really *Is* When Separated from Fact

14.2.1 The Logical Form of Positive Contract Law

Law professors often congratulate themselves on teaching their students to "think like lawyers." But to have a businessperson in the real world suggest you are "thinking like a lawyer" is generally no compliment. At least that is my casual empiricism over the course of a long career as a litigation and transactional lawyer in a large firm and as the general counsel of two substantial industrial businesses. In the process of becoming an academic, I have struggled to reconcile what I experienced as a lawyer-businessman with the pure legal doctrine I teach, particularly in courses on contract and business association law. What I have come to realize is that Kelsen was correct: there is a separation of fact and law, although perhaps not in the way he meant it. Kelsen wanted to acknowledge law's normativity, but nevertheless be able to isolate the norms of positive law from all others. To me, law, legal systems, and their constituent elements (things like contracts, corporations, limited liability companies and other abstractions) are something other than fact. That is because they are creations of mind, simply one way among many of organizing the manifold experience of the world. The "science," if any, comes about because law consists not just of concepts but systematized concepts. They may or may not correspond to facts on the ground, and what lawyers think is important to the coherence of those structures may have little to do with what their clients consider valuable.[11]

Not every bit, but much of the language and logic of contracts as the parties or their lawyers write them when undertaking transactions ("before-the-fact" of a disagreement) and of the law of contracts employed in dispute resolution ("after-the-fact" of a disagreement) indeed takes the form of Kelsen's basic norm of positive law: the imputation of a legal consequence arising as a result of particular antecedent conditions.[12] The logic of the basic norm and all law deriving from it is *modus ponens*. As Louis Wolcher (2008: 93) observed, that exercise is not necessarily a search for empirical truth.[13]

---

[11] Thus Peter Goodrich (2009: 480) has criticized traditional legal theory, insulated from the other disciplines, as "a normative order that is predominantly choral and liturgical, as much propelled by acclamation as celebration."

[12] Kelsen encapsulated the basic norm:

> The basic norm confers on the act of the first legislator—and thus on all other acts of the legal system resting on this first act—the sense of 'ought', that specific sense in which legal condition is linked with legal consequence in the reconstructed legal norm, the paradigmatic form in which it must be possible to represent all the data of the positive law (Kelsen 1934: 58).

[13] To be clear, I am reticent to apply the adjectives "true" or "false" to all but the most obvious and intellectually trivial statements about what the law "is." I know the United States Code and the language of Restatement of Contracts (Second) § 90(1) in Georgia (it was codified) are law as an empirical matter, but any proposition of law seems to me to be not so much meaningless as sterile

> In the usual case, an expression of the law and an expression of the facts will *eventually* be brought together as the major and minor premises of the *modus ponens*, which constitutes the ideal-typical final form of normative justification in general. An expression taking the form of the *modus ponens* typically characterizes the end-moment of legal justification regardless of what went before—that is, regardless of how elaborate, messy, and/or confused the actual process of judicial decision making may have been.[14]

What contract lawyers do before the fact is to translate messy experience (or the contingencies of future experience) into models (some more complex than others) consisting of premises that would support after the fact use of *modus ponens* logic to resolve disputes: If *A*, then *B*. *A*. Therefore *B*. That is no less the case in contract law than in any other form of law, notwithstanding the fact that the parties may have had something to do with the creation of the law. For example, in a merger agreement, the indemnification clause deals with breaches of warranty. If there is a breach of warranty, then Seller shall indemnify Buyer (If *A*, then *B*). There was a breach of warranty (*A*). Therefore Seller shall indemnify (*B*).

There is little doubt these are synthetic judgments. Are they, however, in Kantian terms, *a priori* as well as synthetic? One of the problems with analogy between the Kantian conception of causation and Kelsen's of legal imputation is that the *a priori* aspect of law in action is limited to the most general logical relation between the "if" and the "then" statements in the modus ponens inference. To give appropriate credit to the basic norm and rules that take its form, there is a seed of *a priori* judgment in what we do to apply the law. Regardless of the subject matter to which we apply *modus ponens*, we cannot determine *B* merely as something contained within *A*. If "the predicate *B* belongs to the subject *A* as something that is (covertly)

---

without its application to something in the world. The closest view to my own is Dennis Patterson's (1999) conception of law as argumentation—what lawyers do. That is, worrying about whether a proposition of law is true is largely a waste of time. Patterson's assessment largely concerns itself with the usual stuff of jurisprudence, constitutions, statutes, and judicial decisions, and not the private law the parties create for themselves in a contract. In the spirit of a Kantian analysis, I suggest that what lawyers do when they create private law or when they argue to a judge is to use reason to make demands upon experience—they are either applying theoretical reason to construct a model of experience or possible experience (ie, drafting a contract) or practical reason to determine or argue what it is that somebody ought to do.

[14] Getting to the operative expression of the law for purposes of the important *modus ponens* inference may take some unpeeling. For example, suppose a claimant contended that a promisor committed himself legally by a series of eye blinks. Under the rules in the *Restatement (Second) of Contracts*, we might have the following progression. It is a contract under § 1 if there was a promise for the breach of which the law provides a remedy. But was it a promise? Section 2 tells us a promise is a manifestation of an intention to act in a specified way so made as to justify a promisee in understanding that a commitment has been made. There is no definition in the *Restatement* of a "manifestation" or a "commitment." But one of the issues may be whether the eye blinking constituted a manifestation or a commitment justifiably so understood by another. At some point, there will be a determination in the following form: If A, then B; A; therefore B. If there was a physical movement having a sensible pattern, then it is a manifestation. There was such a physical movement. Therefore, there was a manifestation. There is no getting around the infinite regress of meaning, but at each level it *is* a *modus ponens* exercise. As to the inevitability of the infinite regress, see Stumpff (2013).

contained in this concept *A*," the judgment is analytic (Kant 1781: 141). If "*B* lies entirely outside the concept *A*, though to be sure it stands in connection with it," then the judgment is synthetic (Kant 1781: 141). The *form* of a logical statement, which in *modus ponens* presumes a relation between the subject *A* and the predicate *B*, but which relation does not inhere in the concept of the subject *A* and needs no experience to bear it out, is, like mathematics, the epitome of what Kant terms a synthetic *a priori* judgment (Kant 1781: 145).

So our most fundamental ability to perceive a connection between an antecedent condition and a consequence does strike us as something akin to an *a priori* judgment of cause-and-effect. But that is as far as it goes. It is far more problematic to extend the analogy to the legal rules of inference themselves. It strikes me as the very antithesis of legal positivism to believe that any particular rule, at least in contract and business law, arises independent of experience. That is, all legal rules serving as the major premise of the modus ponens sequence—ie, the statement of the legal consequence that arises from the antecedent condition—must be *a posteriori.*[15] There is simply no necessary reason that the legal consequence of a breach of warranty, for example, is a right to relief. If there is such a right, whether by default rule or private ordering, and whether or not the right accords with a sense of morality, it seems to me beyond any serious debate that it is a contingent and not a necessary happenstance.[16]

14.2.2 The Logical Form of Contract Law in Practice

14.2.2.1 In After-the-Fact Litigation

In my experience as teacher and practicing lawyer, the *modus ponens* form of the basic norm is valuable in characterizing how lawyers think both after the fact of a transaction in litigation and before the fact in writing the contracts. As to litigation,

[15]This is consistent with the dictum in Holmes (1881) about the relationship of logic and experience to the life of the law ("The life of the law has not been logic: it has been experience" (Holmes 1881: 1)). However, Holmes is aware that the mechanism of the law is indeed logic. He concludes his derivation of the modern law of civil liability with this observation:

> The foregoing history…illustrates the paradox of form and substance in the development of law. In form its growth is logical. The official theory is that each new decision follows syllogistically from existing precedents. But…precedents survive in the law long after the use they once served is at an end and the reason for them has been forgotten. The result of following them must often be failure and confusion from the merely logical point of view (Holmes 1881: 35).

How the rules themselves develop and adapt is indeed *a posteriori*, a matter of experience. But their final expression as rules maintains the syllogistic form.

[16]Michael Steven Green (2003: 379) has captured this relationship, perhaps more articulately than I, as one in which the form of legal sentences provide the underlying logic that links the antecedent conditions and the legal consequence, but the content of the sentences is contingent on social facts that provide "primitive legal meaning."

a staple of contract law pedagogy, *Allegheny College v. National Chautauqua County Bank of Jamestown* (246 N.Y. 369, 159 N.E. 173 (1927)), reveals just how powerful *modus ponens* logic is as a fundamental form of expression of the positive law. I enthusiastically teach the case to my first-year law students not because I care particularly about the doctrinal niceties either of consideration or promissory estoppel (to be perfectly honest, I do not), but because the case so clearly demonstrates (a) the basic norm in theory; ie, separation of facts on the ground from the abstract *modus ponens* conceptions of legal analysis, and (b) the basic norm in practice, ie, how two great lawyers (Cardozo and Kellogg) wrestle with drawing legal consequences from the antecedent conditions before them.[17]

The facts were not complex. In June 1921, Mary Yates Johnston subscribed to contribute $5000 to Allegheny College "in consideration of [her] interest in Christian education and others subscribing." The contribution was payable by her executor 30 days after her death. She paid $1000 on account of the subscription in December 1923 but in July 1924 repudiated the subscription. Thereafter she died, and Allegheny College sued her executor for the balance of the contribution. The trial court found for the estate, and the Appellate Division affirmed. On appeal to the New York Court of Appeals, Judge Cardozo, writing for the majority, reversed and ordered judgment for Allegheny College as requested in the complaint, holding:

> We think the duty assumed by the plaintiff to perpetuate the name of the founder of the memorial is sufficient in itself to give validity to the subscription within the rules that define consideration for a promise of that order (*Allegheny*, 159 N.E. at 176).

I am less interested in the precise holding than the method Cardozo used to reach it. There were four possible models or legal theories within which to fit this case from a judicial frame of reference, all of which Judge Cardozo mentioned in the opinion: charitable subscription, promissory estoppel, gift, and contract supported by consideration. Twice Judge Cardozo referred to legal theories as "moulds," first to suggest that the mould as fixed by the old doctrine had been expanded, and second to say that this particular transaction "can be fitted within the mould" (*Allegheny*, 159 N.E. at 175). What is a "mould"? It is a British spelling of "mold," for which the *Oxford Dictionary Online* gives one definition as "a hollow container used to give shape to molten or hot liquid material when it cools and hardens…" The origin of the word is "Middle English: apparently from Old French *modle*, from Latin *modulus*." In short, consideration as a legal doctrine is a model—a mould—into which we pour the facts (Oxford Dictionaries 2014).

We may express each of those moulds in the form of *modus ponens* argument: if *A*, then *B*; *A*; therefore *B*.

---

[17] I am fairly sure that I came to this reading of *Allegheny College* independently, but I have since discovered that Konefsky (1987) anticipated me in large part by about 20 years. I believe Professor Konefsky was correct from stem to stern in his unraveling of Cardozo's supposedly elliptical, convoluted, and incomprehensible opinion. My approach follows his in spirit though it varies in technique, and I credit Judge Kellogg's dissent somewhat more affirmatively than he did.

1. *Charitable subscription.* If there is a promise to subscribe to a charity with or without consideration, the promise will be legally enforceable.

The facts supported the presence of the major premise, a promise to subscribe, but Cardozo's view was that New York law did not support the necessary rule of inference; ie, he did not conclude that the mere antecedent charitable promise led to the legal consequence of enforceability. He could have found for the estate on this basis, but it was troubling: to back out even from a charitable gift on the basis of there being no deal amounted to "breaches of faith toward the public, and especially toward those engaged in the same enterprise, and an unwarrantable disappointment of the reasonable expectations of those interested" (*Allegheny*, 159 N.E. at 175). So one avenue would have been to adopt a very controversial rule of inference: endowment or charitable gifts are so important that we would enforce them merely on the promise itself, without regard to whether there has been consideration or reliance. But Cardozo declined to take that route.[18]

2. *Promissory estoppel.* If the promisor promises a charitable subscription and the charity relies on the promise to its detriment, then the promise is legally enforceable.

Cardozo accepted the rule of inference. This was the legitimate use of promissory estoppel theretofore established under New York law. In *Barnes v. Perine* (12 N.Y. 18 (1854)) and *Presbyterian Society of Knoxboro v. Beach* (74 N.Y. 72 (1878)), the Court of Appeals applied the doctrine of promissory estoppel because "the church did incur expense to the knowledge of the promisor, and in the reasonable belief that the promise would be kept" (*Allegheny*, 159 N.E. at 175). The problem with the promissory estoppel mould in *Allegheny College* was that there was simply no evidence that the donee relied on the promise to its detriment.[19] Cardozo ducked the issue by stating that the holding on the application of consideration theory made it unnecessary to consider the mould of promissory estoppel (*Allegheny*, 159 N.E. at 177).

3. *Gift.* If a conditional promise does not invite a bargain (ie, it merely induces the promisee to act or refrain from acting without the promise and the act having been motive for each other), then the conditional promise constitutes a gift and is not legally enforceable.
4. *Consideration.* If a conditional promise (ie, to contribute) invites a bargain by way of a return promise (ie, if the promisee promises to perpetuate the name of the donor of the scholarship), and the promisee "subjected itself to such a duty at

[18] "The law of charitable subscriptions has been a prolific source of controversy in this state and elsewhere. We have held that a promise of that order is unenforceable like any other if made without consideration" (*Allegheny*, 159 N.E. at 174).

[19] The best Cardozo could come up with was the notion that, absent the promise, the college might have simply applied the funds to purposes specified under its charter, and not have created a special fund that would only become sufficient to make the scholarship if others contributed to it after Mrs. Johnston's death (*Allegheny*, 159 N.E. at 177).

the implied request of the promisor," then the conditional promise is legally enforceable, ie, "the result was the creation of a bilateral agreement."

The "if/then" statements for consideration and gift are reverse images of each other. Either the promise invites a bargain or it does not. The consequence of the former is a contract; the consequence of the latter is a gift. It is clear that Cardozo did not like the implications of imposing the "gift" mould over the transaction for the same policy reasons that he believed promissory estoppel arose in the charitable subscription context: these were important promises for which the promisor ought not easily be let off the hook. So if he was not inclined to let the estate renege, the moulds expressed in *modus ponens* logic gave him three choices, two of which—charitable contribution without reliance and promissory estoppel—he did not want to apply either for policy reasons or because the fact needed to supply the antecedent condition of reliance was so weak.

The facts *did* support the idea that the college promised *something*, even if the something was as fleeting as naming the fund for her as a memorial. Mrs. Johnston's conditional promise was to the effect, "If you name a fund for me, I will contribute to the college." When the college promised to do so, it made a bargain. Because the bargain came about as the result of a promise in exchange for a promise, it was a bilateral agreement and, under the appropriate rule of inference for such agreement, legally enforceable from the moment of the return promise.[20] And for Cardozo, that concluded the overlay of theories of positive law—expressed in the form of the basic norm—upon these facts.

That law is separate from fact is apparent from Judge Kellogg's dissent. There was no dispute over the facts; the only question was the appropriate insertion of those facts into the moulds of positive law theories, those *a posteriori* rules of inference that constitute the common law. Judge Kellogg focused on two.

3. *Gift.* If a conditional promise does not invite a bargain (ie, it merely induces the promisee to act or refrain from acting without the promise and the act having been motive for each other), then the conditional promise constitutes a gift and is not legally enforceable.

Judge Kellogg was not inclined in the first instance to see Mrs. Johnston's promise even as stating a condition capable of inviting a bargain. She stated merely that "this gift shall be known as the Mary Yates Johnston Memorial Fund," and the college "was not requested to perform any act through which the sum might bear the title by which the offeror states that it shall be known. The sum offered was termed a 'gift' by the offeror" (*Allegheny*, 159 N.E. at 177).

But even if the court were to use consideration theory, in Judge Kellogg's view, the facts still did not justify a legal conclusion that there was a contract. There are two rules expressible in the form of *modus ponens* rules for contract *formation* in

[20] "A bilateral agreement may exist though one of the mutual promises be a promise 'implied in fact,' an inference from conduct as opposed to an inference from words.... The fair implication to be gathered from the whole transaction is assent to the condition and the assumption of a duty to go forward with performance" (*Allegheny*, 159 N.E. at 176).

the classical expression of the common law. These rules operate to supply a conclusion whether the parties actually formed, in an objective sense, a mutual understanding, regardless whether the understanding related to what turns out to be an enforceable contract or an unenforceable gift. The naked offer is simply a promise to enter into a contract if the promisee accepts according to the terms of the offer.[21] The offer becomes binding if the offeree accepts by exercising the power of acceptance that the offer creates in the offeree.[22]

The two rules on formation differ, and they depend on the nature of the consideration for the offeror's otherwise unenforceable promise, ie, whether the original offer invites acceptance by way of a return promise or return performance,[23] or is silent on the manner of acceptance.[24] Cardozo applied the former.

5. *Bilateral contract.* If a conditional promise (ie, to contribute) invites a bargain by way of a return promise (ie, if the offeree *promises to perpetuate* the name of the donor of the scholarship), and the offeree "subjected itself to such a duty at the implied request of the promisor," then the conditional promise is legally enforceable, ie, "the result was the creation of a bilateral agreement."

Judge Kellogg's objection was that there was no evidence of the required antecedent condition, namely a return promise from Allegheny College so as to form an immediately enforceable promise-for-promise bilateral contract. If the transaction fit into any mould of contract formation, it would have been promise-for-performance—a unilateral contract.

6. *Unilateral contract.* If a conditional promise (ie, to contribute) invites a bargain by way of a return performance (ie, if the offeree *perpetuates* the name of the donor of the scholarship), and the offeree "subjected itself to such a duty at the implied request of the promisor," then the conditional promise is legally enforceable, ie, the result was the creation of a unilateral agreement.

As Judge Kellogg observed, "she proposed to exchange her offer of a donation in return for acts to be performed" (*Allegheny*, 159 N.E. at 177). Allegheny College never actually named a scholarship for her. Thus, "although a promise of the college to make the gift known, as requested, may be implied, that promise was not the

[21] Compare the definition of "promise" in *Restatement of the Law Second, Contracts* § 2 ("A promise is a manifestation of intention to act or refrain from acting in a specified way, so made as to justify a promisee in understanding that a commitment has been made") with the definition of offer in § 24 ("An offer is the manifestation of willingness to enter into a bargain, so made as to justify another person in understanding that his assent to that bargain is invited and will conclude it"). See also Hogg et al. (2008: 148–149).

[22] *Restatement of the Law Second, Contracts* §§ 38, 50. See also Hogg et al. (2008: 154).

[23] *Restatement of the Law Second, Contracts* § 30(1) ("An offer may invite or require acceptance to be made by an affirmative answer in words, or by performing or refraining from performing a specified act, or may empower the offeree to make a selection of terms in his acceptance.").

[24] *Id.* § 30(2) (1981) ("Unless otherwise indicated by the language or the circumstances, an offer invites acceptance in any manner and by any medium reasonable in the circumstances.").

acceptance of an offer which gave rise to a contract" (*Allegheny*, 159 N.E. at 177). But there is one more link in the logical chain.

7. *Revocation of offer in unilateral contract.* If (a) an offeree under a power of acceptance created by an offer that invites performance has not performed the requested act, and (b) the offeror receives a manifestation of an intention not to enter into the proposed contract from the offeree, then the offeree's power of acceptance is terminated.[25]

In July 1924, Mrs. Johnston repudiated the gift. As Judge Kellogg would have applied the rules of inference, because she revoked her offer before the rules would have caused the legal consequence of a binding contract, there was no contract and she was not obliged to contribute: "the donation was not to take effect until after the death of the donor, and by her death the offer was withdrawn" (*Allegheny*, 159 N.E. at 177).[26]

What separates law from fact is the judges' post hoc application of logical sentences in the form of the basic norm to the narrative. Nobody knew or could know, except by extrapolation and interpretation, what either Mrs. Johnston or the officials of Allegheny College meant to have happen immediately after she made her original statement public. Perhaps she never thought about revocability at all. The process of legal judgment only takes account of any of that to the extent that the underlying facts satisfy (or not) the *modus ponens* logic of the *a posteriori* rules constituting the proffered legal theories.

14.2.2.2 In Before-the-Fact Contracts

The form of the basic norm, its modus ponens logic, is no less significant on the transactional side of the lawyering house. To be sure, some of what we do as lawyers is to create artifacts that have meaning wholly independent of the language employed in the artifacts (Suchman 2003). The Jewish marriage contract hanging in our home is significant as ritual and not because we refer to it as a guide to our spousal duties. In my experience, even the execution of a corporate acquisition agreement—something for which the linguistic content ought to be paramount—has a ritual or symbolic meaning (Lipshaw 2012b). Whether the contract is ritual or metaphoric map of the transaction, and even considering that the longest contract will still fail fully to embody all of the understandings of the parties, the contract is still an artifact the form of which is set in language, a narrative, part of which the

[25] Restatement of the Law Second, Contracts § 42 ("An offeree's power of acceptance is terminated when the offeree receives from the offeror a manifestation of an intention not to enter into the proposed contract.")

[26] There is the question of the $1000 Mrs. Johnston paid on account before she died. Judge Cardozo cites this as evidence a bilateral contract had been previously formed, and that by accepting it, the college was saying implicitly that it would fulfill its promise to name the scholarship fund after her. (*Allegheny*, 159 N.E. at 176–177). Judge Kellogg must have considered the $1000 as a gratuity, given that Allegheny College had not yet performed the act invited in the offer.

drafters express in series of "if-then" propositions. The propositions—almost always designed to work in the form of *modus ponens*—ideally control the contingencies and subsequent conditions the drafters anticipate. They are privately enacted rules of law the drafters hope will determine the legal consequences of the relationship even if the parties never litigate them.

- "If tenant fails to pay rent, Landlord may evict."
- "If the product is defective on account of materials or workmanship, Seller will repair or replace it".
- "If the Net Equity on the Closing Balance Sheet exceeds the Net Equity on the Reference Balance Sheet, Buyer shall pay Seller the dollar amount of such difference within 90 days."

The last example reflects my experience as a transactional lawyer doing complex deals, and seeking to create algorithmic contract models that anticipate the most likely contract contingency. We draft covenants and conditions applicable both before and after the consummation of the deal, the primary difference being that the legal consequence of a breach of covenant is generally a claim for damage or other legal remedy, and the failure of a condition excuses one or more of the parties' performance of its obligations.

Some of the covenants and conditions are more sophisticated than others. The recitation of the purchase price, for example, is really an expression of the following relatively simple proposition: "If all of the conditions to the closing are satisfied, then Seller will pay Buyer $X." A condition can be relatively simple in its expression, yet complex in determination. In the *modus ponens* logic of the expression, "If there is a Material Adverse Change (*A*), then Buyer shall not be obliged to consummate the transaction (*B*)," whether the facts support the existence of *A*—ie, whether something important happened that excuses the Buyer's performance—can be the subject of some significant litigation.[27] For example, did the agreement mean to limit such changes to those intrinsic to the target company, or did it include exogenous changes, such as a downturn in the economy? To deal with that, the seller may try to add another "if/then" clause to make that limitation express rather than implied. And in any agreement of more than passing complexity, the *modus ponens* exercises will pile on top of each other in just this way, whether the subject matter is the commercial tenant's right to renew a lease, the allocation of risk in the event of full or partial destruction of the leased premises, the adjustment of an acquisition purchase price on account of balance sheet changes after a certain date, or the respective indemnification obligations of seller and buyer for liabilities created by the acquisition target before or after the closing date (something mergers and acquisitions lawyers know as "caps, baskets, and survival periods").

The point here is that, as an empirical matter, transactional contract "law"—ie, the rule of inference connecting the *A* condition to the *B* consequence—arises potentially from three sources. The terms or conditions can be *implied in law* as a default. That means there is no evidence the parties agreed to them but an adjudicator

[27] An example is *IBP, Inc. v. Tyson Foods*, 789 A.2d 14 (Del. Ch. 2001).

will read them into the agreement because, in the absence of any indication otherwise, most people in the community would do so as well.[28] The terms or conditions can be *implied in fact*. That means that there is enough evidence to justify to a third party that the parties actually meant the term or condition to be included, even if they did not expressly state it.[29] Or the terms and conditions can be *express*. I often tell my contract law students there are whole sections of the course that they may never encounter in practice (like the doctrine of consideration or promissory restitution), but that the essence of before-the-fact contract lawyering is to substitute express terms for implied terms. There are very few substantive terms or conditions that courts will be willing to imply as a matter of law, and the deal lawyer's nightmare is explaining (either to a court or to one's client) why a term not made express and not so obviously sensible as to be implied in law is one that the court should imply in fact.

The practice of transactional lawyers, then, is to *create* law by using a language, the form of which derives from the basic norm in Kelsen's conception of positive law. The result is an objective manifestation of the parties, one hopes made express but, at the very least, implied in fact.

14.3 Cognition, Reason, and Teleology in Legal Analysis

By examining the Kelsen-Kant connection in the context of contract and business law (ie, law that is not only private but also created in large measured by the parties themselves), I want to (a) offer a somewhat different criticism than heretofore proffered of Kelsen's analogy to Kant's theory of knowledge, (b) yet affirm Kelsen's intuition that there is something essentially Kantian about what contract lawyers and judges do, albeit as a matter of reason rather than cognition. In Sect. 14.4, however, I sound a caution about the same possibilities of transcendental illusion in the law that Kant sounded for all matters of faith.

Having established that contracts and contract law take place in a language that uses sentences that are often in the form of the basic norm, how does this inform our understanding of Kelsen's project of separating law from fact? If we accept the

[28] Judge Cardozo also wrote two of the iconic opinions on this subject. In *Wood v. Lucy, Lady Duff-Gordon*, 222 N.Y. 88, 118 N.E. 214 (1917), he held that an exclusive marketing agent had an obligation to use reasonable efforts when he did not so commit either expressly or "in so many words." In *Jacob & Youngs v. Kent*, 230 N.Y. 239, 129 N.E. 889 (1921), the issue was the extent to which one party had to perform in order to trigger the other party's obligation. Judge Cardozo held that, "where the significant of the default is grievously out of proportion to the oppression of the forfeiture" (*Jacob & Youngs*, 230 N.Y. at 243–44), the implied in law condition was substantial, not perfect performance.

[29] Bloomgarden v. Coyer, 479 F.2d 201, 208 (D.C. Cir. 1973) ("An implied-in-fact contract is a true contract, containing all necessary elements of a binding agreement; it differs from other contracts only in that it has not been committed to writing or stated orally in express terms, but rather is inferred from the conduct of the parties in the milieu in which they dealt.").

Kantian terminology, it is indisputable that to the extent law incorporates *modus ponens* logic, it requires *some* synthetic *a priori* judgments by the very "if-then" relationship of the basic norm, even if the rule of law itself is *a posteriori*. So, as Stanley Paulson (1997: xxxi) observed, Kelsen (like Kant) did not question that such judgments were possible (and indeed were fundamental to thought), but wanted to deduce *how* they were possible. Kelsen posited the logical "if-then" imputation of the basic norm as an analogy to the Kantian categories that make cognition possible. In Kantian epistemology, the categories are the "perfect concepts of the understanding" (eg, causality, unity, plurality, negation, etc.) that give order *a priori* to sensible experience—we would have no ordered cognition of reality without them. Having enumerated the categories, the concept of pure understanding that are the basis of synthetic *a priori* judgments, Kant proceeded to the "Transcendental Deduction," an extended argument demonstrating that the skeptic would need to make the kind of *a priori* judgments the categories permit even to ask the skeptical question about how we can know anything.[30]

There is nothing new in my merely criticizing the Kant-Kelsen connection. Professor Paulson (1997: xxix–xlii) has argued persuasively that Kelsen's attempt to resolve the question "how is a pure legal science possible?" by analogy to Kant's resolution of the questions "how is pure mathematics possible?" and "how is pure science possible?" simply does not work. Alida Wilson showed that Kelsen's imputation in law is nothing like Kant's causality in nature (Wilson 1986).[31] To me, however, the real problem with Kelsen's analogy to the categories is that the kind of knowledge we have by their operation—mere cognition—is low-grade at best. Kelsen asserted law, distilled into something "pure," is capable of analysis like a science, even if it is normative, ie, different from something empirical, and even if that normativity is not necessarily based in morality. I think the "is-ought" dichotomy in legal argumentation—at least in the realm of contract and business law—is far less crisp than either Kelsen (at least in the pure theory) or his critics make it out to be.[32]

---

[30] Making one's way through the Transcendental Deduction is notoriously difficult, but Michael Steven Green's (2003: 389–395) synopsis is very good.

[31] Professor Wilson delivered a devastating critique of Kelsen's analogy between "imputation" (in German, *Zurechnung*) and Kant's categories (Wilson 1986: 54–58). She then proceeded to a discussion of the difficulties in Kelsen's attempts to ground the science of law in Kant's insights as they pertain to the kind of systematic knowledge that we would call science (as opposed to mere perception) (Wilson 1986: 58–61). I think her primary point was that, tracking what Kelsen wrote over the years, *Zurechnung* was a moving target, at least in the analogy to causality. Professor Wilson touched briefly, however, on what I am saying more fully here: Kant's categories may be the *a priori* faculties by which the human mind puts any order at all to sensible intuition, but they "are not co-ordinating concepts…in the way some scientific concepts are" (Wilson 1986: 61, quoting Walsh 1975: 42). In short, if we really want to talk about contract law in Kantian terms, then we need to be focusing on reason and not cognition.

[32] Professor Wilson (Wilson 1986: 38–45) also delivered a devastating critique of Kelsen's adherence (or lack thereof) to the "is-ought" distinction, namely that in Kant's practical philosophy, a rational being's "ought" implies freedom from compulsion or constraint of the natural world, and Kelsen seems to adopt a kind of moral determinism.

Moreover, the observation that law requires judgments having a synthetic *a priori* component (ie, the *modus ponens* form) does not in itself vindicate Kelsen's analogy to Kant. One could observe that a moral or other practical judgment also boils down to a *modus ponens* expression, except that a moral or practical, rather than legal, rule of inference applies. If there is no *a priori* basis for distinguishing a legal rule of inference from a moral or practical one, then the answer would indeed seem to be that Hart's reduction of law to the Rule of Recognition by way of commonly accepted social facts must necessarily trump Kelsen's derivation (Hart 1997: 94–95). But we ought not end there. We might instead assess the kind of judgment one makes when one distinguishes a legal rule from a moral rule, the whole point of the Kelsenian and Hartian exercises. Is that a synthetic *a priori* judgment of cognition alone? Or is it the exercise of reason? So what we are analyzing now is a sentence like:

8. The inference from antecedent facts to consequence in connection with the application of UCC 2-207 [to take an example of a contingent rule of law without a shred of morality attached to it] to circumstances is necessarily legal and not necessarily moral.

That is clearly a synthetic judgment. Is it *a priori* or *a posteriori*? Do we "cognize" the difference between legal and moral without more, or do we have to proceed to integrate contingent facts and other cognitions to draw a conclusion? My inclination is to say that we have now started down an infinite regress, looking for the rule for following a rule, and will return ultimately to a seed of synthetic *a priori* cognition from which we then reason our way to a conclusion about the rule that determines the difference between an inference that is legal and one that is moral. Kant himself recognized that these questions take us to the very edge of our ability to talk at all about things like pure reason or freedom at all: "But Reason would overstep all its bounds if it undertook to explain how pure reason can be practical, which would be exactly the same problem as to explain how freedom is possible" (Kant 1785: 216).[33]

To give full credit to Kelsen, and to say why his pure theory struck a chord in me, it is indeed his recourse to Kant as a way of dealing with the subjective or internal point of view that is a hallmark of something being law rather than a mere pattern of behavior. Even from his more sociological perspective, Hart's later articulation of the "internal point of view" was an attempt at reconciling the objective reality of positive law as social fact with the subjective processes that legal actors undertake when *doing* law.[34] Kelsen, like Hart, saw that law had something to do with how

[33] I suspect it is precisely this regress that leads many to conclude pursuing it is a waste of time, to abjure the smell of metaphysics, and to turn to sociology (read: Hart).

[34] A nice summary consists of the essays collected in connection with the Fordham Law Review's 2006 symposium, and introduced by Benjamin Zipursky (2006). Richard Holton (1998) made a brief and prescient remark at the end of his essay on the seeming schizophrenia of legal positivism. Referring to the semantic thesis of legal positivism, ie that "the sense of normative terms in legal claims is different from their sense in moral claims" (Holton 1998: 609) he asked why it should be the case that to have a legal system (in Hartian terms) it is even necessary to have participants who

actors (whether state officials or private parties) perceived it, and could not be satisfactorily understood merely by observation of the actors. The problem, however, with the Kantian analogy in Kelsen's pure theory lies in his focus on cognition rather than *reason*. Reason is the Kantian faculty by which we systematize cognitions into something we might call science. And it is the teleological impulse of reason—its inclination to see purposiveness in the "is" of nature *as well as* the "ought" of morality—that muddies the dichotomy. My proposal is that we will far better understand what contract and business lawyers do in their lawyering—to explore if there is anything like science to it—if we rethink the analogy between the basic norm and Kantian cognition, and focus on how thinking legally is an exercise in Kantian reason, of which the law's use of *modus ponens* logic (deftly applied in *Allegheny College*) is perhaps one of the best examples. Contract law provides a nice laboratory for this for the very reason so little of it has to do with the commands of a sovereign, and so much has to do with the rules the parties would have seemed to legislate for themselves.

Let us consider this in the context of a common and powerful metaphor in contract law and interpretation, the notion that the objective manifestation of the parties in a contract reflects a "meeting of the minds." The metaphor suggests that there really was some objective joinder of hitherto subjective intentions, a kind of Vulcan mind-meld of self-legislated norms that the litigation process is capable of uncovering. If we take the metaphor seriously, this is not a normative "ought" exercise, but instead an exercise of constitutive knowledge—an example of phenomenological experience, whether the source of our knowledge is words on paper or actions of the parties from which we can imply the "meeting."

What is our best theory about the shared intentions (if any) of Mrs. Johnston and Allegheny College regarding the contribution? Judges Cardozo and Kellogg each wanted to establish what was true about the transaction between Mrs. Johnston and Allegheny College. But, as a matter of Kant's epistemology, the real work in acquisition of that constitutive knowledge occurs not in the process of *cognition*, to which the categories apply, and which was the basis of Kelsenian analogy for the basic norm. The work of the categories in simple cognition (ie, cognitive judgments) is merely to permit the subjective perception of objective reality. The Kantian question there is "how can there be knowledge in principle of empirical objects or of objective happenings at all?" (Buchdahl 1969: 483). As Buchdahl noted:

> This question is answered by [Kant's] claiming that we ourselves necessarily inject the logical character corresponding to this objectivity (the categories) into the perceptual situation.

---

take the internal point of view. And, assuming that it is necessary, why is the internal point of view so central? Holton answers his own question:

> I suspect the answer lies in the role that we want the notion of law to play in our account of practical reasoning. We want to explain the distinctive way that the law guides action; and we want to explain the kinds of pressures that lead practitioners to reform the law (Holton 1998: 625).

That is precisely the kind of answer, unsatisfying as it may be, I am trying to provide here.

> At the same time, the *empirical* significance of this logical character (here: the categories) is entirely linked to, and exhausted by, the injective function (Buchdahl 1969: 483).

In other words, what we might perceive by operation of the categories is the most obvious (and trivial) physical aspects of making contracts: the conversation, the fax, the e-mail, execution of a written document, Mrs. Johnston's letter, her statements constituting repudiation, or the handshake.

Distinguishing reason from the faculties of cognition in Kant's epistemology is significant. The knowledge the categories permit is minimal. The categories permit us to know (ie to make judgments) sufficient enough to make to make our way through the physical world.[35] Susan Neiman (1994: 58–59) observes that without reason we might still make causal judgments, for example, that one billiard ball caused another to roll. But it would take reason (for example, the exercise of inductive logic) to assess whether the next collision would have the same result (Neiman 1994: 58). When I assert that knowledge in the sense of Kantian cognition is trivial in business or contract, I mean that Kant's categories are the basis upon which we have any public language in which to express our commonly held subjective perceptions of objective things in the world.[36] For example, we know the legislature enacted the Uniform Commercial Code and it is located in the state's general laws, a phone conversation took place, two people signed a paper, a truck loaded with orange crate traveled from Florida to Massachusetts, and the oranges got sold at the Whole Foods in Cambridge. In contrast, however, what all that means *legally*, if anything, goes beyond the mere cognition in which the categories do their conceptual work of ordering perceptions.

The assertion that we can know something like the "meeting of the minds" or "mutual intention of the parties" is far more sophisticated in Kantian terms than the knowledge provided by mere cognition. To take Kelsen at his word, the creation of a legal science (at least if we are going to be Kantian about it) means systematization of our perception of events in the real world such that we are able effectively and seriously to use metaphors like "meeting of the minds" to describe what has happened.[37] *Scientific* claims of knowledge are something quite different from the kind of knowledge, for example, that allows us to walk down a sidewalk and process the information of the world so as to avoid bumping into others or wandering into the street. Mere cognition, in the sense of the application of Kantian categories of *a*

---

[35] Understanding is incapable of anything other than this meager performance because it lacks autonomy, and its mechanical nature is inseparable from the abstractness of its results. Routinely and automatically, understanding applies the twelve categories to the given manifold (Neiman 1994, 59).

[36] [W]ithout conceptual principles (whose domain is the field of what Kant calls 'the understanding') there would be no public language, no 'nature,' regarded as the concatenation of things and happenings, nor any 'pure science'… (Buchdahl 1969: 476).

[37] As Michael Steven Green points out, Kelsen did not think primitive legal meaning, as the analog to mere cognition, was the end of the story. "Kelsen's goal is instead to show how the primitive meanings can be conjoined, through rules of imputation, to generate complex legal meanings or sanctionability conditions" (Green 2003: 379). My argument, however, is that we cannot be true to Kant without assessing the role of reason in generating those meanings.

priori synthetic judgments by which we order the objective world, and thereby walk down the street, is not enough for science.[38] Science is not mere cognition, but instead the exercise of theoretical *reason*, a series of reflective judgments in which we apply generalizations about cause-and-effect to empirical circumstances in the real world. Hence, when we engage in something like an empirical reconstruction of the parties' own private legislation to assert they had a "meeting of the minds," we use reason to make theoretical claims upon experience, that either what did happen or what ought, under normal expectations, to have happened, or what will happen is explicable by natural or social systems.[39] As Buchdahl noted, "The existence of such systems…is not 'given' but merely 'demanded' by the searching (or 'regulative') activity of the scientist, of what Kant calls 'theoretical reason'" (Buchdahl 1969: 476). For all Kant's extensive critique of the illusions that pure reason could create when divorced from experience or possible experience, he viewed *this* as reason's legitimate knowledge-creating use.[40]

In Kantian epistemology, science is the far more advanced and subtle capability of determining not just what is, but why it is, and what things could be. Science calls on the scientist to do something more than merely observe occurrences in the world. This is the critical difference between Kant's approach to science and that of Hume. Hume rejected any metaphysical connection (as, say, in the principle of sufficient reason articulated by Leibniz) between antecedent and consequent events. That is, Hume believed there was no metaphysical (or sufficient) reason for something else to *have been* just because something *is* now. Instead, we perceive and attribute cause and effect merely by the repetitive and constant conjunction of such seemingly cause-and-effect events (Buchdahl 1969: 473). Kant's view, on the other hand, was that empirical science, ie, the subsuming of experience under scientific laws, requires more than merely the observation of constant conjunction of cause-and-effect events. Rather, the work of the scientist involves mental activity that operates *a priori* and separate from the observations that may or may not bear out the thinking. This is what distinguishes scientific knowledge from mere cognitive ordering of

[38] Buchdahl (1967: 210) suggests the notion that the categories of the understanding supply a justification for science, rather than merely the basis for a public language for reporting on events in the real world, arises from concentration on the Transcendental Aesthetic and Transcendental in the Critique of Pure Reason rather than the Transcendental Dialectic and its "Appendix" wherein Kant explains the role of reason in providing foundations for scientific laws.

[39] It is not so different, in a far less sophisticated way, than observing that microwave radiation at far ends of the cosmos is uniform, despite the theory that that universe was already so big when the radiation was released that there was insufficient time for the ends of the cosmos to communicate with each other. So despite the absence of evidence and the apparently implausibility of the hypothesis, Alan Guth suggested in 1980 there was a period of "inflation" when the universe expanded faster than the speed of light. Other scientists first observed empirical evidence consistent with the inflation theory in 2014 (Overbye 2014).

[40] It is easy to miss. In the 1998 Guyer and Wood translation of the *Critique of Pure Reason*, Kant's exposition of the problems created by the exercise of pure reason—the "transcendental dialectic"—runs 205 pages. Kant relegated his discussion of the appropriate use of reason in science, however, to a mere 33 pages in an "appendix to the transcendental dialectic" (Kant 1781: 384–623).

the world: "the construction of theoretical systems [an interconnected system of things and happenings], involving the addition of theoretical concepts in no way reducible to the purely observational basis of the empirical domain of science" (Buchdahl 1969: 476).[41]

The idea that we actually locate a physical "meeting of the minds" (at least when the parties dispute the terms of the meeting) is as fanciful as the Vulcan mind-meld itself.[42] If we imply a term (say, that the risk of loss passed to the buyer when the oranges got loaded on the truck) as a matter of fact, we are theorizing that the parties ought to have made that agreement in fact based on the other circumstances of the transaction. If we imply the term in law, we do so because, even if it cannot be implied in fact from this transaction, nevertheless, that is the way the world usually works as a rule, or we have concluded that as a matter of experience the world works better if we do it that way. In either case, the inquiry is not merely normative, but also asks us to make theoretical (not merely cognitive) judgments as a matter of constitutive experience. In other words, we do not make a *theoretical* (ie, reasoned) judgment about "mutual intention of the parties" in the same way we make the *cognitive* judgment that one billiard ball caused the other one to move.

If we focus on reason rather than cognition, and put aside Kelsen's desire to separate factual description from the normativity of law, it helps resolve some of the problem of translating Kantian epistemology into Kelsenian positivism. When we use theoretical reason to undertake a putatively descriptive inquiry into the "meeting of the minds," it *is* normative as well, but it is a funny and nuanced kind of normativity that is particularly Kantian. When we make a theoretical judgment through the exercise of reason (as opposed to a judgment that is the product of mere cognition) the distinctions blur between fact and value, description and normativity, or law and fact. The usual focus of normativity in discussions about Kant is *moral* and revolves around the use of *practical* reason to determine the "ought" of an autonomous agent. It *is* possible that the positive law of contracts forthrightly incorporates the subjective moral ought of an autonomous agent in, for example, the law of unconscionability. But resolving issues in contract disputes can also invoke the *teleological* normativity within *theoretical* reason. When we think about default rules—terms implied in law—or the interpretation of the agreement, whether before the fact of

[41] Buchdahl (1969: 495–506) also offers a detailed account of Kant's distinction between mere cognition of nature and theorization by way of reason.

[42] Larry Solum (2014: 84) has recently published an insightful essay on this point. The meaning of a legal text created by a group of individuals has, in his coinage, artificial meaning, ie, a meaning that is something other than the natural meaning we would impute to speech uttered by a natural person. Professor Solum focuses on public law—the text of constitutions, statutes, regulations, and ordinances—but the point applies equally to the text of a negotiated contract. Indeed, consider the following insight as applied to the putative "mutual intention of the parties" that courts regularly invoke as the goal of contract interpretation and enforcement:

> Legal interpretation is (usually) the parsing of artificial meanings. Grasping these meanings is not a matter of inferring the mental states of a particular individual or group of individuals. When it comes to group agents, mental states play a role in the production of artificial meanings, but the meanings themselves cannot be reduced to those mental states.

the deal or after the fact in resolving disputes about it, we are making empirical judgments about what happens as a rule. In contract litigation, what the parties seek to determine is not just "what was?" but often an imputation of "what should have been," based on our experience of the world given the objective manifestations of the parties to the transaction.

In Kantian terms, whether theoretical or practical, it is the same faculty of reason applied to different ends. Kant (1790) treated the implicit "ought" of legitimately employed theoretical reason (ie, in deriving empirical laws) most significantly in the *Critique of Judgment* (and particularly the critique of teleological rather than aesthetic judgment that constitutes the final third of the work). This normativity reflects either (i) the "ought" of prediction arising from an observer's reasoned expectations about how the world usually operates empirically, and/or (ii) the "ought" of the observer's sense of a well-ordered empirical world. As Susan Neiman (1994: 6) elucidates, proposing ends beyond experience is the fundamental human capability, and reason, rather than mere cognition, is the means by which the observer so proposes. Reason stands apart from mere experience and makes demands upon it, not only morally but theoretically as well. The concepts of the understanding—our judgments of mere cognition—allow us to synthesize objects in the world, and to make our way in it, but "reason's province is freedom." By that, Neiman means that freedom is not just the freedom of the autonomous moral agent to make a moral choice. Reason's freedom from experience is precisely what allows us to theorize, to take the data of experience and to impute regularities. The difference between reason's operation in the moral and theoretical spheres is the difference between its constitutive and regulative use. In the moral sphere, reason is free, "without depending on any purpose as material condition," to permit us to fathom the constitutive practical ends to which we strive (Kant 1790: 225).[43] But in the theoretical sphere, reason only serves regulative purposes, even if the nature it seeks to explain appears to be the product of an intelligent being's design.[44] We seem to be able to theorize effectively about nature, using reason's power, because nature seems to have a purposiveness to it that is comprehensible by human judgment, even though we have no basis whatsoever for believing that causality in nature has anything to do with subjective purposiveness. In other words, it is fine to presume what looks like a subjective purpose to create order when we investigate nature, but

[43] Pure Reason, as a practical faculty, *i.e.*, as the faculty of determining the free use of our causality by Ideas (pure rational concepts), not only comprises in the moral law a regulative principle of our actions, but supplies us at the same time with a subjective constitutive principle in the concept of an Object which Reason alone can think, and which is to be actualised by our actions in the world according to that law. The Idea of a final purpose in the employment of freedom according to moral laws has therefore subjective *practical* reality (Kant 1790: 227).

[44] But a final purpose is merely a concept of our practical Reason, and can be inferred from no data of experience for the theoretical judging of nature, nor can it be applied to the cognition of nature (Kant 1790: 228).

we need to make sure we remember that we are merely analogizing to such a purpose, and have no empirical basis for assuming one (Kant 1790: 153–154).[45]

It is not surprising, then, that we conflate the descriptive and the normative, the "is" and the "ought," when we deal with the law of contracts. Debates over, say, the common law mirror image rule versus UCC 2-207 have little to do with the *ought* of morality as might, for example, a discussion of unconscionability. In the latter instance, the positive law incorporates a moral imperative: contracts ought not to be enforced when they reflect, among other things, a gross imbalance of bargaining power, information, consideration, etc. The former instance has far more to do with a view of how the rules *ought* best to reflect the empirical realities of the business world. In other words, in any dispute over a contract, we can never really know what the parties intended subjectively (even what they say they intended is an objective manifestation), and the notion of an inter-subjective intent is little more than mystical nonsense. Hence, contract litigation is rarely about knowing the positive law in the sense of Kantian cognition; instead it is about employing reason in the application of legal rules to theorize what did happen or what *normally* (and, in that sense, normatively) ought to have happened.

In short, the "ought" of normativity expressed in moral or legal imperatives, and the "ought" of description expressed in theory, spring from the same source: the freedom reason affords us not just to perceive but also to adjudge experience. That is the important Kantian insight.

14.4 Implications of the Jurisprudential Point: The Illusory Noumena of Positive Contract Law

What, if any, are the implications of these somewhat arcane distinctions for contract law teachers and practitioners? I do believe there is a payoff. We need to tweak Kelsen's positivism to account for the little about contract law *itself* that is really knowable in Kantian terms through the faculties of cognition. We do not know the law; we use its tools to reason to conclusions about experience or possible experience, to create theories that explain descriptively or theories that adjudge normatively. And because reason itself does not distinguish between descriptions of experience and normative imperatives, our understanding of the kind of law the parties make for themselves quite naturally melds the empirical and the ideal. For

[45] ...[T]here must then have preceded a rationalising subtlety which only sportively introduces the concept of purpose into the nature of things, but which does not derive it from Objects or from their empirical cognition. To this latter it is of more service to make nature comprehensible according to analogy with the subjective ground of the connexion of our representations, than to cognise it from objective grounds (Kant 1790: 153).

Kelsen, then, to speak oxymoronically of law as ideal *reality*—something noumenal—is to raise the hair on the back of my somewhat Kantian neck.[46]

One might think that talk of cognition, reason, and noumena is purely academic, but my experience is that one of the hardest things in the practical world of business is to face reality when it is time to make a decision.[47] If we are faithful to my reading of Kant, the physical aspects of law we know by perceiving them via the categories are this trivial: We shook hands. We wrote something on a piece of paper. We signed our names. What is truly meaningful for lawyers and their clients about contract law comes not from this mere cognition. Instead it comes from the exercise of theoretical and practical reason, something Kelsen did not incorporate into the pure theory. Ironically, in focusing on cognition rather than reason, Kelsen obscured his own project of distinguishing positive law from natural law. That is, the pure theory meant to knock down the ephemeral metaphysics of natural law in favor of positive law, but set up the possibility of seeing positive law as a thing in itself—mistaking the fruits of pure reason—the regulative—for something constitutive of reality. Law (other than as a physical artifact) *can* be real, but only in its application to facts on the ground, and not as some ideal and coherent body of doctrine—a kind of natural law of contracts as it were.

Kelsen was right in separating law from fact to the extent that law is an exercise in reason and therefore merely regulative. What makes adhering to the separation difficult (at least in contract law) is the very unity of reason as Kant describes it. Kant's cautionary advice on the legitimate role of reason in science did not appear in the Transcendental Analytic, the source of cognitive faculties to which Kelsen analogized. Rather, Kant discussed it in the *Appendix* to the Transcendental Dialectic, after having inveighed for better than 300 pages on reason's capacity for creating transcendental illusion—the mistaking of reason's product for knowledge. The transcendental ideas, which are the purview of reason, can have a benign use, so long as they are not taken for concepts of real things; thinking something transcendent is real by application of those ideas is an illusion and deceptive. It is the use of the idea that is important—the use can be extravagant if directed to supposed

---

[46] Alida Wilson (1986: 49–50) suggests that Kelsen's commitment to the idea of law as an "ideal reality" was fleeting. As she correctly points out, the first line of both versions of the introduction to the *Critique of Pure Reason* is Kant's statement to the effect that all cognition begins with experience.

David Gray Carlson (2009: 23–24) has made a similar point regarding H.L.A. Hart's expression of positivism—one that has largely crowded out Kelsen's in Anglo-American jurisprudence. Professor Carlson's thesis is (a) the core of Hart's positivism is to take the official's internal point of view—her acknowledgment that something is law according to the rule of recognition—as empirically present in the world; (b) making a judgment from an internal (and subjective) point of view is never, in Kantian terms, an empirical matter, but rather "a matter of belief, as licensed by theoretical reason; (c) the Hartian internal point of view *is* morality—ie the exercise of reason with respect to the question "what to do"—from a Kantian perspective; and (d) therefore Hart's separation thesis (of law from morality) fails.

[47] Per one of the leading philosophers of business in the twentieth century, John F. Welch, Jr., the former chairman and CEO of General Electric: "Face reality as it is, not as it was or as you wish it to be" (Welch).

objects corresponding to the ideas, or the use can be appropriate (immanent or indigenous) if directed to what our faculty of cognition tells us about objects (Kant 1781: 590).

Moreover, reason will impel us to make things fit together systematically, whether or not nature is thus systematic. When we classify, for example, the classification is a product of our inherent tendency to look for universals and commonalities among the particulars of our experience. That is the source of all hypotheses and theories: "the particular being certain while the universality of the rule for this consequent is still a problem" (Kant 1781: 592). Importantly, however, there is no reason to think that nature itself abides by the product of what our minds do to classify it: "Such concepts of reason are not created by nature, rather we question nature according to these ideas, and we take our cognition to be defective as long as it is not adequate to them" (Kant 1781: 592). It is our teleological impulse, and one that we simply cannot prove or disprove.

> For the law of reason to seek unity is necessary, since without it we would have no reason, and without that, no coherent use of the understanding, and, lacking that, no sufficient mark of empirical truth; thus in regard to the latter we simply have to presuppose the systematic unity of nature as objectively valid and necessary.[48] (Kant 1781: 595)

And what is the end result of all this hard thinking about nature? Strangely, by the very nature of reason itself, there is always another question to ask, another particular to try to fit within the systematic whole, and our entire experience of seeking reasoned explanation operates "asymptotically, as it were," finding more and more systematic unity, but without ever reaching the final unifying principle of everything (Kant 1781: 601–602). Whether it is making a demand of order upon nature (its appropriate theoretical use) or seeking a correct answer to the practical question "what to do next" (its appropriate practical use), reason looks to subsume the manifold of experience in fewer and fewer rules.

Though I never speak of it in those terms to my first-year contract law students, it is transcendental illusion about which I caution them almost from the first day of class. In the real world of working lawyers and business people, the end of the legal process in contract is something we can know because it is a document or a judgment or an order that has conventional meaning. The legal process itself, in the sense of contracts, pleadings, discovery, motions, trial, and appeals, is as well empirically knowable. Why? Because they are constitutive of experience or possible experience, whether we know them as a matter of cognition or the exercise of theoretical reason. We *employ* the tools of the law in making legal judgments; that employment is the regulative exercise of reason. To mistake either the *a priori* regulative process of reason or the ends to which we can reason for constitutive

---

[48] Even Quine and Ullian, while rejecting synthetic *a priori* knowledge as a helpful concept, thought there were five "virtues" underlying hypotheses: conservatism, modesty, simplicity, generality, and refutability. "Hypothesis, where successful, is a two-way street, extending back to explain the past and forward to predict the future. What we try to do in framing hypotheses is to explain some otherwise unexplained happenings by inventing a plausible story, a plausible description or history of portions of the world." (Quine and Ullian (1998: 405).

knowledge of a thing-in-itself (like law) *is* to fall into the transcendental illusion. In my conception, "knowing" the rules for consideration under *Restatement (Second) of Contract* § 71 (American Law Institute 1932), for example, without knowing how a litigant is employing them in pursuit of an outcome is as arid as understanding the rules of inference in *modus ponens* logic without applying them to solve a problem.[49]

I regularly have conversations, in so many words, usually with my best and deepest-thinking students and usually just before exams, to the following effect.

> Contract doctrine consists of many tools, expressible in theories and their constituent rules, that one uses in after-the-fact litigation to achieve a desired result, or which we try to anticipate in before-the-fact planning to create contracts as congruent as possible with an underlying reality of expectation.
>
> For example, we employ the parol evidence rule if the problem is that there is an advantageous oral exchange not committed to the written document. We argue for implied-in-law terms if the contract is silent on something that otherwise needs to be decided. We employ mistake doctrine if the contract as model turns out not to have reflected the underlying reality (as if the map of Cambridge we were using to guide our transaction mistook Hampshire Street for Harvard Street). We employ frustration doctrine when the contract says what it says, but it is no longer of use to one of the parties.
>
> Think of each of those aspects of doctrine metaphorically as a tool. One is a hammer, one is a wrench, one is screwdriver, one is a pliers. It is productive to consider how we use each of those tools singly or in combination with each other to address a problem. Sometimes more than one tool works to solve it. What is less productive is to spend a lot of time thinking about the theoretical relationship of the wrench to the screwdriver or the hammer to the pliers. And your trying to work out how all the doctrine "fits together" (as though it will give you further insight into resolution of the real-world problem) is analogous precisely to that.

My students are impressionable, I am one of the first legal theorists to get to them, and I am willing to be patient in repeating the "tool metaphor" mantra during the year they are obliged to listen to me, so I may have a fleeting influence on them. To be candid, I hope to give them intellectual ammunition to be true positivists of contract law, and not to succumb to the noumenal, if not natural, law of pure doctrine (the holy text being the *Restatement (Second) of Contracts*). Many academic

---

[49] It is fashionable now to criticize Langdell (1871: vi–vii), but his statement of purpose in the first contracts casebook still resonates with me as an apt description of law as the product of reason, whether applied descriptively or normatively:

> Law, considered as a science, consists of certain principles or doctrines. To have such a mastery of these as to be able to apply them with constant facility and certainty to the ever-tangled skein of human affairs, is what constitutes a true lawyer; and hence to acquire that mastery should be the business of every earnest student of law.…[T]he number of fundamental legal doctrines is much less than is commonly supposed.…If these doctrines could be so classified and arranged that each should be found in its proper place, and nowhere else, they would cease to be formidable in their number.

contract theorists, I think (I am excluding Stewart Macaulay and the "contracts-in-action" school from this), do operate in a kind of transcendental illusion, looking for the coherent noumena of contract law, as though there is some transcendent ideal in which all the doctrine, removed from its application to the real world, fits together.[50]

We can see it in the writing of Karl Llewellyn (2012: 51), who observed 80 years ago, the work of a lawyer or judge in determining the law in the case method proceeds on the assumption "that all the cases everywhere can stand together. It is unquestionably the assumption you must make, at first. If they can be brought together, you must bring them."[51] I very much like the very fine casebook (co-authored by one of my faculty colleagues) that I use to teach contracts. Nevertheless I wholly disagree with the assertion on the third page of the text that one of the reasons to study jurisprudence is to see law not merely as rote doctrine, but, as great lawyers do, to "truly understand[] it as an integrated whole" (Hogg et al. 2008: 3). I see it in many of the debates and discussions that occur on the list-serv the Association of American Law Schools maintains for contract law professors. As one who was strongly influenced by Kant before he ever heard of Kelsen, most of that effort for pure systematization seems to be to be as futile as an empirical search for God. If there is such an ideally coherent doctrine, and it is meaningful, it is only meaningful, like God or justice, as an exercise in pure reason, and therefore suspect.[52]

Nor are practitioners immune. Contract law, as legal scholars have organized it over the last hundred years or so, is a powerful, useful, but sometimes deception-creating theoretical paradigm (Lipshaw 2012b: 989). The ideal paradigm is so powerful that lawyers can come to think that the contract is the deal rather than a mere model of it (Lipshaw 2012b: 1026–1028). I will simply assert here that nothing in my experience as a business lawyer was as frustrating as dealing with a lawyer on

[50] Robin Kar has recently undertaken a thoughtful and original attempt at a unified theory (as well as a summary of the extant descriptive and normative theories) of contract law (Kar 2014). The paper proposes to respond to the observation of Professors Schwartz and Scott that there is no "complete" descriptive or normative theory. What is interesting to me, beyond the specifics of Professor Kar's very interesting take on the philosophical underpinnings of contract law, is the question why we feel the need, as he suggests in the introduction, to "harmonize certain core areas of doctrine," to "provide[] unified answers," or why it is a problem that contract law has no complete descriptive or normative theory, or that the theories "fail to offer a unified understanding of… seemingly disparate features of contract law." As I have made clear here, I believe the answer to that question has less to do with contract law than with our seemingly hardwired inclination to teleology: that there are unified explanations, that doctrine ought to be harmonized, that the world ought to be seen as coherent.

[51] It is the assumption required "at first" because it is possible that the cases may not be reconcilable. "Hence, in your matching of cases, you may, as a last resort when unable to make the cases fit together, fall back upon the answer: here there is a conflict; these cases represent two different points of view" (Llewellyn 2012: 51).

[52] One of the difficulties with Ronald Dworkin's (1996) critique of positivism is the fact that he seems to tap into precisely this kind of noumena as justification for single correct answers in hard cases. Hence, Dworkin seems to believe that single correct answers are possible because we can know objective moral facts (Lipshaw 2006: 991–993).

the other side who seemed to be less concerned about the underlying deal and more concerned about winning the game of contract drafting (ie, outscoring the other lawyer on the number of his or her competing provisions ultimately included).

14.5 Conclusion

Perhaps as the result of a long career in doing law "purely" as a law firm lawyer and "not-so-purely" as an interdisciplinary law-and-business practitioner, I am far more inclined to think of law in the context of lawyering, and thus *doing*, rather than thinking of it as an object of demarcation and classification. This is the conundrum at the heart of the positivist project at least as it appears in the law of contracts: that cognition of the "law" on the books or the physical reality of contracts is each trivial from an epistemological standpoint, and the whole game is in the theories, sometimes descriptive and sometimes normative, that constitute the systematic application of rules to circumstances, whether before or after the fact. No single label serves us particularly well. To call what we are doing mere practical reason, for example, suggests that our only goal is to decide what to do, and fails to acknowledge the descriptive theorizing we often need to do about what actually happened in the creation of the legal norms.[53] "Formalism," for example, in the sense of a presumption that the parties are best served by a derivation of their rights and obligations from the text of the document, is simply a practical guide to the exercise of both practical and theoretical reason in resolving the issue. Even after Hart's overshadowing of Kelsen, the pure theory and the basic norm open the door to an assessment of what it means to *do* law that is, to me, more satisfying than Hart's approach, even if I wonder from time to time about the aridness of the entire philosophical project of distilling legal norms from all the other "oughts" by which we live.

My pluralism as to exploration of the objective and the subjective knows few bounds. Reason may well be the slave of the passions in employment of legal doctrine (and I do teach it that way because we live in a passionate world), but long experience at the intersection of law and business inclines me to think we are free and autonomous moral agents when we make the choice in the first instance to turn to law rather than all the other possible norms that inform relationships. That is, the reasoning we happen to do as lawyers is not particularly privileged, notwithstanding the efforts of Kelsen and others to distill and fence off law as an academic or professional discipline. Kant wanted to deny knowledge of that which is not knowable to make legitimate room for faith; I prefer to deny that law (at least for the business lawyer) is something we know as a matter of *a priori* cognition so as to make room

[53] In other words, I do not believe contract and business lawyering is only an exercise in practical reason, at least in the Kantian sense. I acknowledge there is a long history of jurisprudential debate about law as the product of practical reason or theoretical reason; it should be obvious by this point that I believe it is the product of human reason of some kind, but it is no more or less "real" on either account. For a brief overview of this particular issue, see Burton (1988).

for theoretical and practical reason that takes account of law, morality, principle, compromise, civility, and pragmatism. Even more radically, I see Kant's account of reason itself as merely one of a number of cognitive processes—among them, for example, the kind of metaphoric thinking and cognitive blending proposed by George Lakoff, Mark Turner, Gilles Fauconnier, Mark Johnson, Steven Pinker and others—that mediate between our cognition of the world around us and acting in response to it (Gibbs 2008; Lakoff and Johnson 1980 and 1999; Turner 2001; Pinker 2007).

They will all be on my guest list for the bird-fish wedding.

Acknowledgments This essay is a contribution to *Hans Kelsen in America*, a conference sponsored by the Valparaiso University Law School, supported by a grant from the Botstiber Institute for Austrian-American Studies, and held in Chicago on June 27–28, 2014. I am indebted to Jeremy Telman for the invitation to participate, and to conversation from and with the participants and observers. Thanks to Patrick Shin and Brian Bix for incisive comments on an early draft of the introduction, to Alexander Somek for encouragement about the approach, and to Pierre Schlag and David Gray Carlson for their insights. Finally, I nod gratefully to Michael Steven Green, one of whose articles introduced me to Kelsen, and who influenced my thinking in connection with this essay.

References

American Law Institute. 1932. Restatement of the law second, contracts.

Buchdahl, Gerd. 1967. The relationship between 'understanding' and 'reason' in the architectonic of Kant's philosophy. *Proceedings of the Aristotelian Society* 67: 209–226.

Buchdahl, Gerd. 1969. *Metaphysics and the philosophy of science: The classical origins—Descartes to Kant*. Malden: Blackwell Publishing.

Burton, Steven J. 1988. "Ontological" natural law? *Northwestern University Law Review* 82: 843–850.

Carlson, David Gray. 2009. Hart avec Kant: On the inseparability of law and morality. *Washington University Jurisprudence Review* 1: 21–96.

Craswell, Richard. 1989. Contract law, default rules, and the philosophy of promising. *Michigan Law Review* 88: 489–529.

Dworkin, Ronald. 1996. Objectivity and truth: You'd better believe it. *Philosophy and Public Affairs* 25: 87–139.

Gibbs Jr., Raymond W. 2008. Metaphor and thought: The state of the art. In *The Cambridge handbook of metaphor and thought*, ed. Raymond W. Gibbs, 3–16. Cambridge: Cambridge University Press.

Goodrich, Peter. 2009. Intellection and indiscipline. *Journal of Law and Society* 36: 460–480.

Green, Michael Steven. 2003. Hans Kelsen and the logic of legal systems. *Alabama Law Review* 54: 365–413.

Hart, H.L.A. 1997. *The concept of law*, 2nd ed. Oxford: Oxford University Press.

Hogg, James F., Carter G. Bishop, and Daniel D. Barnhizer. 2008. *Contracts: Cases and theory of contractual obligation*. Minneapolis: West Publishing.

Holmes, Oliver Wendell Jr. 1881. *The common law*. New York: Dover Publications 1991.

Holton, Richard. 1998. Positivism and the internal point of view. *Law and Philosophy* 17: 597–625.

Kant, Immanuel. 1781. *Critique of Pure Reason*. Trans. P. Guyer and A.W. Wood 1999. Cambridge: Cambridge University Press.

Kant, Immanuel. 1783. *Prolegomena to Any Future Metaphysics*. Trans. P. Carus 1949. Chicago: Open Court.

Kant, Immanuel. 1785. Fundamental Principles of the Metaphysics of Morals. Trans. F.M. Muller. In *Basic writings of Kant*, ed. Allen W. Wood, 2001. New York: Modern Library.

Kant, Immanuel. 1790. *Critique of Judgment*. Trans. J.H. Bernard 2005. Amherst: Prometheus Books.

Kar, Robin Bradley. 2014. Contract as empowerment. Social Science Research Network. http://papers.ssrn.com/sol3/papers.cfm?abstract_id=2476148. Accessed 13 Aug 2014.

Kelsen, Hans. 1934. *Introduction to the Problems of Legal Theory*. Trans. B.L. Paulson and S.L. Paulson 1996. Oxford: Oxford University Press.

Konefsky, Alfred S. 1987. How to read, or at least not misread, Cardozo in the Allegheny College case. *Buffalo Law Review* 36: 645–700.

Lakoff, George, and Mark Johnson. 1980. *Metaphors we live by*. Chicago: University of Chicago Press.

Lakoff, George, and Mark Johnson. 1999. *Philosophy in the flesh: The embodied mind and its challenge to western thought*. New York: Basic Books.

Langdell, C.C. 1871. *Selection of cases on the law of contracts*. Clark: The Lawbook Exchange, Ltd.

Lipshaw, Jeffrey M. 2006. Law as rationalization: Getting beyond reason to business ethics. *University of Toledo Law Review* 37: 959–1020.

Lipshaw, Jeffrey M. 2007. Freedom, compulsion, compliance and mystery: Reflections on a duty not to enforce a promise. *Law Culture and the Humanities* 3: 82–101.

Lipshaw, Jeffrey M. 2012a. Contract as meaning: An introduction to "Contract as Promise at 30". *Suffolk Law Review* 36: 601–625.

Lipshaw, Jeffrey M. 2012b. Metaphors, models, and meaning in contract law. *Penn State Law Review* 116: 987–1042.

Llewellyn, K.N. 2012. *The bramble bush: On our law and its study*. New Orleans: QuidPro Books.

Neiman, Susan. 1994. *The unity of reason: Rereading Kant*. Princeton: Princeton University Press.

Overbye, Dennis. 2014. Space ripples reveal big bang's smoking gun. *New York Times*, March 18.

Oxford Dictionaries, s.v. "Mould". Accessed 13 Aug 2014. http://www.oxforddictionaries.com/definition/english/mould.

Patterson, Dennis. 1999. *Law and truth*. Oxford: Oxford University Press.

Paulson, Stanley. 1997. Introduction. In *Introduction to the Problems of Legal Theory*. Trans. B.L. Paulson., and S.L. Paulson, 1996. Oxford: Oxford University Press.

Pinker, Steven. 2007. *The stuff of thought: Language as a window into human nature*. New York: Penguin.

Quine, W.V., and J.S. Ullian. 1998. Hypothesis. In *Introductory readings in the philosophy of science*, 3rd ed, ed. E.D. Klemke, Hollinger Robert, and Rudge David Wÿss, 404–414. Amherst: Prometheus Books.

Solum, Lawrence B. 2014. Artificial meaning. *Washington Law Review* 89: 69–86.

Stein, Joseph, Jerry Bock, and Sheldon Harnick. 2004. *Fiddler on the roof: Based on Sholom Aleichem's stories*. Milwaukee: Limelight Editions.

Stumpff, Andrew Morrison. 2013. The law is a fractal: The attempt to anticipate everything. *Loyola University Chicago Law Journal* 44: 649–682.

Suchman, Marc C. 2003. The contract as social artifact. *Law and Society Review* 37: 91–142.

Turner, Mark. 2001. *Cognitive dimensions of social science: The way we think about politics, economics, law, and society*. Oxford: Oxford University Press.

Walsh, W.H. 1975. *Kant's criticism of metaphysics*. Edinburgh: Edinburgh University Press.

Weinrib, Ernest J. 1987. Law as a Kantian idea of reason. *Columbia Law Review* 87: 472–508.

Welch, Jack, Goodreads, https://www.goodreads.com/author/quotes/3770.Jack_Welch.

Williams, Garrath. 2013. Kant's account of reason. In *The Stanford encyclopedia of philosophy*, 2013 ed., http://plato.stanford.edu/archives/spr2013/entries/kant-reason/.
Wilson, Alida. 1986. Is Kelsen really a Kantian? In *Essays on Kelsen 37–64*, ed. Richard Tur and William Twining, 37–64. Oxford: Oxford University Press.
Wolcher, Louis. 2008. *Law's task: The tragic circle of law, justice, and human suffering*. Burlington: Ashgate Publishing Company.
Zipursky, Benjamin. 2006. Introduction—symposium, the internal point of view in law and ethics. *Fordham Law Review* 75: 1143–1156.

Chapter 15
Kelsen's View of the Addressee of the Law: Primary and Secondary Norms

Drury D. Stevenson

15.1 Introduction

Hans Kelsen argued that all individual laws primarily address state actors rather than the citizens. Ancient edicts or imperatives, such as, "Thou shalt not murder," address the whole citizenry. Modern laws, in contrast, address state actors who must execute, apply, or implement the law. For example, consider the opening line of New York's first-degree murder statute: "A person is guilty of murder in the first degree when, with intent to cause the death of another person, he causes the death of such person or of a third person, and…the defendant was more than 18 years old at the time of the commission of the crime" (N.Y. Penal Law § 125.27). Kelsen's observation, even taken in isolation rather than as a component of Kelsen's grand theories, has significant implications; it has received too little attention in the academic literature in the United States.[1] The point also presents some difficult challenges to popular American ideas about the law, so it may help explain why Kelsen's works have not gained more traction among American legal theorists.

Kelsen's view of the addressee of laws is also important for understanding Kelsen's larger theories overall. On the one hand, the passages where Kelsen bears down on the point are those where he comes closest to solving Hume's "is-ought" problem—he verges on describing an "ought" (a legal norm) without invoking another "ought" besides the Grundnorm. These are passages where the discussion becomes purely positive. On the other hand, Kelsen often lapses from this rigorous position throughout his writings and routinely gives examples of norms

[1] For a typical criticism, see Ota Weinberger (Weinberger 1985: 321), "strongly opposing" Kelsen's view.

D.D. Stevenson (✉)
Hutchins Research Professor, South Texas College of Law, Houston, TX 77002, USA

James A. Baker III Institute, Rice University, Houston, TX 77005, USA
e-mail: dstevenson@stcl.edu

D.A.J. Telman (ed.), *Hans Kelsen in America - Selective Affinities and the Mysteries of Academic Influence*, Law and Philosophy Library 116,
DOI 10.1007/978-3-319-33130-0_15

communicating rules directly to the citizens, a contradiction that makes his work confusing.[2] Kelsen himself attempted to smooth over this problem by suggesting that every law actually contains two inherent legal norms: a primary norm (instructing a state actor to sanction certain conduct) and a secondary norm (deterring citizens from engaging in sanctionable conduct, or committing the delict).

From a formalist perspective, Kelsen's observation is robustly descriptive of modern statutes (legislative laws), which nearly all use indicative rather than imperative verbs forms. Earlier legal philosophers, such as Bentham[3] (Bentham 1999: 119–123) and Austin (Austin 1832: 12–20), had recommended a shift from imperative to indicative verbs, but were unwilling to concede that the primary addressee of each law is the government organ that must apply or execute it, rather than those whose conduct the law ultimately seeks to control. This author has traced the historical development of these concepts elsewhere (Stevenson 2003: 105).

My discussion fleshes out these points, and develops Kelsen's addressee concept a bit further. Section 15.2 surveys what Kelsen actually said about this issue. This concept is not one of Kelsen's better-known tenets, and even some readers who consider themselves Kelsenians might benefit from reviewing these oft-ignored excerpts. Section 15.3 explores the implications of Kelsen's addressee concept for understanding the persistence of technical terms and jargon within laws, for understanding certain interpretive rules pertaining to legislative delegations to executive agencies, and for understanding the boundaries of executive and judicial power. Section 15.4 applies the concept to the inherent problems with executive subdelegations of state functions to private corporations.

15.2 Kelsen's Writings on the Addressee of the Law

Kelsen's major works show a development or evolution of his thinking—and terminology—when discussing the addressees of the law. Over several decades, his thinking became increasingly developed on this point, and his terminology more nuanced. Some of his points are consistent, of course—such as his repeated use of the word "superfluous" for binary articulations of a law's addressees.

---

[2] The same problem seems to beset those who write about Kelsen's ideas, referring to the citizenry as the "addressees" of the law under Kelsen's system (Somek 2006: 765–772; Stewart 1990: 284; Wilson 1981: 275).

[3] Bentham believed that his great project for modern codification would only work if the citizens knew exactly what was expected of them" (Bentham 1999: 122). To this end, he proposed that codes follow a logical organization, in part to facilitate memorization by those governed (Bentham 1999: 119–123). Part of his attempt to create a comprehensive utilitarian code was the division of laws into categories of those that affect everyone and those that affect only some people, so that people could readily identify the sections that they should know by heart regardless of their situation.

15.2.1 Pure Theory of Law

In Kelsen's magnum opus, *Pure Theory of Law*, he introduced the concept of the law's addressee (without using that term in this book) by observing that each statute technically contains two "norms"—one commanding certain behavior from the citizenry, and another directing legal organs, such as the executive or courts, to sanction violations (Kelsen 1960: 55). The latter, he maintained, was the one that truly mattered and that could stand alone in the legal formulations of modern laws. The former (the "command" or prohibition that is what most people mean when they speak of a "law") is impliedly (even tacitly) present in the latter (the sanction provision), making the former "superfluous" or unnecessary verbiage in a modern code. Kelsen's argument in *Pure Theory* on this point unfolded as follows: suppose that a statute contains two legal norms, one prescribing certain behavior by the citizenry, and another norm imposing sanctions when citizens violate the first norm. In this case, Kelsen says, the first norm is inherently dependent on the second norm—the proscribed behavior is merely a triggering condition for the imposition of a punishment by the state. Taking the point a step further, Kelsen then says, "[T]he first one is superfluous from the point of view of the legislative technique" (Kelsen 1960: 55). As an example, Kelsen posits a debtor with a legal obligation to repay a creditor; the relevant statute directs the courts to execute judgment on the possessions of the delinquent debtor in order to repay the debt, at least under certain circumstances. The fact that a statute orders execution on debtors under certain circumstances automatically implies (or "contains," as Kelsen says) the fact that the debtor has an obligation to repay the debt under those circumstances (Kelsen 1960: 55). In fact, including statutory language declaring debtors' legal duties would be superfluous, because the sanctioning provision is sufficient standing alone. Modern statutes, unlike ancient codes, favor the succinct sanctioning form and often skip the commanding language that would address the citizens directly. Kelsen reaches a rather dramatic conclusion: "This shows clearly that a norm like, 'You shall not murder,' is superfluous, if this other norm is also valid: 'He who murders ought to be punished'" (Kelsen 1960: 55). In other words, a legal order prohibits behaviors merely by imposing sanctions for their occurrence, and requires whatever behavior is the opposite of that which triggers the statutory punishments.

Kelsen's terminology evolved over time—here, he uses "independent norm" and "dependent norm" for what he would later call "primary" and "secondary" norms, respectively. Yet the core idea is that the real "law" is the rule directing the state actor to carry out a certain action (sanction) against certain individuals (those who commit the delict). While he seems to be focusing on "legislative technique," that is, stylistic conventions in drafting, the forcefulness of his argument hints that there is something more profound at work here, something closely tied to his overall theory about the state and the nature of law. What most people call "the law" is merely the dependent norm of a given statute, and the fact that it is "superfluous" suggests that intuitions (or common parlance, if the two are distinguishable) about the "law" are commonly mistaken.

As a side note, Kelsen's reference to the Ten Commandments is helpful for purposes of clarifying his point—most readers are at least vaguely familiar with the "thou shalt not" imperative mood of the Decalogue, and can see how it contrasts with the indicative mood of modern legislation. Yet even within the Mosaic Law, one can find imperative-mood commands that are more akin to modern laws, as the conduct rule for the citizenry is a dependent norm. For example, *Exodus* 21:12 (the next chapter after the Ten Commandments) says, "Anyone who strikes a person with a fatal blow must be put to death." This clearly implies an absolute ban on murder for the citizens of ancient Israel, even though the imperative merely requires a sanction, presumably for the community rulers or leaders to impose. Similarly, *Exodus* 21:16 commands, "Anyone who kidnaps someone is to be put to death, whether the victim has been sold or is still in the kidnapper's possession." This does not use the form "thou shalt not kidnap," and we should not make the mistake of thinking all ancient codes used the immediate-command form. Other examples run throughout the Mosaic law.[4]

15.2.2 The General Theory of Law and State

In *The General Theory of Law and State*, Kelsen develops the idea more extensively, beginning with his point from *Pure Theory* that it was superfluous to include the part of a law directed at the would-be offender (Kelsen 1945: 61–62). The "ought" of any legal norm, Kelsen claims, is "an epiphenomenon of the 'ought' of the sanction" (Kelsen 1945: 61). He challenges the conventional notion that legal norms

[4] *See, eg*, other examples of imperatives to the rulers that imply a dependent norm, such as *Exodus* 21:15 ("Anyone who attacks their father or mother is to be put to death."); *Exodus* 21:29 ("If, however, the bull has had the habit of goring and the owner has been warned but has not kept it penned up and it kills a man or woman, the bull is to be stoned and its owner also is to be put to death."); *Exodus* 22:18 ("Do not allow a sorceress to live."); *Exodus* 22:19 ("Anyone who has sexual relations with an animal is to be put to death."); *Exodus* 31:15 ("Whoever does any work on the Sabbath day is to be put to death."). Lest the reader think that all Old Testament sanctions involved death, there are many requiring restitution instead. *See, eg*, *Leviticus* 24:21 ("Whoever kills an animal must make restitution, but whoever kills a human being is to be put to death."); *Exodus* 22:3 ("Anyone who steals must certainly make restitution, but if they have nothing, they must be sold to pay for their theft."); *Exodus* 22:6 ("If a fire breaks out and spreads into thornbushes so that it burns shocks of grain or standing grain or the whole field, the one who started the fire must make restitution."); *Exodus* 22:14 ("If anyone borrows an animal from their neighbor and it is injured or dies while the owner is not present, they must make restitution").

More interesting, from the standpoint of Kelsen's view of norms and the state, are divine edicts that are general rules or limitations on sanctioning, without any "secondary" or "dependent" norm for the citizenry. *See, eg*, *Numbers* 35:30 ("Anyone who kills a person is to be put to death as a murderer only on the testimony of witnesses. But no one is to be put to death on the testimony of only one witness."); *Deuteronomy* 17:6 (same); or *Deuteronomy* 24:16 ("Parents are not to be put to death for their children, nor children put to death for their parents; each will die for their own sin."). All foregoing biblical quotes are from the New International Version. Other modern writers have developed more thorough literary discussions of other Old Testament mandates (Bartor 2012: 292).

contain two "ought" statements, one directed at the citizenry (mandating or forbidding some action on their part), and one for the state officials with a duty of enforcement, that is, a first norm and a second norm. In rebuttal, Kelsen invokes an example of theft, similar to his use of murder as an example previously in *Pure Theory*: "One shall not steal; if somebody steals, he shall be punished. If it is assumed that the first norm which forbids theft is valid only if the second norm attaches a sanction to theft, then the first norm is certainly superfluous in an exact exposition of law." Kelsen concludes that the supposed first norm (the rule the citizen must obey) is already contained in the second norm (the imposition of punishment when certain conduct has occurred). This second norm, Kelsen insists, is truly "the only genuine legal norm" (Kelsen 1945: 61). Kelsen argued that the "law" is not the prohibition of a given act, but the mandate to the state to sanction the act, because the former cannot exist without the latter (Kelsen 1945: 61).

In the same chapter, Kelsen then introduces the terms "primary norm" and "secondary norm," which are somewhat counterintuitive, or at least run counter to usual conventions of writing or parlance, conceding that it greatly facilitates legal discussions "if we allow ourselves to assume also the existence of the first norm. To do so is legitimate only if one is aware of the fact that the first norm, which demands omission of the delict, is dependent upon the second norm, which stipulates the sanction" (Kelsen 1945: 61). Somewhat confusingly, Kelsen proposes designating "the second norm as the primary norm, and the first norm as the secondary norm" (Kelsen 1945: 61). The former refers to the citizens' behavior that the law seeks to incentivize by threat of sanctions (what we normally refer to as the "unlawful behavior," or in Kelsen's jargon, the "delict"). Kelsen contends that it is untenable to have a legal system comprised only of these secondary norms; instead, law in reality is "a coercive order which stipulates sanctions," not merely prohibitions, or actions that elicit punishment (Kelsen 1945: 61).

Kelsen then takes a strong turn, designating law itself as "the primary norm, which stipulates the sanction, and this norm is not contradicted by the delict of the subject, which, on the contrary, is the specific condition of the sanction" (Kelsen 1945: 61). A state entity or official is the only actor that can truly "counteract" a law, by refusing to implement or apply it. Even so, Kelsen concedes, when we speak of an act as "unlawful," we normally do not have in mind the behavior of the state actors who apply and enforce the law, but the citizen whose behavior has triggered the sanctions prescribed by the law (Kelsen 1945: 61).

Kelsen argues that the technical obligation or duty imposed by the law itself is toward state actors; the idea that a citizen "ought" to avoid a prohibited act is an indirect implication of the statute's plain language requiring the state to impose a penalty on individuals engaged in the prohibited act. Only by referring to a "secondary norm" can one say that a citizen "ought" to do something required by the law (or avoid something prohibited) (Kelsen 1945: 61). The governmental entity or officials entrusted with applying and implementing the law are those who truly obey or disobey the primary legal norm. Moreover, Kelsen says that it is necessary to use this terminological distinction to define the law's relationship to the citizens and the state (Kelsen 1945: 61). From this vantage point, the law "is efficacious if it is applied by the organ—if the organ executes the sanction. And the organ has to apply law precisely in the case where the subject 'disobeys' law: this is the case for which the sanction is stipulated" (Kelsen 1945: 62).

15.2.3 General Theory of Norms

Years later, in the posthumously published *General Theory of Norms* (Kelsen 1979),[5] Kelsen returned to this point with some clarifications, and wrote in much more detail about this point, adding the terminology "addressees" and "immediate/mediate." Kelsen explains, "The immediate addressees of general hypothetical legal norms are thus the individuals who are empowered—and in certain circumstances, also obligated—to order concretely and to execute the coercive acts which serve as sanctions" (Kelsen 1979: 52). Kelsen calls the citizenry "merely mediate addressees"—those whose behavior could trigger state sanctions (Kelsen 1979: 52). He goes on to explain that only a governmental organ can "obey" or "disobey" the law in this sense, as the law itself directs state organs to impose coercive sanctions in certain circumstances. The performance of the law may fall upon two different branches of government in different stages—the judiciary (or regulatory agency) makes a determination that an individual qualifies for sanctions under the law, and the executive organ imposes the sanction on the individual (Kelsen 1979: 52–54). Kelsen concludes the section by observing that if the true addressee of the law is the state (or state actors), and that the citizenry are only indirect addressees, the law becomes truly "autonomous"[6] (Kelsen 1979: 54).

In the subsequent chapter, Kelsen briefly attacks a common misunderstanding of this position, which in the United States was most famously championed by law professor Meir Dan-Cohen (Dan-Cohen 1984) in his widely cited article on "acoustic separation" in the law.[7] Kelsen explains that the decision about whether a violation occurred is solely in the hands of the adjudicator (the state), and the individual citizen could trigger sanctions under the law even without knowing about the law (Kelsen 1979: 56–57). He concedes that people usually support the view that "that legal norms are commands addressed in the first instance to legal subjects and only secondarily to legal organs," but explains that this cannot be true because "it is of the essence of a command that it be known to the addressee is clearly untenable.

[5] The original title was *Allegemeine Theorie der Normen* . This lengthy work was among Kelsen's unpublished papers at the time of his death in 1973, and first appeared in German in 1979.

[6] Kelsen goes on to say that no subject of the law can decide whether she has obeyed or violated the law. Rather, only the relevant legal organ can make that determination (of compliance or violation)—at least, a determination that is legally relevant (Kelsen 1979: 54–55).

[7] I have written an extensive refutation to Dan-Cohen's article elsewhere (Stevenson 2003: 132–36).

This is true not only of the general legal command of the legislator, but also of the individual legal command of the judge"[8] (Kelsen 1979: 57).

Near the end of *General Theory of Norms*, Kelsen returns to this point, explaining why the norm addressed to the legal organ is "primary" and the indirect norm for the citizenry is "secondary," rather than the other way around[9] (Kelsen 1979: 142–143). Kelsen's concluding point seems to be that law without a sanction is not really law, but he addresses this point in his other works, explaining that sanctionless norms can still induce behavior because adherents want social approval, credibility, and so on. *General Theory of Norms* also develops a detailed theory of desuetude for laws that state officials or judges no longer follow or enforce.

To summarize, Kelsen's discussion of this point became increasingly detailed through the years as he wrote subsequent books. By the end, he recognized that this point—that laws are addressed to the judiciary and executive organs—is necessary for understanding that law is autonomous. This appears to be an under-appreciated component or feature of Kelsen's overall system, a point to which he returned repeatedly, and a point he seemed to consider inseparable from the rest of his theory.

15.3 Plain Language, Legal Jargon, and Legal Complexity

This Part explores the implications of Kelsen's addressee concept for understanding the persistence of technical terms and jargon within laws. It also discusses interpretive rules pertaining to legislative delegations to executive agencies, and for understanding the boundaries of executive and judicial power.

15.3.1 Plain Language

Given that the addressee of the laws (or at least primary addressee) is a state organ, like courts or bureaucrats, then it is unimportant to have laws in language that is easily understandable to laypersons or the citizenry overall. The plain language

[8] Kelsen concludes that objectively observing or violating a command occurs when the behavior addressed by the law comports with the law's prescription, regardless of the knowledge of the actor, while subjectively obeying or violating a law requires knowledge and intent on the part of the actor concerning compliance.

[9] The translator's Introduction to *General Theory of Norms* observes the following about this aspect of Kelsen's thought in the book:

> *ATN* [?] clarifies things considerably; a legal norm has two addresses, one immediate (the official) and the other mediate (the person liable to the sanction), and both addressees can observe or violate the norm; this implies that the effect of the norm on *both* addressees is one of commanding. It imposes a legal duty on the mediate addressee, and on the official it imposes some sort of requirement which is something other than a legal duty but which is never explained.

Id. at xl.

movement is as old as Moore's *Utopia*, Moore (1901: 88–89) but is somewhat misguided. There is little value in expunging useful technical terms in order to make the laws easier for laypersons to read (Stevenson 2003: 148–151; Crump 2002).

The Plain English Movement (or Plain Language Movement) has grown in recent decades, demanding simplification of statutes and regulations into common parlance so that average citizens can easily read and comprehend them; this has affected consumer documents, jury instructions, and even court documents and statutes (Solan 1993: 133–138; Tiersma 1999: 211–230; Gallacher 2013: 451 et seq.; Serafin 1998; Hathaway 1994; Gopen 1987). A popular "TED Talk" by Alan Siegel (who has spearheaded the Plain English Movement for decades)[10] calls for the elimination of "legal jargon" (Siegel 2010). During the talk, Siegel exclaims, "There is no way that we should allow government to communicate the way they communicate. There is no way we should do business with companies that have agreements with stealth provisions and that are unintelligible.…Make clarity, transparency and simplicity a national priority."

At the same TED conference in 2010, Philip K. Howard gave a presentation entitled *Four Ways to Fix a Broken Legal System* (Howard 2010), also largely decrying the prevalence of legal jargon, complexity, and technical terms in statutes, regulations, contracts, and government documents; and he promises (to the delight of his TED Talk audience) to make lawyers unnecessary. Howard has a nonprofit, Common Good, devoted to reforming the legal system so that it will be more accessible to the citizenry.[11]

Superficially, it may seem self-evident that certain consumer contracts, such as leases, insurance policies, and home mortgages, should use terminology intelligible to the average consumer, so that the contract embodies a meeting of the minds. Yet the purpose of these legal instruments is not to provide the parties (the consumer or the firm) with guidelines to follow, but rather to inform a court about how to resolve disputes that may arise (but which both parties hope to avoid). Even with private contracts, which epitomize private law, the written instruments have the courts as their anticipated audience, not the parties themselves. The purpose of formalizing an agreement in writing, in fact, is for the convenience of the potential judge who would otherwise face evidentiary problems with determining the terms of an ephemeral oral agreement. From a Kelsenian point of view, there is no problem with consumer contracts containing terms and phrases that are unintelligible to the consumer, because the text is for a judge to read and decide which side should prevail. In the vast majority of cases, the parties will fulfill their agreement and no litigation will result, making the contract language moot. Its language has no direct relevance to the parties themselves—the only significance for the parties is indirect, secondary, or dependent, to use Kelsen's three alternating terms for the derivative interest that citizens have in a legal text.

---

[10] *See, eg*, Siegel's biographical summary at http://www.siegelgale.com/team_member/alan-siegel/.

[11] *See also* www.commongood.org.

The Plain English Movement has perhaps its most appealing argument when it comes to jury instructions. The legal system intentionally includes layperson-citizen jurors in litigation decision-making. There is an easy, intuitive appeal to the idea that jury instructions about the law need to be in terms the jurors comprehend. Legal language reformers insist that jurors find the judge's explanation of the law incomprehensible, especially if the judge uses technical legal terms or jargon (likely to occur if the judge quotes the relevant statute or caselaw itself). Yet even here, recent empirical studies demonstrate that that the Plain English advocates are mistaken. In a recent study by Shari Siedman Diamond, Beth Murphy, and Mary R. Rose, in which they observed and analyzed the deliberations of 50 real juries in actual trials, it appears the traditional jury instructions were not the problem. "[W]hen communication breaks down, the breakdown stems from more fundamental sources than simply opaque legal language.…We conclude that it will take more than a 'plain English' movement to achieve genuine harmony between laypersons and jury instructions on the law" (Diamond et al. 2012: 1537).

The Plain English movement seems even more misguided in pushing for the redrafting of statutes and regulations in "user-friendly" English, as this endeavor seems premised upon an ideological commitment to having citizens read the laws. A number of sections of the modern Code of Federal Regulations (C.F.R.) contain repeated use of "when you do this," and "we will try to do this."[12] It is futile to rewrite laws in non-legal language merely to make the laws "accessible" to the citizenry, as the citizenry is not the real addressee. This is not to say that we should favor grandiloquence, anachronisms, or poor grammar. The law serves its purpose when it is understandable to agency officials, judges, law enforcement officers, and perhaps (but not necessarily) lawyers.[13] The efficient course would be to cast the law in terms both familiar and facile to this group. Clarity and precision are helpful to courts and officials as much as for others. Judges and officials live in the modern era, and overly antiquated language may hinder, rather than facilitate, their tasks. Cumbersome language consumes time in deciphering and explaining, and can be a waste of judicial resources, whether in statutes or older court opinions. Even so, the benchmark should be the readability for a judge (most of whom have law degrees) or the relevant government official (usually experienced and specialized in that field).

[12] *See, eg*, 20 C.F.R. §404.1530 (2002) ("In order to get benefits, you must follow treatment prescribed by your physician if this treatment can restore your ability to work").

[13] Maley observes that the grammatical layout of statutes, which are generally one continuous sentence, was historically motivated by the belief in the legal community that "it is easier to construe a single sentence than a series of sentences, and that there is therefore less potential for uncertainty" (Maley 1994: 24). While this belief may be mistaken, it has led draftsmen to use complex patterns of subordinate clauses, making for greater lexical density. Maley notes that even with modern formatting, such as indentation of subordinate clauses, "the syntactic complexity -probably more than technical terms -renders legislative texts incomprehensible to all except the specialist reader." He notes that drafters prefer repetition of nouns rather than employing pronouns for the same reason (Maley 1994: 25).

It makes little sense to talk about citizens "interpreting" the ambiguous statutory language, as a private individual's personal interpretation of a statutory term would not be recognized in our courts. Certainly, a legislature would not leave ambiguity in a statute in order to delegate discretion or power to individual citizens, which would be result of the citizens having legal rights to make authoritative interpretation of the law, even for oneself. Kelsen discusses this idea and argues that whatever discretion that may appear to be left to citizens themselves is not "authentic, because it is not binding on the state agents responsible for enforcement and punishment[14] (Kelsen 1960: 355). Interestingly, Kelsen distinguishes state interpretation of legal texts from interpretations by the citizenry in stark terms: "The interpretation by a law-applying organ [of the state] is different from any other interpretation—all other interpretations are not authentic, that is, they do not create law" (Kelsen 1960: 355).

Jargon or "legalease" is appropriate and efficient where the primary interpreters or recipients of the communication are familiar with the nomenclature or shorthand for complex concepts. The "law" directed at the citizenry is not, in fact, the text of the statute or regulation, but the sanction of the state organ against those who engage in the delineated behavior. There is obvious utility in technical vocabulary, as every profession develops its own shorthand expressions, technical terms, acronyms, and other jargon (Maley 1994: 24–25). One word, such as "domicile," "Mirandize," "bailment," or "assignee," can capture and communicate an entire phrase or set of ideas to one trained in the profession. It does not undermine democracy that a person on the street does not understand "bailments" or know that "consideration" in a contract does not mean altruism, neighborliness, or contemplation (Tiersma 1999: 106–110). Such terms are for individuals empowered to implement the legal text with the force of the state. Similarly, legal complexity (volume of laws and provisions, intricacy of legal procedures, and systemic redundancies (checks and balances) are appropriate despite being the target of perennial complaints from would-be reformers.[15] The systematization and compilation of laws inherent in

[14] In the same section, Kelsen argues that an attorney who, in the interest of his client, propounds to the judge only one of several possible interpretations of the legal norm to be applied in the case, or a writer who in his commentary extols a specific interpretation among many possible ones as the only correct one, does not render a function of legal science, but of legal politics.

[15] The plight of an average citizen has become an issue in Supreme Court decisions—*Citizens United v. F.E.C.*, 130 S. Ct 876 (2010), being the prime example. There, the majority based its holding in part upon the prolixity of campaign regulations, apparently adopting a void-for-verbosity rule:

> These entities are subject to separate rules for 33 different types of political speech. The FEC has adopted 568 pages of regulations, 1278 pages of explanations and justifications for those regulations, and 1771 advisory opinions since 1975…Prolix laws chill speech for the same reason that vague laws chill speech: People 'of common intelligence must necessarily guess at [the law's] meaning and differ as to its application.'

Citizens United< 130 S. Ct. at 888–889. Professor Mila Sohoni recently commented that this "may be the first modern instance of the Supreme Court treating the volume and complexity per se of a federal regulatory scheme as an unacceptable burden on the exercise of a fundamental right" (Sohoni 2012: 1600). Similarly, in *Sampson v. Buescher*, 625 F.3d 1247, 1259 (10th Cir. 2010), the

modern codification produce law designed for the efficient implementation by the state-organ recipient, not the citizenry.

15.3.2 How Do Citizens Obey?

In *The Concept of Law*, H.L.A. Hart included a lengthy attack on Kelsen's concept of the law's addressee (Hart 1961: 35–40). The thrust of his argument is that there must be some way for citizens to discover or know their legal duties, so that they can conform their behavior accordingly. Thus, he concludes, the law must primarily address those whose behavior it seeks to control (Hart 1961: 40). In fact, Hart flips Kelsen's nomenclature of "primary" and "secondary" laws. He uses the former to refer to the citizen-targeted aspect and the latter refer to the instructions to judges and officials about application and implementation (Hart 1961: 94–97). Hart criticizes Kelsen's point that the citizen-oriented norm is superfluous and can be missing entirely from statutory text. He ignores the important fact that most modern statutes are, in fact, written in the indicative mood using the very form that Kelsen recommended—that is, free from the superfluity that Hart thinks is the "primary" part of the law.

I have written an extensive answer elsewhere to the question of how the laws deter citizens, in practice, from the sanctioned behavior (Stevenson 2005: 1535 et seq.); here I will merely summarize the argument. The critical problem with Hart's view—which is the prevailing view—is that citizens do not read the law; most citizens will go through their whole lives without ever reading a single statute. They see signage announcing speed limits, forbidden access, and so forth, and some signs actually include a citation to a statute or ordinance. During the era of Blockbuster video, people would see (and usually fast-forward through) a display of the F.B.I.'s warnings about copyright violations (pirated video), which included a quote from a statute. Most of the population is able to conform their behavior to the requirements of the law reasonably well without ever reading the statutory text itself. If, as Hart claims, the law must address the citizens if they are to conform their behavior to it, how does this communication occur when we can easily observe that almost nobody reads the laws?[16] How does a law deter behavior without the deterred individuals ever reading the laws?

---

court said, "The average citizen cannot be expected to master on his or her own the many campaign [laws and regulations]. Even if those rules that apply to issue committees may be few, one would have to sift through them all to determine which apply." In *Doctor's Hospital of Hyde Park v. Appeal of Daiwa Special Asset Corp.*, 337 F.3d 951 (7th Cir. 2003), the court declared, "There are an enormous number of state laws, and it might be unreasonable to expect a person…to determine in advance the possible bearing of all of them."

[16] Some may answer that people ask lawyers to read the law for them, and inform them of its content, but most individuals in society do not consult lawyers before they make decisions—that luxury is largely reserved for corporations and wealthy individuals. For a recent article recognizing that those who end up being liable for patent infringement never read patent laws themselves, in a

A variety of possible explanations are available for this phenomenon, but regardless of the mechanism, the point is clear that most people conform to the law most of the time without ever reading it, so it is not necessary to posit that law address the citizens directly in order to explain the survival of civic society. People often have a vague notion about the laws pertaining to their activities, and in the presence of uncertainty about the particulars, they steer clear of the imagined outer limits of whatever the rules might be (Stevenson 2005: 1584–1585). We are social creatures, and much of our behavior is merely mimicking the behavior of those around us, so if even a few people are aware of things that trigger legal sanctions (even without reading the law), this influences others. Some sanctions, like incarceration, remove lawbreakers from society, thereby subtracting their example from the pool of influences on the rest of us. Many laws reflect societal values and morals—most people would refrain from rape, burglary, and murder even if the law did not sanction it—these are socially taboo actions, and they can be very risky for the perpetrator (Stuntz 2000, discussing the complex relationship between popular norms and criminal statutes). The extensiveness or comprehensiveness of modern codes (statutes and regulations) means that one individual's entire life (work, family, and other activities) will fall outside the ambit of most of laws—only a fraction of the existing laws in any jurisdiction would be relevant to any given individual. Even lawyers know only a few laws that pertain to their area of practice, a fraction of the whole body of laws that govern their jurisdiction. In any case, laws "work" without most people ever reading the legal texts, so the addressee of the text does not affect whether, or how, the laws "work" as far as controlling behavior of the citizens.[17]

15.3.3 Judicial Interpretation

Kelsen's view about the addressee of the law is also illuminating for our understanding of judicial interpretation. When faced with ambiguous provisions or multiple possible meanings, we should favor the one that fits with the recipient's common usage of that language. In the case of statutes, that recipient is the judiciary or an administrative agency; in the case of agency-promulgated regulations, it is typically the agency itself. This view runs counter to traditional academic theories of interpretation, which focus almost exclusively on the intent of the author (in the case of laws, the legislature). Yet it does fit neatly with the most robust interpretive norms

similar vein to the arguments in this paper, *see* Janis and Holbrook (2012: 72). Janis and Holbrook argue for better use of "intermediaries" (presumably lawyers) to bridge the communication gap between the law's actual audience and those whose conduct will trigger sanctions under the law.

[17] Even in the case of so-called "legislative threats," wherein a regulator or legislator communicates directly to the leaders of a targeted industry that they need to self-regulate to a requisite level or else face draconian legislation (not yet enacted), the deterrence is not through the legislative text itself. Rather, the deterrence comes through the orally-transmitted threat of a sanction that contemplated legislation will authorize unless the audience preempts this move by voluntarily changing their behavior (Halfteck 2008).

used within the American judiciary, related to judicial deference to administrative agencies when the agency is interpreting its own governing statute or its own regulations: these are the *Chevron*, *Skidmore*, *Auer*, and *Hearst* doctrines, rules of judicial deference to administrative agencies.

At the outset of this discussion, however, it is appropriate to note that Kelsen himself eschewed interpretive theories or systems, considering them merely political. As he explains in *Pure Theory of Law*, ambiguity in statutory language may often be unintentional on the part of the lawmaker, and in some instances, even clear language may inaccurately represent the lawmaker's intention (Kelsen 1960: 350). Kelsen explains interpretation in terms of legal "frames." Ambiguous provisions in a statute are merely "frames" within which the legal organ applying it could choose one of several plausible options, such as the perceived intent of the legislator, or one of the possible literal readings of the text. An ambiguous provision can even be interpreted by reference to other clearer laws (Kelsen 1960: 351). Kelsen rejects the idea that there is a single "right" answer to the interpretation of a statute, because a legal organ inevitably will have several viable alternatives, and its decision becomes positive law in that case (Kelsen 1960: 351). He notes that "traditional jurisprudence" wants more: "Traditional theory will have us believe that the statute, applied to the concrete case, can always supply only *one* correct decision and that the positive-legal 'correctness' of this decision is based on the statute itself" (Kelsen 1960: 351). Kelsen portrays this as pure folly, a "futile endeavor" (Kelsen 1960: 352).

"From the point of view of positive law, one method is exactly as good as the other—to neglect the wording and adhere to the presumed will of the legislator or to observe strictly the wording and pay no attention to the (usually problematical) will of the legislature" (Kelsen 1960: 352–353). Reasoning by analogy, Kelsen observes, does not resolve this decision, nor does "weighing the interests," analyzing social costs, or balancing the costs and benefits, all of which he sees as merely political decisions (Kelsen 1960: 354).

The implication of Kelsen's concept of the law's addressee for interpretation then becomes clear: "In the application of law by a legal organ, the cognitive interpretation of the law to be applied is combined with an act of the will by which the law-applying organ chooses between the possibilities shown by cognitive interpretation" (Kelsen 1960: 354). In other words, "This act of will differentiates the legal interpretation by the law-applying organ from any other interpretation, especially from the interpretation of law by jurisprudence" (Kelsen 1960: 354).

If judges and regulators (and perhaps other executive branch officials) are the primary addressees of legislation, then the textualist-intentionalist debate is somewhat illusory or misguided. The assignment of these adjudicative or other official duties inherently delegates some degree of discretion to these officeholders, and their "interpretive" acts are exercises of official discretion rather than a mere act of comprehension, as interpretation would normally be in other contexts. The judge's decision to take a text literally or to apply the "spirit of the law" is either an *ex ante* political decision or an *ex post* justification of the judge's act of discretion. If the former, there could be a number of reasons for a given choice—to give an expansive reading to a law the judge likes or a narrow reading to a law the judge disdains; a decision about institutional competencies that either leads a judge to use textualism as a second-best rule or intentionalism as a faithful-agent rule; or even a theory that links an interpretive "approach" to a particular view of the separation of powers or checks and balances. Both textualism and intentionalism elicit charges of "judicial activism" from those who take the opposing view, which Kelsen would have predicted. *Ex ante* commitments to an interpretive approach, he observes, are inherently political. From an *ex post* perspective, a judge may exercise her discretion and then appeal for support to legislative history, dictionary definitions of words, cost-benefit analysis, *stare decisis*, or other justifications to deflect criticism and add credibility and gravitas to the decision. Perhaps some or all of these things indeed influenced the judge in choosing one alternative over the other—but it was still a choice nevertheless, and another judge could have chosen the other alternative in that case and then could have found supporting arguments and rationalizations.

To take Kelsen's argument a step further than he did, a judge or official who embraced the concept of being the addressee of the law (rather than the citizenry being the addressee) could find certain interpretive assumptions to be more consistent with that view than others. If the courts or other government organs are the addressee of the law, then it seems inconsistent for a judge or official to insist that the "plain meaning" of the legal text is the one that should control—if, by this, we mean the common or vernacular meaning of terms, as used by the general population. The general population does not read the laws, and has no power to "interpret" laws in any authentic sense. Rather, it would be more consistent to presume that the technical or judicial usage of the term is the best—the addressee furnishes the essential "audience design" of the legal text[18] (Bell 1984: 145). Speakers and writers tailor their communication to how the addressee is likely to understand it (Lotman and Shukman 1982: 81). When discussing meaning and interpretation, we should be looking not only at the intent of the legislative author(s), or even at the text itself as it might be understood by the general culture but as the intended audience would understand it. Legislators do indeed consider judicial precedent and word usage in drafting laws, and regulators interact with legislative committees during the drafting stage of laws that they will have to implement (Bressman and Gluck 2014: 725). Even though Kelsen eschewed any type of interpretive ideal, his concept of the law's addressee suggests at least that it is appropriate for courts and officials to work within the indigenous linguistic context of those in that position. Instead of asking what the legislature probably meant by certain words (assuming that collective semantic intent is even possible), a judge could ask how the judiciary itself typically uses such words or phrases.

---

[18] Bell surveys several studies in this area, and explains how the primary addressee exerts the most influence over the crafting of the communication, relatively speaking, while known overhearers have a relatively small effect on the design of the speech or writing. Bell calls non-addressee recipients of the communication "auditors," which would correspond to the role of the citizenry regarding the law under Kelsen's theory. I am indebted to Professor Henry E. Smith for some of these core insights (Smith 2003).

This brings us to the most robust interpretive norms (as Kelsen would call them) used by American courts—those requiring (non-absolute) judicial deference to the legal interpretations of regulatory agencies. These are the *Chevron* doctrine,[19] the *Skidmore* doctrine (Skidmore v. Swift & Co., 323 U.S. 134 (1944)) (used when the court finds that the agency interpretation does not have the force of law), and *Auer* deference[20] (agency interpretations of the agency's own promulgated regulations), each named after the seminal Supreme Court case that made the rule binding on lower federal courts. The logic undergirding these supremely important doctrines, or norms in Kelsenian nomenclature, is very close to the idea that the laws have the government agencies as their addressee. Under *Chevron*, if a statute is facially ambiguous and the relevant agency's interpretation is not far-fetched, the agency's interpretation trumps any other. *Chevron* deference does not apply to agency interpretations of statutes other than their own governing statutes—that is, statutes not addressed specifically to that agency.[21] *Chevron* essentially recognizes that the primary addressee of a law is its intended interpreter, which has delegated authority and responsibility to exercise discretion and make positive law in its field. Moreover in line with Kelsen's view, *Chevron* recognizes that a range of possible

---

[19]The doctrine takes its name from the landmark case *Chevron U.S.A., Inc. v. Natural Resources Defense Council, Inc.*, 467 U.S. 837 (1984). The decision laid down a two-step rule for courts to use in deciding whether to defer to an administrative agency's interpretation:

> When a court reviews an agency's construction of the statute which it administers, it is confronted with two questions. First, always, is the question whether Congress has directly spoken to the precise question at issue. If the intent of Congress is clear, that is the end of the matter; for the court, as well as the agency, must give effect to the unambiguously expressed intent of Congress. If, however, the court determines Congress has not directly addressed the precise question at issue, the court does not simply impose its own construction on the statute, as would be necessary in the absence of an administrative interpretation. Rather, if the statute is silent or ambiguous with respect to the specific issue, the question for the court is whether the agency's answer is based on a permissible construction of the statute.

Chevron, 467 U.S. at 842. Note that the Supreme Court recently announced in an immigrant removal case that *Chevron* Step Two and the "arbitrary and capricious" standard are the same and yield identical results. *See Judulang v. Holder*, 132 S. Ct. 476, 484 n.7 (2011).

[20]*See* Auer v. Robbins, 519 U.S. 452 (1997). This is the same as the older rule in *Bowles v. Seminole Rock & Sand Co.*, 325 U.S. 410 (1945), and courts and writers sometimes call this the *Seminole-Auer* Rule (or the *Auer-Seminole* Rule).

[21]H.L.A. Hart's rejection of Kelsen's views about the addressees of the law make a large omission of this type of legislation—delegating tasks to government agencies—that are extraordinarily common today. Though an individual agency may not receive deference when interpreting a law not addressed to that agency, the norm of *Chevron* deference is universal in that the same rule (with the same contours and exceptions) applies to all agencies. In *Mayo Foundation for Medical Educ. and Research v. United States*, 131 S. Ct. 704 (2011), the Supreme Court held that the *Chevron* approach should apply uniformly across agencies, rather than having special rules (or varying levels of scrutiny) for certain agencies like the Internal Revenus Service.

interpretations are inherent in a law and are equally permissible for the intended addressee (the agency).[22]

Skidmore deference[23] applies in situations where the agency is not making positive law but nonetheless must implement legislative norms addressed to it. The analysis is similar to *Chevron*, and the ultimate outcome is nearly always the same—the agency typically prevails—but there are some subtle differences. *Skidmore* involves judicial inquiry into the circumstances of the agency's decision, a host of factors for courts to weigh. Was this decision within the agency's area of specialization and expertise? Did the agency study the question and consider alternatives, or was it a more spontaneous decision? Was the decision consistent with prior decisions of the agency in similar cases? What was at stake for the private party involved in the case? Again, the underlying assumption is that the agency is the intended addressee of the law, and the judicial inquiry focuses on the reliability of the agency's decision-making in this instance.

Similarly, *Auer* deference rests on an assumption that agencies must promulgate norms that govern its own future decisions in individual cases—that is, regulations rather than statutes. Even though the agency is the lawmaker in these instances, it is also the primary addressee of its own regulations, and courts therefore yield to the agency's official interpretation of its own promulgated rules and regulations. This is a rule of super-deference, at least in its wording or formulation, it is *stronger* than *Chevron* because the agency wins unless it is "plainly erroneous."[24] Most empirical studies indicate the Supreme Court affirms the agency 90 % of the time when it invokes *Auer.*

Significantly (for Kelsenian analysis), *Auer* deference usually comes up in cases in which the agency is not a party, but instead has filed an amici brief or has otherwise sought to intervene in a case between two private parties whose dispute would

[22] At the same time, entrenched judicial precedents can trump the agency's interpretations in certain cases, according to a recent decision from the Supreme Court. The Court held that the recently promulgated agency regulation equating an overstatement of unrecovered cost or other basis with an omission from gross income was not entitled to deference under *Chevron* based on ambiguity in the statute. Precedent has already interpreted the statute and there was no longer any different interpretation, which is consistent with the precedent and available for adoption by the government. *See U.S. v. Home Concrete & Supply, LLC.*, 132 S. Ct. 1836 (2012). On the other hand, long-standing agency interpretations (which the courts have not challenged) receive heightened deference under *Chevron*. *See Astrue v. Capato ex rel. B.N.C.*, 132 S. Ct. 2021 (2012), holding that the Social Security Administration's (SSA) interpretation of the Social Security Act governing determination of the status of posthumously conceived children was entitled to *Chevron* deference; SSA's interpretation of the relevant provisions, adhered to without deviation for many decades, was reasonable, and was therefore entitled to deference.

[23] The trigger for applying *Skidmore* deference, rather than *Chevron*, is the *Mead* case's rule about whether the relevant legislative norm (the statute) creates a situation where the agency is supposed to make positive law, or where the agency merely implements the law. Most scholars call this "*Chevron* step zero."

[24] Justice Scalia, the author of the majority opinion *Auer v. Robbins*, worried in his dissent in *Mead* that agencies would start promulgating vague rules for the strategic reason of getting *Auer* super-deference to whatever interpretation they want to adopt later.

require an interpretation of an agency regulation as part of the resolution of the matter.[25] Such cases serve as a poignant illustration of Kelsen's point about primary and secondary norms. Even in a case between private parties, without the government as a party, courts recognize that the primary norm of the relevant statute is the rule addressed to the government organ; the rule for the private parties is a dependent or secondary norm.

To anticipate a likely objection, I concede that in the penal context, the courts have no interpretive rule of deference to the executive—that is, to the prosecutor's interpretation of the law. There is no *Chevron*-style rule for criminal law; in fact, the Rule of Lenity produces nearly the opposite effect. To apply Kelsen's addressee concept in reverse, then, we might say that penal codes (criminal statutes) have the judiciary as their addressee rather than the executive. A more plausible explanation would be to treat the doctrine of prosecutorial discretion—nearly absolute in terms of judicial deference—as an interpretive norm, and to treat the Rule of Lenity as a safeguard of the courts against the *legislature* rather than against prosecutors. The (inconsistently applied) Rule of Lenity gives criminal defendants the benefit of the doubt when multiple interpretations of a criminal statute are possible. Yet this does not keep the prosecutor from exercising nearly absolute discretion in deciding what cases to prosecute or whom to arrest; instead, it allows a court to justify its decision to choose one of the alternative meanings within a frame (to use Kelsen's term), and to choose one that minimizes the reach or scope of the legislature's enactment. As Kelsen said, this is essentially a political move. The Rule of Lenity is far less robust (less consistently or stridently applied) than the doctrine of prosecutorial discretion. To the extent that decisions about whether to prosecute certain defendants necessarily involve interpretation of the penal code by the prosecutors, their exercise of discretion is generally unassailable.

In other words, doctrines of judicial deference are actually a choice about the addressee of a law rather than about its meaning. Once a court decides that the law or rule primarily addresses a government entity, it defers to any interpretation of that entity as a legal exercise of its discretion—unless the interpretation is so unfaithful to the law as to be illegal, a true "violation" of the law in the sense that Kelsen discussed.

A less robust interpretive norm among the American judiciary is the nondelegation doctrine, which involves a judicial inquiry into the amount of interpretive leeway that a statute gives to an agency. The clear implication of the doctrine is that the legislature addresses these laws primarily to the agency, but in some cases it does so without articulating an "intelligible principle" (any norm whatsoever) to guide the agency as it makes positive law, which makes the law constitutionally invalid.

---

[25] The Supreme Court began applying *Auer* more often starting in 2007, and it has become an important doctrine now. The Department of Justice and other agencies are filing a lot more amicus briefs in cases around the country urging the Court to adopt agency interpretations rather than those proposed by the parties. *See* Decker v. Northwest Environmental Defense Center, 133 S. Ct. 1326 (2013); Christopher v. SmithKline Beecham Corp., 132 S. Ct. 2156 (2012); PLIVA, Inc. v. Mensing, 131 S. Ct. 2567 (2011); Talk America, Inc. v. Michigan Bell Telephone Co., 131 S. Ct. 2254 (2011); Chase Bank USA, N.A. v. McCoy, 131 S. Ct. 871 (2011); Kennedy v. Plan Adm'r for DuPont Sav. and Inv. Plan, 555 U.S. 285 (2009); Long Island Care at Home, Ltd. v. Coke, 551 U.S. 158 (2007); National Ass'n of Home Builders v. Defenders of Wildlife, 551 U.S. 644 (2007).

Most academics talk about the nondelegation doctrine merely as a limitation on executive power—that is, a rule against the agencies having too much discretion. Using the lens of Kelsen's theory, the nondelegation doctrine is a strong recognition that laws must transmit a discernable norm to a state organ in order to be valid—that is, in order to qualify as "law." Nondelegation analysis essentially asks whether the law sufficiently addresses its true addressee.

15.4 Privatized Delegations

This Part applies the concept to the inherent problems with executive subdelegations of state functions to private corporations. Such outsourcing began primarily in the defense industry, but it has now spread to most areas of civilian governance.

A problem arises when the state actors, who are the primary addressees of the law, subdelegate their functions to private for-profit firms via public contracts. This is an increasingly widespread practice—with privatized prisons, privatized parking meter enforcement, privatized welfare services, privatized foster care systems, privatized motor vehicle licensing bureaus, and so on. The inherent delegation of discretion in the statutes, which originally conferred discretion on the officials, passes imperfectly through the contract with the private party now carrying out the legal organ's responsibilities (Metzger 2003). While there may be some supervision of the contractor by the official, agency costs and monitoring costs necessarily render such supervision imperfect, meaning the private contractor—not a public servant—will exercise some of the discretion delegated through the law in implementing it. Moreover, any ambiguous provisions in the contract itself necessarily create additional room for the exercise of discretion by the contract worker.

In this situation, a tension can arise between the interpretive norms in the legal system governing the application of statutes by officials, and the different interpretive norms governing the construction of contracts. Interpreting the terms of a contract is almost completely "intentionalist"-driven; the courts attempt to read each word as the parties would presumably have understood it. In contrast, when it comes to statutory interpretation and construction, legislative intent is only one of the array of interpretive tools courts employ. The statute and a contract are different genres of legal text, and indeterminacy or imprecision can function differently in each. Courts are likely to interpret privatization arrangements according to contract principles (Freeman 2000: 176–83),[26] leaving potential for violations or noncompliance with the legal norms in the sense that Kelsen described.

[26] Another significant difference between the operation of contracts and regulations is that agencies are generally free to change or amend problematic regulations (as long as proper procedures are followed), while contracts cannot be freely revoked by states (although the federal government can claim sovereign immunity when it breaches a contract). Freeman notes that "an agency may find itself, even if only temporarily, bound to a bad bargain and unable to alter it through a simple interpretive decision or rulemaking process. States may choose to avoid these complications by codifying contractual terms in state law or promulgating them as regulations." (Freeman 2000, 183).

Government agencies use privatization or outsourcing not only to try to lower costs, but also to avoid a number of norms targeted at officials that bureaucrats find inconvenient, such as Freedom of Information Requests, as the private entity can often claim immunity from norms that place burdens specifically on officials. An advantage of the theory of the identity of the law and state is that it implies accountability or responsibility for those wielding power. Outsourcing of the tasks to private parties can thwart the operation of useful norms by diluting the responsibility of the officials and deflecting the sanctions that the norm prescribes.

In any case, once we embrace the concept of the law addressing state officials and judges, rather than the citizenry directly, it casts the outsourcing of official duties in a different light. The discretion that the legislature intended to delegate to public officials ends up being the purview of private for-profit contractors, who have a different set of influences on their choices when they implement ambiguous provisions (or work within the "frames," as Kelsen would say) than would the state officials. Moreover, they escape the control of certain norms that would govern the behavior of the officials, especially safeguards designed to ensure transparency and political accountability. The dependent or secondary norms that are supposed to deter the citizenry from sanctionable conduct become filtered through the intermediary of the private contractor.

15.5 Conclusion

Kelsen argued convincingly that the written formulations of the law address the state and its actors, not the citizenry in general nor the segment of the population whose conduct the law potentially sanctions. This concept has significant implications for legal reform movements calling for "simple English" in statutes and regulations, for doctrines of judicial interpretation, and for delegations of governmental power to private parties. Nevertheless, some of these implications run counter to populist American ideals about democracy and civic responsibility. Kelsen's view of the law's addressee is an important component of his overall system of identifying the law with the state, so his arguments in this regard are an obstacle to acceptance of his larger work by American jurists and legal commentators.

Acknowledgments This chapter was occasioned by the "Hans Kelsen in America" conference in Chicago on June 27–28, 2014. Valparaiso University Law School sponsored the event, with support from a grant by the Botstiber Institute for Austrian-American Studies. Many thanks to Jeremy Telman for inviting me to participate, and to the other participants for thoughtful comments and suggestions. I am deeply indebted to Dr. Henry Smith (currently at Harvard Law School) for introducing me to both the sociolinguistic concept of addressees and to Hans Kelsen's work on legal theory.

References

Alan Siegel, *Let's simplify legal jargon!*, TED talk video. http://www.ted.com/talks/alan_siegel_let_s_simplify_legal_jargon. Accessed on Feb 2010.

Austin, John. 1832. *The providence of jurisprudence determined.* Amherst: Prometheus Books 2000 ed.

Bartor, Assnat. 2012. Reading biblical law as narrative. *Prooftexts* 32: 292.

Bell, Allan. 1984. Language as audience design. *Language in Society* 13: 145.

Bentham, Jeremy. 1999. In *'Legislator of the world': Writings on codification, law, and education*, ed. Schofield Philip and Harris Jonathan. Oxford: Oxford University Press.

Bressman Lisa, Schultz, and R. Gluck Abbe. 2014. Statutory interpretation from the inside—An empirical study of congressional drafting, delegation, and the canons: Part II. *Stanford Law Review* 66: 725–801.

Crump, David. 2002. Against plain English: The case for a functional approach to legal document preparation. *Rutgers Law Journal* 33: 713–744.

Dan-Cohen, Meir. 1984. Decision rules and conduct rules: On acoustic separation in criminal law. *Harvard Law Review* 97: 625–677.

Diamond, Shari Seidman, Beth Murphy, and Mary R. Rose. 2012. The "Kettleful Of Law" in real jury deliberations: Successes, failures, and next steps. *Northwestern University Law Review* 106: 1537–1608.

Freeman, Jody. 2000. The contracting state. *Florida State University Law Review* 28: 155–183.

Gallacher, Ian. 2013. "When Numbers Get Serious": A study of plain English usage in briefs filed before the New York Court of Appeals. *Suffolk University Law Review* 46: 451501.

Gopen, George. 1987. The state of legal writing: Res Ipsa Loquitur. *Michigan Law Review* 86: 333–380.

Halfteck, Guy. 2008. Legislative threats. *Stanford Law Review* 61: 629–710.

Hart, H.L.A. 1961. *The concept of law*. Oxford: Oxford University Press.

Hathaway, George. 1994. The plain English movement in the law. *Journal of the Missouri Bar* 50: 19–21.

Howard, Philip K. 2010. *Four ways to fix a broken legal system.* http://www.ted.com/talks/philip_howard. Accessed on Feb 2010.

Janis, Mark D., and Timothy R. Holbrook. 2012. Patent law's audience. *Minnesota Law Review* 97: 72–131.

Kelsen, Hans. 1945. *General Theory of Law and State*. Trans. A. Wedberg 1945. Cambridge: Harvard University Press.

Kelsen, Hans. 1960. *Pure Theory of Saw, Second ed.* Trans. M. Knight 1967. Berkeley: University of California Press.

Kelsen, Hans. 1979. *General Theory of Norms*. Trans. M. Hartney 1991. Oxford: Oxford University Press.

Lotman, Yury M., and Ann Shukman. 1982. The text and the structure of its audience. *New Literary History* 14: 81.

Maley, Yon. 1994. Language constructing law. In *Language and the law*, ed. Gibbons John, 24–25. London: Routledge Publishing.

Metzger, Gillian E. 2003. Privatization as delegation. *Columbia Law Review* 103: 1367–1502.

Moore, Sir Thomas. 1516. *Utopia*. London: Cassell & Co., 1901.

Serafin, Andrew. 1998. Kicking the legalese habit: The SEC's plain English disclosure proposal. *Loyola University of Chicago Law Journal* 29: 681–717.

Smith, Henry E. 2003. The language of property: Form, context, and audience. *Stanford Law Review* 55: 1105–1191.

Sohoni, Mila. 2012. The idea of "too much law". *Fordham Law Review* 80: 1585–1632.

Solan, Lawrence. 1993. *The language of judges*. Chicago: University of Chicago Press.

Somek, Alexander. 2006. Stateless law: Kelsen's conception and its limits. *Oxford Journal of Legal Studies* 26: 753–774.

Stevenson, Drury. 2003. To whom is the law addressed? *Yale Law and Policy Review* 21: 105–167.
Stevenson, Dru. 2005. Toward a new theory of notice and deterrence. *Cardozo Law Review.* 26: 1535–1594.
Stewart, Iain. 1990. The critical legal science of Hans Kelsen. *Journal of Law & Society* 17: 273–284.
Stuntz, William J. 2000. Self-defeating crimes. *Virginia Law Review* 86: 1871–1899.
Tiersma, Peter. 1999. *Legal language*. Chicago: University of Chicago Press.
Weinberger, Ota. 1985. Freedom, range for action, and the ontology of norms. *Synthese* 65: 307–324.
Wilson, A. 1981. The imperative fallacy in Kelsen's theory. *Modern Law Review* 44: 270–281.

Chapter 16
Kelsen, Justice, and Constructivism

Joshua W. Felix

16.1 Norm and Philosophy

Hans Kelsen's final and posthumously published work, *General Theory of Norms*, has been a puzzle for Kelsen scholars. It is an extended treatment of arguments that Kelsen first presented in *Derogation* (reprinted in Kelsen 1973: 261–275) and *Law and Logic* (reprinted in Kelsen 1973: 228–253): the critique of practical reason and deontic logic. On the one hand, the work provides a general philosophical treatment of norms and normative science. These are important and familiar themes from the pure theory of law. It elaborates much of the metaethical and social scientific framework of normative science. On the other hand, it has generally been received as a failure and a radical departure from his previous work. For Michael Hartney, Kelsen's arguments are fallacious and conflate problems of logic and ontology (Hartney 1993: 16). For Deryck Beyleveld, Kelsen's critique of practical reason results in "normative irrationalism," altering a phrase of Ota Weinberger (Beyleveld 1993: 104). For Stanley Paulson, Kelsen's arguments undermine the basis for normative science (Paulson 1992: 273).

This chapter makes two claims. First, Kelsen's critique of practical reason and deontic logic is best understood as a response to constructivism. These arguments should not be viewed as a radical departure from his previous work, but as an attempt to defend his skepticism about justice from a constructivist challenge. Second, these arguments are not fallacious and may be of interest in contemporary debates about constructivism.

Section 16.2 provides a general overview of Kelsen's idea of normative science. It covers the distinction between facts and norms, normative science and sociology,

J.W. Felix (✉)
Department of Philosophy, Binghamton University/SUNY, Binghamton, NY, USA
e-mail: jfelix1@binghamton.edu

D.A.J. Telman (ed.), *Hans Kelsen in America - Selective Affinities and the Mysteries of Academic Influence*, Law and Philosophy Library 116,
DOI 10.1007/978-3-319-33130-0_16

positivity and validity, psychological and real volition, and objective and subjective value.

Section 16.3 presents Kelsen's general case for skepticism about justice. Justice is a subjective value that originates in the hope for a society in which there is a harmony of interests. For Kelsen, this hope is irrational because its end is impossible. Conflicts of interest are inevitable and intractable. Moreover, the idea of justice is ideological: it inverts the relation between norms and normative orders.

Section 16.4 introduces constructivism and the challenge it poses for skepticism about justice. Classical constructivism relies on an analogy between incompossibility and logical contradiction. Kelsen argues that there is no such analogy.

Section 16.5 introduces John Rawls' version of constructivism and its relation to Kelsen. Rawls attempts to circumvent positivist conceptions of objective value by means of a decision procedure to identify rational criteria for validity.

Section 16.6 assesses the critique of practical reason and deontic logic. Kelsen sets up a dilemma for practical reason: either it leads to the absurdity that reason and will are identical, or reason cannot posit norms. This dilemma is supplemented by two arguments: that validity is not a property and that norm conflict is not a logical contradiction. The section also considers and responds to the objections of Hartney and Beyleveld.

Section 16.7 concludes the chapter with a reconsideration of the Kelsen's view that validity is the existence of a norm. For Kelsen, the possibility of normative science rests on the realist conviction that validity is existence.

16.2 Norm and Interest

Normative science is the science of objective value. However, there are two kinds of value judgment: factual value judgments and normative value judgments. Factual value judgments are propositions about facts. Normative value judgments are propositions about norms. Nevertheless, only norms can be the basis of objective value. Factual value judgments are about subjective value and normative value judgments are about objective value (Kelsen 1991: 185). The method of verification for each kind of value judgment is essentially different. Factual value judgments are verified when the corresponding fact is the case. Normative value judgments are verified when the corresponding norm is valid (Kelsen 1991: 180). Positivity is a necessary condition for the validity (existence) of a norm (Kelsen 1991: 251). It follows that all valid norms are positive norms, and that normative science is a positive social science.

There are two kinds of positive social science. Sociology is the science of positive facts. Normative science is the science of positive norms. However, the positivity of a fact is different from the positivity of a norm. A fact is positive if it is the case. A norm is positive if it has been posited (Kelsen 1991: 4). The existence of a fact is its positivity, whereas the validity (existence) of a norm is a consequence of its positivity.

Sociology and normative science both explain value in terms of volition. There are two kinds of volition: psychological volition and real volition. These differ in their content and mode of address. Psychological volition is an act of will that posits an interest (Kelsen 1957: 211). Real volition is an act of will that posits a norm (Kelsen 1991: 27). Psychological volition is an act of will directed to one's own behavior, whereas real volition is an act of will directed to the behavior of another (Kelsen 1991: 31–32). Interests are the objects of factual value judgments. Norms are the objects of normative value judgments. It follows that subjective value is reducible to facts about acts of psychological volition, whereas objective value is reducible to facts about acts of real volition.

Sociological theories of value are interest theories. Interest theories of value hold that something is valuable because someone takes an interest in it. Therefore, all value is reducible to facts about acts of psychological volition. Interest theories are appropriate for subjective value but not objective value. When interest theories are applied to objective value, they entail the absurdity that norms are interests, or that norms are posited by psychological volition.

Consider the absurd consequences of interest theories of value in ethics and jurisprudence. Classical interest theories in ethics are those of Hobbes and Hume. These theories maintain that the validity of moral norms depends on individual or general interests (Stevenson 1937: 15–16). The classical interest theory in jurisprudence is that of Austin. That theory maintains that the validity of legal norms depends on the interests of the sovereign or legislating body (Kelsen 1957: 212–214). If moral and legal validity depend on interests, ethics and jurisprudence are forms of applied psychology. This is absurd because the ethicist and the legal scientist are concerned with norms. The ethicist is concerned with valid moral norms (Kelsen 1991: 359). The legal scientist is concerned with valid legal norms (Kelsen 1957: 273). The study of objective value requires normative science.

16.3 The Irrational Ideal

For Kelsen, justice is an "irrational ideal" (Kelsen 1945: 13). Justice is supposed to resolve conflicts of interest. But conflicts of interest are inevitable and intractable. They can only be resolved "by an order that either satisfies one interest at the expense of the other, or seeks to achieve a compromise between competing interests" (Kelsen 1945: 13). Moreover, although justice purports to be an objective value it is in fact a subjective value (Kelsen 1945: 49). It follows that justice is a topic for sociology.

Accordingly, Kelsen provides a sociological analysis of justice. He claims that justice as an idea that originates in the hope for a society in which there is a harmony of interests: "Justice is social happiness" (Kelsen 1957: 2). This hope is irrational because its object is impossible: it is the hope for a social order in which all interests are satisfied (Kelsen 1957: 3). This hope can only be made rational by abandoning the ideal of satisfying interests, and replacing it by the ideal of satisfying needs.

Needs are socially recognized interests established by a normative order (Kelsen 1957: 4).

The irrationality of the ideal of satisfying interests also informs Kelsen's defense of democratic politics. For Kelsen, political forms are distinguished by their mode of legislation. Democracy is government by the people, not government for the people. Government by the people occurs when the mode of legislation is one of "universal, equal, free, and secret suffrage" (Kelsen 1955: 3). Government for the people is legislation in accord with the general interest (Kelsen 1955: 2). But government for the people is irrational and ideological. It is irrational because it is impossible: there is no general interest because conflicts of interest are inevitable and intractable. It is ideological because it conceals the distinction between a rational ideal and an irrational ideal. Every government claims to be government for the people (Kelsen 1955: 2). But only government by the people is democratic.

Likewise, the idea of justice is ideological because it inverts the relation between norms and normative orders. Justice purports to be a norm that is independent of and prior to a normative order. Kelsen argues that it is the other way around. Norms are the product of normative orders. Only a normative order can establish norms so that the irrational ideal of satisfying interests can be replaced by the rational ideal of satisfying needs.

16.4 Constructivism

Constructivism poses a challenge to the thesis that justice is an irrational ideal. Constructivism can refer to distinct positions in several subjects, such as mathematics, philosophy, and jurisprudence. For example, Paulson identifies an early version of the pure theory of law as a form of legal constructivism (Paulson 1996: 801). The common thread among these positions is that certain ideas are regarded as constructions of reason. For the purposes of this chapter, constructivism is the thesis that objective values are constructions of reason and that validity is determined by rational criteria. On this view, validity can either be discerned by reason or by means of a rational procedure.

Classical constructivism accounts for the dependence of validity on rational criteria through an analogy between incompossibility and logical contradiction. The two main classical constructivist accounts of justice are those of Hume and Kant. For Hume, justice resolves conflicts of interest by determining which interest is to be satisfied (Hume 1983: 20–23). Conflicts of interest occur when there are incompossible interests: there are at least two interests, and it is not possible to satisfy both interests, either at some particular time, or generally. For Kant, justice resolves conflicts of rights by determining which right is to prevail (Kant 1996: 387–389). Conflicts of rights occur when there are incompossible rights: there are at least two rights, and it is not possible for both to prevail, either at some particular time, or generally. Both regard such conflicts as contradictions that can be resolved by justice.

In earlier writings, Kelsen responds to these constructivist positions by emphasizing the inevitable and intractable nature of conflict. Such conflict can only be resolved by determining which interest is to be satisfied or which right is to prevail (Kelsen 1957: 4). If both interests may be satisfied or both rights may prevail, interests are compossible and there is only pseudo-conflict. In that case, the idea of justice is superfluous and resolves nothing. But if only one interest may be satisfied at the expense of the other, or only one right may prevail over the other, then the idea of justice is useless and resolves nothing.

However, *General Theory of Norms* contains a general argument against the analogy between incompossibility and logical contradiction. Part of the problem of deontic logic is whether norm conflict is analogous to logical contradiction (Kelsen 1991: 191). Norm conflict occurs when there are incompossible norms: there are at least two norms, and it is not possible to comply with both norms, either at some particular time, or generally (Kelsen 1991: 123). First, norm conflict can only occur between valid norms, so if incompossibility is analogous to logical contradiction, it cannot be a contradiction in validity (Kelsen 1991: 213). Only valid norms can be incompossible norms. Second, the analogy between incompossibility and logical contradiction treats norms as though they are propositions about the consequences of their observation. However, "the fact that the logical principle of contradiction is applicable to statements about the observance of conflicting norms does not entail that it is applicable to the conflicting norms themselves" (Kelsen 1991: 222–223). This clarifies the association between incompossibility and logical contradiction, while at the same time demonstrating the disanalogy.

16.5 Decision Procedure

Rawls revives constructivism through the notion of a decision procedure that determines the criteria of validity rather than the analogy between incompossibility and logical contradiction. The most comprehensive version of this view is presented in *A Theory of Justice* (Rawls 1971: 118–136), but it was initially worked out in his doctoral dissertation and early publications. Important for our purposes, Rawls had more than a passing familiarity with the work of Kelsen. Early in his career, Rawls sought to use the pure theory of law as a model for a normative science of ethics (Reidy 2014: 15–16). However, by the time Rawls finished his doctoral dissertation, his attitude toward positivism in moral and political theory had soured.[1] Rawls' mature work was developed against the background of his dissatisfaction with positive social science.

Rawls came to accept the view that positive social science has the wrong account of the objectivity of value. Sociology presents subjective value as objective value:

[1] Rawls' dissertation references the first edition of the *Reine Rechtslehre*, *General Theory of Law and State*, and *The Pure Theory of Law and Analytical Jurisprudence* (Rawls 1950: 4). Of note is that the dissertation predates Rawls' time at Oxford, where he was in contact with H.L.A. Hart.

the objectivity of value ultimately depends on our psychology and emotional states. Normative science presents objective value as a problem of ontology: the objectivity of value ultimately depends on the validity (existence) of norms. However, for Rawls,

> the objectivity or the subjectivity of moral knowledge turns, not on the question whether ideal value entities exist or whether moral judgments are caused by emotions… but simply on the question: does there exist a reasonable method for validating and invalidating given or proposed moral rules and those decisions made on the basis of them? (Rawls 1951: 177)

Rawls' solution is to set aside the presumption that validity depends on psychology or ontology. This puts out of play the key considerations that entail that justice is a subjective value and an "irrational ideal" (Kelsen 1945: 13). Rawls' approach is to make use of a decision procedure in order to identify rational criteria for validity. The rational criteria for validity are analogous to rational criteria for inductive inference (Rawls 1951: 177). Therefore, in contrast with classical constructivism, the decision procedure models validity in terms of inductive logic rather than deductive logic.

On this view, the idea of justice is a construction of reason. The elements of construction are ideas about the characteristics of competent judges, the scope of probative judgment, and the context of impartial adjudication (Rawls 1951: 178–186). The construction can then be used to "determine the manner in which competing interests should be adjudicated, and, in instances of conflict, one interest given preference over another" (Rawls 1951: 177).

16.6 Practical Reason

General Theory of Norms is a critique of practical reason and deontic logic. However, there are at least three powers of reason that may be described as practical reason: discernment, deliberation, and postulation. Discernment is the power to discern the validity of norms and when norms apply to the case. Deliberation is the power to deliberate about and determine when and whether to comply with a norm. Postulation is the power to posit norms. Kelsen recognizes discernment and deliberation as ordinary powers of reason, although not as practical powers (Kelsen 1991: 15, 165, 252–253). For Kelsen, practical reason is postulation (Kelsen 1991: 80–81).

The critique of practical reason is necessary in order to defend the thesis that justice is a subjective value. Constructivism blurs the distinction between discernment and postulation. This is the case because validity is existence, and positivity is a necessary condition for validity. For Kelsen, even if validity were subject to rational criteria, valid norms must be positive.

Kelsen presents a dilemma for the view that practical reason posits norms. Recall that a norm is positive if it is posited by an act of real volition (Kelsen 1991: 234). On the one hand, if practical reason can posit norms, it can only do so because an act of thought is also an act of real volition (Kelsen 1991: 80–81). But this is absurd, since reason and will are distinct faculties. On the other hand, if practical reason is not an act of real volition, then practical reason cannot posit norms.

The critique of deontic logic is necessary to demonstrate that there is no analogy between validity and truth. For Kelsen, the problem of deontic logic concerns whether norm conflict is a logical contradiction and whether the rule of inference from the general to the particular applies to norms (Kelsen 1991: 191).

Kelsen argues that validity is not a property of a norm and that norm conflict is not a logical contradiction. First, validity is not a property of a norm because validity is the existence of a norm, and existence is not a property (Kelsen 1991: 383). Second, norm conflict is not a logical contradiction for reasons presented in Sect. 16.4: there is no analogy between incompossibility and logical contradiction.

Hartney argues that Kelsen's critique of deontic logic is based on a mistake. The mistake was to conflate logic and ontology: Kelsen does not distinguish between norms as imperatives from norms as entities (Hartney 1993: 16). Consequently, Kelsen came to believe that "the only way of preserving the law-making monopoly of legal authorities is to deny that norms can be derived from other norms" (Hartney 1993: 15). For Hartney, Kelsen would not have involved himself in the quagmire of deontic logic had he had a clearer sense of the distinction between logic and ontology.

But Kelsen had good reason to believe that the problem of deontic logic is relevant to whether norms may be valid for reasons other than having been posited by competent authorities. Part of the problem of deontic logic is whether validity is a logical property such that there can be a deontic logic analogous to propositional logic. More generally, it concerns whether there is an analogy between validity and truth. As shown in Sect. 16.4, classical constructivism makes much of the analogy between incompossibility and logical contradiction in order to motivate the position that validity is a logical property. Likewise, Rawls' constructivism presents validity as a logical property.

Moreover, Kelsen does not emphasize the distinction between imperatives and entities because he rejects the thesis that deontic logic is imperative logic (Kelsen 1991: 150). For Hartney, the difference between facts and norms is a formal one: facts and norms are expressed by different sentence forms. Facts are expressed in the form of propositions and norms are expressed in the form of imperatives. On this view, deontic logic is imperative logic. Therefore, he believes that Kelsen's failure to discuss imperatives belies an essential misunderstanding of deontic logic. For Kelsen, the difference between facts and norms is a modal one: facts and norms can only be expressed in sentences with different modal operators (Kelsen 1991: 195). Norms can be expressed by imperatives and *sollen*-sentences (Kelsen 1991: 149). It is the modal operator and not the sentence form that counts (Kelsen 1991:155).

In fairness to Hartney, his point is that logic concerns relations between sentences, not relations between entities (Hartney 1993: 18). Hartney is right to emphasize that Kelsen is inconsistent in his use of terms. Kelsen frequently uses "norm" to refer to both entities and to sentences. Consider the analogy he frequently draws between facts and norms. According to Kelsen, norms are no more subject to logical relations than facts are because both norms and facts are entities and not sentences (Kelsen 1991: 17, 181). Nevertheless, Kelsen often compares norms with propositions, especially when discussing the disanalogy between truth and validity (Kelsen 1991: 163–165, 170–174).

On account of this inconsistency, Kelsen makes two different kinds of arguments about norms and deontic logic. First, insofar as norms are entities, there can be no logical relations between norms. It follows that a logic of norms in the strict sense is not possible. If there is a deontic logic, it cannot be a logic of norms. Second, insofar as norms are sentences, there are no relations between such sentences analogous to those between propositions. This is the case because validity is not a property and, even if it were a property, it would not be the kind of property that would be the basis of a deontic logic analogous to propositional logic. Hartney finds the first kind of argument unimpressive and misleading because it conflates logic and ontology. Hartney thinks the second kind of argument is also ultimately about ontology because, for Kelsen, validity is existence. Although the success of the second kind of argument depends on the definition of validity as existence, it does not conflate logic and ontology.

Beyleveld argues that Kelsen's critique of deontic logic begs the question about whether validity is a logical property (Beyleveld 1993: 115). For Beyleveld, the problem of deontic logic is whether validity is a logical property. As he presents it, Kelsen argues that validity is not a logical property by appeal to the fact of norm conflict. But this begs the question, since appeal to the fact of norm conflict is to assume that validity is not a logical relation (Beyleveld 1993: 115).

Like Hartney, Beyleveld thinks there is something problematic with the idea that validity is existence. For Beyleveld, validity is the binding force of a norm and not its existence. The problem of deontic logic is whether binding force is a logical relation between sentences that express norms. Kelsen's view entails that norms are binding because they exist (Beyleveld 1993: 113). However if existence is the same as binding force, appeal to the fact of norm conflict to demonstrate that validity is not a logical property begs the question.

This criticism conflates Kelsen's two arguments against deontic logic. The argument that norm conflict is not a contradiction is distinct from the argument that validity is not a property. The former argument does not depend on the fact of norm conflict, but on the definition of norm conflict. Since all norms are valid norms, norm conflicts can only occur between valid norms. The latter argument holds that validity is not a logical property because it is the existence of a norm and existence is not a property.

Beyleveld also argues that Kelsen's critique of practical reason undermines the basis of normative science. For Beyleveld, empowering norms must function through an application of the rule of inference from the general to the particular to sentences that express norms. Since Kelsen denies that the rule of inference applies to norms, he must account for empowering norms by making positivity and validity identical (Beyleveld 1993: 115). But if positivity and validity are identical, there is no distinction between sociology and normative science.

Custom appears to be a case in which positivity and validity are identical, since it is a norm that originates in convergent behavior rather than real volition. Convergent behavior becomes custom by virtue of an empowering norm (Kelsen 1967: 9).

However, this critique fails to show that the rule of inference for empowering norms is an exercise of practical reason. Recall that Kelsen recognizes discernment as a power of reason. He only denies that discernment is a form of practical reason. The rule of inference can apply to norm propositions: from the fact that an empowering norm is valid, and that convergent behavior is sufficient to be custom, it follows that custom is valid (Kelsen 1991: 252–253). It can also apply to the "modally indifferent substrate" (Kelsen 1991: 60–61). The modally indifferent substrate is the part of a sentence that expresses a norm that is distinct from the modal operator. There are further questions about Kelsen's notion of custom, but they are distinct from Beyleveld's argument about empowering norms.

16.7 Validity Reconsidered

Much of what is puzzling about *General Theory of Norms* turns on the realist conviction that validity is existence. As we have seen, both Hartney and Beyleveld find something suspect with this account of validity, even if they do not successfully show that it is blatantly false. Likewise, Rawls' constructivism attempts to circumvent this realist view by presenting an alternative conception of validity based on rational criteria.

Unfortunately, Kelsen does not directly argue for this notion of validity. But it is worth recalling the first horn of the dilemma about practical reason. For Kelsen, practical reason is the power of postulation: it is the identification of reason and will. If such an identification is not absurd, it is only possible insofar as human reason is divine reason. Practical reason is essentially a theological notion (Kelsen 1991: 4–6). This hardly demonstrates that validity cannot be determined by rational criteria. However, it illustrates what is at stake if this notion of validity is denied.

Briefly, if validity is distinct from existence, objectivity is unhinged from actuality. Rawls' later formulations of constructivism drive a wedge between validity and truth: the validity of a conception of justice is a matter of its reasonableness, which is distinct from its truth (Rawls 2005: 128–129). But for Kelsen, notwithstanding the disanalogy between validity and truth, to disconnect the validity of a norm from the truth of a norm proposition is to abandon the scientific enterprise. The need to defend normative science is what stands behind Kelsen's conviction that one can no more derive an ought from an ought than an ought from an is.

Acknowledgements Thanks to George Mazur for an informative discussion and for pointing me in the direction of *Foundations of Democracy*. Thanks to Jeremy Telman and Valparaiso University Law School for organizing *Hans Kelsen in America*. Finally, thanks to Jessica Wielgus for her hospitality during my stay in Chicago.

References

Beyleveld, Deryck. 1993. From the 'middle way' to normative irrationalism: Hans Kelsen's General Theory of Norms. *The Modern Law Review* 56: 104–119.

Hartney, Michael. 1993. The death of practical reasoning in Kelsen's later theory of norms. In *Sociological jurisprudence and legal philosophy: Random thoughts on*, ed. K.B. Agrawal and Rajendra Kumar Raizada, 11–18. Jaipur: University Book House.

Hume, David. 1983. *An enquiry concerning the principles of morals*. Indianapolis: Hackett Publishing Company.

Kant, Immanuel. 1996. *Practical philosophy*. Trans. M. Gregor. Cambridge: Cambridge University Press.

Kelsen, Hans. 1945. *General theory of law and state*. Trans. A. Wedberg. Cambridge: Harvard University Press.

Kelsen, Hans. 1955. Foundations of democracy. *Ethics* 66: 1–101.

Kelsen, Hans. 1957. *What is justice? Justice, law, and politics in the mirror of science*. Berkeley: University of California Press.

Kelsen, Hans. 1967. *The pure theory of law*. Trans. M. Knight. Berkeley: University of California Press.

Kelsen, Hans. 1973. *Essays in legal and moral philosophy*. Trans. P. Heath. Boston: D. Reidel Publishing Company.

Kelsen, Hans. 1991. *General theory of norms*. Trans. M. Hartney. Oxford: Oxford University Press.

Paulson, Stanley. 1992. Kelsen's legal theory: The final round. *Oxford Journal of Legal Studies* 12: 265–274.

Paulson, Stanley. 1996. Hans Kelsen's earliest legal theory: Critical constructivism. *The Modern Law Review* 59: 797–812.

Rawls, John. 1950. *A study in the grounds of ethical knowledge: Considered with reference to judgments on the moral worth of character*. Ph.D. Thesis, Princeton University.

Rawls, John. 1951. Outline of a decision procedure for ethics. *The Philosophical Review* 60: 177–197.

Rawls, John. 1971. *A theory of justice*. Cambridge: Harvard University Press.

Rawls, John. 2005. *Political liberalism: Expanded edition*. New York: Columbia University Press.

Reidy, David. 2014. From philosophical theology to democratic theory: Early postcards from an intellectual journey. In *A companion to Rawls*, ed. Jon Mandle and David Reidy, 9–30. Chichester: Wiley Blackwell.

Stevenson, C.L. 1937. The emotive meaning of ethical terms. *Mind* 46: 14–31.

Part V
Conclusions

Chapter 17
In Defense of Modern Times: A Keynote Address

Clemens Jabloner

17.1 Introduction

Recently, the Hans Kelsen Institute in Vienna published Kelsen's opus posthumous *Secular Religion—A Polemic against the Misinterpretation of Modern Social Philosophy, Science and Politics as "New Religion"* (Kelsen 2012). The work is the final chapter in Kelsen's serial critique (Kelsen 2004) of his former pupil Eric Voegelin's *New Science of Politics* (Voegelin 1987). It is illuminating that previous versions of Kelsen's work bore the titles *Defense of Modern Times* and *Religion without God?*[1] Both alternatives seem highly significant: Kelsen as a "champion of modernity" serves quite well as a *Leitmotiv*—and therefore as the title of my short address.

Then again, *Religion without God*—with a question mark—is almost identical to the title of Ronald Dworkin's last monograph, *Religion without God* (Dworkin 2013). The two similar titles offer an occasion for putting these two eminent scholars into conversation with one another. At the same time, it might be of interest to focus a little on Kelsen's concept of religion, with a view to his Jewish background.

[1] For the complicated pre-history of this publication see the editorial remarks in Kelsen (2012, 11) and Di Lucia/ Passerini Glazel (2014, XIX).

C. Jabloner (✉)
University of Vienna, 1010 Wien, Austria
e-mail: clemens.jabloner@univie.ac.at

D.A.J. Telman (ed.), *Hans Kelsen in America - Selective Affinities and the Mysteries of Academic Influence*, Law and Philosophy Library 116,
DOI 10.1007/978-3-319-33130-0_17

17.2 Combatting Premodernism

17.2.1 Viennese Modernity

The enlightenment is understood as a process of secularization, in which science and human autonomy displace religion as the general source for both truth and justice. But the confidence of the Enlightenment in the powers of reason gave rise to a new natural law—rational law (see Bräuer (2013: 166)).

The efforts to realize a scientific conception of the world gained a new intensity in the so-called era of Viennese Modernity (see Janik/Toulmin (1973); Schorske (1980)). Kelsen's Vienna years[2] fell within the heyday of this period, which continued for the first three decades of the last century. The Austro-fascist "corporate state" brought it to an abrupt end in 1933. In recent years, numerous publications have appeared addressing the social and historical conditions of this intellectually progressive period, the diverse links between its leading figures and, finally, the cultural exodus from Austria.[3] An important characteristic of Viennese modernism was the way it encompassed both culture—understood in a narrow sense—and science. This may explain why there was a "scientific" streak in the rational "coolness" of the Vienna School's 12-tone music, why the development of psychoanalysis transcended the boundaries of science and culture, and why even the iron core of Viennese modernism, the logical positivism of the Vienna Circle, might be seen today as a cultural phenomenon.[4]

A further element of Viennese Modernity was a certain sense of mission (*Sendungsbewußtsein*) on the part of some of its leading exponents, including, for instance, Freud, Loos, Wittgenstein, as well as the dubious Otto Weininger. Various "circles" and "schools" overlapped and influenced one another. Kelsen was a friend of Otto Weininger (Mètall 1969: 6). and later participated in Freud's "Wednesday meetings" (see Jabloner (1998: 382)). Ludwig von Mises was Kelsen's schoolmate and lifelong friend; Kelsen was Josef Schumpeter's best man, to name just some relations (Mètall 1969: 32).

With his pure theory of law, Kelsen subjected the theoretical underpinnings of jurisprudence—practiced for centuries—to a fundamental critique, while at the same time constructing a new foundation for legal theory. Both in his life and his work, Kelsen conformed to a pattern often found in the leading figures of Viennese modernism: a family background of assimilated Judaism, Viennese gymnasium schooling, involvement in the most progressive intellectual movements of the time, radicalism and acuity in his particular revolutionary approach, a unique combination of rationalism and an ethic of the scientific conception of the world, the development of a "theory," the founding of a "Viennese school," world fame, and immigration—namely to the United States of America.

---

[2] For the following, compare in more detail Jabloner (1998).

[3] Cp. the collected essays in Stadler (2004).

[4] Cp. the collected essays in Stadler (1997).

17.2.2 Critique of Ideology

Kelsen embarked on his undertaking within the realm of legal science, which always remained his main concern. On the one hand, he combatted natural law doctrines, including rational law. On the other hand, he condemned the contamination of legal science with a false understanding of legal sociology. As is often pointed out, Kelsen aimed at—and succeeded in—the construction of a normative as well as a positivist legal theory (see Dreier (1990: 27); Paulson (2006: passim)). In his critique of natural law, Kelsen not only attacked the phenomena of explicit natural law, but he also reached out to identify the residua of natural law, especially in the *Staatslehre* of his age. It is not surprising that the concept of the "state" itself, as an essence beyond the law, served as the primary target for Kelsen's deconstruction (see Dreier (1990: 208; Feichtinger 2010: 369): "Funktionen statt Substanzen").

It is rather surprising that Kelsen's critique of ideology found its inspiration not least in Sigmund Freud, perhaps as the result of their personal interactions (see Jabloner (2014: 138); Feichtinger (2010: 385)). In his essays *Der Staatsbegriff und die Psychoanalyse* and *Gott und Staat* (Kelsen (1922/23, und 1927)). Kelsen made an extremely bold attempt as a legal theoretician to apply Freud's theory of totemism—that is, a tribal community's collective consumption of a sacrificed animal as an act of identification—to legal theory. Kelsen recognized that the idea of the state as person, the "illustrative personification of the legal order constituting the social community and founding the unity of a diversity of human behaviour" was an example of a reification. He replaced that idea with the recognition of the state as a legal function. Kelsen saw parallels with other concepts of substance, such as "force" in physics or "soul" in psychology, and recognized in such residua the piece de résistance of metaphysical thinking. According to Kelsen, in the "totem-meal," the primal image of any conception of substance comes to light. Undoubtedly, Kelsen's deconstruction of the state as a superior and obscure entity is sufficient to qualify him as a modern thinker. His recourse to Freud's phylogenetic fable could today be questioned as an act of "re-mythologizing,"[5] but I will leave this open.

17.2.3 Positive Law and Democracy

In a political sense, Kelsen's modernity centers on the fact that man-made positive law could take the place of the instructions derived from religious or metaphysical worldviews. In a society in which the law is explicitly and centrally set, the positivization of the law, therefore, also entails the ongoing opportunity to change it. In this way, the law becomes an instrument to shape society. Still, this displacement of religious or metaphysical perspectives tells us nothing about who should legislate. This is where Kelsen's theory of democracy applies: Kelsen analyzed democracy as

[5] For an early critique on Freud's fable, compare Kroeber (1920), passim.

a political idea. We are referring here to Kelsen's famous essay *Vom Wesen und Wert der Demokratie*, first published in 1920 and expended in 1929. It is surprising that the first English translation of this important—and famous—work only dates from 2013 (Kelsen 1929).

As a way of creating law, democracy best realizes the idea of freedom. In order to function, democracy must, as parliamentarism, accept a compromise with the division of labor that is a condition of all social and technical progress. Kelsen showed the degree to which this compromise requires fictions—a concept he used neutrally—in order to achieve the desirable identities of rulers and ruled.

The element that connects Kelsen's pure theory of law with his theory of democracy is value relativism (see Dreier (1990: 249); Jestaedt and Lepsius (2006: XVIII)). The main concern of Kelsen's legal theory is that the validity of the law cannot be based on pre-positive values or norms, while the main concern of his theory of democracy is not to impose limits on the decisions made by the people—that is, by the majority.[6] Such limits are frequently called for with the argument that it is by no means certain that the majority will recognize what is right. However, according to Kelsen, such limits on democracy assume insight into absolute values and are ultimately possible only within the framework of a "metaphysical, and especially religious and mystical, *Weltanschauung*" (Kelsen 1929: 225).

For Kelsen, however, democracy is not only a convenient form of producing laws to optimize individual freedom in mass society. Rather, he is looking for the corresponding conception of man as one functional condition for democracy.

His relevant social-psychological considerations can be found in particular in his *Staatsform und Weltanschauung* from 1933. Although he does not mention Freud in that work, his influence is manifest (Freud 2000, 120 seqq.). Using Freud's structural model of the human psyche, Kelsen opposes the democratic to the authoritarian character. The authoritarian subject identifies with his superego, his ego-ideal, which is represented in the mighty dictator. Consequently, this *typus* adores the blind obedience and finds happiness in dictating as well as in obeying: "The identification with the authority: this is the secret of obedience" (Kelsen 1929: 13). By contrast, the democratic subject is inclined to find his ego-ideal in equality with the other (Kelsen 1929, 11). Thus, Kelsen recognizes the democratic character in the type of person who has a relatively reduced sense of ego—a type of sympathizing, peace-loving, non-aggressive *Epson*—a person whose primary aggressive drive is not so much directed to the outside world but rather inwards, manifesting itself as a tendency to self-criticism and a heightened sense of guilt and responsibility. We can say that in Kelsen's view the democratic-tempered individual and the—well-functioning—democratically organized state are interdependent because a well-functioning democracy does not create a favorable terrain for the principle of authority. Now we understand why Kelsen—from his very beginnings—laid so much weight on education and *Volksbildung* (Kelsen 1913).

[6] Against the background of the inter-war-period Feichtinger (2010, 373) sees the function of a Kelsenian purified legal theory as a "guardian of democracy."

17.3 Defending Modernism

17.3.1 Voegelin's Gnosis

Kelsen's jurisprudence was already contrary to traditional legal dogma—we need only take a look at his preface to the second edition of the *Pure Theory of Law* from 1934 (Kelsen 1934, Vorwort). His relativism and his advocacy of democracy in the short years between the World Wars naturally met fierce resistance. In Kelsen's defense of "Weimar," his harshest—but by no means his only—opponent was Carl Schmitt.

The dispute with Eric Voegelin—which I would like to address now—had a distinctive character, as Voegelin was part of Kelsen's Vienna Circle (Arnold 2008: 513). After 1933, he accommodated himself the Austro-fascist system (Voegelin 1997). Cp. Feichtinger (2010: 345); Arnold (2008: 516), but he bet on a wrong horse and had to immigrate to the United States in 1938 (Arnold 2008: 517). There, Voegelin developed his "New Science of Politics" (Voegelin 1987/1952), which is characterized by its anti-positivism, its aggressive anti-modernity and its hostility to democracy. At its core, it is about the supposed need for a mythical foundation for a political order, which Voegelin sees in the Christian religion and in ancient philosophy. Voegelin attacked conflicting ideas as forms of "Gnosticism." By gnostic aberrations—signifying "false" religions—Voegelin meant not only those totalitarian ideologies to which religious traits are so often attributed—such as Communism or Nazism—but also the "heresies" of liberal democracy, or indeed any modern, scientifically influenced worldview (Arnold 2008: 518).

17.3.2 Kelsen's Critique

Kelsen saw Voegelin's attack as a threat to the scientific perception of the world: "If any criterion distinguishes modern times from the Middle Ages, it is—in Western Civilization—the existence of objective and independent science" (Kelsen 2012: preface, 4). Voegelin's thinking offered Kelsen a number of points of attack and plenty of space for immanent criticism. For our context, it is essential that Kelsen fixated primarily on the abuse of the concept of religion, and it is remarkable how important this—perhaps merely conceptual—question was for him. The transfer of the concept of religion to "moral-political doctrines," such as Marxism, was, for Kelsen, based on a confusion of the intensity of feelings that people can have for ideas with the "nature of the feelings." Arguing against Raymond Aron, who regarded Marxism as a political religion, Kelsen declared Aron's argument to be the product of an erroneous identification of religious and moral systems of belief: "Such a system is not necessarily religious. Some moral systems have no relation to any religion. The moral values of a religion are characterized by the belief that they are established by the will of god or a godlike transcendent being and hence are absolute" (Kelsen 2012: 25). The—at first glance affirmative—title *Secular Religion* is misleading. Kelsen's aim was to show the absurdity of this concept.

17.4 Concepts of Religion

17.4.1 Kelsen—A Jewish-Inspired Thinker?

As I mentioned at the beginning, Kelsen came from a Jewish family and he developed in an intellectual climate in which assimilated Jews played an important role. He himself was probably more agnostic than atheist. He did not oppose religions as such in the sense of subjective beliefs. He also said in the preface to *Secular Religion* that his writing is not directed against theologians (Kelsen 2012: preface, 3). He viewed his own religious association pragmatically, as attested by his two religious conversions—first to Roman Catholicism, then to the Protestant faith (see Staudacher (2009), passim). Certainly he remained aware of his Jewish ancestry, and it influenced some of his personal decisions. Kelsen's very late reflection on his Judaism, reported by Max Knight, may be semi-apocryphal (Knight 1973).

Furthermore, there is no sense in seeking to detect "Jewish" characteristics in the pure theory of law. Such an endeavor would be highly ambivalent in itself and, besides, while Kelsen and many other scholars from his circle did have Jewish family backgrounds, many other outstanding minds of the time did not. Alfred Verdross and Adolf Julius Merkl, two of Kelsen's earliest companions, came from bourgeois non-Jewish families.[7]

It is wrong to say that the pure theory of law—as a general legal theory—has been inspired by Jewish law or legal thinking. The question of whether the pure theory of law is compatible with Jewish law would be just as misguided, as Itzhak Englard impressively demonstrated at the Vienna Symposium on *Secular Religion* (Englard 2013, passim). Gustafsson's recently uttered thesis that there was a school of "distinctly 'Jewish Legal Positivism,'" inspired by Hermann Cohen, which included the Jellineks, Kelsen, Hart and Raz, is also rather embarrassing (Gustafsson 2010: 330).[8]

Admittedly, in the preface to the 1923 second edition of his *Hauptprobleme der Staatsrechtslehre* Kelsen mentioned that he had become aware of the extensive parallels between his own work and Cohen's *Ethics of Pure Will*, with regard to the concept of the legal will (Kelsen 1923: XVII). Here Kelsen admitted his neo-Kantianism, "according to which the epistemic orientation determines its object, and the epistemic object is generated logically from an origin." Kelsen also wrote some time later in a letter to Renato Treves that Cohen's "théorie de la conaissance" had a lasting influence on him (Kelsen 1992). But Kelsen does not cite Cohen's

[7] For more details, see Jabloner (1998, 370).

[8] Englard (2013, 105) calls Gustafsson's attempt "absurd."

work on the philosophy of religion, *Religion der Vernunft aus den Quellen des Judentums* ("Religion of Reason from the Sources of Judaism"), first published 1919 and reissued in 1928, and it is by no means established that he read it at all. Some possible analogies may be found, but they remain superficial.[9]

I cannot close this section without reflecting on the fact that Kelsen was indeed particularly subjected to anti-Semitic attacks, in which the *Pure Theory of Law* was reviled as a typical Jewish product. At the forefront of this agitation was the sharp-tongued and malicious Carl Schmitt, whose anti-Semitism was not just an ingredient in his work, but was at its center (Gross 2000, passim). Thus Schmitt spoke after 1933 of the "Vienna School of the Jew Kelsen" (Schmidt 1936: 1195). Kelsen's central elements—normativism, universalism, pacifism—can only be tools of Jewish decomposition for Schmitt: "normativity," because it destroys the original unity of the "Nomos"; universalism, because "whoever invokes humanity wants to cheat"[10]—and pacifism in any case. Schmitt was part of the phalanx of those German *Meisterdenker* who dressed up their anti-Semitism as the opposition of soul and spirit, essence and form; Heidegger was another one—as has become even clearer today (Wenzel 2014).

There is the temptation to follow this identification of Jewish elements, which was originally made with anti-Semitic intent, but to re-evaluate it positively, in accordance with a popular contemporary consensus. Then one would have a "secular Judaism," based on strong self-control, the equality of all men and peacefulness acquired through civilization. I would urge not to give in to this temptation. Indeed, secular Jews might often embrace such values, but they are not specifically "Jewish."

17.4.2 Kelsen's Concept of Religion

Now, the fact that Kelsen was fascinated by religious subjects should not be overlooked (Dreier 2009: 13; Englard 2013: 106). The concluding sentences of *Vom Wesen und Wert der Demokratie*, in which Kelsen recounts the scene of "Jesus before Pilate" from the Gospel of John, are very well known. According to Kelsen, this encounter has become "a tragic symbol for relativism and democracy." Kelsen ends with the following:

> Believers—political believers—may object that precisely this example argues against, rather than for democracy. This objection must be granted, but only under one condition:

[9] Cohen (1928: 66) speaks about the image of God as follows: "…so lehrt dagegen der Monotheismus, daß Gott schlechterdings kein Gegenstand sei, der nach Anleitung eines Bildes gedacht werden könnte. Und es ist die Probe des wahren Gottes, daß es kein Bild von ihm geben kann (spaced by Cohen). Er kann nie durch ein Abbild zur Erkenntnis kommen, sondern einzig und allein nur als Urbild, als Urgedanke, als Ursein." Here we are invited to speculate about a certain analogy to Kelsen"s Basic Norm, which is—in its final version—by no means a norm but is to be understood as a mandatory assumption for objective normativity, cp. Walter (1992: 56).

[10] Schmitt (1932, 55): "Wer Menschheit sagt, will betrügen".

> that these believers are as certain about their political truth, which they will enforce by violence if necessary, as the son of god was about his (Kelsen 1929: 103; see the cited English translation, 104).

Kelsen therefore does not rule out the possibility of faith; rather, he regards it as an expression of subjective certainty, which can even be realized if the believer does not at the same time consider his experience to be objectively true—and thus binding for all. Value-relativism—as particularly elaborated by Horst Dreier—is therefore by no means a value-nihilism (Dreier 2013: 18).

Kelsen understood religion as a system of norms, the validity of which is attributed to the will of God (Kelsen 1963a: 4, 7). I emphasize two aspects of Kelsen's view of religion that are not always easy to tell apart. First, if religious norms are described in a scientific manner—which is the task of theology—this can only be done under the condition that a "basic norm," which is to obey God's commandments, is established. Only in this way can the objective "ought" of religious norms—their "validity"—be achieved.

Second, the later Kelsen's fundamental principle, "No imperative without an imperator," also breaks new ground here. In his *General Theory of Norms*, Kelsen made clear that the positivity of the law depends for Kelsen particularly on the fact that it is based on real acts of will set by certain people. This remains true even "if the authority's act of will of which the merely thought norm is the meaning is fictitious.…In general terms: No Ought without a will (even if it is only fictitious)" (Kelsen 1979: 186 seq.). Because—according to Kelsen—one can think of such a norm only as the meaning of an act of will that has to be assumed at the same time. Transferred to a religious system of norms, acts of will have to be assumed and/or believed in their fictive setting, but the idea of a personal God is essential. For Kelsen, the conception of a religion without god must inevitably be absurd. According to Englard's cautious remark, Kelsen developed here, in a nutshell, something like "A Pure Theory of God."[11]

It should not be neglected to note that Kelsen's late view on norms brings with it a series of questions, especially with regard to his naturalistic concept of the "will-act" and in the light of customary law (Cp. Jabloner 1988: 78, 84). But the point here is to illuminate the consistency of his thinking.

17.4.3 Dworkin's Religion

Obviously, Ronald Dworkin has nothing in common with Voegelin's extremely reactionary positions. Dworkin insisted on a jurisprudence oriented at objective values in order to defend jurisprudence against postmodern relativism. However, with his concept of religion, Dworkin becomes—in my interpretation—the unforeseen target of Kelsen's critique.

[11] "…man könnte fast sagen, es sei eine reine Gotteslehre" (Englard 2013, 110). Kelsen referred to himself—perhaps ironically—once even as an "advocatus Dei" (Kelsen 1963b: 711).

Dworkin expresses the firm opinion that "religion is deeper than god," according to the first sentence of his lecture, and he explains that a "belief in a god is only one possible manifestation or consequence of that deeper worldview." In a sharp contradiction to Kelsen, Dworkin says that the "conviction that a god underwrites value… presupposes a prior commitment to the independent reality of that value" (Dworkin 2013: 1–2). Only consequently does Dworkin presuppose "the objective truth of two central judgments about values:" "Life's intrinsic meaning and nature's intrinsic beauty" (Dworkin 2013: 10). But how does one get this security without the authority of a god? Dworkin argues that there is a need for basic assumptions in science and mathematics as well, because without the shared assumption that there is an external world or without accepting the axioms of mathematics, science cannot certify itself (Dworkin 2013: 17). Dworkin does not aim at verification through interpersonal agreement but through personal evidence. This is not to be understood in a merely subjective manner, however, as Dworkin notes "that we cannot have that conviction without thinking that it is objectively true" (Dworkin 2013: 20).

Now, Dworkin, as a rational thinker, has to draw a line between general religious worldviews and—for instance—creationist beliefs. For that purpose, Dworkin differentiates between two parts of the traditional theistic religions, "a science part and a value part"—and for him "as a religious atheist," only the second part matters (Dworkin 2013: 23). Dworkin then embarks on the fundamental theistic problem: the image of god, about which he says—and in this point he is in agreement with Kelsen—that a non-personal god is an "obscure idea" that we no longer need (Dworkin 2013: 43).

We have to appreciate Ronald Dworkin as a deeply human scholar, who wrote this rather moving essay at the very end of his life. However, the analogy between the certainty concerning the real world and the evidence of values does not convince me. The first may be—in Dworkin's words—an implicit "assumption" that we make while we are acting in and speaking about reality. The second seems to me just an individual experience of evidence, a rather romantic way of "beholding" values (*ein Erlebnis des "Erschauens" von Werten*). Furthermore, it does not make a difference in one's actual experience whether one believes in reality or not, which is manifestly not the case with values (A solipsist may argue that, if reality is only an illusion, then there is no reason not to murder, but this is an expression of a mental insanity).

Concerning the second argument, the objectivity of values, Kelsen and Dworkin are indeed just as divided as they are in their respective legal theory. As far as the interpretation of general legal norms is concerned, legal science could only offer, according to Kelsen, a framework of possible interpretations; it remains for the judge to decide among those possibilities. Kelsen called this—not very conveniently—an "authentic interpretation" (Kelsen 1960: 346). In Dworkin's theory, it is precisely the most important exercise of the judge to find the legally correct interpretation. Therefore, in Kelsen's view, the famous "hard cases" are outside the "law's empire," but in Dworkin's view, they are its very heart. Dworkin's foremost argument is that the judge cannot think of his opinion as one of many possible solutions, but has to be convinced of having found the right solution—the "interpretation aims at truth" (Dworkin 2011: 126).

Here we do not intend to contribute to this basic question of legal interpretation. Kelsen's attitude towards interpretation, and its further development in the post-Kelsenian Viennese school, is a chapter of its own. My concern here is only to point out that Kelsen and Dworkin consequently followed their respective methods.

However, we perhaps should not neglect the fact that Kelsen and Dworkin are not addressing the same people. Dworkin has in mind the judge applying the law, while Kelsen addresses the legal scholar, prohibiting him from selling his opinion as scientific truth. In addition, on the religious level, Kelsen is thinking of the theologian who reaches out for a scientific description of his (or one's) faith rather than the believer himself, who is most certainly Dworkin's mainspring.

References

Arnold, Eckhard. 2008. Erich Voegelin. In *Der Kreis um Hans Kelsen*, ed. Robert Walter, Klaus Zeleny, and Clemens Jabloner, 513–552. Wien: Manz.

Bräuer, Stefan. 2013. Hans Kelsen als Aufklärer –Einsichten und Grenzen. In *Secular religion. Rezeption und Kritik von Hans Kelsens Auseinandersetzung mit religion und Wissenschaft*, ed. Clemens Jabloner, Thomas Olechowski, and Klaus Zeleny, 165–168. Wien: Manz.

Cohen, Hermann. 1928. *Religion der Vernunft aus den Quellen des Judentums*, 2nd edn, reprint 1995. Wiesbaden: Fourier.

Di Lucia, Paolo, and Passerini Glazel, Lorenzo. 2014. Prefazione all'editione Italiana. Religione senza un Dio. In Kelsen, Hans. 2014. *Religione secolare. Una polemicva contro l'errata interpretation della filosofia sociale, della scienza e della politica modern come "nuove religioni"*. A cura di Paolo di Lucia e Lorenzo Passerini Glazel, IX–XXIII. Milano: Raffaello Cortina Editore.

Dreier, Horst. 1990. *Rechtslehre, Staatssoziologie und Demokratietheorie bei Hans Kelsen*, 2nd ed. Baden-Baden: Nomos.

Dreier, Horst. 2009. Joh 18, Wertrelativismus und Demokratietheorie. In *Reflexionen über Demokratie und Recht*, ed. Robert Walter and Klaus Zeleny, 13–31. Wien: Manz.

Dreier, Horst. 2013. "Secular Religion" im Kontext von Kelsens Gesamtwerk. In *Secular religion. Rezeption und Kritik von Hans Kelsens Auseinandersetzung mit religion und Wissenschaft*, ed. Clemens Jabloner, Thomas Olechowski, and Klaus Zeleny, 1–18. Wien: Manz.

Dworkin, Ronald. 2011. *Justice for hedgehogs*. Cambridge, MA/London: The Belknap Press of Harvard University Press.

Dworkin, Ronald. 2013. *Religion without god*. Cambridge/London: Harvard University Press.

Englard, Izhak. 2013. Haben Kelsens Reine Rechtslehre, seine Faszination für Religion und sein Religionsverständnis einen jüdischen Hintergrund. In *Secular religion. Rezeption und Kritik von Hans Kelsens Auseinandersetzung mit religion und Wissenschaft*, ed. Clemens Jabloner, Thomas Olechowski, and Klaus Zeleny, 101–111. Wien: Manz.

Feichtinger, Johannes. 2010. *Wissenschaft als reflexives Projekt. Von Bolzano über Freud zu Kelsen: Österreichische Wissenschaftsgeschichte 1848–1938*. Bielefeld: transcript.

Freud, Sigmund. 2000. Massenpsychologie und Ich-Analyse (1921). In Freud, Sigmund. *Studienausgabe*, ed. Alexander Mitscherlich et. al., vol. IX: Fragen der Gesellschaft. Fragen der Religion. Special edition. Frankfurt: S. Fischer.

Gross, Raphael. 2000. *Carl Schmitt und die Juden. Eine deutsche Rechtslehre 2000*. Frankfurt/Main: Suhrkamp.

Gustafsson, Hakan. 2010. Fiction of law. *Rechtstheorie* 41: 319–363.

Jabloner, Clemens. 1988. Kein Imperativ ohne Imperator. In *Untersuchungen zur Reinen Rechtslehre II*, ed. Robert Walter, 75–95. Wien: Manz.

Jabloner, Clemens. 1998. Kelsen and his circle: The Viennese years. *European Journal for International Law* 9: 368–385.

Jabloner, Clemens. 2014. Menschenbild und Friedenssicherung, Reprint. In *Hans Kelsen: Die Aktualität eines großen Rechtswissenschafters und Soziologen des 20. Jahrhundert*, ed. Nikitas Aliprantis and Thomas Olechowski, 133–149. Wien: Manz.

Janik, Allen, and Stephen Toulmin. 1973. *Wittgenstein's Vienna*. New York: Simon and Schuster.

Jestaedt, Matthias, and Oliver Lepsius. 2006. Der Rechts- und der Demokratiekritiker Hans Kelsen—eine Einführung. In *Hans Kelsen. Verteidigung der Demokratie*, ed. Matthias Jestaedt and Oliver Lepsius, VII–XXIX. Tübingen: Mohr Siebeck.

Kelsen, Hans. 1913. Politische Weltanschauung und Erziehung. *Annalen für soziale Politik und Gesetzgebung* 2(1913): 1–26.

Kelsen Hans. 1922/1923. Gott und Staat. *Logos* 11: 261–284.

Kelsen, Hans. 1923. Vorrede. In *Hauptprobleme der Staatsrechtslehre entwickelt aus der Lehre vom Rechtssatze*, 2nd ed, ed. Hans Kelsen, V–XXIII. Tübingen: J.C.B. Mohr.

Kelsen, Hans. 1927. Der Staatsbegriff und die Psychoanalyse. In *Almanach für das Jahr 1927*, 135–141. Wien: Internationaler Psychoanalytischer Verlag.

Kelsen, Hans. 1929. *Vom Wesen und Wert der Demokratie*. 2nd. Ed. Tübingen: J.C.B. Mohr (Paul Siebeck). English translation: Kelsen, Hans. 2013. *The Essence and Value of Democracy*, ed. Nadia Urbinati, Carlo Invernizzi Accetti. Trans. B. Graf 2013. Plymouth: Rowman & Littlefield Publishers.

Kelsen, Hans. 1934. *Reine Rechtslehre. Einleitung in die rechtswissenschaftliche Problematik*, 1st ed. Leipzig/Wien: Deuticke.

Kelsen, Hans. 1960. *Reine Rechtslehre*, 2nd ed. Wien: Deuticke.

Kelsen, Hans. 1963a. Politics, ethics, religion and law. In *Faktoren der politischen Entscheidung. Festgabe für Ernst Frankel zum 65. Geburtstag*, ed. Gerhard A. Ritter and Gilbert Ziebura, 3–10. Berlin: Walter de Gruyter & Co.

Kelsen, Hans. 1963b. Die Grundlagen der Naturrechtslehre. *Österreichische Zeitschrift für öffentliches Recht* XIII/1–2: 1–37.

Kelsen, Hans. 1979. *Allgemeine Theorie der Normen*. Wien: Manz.

Kelsen, Hans. 1992. Reine Rechtslehre, "Labandismus" und Neukantianismus. Ein Brief an Renato Treves (3. August 1933). In *Kelsen, Hans/Treves, Renato. Formalismo Giuridico e realtá sociale*, ed. Stanley L. Paulson, 55–58. Napoli/Roma: Edizioni Scientifiche Italiane.

Kelsen, Hans. 2004. *A new science of politics. Hans Kelsens reply to Erik Voegelin's "New Science of Poltitics". A contribution to the Critique of Ideology*, ed. Eckhart Arnold. Frankfurt/ Lancaster: Ontos.

Kelsen, Hans. 2012. *Secular religion. A polemic against the misinterpretation of modern social philosophy, science and politics as "new religion."* Wien/New York: Springer. Italien translation: Kelsen, Hans. 2014. *Religione secolare. Una polemicva contro l'errata interpretation della filosofia sociale, della scienza e della politica modern come "nuove religioni"*. A cura di Paolo di Lucia e Lorenzo Passerini Glazel. Milano: Raffaello Cortina Editore.

Knight, Max. 1973. Erinnerungen an Hans Kelsen. *Aufbau*, 4 March 1973.

Kroeber, A.J. 1920. Totem and taboo: An ethnologic psychoanalysis. *American Anthropologist* 22(1) (January–March 1920): 48–55.

Mètall, Rudolf Alàdar. 1969. *Hans Kelsen. Leben und Werk*. Wien: Deuticke.

Paulson, Stanley. 2006. Der Normativismus Hans Kelsens. *Juristenzeitung* 61: 531–536.

Schmitt, Carl. 1932. *Der Begriff des Politischen. Text von 1932 mit einem Vorwort und drei Corollarien*. Berlin: Duncker & Humblodt.

Schmitt, Carl. 1936. Die deutsche Rechtswissenschaft im Kampf gegen den jüdischen Geist. Schlußwort auf der Tagung der Reichsgruppe Hochschullehrer des NSRB vom 3. und 4. Oktober 1936. DJZ 1936: 1193 seqq.

Schorske, C.E. 1980. *Fin de Siècle Vienna. Politics and culture*. London: Weidenfeld and Nicolson.
Stadler, Friedrich (ed.). 1997. *Wissenschaft als Kultur. Österreichs Beitrag zur Moderne*. Wien/New York: Springer.
Stadler, Friedrich (ed.). 2004. *Vertriebene Vernunft. Emigration und Exil österreichischer Wissenschaft [1988]*, 2nd ed. Münster: LIT.
Staudacher, Anna L. 2009. Zwischen Emanzipation und Assimilation: Jüdische Juristen im Wien des Fin-de-Siècle. In *Hans Kelsen: Leben—Werk—Wirksamkeit*, ed. Robert Walter, Werner Ogris, and Thomas Olechowski, 41–53. Wien: Manz.
Voegelin, Eric. 1987. *The new science of politics. An introduction [1952]*, 2nd ed. Chicago: The University of Chicago Press.
Voegelin, Eric. 1997. Der autoritäre Staat. Ein Versuch über das österreichische Staatsproblem [1936]. Wien/New York: Springer.
Walter, Robert. 1992. Entstehung und Entwicklung des Gedankens der Grundnorm. In *Schwerpunkte der Reinen Rechtslehre*, ed. Robert Walter, 47–59. Wien: Manz.
Wenzel, Uwe Justus. 2014. Das Schwarz der Seele. Ein Versuch, Martin Heideggers "Schwarze Hefte" zu lesen. *Neue Zürcher Zeitung*, 12. April 2014: 25.

Chapter 18
The Free Exercise Clause and Hans Kelsen's Modernist Secularism

D.A. Jeremy Telman

18.1 Introduction

Hans Kelsen's most recent book, *Secular Religion* (Kelsen 2012) is a passionate confrontation with leading mid-century thinkers who chose in various ways to equate intellectual and political movements with religion or at least analogize them to religion. Kelsen's abreaction against this characterization marks him as both a representative and a defender of the high modernism that shaped the social sciences and humanities while also paving the way for the more pronounced forms of skepticism associated with post-structuralism. The publication of Kelsen's work is especially timely for the U.S. legal academy, as numerous U.S. and Canadian scholars, from a number of perspectives, have similarly grappled with the troublesome but, as recent U.S. case law indicates, momentous distinction between religious conviction and other forms of deeply held belief.

Section 18.2 of this Article summarizes Kelsen's argument in *Secular Religion*. First, Kelsen objects to commentators who have characterized modern systems of scientific[1] and political belief as either religious in form or as substitutes for religion. Second, Kelsen bristles when contemporary commentators claim that individual enlightenment and post-enlightenment figures, many of whom are renowned for their religious skepticism or avowed atheism, structured their thoughts in fundamental ways according to religious modes of thinking, incorporating teleology and eschatology borrowed from Christian theology. Kelsen attacks both modes of

[1] I use "scientific" here in the sense of *Wissenschaft*. The European concept is broader than the American concept of science. The word encompasses the natural sciences and the social sciences and even the humanities to the extent that they encompass systematic approaches to knowledge and information.

D.A.J. Telman (✉)
Valparaiso University Law School, Valparaiso, IN 46383, USA
e-mail: Jeremy.telman@valpo.edu

D.A.J. Telman (ed.), *Hans Kelsen in America - Selective Affinities and the Mysteries of Academic Influence*, Law and Philosophy Library 116,
DOI 10.1007/978-3-319-33130-0_18

analysis and points out how easily the distinction between analogy and identity melts away.

Section 18.3 briefly addresses Kelsen's reasons for electing not to publish the book during his lifetime. Section 18.4 places *Secular Religion* in the context of the times in which it was finally published. In the U.S. context, the book is at least as timely now as it was in the 1960s, as it lands in the midst of a wave of recent publications and court opinions addressing the legal protections available for the free exercise of religious belief and religious practices.

18.2 Religion and Other Systematic Approaches to Knowledge and Belief

Kelsen characterizes the twentieth-century writers addressed in *Secular Religion* as doing one of two things. Sometimes they point to ways in which modern belief systems are analogous to religions. At other times, they argue that modern belief systems, even while proclaiming their hostility to all religion and metaphysics, are in fact ersatz religions. For Kelsen, whether these works assert that science and politics are actually new religions or mere analogues to religion, they misunderstand modern science and politics. They either ignore or deny the anti-metaphysical impulse that is the very essence of modern approaches to belief and knowledge. For Kelsen, the stakes were very high:

> If any criterion distinguishes modern times from the Middle Ages it is—in Western civilization—the existence of objective and independent science. A retrogression of science to metaphysics and theology means the return to the spirit of the Middle Ages. The literature against which this book is written seriously endangers the existence of an objective and independent science and therefore the spirit of modern times (Kelsen 2012: 4).

In defending modern science against the claim that it is either a religion or a substitute for religion, Kelsen was defending the modernist movement, of which his pure theory of law is a part.

For Kelsen, both scientific and political beliefs are based in human reason. They are subject to proof and disproof, and upon disproof, they are discarded or revised. Religious belief, by contrast, is based on faith and is impervious to demonstration or counter-demonstration. His polemic is a defense of modern science and modern politics, which are based not in faith in ultimate, transcendent and revealed truth but in the human capacity to reason and understand one's surroundings.

18.2.1 Modern Science and Modern Politics as Ersatz Religion

Secular Religion is often characterized as Kelsen's most extended response to the views of his one-time pupil Eric Voegelin (Arnold 2013: 24–37; Potz 2012: vii), especially as articulated in Voegelin's *The New Science of Politics* (1952). However, while Voegelin is clearly one of Kelsen's targets, the book is far more ambitious, taking on a wide range of mid-twentieth-century intellectuals who, for various reasons, and to differing extents, analogized or equated modern political and social scientific movements to religion. Kelsen objects to Carl Becker's and Ernst Cassirer's interpretations of the Enlightenment that sought to strip it of its association with secularism (Kelsen 2012: 5–6). He opposes with equal vehemence all attempts (including those of Karl Löwith, Antonin Gilbert Sertillanges, Reinhold Niebuhr, Rudolf Bultmann, Arnold Toynbee, Karl Jaspers, Raymond Aron, Martin Buber, and Crane Brinton) to treat nineteenth-century philosophies of history, encompassing the German traditions of Herder, Hegel and Marx, as well as the French traditions of Condorcet, Voltaire, St. Simon, Comte and Proudhon, as heretical forms of a Christian theosophy of history (Kelsen 2012: 6–12). This tradition seems to culminate in Voegelin's work, which builds on that of others who have treated modern political and social movements as heretical forms of theological thinking (Kelsen 2012: 13–15).

Voegelin regarded a concept of the transcendent as indispensable to a well-ordered political community. Any attempt to circumvent transcendence leads to the divinization of humankind and a descent into some version of totalitarianism (Potz 2012: vii). Kelsen regarded Voegelin as an influential figure whose attacks on modern social science could not go unanswered. From Kelsen's perspective, Voegelin stood for an anti-modern and elitist Romanticism, militarism and authoritarianism that rejected both democracy and modernity (Arnold 2013: 22, 24–25). In the end, Kelsen believed, Voegelin and others like him sought to restore the hegemony of theology over science (Kelsen 2012: 53).

> "Go back to God!," these writers call to modern science. But God seems to be more progressive than they are. For when there was darkness upon the face of the deep, he said: Let there by light! Whereas they want darkness to prevail again. This attempt must not go unchallenged (Kelsen 2012: 54).

Voegelin denounced positivist approaches to the social sciences (Voegelin 1952: 4) and equated such approaches with "Gnosticism" (Voegelin: 107), because they prohibit ultimate questions as beyond the reach of science. But Kelsen is adamant that modern social science does not concern itself with the world of theology, encompassing such matters as the transcendent source of being. Such matters are beyond our knowledge, and any claim to "knowledge of something which, by its nature, transcends our knowledge is a meaningless contradiction in terms" (Kelsen 2012: 51).

One could define "religion" in such a way so as to encompass many modern belief systems that view themselves as anti-theological. And in fact, modern social philosophers, beginning with the *Philosophes*, occasionally described their systems in religions terms. As Kelsen explains, those Enlightenment figures who were not outspoken atheists described themselves as deists who rejected Christianity but retained the concept of a Supreme Being. Their "natural religion" had no theological content; it was a moral system (Kelsen 2012: 91). Rousseau distinguished his "civil religion" from what he termed "true religion" because he considered the latter to be destructive to the civil spirit. God plays no role in Rousseau's civic religion; it is strictly a moral code (Kelsen 2012: 172).

Auguste Comte and Friedrich Engels, embraced the view that the sciences that they created were forms of anti-religious religion (Kelsen 2012: 159). Comte consciously modeled his society of the future on the Catholic Church, but he did so because he thought the Church's organization was efficient, not because he accepted any part of the Church's ideology (Kelsen 2012: 162–63). If one thinks of religions as mainly being systems of thought that provide moral codes for behavior in this world and hope for a better world to come, one can easily claim that modern approaches to philosophy, beginning with the Enlightenment association of history with progress, and political ideologies, ranging from communism to nationalism, serve the same role for their adherents that religious belief serves for believers. Kelsen notes the obvious difference: religion defers the hopes for a perfect world through a separate existence and relies on supernatural intervention to bring that world about, while modern science and politics believe that human beings can create a perfect world here on earth simply through the exercise of our reasoning powers (Kelsen 2012: 91–128). Kelsen acknowledges chiliastic movements within the Christian tradition, which, while not eliminating God from the equation, did postulate a second earthly paradise (Kelsen 2012: 117). Still, Kelsen insists on an unbridgeable gap between religious modes of thinking and his understanding of modern science, which provides us no path from the "is" to the absolute "ought" (Kelsen 2012: 42–43).

18.2.2 Metaphorical Relations Between Science, Political Movements, and Religion

One can easily understand the attraction of the analogy. Modern political movements substitute a "heaven on earth" for the heavenly kingdom. Works such as Crane Brinton's *A History of Western Morals* replace the messiah with a messianic belief in human progress (Kelsen 2012: 31–32). In the secular religion in which man is the measure of all things, human lawgivers displace the sovereign Lord, and morality derived from human reason replaces divine law. And yet, Kelsen finds the analogy fundamentally misleading in that it ignores the extent to which modern scientific inquiry, including modern social scientific inquiry and the modern political movements that derive from such inquiry, is fundamentally a-religious or even anti-religious in nature.

Moreover, the penchant for analogy can lead into intellectual cul de sacs. First, some scholars characterize a modern thinker as a prophet of a new religion. Next, if they themselves are invested in a certain religious perspective, they denounce the modern thinker as a heretic. Finally, they debate which sort of heretic the modern thinker is. Kelsen cites the example of Fritz Gerlich, who focuses on the Marxist belief in progress. Gerlach declares communism a "secularized religion of redemption" and a chiliastic movement, but he concludes that Marxism is a corrupted version of the Christian idea (Kelsen 2012: 163). Crane Brinton blames modern natural science for giving rise to the "heresies of materialism, rationalism, humanism, scientism, naturalism, secularism, evolutionism, positivism and ethical culture" (Brinton 1959: 275). These heresies are, for Brinton, "great secular religions" associated with the likes of Galileo, Newton, Darwin, Locke, Spencer and Marx (Brinton 1959: 277). Voegelin calls both Marx and Nietzsche "speculative Gnostics," and calls Marx a Gnostic magician, and Jakob Taubes points to Marx's dialectics as the evidence of his Gnosticism (Kelsen 2012: 181, 213). Karl Löwith sees Comte as a philosophical priest whose scientific age realizes Joachim of Fiore's vision of a Kingdom of God on earth, and Voegelin views Comte as in the tradition of Joachim but also as a "volitional Gnostic" like Marx and Hitler (Kelsen 2012: 148).

It is not surprising that one can identify non-religious thinkers with certain types of heretical thinkers, but this would only be relevant if they were attempting to contribute to a theological discourse. This manner of characterizing modern social scientists in terms of Christian doctrines does not add anything to our understanding of their perspectives. Worse, it obscures the fundamentally a-religious or anti-religious impetus that animates so much of modern social thought and suggests that there is no escape from religious modes of inquiry.

Kelsen is more suspicious of analogies than most. He cites approvingly Hobbes's categorization of metaphor as an abuse of speech in which words are used "in other sense than that they are ordained for, and thereby deceive others" (Kelsen 2012: 162). Raphael Gross suggests that Kelsen was especially wary of analogies applied to modes of thought because, throughout his career, Kelsen was dismissed as a Jewish thinker, and his anti-Semitic adversaries attempted to establish analogies between Talmudic thought and the pure theory of law (Gross 2013: 113, 119). In *Secular Religion*, Kelsen specified the tendency of analogies to exaggerate similarities while downplaying differences and to ignore the ways in which similar terminology can have completely different meanings in two analogized systems of thought (Gross 2013: 113, 119).

Another reason for Kelsen's hostility to metaphor might lie in his intellectual antipathy for Carl Schmitt, whose work on political theology (Schmitt 1922) Kelsen holds up as an example of the dangers of inappropriate analogical reasoning. Kelsen accuses Schmitt of confusing analogy and identity in his political theology (Kelsen 2012: 17). In particular, Schmitt equates the omnipotence of God with the omnipotence of the legislature. However, Kelsen points out, God's omnipotence is unlimited, while the legislature is only omnipotent with respect to its power to promulgate positive law, a much more modest power (Kelsen 2012: 18).

But Schmitt was by no means alone in mistaking analogue for identity. For Kelsen, Karl Löwith's approach to history merges the human-centered philosophy of history with God-centered theology of history by contending that teleological philosophies of history that regard history as progressing towards a utopian future are in fact secularized theologies featuring secularized eschatologies. These concepts are for Kelsen contradictions in terms, as the very essence of secularism is the elimination of supernatural religious and eschatological elements (Kelsen 2012: 20–21). Thus Kelsen rejects Löwith's interpretation of Comte's political philosophy as eschatological:

> But how can Comte's philosophy be eschatological if he does not and cannot accept the Christian idea of salvation of the individual soul? The only element that positive philosophy and the Christian scheme of salvation have in common is the idea of improvement, which is certainly not a monopoly of the Christian religion (Kelsen 2012: 156).

Kelsen is willing to acknowledge only surface similarities between Christian theology and modern social science, and he rejects the assumption that the similarities are proof of a connection.

Kelsen finds the false equivalence between modern political movements and religion objectionable, "not because it wounds religious feelings, but because it is logically inadmissible, implying a contradiction in terms" (Kelsen 2012: 29). In particular, as becomes clear in Kelsen's critique of Raymond Aron, modern political movements are not eschatological in that the ends they seek are of this world and they are obtained through human, not divine, power (Kelsen 2012: 22–23). It is true that both theologies and philosophies of history embrace notions of progress, but the concepts of progress are fundamentally different. Marxist or Comtian ideas of progress in history are merely predictions of future probabilities; contrarily, religious notions of progress entail ultimate truths (Kelsen 2012: 41).

Moreover, when Aron identifies Marxist perspectives as "dogma," he ignores the fundamental epistemological chasm separating modern political movements from religion. Dogmas are revealed truths that are not susceptible to proof or disproof. They are simply to be believed, unless one chooses the life of the heretic. But Marxist maxims are not dogma in the proper sense. They are derivations of reason that can be challenged on their own terms (Kelsen 2012: 26). Having no dogma, Marxism also has no cosmology, and so Crane Brinton errs in treating Marxism as a religion "without a supernatural godhead" (Brinton 1959: 106). Kelsen treats Marxism in its own terms, as a social science, and the social sciences assign to the natural sciences the task of undertaking a scientific description of the world and to religion the task of undertaking an extra-scientific explanation of the natural world. Brinton errs to the extent that he conflates these two very different cosmological projects (Kelsen 2012: 28–29, 31–32).

Kelsen's opposition, even to those scholars who merely pointed out analogies between religious and non-religious systems of thought, suggests the limits of his own tolerance for metaphorical thinking. From this perspective, Kelsen's polemic seems to be a product of a misunderstanding that derives from Kelsen's literal-mindedness and suspicion of both metaphor and analogy. Crane Brinton actually anticipated a perspective very much like Kelsen's in defending the extended analogy in his work between modern political movements and religions. Kelsen cites to Brinton as acknowledging that, if nationalism is not a theistic religion and that, if you regard "a *theos* and a supernatural view of the cosmos an essential mark of a religion, you must abandon the analogy between religion and nationalism. You will, however, have thereby abandoned a useful tool for understanding human conduct" (Kelsen 2012: 269). But Kelsen has a ready response. Brinton cannot decide between analogy and identity: "He again and again asserts that the Enlightenment and its offspring *are* religions" Kelsen has no regrets about abandoning "a highly dangerous misinterpretation of the essential elements of modern civilization" (Kelsen 2012: 270).

18.2.3 Science as Anti-theological

Make no mistake. Analogies are powerful, and they threaten to rob modern science of its main intellectual legacy: the liberation of human thought from religious modes of thinking. Kelsen explains that the attacks on modern social theory as "secular religions" threaten to re-subordinate science to theology. He cannot specify cause and effect, but he does note "the work of theologians who welcome this misinterpretation of modern philosophy and science, who want us to go back to religion, to let theology again rule over science" (Kelsen 2012: 29). Kelsen points to the writings of Antoine-Gilbert Sertillanges, Reinhold Niebuhr and Arnold Toynbee. Sertillanges clearly wanted to subordinate science to faith (Kelsen 2012: 43). In Niebuhr and Toynbee, where one might simply see Cold War denunciations of Communist misreadings of history, Kelsen sees similar attempts to subordinate scientific to theological understandings of history (Kelsen 2012: 44).

Indeed, Kelsen imagines that the wedge created by the idea that modern social theory and political movements are ersatz religions can open a space for the eradication of a-religious thought:

> If modern social theory is secularized theology and if political ideologies are disguised or degenerated religion, are we then to think that this secularization, disguise or degeneration are the fundamental errors of modern civilization, that our social theory and politics are moving in a wrong direction and should return to their original, but forgotten or wrongly denied model? As a consequence of this doctrine a desecularization of science and political ideologies is necessary. Only then will they be able to reach the truth, which, of course, can only be the truth of God. Thus the emancipation of science and political ideology from theology and religious authority, to which modern civilization owes its existence, shall be undone (Kelsen 2012: 43).

Having laid out the fundamental opposition between theological and scientific modes of inquiry, Kelsen then presents his own readings of the most important representatives of modern social thought. In each case, his aim is to demonstrate that these thinkers consciously sought to and succeeded in eliminating theological modes of inquiry from scientific methods.

Kelsen begins this part of the book with a brief chapter on Thomas Hobbes. In a few pages, he refutes Voegelin's characterization of Hobbes as a Gnostic thinker (Voegelin 1952: 152). Hobbes cannot be a Gnostic, according to Kelsen, because his was among the first "attempts to establish a positivistic political and legal theory at a time when theological speculation and natural-law doctrine were prevailing" (Kelsen 2012: 85). Voegelin thought that because Hobbes wrote of the "law of nature" that he was part of that natural law tradition, but Voegelin misread Hobbes. Hobbes characterizes the state of nature as one in which law is absent. Law only comes into being with the advent of the state, and the state, as a product of mortal men, like them, is only a transitory, earthly order (Kelsen 2012: 85–86). On Kelsen's reading, Hobbes regarded speculation on eternal legal or cosmological orders as beyond the scope of his inquiry (Kelsen 2012: 86–87).

The chapter on Hume and Kant is also very short. Apparently, none of Kelsen's main interlocutors dared claim Hume as a theological thinker. Although the point seems unnecessary to Kelsen's broader argument in *Secular Religion*, Kelsen's discussion of Hume emphasizes the extent of Hume's rejection of revealed religion, which Kelsen insists is the "inevitable consequence" of Hume's empirical skepticism (Kelsen 2012: 131). His brief discussion of Kant stresses that Kant's transcendental philosophy of epistemology built on Hume's skeptical empiricism and thus ruled out any eschatological speculations (Kelsen 2012: 134–135).

Given the patently anti-theological nature of their works, one would think that Saint-Simon and Proudhon would be unlikely candidates for the title of prophets of new religions. Nonetheless, Kelsen takes on Etienne Gilson's treatment of Saint-Simon's philosophy as "a new Christianism of science" (Kelsen 2012: 137). Although Proudhon was an avowed atheist, Karl Löwith characterized him as a "theologian of progress" and a "religious soul." Kelsen refutes these views with numerous quotations from Proudhon evidencing his atheism and his hostility to religion (Kelsen 2012: 139–40).

Kelsen provides a far more extensive refutation of scholars who have characterized the Enlightenment as a religious movement or as an ersatz religion. Ernst Cassirer errs, in Kelsen's view, in conflating the Enlightenment fascination with the problem of evil with theodicy, which is a specifically religious "problem of how moral evil comes into this world created and governed by an all-good and all-powerful God" (Kelsen 2012: 94). Enlightenment thinkers regarded evil as a fact in existence in this world, and it was to be subjected to the same sort of inquiry as any other fact (Kelsen 2012: 95–96).

In Kelsen's estimation, Carl Becker's work on *The Heavenly City of the Eighteenth Century Philosophers* (1932) "obliterates the essential difference between reason and faith" (Kelsen 2012: 97). As a result, he misreads the enlightenment project as one consistent with Christian ideas of service and commitment to "the humanitarian impulse to set things right" (Kelsen 2012: 98; Becker 1932: 41). Kelsen objects that Christianity has no monopoly on commitment to service and humanitarianism, and that moral and political perspectives derived from human reason animated the *philosophes* (Kelsen 2012: 98). Rather than putting their faith in some superhuman theological order, the *philosophes* aspired for humankind, through progressive improvements on its past endeavors and the exercise of human powers, to create the ideal society. For Kelsen, this mode of thinking was as far from religion as black is from white (Kelsen 2012: 101).

Charles Frankel's work on the Enlightenment (1948) assumes that the *philosophes* made metaphysical assumptions because they thought that they could establish absolute truths. Kelsen points out that the *philosophes* were empiricists and believed (mistakenly in Kelsen's view) that they could arrive at absolute truths without resort to metaphysical claims (Kelsen 2012: 102–03). Crane Brinton similarly mistakes the *philosophes'* penchant for the teleological to be a rough equivalent of Christian eschatology (Kelsen 2012: 114). But Kelsen regards the *philosophes'* perspective to be essentially the opposite of eschatology, because it substitutes belief in progress through human ingenuity for Christian faith in supernatural intervention in human affairs. Moreover, the Enlightenment *telos* does not entail any ultimate day of judgment. There is to be neither reward for good behavior nor retribution for evil. Rather, the Enlightenment foresaw progress towards a world in which one received according to one's needs (Kelsen 2012: 116).

It is somewhat surprising that Kelsen felt the need to devote two entire chapters to the refutation of claims that Friedrich Nietzsche, who called himself the Antichrist, was either a Christian or a metaphysician. The extensive treatment was necessary because major authorities had claimed him as both a Christian and a metaphysician.

Karl Jaspers argued that Nietzsche's passionate attacks on Christianity sprang from his own Christianity (Kelsen 2012: 199). Jaspers located Nietzsche's Christianity in his "boundless will to truth," but Kelsen was no more willing to acknowledge a Christian monopoly on truth-seeking than on belief in progress (Kelsen 2012: 200–201). Indeed, although they are distinct in many ways, both Kelsen and Nietzsche see Christian methods of truth-seeking as antithetical to their own: "If truth is a value recognized by Christianity, it is not truth in the sense of science, that is, truth accessible to human reason" (Kelsen 2012: 206). Kelsen also noted that, if some impulse gave rise to the Nietzschean idea of eternal recurrence, the impulse would have to be classical, not Christian (Kelsen 2012: 204).

In Kelsen's view, "Nietzsche's philosophy clearly, incontestably, passionately rejects Christian metaphysics" (Kelsen 2012: 222). Kelsen makes this point emphatically in order to refute scholars who have attempted to claim "a close affinity" between Nietzsche and Kierekgaard (Kelsen 2012: 222–223). But in response to Heidegger's treatment of Nietzsche, Kelsen also makes broader claims, rejecting Heidegger's suggestion that Nietzsche is a metaphysician (Kelsen 2012: 230). Kelsen contends that Nietzsche's relativism is incompatible with any form of metaphysics (Kelsen 2012: 227). Nietzsche, Kelsen says, could not engage in metaphysics because he has no concept of transcendent truth. Just as one cannot have religion without God, Kelsen observes that there can be no metaphysics without a concept of transcendence (Kelsen 2012: 231).

In fairness to Heidegger, as the quotations that Kelsen provides make clear, he acknowledges that Nietzsche is attempting to combat metaphysics. Heidegger, however, contends that metaphysics is inescapable and Nietzsche, in attempting to overcome metaphysics, can only enact and re-inscribe it (Kelsen 2012: 234, n.878). Kelsen recognizes that Heidegger's project is not to explicate Nietzsche in his own terms but to expose the limitations of Nietzsche's anti-metaphysical project. But Kelsen contends that Heidegger's project results in a gross misinterpretation of Nietzsche (Kelsen 2012: 249).

18.2.4 Kelsen's Conclusions

Kelsen's explication of modern social science and political theory is clear and consistent throughout. He views modernity as an escape from religious modes of thought. Modernity replaces a belief in God with a faith in human resourcefulness. It replaces a hope for the afterlife with an optimism that reason can lead in this world to solutions to human problems. Modernity need not be anti-religious, although it often combats the distortions of logic that emanate from religious perspectives. Rather, scientific approaches bracket the questions that religion addresses. Reason lacks the tools to resolve those issues and thus finds reasoned inquiries into the traditional subject matters of religion to be pointless.

Contemporary writers who identify modernity with or analogize modernity to religion err in two ways. Some, trapped within their own Christian perspectives, fail to grasp the extent to which modernity has liberated itself from such perspectives. Others, more ominously, resist modernity and mischaracterize it in an attempt to drag social, scientific, and political discourse back into the traditional modes of thinking from which modernity liberated them.

18.3 Why Did Kelsen Decide Not to Publish *Secular Religion*?

In *Secular Religion*, Kelsen goes to war on behalf of his high estimation of the value of science. He regards the scholars to whom he is responding as posing an actual danger to the progress of modern science. Given how strongly Kelsen felt about the subject matter of *Secular Religion*, it is curious that he decided not to publish the book during his lifetime.

No writings of Kelsen's explain his decision not to publish *Secular Religion*. Scholars have offered numerous explanations for Kelsen's decision not to publish *Secular Religion* in the 1960s. In defending his book in its concluding chapter, Kelsen himself offered the simplest explanation for its non-publication—the entire book was an overreaction to a mere manner of speaking that posed no serious consequences to readers who would not confuse analogies and identities. But Kelsen insisted that the stakes remained high: he regarded the writers addressed in his book as one part of a movement aimed "at returning religion to politics, and theology to science" as the only mechanism by which to safeguard capitalism and democracy against the communist threat (Kelsen 2012: 271).

18.3.1 Religion Without God?

It appears that Kelsen had originally planned the title *Religion without God*? for the book that became *Secular Religion* (Jabloner 2012: XIII). According to Kelsen's biographer, Kelsen regretted that title and the narrowness of the definition of religion that the work entailed. He recognized that some thinkers to whom he was sympathetic, Julien Huxley and Bertrand Russell, believed in the possibility of religion without metaphysics or belief in a supreme being (Métall 1969: 91). Kelsen came to doubt the operative assumption in *Secular Religion* that religion is impossible without belief in God (Arnold 2013: 38). In defending modern science against a retreat into theology, Kelsen treated committed atheists who saw social science as analogous to religion no differently from genuine enemies of modern social science who derided it as a false religion (Arnold 2013: 38).

As Michael Potacs has pointed out, Raymond Aron was quite clear-eyed about the ways in which Marxism could be analogized to religion and the ways in which it was distinct from religion. The analogy was useful to Aron because it helped him specify the ways in which Marxism, like religion, built up a self-contained and self-reinforcing system of ideas and thus insulated itself against external critique (Potacs 2013: 98). On the other hand, Aron recognized that Marxism remained anchored in an empirical reality while religions recognize a transcendental godly realm. Aron made this difference clear in referring to Marxism as a *secular* religion (Potacs 2013: 99). This was not enough for Kelsen. For Kelsen, Marxism could be discredited through rational discourse, while religion operated on a separate plane. Still, the distinction was really a matter of argumentative strategies, and Potacs specultates that Kelsen came to doubt whether he needed to publish an entire book refuting people over word choice (Potacs 2013: 99).

18.3.2 Concern About Voegelin's Response

We know that Kelsen and Voegelin corresponded about Kelsen's response to Voegelin's *New Science of Politics*. According to the editors of *Secular Religion*, no writings by Voegelin relating to this subject matter have survived; it appears that he "warned" Kelsen that if Kelsen were to publish the review of Voegelin's book, much of which found its way into *Secular Religion*, Kelsen's reputation would suffer as a result (Jabloner 2012: XII). Although it seems unlikely, it is possible that some of Voegelin's points sufficiently resonated with Kelsen as to dissuade him from publishing *Secular Religion*. After all, Kelsen also never published during his lifetime his book-length review of Voegelin's *New Science of Politics*, although that book, like *Secular Religion*, was published after Kelsen's death (Kelsen 2004).

At least one Voegelin scholar disputes this version of events. Bjørn Thomassen (2013) cites to a letter that Voegelin wrote to Alfred Verdross in 1956 in which Voegelin wrote that Kelsen could "publish anything about me that he wishes." Voegelin's only objection was that Kelsen could not expect that Voegelin would respond to Kelsen's criticisms (Voegelin 2007: 270). The letter does not really illuminate the mystery. Voegelin's letter comes nearly a decade too early to shed light on Kelsen's decision not to publish *Secular Religion*. Voegelin's haughty and dismissive tone in his letter to Verdross suggests a great deal of resentment towards his former mentor and actually suggests that Voegelin would be quite annoyed by the prospect of a publication like *Secular Religion*.

18.3.3 Cold War Concerns About Kelsen's Positive Evaluation of Marxism

One refreshing aspect of *Secular Religion*, written as it was during the chilliest parts of the Cold War, is Kelsen's appreciation of Marx's and Engels' work. But perhaps Kelsen, who was already an exile, decided that, given the political climate in the United States in the 1960s, this was not the time to defend dialectical materialism (Gross 2013: 121). Voegelin's warning to Kelsen may have related to Kelsen's positive depiction of Marx and Engels. But Kelsen wrote two books criticizing Bolshevism as a political system and the communist theory of law (Kelsen 1948, 1955).[2] In the former, Kelsen set out to show "the paradoxical contradiction which exists within Bolshevism between anarchism in theory and totalitarianism in practice and to defend the true idea of democracy against the attempt to obliterate it and adulterate it by presenting a party dictatorship as the political self-determination of a free people" (Kelsen 1948: 1–2). One might think that such writings would put Kelsen's anti-communist bona fides beyond peradventure. Still, Kelsen might not have wanted to take the risk.

As in his treatment of other major figures in the history of modern social science, Kelsen focuses, in his discussion of Marx and Engels, on their anti-metaphysical, empirical approach to the studies of history of and economics. Kelsen rejects Robert C. Tucker's claim that Marxism is a religion because it puts man in the place of God as a "supreme being." Marxism is for Kelsen simply a "system of morals" without any religious character (Kelsen 2012: 179–80). Attempts to read a religious impulse back into Marx (or Feuerbach) undercuts the fundamentally anti-religious nature of their thought:

> According to these anti-religious thinkers, what man should draw back to himself is not and cannot be God—whose existence they denied—but all that is best in man and which the

[2] I am grateful to George Mazur for calling my attention to these works.

> Christian religion has projected into an imaginary beyond...By drawing back what is best in man to himself, man abolishes the religious self-alienation, in the same way as by the proletarian revolution he abolishes his economic self-alienation (Kelsen 2012: 193).

Those who characterize Marx as a religious or metaphysical thinker do so in part based on his refusal to say anything about the world after the proletarian revolution. But Kelsen rejects any contention that Marx was predicting an apocalyptic end of days or even an end of history (Kelsen 2012: 194). On the contrary, Marx was being a good social scientist, refusing to make predictions about an era for which he had no useful data.

18.3.4 Was the Book Too Personal?

On the face of things, Kelsen intervenes to correct what he describes as a misinterpretation of the writings of these leading figures. However, the length of the work suggests that Kelsen's investment in the issue encompasses a defense of his own legal positivist project and perhaps even more. Raphael Gross has suggested that the book was Kelsen's "most intimate autobiographical text," in which he defends not only his pure theory of law but also his conception of science and even himself (Gross 2013: 122). The length, vehemence and passion of Kelsen's approach in *Secular Religion* all suggest the power of Gross's reading of the work. *Secular Religion* was a very personal defense of Kelsen's work. Given how bound up the book was with Kelsen's intellectual biography, discouraging or even threatening words from Voegelin or others might have been enough to persuade Kelsen not to publish.

18.4 The Contemporary Relevance of Kelsen's Work

The publishers of *Secular Religion* had their own reasons for publishing the work decades after Kelsen had abandoned it (Jabloner 2012: XIV–XV), but the timing of the publication was serendipitous, as Kelsen's work constitutes a useful intervention in an on-going debate about the status of religion in a secular society. Recently, legal scholars have focused on the question of the special legal status accorded to religious belief. But their work builds on more fundamental philosophical inquiries into the nature of religious belief and the status of such belief in a secular society. Following Jocelyn Maclure and Charles Taylor, I will use the phrase "secular society" to connote "a political and legal system whose function is to establish a certain distance between the state and religion." (Maclure and Taylor 2011: 2–3). Maclure and Taylor identify two aims and two modes of secularism. The aims are respect for the moral equality of individuals and protection of freedom of conscience and of religion; the modes are the separation of church and state and state neutrality towards religions (Maclure and Taylor 2011: 20).

The two aims come into conflict when adherents of recognized religions are accorded certain accommodations or exemptions (Maclure and Taylor 2011: 4). While some scholars argue that non-religious or non-traditional belief systems are entitled to exemptions as much as are religious belief systems (Dworkin 2013; Maclure and Taylor 2011); others argue that no belief systems should be entitled to such exemptions (Leiter 2013).

Christopher Eisgruber and Lawrence Sager take a somewhat different approach, focusing not on religious exemptions from generally applicable laws but on a system of laws that guarantees the free exercise of religion while retaining its commitment to equal treatment (Eisgruber and Sager 2007). Their principle of Equal Liberty "insists that no member of the community ought to be devalued on account of the spiritual foundations of his or her basic commitments" (Eisgruber and Sager 2007:18). On the subject of religious exemptions from generally applicable laws, Eisgruber and Sager propose that such exemptions be available on religious grounds where they are also available on other grounds:

> Hence the conclusion that the City of Newark had to permit Muslim police officers to wear beards on grounds of religious necessity, just as it had already permitted other officers to do so on medical grounds; and hence the conclusion that a high school basketball association that permitted players to wear eyeglasses was obliged to make a comparable concession to Orthodox Jews whose religion required that they wear yarmulkes (Eisgruber and Sager 2007: 279–280).

Eisgruber and Sager thus seek to arrive at practical results through a "principled moderation" (Eisgruber and Sager 2007: 280) that rejects both those who would strictly separate law and religion and those who would always seek to accommodate those who claim entitlement to religious exemptions from generally applicable laws.

Kelsen's *Secular Religion* does not directly address the question of religious exemptions from generally applicable laws. However, like Brian Leiter's work. it helps us focus on what may set religious beliefs apart from other belief systems. Kelsen's understanding of religion places religious sensibilities at odds with modernity and thus raises interesting challenges for those who would preserve special exemptions for adherents of religions while also embracing other aspects of the modern outlook.

18.4.1 The Renewed Interest in Secular Religion

A number of recent works by secular scholars have embraced the concept of secular religion or religion without god. Maclure and Taylor contend that, in countries like France and Turkey, where secularism arose after "a bitter struggle against a dominant religion," the temptation is far stronger to make secularism "the equivalent of religion" in the tradition of Rousseau's civil religion (Maclure and Taylor 2011: 14).

Maclure and Taylor's project is to determine the extent to which, in keeping with the principle of moral autonomy, a secular society must accommodate religious practices that might otherwise violate laws of general applicability. For example, Maclure and Taylor cite with approval a 2004 decision of the Canadian Supreme Court in which it embraced a justification grounded in moral autonomy for the accommodation of religious practices (Maclure and Taylor 2011:81–82). However, the same principle of moral autonomy leads Maclure and Taylor to advocate accommodations of all practices, whether religious or not, that derive from "core commitments."

The important distinction for them is not between religious and secular core beliefs but between core commitments and "personal preferences that are not intimately connected to my self-understanding as a moral agent" (Maclure and Taylor 2011: 91). Maclure, and Taylor fuss about mechanisms for preventing excessive claims of entitlement to special treatment. They would allow a government to refuse requests for accommodation that: (a) significantly hinder the realization of institutional aims; (b) are excessively costly or burdensome; or (c) impinge on the rights and freedoms of others (Maclure and Taylor 2011: 100–101). They conclude that "[t]here do not seem to be any principled reasons to isolate religion and place it in a class apart from the other conceptions of the world and of the good" (Maclure and Taylor 2011:105). Thus, religious practices ought to be entitled to no special protections not accorded to core commitments that derive from secular belief systems.

Ronald Dworkin arrives at a similar solution from a different direction. Rather than calling for equal treatment of all deeply-held beliefs and practices, whether religious or secular, Dworkin adopts a broad understanding of religion. While Kelsen rejected the possibility of a religion without God, Dworkin embraced it, titling his last book, *Religion without God* (2013). As Dworkin explains at the outset, his view is that "religion is deeper than God" (Dworkin 2013: 1). Dworkin defines religion as encompassing two views: first, that human life has objective meaning or importance, with each person carrying a special responsibility to make her life a successful one; and second, that "the universe as a whole and in all its parts…is itself sublime: something of intrinsic value and wonder" (Dworkin 2013: 10). Thus Dworkin disagrees with Richard Dawkins, who thought Einstein's references to God were misleading (Dawkins 2006: 8). Einstein may not have believed in god, but that, in Dworkin's view would not disqualify him from being a deeply religious person (Dworkin 2013: 5–6).

Dworkin, like Maclure and Taylor,, applauds the U.S. Supreme Court's decision in *United States v. Seeger* (380 U.S. 163 (1965)) to recognize the right of an atheist to protection as a conscientious objector (Dworkin 2013: 119–20). But he dislikes the Court's willingness to protect any "sincere and meaningful belief which occupies in the life of its possessor a place parallel to that filled by the God of those admittedly qualifying for the exemption" (*Seeger*, 380 U.S. at 176). Dworkin expresses concern that the Supreme Court's approach would protect a worshipper of Mammon, and so he would limit protections to beliefs that are "part of and drawn from a general, sincere, coherent, integrated and comprehensive account of why it is important for people to live well and what it is to live well" (Dworkin 2013: 122).

Brian Leiter devotes an entire chapter of his *Why Tolerate Religion* (2013) to the project of identifying criteria that capture all religions and exclude all non-religions (Leiter 2013: 31–53). He concludes that all religions: (1) make categorical demands on their adherents; (2) are insulated, by virtue of being based on faith, from ordinary standards of evidence and rational justification applicable to both common sense and science (Leiter 2013: 34); and (3) offer existential consolation to their adherents (Leiter 2013: 53). Given the way he has defined religion it comes as no surprise that Leiter concludes that "there is no moral or epistemic consideration that favors special legal solicitude toward beliefs that conjoin *categorical commands* with *insulation from evidence*...(Leiter 2013: 67). It follows that there is no reason to "tolerate" deviations from laws of general applicability based on religious belief, nor should we respect religious belief (Leiter 2013: 90–91), if by "respect" we mean "an attitude of positive appraisal of [a] person either as a person or as engaged in some particular pursuit" (Leiter 2013: 70).

By contrast, Maclure and Taylor refuse to adopt any definition of religion for legal purposes. They observe that such definitions tend to lean toward the "three major monotheisms," excluding eastern spiritual philosophies, "something that seems hardly seems justifiable" (Maclure and Taylor 2011: 84). Dworkin goes in the opposite direction, adopting a definition of religion so broad as to encompass even the beliefs of some who may not think of themselves as religious or would even emphatically reject the label.

Dworkin recommends the abandonment of the idea of a special right to religious freedom. Instead, echoing Maclure and Taylor's embrace of the moral autonomy argument, he calls for the recognition of a right to "ethical independence" (Dworkin 2013: 132). Dworkin's and Maclure and Taylor's approaches are consistent with that of the Human Rights Committee in its construction of Article 18 of the International Covenant on Civil and Political Rights, which guarantees "freedom of thought, conscience and religion" (ICCPR 1966: Art. 18.1). The Human Rights Committee commented that Article 18 "protects theistic, non-theistic and atheistic beliefs, as well as the right not to profess any religion or belief" (General Comment 22 (1993: 2). The U.S. Supreme Court had some latitude to define conscientious objection broadly in the *Seeger* case, in which the Court construed a congressional enactment, but the U.S. Constitution's protections of religious freedom pose special challenges to those who want to erase the distinction between religious and non-religious convictions.

18.4.2 The Establishment Clause Issue

The U.S. Constitution's First Amendment states that Congress shall make no law establishing a state religion, nor may it interfere with any person's free exercise of religion (U.S. Const, amend. I). This Amendment has been incorporated through the Fourteenth Amendment's Due Process Clause and thus also prohibits state governments from establishing a religion or infringing upon the free exercise of religion.

In light of these constitutional provisions, quite a bit turns on whether or not a set of beliefs is religious in nature. For example, the U.S. Supreme Court recently exempted religious organizations from the duty to comply with prohibitions on workplace discrimination so long as the affected employees do "ministerial" work, and the Court deferred to the defendant congregation's definition of which employees can be counted as a minister, so long as the evidence supports that designation (*Hosanna-Tabor Evangelical Lutheran Church & School v. EEOC*, 132 S. Ct. 694 (2012)). More recently still, the Court determined that corporations can avail themselves of protections of religious liberty under the Religious Freedom Restoration Act (RFRA) (107 Stat. 1488, 42 U.S.C. § 2000bb, *et seq.*, 1993).

RFRA provides that, where a federal regulation imposes a substantial burden on religious exercise, that regulation must both serve a compelling government purpose and also constitute the means for achieving that purpose that impose the least possible restriction on religious exercise (*Burwell v. Hobby Lobby*, 134 S. Ct. 2751, 2759 (2014)). At issue in *Burwell* were regulations passed by the U.S. Department of Health and Human Services intended to implement the Patient Protection and Affordable Care Act of 2010 (124 Stat 119). These regulations required employers with 50 or more full-time employees to provide health care coverage for their employees, including coverage of forms of contraception approved by the Food and Drug Administration (77 Fed.Reg. 8725–8726 (2012)).

In *Burwell*, the Court struck down these regulations on the ground that they violated RFRA. The Court assumed that the government had a compelling interest in guaranteeing access to the forms of contraception at issue in the case (*Burwell*, 134 S. Ct. at 2779–2780). It nonetheless found that the regulations violated RFRA because they were not the least restrictive means available to the government for achieving its ends (*Burwell*, 134 S. Ct. at 2781–2782). In so doing, the Court also ruled that the closely-held plaintiff corporations were "persons" who could avail themselves of RFRA's protections of religious freedom. This made sense, according to the *Burwell* majority, because protecting the religious freedom of closely-held corporations like the plaintiffs "protects the religious liberty of the humans who own and control those companies" (*Burwell*, 134 S. Ct. at 2768).

RFRA, and the various state RFRAs that have extended it, exempt religious humans, religious institutions, and now also close corporations held by religious humans from a wide range of generally applicable laws. In her *God vs. the Gavel* (2014), Marci Hamilton has catalogued the consequences of such exemptions. Hamilton's book "describes six arenas where religious individuals and institutions have insisted on the right to avoid the law as they have harmed others: children, marriage, schools, land use in neighborhoods, prisons and the military, and anti-discrimination laws" (Hamilton 2014: 36). Her book highlights the many areas in which the modernist project that Kelsen defends in *Secular Religion* can be thwarted by exemptions based on religious belief.

18.4.3 The Establishment Clause and Secular Religion

In *Religion without God*, Dworkin attempts to bridge the gap between the secular and the religious by means of a definition that most adherents of religion would find too broad and that some agnostics and atheists would still find ill-suited to describe their deeply-held commitments. One review of *Religion without God* concludes that "the company to which Dworkin belongs or belonged must still converse with more traditional theists from opposite sides of [a] chasm" (Smith 2014: 1355).

In *Secular Religion*, Kelsen celebrated determinedly materialist, anti-metaphysical thinkers, and he energetically opposed any characterization of their philosophical systems as religious in nature, even if religion is defined as broadly as Dworkin defines it. That is, the heroes of Kelsen's narrative are not only without God.; many of them reject Dworkin's embrace of objective value, human purpose and an ordered universe.

Compared with Dworkin and with Kelsen's various mid-century nemeses (Voegelin, Löwith, Cassirer, Aron, Brinton), Kelsen defines religion very strictly. Kelsen seems to have grown so frustrated with the post-war ubiquity of the concept of ersatz religions that he could no longer tolerate even extended metaphors or analogies between modern philosophical or political movements and religion. For Kelsen, a religion must entail a belief in a superhuman being and an end of days in which either an earthly or an ethereal paradise awaits. Like Leiter, Kelsen associates religion with a set of beliefs that defy traditional modes of verification.

18.5 Conclusion

Based on *Secular Religion*, it seems that Kelsen would side with Brian Leiter and not with Ronald Dworkin or Taylor and Maclure. Kelsen thought that religious modes of belief are radically different from at least certain non-religious modes of belief. The Kelsen of the pure theory of law could thus imagine a perfectly coherent legal system in which religious beliefs are accorded special protections. However, like Brian Leiter, the Kelsen of *Secular Religion* seems to think that there are good reasons for a modern society to reject special protections for religious belief. Kelsen's defense of modernity encompasses a rejection of the power of theology in legal affairs and in other realms of society that, *Secular Religion* strongly suggests, are better governed by Enlightenment and post-Enlightenment modes of reasoning that reject metaphysics, supernaturalism, eschatology and other variants of pre-modern irrationalism. But Kelsen does not specify those conclusions in the book. He restricts himself in *Secular Religion* to a defense of modern science and politics as projects that define themselves in crucial ways as antithetical to religious modes of discourse.

Acknowledgments I am indebted to George Mazur for his careful attention to and instructive comments on multiple drafts of this chapter. I would also like to thank Karen Koelemeyer for her extraordinary editorial efforts in bringing this chapter and this volume into being. Finally, my work on this chapter and this volume were made possible with the support and encouragement of the Hans-Kelsen-Institut in Vienna and through a grant from the Dietrich W. Botstiber Foundation's Institute for Austrian-American Studies.

References

Arnold, Eckart. 2013. Bedarf die politische Ordnung einer spirituellen Grundlage? Kelsens Kritik an Voegelins autoritärer politischer Theologie. In *Secular Religion: Rezeption und Kritik von Hans Kelsens Ausinandersetzung mit Religion und Wissenschaft*, ed. Clemens Jabloner et al., 19–42. Wien: Mainz.

Becker, Carl. 1932. *The heavenly city of the eighteenth century philosophers*. New Haven: Yale University Press.

Brinton, Crane. 1959. *A history of western morals*. New York: Harcourt Brace.

Dawkins, Richard. 2006. *The God delusion*. Boston: Houghton Mifflin.

Dworkin, Ronald. 2013. *Religion without God*. Cambridge, MA: Harvard University Press.

Eisgruber, Christopher L., and Lawrence G. Sager. 2007. *Religious freedom and the constitution*. Cambridge, MA: Harvard University Press.

Frankel, Charles. 1948. *The faith of reason: The idea of progress in the French enlightenment*. New York: Columbia University Press.

Gross, Raphael. 2013. Der Parallelismus als Gefahr: Zur "jüdischen Biographie" von Hans Kelsen. In *Secular Religion: Rezeption und Kritik von Hans Kelsens Ausinandersetzung mit Religion und Wissenschaft*, ed. Clemens Jabloner et al., 113–129. Wien: Mainz.

Hamilton, Marci A. 2014. *God vs the gavel: The perils of extreme religious liberty*, 2nd ed. Cambridge: Cambridge University Press.

Human Rights Committee, General Comment 22. 1993. U.N. Doc. CCPR/C/21/Rev.1/Add.4.

International Covenant on Civil and Political Rights. 1966. 999 U.N.T.S. 171.

Jabloner, Clemens, et al. 2012. Editorial remarks. In *Secular religion. A polemic against the misinterpretation of modern social philosophy, science and politics as "new religion"*, ed. Hans Kelsen, IX–XV. Wien/New York: Springer.

Kelsen, Hans. 1948. *The political theory of Bolsheivism. A critical analysis*. Berkeley/Los Angeles: University of California Press.

Kelsen, Hans. 1955. *The Communist theory of law*. London: Stevens & Sons.

Kelsen, Hans. 2004. *A new science of politics: Hans Kelsen's reply to Erik Voegelin's "new science of politics."* Edited by Eckhart Arnold. Berlin: De Gruyter (Ontos).

Kelsen, Hans. 2012. *Secular religion. A polemic against the misinterpretation of modern social philosophy, science and politics as "new religion"*. Wien/New York: Springer.

Leiter, Brian. 2013. *Why tolerate religion?* Princeton/Oxford: Princeton University Press.

Maclure, Jocelyn and Charles Taylor. 2011. *Secularism and Freedom of Conscience*. Trans. J.M. Todd. Cambridge, MA: Harvard University Press.

Métall, Rudolf Aladár. 1969. *Hans Kelsen: Leben und Werk*. Vienna: Verlag Franz Deuticke.

Potacs, Michael. 2013. Marxismus als "säkularer" Religion? Kelsen und Aron. In *Secular Religion: Rezeption und Kritik von Hans Kelsens Ausinandersetzung mit Religion und Wissenschaft*, ed. Clemens Jabloner et al., 89–99. Wien: Mainz.

Potz, Richard. 2012. Introductory remarks. In *Secular religion. A polemic against the misinterpretation of modern social philosophy, science and politics as "new religion"*, ed. Hans Kelsen, VII–X. Wien/NewYork: Springer.

Schmitt, Carl. 1922. *Politische Theologie: Vier Kapitel zur Lehre von der Souveranität*. Berlin: Duncker und Humblot.
Smith, S. 2014. Is God irrelevant? *Boston University Law Review*, 94: 1339–1355.
Thomassen, Bjørn. 2013. Review of Hans Kelsen. *Secular religion. A polemic against the misinterpretation of modern social philosophy, science and politics as "new religion". Plurilogue: Politics and Philosophy Reviews*. Available at http://www.plurilogue.com/2013/01/secular-religion-polemic-against_28.html.
Voegelin, Eric. 1952. *The new science of politics: An introduction*. Chicago: University of Chicago Press.
Voegelin, Eric. 2007. *The collected works of Eric Voegelin: Selected correspondence, 1950–1984*. Edited by Thomas Hollweck. Columbia/London: University of Missouri Press.

Index

D.A.J. Telman (ed.), *Hans Kelsen in America - Selective Affinities and the Mysteries of Academic Influence*, Law and Philosophy Library 116,
DOI 10.1007/978-3-319-33130-0

MIX
Papier aus verantwortungsvollen Quellen
Paper from responsible sources
FSC® C105338
FSC
www.fsc.org

If you have any concerns about our products,
you can contact us on
ProductSafety@springernature.com

In case Publisher is established outside the EU,
the EU authorized representative is:
Springer Nature Customer Service Center GmbH
Europaplatz 3, 69115 Heidelberg, Germany

Printed by Libri Plureos GmbH
in Hamburg, Germany